THE ENCYCLOPEDIA
OF WORLD BOXING CHAMPIONS

Books by John D. McCallum

The World Heavyweight Boxing Championship: A History
College Football, U.S.A.
Boxing Fans' Almanac
Everest Diary
Going Their Way
Dumb Dan
The Tiger Wore Spikes
That Kelly Family
Six Roads from Abilene
The Story of Dan Lyons, S.J.
Not by Bread Alone
This Was Football
Scooper
The Gladiators: A Chronicle of Pacific Lutheran University Sports
How You Can Play Little League Baseball

and other books . . .

THE ENCYCLOPEDIA OF WORLD BOXING CHAMPIONS

SINCE 1882

JOHN D. McCALLUM

CHILTON BOOK COMPANY · Radnor, Pennsylvania

Copyright © 1975 by John D. McCallum
First Edition *All Rights Reserved*
Published in Radnor, Pa., by Chilton Book Company
and simultaneously in Don Mills, Ont., Canada
by Thomas Nelson & Sons, Ltd.

Manufactured in the United States of America
Designed by Donald E. Cooke

LIBRARY OF CONGRESS CATALOGING IN PUBLICATION DATA

McCallum, John Dennis, 1924–
The encyclopedia of world boxing champions since 1882.

1. Boxing—Biography. I. Title.
GV1131.M32 1975   796.8′3′0922 [B]   75-19012
ISBN 0-8019-6161-7

To
JAMES WARNER BELLAH,
*one who brought the true cavalry
to Literature—
and the best damn writer I know
about fighting men*

CONTENTS

Foreword xiii

HEAVYWEIGHTS
John L. Sullivan 2
James J. Corbett 5
Bob Fitzsimmons 7
James J. Jeffries 11
Tommy Burns 15
Jack Johnson 16
Jess Willard 20
Jack Dempsey 22
Gene Tunney 29
Jack Sharkey 32
Max Schmeling 35
Primo Carnera 38
Max Baer 40
James J. Braddock 43
Joe Louis 45
Ezzard Charles 51
Jersey Joe Walcott 52
Rocky Marciano 55
Floyd Patterson 60
Ingemar Johansson 63
Sonny Liston 66
Cassius Clay (Muhammad Ali) . . 68
Joe Frazier 74
George Foreman 77

LIGHT-HEAVYWEIGHT
Jack Root 81
George Gardner 82
Philadelphia Jack O'Brien . . . 82
Jack Dillon 84
Battling Levinsky 85
Georges Carpentier 88
Battling Siki 91
Mike McTigue 94
Paul Berlenbach 95

Jack Delaney	96
Tommy Loughran	97
Maxie Rosenbloom	100
Jimmy Slattery	102
Bob Olin	103
John Henry Lewis	103
Melio Bettina	103
Billy Conn	104
Anton Christoforidis	107
Gus Lesnevich	108
Freddie Mills	109
Joey Maxim	110
Archie Moore	113
Harold Johnson	117
Willie Pastrano	118
Jose Luis Torres	120
Dick Tiger	122
Bob Foster	123

MIDDLEWEIGHTS

Jack Dempsey, the Nonpareil	124
Tommy Ryan	125
Stanley Ketchel	126
Billy Papke	132
Frank Klaus	134
George Chip	135
Al McCoy	135
Mike O'Dowd	135
Johnny Wilson	136
Harry Greb	136
Theo (Tiger) Flowers	141
Mickey Walker	142
Gorilla Jones	146
Ben Jeby	147
Marcel Thil	147
Vince Dundee	148
Teddy Yarosz	149
Eddie (Babe) Risko	149
Freddie Steele	151
Fred Apostoli	155

Al Hostak	157
Solly Krieger	160
Ceferino Garcia	161
Ken Overlin	161
Billy Soose	161
Tony Zale and Rocky Graziano	161
Marcel Cerdan	169
Jake LaMotta	170
Sugar Ray Robinson	172
Randy Turpin	176
Carl (Bobo) Olson	177
Gene Fullmer	180
Carmen Basilio	181
Terry Downes	185
Paul Pender	185
Joey Giardello	186
Emile Griffith	187
Nino Benvenuti	188
Carlos Monzon	188

WELTERWEIGHTS

Mysterious Billy Smith	189
Kid McCoy	190
Matty Matthews	192
Rube Ferns	193
Joe Walcott	193
Dixie Kid	194
Billy (Honey) Mellody	194
Mike (Twin) Sullivan	195
Jack Britton and Ted (Kid) Lewis	195
Pete Latzo	200
Joe Dundee	201
Young Jack Thompson	201
Lou Brouillard	202
Jackie Fields	202
Tommy Freeman	203
Young Corbett III	203
Jimmy McLarnin	204
Barney Ross	208
Henry Armstrong	211

CONTENTS

Fritzie Zivic	213		Lauro Salas	256
Freddie Cochrane	215		Paddy DeMarco	258
Marty Servo	216		Wallace (Bud) Smith	258
Johnny Bratton	216		Carlos Ortiz	258
Kid Gavilan	216		Carlos (Theo) Cruz	259
Johnny Saxton	219		Armando (Mando) Ramos	259
Tony DeMarco	219		Ismael Laguna	259
Virgil Akins	220		Ken Buchanan	260
Don Jordan	220		Roberto Duran	260
Benny (Kid) Paret	221			
Luis Rodriguez	221		**FEATHERWEIGHTS**	
Curtis Cokes	222		Ike Weir	261
Jose Napoles	223		Torpedo Billy Murphy and	
Billy Backus	223		Young Griffo	261
			George Dixon	264
LIGHTWEIGHTS			Solly Smith and Dave Sullivan	265
Arthur Chambers	224		Young Corbett II and	
Jack McAuliffe	225		Terry McGovern	265
George Lavigne	227		Abe Attell	268
Frank Erne	227		Johnny Kilbane	269
Joe Gans	229		Eugene Criqui	271
Battling Nelson	231		Johnny Dundee	271
Ad Wolgast	233		Louis (Kid) Kaplan	273
Willie Ritchie	235		Benny Bass	274
Freddie Welsh	236		Andre Routis	274
Benny Leonard	237		Christopher (Bat) Battalino	274
Jimmy Goodrich	242		Kid Chocolate	276
Rocky Kansas	242		Freddie Miller	276
Sammy Mandell	243		Petey Sarron	277
Al Singer	243		Joey Archibald	277
Tony Canzoneri	244		Harry Jeffra	279
Lou Ambers	246		Albert (Chalky) Wright	279
Lew Jenkins	248		Petey Scalzo	280
Sammy Angott	250		Phil Terranova	280
Beau Jack	251		Sal Bartolo	281
Bob Montgomery	252		Willie Pep	281
Juan Zurita	253		Sandy Saddler	284
Ike Williams	253		Hogan (Kid) Bassey	285
Jimmy Carter	254		Davey Moore	286
Joe Brown	256		Sugar Ramos	287

CONTENTS

Johnny Famechon	287
Vincente Saldivar	287
Kuniaki Shibata	288
Clemente Sanchez	288

BANTAMWEIGHTS

Jimmy Barry	289
Harry Harris	289
Harry Forbes	290
Frankie Neil	290
Joe Bowker	290
Jimmy Walsh	291
Johnny Coulon	291
Kid Williams	291
Pete Herman	291
Joe Lynch	293
Johnny Buff	294
Abe Goldstein	294
Eddie (Cannonball) Martin	295
Charley Rosenberg	295
Bud Taylor	295
Bushy Graham	295
Panama Al Brown	295
Baltazar Sangchilli	296
Tony Marino	296
Sixto Escobar	296
Lou Salica	296
George Pace	297
Harold Dade	297
Manuel Ortiz	298
Vic Toweel	299
Jimmy Carruthers	300
Robert Cohen	300
Mario D'Agata	300
Alphonse Halimi	300
Jose Becerra	301
Masahiko (Fighting) Harada	302
Eder Jofre	302
Lionel Rose	302
Chucho Castillo	303
Ruben Olivares	304

Rafael Herrara	304
Enrique Pinder	304
Romera Anaya	304
Arnold Taylor	304

FLYWEIGHTS

Jimmy Wilde	306
Pancho Villa	308
Frankie Genaro	310
Emile Pladner	310
Fidel LaBarba	311
Albert Belanger	311
Izzy Schwartz	311
Victor (Young) Perez	312
Midget Wolgast	312
Jackie Brown	312
Benny Lynch	313
Small Montana	313
Peter Kane	314
Jackie Paterson	314
Rinty Monaghan	314
Terry Allen	315
Dado Marino	315
Yoshio Shirai	315
Pascual Perez	315
Hiroyuki Ebihara	318
Pone Kingpetch	318
Salvatore Burruni	318
Walter McGowan	319
Alacran (Efren) Torres	320
Chartchai Chionoi	320
Erbito Salvarria	320
Venice Borkorsor	320

APPENDICES

Boxing Hall of Fame	321
States in U.S. Producing Most World Champions	322
Rating the All-Time Champions	322
Heavyweight Championship Bouts	323

CONTENTS

Fight Records of the Champions. 326
   Heavyweight Champions . . 326
   Light-Heavyweight Champions 327
   Middleweight Champions . . 327
   Welterweight Champions . . 328
   Lightweight Champions . . . 328
   Featherweight Champions . . 329

Bantamweight Champions . . 329
Flyweight Champions . . . 330
Principal Rules of the
   Prize Ring 331

Index 335

FOREWORD

ONCE, some years ago, Dumb Dan Morgan, the non-stop septuagenarian, lost his voice temporarily. Without his well-worn pipes the fight world would be reduced to the bleakest sort of silence, for old Dan's was one of the few voices left among the fight crowd that carried the qualities of wit, honor, courage and experience. As an old-line manager of three bona fide world champions, as adviser or trainer to dozens more, he had brightened the dim, disreputable ring racket for more than 60 years. It seemed urgent to look in on him.

This was on the eve of the New York Boxing Writers' annual dinner, at which Morgan was to receive the Walker Memorial Award for meritorious service to prizefighting, and I rushed to his bedside on the West Side of upper Manhattan to bombard him with neutrons and throat drops.

"What will happen," I asked the veteran free-style monologist and unreclaimed horseplayer, feverishly wrapping flannel around his pencil-thin neck, "if you never speak again? Who will describe the twenty-first fight between Jack Britton and Ted Kid Lewis? Who will tell us what Dempsey would have done to Louis? Who'll give us the *angle?*"

The thought of the impending gap was so horrible that Morgan recovered his voice on the spot.

"I will," he said, perking up. And he did— and he continued to do so until the day of his death in 1953. But before he passed on, I wrote a book with Morgan based on his memories of the fight racket. On the eve of publication, he rushed out and wired all his friends: "Please come and help me celebrate the publication of my bestseller." Although Chamberlain, Gannett, Wilson, North, Hansen and the other metropolitan critics mysteriously absented themselves, Musky Jackson, Evil Eye Finkle, Fatso Zuckerman, Hot Horse Andy and Mushky McGee of the Jacobs Beach literati were generous in their praise.

The volume was written almost totally in English rather than lower East Side Gaelic. This was the result of careless hospital proce-

xiii

dure some years previously, when Morgan was ill and getting blood transfusions. Blood of all kinds was contributed in the rush by the boxing mob.

"You shoulda seen the gang comin' in," Dan beamed. "Frank Mantell, one of the first I managed. He fought Wolgast and Klaus and Papke and now he's sixty-one and looks great. Right downstairs he goes to the blood bank and he gives a pint. This fella Pete Montesi—lost a leg and an arm in the war—and he gives, too. Then five of them walk into my room together. I look at them and say, 'Listen, four of you guys scram. You're horseplayers and you need it more than I do.' There was even an *Englishman* among the donors, sad to say, but much obliged to him anyway. I haven't talked the same way since."

In his conversation, old Dan was as direct and forceful as a left jab to the mouth. He criticized challengers and champions to their faces and had outspoken contempt for most modern managers, but he mixed his criticisms and opinions with old-fashioned Irish wit that at once won him the attention of his audience and the respect of America's boxing writers. In appearance, he suggested a clergyman, a schoolmaster, or the faithful old bookkeeper who is just about eligible to receive a watch from the company for his lifetime of faithful service.

Old Dan was no bigger than a sack of popcorn. He stood 5 ft. 6 in. and weighed 120 lbs., topped off with an ever-present derby hat and high, stiff collar. Sports writers nicknamed him "Dumb Dan." They learned that

In a photo taken in 1951, Dumb Dan Morgan, then eighty-one, took stance to show author John McCallum what Jack Dempsey would have done to Joe Louis. (UPI)

when contradicted or ribbed he would talk for several hours at a stretch, with much resultant hot copy for their newspapers.

Citizens walking along Broadway in New York often were shocked to see a meek-looking little old man back away from a group of conversationalists and begin shadowboxing furiously on the sidewalk. That was Dumb Dan. Hands held in orthodox boxing position, he'd hook an imaginary opponent with a left to the jaw, follow through with a right cross, lunging at one of his listeners. Then he'd dance away to his right, bobbing and weaving, and dart in again.

"I get plenty of exercise that way," Morgan would say. "Maybe that's the reason I've lived so long."

All through World War II and the postwar period, Morgan organized boxing shows and entertained at veterans' hospitals with them. Once in a while, it got quite rugged for him.

"Like that time I hadda use my head to keep from freezing," Dumb Dan recalled. "I was all alone goin' to keep a speaking engagement at this Army hospital out on Long Island. It was below zero and two volunteer Red Cross ladies picked me up in a car and I sat in the back. The car was unheated. I looked at the women in the front seat and they were kitchen types with plenty of spread to them. They were light-heavyweights. The wind was blowing hard and I was shivering and freezing. I said stop the car. I got in between them in the front seat. There wasn't much room but I squeezed in right between them. I had one on each side of me and I was warm as toast. They protected me and I didn't even catch cold, let alone pneumonia. Most modern fight managers would have died of the cold in the back seat. Not me. I used the old head for something besides a hatrack."

They were a great and colorful crew, Morgan and his fellow fight managers. I mean, oldtimers like Jimmy Johnston and Silvey Burns and Eddie Mead and Charlie Harvey and Scotty Monteith and Billy Gibson and Leo P. Flynn and Prof. Billy McCarney and a slew of others of that era who will not pass this way again. They came up over a rough and tumble course and were perfectly at home in a rough and tumble business. The difference between them and those who followed was that they had something to contribute to the prize ring and were not content merely to take out of it all they could and give nothing in return but a smirk.

The oldtimers played hard. They played for keeps. They carried on feuds. But they knew a fighter when they saw one and they knew what to do with him when they got their hands on him. They worked over him and taught him and sweated with him. They made the right matches for him. They made money for him and, of course, for themselves. They helped to create an era that was perhaps the greatest in prize ring history.

In W. S. Davis's long-forgotten *The Sportsman's Manual*, published in 1885, the author recalled covering a prizefight between one Deaf Burke and Sam O'Rourke, in 1838, with Burke getting in his licks in the early rounds. "Burke was getting along just fine until O'Rourke's gang drew bowie knives and pistols and cleaned things out in a hurry," reported Davis.

In 1869, author Davis recollected, Tom Allen and Bill Davis fought for a $2,000 purse. In the words of *The Sportsman's Manual*: "Mr. Davis looked like a man in the last stages of a busted constitution and was only living to save funeral expenses after he and Mr. Allen had been together in the ring for awhile."

Two years later, Jem Mace met Joe Coburn for a purse of $2,500 in what *The Sportsman's Manual* described as a very dull, unsatisfactory performance. "Considerable monkeying was done in the mill," Davis wrote. "In fact, both fighters fooled around from 5 minutes to an hour without pitching a blow. After 3 hours and 38 minutes, the referee finally informed the crowd that 'one is afraid and the other daresn't' and called it a draw."

When "glove" fighting replaced the bareknuckle breed, the purists, brought up in the old way, lamented the coming of the "knockout" punch era. "There's more luck and less generalship in the new way," author Davis quoted one oldtimer as saying. "Sure, it makes shorter fights. One man or the other has got to run very soon from something that'll put him to sleep, when men are wildly swinging. Excuse me if I don't see the science of it. When I see one of these slugfests I always think of the collision of two locomotives coming together, head to head, at full speed on a single track. It makes a very lively and smashing event with a good deal of execution done in a very short metre, but where the science of such encounters comes in you'll have to tell me."

Major historians, as once pointed out by the late John Lardner, seldom write of it, but at the popular level, prizefighting has played as strongly as any factor in non-military life on the emotions of nations and peoples. Feeling was intense, for example, when Tom Sayers, champion of England, fought John C. Heenan, the Benicia Boy, of California. French emotions ran high at the time of the Dempsey-Carpentier fight. Feeling among whites against Negroes was strong at the time when John L. Sullivan invented the so-called "color line," and at a time when Jack Johnson crossed the line, some years later, and knocked out Jim Jeffries. Adolph Hitler personally ordered the German heavyweight, Max Schmeling, to flatten Joe Louis, "that non-Aryan!"

A curious thing about boxing is that most matches are interesting only to seasoned and expert fans. The general public is largely concerned with the issues behind them, and with the flavor of the characters involved. Each big bout is a climax in a story, or series of stories, about people. Some of the important matches down through history belong in the annals solely on their physical action, of what happened in the ring. But, generally, prizefight life outside the ring is more entertaining than prizefight life inside it.

There have been periods in American history when a heavyweight boxing champion outranked the President in public interest.

Muhammad Ali's impact on popular feeling in America was often sharper than Lyndon B. Johnson's, I'm sure. Before him, Jack Dempsey overshadowed Calvin Coolidge, and Jack Johnson surpassed William H. Taft. Any fighter, champion or not, provided he is famous, enjoys a special kind of power and prestige.

Years ago, Luis Firpo, the Argentine heavyweight, was introduced to President Coolidge.

"Well," the President told him, admiringly, "you seem to be everything I've heard about you."

"Who was that fellow?" Firpo asked later.

For some reason, the prizefight crowd instinctively think of the White House when making comparisons with their profession.

"My tiger," said Jimmy Johnston, a gifted manager, speaking of "Fainting" Phil Scott, "just sitting on the floor grabbing his groin, made more money in one year than the President of the United States."

The prize ring always has been the refuge of the underprivileged. The pattern of social persecution in America is traced in the names and records of the great Irish, then Jewish, Italian, Negro and Puerto Rican fighters who have graced the game.

In this vein, Dr. Charles P. Larson and I sat in his office one day recently, engaging in a roundtable discussion dealing with the dominance of blacks in modern prizefighting. Dr. Larson's credentials are impressive. He is past President of both the College of American Pathologists, and of the International Congress of Forensic Pathology. In 1961, he was elected President of the National Boxing Association, and served as the W.B.A.'s first President the following year.

On the subject of boxing, the doctor was precise and confident. For 35 years, he conducted clinical studies and investigations relating to boxing fatalities. His research covered a large number of reports from the New York Medical Examiner's Office, as well as many other state medical examiners' and coroners' offices in the United States and in Europe.

"People ask me to explain why only two white men have held the world heavyweight championship since Jim Braddock," he said, addressing himself more to my tape recorder than to me. "They seem to think that a doctor has the answer. The fact that 8 of the last 10 heavyweight champions have been black is no mystery."

"Why?" I said. It's a writer's best word.

"In symposiums I've listened to the same old tired theories," Dr. Larson said. "The black fighter is hungrier than the white. The black has more rhythm. The black has a harder head. The black's got this one muscle in his leg that's longer than anybody else's. I've been studying prizefighters for three-and-a-half decades and can't find where blacks are physically superior to whites."

"Then why this preponderance of black champions?" I asked. Dr. Larson glanced at the ceiling, mouth pursed.

Jack Dempsey gets together with Harry Falk, left, and Dr. Charles P. Larson, former President of both the N.B.A. and W.B.A. Picture was taken in Dempsey's Broadway restaurant, which closed its doors in 1974, another indication of boxing's changing times. (Photo from Arch Hindman collection)

"Because they have more ambition, more desire to win," he said. "It's their primary route to eminence and riches. Subsequently, more of them go into the business. Their strength is in numbers. Blacks invariably outnumber white fighters all the way from 2–1 up to 10–1. I discovered this when I was N.B.A. and W.B.A. President and traveled around the country visiting boxing clubs and gyms. So what does it mean? It means that if you have 10 good young men of equal ability and opportunity—and 9 of them are black and only 1 is white—you have only a 10 percent chance of turning out a white champion and a 90 percent chance of turning out a black one. This is what has happened at every boxing club across the U.S. Even in the amateur ranks, the majority of candidates are black."

"White racists claim they are more intelligent than blacks—that black athletes win on brute strength," I said. "How do you answer them?"

"They base their arguments on the blacks' lack of schooling," Dr. Larson said. "But you don't need a lot of formal education to prizefight. *Intelligence*, yes. When a fighter has native intelligence, he'll go farther than the fighter with a low-grade I.Q."

"Like Dempsey."

"Yes. Dempsey didn't go far in school, but he's one of the most intelligent men I've ever met. So is Tunney . . . and Muhammad Ali. In fact, there have been very few champions—black or white—who didn't have a *high* I.Q. Even Sonny Liston. Sonny was one of the most uneducated men I've ever known—he had to be taught to read and write after he became champion—yet he possessed enough basic intelligence to win the world title."

"Between John L. Sullivan and Joe Louis, only one black man, Jack Johnson, held the heavyweight crown. Why did it take Negroes so long to gain control?"

"Historically, until the reign of Louis, the black fighter was simply overawed by his white opponents," Dr. Larson said. "Do you remember Bill Brennan, the former President of the W.B.A.? Well, Bill was a pretty fair professional boxer himself. He once told me, 'Charley, let me tell you how I won all those fights with black boys. I walked into the ring with a scowl on my face, as if I owned the world. Then I'd walk over to the other man's corner and snarl: Ya black sonofabitch, I'm gonna kill ya! I'm gonna split ya open and feed ya to the fish! That scared hell out of them. Intimidation. They were so confused they couldn't concentrate on attack. I psyched them to death.'"

"That wouldn't work today," I said.

Dr. Larson nodded. "Of course not," he said. "Louis, Robinson, Charles, Walcott, Patterson, Liston, Ali, Frazier and Foreman—they've shown their black brothers that black is beautiful. Now it's the other way around. The black man has the white man psyched into thinking that blacks are physiologically superior. Now he believes he is better. Now he *knows* he is better. This positive attitude has been turned into an advantage for blacks at all levels of sport."

"Will the white champion ever return in numbers?"

"A Depression might do it. Bring hunger back to America and I predict you'd find Jewish fighters dominating. Back in 1928–30, the champions were largely Jewish. Anti-semitism was rampant—economic advancement was slim—and so the Hebrew was forced to use his fists professionally to club his way out of the ghetto. He developed into a tremendous boxer."

"There have been few Jewish prizefighters since the 1930s. What happened?"

"Few go into boxing anymore," Dr. Larson said. "They make a very comfortable living in other fields now, where the standards are far less risky, require much less physical training, and life is better. The life of a prizefighter is not easy. It requires lots of work and self-sacrifice. Few whites want to live that way anymore."

Example: In late June, 1974, as a fighting-mad heavyweight Jerry Quarry weighed in at Madison Square Garden for a bout with former world champion Joe Frazier, his wife Charlie weighed in with comments on their sex life for NBC's *Today* show.

"We have a two-week curfew," explained the blonde former Miss Indiana. "Gil Clancy, Jerry's manager, is in the room right next to us, and his ear is glued to the wall. If there's a cough in the middle of the night, Gil says, 'What are you doing in there?'"

On the way up the ladder, Angelo Dundee says a fighter must be willing to make sacrifices.

"It takes a while for a fighter to develop," the famous trainer explained. "He needs patience. Money won't be plentiful for a long time. He'll have to give up drinking and smoking and other pleasures and devote a good deal of his life to really hard physical work and training. And he'll have to be ready to accept pain. Boxers get hurt. They have to be strong enough to take the pain without letting it confuse them or create any fear in them. If they have enough dedication to accept all this and work hard for two or three years, there is still the possibility that they will be just short of good enough to make a respectable living in the ring. I don't mean win a championship—the odds against that are so tough that most kids would run like bandits if they realized what they were. Just to be good enough to fight in main events requires a truly exceptional man."

What does it mean to be a champion of the world? Well, this was a little after noontime of June 17, 1954, in New York, and Rocky Marciano, who was fighting Ezzard Charles for the heavyweight championship at Yankee Stadium that night, was leaving the weigh-in ceremonies with his handlers. The entourage hesitated just inside the windowed doors of old Madison Square Garden, as though shrinking back from the crowds on the sidewalk. They chose the door closest to the auto waiting at the curb, and plunged for the car in a flying wedge formation. A burst of shouting rose in 50th Street.

"Hey, Rock!"

"Hiya, Rocky boy!"

"Yay, Champ!"

Red Smith, in the foyer, listened and smiled appreciatively.

"There's a sound," he said, "that will stay with him all his life."

Better than a volume of words, Red Smith

summed up what it is like to be a prizefight champion of the world. In all sports there never has been another thrill quite like it.

Once there were more than 400 fight clubs in the U.S.; in 1974, there were only a handful. Fifteen years ago the files of *The Ring*, boxing's leading publication, held the cards of 12,000 active professional fighters, 9,000 of them in this country. In '74, there were cards for less than 2,000 boxers in all the world.

Walter E. Magnolia, of Hewlett, New York, the son of the late Lou Magnolia, who refereed several Jack Sharkey fights and such world championship bouts as Jimmy McLarnin vs. Sammy Mandell and Izzy Schwartz vs. Bushy Graham, remembers the time when his father officiated in three title matches in four days.

"Those days are gone forever," Walter told me. "Now there isn't enough business around to keep a referee in meal money."

With so few small boxing clubs operating today, where are you going to take a young fighter so he can make some money and so he can learn?

"Learn?" said the late Doc Moore one time. Doc had been around boxing since 1905. "Today most of them managers and trainers sic a fighter like he was a dog. You go in each corner, and they're sayin': 'Go in there and get him.' They destroy fighters."

A few years ago, Jersey Jones, then Assistant Editor of *The Ring*, pointed out that there was too much work around. "A kid doesn't have to become a fighter," he said. "And in the old days, what did the average boy in the street have to look forward to? Baseball, if he lived near a vacant lot, or boxing. Golf was for old men, tennis for sissies, football was for college, and basketball was a Y.M.C.A. and settlement-house game. Now a kid says, 'Pop, how about the car tonight and 10 bucks?' Boxing, as we have known it, is all washed up."

There is no endeavor where the passing of prizefighting is more apparent as when one sits down and compiles a work such as this. The characters are gone, the *fun* has vanished. Except for an occasional Ali, the principals lack originality and personality.

Eavesdropping on a conversation between Dumb Dan Morgan and Francis Albertanti was like living something Damon Runyon had written. Bill Heinz remembered overhearing Morgan saying to Francis: "Let us talk about the oldtimers. Napoleon and Brian Boru and . . ."

"Pete the Goat," said Albertanti.

Morgan kept on, "And what was the name of that guy at the bridge?"

"What guy?"

"The big gossoon who stood at the bridge and fought off the mob."

"Horatius," Albertanti said.

"That's right, and he ended up takin' a dive, didn't he?"

"Into the river," Francis Albertanti said. "But one day Pete the Goat . . ."

Now Morgan and Albertanti are gone, the wreckers tore down Stillman's Gym, most of the old clubs have disappeared, and all we have left are the memories of better days and better fighters.

Sweet dreams.

HEAVYWEIGHTS

THERE never has been a standardized type among heavyweight champions. Perhaps that's just as well, because the idols of the division have made their class larger than life by the very divergence of their personalities.

Thumbing down the list, you have had the intemperate John L. Sullivan, the impeccable Jim Corbett, the quaint Bob Fitzsimmons, the sullen Jim Jeffries, the flamboyant Jack Johnson, the dull Jess Willard, and the tenacious Jack Dempsey. There was Gene Tunney's calm assurance set against Primo Carnera's fantastic fumblings, and Max Baer's buffoonery as opposed to Jim Braddock's businesslike manner.

In style, Dempsey always bounded up and down on the balls of his feet in a nervous sort of pre-fight jig. Tunney wore a broad, fixed smile, acknowledged greetings from friends close up and was consistently unperturbed. Sharkey had a way of crunching the padding in the forepart of his gloves back toward his wrists. If the preliminary rituals were overly long, he'd have the gloves quite out of shape and there would be very little padding over his middle knuckles. As for the phlegmatic Joe Louis, he always appeared bored, as if on the verge of sleep. Once, Rocky Marciano *did* fall asleep—a half-hour before his fight with Ezzard Charles!

This diversity among the big men has added tremendous spice and drama to the prize ring.

The evolution of the sport's most popular class parallels that of society. From a sordid background of surreptitious bouts in smoke-filled rooms, scraps in frontier boom towns, in barns, aboard ships and barges, in gambling houses or as part of a circus sideshow, the heavyweight division's character has been tempered, its motives diverted to loftier ends.

Two dropouts—George Foreman and Muhammad Ali—were proof positive in 1974, when they split a $10,000,000 guarantee for a *single* fight, that no class is so filled with opportunity. Wealth, education, inherited privilege and superficial cleverness have no place among the heavies. Such qualities as brute force, muscular prowess, nervelessness and sharp thinking are at a premium. The man who combines them usually wins wealth and international adulation.

Most of our most compelling heavyweight champions rose from abject poverty, fought their first fierce battles in the shadow of a slum tenement, and, once in the prize ring, struck with the consummate fury of men whose iron fists offer the only escape route from a lackluster environment.

Fitzsimmons was a blacksmith, for example. Jeffries was a boilermaker and toiled in California mines. Dempsey was a hobo fighting for $2.50 purses, Tunney was a stevedore at the age of fourteen, Max Baer slammed beef around in a slaughterhouse, and Louis was the son of a poor family from the cotton fields of Dixie. Sonny Liston, from a fatherless family of 25 children, grew up thinking criminals were great guys.

Gene Tunney once said that a heavyweight is at his best when he scales between 185 and 195 pounds. After he tops the 200 figure the weight, in most cases, deters him. "At the 185–195 pound mark a heavyweight can hit hard enough to knock out any man," Tunney said. "Louis proved this when he K.O.'d Carnera, 65 pounds heavier than he. And a fighter is definitely faster on his feet at the lower weight than at the heavier."

Tunney, the first heavyweight champion to retire undefeated, made that observation in 1955. Since then, only Rocky Marciano (184), Floyd Patterson (190) and Ingemar Johansson (197) have approximated the erstwhile Fighting Marine's measurements for the *ideal* heavyweight champion. The others—Liston (212), Ali (215), Frazier (202), and Foreman (220)—have tended to lean toward more muscle. And yet Muhammad Ali is generally believed to be the *fastest* heavyweight champion in history. At the other end of the spectrum, Tommy Burns stood a mere 5 ft., 7 in. and weighed 175, ten pounds heavier than Bob Fitzsimmons.

Ex-Marine fighter pilot Dick Francisco, who was All-Service Light-Heavyweight Champion in World War II, and who tutored Rocky Marciano when PFC Marciano was stationed at Fort Lewis, Washington, in 1946, doesn't share Tunney's view. "I like my heavyweights *big*," the Seattle restauranteur told me. "If I was going to set out to breed a heavyweight champion, I could do no better than make a photo copy of George Foreman. Physically, he's the model of the perfect specimen: big legs, fast, a shattering puncher, with a killer's instinct. I'm one of those who believes that a good big man can whip an excellent little man every time."

The heavyweight division dates back to ancient Greece, but the first record of it started with James Figg, who opened a boxing school at Gottenham Court Road in London in 1719. Since 1800, the United States has virtually dominated the heavies. Only Bob Fitzsimmons of England (who later became a U.S. citizen), Tommy Burns of Canada, Max Schmeling of Germany, Primo Carnera of Italy, and Ingemar Johansson of Sweden ever have been able to break through the American monopoly since 1882.

Jim Corbett is frequently credited as the man who first introduced gloves and ring cleverness to boxing. Both are fallacies. Prizefighters wore gloves long before Gentleman Jim flattened the Great John L. to win the title in 1892. It is true, however, that that was the first time a world heavyweight championship match had been fought with gloves. As for speed and cleverness, oldtimers testified that the Sullivan of the early 1880s was surely comparable to the Corbett who out-foxed and out-boxed him in New Orleans in 1892.

It was John L. who did more than anyone else to popularize the boxing glove. He clearly demonstrated that boxing is a raw, rough sport in which the fittest survive to be legends.

PUBLISHER'S NOTE:
What follows are mini-biographies of the 24 men who have held the world heavyweight championship. For a more complete picture, read John D. McCallum's *The World Heavyweight Boxing Championship—A History*, published recently by Chilton Book Company. It's a Literary Guild Alternate Selection.

JOHN L. SULLIVAN
(1858–1918)

Was John L. Sullivan a myth? Of course. Every commanding figure—in politics, business, literature, movies, sports—becomes something of a myth, bigger than life-size.

They shoot up, they die down, and very few survive the cruel process of overnight fame and then back to overnight obscurity again.

Americans always have had a hunger for outsized figures. To say that a man is a myth doesn't mean he's a *fake*, but only that we have an investment of belief in him. So in that sense then, John L. was our first great "myth" in sports. He was a folk hero—Superman, Victorian style.

John L. Sullivan, the last bareknuckle champion. (UPI)

Generally, the image of Sullivan is that he had a handlebar mustache, a large belly full of champagne, and a conviction that he could whip any so-and-so in whatever saloon he happened to be patronizing. He was a powerfully built man, slightly under six-feet, bull-necked, a Sandowlike torso—190 pounds of dynamite by early-day standards. He was the first to admit, however, that he was not a *big* man. "I was no superman physically," he said. "That Great John L. myth started because I *looked* big compared to the rather light chaps of the day."

Sullivan once estimated he had earned between $500,000 and $600,000 in the 1880s; more than $125,000 of that was made between September 26, 1883, and May 26, 1884, when he went around the U.S. offering $1,000 to anyone he couldn't knock out in four rounds. His total prize ring earnings amounted to $1,211,470.

John L.'s fighting attire usually consisted of knee breeches, stockings and shoes, no shirt. His ring shoes had three big spikes in them to prevent slipping. To harden his skin, he washed his hands and face in a mixture of rock salt, white wine, vinegar and several unidentified ingredients. Asked if he felt sorry for an opponent he'd hurt, Sullivan replied: "I never feel sorry until the fight is over."

For his famous bareknuckle fight at Richburg, Mississippi, with Jake Kilrain, on July 8, 1889, Sullivan dropped from 237 pounds to 195. Years later, he said, "I trained hard, I got up at 6 A.M. every day and got rubbed down. Then Billy Muldoon, my trainer, and I walked and ran a mile or a mile-and-a-half and then back. Just as soon as we'd get back to camp I was given a showerbath, and after being thoroughly rubbed down again I put on an entire fresh outfit—a heavy sweater and a suit of heavy corduroy buttoned tightly. I also wore gloves. After my daily walk I put on a fresh sweater, so I wouldn't take cold. I walked so much to reduce my fat and to harden my muscles. I never took a cold showerbath. I didn't believe in cold water, it chills the blood. I preferred warm water. Two men rubbed me down briskly with a mixture of ammonia, camphor and alcohol.

"In my daily diet, I ate nothing fattening. I had oatmeal for breakfast and meat and bread for lunch, and cold meat and stale bread for supper. I ate no sweets or potatoes. Between matches I smoked cigars, but usually gave them up for training. I drank an occasional glass of ale, though it didn't average one a day. I always hated training. I'd have rather fought 12-dozen times than train once.

"At 10:30 each morning, I ran and walked another 12 miles, covering the distance in about two hours. Then I came back for another rubdown and 1 o'clock lunch. Afternoons were spent doing more exercises. I'd wrestle with Billy Muldoon, punch a bag, throw a football, swing Indian clubs and dumbbells, and then more body exercises until supper. Lifting kegs of nails over my head was my favorite exercise."

In 1889, the wear and tear of the prize ring began to show on John L. "I once liked prizefighting," he said. "I was fond of traveling and the excitement of the crowds, but no more. Now I am tired. I am growing old. Now I fight only for money. I made plenty of money in my prime, but I have been a fool and today I have nothing. It came easy and went easy."

They used to tell a story about how John L. walked out of a saloon long after midnight and saw an old woman selling newspapers on the corner. "Here," said Sullivan, gruffly, "I'll buy your papers. It's too late for an old woman like you to be out this late. Give me your papers and go home." Taking the papers, he reached into his pocket and pulled out a crumpled wad of bills and loose change and dumped them into the old woman's lap, and then went back into the saloon. When the woman counted up the money, it amounted to more than $200!

John Lawrence Sullivan was born on October 15, 1858, in Boston, across the street from what was then Boston College. His parents were Irish, from the old country, who had met in America. Ma Sullivan stood 5 ft., 10½ in., exactly the height of son John L. at his peak, and she weighed 180 lbs. Pa Sullivan stood 5 ft., 3 in., and weighed 125.

Almost from the beginning, John L. Sullivan was called "John L.," or "Mr. Sullivan." He was never called Jack, never Sully. His mother wanted him to be a priest, but he gave up the idea after attending only a few classes at Boston College. He said he lacked the discipline for so much study.

John L. always was fond of baseball; he played semi-pro ball for teams around Boston, was paid $25 a game, twice a week. At nineteen, he rejected an offer of $1,300 a season to play for a Cincinnati team. "By then," he explained, "I had drifted into the occupation of boxer."

Starting in 1878, Sullivan's career went on to overlap the bareknuckles and gloves eras, bridging the gap between those contrasting styles. In 1882, he notched his name in ring history as the last bareknuckle champion, by knocking out Paddy Ryan in nine rounds, at Mississippi City, Mississippi, for a purse and side bet totalling $5,000. Ten years later he became the first man to lose the world heavyweight title under Marquis of Queensberry rules, when James J. Corbett knocked him out in 21 rounds in New Orleans, on September 7, 1892. But he carried his London Prize Ring (bareknuckle) championship with him to the grave.

John L. fought for 27 years (1878–1905). Only 16 men ever campaigned longer professionally; Jem Mace was tops with a record of 34 years. In 1889, Sullivan fought 75 rounds (bareknuckle) with Jake Kilrain under a sweltering sun at Richburg, Mississippi, which stands as the twelfth longest match since 1887.

Nicknamed "The Boston Strong Boy," John L. was the first barnstorming champion, knocking out 49 of 50 challengers. He was the real pioneer of boxing gloves, never fought to a losing gate, and was champion of the world at twenty-four. He was also the first champion to draw the "color line." In January, 1892, eight months before losing his title to Corbett, he turned up in Tacoma, Washington and talked to the local reporter from *The Ledger*. In the interview, he said, "Any white fighter who'd get into the same ring with a black loses my respect." He was also contemptuous of South Americans: "In case of war with Chile, I'd like to take a crowd of men down there and whip them so thoroughly they'd never forget it."

John L. wore a little black mustache, had high cheekbones and sunken cheeks. He was taught to box by Mike Donaldson. A fine, stand-up fighter and extremely clever for a heavyweight, he knew how to feint and had a marvelous one-two punch. He was the first to discover that the point of the jaw was vulnerable. It is believed that an old Irish physician showed John L. in great detail that the real nerve center is on the left side of the nose just below the eye. Until Sullivan began hitting to the chin or under the eye, fighters went for the temple or a point behind the ear. John L. mastered this new lethal punch and toured the country, flattening one comer after another.

In 1880, John L., twenty-two years old and at his prime, inserted an advertisement, from a "modest and unassuming man," in the daily press, which read: "I am prepared to fight any man breathing for any sum from $1,000 to $10,000 at catchweights. This challenge is especially directed at Paddy Ryan and will remain open for a month if he should not see fit to accept it." The ad was signed, "Respectfully yours, John L. Sullivan."

Ryan had ascended to the heavyweight championship six months before by beating Joe Goss in 87 grueling rounds. Sullivan had boxed half a dozen men and two short exhibitions with Mike Donovan and Goss. His first bout, in '78, had been with Cocky Woods. Thus he didn't have much of a reputation and Ryan ignored the challenge.

Shortly thereafter, Sullivan accepted an open challenge tendered by Professor Mike Donaldson in Buffalo to meet anyone for a purse. The professor took one look at John L. and retired from the scene.

Donaldson was so goaded by criticism, however, he finally agreed to meet John L., on December 24, 1880, in Cincinnati. Sullivan kayoed him in 10 rounds. The following May 16th, Sullivan flattened John Flood in eight rounds in their famous battle on the barge anchored off Yonkers. Following more victories, Paddy Ryan finally agreed to fight Sullivan. After the bout, Ryan said, "John L. has arms like sawed-off telegraph poles. He hits like a piledriver."

Champion of the world now, Sullivan later toured England, Ireland, Scotland, the continent. Wherever he went, his personal magnetism won the crowd. He was the first really good fighter to visit Australia. His supreme confidence in his ability to lick any man in the world carried him on to victory—often over considerably awed opponents. He lost none of his self-assurance outside the ring and was as unflustered before world greats as he would have been in a Boston pub.

John L. had many fair-weather friends, among them old John Barleycorn, and with them led a roistering, swashbuckling life. Yet for all his roughness when in his cups, he disliked the brutality of bareknuckle fighting under London Prize Rules and inveighed against them.

"Fighting under the Marquis of Queensberry Rules before gentlemen is a pleasure," he said. "To the other element it becomes a brawl."

As he entered the ring at the New Orleans Olympic Club, September 7, 1892, to defend his crown against Gentleman Jim Corbett, Sullivan weighed 212 pounds, or 22 pounds more than his normal fighting weight. Fat and flabby, he had only his great fighting heart and determination left. Fighting with five-ounce gloves for a $25,000 purse and a $20,000 stake, the fighters battled 21 rounds before John L., gory and exhausted, succumbed to Corbett's dancing, jabbing attack.

Except for two subsequent fights, which were in the nature of exhibitions, Sullivan retired from the ring. In his later years, he became a staunch advocate of temperance and lived out his life lecturing on the evils of drink.

He also had some very definite opinions about the way boxing was being run, and opted for the following:

"Keep politics out of the fight game—the prize ring is no place for politicians.

"Place in power men who would control the sport with fearlessness and honesty.

"Have strong rules against fouls.

"Fifteen rounds should be enough to decide any fight, no matter how important.

"Five-ounce gloves are the correct size for all fighters to wear.

"Make it compulsory to have all contestants examined by competent physicians before entering the ring.

"*Keep all crooks out of boxing.*"

A great era in the prize ring ended with Sullivan's death at Abingdon, Massachusetts, on February 2, 1918, but its memories lingered on, and many a man went around and proudly said: "Shake the hand that shook the hand of John L. Sullivan."

JAMES J. CORBETT
(1866–1933)

Gentleman Jim Corbett was a turning point in prize ring history. He was the first world heavyweight champion to win the title with gloves under Marquis of Queensberry Rules. He was also the first heavyweight titleholder ever to twice try to regain his crown. Each time he was knocked out by Jim Jeffries.

Corbett was derided as a dancing master, a slick guy who would not stand still and fight the great John L. He was branded as a dandy, a dude, an over-educated fop. He was none of these things, of course, as the public slowly came to realize. Dumb Dan Morgan listed him as the fifth greatest heavyweight champion in history, behind Jim Jeffries, Sullivan, Jack Johnson, and Bob Fitzsimmons.

Handsome, pompadoured and blue-eyed, the articulate Gentleman Jim brought an aura of respectability and dignity to the prize ring. At sixty-four, he was still slim, clear-skinned, alert and in good shape. In 1925, when he was fifty-nine, Corbett fought a three-round exhibition behind closed doors with Gene Tunney. Afterward, Tunney said, "He was brilliant. He still had bewildering speed. He mixed up his punches better than practically any fighter I've seen. Imagine, fifty-nine years old! It was the greatest demonstration I've ever seen in the ring. I learned plenty."

Corbett was twenty-six when he won the title from Sullivan. He was boxing's first "Fancy Dan" to hold the heavyweight championship and did not meet with instant public approval. He was not a popular draw at the gate, at first. People resented the downfall of John L., their idol. They wanted a heavyweight champion of brawn, not a boxing artist.

Gentleman Jim gained in stature, however, when he stopped Charley Mitchell in three rounds in Jacksonville, Florida, on January 25, 1894, to become undisputed heavyweight champion of the world under Marquis of Queensberry rules.

Corbett was proudest of being called a "gentleman." He was obsessed with his own urbanity. He even enjoyed a measure of success in musical comedies and vaudeville, though always in supporting rather than leading roles.

"In 1910," he recalled in 1930 to Anthony Petronella, who later became President of the N.B.A., "I was doing an act in the American Theatre in New York. My car was parked outside on the street. It was one of the few automobiles that existed then. People would gather around it and just stare at it in awe. I paid this clean-cut kid to mind it for me. He'd sit behind the steering wheel and gloat. Well, 13 years later, Johnny Dundee whipped Criqui to win the world's featherweight title and I went to his dressing room to shake his hand. Johnny's face lit up like the Cheshire cat when he saw me. It was then that the truth came out. He confessed that he'd been that clean-cut kid who used to watch my car for me!"

Corbett was born on September 1, 1866, in San Francisco. He was one of eleven children. At his prizefighting best he stood 6 ft., 1 in. and scaled 178. "When I was seventeen, I was the amateur heavyweight champion of the Pacific Coast," he recalled once. "Nine years after that, I won the heavyweight championship of the world. It just goes to show you what a boy can do when he just takes care of himself."

Jim Corbett was the first world heavyweight champion to win the title with gloves under Marquis of Queensberry Rules. (UPI)

Jim graduated from high school (in those days quite an achievement) and then worked around the San Francisco docks before taking a job in a bank, where his mastery of mathematics served him well. He later joined the famed Olympic Club in San Francisco to "meet important people." The Club's boxing instructor was Professor Walter Watson, a fifty-five-year-old Englishman. He saw in Corbett the makings of a great prizefighter. Corbett spent long hours practicing in front of a full-length mirror so he could quickly spot any visible flaws.

Fighting only in and around San Francisco, Corbett built up a big reputation and a large following. He proved himself a conqueror. He destroyed Joe Choynski, Jake Kilrain, Mike Donovan and Dominick McCaffrey, four excellent contenders, one after the other in a carefully thought-out campaign. That left only Peter Jackson and Sullivan standing in his path to the world championship. He battled Jackson for 61 rounds to a draw, and received only $3,000. But with his victory over John L. came riches.

The end came on March 17, 1897, at Carson City, Nevada, four and a half years after winning the title. He gave in to public demand and put his crown on the line against Bob Fitzsimmons. An odd angle to the training camp activities was that Jim Jeffries had been engaged as rubber and trainer for Corbett. Jeff was given the job of keeping one of the champion's legs in shape, a different rubber being assigned to each arm and the other leg. Jeff was a big willing fellow, and often boxed with Corbett during the training period.

On the afternoon of the fight, there were two gangs at the ringside. In Corbett's corner was a delegation of six-gun manipulators headed by Wyatt Earp, known as "the quickest man on the draw in the West." Behind Fitzsimmons was an equally large delegation led by Bat Masterson, on whose gun were 18 *notches*.

The fight appeared to be Corbett's, right up to the 14th and last round. He dealt Fitz terrific punishment. In the sixth round, Fitz, groggy from body blows, dropped to the floor. Crouching, he wrapped his arms around Corbett's legs.

There was a situation for George Siler, the referee. Corbett called for him to count. If he allowed a foul, guns would roar across the crude ring. If he broke Fitz's grip on Corbett's legs, there would be just as heavy a barrage. He hesitated—then Fitz let go and sat down. And Siler began to count. Fitz was back on his feet at nine. Afterward, Corbett insisted that Fitz was on the floor fully 15 seconds.

Corbett had shot the works on the chance for a knockout. When he came out for the seventh he was tired. It was give and take for the next six rounds. Finally, in the 14th, a long swing by Fitz caught Corbett in the pit of his stomach. He went down, still conscious. He reached vainly for the ropes, and fell on his face. Bob Fitzsimmons was the new heavyweight champion of the world.

Gentleman Jim twice fought for the crown again—but not against Fitz. Ruby Robert wouldn't fight him. Jim Jeffries, by then champion, gave Corbett two chances to win the title back, and knocked him out each time. The first bout lasted 23 rounds, the second 10.

Jim Corbett had one weakness as a fighter. He lacked the killer instinct. There was nothing very brutal about him. He was fast physically and mentally, yet slow and deliberate in his speech. In and out of the ring he was always a great actor.

In 1928, when promoters were working overtime trying to build interest in the dismal Gene Tunney–Tom Heeney match, a boxing writer called on Billy Brady at his theatre in midtown Manhattan.

"I understand, Mr. Brady, that all old fighters are seen in the flattering light of distance, but can't you by some stretch of the imagination see Tunney as Corbett's equal as a boxer?" the reporter asked.

A look of utter disgust came over Brady's face.

"Young man," he said, "did you ever see Jim Corbett box?"

BOB FITZSIMMONS
(1862–1917)

Robert Prometheus Fitzsimmons, boxing's first triple titleholder, had iron in his system. Born at Cornwall, England, on June 4, 1862, and reared in New Zealand, although he is usually referred to as an Australian, Fitz was fighting bouts at eighteen and didn't stop until he was fifty-two. He fought for 34 years.

Ruby Robert won the middleweight championship from the Nonpareil Jack Dempsey in 1890, the heavyweight title from Jim Corbett when he was thirty-five, and in 1903, at the age of forty-one, took the light-heavyweight crown from George Gardner. He was still winning at forty-six. His last bout was a no-decision affair of six rounds against K.O. Sweeney at Williamsport, Pennsylvania, in 1914—at the age of fifty-two!

Fitz might not have looked like your idea of a heavyweight champion. From toenails to torso he would evoke only laughs in a bathing suit—knock-kneed, pipestem legs, hairy barrel chest, topped off by a freckled face, garnished with sparse red hair. His looks were deceiving, of course, for his heavyweight arms could deliver blows as devastating as sticks of dynamite.

"It has been written that Bob was hardly more than a middleweight and never more than a light-heavy when he fought the big fellows," Moose Taussig said once. "Don't you believe it. I remember when he was training with Jim Jeffries, and he tried to put big Jeff's coat on and found it too tight across the shoulders. Bob might have looked like a featherweight from the beltline down—but he was all heavyweight from the waist up."

Fitzsimmons had those belligerent qualities found in only two types of fighters: those who have had to club their way up through life, and those who have an inherent streak in them that makes it possible for them to shed their normal personality once the fight starts.

This inner viciousness even was apparent in Bob around the house, where he frequently slugged it out with a pet tiger cub that grew into dangerous maturity. When the beast would snap or snarl old Fitz would smash it. He'd fight it until it quit and often he came out with both arms badly clawed. Fitz was mean and tough when he was mad. He also had a curious sense of humor. He loved practical jokes, the cruder, the better. He delighted in frightening visitors half to death with his tiger. He wrestled with the beast until the rough and tumbles finally killed the jungle beast. Fitz had him stuffed. Man or beast, he was afraid of nothing.

By nature, however, Fitz was quite a sentimental, even-tempered man, slow to anger and swift to forgiveness. Rancor, hatred and enmity had no part of him. Unlike Sullivan, he admitted he felt sorry for opponents he knocked out. In his fight with the first Jack Dempsey at New Orleans, in 1891, when the Nonpareil was staggering around the dirt arena helpless and facing certain defeat, Fitz begged him to quit.

"The champion never quits," retorted Dempsey, puffing a red spray from his bloody lips. "You've got to knock me out first."

Fitz considered it an act of mercy to put him out of his misery by knocking him out. Dempsey fell face forward with his shattered mouth in the mud.

"To my dying day," Fitz said later, "I'll see Dempsey lying there with the little red bubbles busting as 'e breathed heavily into the red earth. I picked 'im up and 'elped carry 'im to 'is corner. I never lifted a braver man to 'is feet."

It was on February 21, 1896, when Fitz met Peter Maher on the Texas-Mexican border, that the term "ghost writer" first showed up on the American sports scene. An ex-prizefighter had been sent down by a Boston newspaper to cover the match, and he took a student from Harvard to do the writing for him. The fight lasted two punches. Maher floored Fitz with the first punch and Fitz knocked Peter out with the second. The Boston correspondent's lead (as written by his Harvard ghost) came out this way: "E'en as the mantle of the dewey eve settled over the silvery Rio Grande tonight . . ." It was signed by John Lawrence Sullivan!

There always has been a dispute among experts whether or not Fitz was really a very good boxer. Some argue that he lacked grace and was unscientific. Whatever his shortcomings, few fighters have been better equipped to mix and give and take. He moved with a shuffling, gangling gate. He stood flatfooted. His timing was perfect. He was a superb judge of distance. His punching, therefore, was deadly accurate.

For his championship fight with Corbett, Fitz weighed exactly 156½ pounds. He said one of the reasons he took the fight was to prove to the world that a middleweight could beat a heavyweight. Ironically, rumors circulated during the pre-fight buildup that Fitz had accepted a bribe to throw the fight. Fitz blamed the stories on enemies. "It's true I was offered $500,000 by some San Francisco gamblers to take a dive," Fitz admitted later, "and $250,000 by a bloke in New York. But I made up my mind to win, that if they carried me out a loser it'd be as a dead man."

Five weeks before the match, Fitz told the press he dreamed he would beat Corbett in seven rounds. "I dreamt I pasted Corbett a corker on the button and 'e went dead out," Fitz told them. "I often dream about my fights, and I 'ave never been wrong. Whenever a big fight is coming up, I always dream about 'ow it will end. It was so with poor Jack Dempsey, Maher, Hall, Creedon and all the rest. I dreamed each time that I won, even to the number of rounds. Before all my big bouts, I'm always going to bed nights looking for the Big Dream. Now I've dreamed of knocking Corbett out in the seventh round, and the applause in my dream was so loud it woke me up. So paste this in your hats and then watch me paste Corbett."

Fitz trained hard for Corbett. He was a big eater, even in training. An average training meal for him was half a chicken, two vegetables, and a rice or custard pudding. He also had an obsession for calf's foot jelly, which he consumed by the pound. For breakfast he ran to eggs, toast and coffee, ham and eggs, bacon and eggs, and lamb chops. His roadwork was systematic: 10, 12 or 15 miles a day were nothing to him. He didn't like training before crowds; he usually worked in private and hired sparring partners who would go at it hammer and tong. Robert Edgren, a sports writer of the day, once recalled seeing one sparring mate try to knock out Fitz. "He was cocky and sure he could outslug Bob," Edgren said. "He charged in head down, both arms pumping. Finally, just to teach him a lesson, Bob hit him on top of the head, knocking him cold for 10 minutes. Fitz was a rough bird in training, yet he thought it a big joke when any sparring partner managed to sock him."

In the Corbett fight, Fitz introduced Gentleman Jim to the left hook to the body, and Bob Davis, the New York correspondent who helped out in Fitz's corner during the bout, later heard two San Francisco doctors talking about the blow, and in one of his dispatches back to his paper introduced the "solar plexus punch" to the lexicon of boxing. Thus the Corbett-Fitzsimmons title fight of March 17, 1897, always will be remembered as "The Birth of the Solar Plexus Punch." It remains the most famous single punch in the long history of boxing.

Journalists of the period waxed poetic in their coverage of the fight. One Eastern writer compared the event with the "bloody carnivals of Julius Caesar and Titus Flaminius—when Trajan in one triumphal show exhibited 5,000 pairs of fighting men . . ."

Writing in the Thursday (March 18, 1897) edition of *The Boston Daily Globe*, correspondent J. N. Taylor called the fight "the most amazing match ever seen in America." He reported that the crowd was composed of people of every stripe: business and professional men from the East "who suddenly were called to Carson City on important business"; ranchers, cow punchers and card sharps, gun-toting bad men, buck riders, surething bettors, thugs, pickpockets, garroters—and "ladies." Yes, there were some women in attendance, causing Bill Madden, the ring announcer, to ask the gents to please be on their best behavior "and not forget that fact." Taylor described Corbett as "handsome, with the look of an athlete. His intelligent face suggests the actor rather than the pugilist. His skin is as white as marble, and muscles play over his body like quicksilver. His powerful legs taper down like the limb of an elk . . ."

Corbett went over to Fitz's corner before the fight and extended his hand, but Martin Julian, Fitz's manager, said, "No," and there was no handshake. "All right," Corbett said to him, "just as you like!"

Dan Steward, the promoter of the fight, asked Fitz one question: "Are you all right?"

"Never better," Fitz said.

Earlier that morning, Fitz calmly repeated the prediction he had made five weeks before: "I'll win in seven rounds."

"Which hand?" he was asked.

"Left 'and," he said.

"Chin or body?"

"I'll 'it 'im somewhere in the body," he said. "It ain't so easy to 'it 'is chin."

The bout was fought under a clear sky and blazing Nevada sun at Carson City. It began at high noon.

In the first three rounds, Corbett was all over Fitz with lefts and rights—"like a jealous terrier at an intruder," in the words of Taylor. "The fourth and fifth rounds were Corbett's with lots to spare." Taylor reported that Corbett had Fitz's face in the condition of "raw beef." In the sixth, Corbett knocked Fitz down for a count of nine, but couldn't finish him. Fitz's wife jumped out of her seat, rushed to ringside and called to her husband: "Come on, Bob, get up! Hit him in the slats!"

Between the sixth and seventh rounds, as Fitz sat in his corner, he confessed, "I can't get at 'im. 'E's too fast. Wait."

John L. Sullivan sat at ringside, convinced that Corbett would outdistance Fitz. John L. noted that Corbett's "spiteful little jabs in the face are weakening Fitz." He turned to Frank B. Dunn, of Boston, and said, "It was those same little punches that beat me in New Orleans. I couldn't find him (Corbett), and those punches not only wounded me but made me so mad I could have eaten a pound of tenpenny nails."

Corbett held the edge for 12 rounds, when Fitz started finding the range. In the 13th, he knocked out one of Corbett's front teeth with a sizzling left half-arm punch.

Just before the 14th round started, Fitz told one of his cornermen, "'Ave you got any money on you?"

"Eighty dollars in gold."

"Bet it all on the next round," Fitz said. "I am going to knock 'im out."

This time Fitz was correct. In a flash he saw a clean opening on Corbett's stomach and put all his weight behind a left-hand smash. "It was vigorous with pent-up energy," wrote Taylor. "It landed just under the ribs where they curl away from the breastbone. It was partly on the mark and partly under the heart. It was deadly. Corbett went down on his hands and knees, not in a fall, but he sank down like a person overcome by a great bodily weakness. His face became grizzly with

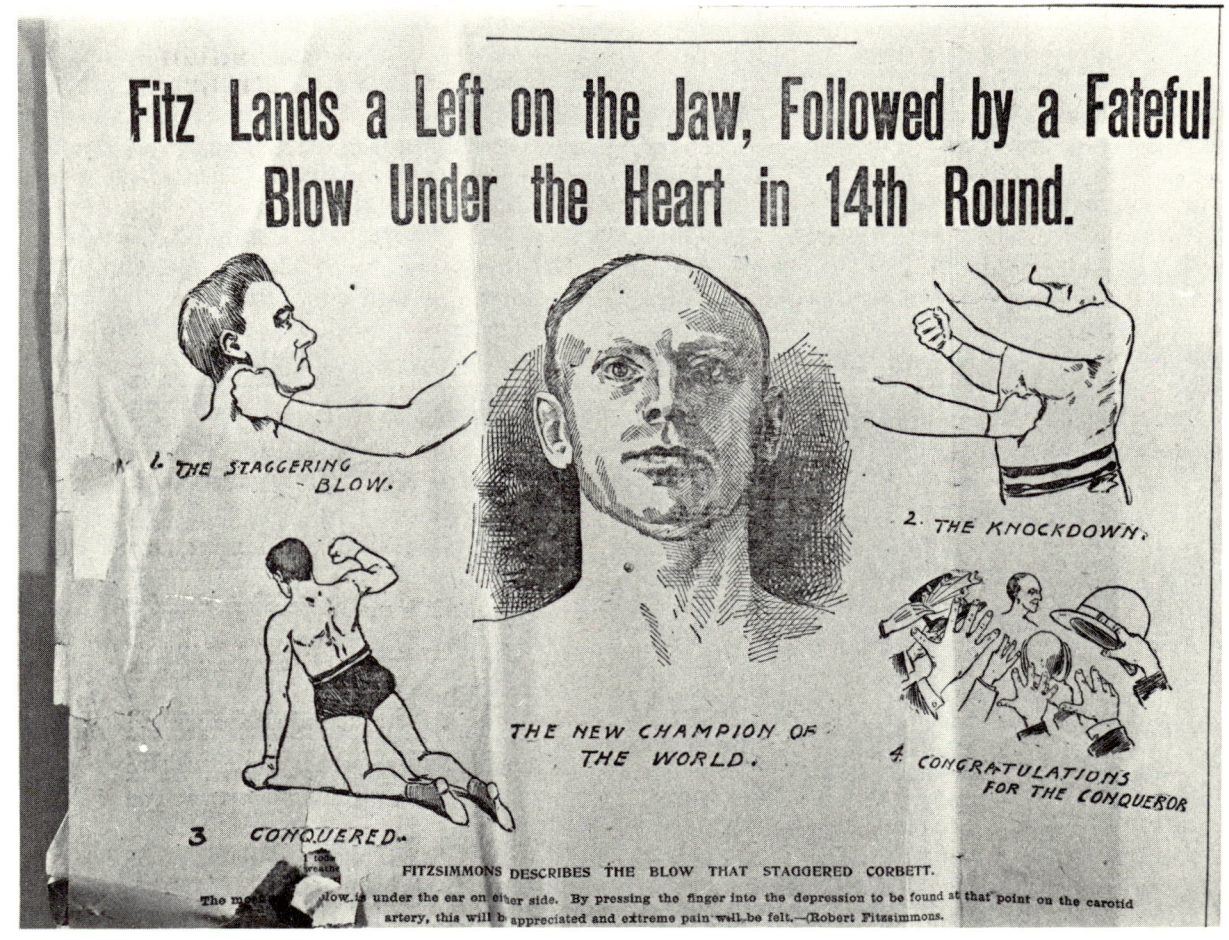

This is the way the March 18, 1897, *Boston Daily Globe* headlined Bob Fitzsimmons' 14th-round K.O. of Jim Corbett.

the ashen hue, superinduced by a tardy action of the heart. He groped with one hand, stretched and strained and groaned. He tried to rise, but the effort was painful. He couldn't get back on his feet before the toll reached the fatal 10. Bob Fitzsimmons was the new heavyweight champion of the world."

And then a crazy thing happened. Suddenly, Corbett, coming out of his fog, rushed across the ring and tried to smash Fitz in the face, demanding a return match. Taylor reported: "There were suspicious hip-pocket movements on every side of the ring. Several blackjacks were drawn. Then Corbett came to his senses and permitted himself to be led away to his dressing room."

After the fight, Fitz talked to reporters. "There were moments when my chances appeared very dim," he told them. "I was pretty distressed at times. But I finally got to 'im, and now I've evened up old scores with 'im."

Bill Brady, Corbett's manager, refused to accept defeat. When Fitz left the ring, Brady stood in center stage and shouted at the departing audience: "Ladies and gentlemen, I have $10,000 that says James J. Corbett can whip Robert Fitzsimmons in this same ring and any time Fitzsimmons is ready to make such a match."

A chorus of approval greeted the offer: "Good boy, Brady! We are still with you!" Brady turned to go, then turned suddenly and shouted: "I'll raise the amount to $20,000!" He climbed down off the stage a more dejected man than Corbett. He broke into tears. "This is terrible," he cried. "I never thought I'd see the day that Gentleman Jim would be laid out in the ring. But from the time my wife died I knew bad luck was coming. I've seen the cloud hovering over us, yet I had faith to the very last, and bet my money 8 to 5 on Jim." He broke out in another fit of tears.

Fitz won a total of $37,500 on the fight.

Later, Corbett met Fitz on the street. He told him he wanted a return match. "You've got to fight me again!" he shouted. "I'm entitled to another chance."

"I am through with the ring," said Fitz.

"If you don't fight me," said Jim, 'I'll lick you every time I meet you in the street."

"If you ever lay a hand on me outside the prize ring," Fitz replied very earnestly, "I'll kill you."

The threat was not repeated again.

Fitz did go on fighting, however. Matter of fact, he fought for another 17 years. On April 30, 1900, he established another record when he K.O.'d the 312-pound Ed Dunkhorst in two rounds in Brooklyn. Dunkhorst's 140-pound advantage stands as the biggest weight difference in history in a major prizefight.

Fitz did not coin the expression, "The bigger they are, the harder they fall," but he certainly acted on Joe Walcott's famous epigram.

Fitzsimmons finally retired in 1914, and died three years later of pneumonia at the age of fifty-five.

Despite stories to the contrary, he was not the first foreigner to win the heavyweight championship. He had already become a naturalized citizen of the United States by the time he won the title from Corbett.

JAMES J. JEFFRIES
(1875–1953)

Boxing skill relates inversely to age. The older a man gets, the better a fighter he was when young, according to the watery eye of memory. By reputation, Jim Jeffries could endure more punishment than any prizefighter since the cruel days of the cestus. Never beaten, never off his feet, until Jack Johnson did away with him in 1910 at Reno, he remains the tantalizing central figure in boxing's non-stop argument. Was he the greatest of them all? Maybe so, maybe not.

Oldtime referee Billy Roche, who bridged the gap between boxing generations, once told me that Jeff's iceberg bulk (220 lbs.) made him appear slower than he really was. His legs measured 25 inches at the thigh, 10 inches at the ankle. His size and rough manner gave him the title of "The Beast," and effete New Yorkers looked upon him as a throwback to primeval man.

"Jeff's looks were belying," Roche said. "Before age got to him, he had the acrobatic springiness of a circus tumbler in his legs. He was no lumbering ox, anchored to one spot, but a natural athlete who kept himself in shape by tramping through the Sierra Madre Mountains. Big as he was, he was agile enough to run 100 yards in 11 seconds, high jump 5 feet, 10 inches and hold his own in rough-and-tumble wrestling."

Dumb Dan Morgan went even further.

"Jeffries was my Champion of Champions," Dan said. "I firmly believe Big Jeff could have beaten any fighter who ever lived, with the exception of Brian Boru, the famed Irish hero-king. What a broth of a lad, that Baru! But outside of him—Jeffries. He was a great fighter. He beat Fitzsimmons, the greatest one-punch slugger, twice; and he also outboxed and knocked out the father of American boxing, Jim Corbett, twice. He fought anyone they wanted to match him with."

Ned Brown, one-time Sports Director-columnist for the old *New York World*, and later Jack Dempsey's press agent, tended to hedge when I asked him to name the greatest heavyweight of all time. Ned covered the Jeffries years.

"Jim Jeffries may not have been the greatest heavyweight champion who ever lived, but he wasn't the worst, either," Ned told me. "When he finally did reach his peak, he was far and away the best heavyweight in the world at the time. He was one of the most powerfully built, could take a solid punch, and had acquired a fair amount of boxing skill by the time he tangled with Jim Corbett in their second match. Jeff had as deadly a wallop as any I've ever seen. Like Roche and Morgan, remember, I, too, *saw* Jeffries fight, when he was good. Even when he was the famous 'hollow shell' in Reno, he was able to stand up under the heavy barrage of punches by Jack Johnson, himself a real terrific heavyweight.

"But you can throw out that Reno affair. That wasn't the real Jeffries. I wish they had fought earlier. In August, 1904, they nearly did. The two had first met in a San Francisco saloon. Johnson demanded a chance at the title, accused Jeff of ducking him and received an interesting invitation. 'There's a cellar in this place,' Jeff said. 'Tell you what I'll do. I won't meet you in a ring because you've got no name and we wouldn't draw flies. But I'll go downstairs with you and lock the door on the inside. The one who comes out with the key will be the champ.' Johnson told Jeff he must be nuts. 'I'm serious,' Jeff said. 'I'll go downstairs with you right now.' Johnson walked out.

"It was a different story, six years later, when Tex Rickard lured Jeff from retirement to fight Johnson as a white hope. Johnson was now champion. He was 26, in his prime. By this time, Jeff was portly, bald, far over the hill and forced to train off 65 pounds in three months. It was widely reported that Jeff was 'doped' at Reno against Johnson, but I was there and can truthfully say he was suffering from a dysentery attack and was so weak he spent the final pre-fight hours in bed. Even then it took Johnson 15 rounds to put Jeff off his feet. He took nine counts and got up. He was dropped twice more and got up. Finally, his seconds leaped into the ring and it was all over. Jeff got $177,000 for the fight, but he said it wasn't worth it. Johnson never licked him, he said, age did.

James J. Jeffries' size and rough manner gave him the title of "The Beast." (UPI)

"About the most futile thing to do is try to compare heavyweight champions. Boxing is a sport that cannot be accurately measured by the clock, scale or tape, like some games. It just can't be done, because there's no real yardstick for comparison. Besides, it's usually largely a matter of personal opinion, plus prejudice, for or against. But if you want to talk about *good* fighters, give me Ketchel, Papke, Sam Langford, Joe Gans and Benny Leonard and Dempsey—and you can have all the rest."

From Carroll, Ohio, where Jim was born, April 15, 1875, the Scotch-Irish Jeffries moved to southern California a few years

HEAVYWEIGHTS

later. His father was a Bible-shouting, itinerant revivalist, always on the road; Ma Jeffries was the family anchor. Jim weighed 200 lbs. when he was fifteen. At seventeen, he was a good journeyman boilermaker. From there he drifted into the mines at Temecula.

Returning to Los Angeles, Jim started hanging around the old Los Angeles Athletic Club on Spring Street. That's how he met Van Court, the silver-haired boxing instructor who had taught Jim Corbett.

"I saw him playing handball and noticed how remarkably he handled his huge frame— he was but a big kid then," Van Court recalled once. "After talking with him I learned he'd been a boilermaker and was interested in boxing and wanted to join the Club. Right then and there I told some of the Club officials that Jeff had the makings of a world's champion, but they showed little interest. A few months later, Billy Gallagher took Jeffries to San Francisco and matched him against Dan Long, who was later a Los Angeles police lieutenant. Jeff fought him on July 2, 1896, and knocked him out in the second round. Every time Long saw Jeff in Los Angeles after that he shook his fist angrily at him. He never forgot that punch Jeff gave him 30 years before.

"Well, Gallagher finally arranged for Jeff to help Corbett prepare for his fight with Fitzsimmons. They told Jeff a lot of bunk about

Jack Johnson was first black to hold the world heavyweight championship. In 1910, at Reno, Nevada, an aging Jim Jeffries, who had retired as champion in 1908, returned to the ring and was knocked out in the 15th round in futile attempt to dethrone Johnson. (UPI photo)

Corbett and scared the daylights out of the big fellow. So instead of going to Corbett's training camp, he returned to L.A. I got busy and wrote to Corbett and he wrote back and said to send Jeff on."

In March, 1897, Jeffries was officially hired as a sparring partner for Corbett. In the privacy of a walled-in handball court, the two men squared off for the first time. Exactly what happened has many versions; it made good boxing gossip for many years. The truth, Jeffries revealed before his death, was this:

"I was a greenhorn and didn't expect Corbett to do more than box and take it easy. But

Garbed in what the well-dressed referee of 1908 wore, champion Jim Jeffries officiated a battle between Phil Schlossberg, light-heavyweight champion of the Navy, and the U.S.S. Missouri's W. Alteri before packed house in Los Angeles. (From author's collection)

the first time I led my right, he countered with a real smash to the mouth. Then he let me have it again. It hurt and I went wild. I grabbed Corbett and threw him into a corner of the court and when he bounced out I took a swing and knocked him right back again. Billy Delaney, my trainer, grabbed me. Charlie White, Corbett's second, began cursing me. Corbett covered up fast. He laughed and said we'd had enough. He'd have fired me, I think, only it would have made too much talk."

Manhandling the world's champion hadn't been Jeffries' aim, but it made him a curiosity item and opened the door of boxing arenas in San Francisco to get some fights.

Jeffries fought only one preliminary bout in his entire career. He won the world championship from Bob Fitzsimmons, the 3–1 favorite, at Coney Island, June 9, 1899, when Fitz went down in a heap in the 11th and didn't get up.

Jeffries started out as a stand-up fighter, was doubled up by a blow above the liver by Joe Choynski, a triphammer puncher, in his seventh bout, and continued to fight after that in a crouch. That was in 1897. Never again did Jeffries rush in as a stand-up target. He came out in the "Jeffries crouch"—kids everywhere imitated it—with left arm extended in a swinging boom movement, body protected. He could hook the left or throw a long right with equal power from the crouch. As defenses go, it was fairly elemental, yet served the purpose.

Within 20 months after Choynski, Jeffries was champion of the world.

Weighing 220 at his peak, Jeff broke three of Tom Sharkey's ribs, laying him up for months; Joe Goddard, the Australian Iron Man, was a hospital case after being floored four times in the first round; Fitzsimmons suffered two cracked ribs in one of his two losing bouts against Jeff; and Mexican Pete Everett, who was supposed to be fearless, fled from him and was stoned cockeyed with a piledriver right to the middle of his back.

"No style to him," Tex Rickard spoke of Jeffries, "but he's the hardest hitter I ever saw. And that includes Dempsey."

Jeffries, himself, ignored the rating polls. He thought they were damned nonsense. He had fought the best of the heavyweights of his era, defended his title eight times, without loss or even being on the canvas. Twice he K.O.'d Corbett and twice he K.O.'d Fitzsimmons.

Jeff had the most unfortunate personality of all the big-boy champions. Untalkative, disliking crowds, a poor public speaker, he was only respected by the country, never idolized. However, he is best remembered as a man of character. Gamblers admitted he was untouchable. No scandal ever touched him. He married once, in 1904. It lasted 37 years, until Freida Jeffries' death in a traffic accident in 1941. Billy Delaney trained him all the way. Their only contract was a handshake.

James Jackson Jeffries died a near-millionaire in 1953 at Burbank, California.

TOMMY BURNS
(1881–1955)

Shortness figured prominently in the career of Tommy Burns. He was the shortest (5 ft., 7 in.) man ever to hold the world heavyweight crown—and he won the shortest world heavyweight title fight on record when he K.O.'d Jem Roche in 1 minute, 28 seconds in Dublin, Ireland, on March 17, 1908.

Labeled a "chump among champs, and a champ among chumps," chunky (175 lbs.) Tommy made a little ability go a long way. He was boxing's original globetrotter, was highly adept at the game of tag. He led Jack Johnson on a merry chase around the world for several years before Li'l Arthur caught up with him in 1908 and knocked him out.

Christened Noah Brusso, Tommy was born at Hanover, Canada, on June 17, 1881. One of the few fighters who fought without a manager, he started out as a welterweight, and gradually built his body up to heavyweight class by playing lacrosse.

Despite his size, Burns harbored tremendous self-confidence and courage. He flourished in an age when the heavyweights were at an extremely low ebb. Jim Jeffries had retired after destroying all solid opposition, leaving the title to Marvin Hart, at best a third-rater. Tommy's claim to the crown was based on his 20-round decision over Hart in 1906, and another 20-round victory a year later over light-heavyweight Philadelphia Jack O'Brien.

Little Tommy Burns was thus a heavyweight champion of dubious authority.

Between October 2, 1906, and December

26, 1908, Burns defended the championship 11 times, mostly in Europe. In his final defense, in Sydney, Australia, Jack Johnson toyed with him from the opening bell to the finish. The bout lasted 39 minutes, when Johnson finally grew bored by the travesty and knocked "Tahmy" out in the 14th.

Little Tommy Burns lost his claim to world heavyweight title in 1908, when Jack Johnson here kayoed him in the 14th round in Sydney, Australia. (Photo from Ernie Jensen collection)

While there is plenty of room for argument as to who was the greatest heavyweight champion up to the retirement of Gene Tunney in 1928, there's very little doubt that Burns was the worst. Nonetheless, Tommy had a keen business sense and got a lot of mileage out of what he had. Not even Luis Firpo, a champion pinchpenny, was able to hold a candle to Burns when it came to extracting the last dollar out of ring purses. Tommy received $30,000 for the Johnson fight, for example, while Jack had to be satisfied with $5,000.

Following retirement from the ring (he fought only six times in his last 11 years), Tommy settled down at Bremerton, Washington, and ran a pub. Jim Rondeau, the referee, remembers the Burns of the pre-World War II era. "He certainly didn't resemble an ex-heavyweight champion of the world," Rondeau said. "He was more like an ex-middleweight. I grew up in Bremerton and remember Tommy as a stately man, very soft-spoken, friendly. He didn't even look like a fighter. His nose wasn't even bashed. Everybody at home loved him. He was well-fixed financially, was a good businessman, and had the respect of everyone."

Tommy Burns later heard the "call." He entered the ministry, traveled diligently in the Pacific Northwest as an evangelist. He moved to Vancouver, British Columbia, where he succumbed to a heart attack in 1955.

JACK JOHNSON
(1878–1946)

Till the very end, Jack Johnson the man and Jack Johnson the legend flourished. At his peak, he was Li'l Artha, the Black Avenger—a big, flamboyant, fun-loving, lecherous rebel who took and gave what he wanted, when he felt like it. He was everything that society of 60 years ago couldn't tolerate: the son of a slave who became king.

Al Stump, a major biographer of legendary heroes of sport, once zeroed in on the Galveston giant, concluding that historians heretofore had been too soft on him. "Johnson was a rake and riot-maker, perjurer, cheat, fornicator, jail-dodger, and lover of white women almost unequaled in American history," Al wrote harshly. "Most white people wanted to hang him from the highest tree."

Stump went on to point out that Li'l Artha broke a few other taboos as well, such as the code handed down from John L. Sullivan which prohibited a Negro from holding the heavyweight championship of the world. While he held it, from 1908–1915, some 19 persons died in race riots caused by Johnson's activities. "As for white women," Stump wrote, "he loved them freely and married three of them."

"The public fails to understand my feelings toward different kinds of women," Johnson said once. "I didn't court white women because I thought I was too good for the others. It was just that they always treated me better. I never had a colored girl that didn't two-time me."

Li'l Artha's guile and urbane manner fascinated almost every female he met. "His great, staring eyes simply devoured one," sighed Gaby Deslys, the French actress. "His wit—*enchantement!*" In conning them, he had other weapons—a supreme arrogance, recklessness, and beyond all else a driving need for social equality. As a scullery boy in Galveston, in his youth, he used the "coon walk," or dirt area bordering the street. As a man, he drove the flashiest cars, owned a Chicago saloon called the Cabaret du Champion, played in *Aida* in grand opera and plated seven of his top teeth in 14-karat gold. He owned trotting horses, suits of silk and velvet, and thumped the bass viol with Johnson's Troubadours, his personal jazz band. Once he spent six weeks as a paid companion of a famous female silent film star.

"I'll make them (white people) kow-tow to me," he promised, after winning the heavyweight crown from Tommy Burns. "I'll make them small beer."

Of his three white wives, one became an alcoholic, one was cast out by her friends, and one killed herself within 11 months of the ceremony.

"The man was a disaster to anyone who came near him," remarked Archie Moore. "American blacks are still paying for him."

"He was a bum—a dead loss," said Jim Corbett. "He hated everybody—his managers, Tex Rickard, who made him rich, his women. He even hated himself. It isn't generally known, but three times Johnson tried to commit suicide, but couldn't pull the trigger."

For seven years, Li'l Artha was a fugitive, on the dodge in Europe and Latin countries from a Mann Act white-slavery conviction and owing his government one year and a day in the jug. The indictment, handed down by a Chicago federal jury in 1912, accused him of transporting a white girl, Lucille Cameron, across a state line for immoral purposes. She later married him. Johnson was convicted anyway. He always denied his guilt, claiming he'd been framed by a moral-welfare group. To avoid imprisonment, he fled to Paris.

No one of his era dared to broach the subject of integration—but Johnson did. He made his own rules, beginning in Sydney, Australia, in 1908, when he knocked out Tommy Burns in 14 rounds, for the title, and continuing into the 1920s.

The 220-pound, catfooted John Arthur Johnson came about as close to being an unbeatable fighter as ever lived. Once on the same night, he met and walloped two tough punchers, Joe Jeanette and Walter Johnson. Twice within 10 days he met the great Sam Langford, and both times left Langford hanging on the ropes, limp and bloody. The so-called "white hopes" fell apart when he struck—Fireman Jim Flynn with a cracked jaw, Bob Fitzsimmons glassy-eyed, Stanley Ketchel talking to himself, and old Jim Jeffries, never before on the floor, blindly appealing to his cornermen to come rescue him. In 1921, at the age of forty-four, Johnson boxed the ears off Luis Angel Firpo, 25, in two rounds and had him hanging on. At almost fifty, he went 15 rounds and whipped Pat Lester, a good heavyweight.

Many critics still class Johnson as the best boxer-counterhitter combination of all time, as vicious as Dempsey, and faster; smarter, more powerful than Joe Louis. When the Boxing Hall of Fame opened in 1954, Johnson's was the first name ratified.

Johnson was a reputation-breaker. He could make almost any opponent look bad, without looking invincible himself. It is doubted if the prize ring has known of a more muscular champion. Yet despite his size, he used his colossal strength chiefly for defensive purposes. He gave the lasting impression of always fighting under wraps, of never going all-out.

"I had the feeling he could demolish an opponent any time he chose," Dumb Dan Morgan said. "And yet it is difficult to really rate him, because he never fought a first-class white heavyweight. You can throw out the so-called Jeffries match. That dull-eyed, flabby man he beat was Jim Jeffries in name only. But of all the heavyweight headliners, Johnson would have given the real Jeffries his greatest battle."

"I won't argue with that," added Jack Dempsey. "The farther back you go, the tougher fighters were, and Johnson was the top guy among the oldtimers. He was all elbows and arms, the greatest catcher of punches who ever lived. And he could fight all night. He was a combination of Jim Corbett and Louis. I'm glad I never had to fight him."

Li'l Artha's mother was a very small woman, 4 ft., 8 in., who bore nine children in a Galveston shacktown, aided only by a midwife. Jack was born—he always claimed—in 1878. There were those who insisted he had shaved five or six years off his age. His father, also pint-sized, was a former Tennessee slave and a janitor by trade.

Johnson began his professional career in 1897, and was still fighting exhibitions in 1945. Only Fitzsimmons fought longer. Most of his victories as champion were handy but unviolent. He avoided scoring knockouts, as a rule, because he preferred to demonstrate his defensive speed of hand and eye. An exception was his bout with Ketchel. Johnson had understood that the match was to be nothing more than an exhibition of sparring between a famous big fighter and a famous little fighter. So when Ketchel swung his right hand full force and floored Johnson in the 12th round, Johnson got back up and hit Stanley in the face so hard that his lips were impaled on his teeth. Ketchel was 10 minutes regaining consciousness.

The Ketchel fight convinced everyone, including Jim Jeffries, that Jeff would have to come out of retirement to redeem the white race's honor in person. The bout took place in Reno, on July 4, 1910. George L. (Tex) Rickard was the promoter and referee. Jeffries was then thirty-five, three years older than Johnson. He was slow and rusty. The betting favored him at odds of 10–7, however. Johnson won the fight easily. He kept up a steady, teasing chatter, chopped away at Jeffries at will, and knocked him out in the 15th. On the levees and in Darktown slums, he was now the Black Avenger, come to raise an abject race from its knees, and black people everywhere celebrated like it was the first day of the world.

As the first black man to hold the world heavyweight championship, Jack Johnson went on to earn an estimated $1,000,000. Much of it went into lavish night clubs and cafes in Chicago, Paris, Juarez, Barcelona and Los Angeles. Each had attached to it what Johnson (a fluent linguist, speaking French, German and Spanish) called his *"joie de fille room,"* or harem quarters. Li'l Artha was studious and widely read. He drank beer or vintage wines through a straw and loved to tell tall stories about himself. He claimed, for example, that before the Tommy Burns fight in Australia, on a bet, he chased a kangaroo—an animal famous for its speed and endurance—until the kangaroo, finding itself outclassed, dropped dead.

With jail always beckoning at home, Johnson played the roaming rake for seven years. If he ever repented, the record fails to show it. "I'm so damned illegal back home," he told friends in Heidelberg, "that they even cut my picture out of all the school books."

Because of his exile, Johnson had to fight Jess Willard outside the U.S., in Havana, on April 5, 1915. The bout was advertised for 45 rounds. Johnson was guaranteed $30,000, plus the European and South American rights to the motion pictures of the match. In return, he claimed later, he had agreed to lose, in the 10th round. He also hinted that the U.S. Government would be inclined to make a deal (he never revealed who his authority was) and not send him to prison if he let Willard win.

"I was willing to make any sacrifice," wrote Johnson in his autobiography, later. "I did not really expect to go to prison when I returned to the United States. The main thing against me was that I, a black man, held the championship."

Whatever the merits of Johnson's account, the fight was a sluggish one for the first 25 rounds. No important blows were struck by either man. Johnson tired in the 25th round, however. Referee Jack Welsh had to "call" him out from his corner at the start of the 26th round, and Johnson "tottered" to the center of the ring. Willard landed two light punches, and then a right uppercut. Johnson fell to the floor, rolled over on his back, one glove shielding his eyes from the blazing sun, and was counted out.

The following day, Johnson gave out a number of moody statements to the press. He said it was "the old story of age." He said that Willard was "too big for the average-sized heavyweight ever to beat." He spoke of "getting away from crowds." He spoke of "going to China."

Thus ended the "white-hope era" in boxing.

Johnson spent most of the period from 1916 to 1918 in Spain, where he won a few fights. In 1919, he went to Mexico, to make a try for a pardon from the American government on his Mann Act sentence. He was turned down. On July 20, 1920, he surrendered to federal authorities in San Diego, California, and was taken to Leavenworth Prison, in Kansas, where he served all but a few days of his sentence. He was released on July 9, 1921. His last *official* prizefight was in mid-May, 1928, when one Billy Hartwell kayoed him in six. After that, all of his ring appearances were listed as "exhibitions."

Li'l Artha spent the Thirties appearing as a

sideshow attraction at Hubert's celebrated museum and flea circus on West 42nd Street, in Manhattan. John Lardner said he used to call on Johnson at the museum occasionally. Johnson talked freely, and with a fine, romantic feeling, about his life. Once, he paused, stared coldly at Lardner, and said, "Just remember, whatever you write about me, that I was a *man*—and a good one."

One afternoon, Dumb Dan Morgan dropped down at Hubert's Museum and Flea Circus and caught Johnson's itchy act. Li'l Artha was an expert on fleas and had trained them to do everything but close-order drill. But Morgan was unimpressed.

"Jack, what are you wasting your time with fleas for?" Morgan asked. "Why don't you get yourself a heavyweight and make him into a champion and get rich again?"

Johnson flashed that golden grin.

"Listen, Morgan," he said, "these fleas can think better than the heavyweights around today."

In his final, downhill years, J. J. was "needy" much of the time. For a while, he considered himself haughtily above the handouts customarily given ex-pugs. In the 1920s and part of the 1930s, he traveled the revival circuit, urging more hygienic and moral behavior by Americans. He was all action then—preaching Confucianism, operating a cabaret in Hollywood, squiring actress Lupe Velez around town, selling rubbing liniment, and, of course, training his fleas.

He was always himself, believing fully that the good man takes what he wants, to the last. But in a career shot through with larceny and lies, nowhere, during his final struggle for survival, is there any evidence of just how broke Li'l Artha was.

This reminded Freddie Steele, who enjoyed moderate success in motion pictures after holding the middleweight championship (1936–38), of an incident that happened on his Hollywood set in '45.

"In the middle of filming, one day," Freddie recalled recently, "one of the script girls told me I had a visitor waiting at the main

Because of his exile, Jack Johnson had to fight Jess Willard outside the U.S., in Havana, on April 5, 1915; fight was a sluggish one, Willard winning questionable K.O. in 26th round. (Photo by UPI)

gate. Since I wasn't needed in that particular scene, I went out to see who it was. This big black put out a gnarled hand to shake mine, and said, 'Freddie, I'm broke and need a job bad. I'll take anything. Can you use your influence and get me a job as an extra?' He looked terrible. He was unshaven, haggard, his clothes wrinkled. 'Wait here, Jack,' I told him, 'I'll talk to the producer.' I went to the producer but he brushed me off, saying it was against studio policy to hire blacks. So I had to go back to Jack and tell him a phony story that there was no work available. As he turned to leave, head bowed, I then slipped Jack Johnson a $20 bill. Eight months later, he was dead."

Jack Johnson always had a prophecy about the way the end would come. "I'll die in an auto accident," he told Dan Morgan. That famous golden smile was clenched tightly in place at around 5:30 P.M. of June 10, 1946, when he drove his Lincoln Zephyr at a furious speed over the white dividing line on U.S. Route 1, 20 miles north of Raleigh, North Carolina, and skimmed a truck, hit a ditch, then a power pole. At sixty-eight, Jack Johnson had crossed the white line for the last time.

JESS WILLARD
(1881–1968)

Several thousand people attended the funeral of Jack Johnson in Chicago, among them Jess Willard. When Jess was asked by a reporter to comment on Li'l Arthur's death, he said that Johnson had been the greatest of all heavyweight champions.

"What happened in Havana, then?" the reporter wanted to know.

"I hit him with a good uppercut," said Willard calmly.

Twenty-two years passed between Johnson's defeat by Willard and the accession of the next black heavyweight champion—Joe Louis.

At 6 ft., 6¼ inches, Jess Willard was the tallest man ever to hold a world boxing title. This was ½-inch taller than Primo Carnera.

Born on the edge of an Indian reservation in Pottawatomie County, Kansas, on December 29, 1881, Willard ranks close to the top as the rawest contender ever to win the world heavyweight championship. He was twenty-six even before he saw a boxing glove; twenty-nine before he fought in his first professional bout. Until then, he rode wild horses, hunted, developed endurance and worked as a plains teamster in Kansas. Hence his nickname, "Cowboy Jess."

Big Jess Willard was twenty-six years old before he saw a boxing glove; twenty-nine before he fought his first professional bout. (UPI)

Willard was a direct product of boxing's White Hope fanaticism 65 years ago. He had about as much natural fighting instinct as Carnera, who had less than a rabbit.

The late Robert Edgren, syndicated sports columnist-cartoonist, pointed out that Jess was nothing but a big clown at the outset. "Partly because he was embarrassed fighting smaller men, and partly because he liked to get a laugh out of the crowd," Edgren said. "But he cut out all the horsing around when he learned he might get a chance to fight Johnson for the championship. Then he trained seriously for 10 months. The last part of it, at El Paso and Havana, was very earnest indeed. He became so serious in his workouts near the end that his sparring mates were afraid of him. Jim Savage, a very good heavyweight who did most of the work with Jess, told me one day: 'That big lug is getting a

HEAVYWEIGHTS

wild look in his eye. I think he's a bit crazy. I've got to duck quick or he'd take my head off with his punches. He's got us all shell-shocked.'"

There was not much about Willard to grip the public imagination, apart from his size and the fact that he had recovered the heavyweight title for the Caucasian race from Johnson in 1915. Johnson later claimed he'd laid down in that 26th round. As evidence that he told the truth, there is a photograph of Li'l Arthur comfortably sprawled on the floor, shielding his eyes from the bright sun.

Willard robustly denied there was anything tawdry about the way he won the championship. "I hardly think he'd have waited 26 rounds before taking a dive," Jess said, logically. "If he quit I didn't know about it. But if he did, I wish it'd been sooner. It was godawful hot in that Havana sun and he could have saved us both a lot of punishment."

Before his fateful fight with Jack Dempsey, Willard defended his crown only once. He romped 10 rounds of no-decision against Frank Moran in what was the great Tex Rickard's first promotion in New York. Otherwise, Jess remained idle most of his years (1915–1919) as champion. It wasn't until 1918 that he got busy and warmed up in two exhibitions against Jim Golden and Tim Logan for his title match with Dempsey.

Critics of Willard have long argued that his enthusiasm for thrift cost him the world championship. On that July 4, 1919, day in Toledo, he had no smart and seasoned helper or manager in his corner. "Willard managed himself, trained himself, and tossed in his own towel," was the charge against him.

It was the first major outdoor prizefight in the U.S. since 1910, when Johnson knocked out Jeffries in Reno. Promoter Tex Rickard guaranteed Willard $100,000 to fight Dempsey.

Willard decided he had had enough just before the start of the fourth round. The second and third rounds were anti-climatic. Dempsey was arm-weary from punching, and failed to knock Willard down again. Willard frequently charged in later years, and Dempsey just as frequently denied, that much of this arm-weariness could be accounted for by the fact that the tape on Dempsey's hands, beneath his gloves, was smeared with cement.

Walter Monahan and Ray Archer, two of

To his dying day, Jess Willard was convinced that Jack Dempsey's gloves were "loaded" on that hot Fourth of July, 1919, in Toledo, Ohio, as The Tiger Man crushed him in three bloody rounds to win the title. (UPI)

Willard's cut-rate assistants, watched Dempsey put the tape on himself. "Watch close," Dempsey kidded them, "and maybe you'll pick up a tip or two on how this is done. Now I wrap it over here, like this, and then I bring it over here, and then I take some more tape and bring it across here."

Willard's boys stood with their mouths hanging open.

Professor Billy McCarney was another reliable eyewitness to the taping of Dempsey's hands before the fight.

"He had enough black bicycle tape on there, over the bandages, to patch a battleship," McCarney said, "but no cement. He didn't need it."

Dumb Dan Morgan also testified there was no truth in Willard's assertions that Dempsey's hands were loaded. "Monahan was with Dempsey in the dressing room all the time before the fight," Dan told me. "And when Jack got into the ring, Jess carefully walked over and examined his hands. Meanwhile, one of Dempsey's handlers watched every move Willard made. There were no shenanigans, everything was on the up and up."

Willard went broke after losing the title, but became financially secure again in 1923 when he K.O.'d Floyd Johnson and was flattened by Luis Angel Firpo.

Big Jess had height, reach and weight. He seldom cut loose except when hurt. Then he was explosive, especially with a right-hand uppercut. The records bear out that statement: on August 22, 1913, Willard clubbed Bull Young flush on the jaw with that big right fist—and *killed* him.

JACK DEMPSEY
(1895–)

Dan Morgan was asked thousands of questions in hundreds of fistic debates during the 67 years he appeared at benefits, smokers and at veterans' hospitals following World Wars I and II. One question led all the rest: Who would win a Jack Dempsey–Joe Louis fight if both were in their prime?

"That's easy," Morgan told me. *"Dempsey would knock out Louis in a single round!* Here's how. When the bell rang, Louis would move to mid-ring and wait on Dempsey's first move. He'd be straight up, ready to counter any punch thrown at him. Dempsey is a bundle of nerves. Jack stands with his back to Louis till the bell sounds, then is across the ring like a flash, down low and weaving. Joe can't jab, counter or hit him with an uppercut because Dempsey's head is bobbing from side to side. Dempsey would drive left and right-hand smashes to the body. If Joe attempts to block these, Dempsey would paralyze his arm. For the first two minutes,

Jack Dempsey was the most spectacular fighter ever to hold the world heavyweight championship, the first to draw a million-dollar gate, a figure he exceeded five times. When the Manassa Mauler fought, things happened that never happened before. (UPI)

Dempsey has the lead and is throwing knockout punches at Louis' stomach. Joe is finally hurt, backs away and in the final minute of the first round Dempsey shifts from the body to the head. A left hook, a short straight right, one or two more left hooks and another right and Louis is down for the full count. I don't think Louis would hit Dempsey more than two or three real solid shots in the entire fight. Jack's style would completely baffle Joe."

Morgan believed Dempsey had the three qualities which produce greatness in the prize ring and make a man a fighter for the ages. These are: *ferocity, cold-bloodedness* and *gameness*. He also felt that Jack exemplified boxing's cardinal rule: There's no place for pity in the ring. "If he's a good fighter," Dan said, "the most easy-going fellow outside the ring may become the most vicious man alive once a fight starts. That's what makes boxing such a tough game for a real human being. Many fighters can't bear to hammer a helpless, bleeding opponent until he is pulp. They remember him as he looked at the start, fresh, clean, strong. They don't want to *hurt* him. They *can't*. But look at Dempsey. He was probably the greatest rough-and-tumble fighter who ever lived. He might as well not have worn boxing gloves. He was so wild the night he fought Firpo he hit the South American three times while Firpo was on the floor! Referee Johnny Gallagher had to pull Dempsey off him. I thought Jack was going to bite Firpo."

Dempsey had Firpo down nine times and knocked him out in the second round of the wildest, most action-soaked fight in history.

Dempsey once told Ned Brown that he never rated himself much of a fighter. He said he might have been a lot better if there hadn't been so many rules. "You're in there for three-minute rounds with gloves on and a referee," Dempsey said. "That's not real fighting." Like Harry Greb, Jack would have much preferred an "anything goes" policy.

Jack made the starkest picture of a fighting man inside the ropes—scowling, dark-bearded, mahogany-skinned, busted-nose, and hair cropped close and high above his ears. "He had the speed of a lightweight, hand and foot," said Joe Benjamin, the old lightweight contender. "He could run the hundred in close to 10 seconds. From the hips up he was heavily muscled, and he could box with anybody when he wanted. He *had* to be a good boxer to go 15 sizzling rounds with Tommy Gibbons out at Shelby. That took skill. Jack's hands were hard as rocks. He was the perfect fighting machine—hands, legs, fighting brain and disposition. He was simply a superhuman wild man."

Dempsey said he was at his all-time peak the day he won the title from Willard. He was twenty-four and in rawhide condition. He had been fighting regularly since 1910, with or without gloves, and he had learned something in almost every fight. He had a desperate hunger for the championship.

"The fight game is the toughest game on earth," Dempsey said. "I started when I was eight. I had an older brother who was a boxer, so of course I had to get a pair of small boxing gloves and go to it with four or five kids in our neighborhood. Most of it was slugging, swinging with all we had. When you start at eight you feel comfortable with gloves on in a ring. I doubt many people knew when I fought Willard at the age of twenty-four that I'd already had 16 years' boxing experience.

"When I started, I decided to put all I had on offense and let the defensive side of boxing take care of itself. But I studied that phase more than most people knew. In one of my first fights in New York I met John Lester Johnson, a big, rough black man. I was getting along all right until one round when I came in with my left elbow too high. Johnson was smart enough to lift it a little higher and then crack two of my ribs with a terrific body punch.

"That punch didn't do me any good that night but it helped me a lot, later on. It taught me something about body protection. As I went along, every time I got hit I learned something and found ways to improve my defense that wouldn't weaken my attack. I built up my punching power largely through a heavy bag. I don't believe many people appreciate how hard and how long I worked slugging away at that big bag. That wasn't a matter of a few weeks but a hard, steady grind for several years.

"I counted mostly on power and speed. I used to weave and bob to give my opponent a moving target to hit at, but I guess there wasn't much deception about it. My idea was to get in close in a hurry and get in one good punch. If the other fellow started a swing I tried either to beat him to it or to take it and let him have a harder one in return."

The partnership of Dempsey and his manager, Jack Kearns, was one of the closest in the records of sport, while it lasted.

"Doc is my guy," Dempsey often said.

They rode day coaches together in their lean years and shared rooms in fleabag hotels. Until the Willard fight opened the way to wealth, they did not have a quarter between them.

"I didn't know if I was going to be in a fight or a footrace," Dempsey said of the Willard fight. "I thought I could knock him out in the

Grim, dark-bearded, flat-nosed, Jack Dempsey was the starkest picture of a fighting man. He is shown here starting training for Tommy Gibbons bout at Shelby, Montana, in 1923. With him were, left to right, sparring partners George Godfrey, Frank Murray, and Jack Burke. (UPI)

HEAVYWEIGHTS

first round. But I looked over in his corner and saw how big he was and decided I'd better fight for my life. I wondered if I was going to have enough of a punch to knock him out of the picture. He was in great shape and looking very confident. I made up my mind to keep away from him as much as possible and not let him hit me, and do the punching myself. A straight right hand under the heart turned the fight in my favor."

Kearns acquired Dempsey in 1917. He found him working in a San Francisco shipyard. Dempsey was broke and despondent. In 1918, with Kearns handling his business for a one-third interest, Dempsey rolled up a good string of knockouts. In the first five years of their partnership, there was no "paper," or contract, between the two. In August, 1923, they signed a contract on the same two-one basis they had always worked by.

Publicly, Dempsey and Kearns gave a demonstration of perfect harmony. In 1924, when

Dapper Dempsey and manager Jack Kearns get earful from Sunny Jim Coffroth at Tijuana, Mexico, race track. The famous boxing promoter wanted to match Dempsey with Harry Wills, but the 1924 proposal never came off. (UPI)

Dempsey had his nose reconstructed by a surgeon in Hollywood, Kearns had his nose "bobbed," too.

Then, in 1925, Dempsey married actress Estelle Taylor, and rumors began flowing about a breakup between fighter and manager. Dan McKetrick, who was Kearns' New York agent, was quoted in an affidavit a year later as saying that Dempsey once told him that he liked Kearns "and I know he made me money and champion, but my wife can't get along with him."

Before the smoke finally cleared from the ashes of their friendship, Kearns had sued Dempsey, unsuccessfully, for $700,000, and Dempsey had stated on oath that Kearns had forged Dempsey's signature to the contract of 1923–26. Dempsey added that to save face for his manager, he had traced his name in over the bogus signature, and so made an honest man of Kearns.

After their breakup, Kearns wrote a newspaper series about himself and Dempsey. He said that Dempsey was the kind of fighter who needed expert advice. "Sooner or later," he wrote, "Dempsey would come to me and say, 'Doc, how am I going to fight this fellow? What will I do? What's he got, and how do I break it up?'" This made it sound bad for the leaderless Dempsey in the first Tunney fight; yet Kearns was seen in Texas Guinan's, before the fight, offering to bet $10,000 to $4,000 on Dempsey.

In a steady rain, before a record crowd of 120,757 people who paid $1,895,733 in gate receipts, Tunney out-boxed the rusty champion and cut him severely.

"What happened, Ginsberg?" his wife asked Dempsey next day, using her favorite pet name for him.

"Honey," Dempsey said, "I forgot to duck."

Tunney's percentage of his second successful fight with Dempsey, in Chicago in 1927, fell less than $10,000 short of a million. He was able to make the spacious gesture of giving promoter Tex Rickard the difference and accepting a check from him for exactly $1,000,000.

Though people still argue over every aspect

When Jack Dempsey floored Gene Tunney in the 7th round of their second fight (Sept. 22, 1927, Chicago), he ignited one of boxing's all-time controversies—The Battle of the Long Count. (UPI)

of the second Dempsey-Tunney fight—the famous so-called "Battle of the Long Count"— Dempsey was not one of them.

"I was not the timekeeper, so I don't know how long Gene was on the floor," Dempsey said diplomatically. "All I know is that it was a great thing for both of us. Half the folks thought Gene won, and half thought I won. They still talk about it, and it has kept our names alive all these years."

Deep in this vein, long before he made his last landing with fellow Oklahoman Wiley Post, Will Rogers was wild about flying. He was among the few authorized to fly in the mail planes during the Roosevelt administration. Checked out with a parachute—"count 10, then pull the rip cord"—Rogers commented: "Ten will be an awful short count. They gave Gene Tunney a count of 14 against Dempsey."

Dempsey said that there are two things that count in prizefighting: the big punch and the ability to take a big punch. Any genuine champion must have both.

At Chicago, Tunney had Dempsey in trouble. Jack appeared groggy. Tunney was later asked why he hadn't followed up with his right hand.

"Because I knew Dempsey," he said. "Jack could recover faster than any man I ever fought. He was dangerous with a five-second interval."

William Harrison Dempsey was born on June 24, 1895, at Manassa, Colorado—hence his nickname, "Manassa Mauler." The ninth of the 11 children (5 brothers, 5 sisters) of Hiram and Celia Dempsey, Jack's father was a poverty-driven Mormon sharecropper and itinerant railroad hand who moved the family from Uncompahgre to Delta and Montrose, in Colorado, and then to Provo, Utah. At fourteen, Jack was mucking in coal and copper mines. He vagabonded across the Rockies as carnival fighter, fruit-picker, mule-driver, and professional pool-shark. At eighteen, he was a bouncer in a Salt Lake City saloon. It was from there that he left to enter the prize ring, fighting under the name "Kid Blackie." He started out fighting for meal money, went on to earn more than $5,000,000. The most spectacular fighter ever to hold the heavyweight crown, Dempsey was the first fighter to draw a million-dollar gate, a figure he exceeded five times. That magic circle was first drawn on July 2, 1921, in Jersey City, when $1,789,238 was paid to see Dempsey defend his crown against French war hero, Georges Carpentier. Seldom has there been such a taking of sides. By the eve of the fight France was nearly hysterical. French President Alexandre Millerand left orders to be called at any hour for news of the outcome, and airplanes prepared to drop colored flares over Paris to signal the winner. "There are not 50 Englishmen or 10 Americans who understand our pleasure in *Phedre*," wrote the eminently cultured François Mauriac, "but the eloquence of the fist is accessible to all men. Victorious over Dempsey, Georges will be the torch of the modern world. He revives in us the nostalgia of Athens."

But Carpentier, weighing only 167 pounds and with brittle hands, was no match for Dempsey—and he knew it. As he walked through the crowd of 75,000 to the ring, he was thinking: "I don't know where I am. I don't even know if I've come here to fight. I have forgotten everything. I have the feeling that I'm walking on a cotton cloud in a nightmare."

At the opening bell, however, his worries cleared away, and he managed to weather the first three rounds. But in the fourth, Dempsey accelerated with murder in his eye. "He hit me everywhere," Carpentier said later. "On the flanks, arms, shoulders, head. Any place was good for a punch. My legs weakened. I fell. I hurt all over. Yet I was perfectly lucid."

He rose at nine, took a left to the face and a right punch to the heart, and that was the end. From ringside, all French ships at sea received this cable: "Your Frog flattened in fourth"—for a new high in international diplomacy.

Dempsey vs. Carpentier marked the first of the great organized ballyhoos.

Two years later, Dempsey fought Tommy Gibbons at Shelby, Montana, in what has been called "the fight that broke a town." Seven banks went bankrupt. It was the only one of Dempsey's six title fights as defending champion that went the full 15 rounds. Gibbons always said he would fight Dempsey for nothing for a crack at his crown, and that's what his end of the purse came to—*nothing*.

For days after the fight, Gibbons could not

put on his hat because of the bumps Dempsey's fists raised on his head.

"I saw a right hand coming in the first round," Tommy said afterward. "It was too late to do anything else about it, so I dropped my head and took it on the forehead. I didn't know where I was for several rounds. I was forced to hold on a lot in the last three rounds, because Jack belted me in the groin in the ninth and my left leg wasn't much good after that."

When Dempsey fought, things happened that never happened before. His sensational fracas with Luis Angel Firpo at the Polo Grounds, on September 14, 1923, was one of the most thrilling in sports history; his second joust with Tunney—The Battle of the Long Count—was the most controversial in boxing annals.

The second Tunney fight was the beginning of the end for Dempsey. He attempted a short-lived comeback, but retired permanently in 1932. He served as a physical instructor in the Coast Guard during World War II. Age kept him out of the Army.

You won't find it listed in any record book, but Dempsey fought his last "fight" when he was nearly fifty and was on a transport in the Pacific during WWII. It happened while he was refereeing a servicemen's boxing program. He ruled one of the bouts a draw, and one of the boxers fumed and challenged Dempsey to put on the gloves.

"I had no business fighting the man," Jack

When sports writer Hugh Fullerton spotted Tommy Gibbons talking to Blackfoot chief and brave before Dempsey bout at Shelby, he sniffed a good story. In broken Indian dialect, Hugh asked the chief, "Who Big Chief like in fight? Dempsey or Gibbons?" Big Chief replied, in perfect English: "Sir, I happen to like Dempsey. Gibbons has the skill as a boxer. Dempsey has the power. Power usually prevails over skill." (UPI)

said, recalling the incident, "because I was an officer and he was an enlisted man, but the boys started hollering, 'Come on! Come on! Take him on!' So I lost my head, which I never should have done. He was an ex-fighter, this boy—big, but not too much of a fighter. I had no right to do it. The first round went pretty good, and then the second round—I was in fairly good shape—he ran at me with his hands down, and I happened to get lucky and hit him a left hook and it was all over."

Three of the stars of "The Golden Age of Sport" were, left, Red Grange, the Galloping Ghost of football at Illinois; Dempsey; and Bobby Jones, who with his famous putter, "Calamity Jane," ruled golf from 1923 to 1930. (Photo from Jack Dempsey collection)

A highly restless man, Dempsey could not settle down after he retired from the prize ring. Buenos Aires one week, Toronto, Canada, the next and on to Boston or Dallas or San Francisco—refereeing wrestling matches and prizefights or representing some company in an advertising drive. He also took a flier with various circuses, and he loved the work. In one circus he had a chimp that always waited for him. He'd give the chimp a cigar and a bottle of Coke. The monkey would drink the Coke, smoke the cigar and jam the cigar in the bottle for a stopper. He was Jack's pal.

Dempsey was once asked why college athletes seldom made good fighters.

"They're too smart," Jack replied. "The fight game is the toughest game on earth. When I was a young fellow I was knocked down plenty. I wanted to stay down. I couldn't. I had to collect that two bucks for winning—or go hungry. I had to get up. I was one of those hungry fighters. You could hit me on the chin with a sledge hammer for five bucks. When you haven't eaten for two days you'll understand. Few college fellows ever get that hungry. I had one early fight in which I was knocked down eleven times before I got up to win. You think I'd have taken that beating if I had had as much as twenty-five bucks with me? No chance."

But he would have.

GENE TUNNEY
(1898–   )

Gene Tunney made only two mistakes in his life:

1. He soundly trounced the most popular heavyweight champion the world has ever known.

2. He used his head for something more than just to hold his ears apart.

The public never quite pardoned him for either error.

For the longest time after he committed the grievous sin of defeating Jack Dempsey, the prizefight public regarded Tunney as slightly lower in the social scale than the current public enemy No. 1 in the F.B.I. files.

The fact that Tunney read a book or two and could carry on an ordinary conversation without cleaving infinitives all over the place added greatly to the general distrust and dislike of the accomplished heavyweight titleholder.

That the "peepul" should look askance at Gene, whose career somewhat paralleled that of his idol, Jim Corbett, is paradoxical. The Fighting Marine lived out a classic American success story, of the type immortalized by Horatio Alger. Apparently what was lauded in an Alger hero doesn't sit so well in a prizefighter.

Tunney's ring career was a literal example of the triumph of mind over matter. He did not enter the ring with the natural, instinctive fighting equipment of a Jim Jeffries, a Jack Dempsey or a Jack Johnson. He was not a natural-born puncher, his physique was not adapted to fighting and, although he did possess fine reflexes, they had to be adjusted to boxing. Through sheer willpower and mental exertion, Gene converted an ordinary guy into one of the finest fighters the ring has ever known. Those who knew him when he was in the process of converting from a peaceable fellow into a vicious fighting machine can tell you how he carried two rubber balls in his pockets and spent every otherwise idle moment massaging the pellets to toughen his naturally weak and brittle hands. Harry Grayson, one of only two major American sports writers to predict Tunney's startling upset of Dempsey in their first bout, pointed out that Gene had another side to him the public forgot. "He could be cunning and mean in the ring," Harry said. "He liked to break your nose and cut you up. He never cared how much he cut you, he would always take his time. He showed you the difference between great and near-great fighters."

Born in the rough and tumble section of Greenwich Village, in Manhattan, on May 25, 1898, the son of a stevedore, Tunney had a total of 76 prizefights in a career spanning 1915–1928. He joined the Marines in World War I after his first seven pro bouts, won the A.E.F. light-heavyweight title in France, and came back to beat Battling Levinsky for the American light-heavyweight crown (January 12, 1922). He lost the title to Harry Greb in 15 rounds four-and-a-half months later, then won it back from Greb, on February 23, 1923.

After startling the sports world with his upset victory over defending champion Dempsey in 1926, in Philadelphia, Tunney put his title on the block only twice—against Dempsey in '27, and Tom Heeney in '28—before retiring. He was the first heavyweight champion to quit while on top and remain retired.

As a prizefighter, Tunney was unspectacular, but demoniacally efficient. He was a "manufactured boxer—only his spiritual assets were natural," in the words of Tim Cohane, his close friend and former Sports Editor of *Look* magazine. Gene had fragile hands. To strengthen them, he shoveled coal and hoisted five-gallon water jugs. He also used to squeeze those small, hard rubber balls and exercise each finger 500 times a day by using it as a lever to push his body away from a wall.

From Benny Leonard he borrowed the trick of shoving his left jab in a slightly upward plane, to sharpen its cutting edge. This

Promoter Tex Rickard gets the Tunney signature on the dotted line for first Dempsey fight. Manager Billy Gibson witnesses the signing. (UPI)

helped make a mess of Dempsey's eyes. Gene Kessler was even more impressed by Tunney's right-hand snap punch. He named it the "Piston Jab."

"In the first Dempsey fight, that punch saved the day for Gene," Kessler said. "It was a great weapon as a counter to Dempsey's left-handed attack. It scored points, it checked Jack's rushes, and it kept Gene's right arm always in position to fend off blows. I can still picture the charging, half-crouched Dempsey running smack into that short right so much his face was jolted lopsided. Tunney held his right hand high against his chin with his forearm tucked against his side to guard against the Dempsey left hook. Thus he'd snap the right fist downward against Dempsey's face and quickly snap it back in place to protect against a counter. The elbow functioned as a hinge; no sooner did the right fist reach its mark than it was brought back as if attached to a spring. Not many people realized it, but Tunney had invented a new punch."

Few athletes in history ever have been better conditioned than Tunney. He developed stamina enough to step around at top speed every second of every round.

But one of his biggest assets was his nerves of ice.

James Joseph Tunney was the only man ever to master both Jack Dempsey and William Shakespeare. George Bernard Shaw, his friend, once described the Tunney of the Twenties as "an arrant prig." Later, however, Gene received his due as one of the greatest of heavyweight champions. He lost only one pro fight (to Harry Greb) and won much personal popularity.

Tunney's love of the classics was no pose. It stemmed from boyhood, when as a thirteen-year-old in St. Veronica's Parochial School, in New York, he played the Prince in the court scene in *Romeo and Juliet*. He later lectured on the Bard to Professor William Lyon Phelps's English class at Yale.

Tunney was something thunderously beyond the comprehension of the fight mob.

Two of the great boxing writers of the "Golden Age of Sports," Harry Grayson, left, and Westbrook Pegler. Grayson, later author McCallum's boss at NEA in New York, was one of only two major writers to pick Tunney over Dempsey in first match (Harry Keck, of Pittsburgh, was the other). (NEA)

THE ENCYCLOPEDIA OF WORLD BOXING CHAMPIONS

Three great sports writers who frequently covered major championship prizefights together: Frank Graham, left, Grantland Rice, and Red Smith. They knew those they chronicled as intimate friends rather than as impersonal news copy. One of their boxing favorites was Gene Tunney, of whom Granny once observed, "He trained harder than any other ring champ I've known." Graham and Rice have since passed on, but Smith continues to be the most influential single force on American sports writing via his column in *The New York Times*. (Photo by Kay Smith)

Tunney was the only fighter ever to master both Dempsey and William Shakespeare. George Bernard Shaw, his friend here shown, once described Tunney of the Twenties as an "arrant prig." Later, however, Gene won much personal popularity. (From Tunney collection)

By the time he retired from boxing he had read H. G. Well's *Outline of History* and all of Shakespeare several times. His favorite modern authors were Faulkner and Hemingway, who was a good friend.

Gene Tunney was the first heavyweight champion to quit the prize ring while on top and remain retired. (UPI)

Few former champions achieved such distinction as Tunney in other fields. Once a shipping clerk for a steamship line, he had learned early the value of money, and was a full-fledged millionaire by the time he quit the ring. He became director of two banks and eight industries. He topped off his personal version of the Horatio Alger theme by marrying Mary Josephine "Polly" Lauder, of the Carnegie Steel empire.

JACK SHARKEY
(1902–   )

Jack Sharkey had almost everything. He was a 196-pound, 6-footer who was fast of hand and foot. He boxed beautifully and he could punch. But he was probably one of the

HEAVYWEIGHTS

Tunney has his picture taken with other sports greats of the 1920s: back row, left, Babe Ruth, baseball; Tunney; Johnny Weismuller, swimming; Bill Cook, hockey. Front row, left, Bill Tilden, tennis; Bobby Jones, golf; Freddy Spencer and Charley Winter, bike racing. (NEA)

most unstable characters to ever step into a prize ring.

Jack Dempsey, who fought him in 1927, recalled that Sharkey gave him living hell for the first five rounds. "He was as good a fighter as I had ever seen," Dempsey said. "I thought he was going to knock me out."

In the sixth, Dempsey began shifting his attack to the body and by the seventh all fire was directed there with careless abandon. No gentleman was Dempsey. If a punch was low, so what. Then came a right to the groin that was as palpable a foul as ever was thrown. Sharkey pawed at his middle and turned his head to the referee to complain, "He's hitting me low!" His chin jutted out at a perfect and inviting angle.

"What was I going to do—write him a letter of apology?" said Dempsey. "I belted him."

When Sharkey left the Yankee Stadium after the fight, he didn't even know it. He was nearly two hours coming out of the fog.

The Sharkey-Dempsey bout was the only non-title bout ever to draw a million-dollar gate. Had Sharkey won, he would have earned a shot at Gene Tunney's world championship. As it was, he had to wait another five years before winning the title.

There is always a riddle of some sort hooked to the heavyweight crown, and Sharkey goes down as boxing's all-time riddle. No other fighter in the heavyweight class had more chances to scale the top, only to throw most of them away. There were nights when he appeared to be great, but then, as a rule, he blew up with a crash when the big moment finally arrived.

Most fighters climb upward on the ladder of success. Sharkey? He went forward upon one failure after another.

Every fighter has some fetish. Sharkey's was to make himself master of any ring situation by teasing his opponent into abandoning his own style of fighting and falling into traps which Sharkey had set for him. The value of such tactics when they could successfully be carried out was evident. Sharkey was at ease, his opponent was treading unfamiliar territory.

When the opponent was either too wily or too stupid to fall for such tactics, Sharkey didn't look quite so good. Tommy Loughran, according to Sharkey, fell into the trap. Jack teased him with his head until Tommy began to reach and push with his jabs instead of stinging them in.

Sharkey's style was sometimes puzzling. He had a funny motion with his head while waiting in his corner before a fight, a rotating one, with his mouth pulled open. And of course his glare. . . .

"Listen to this," said Sharkey one time, and he suddenly moved his head sharply from right to left. There was a snap. "Hear that? If I'd got hit on the jaw before I did that I'd have been all jarred. I get my neck all loose and limbered up, take all the kinks out of it before I go. Then when I get hit, I'm all set."

Sharkey believed it to be a physiological truth.

"I pull up my eyelids because they get heavy with vaseline sometimes," Sharkey continued. "Then they stick. Huh! That stuff about my glaring. Sure I look at a guy I'm

Moody and temperamental, Jack Sharkey (left) fought best for a cause. He had all the technical equipment to be great. (AP Photo)

going to fight. Sometimes you can find out a lot even before the bell rings. I never once looked at Loughran's face. I looked at his chest. I could see that old heart pumping away as though it were trying to kick its way out through his ribs.

" 'Oh, ho!' I said to myself, 'this guy don't feel so good about this thing. He isn't as cool as he pretends to be.' That put me one up on him."

Sharkey had the technical equipment to be a great heavyweight. He was a brilliant boxer and a terrific hitter, a rare combination. He also loved to fight. His armament included a knowledge of every punch needed in a bout, and his best weapon was his left hand. His left hook was a terrific punch—it stunned, weakened, and could knock a man out. His rasping left jab was meant to cut the skin. His right-hand punch was developed from a looping throw to a straight wallop that started with the hand carried at the chest. There was very little he could not do when he had to do it and wanted to win. He beat K. O. Christner with a right uppercut when he found he could sucker him into lunging at him. His left hook in one round made Dempsey look as though he had been in an automobile accident.

Moody and temperamental, he fought best for a cause. If he could whip himself into a state of nervous frenzy over a match, he was hard to beat. He was the crusader type and in many of his fights he was hysterical. He was K.O.'d only four times in a total of 55 professional fights. But when the cause was lacking or the incentive lacking, or in the doldrums of a fit of just plain laziness, he was terrible. Then he didn't try, he didn't punch and he worked nothing but his left jab. "When I come out hooking," he once said, "you can bet it's going to be a fight."

"He reminds me of a thoroughbred racehorse," once observed Paul Gallico, "a perfect physical specimen with all the necessary attributes of intelligence and courage—but you never know when his owner is going to let him try."

Not that Sharkey's manager, Johnny Buckley, held him back. Sharkey was the one who sometimes lost interest. Easily affected emotionally, any private troubles were instantly reflected in his ringwork.

In action, he argued with himself, debated, and became greatly annoyed when eagerness overcame discretion and he let go a sucker punch such as a right-hand lead and missed. "Sharkey, you damn fool," he'd say to himself, "you ought to be shot. And you think you're smart. A right-hand lead! You ought to get your lug knocked off!"

Born at Binghamton, New York, on October 6, 1902, of Lithuanian lineage, Sharkey's given name was Joseph Paul Zukauskas, or Cuckoshay. His half namesakes for purposes of the prize ring were Jack Dempsey and Sailor Tom Sharkey. He always claimed he could lick an Irishman; most of the time he was right. Names like Muldoon, Maloney, McCarthy, McTigue, and Delaney were listed among his Celt victims.

Sharkey yearned to be the hero of Boston, his adopted home town. He ignored the harsh fact that Beantown resents made-over Irishmen. Bostonians also resented his attitude toward the coveted heavyweight championship. Example: After winning the world title from Schmeling, Jack was asked by news photographers to pose with the traditional championship belt; a mess of silver and gold, strapped around his waist. Someone asked Jack how much he guessed the belt would be worth at a pawnshop. "Probably about twenty-five cents," Sharkey said. "Maybe half a dollar if you knew the guy who ran the place. But you'd have to know him pretty well."

A year after winning the title, Sharkey defended it against Primo Carnera. The Preem, a monster pawn in the hands of racketeers, had no business in the same ring with Sharkey. Even so, on June 29, 1933, he scored a six-round K.O. that was greeted with pinched noses by those who knew the inside story. Sharkey thus was the first heavyweight champion to lose his title in his very first defense.

On August 18, 1936, Sharkey made his farewell appearance from prizefighting. He went out like a lamb in the third round against Joe Louis.

Jack Sharkey's nickname—"The Fighting Fool"—was a misnomer if there ever was one. It takes some fooling to gross a cool million.

MAX SCHMELING
(1905–   )

On June 12, 1930, Germany's Max Schmeling beat Jack Sharkey to become the first and only heavyweight to win the world championship on a *foul*.

This made Maxmillian Adolph Otto Siegfried Schmeling the first continental European to hold the heavyweight title.

Max was also the first to do what no other fighter had yet accomplished—he knocked out the seemingly impregnable Joe Louis.

This latter reminded Jimmy Cannon of the time when he had his choice of two newspaper assignments: Did he want to go West with the baseball Yankees or stay in New York to cover the Schmeling-Louis fight? Cannon decided he would rather travel with Joe DiMaggio and the Yankees. Jimmy confessed later that he'd regarded Schmeling as all washed up. "It won't be much of a fight," Jimmy told his boss.

Cannon and the Yankees were in Detroit on the night of the fight. They sat around the radio listening to Clem McCarthy broadcast the fight. McCarthy's voice rose. "He's down!" Clem shouted.

"I told you," Cannon said to Tony Lazzeri. But it was *Louis* who was down, and he was knocked out in the 12th round that night, June 19, 1936. Cannon never forgot that.

The last publicist to invoke the term "white hope," as used to describe an athlete of so-called Caucasian background who might retrieve the heavyweight championship from a black incumbent, for the honor of his race, was the late Dr. J. J. Goebbels, Hitler's propaganda chief, when he billed Schmeling's second fight with Louis, in 1938, as a mission to restore the championship to "Aryan" control. By then, Louis was champion, and his title was on the line.

Goebbels frowned on Schmeling's partnership with Joe Jacobs, a Caucasian, but non-Aryan, manager.

"But without Jacobs' American connections," explained Max, "I can't get anywhere."

As it turned out, Schmeling kept Jacobs and settled for a big payday in New York, after two minutes of anguish at the Brown Bomber's hands.

It was a source of open discomfort to Goebbels, considered the No. 3 man in Nazi Germany, where relationships between culture and physical strength were emphasized, that Schmeling could not get a return fight with Louis, for the championship, with the help of Joe (Yussel the Muscle) Jacobs. Hitler supported this view. There was national unhappiness in Germany later when Louis K.O.'d Schmeling in the first round. Goebbels reacted officially by pointing out that the U.S., to keep the title, had had to use a member of her "African Auxiliary."

Schmeling hovers over Joe Louis in 12th round on his way to doing what no other fighter had yet accomplished—he kayoed the seemingly impregnable Brown Bomber. (UPI)

Though Max had a polished right-hand punch, he lacked the quality of true greatness. He never seemed to sense the dramatic moment to step in to win, as was demonstrated in his fights with Max Baer in 1933 and with Jack Sharkey in '32.

"He had Baer licked between the 5th and 8th rounds and was chasing him all over the ring," Gene Tunney recalled. "But he was caught flatfooted with an overhand right in the 10th and that ended that. As for Sharkey, he allowed Jack to back all over the ring for 15 rounds and thereby gave Sharkey the title of world champion."

Sharkey loathed Schmeling. You knew by the scorn in his voice and the way his eyes narrowed into mere slits that Sharkey meant it when he said, in 1933: "Schmeling's yellow, he ain't got any moxie. I found it out in our first fight, when he took the title lying on the floor and yelling like a baby. I found it out again last Summer when, with the championship sliding out of his hands, he stood off and wouldn't come in and mix it. If he's such a great hitter why didn't he come in and polish me off? Because he knew if he did I'd knock his head off."

Schmeling grew up in the bitter, poverty-ridden Germany of the Versailles Treaty years. In 1919, he was forced to leave school at the age of fourteen and grub for worthless marks. He worked for three years as an apprentice in the advertising department of a Hamburg newspaper. In 1922, he hit the road, bumming his way from one job to another. He developed his barrel chest by toiling on farms and in foundries, open coal mines, railway shops, and garages.

Max Schmeling, the first Continental European to hold the world heavyweight title, was the division's only contender to win the championship on a foul. (AP)

When he was 18 Max blew into Cologne-Mulheim, became a pumper at the municipal waterworks and joined the Mulheimer Boxing Club and the Benrath Club. By 1924, he had licked all the middleweights in Cologne-Mulheim.

Unlike most foreign fighters who arrive in the U.S. in the full panoply of ballyhoo, Schmeling slipped in on his own, without fanfare, and quietly got lost in Bey's training camp in Summit, New Jersey. He eventually wound up in the hands of manager Joe Jacobs. Jacobs made his first big move when he put Schmeling in with Johnny Risko, the Cleveland Rubber Man. Risko was a great spoiler who had already upset Jack Sharkey. Schmeling stopped Risko in nine rounds. Then came Paulino Uzcudun, whom Max disposed of in 15 rounds.

In the 1930 Sharkey fight to determine a successor to the resigned Tunney, Schmeling fell to the floor in the fourth round from what was claimed to be a low blow. The foul claim by Joe Jacobs was allowed during a few minutes of confusion in which nobody seemed to know what was happening or what to do. Up to that time, Sharkey had been winning big. Then, in the fourth, Schmeling had just driven Sharkey into the ropes with a great right to the jaw when Jack countered with the controversial punch—a wicked left hook to the groin. Max dropped to his knees, clutching his stomach, as Referee Jimmy Crowley counted him out. For the next three minutes, 79,222 customers champed and chaffed as the ring officials haggled like merchants over the contested blow.

Crowley and Judge Charles Mathison had missed the punch. Judge Harold Barnes claimed he saw it, and therefore Crowley disqualified Sharkey. Six days later the New York Boxing Commission elected Schmeling champion by a 2-1 vote, and Max earned the dubious distinction of becoming the first and only heavyweight to win the title by a foul.

Max fought Sharkey again in Long Island, in 1932, and the championship was returned to the U.S. by one of the worst decisions ever perpetrated on an incredulous public. Some critics suspected the conniving hand of old Pete Reilly, who for some unknown reason had soured on Schmeling.

The romanticists claimed that Max descended from "the savage Wends of the Black Forest." Whoever his dark progenitor, he showed a fortuitious combination of strength and cunning. Some experts were inclined to write him off as a plodding, workmanlike heavyweight with a dangerous right. Yet he was truly a great fighter the night he befuddled Joe Louis in one of the classic upsets of all time.

PRIMO CARNERA
(1906–1967)

Six-foot-six Primo Carnera was the all-time physical giant of all the modern heavyweight champions. He was the heaviest (267 lbs.), had the longest reach (85½ in.), the largest neck (20 in.) and the biggest forearm (16 in.). He also boasted the biggest chest size (48 in.), waist (38 in.), biceps (18½ in.), calf (20 in.), and thigh (30 in.).

The Preem's strike zone was so huge, it should have been subdivided. The first time I was introduced to him, I had to resist the temptation to look behind him to see where I'd wind it up. As Jim Murray once wrote about Frank Howard, the Attila the Hun of baseball: "He's so big, he wasn't born, he was founded." Primo was only two stories shorter than the Chrysler Building. He was awesome. It took a fly a week to walk across his fists. He was Gulliver in boxing trunks. He made every other man in the world look like Casper Milquetoast. The only flaw in his makeup is that he couldn't fight. His 350-day reign remains the briefest in heavyweight history.

"Which goes to prove my point," Dumb Dan Morgan told me once. "Bigness alone is more of a handicap than an asset. Any fighter who weighs over 220 pounds can't fight. Look at Jess Willard, Ray Impellitierre, and Buddy Baer. Like Carnera, they were more like Saint Bernards than fist-fighters. The bigger they grew, the more gentle they became. They would have been much better off with a cask of booze around their necks, tracking down drunks in the Alps. So if you have an eight-foot freak hidden away in the mountains someplace, get him a job with the circus and don't bring him around for a crack at the heavyweight title."

In the career of Primo Carnera the fight racket hit its lowest point. His tragic story topped anything that could be invented by a fiction writer. Paul Gallico called Primo's prizefight life the "most scandalous, pitiful, incredible story in all the history of boxing."

Born on October 26, 1906, at Sequals, Italy, Carnera started fighting in 1928. He was taught and trained by a wise, scheming little French boxing manager who had an Oxford University degree, and was later acquired and developed into a heavyweight champion of the world by a group of American gangsters and mob men; then finally, when his usefulness as a meal ticket was outlived, he was shamefully discarded.

The Preem was a masterpiece of stage management. Everything was made to make him appear larger than he really was. Leon See, the Frenchman, was his manager at the outset, and was a small man. The bucket carriers and sponge wielders were chosen for size, too—diminutive men; everything was done to increase the impression of Primo's size.

"Carnera was the only giant I have ever seen who was well proportioned throughout his body for his height," Gallico said. Paul was Sports Editor of the *New York Daily News* during the Carnera era. "His legs were massive and he was truly thewed like an oak.

Primo Carnera was a big but harmless man. At one time, he was moved around by a syndicate of gangsters, and many of his early so-called victories were rigged. He was agile in a big-footed way, but his arms were impotent when they laced the gloves on his hands. He could not punch and what he knew had been taught to him because he had none of the instincts a fighter must have to survive. He was a confused and battered man the night Joe Louis stopped him in the sixth round here. (UPI)

His waist was comparatively small and clean, but from it rose a torso like a Spanish hogshead from which sprouted two tremendous arms, the biceps of which stood out like grapefruit. His hands were like Virginia hams, and his fingers were 10 red sausages. His head was large, and he had a good nose and fine, kind eyes. His skin was brown and glistening and he invariably smelled of garlic."

This was the horror that faced his opponents. That is to say, he was horrible until he commenced to fight, and then there was nothing but bewilderment and complete helplessness. The most dreadful part of the story is that poor Primo was duped along with the public into believing he had a knockout punch. It was not until late in his career that he came to realize that his string of 65 straight "knockouts" had not been on the level. He won those frivolities because of the mediocrity of the opposition, mostly setups.

"But he never could fight," Gallico testified. "In spite of his great size and strength, he remained nothing but a glandular freak who should have remained with the small French traveling circus from which Leon See took him. Still he was brave and game and apparently could take punches to the body all the night long. But one hard, true tap on the chin and he fell down goggle-eyed."

After dethroning Jack Sharkey in 1933, Primo defended his crown only twice over the next 11 months. He won decisions in lackluster matches with Paolino Uzcudun and Tommy Loughran. The latter confessed Carnera hurt him only once. "When he stepped on my foot with one of those size-15 gunboats."

Carnera lost his championship to Max Baer, on June 14, 1934, in New York. He hit the deck 12 times before being counted out in the 11th round.

In his entire career, Primo won no more than a handful of fights on his own merits. While his bouts grossed more than

Carnera hit the deck 12 times before being counted out in the 11th round as he lost his championship to Max Baer. (UPI)

After mobsters stole all of his prize ring earnings, Carnera became a successful wrestler and finally earned some degree of financial security. He was only sixty when he died of sclerosis of the liver, June 28, 1967, in his native Sequals, Italy. (Photo courtesy Arch Hindman)

$3,000,000, he was never known to have more than $500 to call his own after the racket boys who controlled him picked him clean.

Carnera died of sclerosis of the liver, on June 28, 1967. He was only 60. He was not broke, however. After World War II, a Los Angeles wrestling promoter made a small fortune for Primo on the grunt-and-groan circuit—and for the first time in his life, Carnera got to keep his share.

And the greedy vultures who stole the bulk of his boxing earnings? They were either killed by their own kind or put in jail.

"Life has a way of evening things up," philosophized Primo Carnera shortly before his death, in Sequals, Italy. "All that money—what good did it do any of them?"

MAX BAER
(1909–1959)

Max Baer had a wonderful opportunity to become a great champion and flubbed it. He reached his peak when he won the heavyweight title in 1934 from big Primo Carnera, which was no enormous achievement. But Maxie went down gravely after this peak, and lost his world championship only a year less a day later to Jim Braddock.

"Baer was the victim of his own adolescent desires," Gene Tunney said. "Too much night-clubbing and clowning, and not enough serious training."

You had to like Max. He brought laughter to the prize ring at a time when there was nothing funny about the heavies. His huge enjoyment was infectious. Guys and dolls loved him. He was show business and crackling copy.

Baer's best fight was on June 8, 1933, when he knocked out Max Schmeling in 10 rounds. Afterward, Schmeling announced his engagement to Anny Ondra, a German cinema cutie.

"Do you think Schmeling is mad at me for breaking up his engagement party?" Baer asked Joe Williams.

"Why do you ask?" Williams said.

"Well, I kicked him around a little and I don't feel so good about it now myself."

Williams told Baer that there did exist in the German's camp a distinct feeling that he had been a bit rough.

"Rough!" Baer snapped. "Say, a fight's a fight, isn't it? I don't care what they do to me, do I? That's what's wrong with the fight business. There is too much Yoo, Hoo, Sweetie! stuff in it. Why do you think people come to prizefights anyhow—to see a couple of ballroom dancers? They want to see action and they aren't interested in rules. Neither am I."

Then Williams noticed a bracelet that Baer was wearing. "What's that thing you have on your wrist?" Joe asked.

"It's a slave bracelet," Baer said. "June gave it to me a week before the Schmeling fight and I didn't take it off until I got into the ring."

A 203-pound savage of the prize ring wearing a slave bracelet! Joe knew about June. She was June Knight, the musical comedy lovely and Mr. Baer's favorite heart excitement.

"What do the numerals mean?" Williams wanted to know. The bracelet was a delicate thread of gold with a flat centerpiece on which appeared the numbers "143."

"Don't you know what that means?" Baer said. "Where have you been all your life? That means 'I love you.'"

Williams wanted Max to explain.

"Well," Max said, "the '1' means I, the '4' means love, l-o-v-e, and the '3' means you, y-o-u. Get it?"

With all of his braggadocio, fast cars, fast women, flashy clothes and madcap antics, Max Baer was a man difficult to dislike. He possessed a lusty sense of humor, irresistible good nature, and tremendous warmth for people. He chattered and charmed his way into the hearts of just about everybody. Who will ever forget the zany Maxie training for the Schmeling bout by banging his head against a lead pipe to "harden up my noggin for punches"?

Ancil Hoffman, Baer's manager, used to say: "Maxie can do everything but *think*."

"That's right," Baer agreed. "I got a million-dollar body and a 10-cent brain."

The Magnificent Screwball.

From 1930 to '35, it was Baer's showmanship that kept boxing alive. Grantland Rice called him "the New Deal for bored fight fans." His wild escapades were not limited to the prize ring. Women chased him, sued him, swooned over him, threatened him, and one even tried to kidnap him. Standing well over six feet, weighing 203 pounds, with striking, wide shoulders tapering to a narrow waist, gorgeous Maxie was the most handsome heavyweight the world had seen in years.

Though nightclubs were his playground, Baer seldom touched the grog and refrained from smoking. While training for Carnera, a sports writer glimpsed him coming out of a night spot at 3 A.M. and offered him a cigarette.

"No, sir," Max said reprovingly, squeezing his grip on the waist of the blonde at his side, "you know I got to keep in shape for the fight."

Make no mistake, Max Baer could fight. When the mood came over him, which was rare, he was a brutal, savage opponent. He had a stunning right-hand punch; in fact, he was right-hand daffy. And, until he lost confidence in himself, he had the stamina and courage of a bull. He came from behind in the Schmeling fight to give Herr Max a fearful hiding. He battered down the rugged Ernie Schaaf in his prime, reduced the giant Carnera to kindling wood, sent the rough-house Kingfish Levinsky to dreamland in two rounds—and *killed* Frankie Campbell.

In that flashy span between the Schmeling knockout until he goofed away his crown to Jim Braddock, Baer had many championship qualities. He was willing to fight anyone, he believed himself invincible, and was totally unafraid.

Max was born in Omaha, Nebraska, on February 11, 1909. His father, Jacob Baer, was German-Jewish; his mother, Nora Bales Baer, was Scotch-Irish. They both were six feet tall and weighed 200 pounds. Max was the second of five children. He, himself, stood 6 ft., 2 in. and weighed 190 when he was only nineteen.

Max saw his first fight when he was sixteen. At first, boxing didn't interest him. The only fighter he cared about was Jack Dempsey. When Dempsey lost his title to Tunney, Max cried. He never caught the fever of the fight game until he was twenty. He talked his parents into letting him go to Oakland, California, to become a fighter. There, he got a job in the Atlas Diesel engine factory hauling huge iron castings, and spent the evenings training at Jimmy Duffy's gym.

Max got $35 for his first pro fight, all in $1 bills. He knocked out an Indian named Chief Cariboo. Typical of Baer even then, he drank five bottles of soda pop before the bout.

In his second year, Max went right on boffing out all West Coast talent. Now managed by Ancil Hoffman, he piled up 20 K.O.'s in 29 matches, and could demand and get $10,000 a fight without sticking his nose out of California.

Baer's smashing triumph over Schmeling made him the leading contender for the title Sharkey had lost to Carnera. Across the nation, fight fans clamored for Max to meet The Preem and bring the heavyweight championship back to America.

The result was an orgiastic slaughter. Max beat the huge Italian into a bloody pulp, while 50,000 witnesses looked on with mingled emotions of excitement, disgust and pity. As though only one hand was necessary, Max kept pounding Carnera with his powerhouse right, swinging it like a club. Max knocked him down 11 times in 11 rounds to become the 13th heavyweight champion of the world.

Like Jack Sharkey and Schmeling before him, Baer lost his title in his very first defense, a year later. The Braddock fight was a dull, routine affair, a painful spectacle of an

Madcap Maxie Baer brought laughter to the prize ring at a time when there was nothing funny about the heavyweights. (UPI)

over-confident, silly kid losing to an aged, methodical club fighter. "I clowned away the title in 15 rounds," Baer confessed later.

Baer said he was through with fighting. He said his wife, Mary Ellen, wanted him to retire. Then Mike Jacobs offered him $150,000 to fight Joe Louis. The Brown Bomber beat him into bloody, gory submission in four rounds. Baer went on fighting until April 4, 1941, when he joined the Army Air Force. At first, he couldn't pass the physical, but he hollered and whooped it up until the brass let him in. "How could they keep me out?" he demanded. "Why, I started the whole damn war, getting Hitler all riled up by beating Schmeling and then getting Mussolini against us by what I did to poor old Carnera!"

S/Sgt. Max Baer toured around the battle camps teaching physical education with all the color and aplomb of his days as world champion. He had his own private airplane, a captain to fly it, and a first lieutenant to carry his bags. At least, that's the way nutsy Maxie told it. Sure.

JAMES J. BRADDOCK
(1905–1974)

On January 21, 1938, Jim Braddock won a decision over Tommy Farr, the Englishman, and then took his bright green dressing gown that he'd worn into the ring so many times and put it away and hung up his gloves for the last time.

Thus there passed from the scene boxing's all-time Cinderella story. Greater fighters than the Jersey Irishman have held the heavyweight championship, but none of them ever made a deeper impression in his time. For Braddock's influence extended far beyond those who were interested in boxing. He touched those who never saw a bout, wouldn't go across the street to see one and, except for him, had no interest in any prizefighter. The aged and the infirm and out of luck. The forgotten victims of the Great Depression that crushed and tormented them.

It was, of course, Braddock's rise from the docks and the relief rolls to the heavyweight championship that captured the imagination and spurred the hopes of those whose imagination had been dulled and whose hopes had been all but shattered. There is no way of estimating how many persons all over the world must have been inspired by his feat. Many a man, and many a woman, too, must have said: "I can't win the heavyweight championship of the world. But I can do as this man has done. I can attack the forces that are strangling me. I can beat them." Letters came to Braddock from all over the world. Some of them were from small boys who wanted to grow up to be big and strong as their hero. But most of them were from those whom life had treated shabbily. Men who'd had good positions and lost them—whose savings had been swept away by the Wall Street disaster—whose families were in need; from those who had been left alone in the world and who were plodding a weary way, hopeless until this big guy had come swinging back from obscurity to show them how a losing fight could be won.

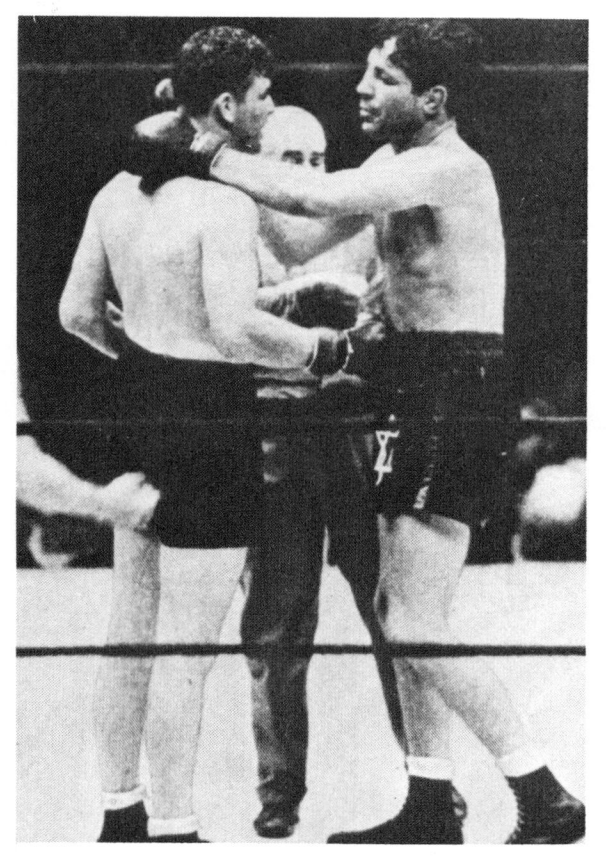

There have been a lot of guys who could fight better than Jimmy Braddock. But there were few who came into the ring the way he did. He approached a fight the way a clerk goes to his desk every morning. It was the job he worked at to make a living for his family and he did the best he knew how. Braddock, on the left here, is shown being congratulated by Max Baer after winning a 15-round decision and the championship in 1934. (NEA)

May Braddock, Jim's wife, remembered that the year before her husband won the title, their gas was shut off, and there was nothing to eat in the house. "Jim went out to see if he could borrow just a few dollars," she said. "And that night, we went on relief. It hurt Jim's pride. After he won the Art Lasky fight, he paid it all back—$240."

Braddock was an 11–2 underdog against Max Baer. The United Press called it "the most one-sided heavyweight championship fight in history." Jim was twenty-nine years old, Baer twenty-six. Newspapers called it "the fight nobody wants." It had been only two years before that Jim was relegated to boxing's dump heap—and then was hauled away from his work as a dock stevedore to fill in as one of the preliminary pugs when Baer won the title from Carnera. Dempsey, Tunney, Sharkey, Carnera, Jim Jeffries, Jess Willard, Tommy Loughran, Benny Leonard and Max Schmeling—they all picked Baer to win.

Harry Grayson, the only syndicated sports writer to pick Tunney to beat Dempsey in their first fight, was sold on Braddock's pre-fight attitude. "When Baer tackles Braddock he'll be facing a fellow who will not be afraid of him, and who can punch more than a lick," Harry wrote. "When Baer hits this fellow, he'll get punched right back as long as Braddock is on his pins. Why, Jim would tackle a freight train if he were in a jam, and give the big engine its first poke."

The Associated Press called Braddock's victory over Baer "the most astounding upset since John L. Sullivan went down before Jim Corbett. Braddock didn't have a chance to cope with the bigger, stronger, harder-hitting

It was Braddock's philosophy that a fighter goes as far as he can. The night Joe Louis took the title from him, in 1937, Jimmy fought with the calmness of a man with great pride in himself. After knocking Louis down in the first round, it was obvious that Braddock didn't have a chance. His handlers demanded he quit. But Braddock said no and Louis gave him a terrible beating. He was still trying to get up in the eighth round here as the referee counted him out. Braddock proved that night he was better than the record in the book. (NEA)

Baer—but he kept fighting, punching, piling up points by paying strict attention to the business of the evening. He earned the unanimous decision of the referee and both judges."

No one was more surprised over Braddock's triumph than Dumb Dan Morgan, who had worked with him at training camp. "Actually," Dan told me, "Jim was all washed up when he won the title. Baer should have chased him out of the ring, but goofy Max had his eyes on the blondes and brunettes and redheads in the audience instead of on Jim. He had dames on his mind, not a million-dollar title. That kind of lady-killer would tip his hat to a clothesline if it had a skirt on it."

Harry Grayson felt that Braddock had brought prizefighting back to the boxing fans. "The fight racket is much better off for having a wholesome chap like Braddock at the head of the procession than a wisecracking clown like Baer," Grayson told his national audience. "Braddock's amazing comeback has more people talking boxing today than at any other time since the Tunney-Dempsey series. Schmeling, Sharkey, Carnera and Baer were unable to resell the more substantial citizen; now Braddock has recaptured them. I'd say that Jim is vastly under-rated. Full credit is denied him simply because the experts cannot imagine anyone coming from such a depth of defeat and disappointment in only a year. I recall the boys referring to Tunney as the 'Greenwich Village Folly' and offering to wager that he wouldn't even show up for his first fight with the mighty Dempsey. And yet, Gene suddenly became a superman when he beat Jack again a year later."

James J. Braddock was the *fourth* "James J." in history to win the world heavyweight prize—James J. Corbett, James J. Jeffries, and James J. Tunney being the others. He had already wound up his career, and was an old man—a *very* old man, of twenty-nine—when he left his Hoboken, New Jersey, waterfront job and climbed in against Baer. It is doubted that promoter Mike Jacobs or anyone else connected with that bout, including Braddock himself, had any idea he could beat Max. But he did, and he wore the crown with dignity and lost it the same way. That night in Chicago, June 22, 1937, he took a frightful beating from Joe Louis, but when Joe Gould, his manager, wanted to toss in a towel for him, he said through the haze of blood in his eyes: "If you do, I'll never speak to you again as long as I live."

Jim's last fight, against Farr, was typical of him. At the end of the eighth round of a 10-round bout at Madison Square Garden, Jim asked Gould: "How am I doing?"

"You're losing, Jim."

"Well," Jim said, "watch me do the big apple in the next two rounds."

And he went back out there and beat Farr in the next two rounds, won the decision, and, in the dressing room afterward, Gould said to him: "That was great, Jim. But that's the end. You'll never fight again." And since Jim Braddock never questioned his manager's judgment, he never did.

JOE LOUIS
(1914–   )

"Nobody hits like Louis," Jimmy Braddock said one time.

"What about Max Baer?" he was asked.

"A joke compared to Joe," Jimmy insisted. "A punch is a punch. But that Louis. Take the first jab he nails you. You know what it's like? It's like someone jammed an electric bulb in your face and busted it."

"What about the right hand?"

"It ain't like a punch," Braddock said. "It's like someone nailed you with a crowbar. I

Training for Carnera, Joe Louis, second from left, sparred with the biggest heavyweights his trainers could find. This trio averaged 6 ft., 4 in. and 250 pounds. (From Joe Louis scrapbook)

thought half my head was blown off. I figured he caved it in. I felt it after he hit me and I couldn't even feel if it was there."

Watching Joe Louis come rushing out of his corner at the work bell was like watching the opening scene of a horror movie. The fans in the front row had to move back when he started swinging his bludgeons. The swish of his fists was like the falling of a sequoia.

There are those who will tell you that Louis was an ordinary heavyweight who was erroneously accused of greatness because of the ineptness of his opposition.

"But don't you believe them," wrote the late Jimmy Cannon, one of the Brown Bomber's most vocal defenders. "There were few as good in any age and that goes for all of them. You can start with John L. Sullivan and come right down the list. There never was a heavyweight champion who took the chances Louis did. They were all alike to him and he fought them all. He never ducked anyone. There were nights when he was slovenly and could not solve the moves of his opponents, but always he went at them and tried to compel them to fight. The only plan he ever had was to go for a guy and stick with him until he could catch him. It always was his theory that a champion does not defend his title. He puts it there for them to take. They never had to search for him. Always he came at them and he tried to get them out of there as fast as he could. There never was any stalling to make the other guy look good. If he caught you he nailed you and his pursuit was always hurried. And so I have to put him down as the greatest champion that ever held the title. No one ever fought more. When I say he was the best I am not defending my generation. The book will tell you how good he was and all the fights were won without the edge most fighters need to build a reputation."

Speaking up for the Old Guard, I once asked Dan Morgan if he thought any of the oldtimers could have licked Louis. Unlike Jim Jeffries, who thought rating the all-time champs was a lot of damned hogwash, Morgan thrived on debate and controversy. His eyes shone brightly as he pondered the question.

"I will give you five men who could have beaten Louis," Dan said. "Jeffries, Fitzsimmons, Johnson, Sam Langford and, of course, Dempsey. Jeff weighed about 215 in shape, was a great boxer and kayoed the greatest slugger, Fitz, twice. He also outboxed and stopped Corbett twice—and Jim was the father of American boxing. As for Fitz, he was a shifty, powerful hitter with both hands; a short-arm puncher. He'd paralyze Louis' body, shift to the head and knock him out.

Joe Louis was an amateur in Detroit when NEA Sports Editor-Columnist Harry Grayson, left, first spotted him and started writing about him in his nationally syndicated articles. Here Harry gets the lowdown from the Brown Bomber. (NEA)

"Johnson would block Louis, counter-punch him, talk to him, confuse him and stop him within five or six rounds.

"Langford, who was a scientific knocker-outer, would crowd Louis, either lead to him or counter him, and take whatever Joe could dish out. I think Sam would finish Joe in about six or seven rounds of real slugging."

You already know what Morgan thought of a Dempsey-Louis match. However, Dan by no means considered Louis a soft touch. He respected Joe's clean fighting and courage, but he recognized his obvious fault—that the Brown Bomber always was a target for a right-hand punch.

"Just look at the guys who hurt him," pointed out Morgan. "After Schmeling came old Jim Braddock. Jim was all washed up when he defended his title against Louis, but before he went out he had Louis on the deck in the first round—from a right hand to the jaw.

"And how about Two-Ton Tony Galento, that spaghetti-mangling bartender from New Jersey? 'Yussel' Jacobs managed him, and before the fight he came to me and asked me what to do. We met up in Yus' office, just like we did before the first Schmeling-Louis fight. I stood this big keg of beer, Galento, in the middle of the room and told him to pay close attention. But he kept muttering, 'Louis is a bum. I'll moider him.' I had to put up with that sort of stuff for half an hour before the lug would pay close attention.

"I told Galento that Louis was a slow starter and expected his opponent to throw a right hand as his first punch. Now, this sawed-off Eyetalian could really belt with either hand. I made Tony swear he would keep his right hand cocked and would keep moving to Louis' left. I told him, if Joe came in close, to grab him and yank him around to the left. This would prevent Louis from hitting him with a right. After Two-Ton had interrupted with several of his own versions of how he would 'moider' Louis, he said okay.

Louis had to wait five years for rematch with Irish Billy Conn after their sensational 1941 meeting. This second fight saw a heavier and not so daring Conn fall beneath Louis' fists in the eighth round. (UPI)

When he figured Louis was confused, I told him, leap in—not with a right hand—but with a left hook to the head. Galento grunted and promised to follow instructions.

"Louis must have been a 12–1 favorite. You recall the fight. Galento rushed across the ring at the first bell and leaped at Louis with a left hook which landed high on Joe's right cheekbone. The blow drove Joe back against the ropes well shaken up. Then Two-Ton lost his head and rushed in wide open. He took quite a beating in the first two rounds, but just kept muttering, 'He's a bum.' In the third, Galento followed instructions. He went into a crouch, his left hand high, his right drawn well behind him as if he intended to throw a roundhouse 'haymaker' at any moment. Louis watched carefully, bewildered by Tony's switch in style. Suddenly this little wild man lunged at Louis. He caught Joe with that left hook on the temple and the champion of the world hit the floor! The crowd was screaming like madmen. This thing couldn't happen. This freakish little fat man could not *possibly* lick the great Joe Louis. We'll never know. Yus Jacobs screamed for Tony to keep his head, but it was like trying to win an argument with your mother-in-law. Tony always thought Louis was a bum—now he knew it. He would knock the bum out. You know what happened. Louis got off the floor, tore into the over-anxious Galento and knocked him out in the following round.

"Joe Louis was a good fighter, sure, but good only for the times. I saw too many second-raters put him on the floor to think he would have had a chance with the great ones of another day. I taught Jersey Joe Walcott to beat him in their first match, and beat him Walcott did, by a city block, though they wouldn't give Jersey Joe the crown.

"I have to rank Louis eighth on my list of all-time heavyweight champs, behind Jeffries, Sullivan, Johnson, Fitzsimmons, Corbett, Tunney and Dempsey. That doesn't mean Joe couldn't fight. Actually, I'm rating him far up the list. He did everything that was asked of him. He fought every leading contender, and gave them all a chance at his title. Along the way, he flattened six other heavyweight champions: Baer, Carnera, Sharkey, Braddock, Schmeling, and Walcott. Boxers, sluggers, maulers, he took them all in stride without a whimper. But Louis was such a fine, sincere man that we were inclined to overglorify his fighting prowess. Seldom has there been a heavyweight champion who has done so much good for the prize ring. Certainly no fist-fighter, and very few men in any walk of life, ever has done so much for his race."

Old Dan Morgan could have gotten quite an argument from Jimmy Jacobs, several times national handball champion and a boxing buff extraordinary. For years, Jimmy went to considerable expense to prove to anyone interested in his crusade that the old-time champs were a bunch of bums. He bought up a collection of old fight films which he felt showed conclusively that Joe Louis could whip Jack Johnson, Rocky Graziano could take Stanley Ketchel, and Ray Robinson could probably chase Bob Fitzsimmons right out of the ring.

He persuaded Jim Murray to view the evidence with him at his home in Brentwood, California one night. Jim had to admit some of it was high comedy.

"Jimmy's most devastating piece of evidence is a staged fight in Edison's kinescope laboratory between Corbett and an Englishman named Peter Courtney," reported Murray. "This Courtney was really something. I only wish my wife were that clumsy in a fight. He fought like he was trying to run up the side of a greased tree. He didn't punch. He just held his arms straight out and ran into the other guy. Corbett didn't look too good, either. He was laughing too hard. In the Fitzsimmons-Corbett title fight, poor old Fitz with his bald head showed up in a long overcoat looking for all the world like a guy who had just come downstairs with a cake of soap and a towel over his arm to get in line in the boarding-house shower. He fought like a stork with a backache. On the other hand, the films were jerky and inconclusive. And something did knock Jim Corbett kicking. He tried to get up and his feet splattered out from underneath him as though he had been lassoed."

Jim Murray confessed later he did not really know what the Jacobs films proved, except that the state of the art of prizefighting was in a primitive stage back in those days of Corbett, Fitzsimmons, Jeffries and that crowd.

"So, for that matter, was the art of the motion picture," Murray concluded. "Between the two, I doubt they did justice to the old fellows."

Tim Cohane, former Sports Editor of *Look*, made the point in his wonderful *Bypaths of Glory* that a boxer cannot become a bona fide champion until he has fought many tough men and learned about punishment.

"Pain and hardship fashioned Dempsey," Tim wrote. "The ordeal of his first fight with Harry Greb, the only bout he ever lost, brought out the gold and steel in Gene Tunney. Joe Louis, who may have been the best of them all, did not really find himself until after he was knocked out by Max Schmeling in their first fight."

After his first professional defeat, Joe had no alibi to offer. "The man just whupped me," he explained to his mother. Someone asked him if he wanted to see the movies of his battle with Schmeling. "No," Joe said, "I saw the fight."

It was the two Schmeling fights that twice changed the character of Louis as a man. From a too-confident, lazy youngster the defeat transformed him into an ambitious hustler who realized that there was no easy road to the top. Even after winning the world championship from Braddock, Louis often remarked, "I won't be champion until I get that Schmeling."

Jimmy Cannon believed Louis was the greatest fighter who ever lived the night he took Schmeling apart, in 1938. The night before the fight, at Pompton Lakes, Jimmy and Joe had dinner together and talked about the fight.

Joe asked Jimmy, "Did you make a pick?"

"Yes," Jimmy said.

"Knockout?" Louis asked.

"Six rounds," Jimmy said.

"No," Louis said. "One." He held up a big finger. "It go one," he said. That's all it went.

Some sports writers, trying to pry a word out of Louis, a school dropout, gave up in despair. They thought him dull and colorless. Overnight, the second Schmeling fight seemed to change all that. Released of the pent-up fury he had harbored, Louis became affable and talkative, self-possessed. Once when he was in the army during World War II and was called upon to acknowledge a tribute to himself before a large audience at a Navy Relief show, soldier Joe, unrehearsed,

HEAVYWEIGHTS

Contenders were all alike to Louis and he fought them all. He never ducked anyone. He packed power in his left here, knocking challenger Tammy Mauriello completely off his feet. (NEA)

fidgeted with his uniform for a second and took the microphone. He spoke clearly: "I want to thank you for such a fine thing you have just said. I'm only doing what any red-blooded American would. We're going to win this war 'cause we're on God's side."

In several ways, Joe Louis was the greatest champion that ever graced the prize ring. He defended the world heavyweight title 25 times, and for 11 years, 8 months and 9 days—more times and longer than any prize ring champion in history. His administration as champion, which began in June, 1937, and ended in 1949 (when he first retired) or in 1950 (when Ezzard Charles beat him), was not only the longest in boxing annals, but one of the most popular with the public. He commanded respect and admiration from nearly all people of all groups who follow boxing closely, and from a good many people who do not.

"Joe Louis," reported the United Press, "was probably the most widely known American black man who ever lived."

Louis once told Jimmy Cannon that the night he beat Max Baer was his finest night in prizefighting. "I felt better that night," he said. "I felt like I could fight for two, three days."

Baer had boasted in his dressing room

about what he would do to Louis. But when the call came to go to the ring, Baer began to pant. "I can't go out there," he cried to Jack Dempsey, who was with him in his corner that night. "I can't breathe." So Dempsey conned him into the ring. "After the first round," Dempsey recalled, "Max came back to the corner and said he couldn't breathe. I told him I'd kill him with the water bottle if he didn't go back out there and get knocked out."

Louis picked the Arturo Godoy fight as his worst. "I guess I tried too hard with him," Joe said. "I was stale. I couldn't do nothing."

The bout was billed as an exhibition and was fought in Santiago, Chile, in 1947. Luis Angel Firpo was the referee. It was the first time Firpo ever saw Louis fight, and Godoy was a very tough man. Unruly, he tried to turn the exhibition into a full-fledged war. After Godoy aimed several savage punches at Louis, Firpo warned Arturo to behave himself. In his irritation, Godoy knocked the referee down. Louis then stepped in and restored calm with several sharp blows to Godoy's head and knocked him out.

Against Ezzard Charles, in 1950, Joe had passed his prime and was trying for the proverbial elusive "comeback." But he was brutally and ignominiously crushed by an underdog in 15 rounds. Charles hammered Joe around as he pleased, punching him as if he were a bean bag. Charles did everything to Joe except knock him out. It was only Joe's second defeat in a career dating back to 1934.

A lot of people felt sorry for old Joe, thirty-six, that night he lost to the twenty-nine-year-old Charles. The blinding speed in his fists was gone. Most of the $4,000,000 he had made as a fighter was gone, too—in taxes, bad investments, bad friends, plain foolishness. He still fought because he needed cash to pay $250,000 in back income taxes.

When the Charles fight was over, Louis, battered but $100,000 richer, told reporters: "I enjoyed the fight and want to thank you all. I done the best I can."

When both were finished with prizefighting, an exhibition match between Louis and Billy Conn was arranged by Frankie Harmon.

Popular with the troops in World War II, Louis said he was "only doing what any red-blooded American would do" when he signed up for the Army. "We're going to win this war 'cause we're on God's side," he told his audiences. (UPI)

"What percentage is Billy getting?" Louis asked the promoter before the match.

Harmon told him. "Take five per cent of my end," Louis said. "Put it on Billy's."

Joe never told Conn that.

Joe Louis improved the fight racket with his presence. There was conceit in him but he controlled it. There was a lot of pride in him, too, but it never took charge of him. He was shy and he hid in silence when there were strangers around, but he was easy-going and good company if you were a friend.

"He was a great champion and I'm glad he was a champion in my time," Jimmy Cannon said. "He was mean at his work but he was able to leave it in the ring. The cruelty was there, all right. He was a fighter—a boy's dream of a fighter—and that's the finest compliment I can give him."

Jim Bishop, the author and syndicated columnist, remembers sitting in Madison Square Garden, on October 26, 1951, and shaking his head in sorrow as he saw Rocky Marciano pummel and knock Louis out in Joe's last official fight. "I saw Joe hit, hit again by Rocky, and fall face down on the canvas and roll outside the ropes," Bishop said. Later, Jim played some golf with Marciano. "You see," Rocky told him, "Joe didn't know he was my hero, when I was growing up in Brockton. The writers said I flattened him and turned my back. They didn't know I was crying."

EZZARD CHARLES
(1921–1975)

Ezzard "Snooks" Charles was perhaps too conservative to be called a great champion, yet he compares favorably with Joe Louis. Charles fought as cleanly as the Detroit Bomber, and was a better boxer. His critics accused him of undue discretion; however, when cornered, he reacted like a catamount. They also claimed he was nothing more than "an overgrown light-heavyweight," and passed him off only as "the best of a bad lot of heavyweights," after he made a mockery of doddering old Louis in 1950.

Poppycock!

The six-foot Charles, who weighed 184, was faster than Louis, who outweighed him by more than 30 pounds when they fought at Yankee Stadium, and unlike Joe, Ezzard could boss the other fellow from start to finish, and make him fight *his* way. Finally, he

Ezzard Charles was the best prizefighter of his particular time. (Photo courtesy Ezzard Charles)

was completely unimpressed by an opponent's credentials, as witness his two fights with Rocky Marciano.

Charles made two attempts in 1954 to win back his world championship from Marciano. The Rock decisioned him the first time in 15, then in the rematch knocked him out in the eighth round. Early in the first fight, Rocky drove a hard right in to the side of Ezzard's head. "That punch was one of Marciano's best," Charles said later, "and I said to myself, 'If that's all he's got, I can stay with him for 15 rounds and maybe knock him out.' I did stay with him 15 rounds, and I almost knocked him out in the middle of the fight."

Ezzard was born at Lawrenceville, Georgia, July 7, 1921, and grew up in Cincinnati. At first, he showed no particular enthusiasm for fighting, though he won 42 amateur fights in a row. He turned professional at eighteen and promptly kayoed one Medley Johnson. Thereafter he won 64 of his next 68 bouts.

In his 69th fight, he decisioned Jersey Joe Walcott in 15 rounds to win the heavyweight championship in Chicago, June 22, 1949. There followed K.O.'s over Gus Lesnevich, Pat Valentino, and Freddie Beshore. And, in the meantime, Louis was wondering if he hadn't been a bit hasty in his decision to retire.

Joe was determined to succeed where Jeffries, Dempsey and others had failed. He was thirty-six and far over the hill; Charles was twenty-nine and getting younger by the minute. The challenge was too much for old Joe to resist.

The bout took place on September 27, 1950, and it was clear from the start that Louis was through. Balding, pot-bellied, his reflexes slowed by time, Joe might better have dressed for the theatre. Gone was the magnificent bombardier of yore. Joe was sluggish and uncertain, Charles quick and confident. At the end of the noble experiment, Grantland Rice scored 13 rounds for Charles, 2 for Louis.

Ezzard successfully defended his crown against Nick Barone, Lee Oma and twice against Jersey Joe. Then an amazing thing happened. In a fourth title match with Walcott, held in Pittsburgh, July 18, 1951, Old Pappy Guy Joe turned on his young tormentor and flattened him in the seventh round! Ezzard had gone to the well of wisdom once too often.

Critics have tried to fault Charles on the grounds he couldn't punch. But he could—43 of his first 73 matches ended in K.O.'s.

Davey Ward pooh-poohs Ezzard's detractors. Davey had a clearer view of Charles in action than the critics. On July 13, 1956, at Tacoma, Washington, Ward refereed the Charles–Pat McMurtry bout.

"I always felt Ezzard was vastly underrated," Davey said. "Even though he was past his peak when he fought Marciano, he gave Rocky a fantastic battle. Charles was great in all departments. He had all the courage in the world, and could take the big punch. He was a terrific puncher himself. In fact, as a middleweight he once killed a fighter in the ring. For a long time, that handcuffed his mental attitude. Many times he had to be hurt himself before he started punching back. But once he found the range, bye-bye baby."

Red Smith, the most quoted sports writer of his time, agreed with the Ward thesis.

"Some day, maybe," Red said, "the public is going to abandon comparisons with Joe Louis and accept Ezzard Charles for what he was—the best fist-fighter of his particular time."

Ezzard Charles spent the last seven years of his life suffering from lateral sclerosis of the spine. He was paralyzed from the waist down. The end came in Chicago on May 28, 1975.

JERSEY JOE WALCOTT
(1914?–)

When you bring up the subject of the greatest fighter in the heavyweight division, a number of names like Jeffries, Johnson, Dempsey, and Louis tend to come up a lot.

When you bring up the subject of the oldest to win the title, there's no contest. It took venerable Jersey Joe Walcott 21 years of seesawing the highs and lows of prizefighting to reach the pinnacle. He was an admitted thirty-seven when he won the title from Ezzard Charles in 1951. Some people swore he was forty-one. There is no birth certificate.

The story of Arnold Raymond Cream (his christened name) was the old heartbreak of boxing. In some ways, the facts were even more remarkable than those behind Jim Braddock. Jersey Joe had hit rock bottom so hard and long he almost dropped clear through. The experts had written him off as "a cutie, a cautious man with little respect for his own ability." His style consisted of no style at all. He would run and hide, skip and loiter, occasionally punch with a right hand, pausing timidly in his constant flight.

"The darkest hour of my career was in 1936," Walcott told me once. "I broke my arm. I couldn't work because of it. There was only $9.50 in weekly relief money to feed my wife and six small kids. I couldn't have gone any farther down, even if I pulled the stopper."

Sixteen years later, after having retired *six* times from the ring and been sidelined for three and a half years, Jersey Joe was champion of the world.

"I want to thank God for helping me win," Joe said afterward. "I've always said that if God's on your side, you're bound to win sooner or later."

That was not idle chatter, for Walcott was a very religious man. The metropolitan press quickly nicknamed him "The Praying Puncher." Prayer to the champion meant sitting down and talking things over with God.

Walcott began his career at sixteen as a middleweight. Jack Blackburn, the old lightweight, had him for a brief spell, being lured away to develop the rising Joe Louis. Then along came James J. Johnston, one of the su-

HEAVYWEIGHTS 53

Arch Hindman, center, Chairman of the Indiana State Boxing Commission, has a few words with Jersey Joe and his manager, Felix Bocchicchio, in Indianapolis. It was Bocchicchio who talked Walcott back out of retirement in 1945 after he had given up on himself for the sixth time. (Photo courtesy Arch Hindman)

perior managers of the day, to pick up where Blackburn left off, but Jimmy lost interest in Joe midway between 1941 and '45, and Walcott fought only two inconsequential matches in tiny Batesville, New Jersey, during those years.

Finally, Felix Bocchicchio picked Joe off the floor. If ever a man had faith in a human being, Felix had it in Walcott. Ironically, Bocchicchio knew nothing about boxing. He was something of a racket guy and boss in Camden. But Felix learned fast. He set sail for potential heavyweight championship challengers whom the Louis camp either politely refused to fight, or just flatly cold-shouldered. One was Curtis Sheppard, the Hatchet Man. Walcott put a lily in his hand in the 10th round in Baltimore. He also out-fenced Lee Oma. Early in '46, Louis predicted that Jimmy Bivins would be the next champion. Joe gave the chill to a $100,000 offer to fight Bivins in Cleveland, so Jersey Joe floored Jimmy and gave him a wicked lacing.

Mushky Jackson dispelled the legend that Walcott knocked Joe Louis down at Lakewood, New Jersey, in early June of '36, when Louis was training for his first and disastrous duel with Max Schmeling. Jackson hustled sparring partners for Louis, and Jersey Joe was one of them.

"Louis half slipped, that was all," Jackson said. "Walcott refused to go another round for $25, so I chased him out of the camp."

Walcott went along with the legend because it was good pre-fight ballyhoo. It was good for business.

Walcott dropping Louis

Jersey Joe Walcott was so lightly regarded that his first fight with Joe Louis, in 1947, was billed at first as an exhibition bout; finally was put on over the 15-round championship distance. A Buffalo firm tried to rent the soles of Walcott's shoes as advertising space for the moment when Louis made his toes turn up. Jersey Joe shocked the crowd when he floored Louis in the first and fourth rounds. At the end of 15 rounds, referee Ruby Goldstein voted for Walcott, but the two judges gave it to Louis, causing considerable wonder as to which fight they were watching. (Photographer unknown)

HEAVYWEIGHTS

Though he'd come back twice to repulse Joey Maxim, Walcott was so lightly regarded still that his first match with Louis, on December 5, 1947, was at first scheduled only as a "10-round, no-decision exhibition." Finally, the promoter agreed to change it to a 15-round championship match, remembering that a heavyweight titleholder brings his crown along every time he's in the ring.

A Buffalo firm had so little faith in Walcott that it tried to rent the soles of his shoes as advertising space should Louis make his toes turn up.

Walcott floored Louis in the first round and again in the fourth. He punched his ears off. After 15 rounds, Referee Ruby Goldstein voted for Jersey Joe, but the judges awarded the decision to Louis, causing great wonder as to which fight they'd been watching. Even Louis himself candidly confessed in his autobiography later that Walcott really won their first match.

Six months later, Louis settled all questions by knocking Walcott deader than last week's newspaper in the 11th round.

Jersey Joe was long overdue when he clipped Ezzard Charles with a left hook, and so was his world championship.

On September 23, 1952, Walcott defended his title against Marciano in Philadelphia in what was described by many experts as "the best heavyweight championship fight" since Jack Dempsey vs. Luis Angel Firpo, 29 years before. The match went a long way toward putting the fight game back on its feet. Marciano had to come from behind to knock out the champion in the 13th round, after being in trouble the previous rounds.

Two fights against the Brockton Blockbuster taught Jersey Joe one of the axioms of prizefighting: *You can't out-smart a sock on the chin!*

Jersey Joe Walcott fought from 1930 to May, 1953. In 67 professional fights, he won 49 of them, 30 by knockouts.

"I had only the deepest respect for Jersey Joe as a man and a champion," Gene Tunney once said. "He boxed well, cutely if not classically, and he had a strong punch in either hand. He was also cautious, but his caution did not prevent him from scoring knockdowns and knockouts. He had Joe Louis on the floor three times, and he knocked out Charles. If Joe had been accorded proper instruction and support earlier in his career, it might not have taken him so long to win the championship."

ROCKY MARCIANO
(1923–1969)

Tim Cohane summed up the Rocky Marciano personality as well as anyone.

"Rocky was a heavyweight champion in the finest sense," Tim said. "He won all his 49 professional fights and his behavior reflected credit on a sport that can always use it. No fist-fighter was more dedicated to his work—and none so glad to hear the last bell that freed him from it for life."

Marciano was the first heavyweight champion in history to retire with a hundred percent perfect professional record. He never lost a fight.

Early in his boxing career, Rocco Francis Marchegiano decided the first thing he would have to do was change his name. He shortened it to Rocky Mack, and then Rocky March. He finally settled for Marciano.

"At least that sounds Italian," Rocky said.

There was no question about the second Louis-Walcott fight, in 1948, at Yankee Stadium. Louis stopped the challenger in the 11th round. Jersey Joe blamed part of his problem on referee Frank Fullam. "The ref kept shouting at me and riding me constantly," Walcott explained. Did this affect the outcome? "Well," Joe said, "it certainly didn't help me." (UPI)

The late Anthony Petronella, former N.B.A. president, gave Rocky the name Marciano. It came about as something of an accident.

"Nine of Rocky's first 11 professional fights were fought in Providence, Rhode Island, our home town," Petronella recalled once. "It was my job to prepare a copy of the matches each fight night for Harold Warman, the ring announcer, and give the list to him prior to the first bout so that he could practice pronouncing the names. Well, the first time Rocky fought there Harold tripped over the name *Marchegiano*. Finally, I told him to call him *Marciano*. 'No one will know the difference, Harold,' I said. So as the new Rocky Marciano, he knocked out Harry Balzerian in the first round. I'll never forget Rocky coming into Rhode Island Auditorium that night, 1948, packing an oil-stained brown paper bag in which his mother had packed three big Italian sandwiches. Win or lose, *her* son wasn't going to starve."

Rocky Marciano went on to take rank with Jack Dempsey as a power-puncher. Gene Tunney agreed that he had at least one asset that matched Dempsey. "Dempsey could take it," Gene said. "He could take it to a full degree—and so could Rocky."

At the beginning, Rocky was as clumsy a novice as anybody ever saw. He either nailed his man with a knockout right hand or fell down after missing. Dick Francisco, the Seattle business man and ex-fighter pilot and prizefighter, used to spar with Marciano, when Rocky was stationed at Fort Lewis, Washington, in 1946.

"I was coaching the Greenwood Boy's Club, in Seattle," Dick said. "Because there were so few heavyweights for Rocky to work out with in nearby Tacoma, Rocky would travel the 45 miles from Fort Lewis to Seattle and train with me at Greenwood. Sometimes I'd go out to the Fort and work with him there.

"After Rocky became champion, it was written that he unquestionably was the crudest heavyweight ever to get a crack at the crown, let alone win it. He was probably the first heavyweight champion who had to be schooled. But this much could be said for him from the start: he was totally unafraid and very aggressive. He hit you as though swinging a baseball bat. When he came to me, he was still an amateur and I'd won the All-Service light-heavyweight title while in the Marine Flying Corps. I recall, however, getting hit by some of his looping right-hand blockbusters on my arms, nearly paralyzing me. I was quite fast and he could never hit me on the head, but I carried my hands pretty high just in case. I never really got nailed by him, but, remember, he was then just a raw beginner. It wasn't until little Charley Goldman got him that he began to learn the art of boxing. Looking back, I saw Rocky as a real tough Italian kid, with all the heart and courage in the world—but a future heavyweight champion of the world, *never*."

Rocky was born at Brockton, Massachusetts, on September 1, 1923. His father was a poor man. He worked in a shoe factory. "When Rocky was still a boy," Pierino Marchegiano recalled, "he told me that when he grew up he'd be heavyweight champion of the world and make a million dollars and take care of all the family." Mr. Marchegiano found it hard to believe the childish prediction even after it came true. "There's something about this that scares me," he'd say, shaking his head.

Rocky was managed by Al Weill, who had also managed other champions—Lou Ambers, Joey Archibald and Marty Servo. Johnny Buckley, who once managed Jack Sharkey, passed up the chance to manage Marciano. Rocky was "cut down the middle" by Weill. That is, Weill got 50 percent of what Rocky earned; Al, however, paid all expenses from his share. In his first 38 fights—including the $50 he was paid for knocking out Lee Epperson at Holyoke, Massachusetts, in his first fight—Rocky's share came to about $750,000. After taxes, he ended up with about $300,000. "In the old days, any fighter who had as many tough fights as I've had—fights that brought in so much money—would have had three times what I have to show for it," Rocky remarked after his retirement in 1956. In his return fight with Jersey Joe Walcott in '53, Rocky's cut amounted to $83,962 less than the challenger's (due to a return-bout clause guaranteeing Walcott 30 percent of the gate).

Although it was not generally known, Frankie Carbo, hoodlum and gunman who wound up serving a long term at McNeil Island, the federal prison near Tacoma, Washington, had a 10 percent cut of Marciano. Carbo controlled many fighters behind the scenes, and Rocky was helpless to prevent the arrangement Weill had with Carbo. But Rocky never allowed the pact to influence his actions in the ring.

Marciano had a relatively short and blocky build for a heavyweight, and his reach of 68 inches was the shortest in championship history. An all-around athlete at Brockton High School, he'd have preferred to be a football (linebacker) or baseball (catcher) player. He once had a tryout in the Chicago Cubs' farm system at Fayetteville, North Carolina, after World War II. He had served overseas with the 150th Combat Engineers.

Marciano reminded oldtimers of Dempsey. He had a knockout punch in either hand. He took a punch beautifully. He had guts, a fighting heart. He feared no man, and would not have feared Dempsey. "I don't want to sound like a loud-mouthed bag o' wind," Rocky commented once, "but I don't think anybody in the world can lick me. I just don't think it'll ever happen." He was right, of course.

Rocky knew only one way to fight: slam in, throw punches, take them. Gene Tunney, for one, believed a Dempsey-Marciano fight would have been a cheek-to-jowl brawl that

Rocky staggers Joe Walcott with his "Suzie-Q" on way to 13th-round K.O. in Philadelphia, in 1952. (UPI)

would have had the crowd hysterical. His guess was that it would have provided the wildest first round since Firpo clubbed Dempsey out of the ring at the Polo Grounds.

I once asked Al Weill to explain his fighter.

"Rocky has something you don't see unless you're around him all the time," Weill said. "After a while, you know it's there, and so do the guys who get in there with him. Nature gave him everything he needs as a champion. He has unusual strength and stamina, a terrific punch and plenty of guts. No one ever trained harder or took better care of himself. Put all that together and you can see why it doesn't really matter who he fights. When he was going to fight Joe Louis, a fellow he worshipped and in a fight he knew would make or break him, he went to sleep in the dressing room. We had to wake him up 10 minutes before it was time to go into the ring."

Marciano's explosive victory over Joe Louis accomplished two things: He succeeded Louis as the biggest heavyweight gate attraction in boxing, and (2) he also succeeded in convincing Joe that the best place for old fighters to court their dreams is beside a fireplace. Louis was thirty-eight.

Against Louis, Marciano was strong, unafraid and a hurtful hitter. He should have been 1 to 10 in the betting. He wagered $1,000 to $10,000 on himself. That was the first time he'd ever bet a quarter on anything. When he tried to bet more, Weill told him: "Listen, Rocky, you do the fighting—and leave the betting to me."

Rocky fought his first pro bout when he was twenty-three-and-a-half years old—one of the latest starts of any champion in boxing history. He was twenty-eight when he won the title from Walcott. He defended his championship six times. All ended in kayoes except his first bout with Ezzard Charles. On September 21, 1955, he finished off Archie Moore in the ninth round, and seven months later announced his retirement. Jim Norris, the millionaire promoter, told Rocky later that he'd write him a check for $1,000,000 if he would come back and fight Floyd Patterson.

"No kind of money can make me fight again," Rocky told Norris. He stuck to his guns, too—even after a Kentucky group offered him $1,250,000 to fight one more time.

Marciano, as mild and soft-spoken out of the prize ring as he was rough and hard in it, once summed up his boxing philosophy this way: "Some people don't understand about professional fighters. We have a job to do. We try to take each other out of there. But once the fight is over, we seldom have any feelings of dislike toward each other. It's usually just the opposite."

Marciano won 43 of his 49 pro bouts on knockouts. One of those kayoes did not come in the above, however, as Ezzard Charles forced Rocky to the limit (15-round decision) in their June 17, 1954, match in New York. (UPI)

Rocky, who died in a plane crash near Des Moines, Iowa, on August 31, 1969, was knocked down only twice in a total of 49 professional fights. After hanging up his gloves, he went on a boat in the Bahamas 500, the toughest race of the offshore circuit. In the first 200 miles the cruel seas decked Rocky 20 times. At Nassau, the refueling point, Rocky announced, "I am getting off here and there are not enough natives on this island to stop me." Safely ashore, he confided to friends, "I have just been in two boat races: my first and my last."

In the prize ring, however, it was another story.

Rocky Marciano is remembered here as one

of the sweetest guys (out of the ring) you'd have ever wanted to know. There was no egotism about him. He never tried to throw his weight around. He was just one of the fellows. Once, Rocky was at Grossinger's training for a fight in defense of his title. Fight-minded guests at the famous resort could see him working out any afternoon for one buck, plus tax. As far as the guests were concerned, he had no identity and no meaning, so hidden had Al Weill kept him from the public.

One day, outside the main building at Grossinger's, Rocky was waiting for his trainer, Charlie Goldman, when a lady came out and said:

"Boy! Get me a cab!"

What did he do?

"I got her a cab," Rocky said.

Did she tip him?

"Not a quarter!" Rocky said.

Another day, he was sitting by the swimming pool. He was wearing slacks and a T-shirt stamped with the name Grossinger's on the chest. He was lying in a deck chair and a man came up to him and asked: "Do you work here?"

"No, sir," Rocky told him.

And the man said: "Then what are you wearing that shirt for? I was going to ask you . . ."

The late Anthony Petronella was credited with changing Rocky's last name from Marchegiano to Marciano. The former President of the N.B.A., here pictured on Rocky's left, listens as Rocky amuses audience at testimonial dinner in Providence, R.I., where the future heavyweight champ fought his early fights. (Photo courtesy Petronella family)

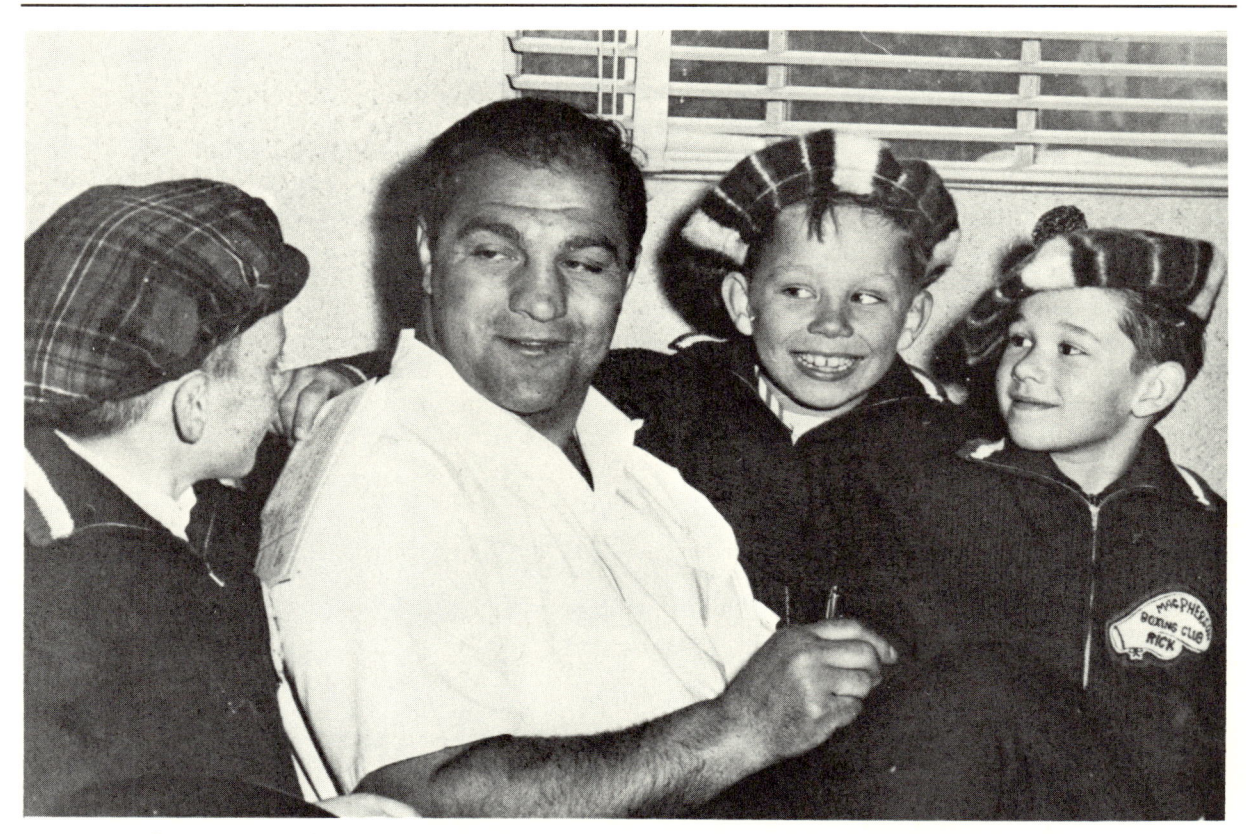

On a visit to Seattle in 1957, Rocky Marciano compared boxing tips with Seattle Golden Glovers Murry MacPherson, Charles Pomianek, and Rick Francisco. (Photo courtesy Dick Francisco)

Thinking about the incident later, Rocky said, "I'll never know what he was going to ask me. I guess I must have upset him. He just walked away."

Then there was this day in Rochester, New York. Rocky had won the Hickok Award as the Professional Athlete of the Year and had gone up there for his dinner, and in the afternoon, he took a long walk, all by himself, and when he came back to the hotel he said:

"This is a real nice town. Everybody is so friendly. I stopped in a drug store for an ice cream soda and the boy behind the counter was swell. We had a long talk. I had two sodas. He asked me if I'd ever been here before and I told him I hadn't and he told me a lot about the town. I certainly enjoyed meeting him."

"He doesn't know who you are?"

"Why, no!" Rocky said. "Why should he?"

"The Rock was a man of gentleness, kindness, compassion and affability," Arthur Daley, of *The New York Times*, said after Rocky died. "He brought dignity to the championship he held with such modest graciousness."

FLOYD PATTERSON
(1935–   )

When Floyd Patterson was 21 years, 331 days old, he won the heavyweight championship of the world. That made him the youngest in history to hold the title. He carved his niche in granite a second time when he defied the maxim "they never come back," and took rank as the first ex-champion to regain boxing's biggest prize.

The trouble with Patterson, however, was that he wasn't cut out to be a prizefighter. He fought 64 times in 20 years, twice earned the championship, narrowly missed winning the W.B.A. piece of it a third time when Jimmy Ellis outscored him in 1968—and yet, somehow, he never truly seemed a part of the violent world of the prize ring. His reputation was that of a bungler.

Among the Patterson detractors, Los Angeles columnist Jim Murray once tweaked his image this way: "Put Floyd in charge of a ship in a storm and he runs it aground. If he was a bloodhound you put on the track of an escaped convict, he'd lead you straight to the warden. And bite him. He's the kind of guy who goes through life spilling soup on the boss' wife. He saves his strikeouts for the ninth inning with the bases loaded. He only fumbles in his own end zone. If he tried to hypnotize you, he'd be the one to fall asleep. If they did his life story, they'd cast Buster Keaton. Floyd's been floored so often, ringsiders can only recognize him by the top of his head or the soles of his feet."

It was sometimes written of Floyd that he "is a kind of a stranger." For the more than two decades he fought he remained an enigma to a multitude of people. They simply could not understand how a man who was something of a mystic could find such gratification in a brutal business where sensitivity is so heavy a liability.

Floyd Patterson, the youngest heavyweight champion of all time, made history a second time when he became the first to regain the title. (Courtesy *Tacoma News Tribune*)

Floyd's evaluation of himself always was important to him.

"The critics may say what they feel, but I cannot think of any fights where I didn't give the fans their money's worth, except in the two Liston fights," he pointed out.

When Sonny Liston stopped him in the first round to win the title from Patterson in Chicago, on September 25, 1962, Floyd drove off into the night back to New York City and hid behind a false beard and mustache because the shame was more than the physical pain. In 1965, when Muhammad Ali tortured him and taunted him through 12 rounds, Patterson's body was hurt but his pride was intact because he had not been counted out. When he became the only man ever to win the heavyweight championship a second time, that should have been his finest hour. But he considered it his most debasing.

"I was filled with so much hate," he said, referring to his five-round K.O. of Ingemar Johansson in 1960. "I wouldn't ever want to reach that low again."

Like Marciano, Patterson had to take boxing lessons in the gym after turning pro. Even though he won the 1952 Olympic Games championship, he had a lot of faults to correct. Cus D'Amato, his manager, noticed that he punched with both feet off the floor. He crossed his right foot behind his left when he stepped to the left. He was easily hit. He didn't follow up an advantage; instead, he stayed back with his hands up. He didn't have the zest for viciousness. But D'Amato stayed with him and saw to it that Floyd mastered the fundamentals. He did an admirable job in bringing young Patterson along. Patterson won his first 13 pro bouts, 8 by knockouts.

Joey Maxim was the first to beat Patterson. Eleven of the 12 boxing writers at ringside thought Patterson won, but the officials voted for Maxim. That was Floyd's only defeat on his way to the heavyweight championship.

Seven months after Marciano retired, Patterson kayoed Archie Moore, the light-heavyweight king, in five rounds to become the youngest man in history to win the heavyweight title. In the first year and a half as champion, he kept pretty much out of circulation, due mostly to D'Amato's bitter feud with James D. Norris and the International Boxing Club. During that period, Floyd defended his crown against only Hurricane Jackson and

THE ENCYCLOPEDIA OF WORLD BOXING CHAMPIONS

In 1957, nearly 17,000 curiosity seekers paid $243,060 to watch a professional heavyweight champion (Patterson) fight an amateur champion (Pete Rademacher) in Seattle. The professional flattened the amateur in the sixth round. Sports writer Red Smith observed that Floyd looked like a man who wanted to carry an opponent and didn't know how. (Photo by Ken Ollar)

amateur Pete Rademacher. The latter was about as bizarre a world title match as ever has been foisted on the public—a case of the heavyweight division coming down to a challenger for the championship who never had had a professional fight. Rademacher's sole credentials were that he won a Gold Medal in the heavyweight division at the 1956 Olympics, and at Washington State University he'd been a rough, tough football lineman. Patterson was guaranteed $250,000 to fight Pete in Seattle.

A total of 16,961 people paid $243,060 to watch a professional champion fight an amateur champion. The professional knocked out the amateur in the sixth round. "Patterson," wrote Red Smith afterward, "looked like a man who wanted to carry an opponent and didn't know how."

When D'Amato refused to do business with the I.B.C., he set up his own private fights for Patterson. He hired fighters, from middleweights to heavyweights, to box Floyd. The idea was to give the champion work and to let him fight under regulation conditions. He fought 22 *secret* bouts. Floyd fought one opponent in secret on three successive days, stopping him in the first round each time.

Jim Murray was still unconvinced.

"Patterson is one of the best gym fighters you will ever see," Jim wrote. "His punching bag hasn't laid a glove on him in a thousand rounds of boxing. He is a heavy favorite over his shadow, and if there was a heavyweight championship rope skip, he'd retire undefeated. But he's not a fighter, he's a situation comedy. Don Quixote in six-ounce gloves."

Ingemar Johansson must have been listen-

HEAVYWEIGHTS

N.E.A. Sports Editor Murray Olderman, left, gets lowdown from Cus D'Amato, who managed Patterson, about his bitter feud with James D. Norris and the International Boxing Club. (Photo courtesy Murray Olderman)

Jim Murray, *The Los Angeles Times'* widely read sports columnist here pictured, once listed Floyd Patterson's reign as heavyweight champion "Top Secret," the phantom of sports. Wrote Murray: "He just bobbed up in odd corners of the world fighting people nobody ever heard of and, once you saw their fighting style, you found out why." (Photo *Los Angeles Times*)

ing. After knocking out Roy Harris and Brian London in defense of his title, Patterson agreed to a match with Johansson in 1959 and had to be revived with smelling salts in the third round.

"Floyd will be the first ex-heavyweight champ to get the title back," D'Amato told reporters after the defeat. Floyd made Cus appear like a resident genius by stopping the Swede in the fifth round 359 days later. In their third and final meeting, in 1961, Patterson stopped Johansson in six. The series between the pair was the first time in boxing history that the same two heavyweights fought in three straight title bouts—1959, '60 and '61.

The championship reign of Floyd Patterson was a sharp departure from the past. A heavyweight champion once was a hero on parade. Wherever he went, crowds followed him. He was here, there, everywhere. Sullivan toured the country, fighting exhibitions against the village blacksmith, guaranteeing him a hundred dollars if he could last four rounds. Jim Corbett, Bob Fitzsimmons, Jim Jeffries, Tommy Burns and Jack Johnson showed in plays, vaudeville or burlesque. Jess Willard was with a circus. Jack Dempsey, Gene Tunney, Max Schmeling, Jack Sharkey, Primo Carnera and Max Baer, they had all the best of it in the way of promotion by their managers.

"You could walk any of them up one side of the street and Patterson down the other and you know whom the crowds would follow, don't you?" asked Frank Graham one time. "Dempsey, naturally. And if Patterson disappeared from the other side of the street and wound up trailing Dempsey, would you be surprised? Floyd could have got lonesome on the other side of the street. After all, who knows him?"

INGEMAR JOHANSSON
(1932–   )

Ingemar Johansson had a stunning right hand. When he swished the air with it and connected, the poor lug on the other end suddenly had the look on his face of a guy who has just stuck his finger in an electric socket he thought was disconnected. Ingo's right flipper did more damage than a crane with an iron ball on the end of it.

Some nights, the handsome Swede ran over

Sweden's Ingemar Johansson brought a whiff of fresh air back to the heavyweight division. (Photo courtesy Johansson)

an opponent so convincingly they had to tear up half the ring apron because they did not know which was resin and which was the adversary. Fourteen of his first 22 opponents had to be excavated.

While Johansson held the heavyweight crown only 359 days, this much can be said for him: His sensational kayo of Floyd Patterson on June 26, 1959, marked the end of an era in the division; an era of American domination. Ingo was the first European to win the heavyweight title since Carnera.

Johansson did not prove to be as great as some of his predecessors, but few of his contemporaries were able to solve his style. Those closest to him claimed his left hook was almost as good as his straight right, and that he adapted to any man's style, moving in on counterpunches as he wisely stayed away from Patterson's attempts to start those swift combinations. His was a cool head in a hot fight.

Johansson brought popularity back to the heavyweight championship. Whereas Patterson was a natural recluse, Ingemar was a natural extrovert. Europe idolized him. American TV and movie audiences applauded him.

Johansson brought a whiff of fresh air to boxing. He staunchly refused to fight for the I.B.C. "I will not have anything to do with gangsters," he declared publicly. He resented the cheap chicaneries of fast-buck hustlers. His true feeling for prizefighting was as amateur as his love of fishing, sports cars, light planes, pretty women, and hacker's golf. He was deeply distressed by the state of boxing in the United States in 1959. His big punch came at a time when prizefighting in America had only two places left to go—up or out. . . . Boxing now had the man who would strike the blow for good against evil.

"When Johansson flattened Patterson so savagely," Harry Grayson wrote, "he gave the heavyweights their biggest boost since Dempsey established the million-dollar gate."

Ironically, Ingemar was as delicately guided as Patterson. The first thing one must question is his number of fights. On his way to the championship, he fought only 21 times in seven years as a professional; only 28 times in his total pro career. After being disqualified for refusing to fight in the finals of the 1952 Olympic Games, he turned professional and was fed a rare assortment of bums from Europe and the British West Indies, with practically all of the action confined to his native Sweden.

The first recognizable name in Johansson's record was Hein Ten Hoff, the towering German whom Ingemar stopped in one round in 1955. Joe Bygraves lasted 10 rounds with him in '56, and then seven months later Johansson won the European championship by knocking out Franco Cavicchi in Bologna. In '57, Henry Cooper was demolished in five rounds, but then Archie McBride, an extremely ordinary American, forced Johansson to go 10 rounds. This was followed by so-so victories over Joe Erskine and Heinz Neuhaus.

Johansson's smashing K.O. of Eddie Machen in 2:16 of the first round in 1958 earned him a shot at Patterson's crown in New York in '59. The fight was a natural. Whether it went long or short there would be suspense in every round. No one had yet hit Patterson hard enough to test him truly. No one the champion had fought since Moore had been able to punch as hard as Johansson.

On fight night, the odds were 3–1 in favor of Patterson. It took Johansson just nine minutes to foil the odds-makers—and Sweden had its first heavyweight champion of the world.

Johansson, born in Goteborg, on September 22, 1932, started fighting as an amateur at thirteen. He went on to win 60 of 71 amateur matches. In 1951, he competed for a European team against an American Golden Gloves team in Chicago and knocked out Ernie Fann in the second round.

Significantly, Johansson was only the fourth heavyweight in history to win the world title without a defeat on his pro record. John L. Sullivan, Jim Jeffries and Rocky Marciano were the other three. When Ingo stopped Patterson, it marked the first time professionally that Floyd had ever been kayoed. He'd won his last 22 straight fights and 16 of his last 17 by knockouts. Patterson admitted he had never been hit so hard before as when Ingo hit him.

Some people got the impression that Johansson did not train seriously for his first and only defense of the title. Whitey Bimstein, who trained him, felt the opposite was true. He believed Ingo trained too hard. "He

Ingemar Johansson won the title from Floyd Patterson on June 26, 1959, but lost the return match 359 days later on a knockout in the fifth round. Here Patterson is lifted in victory on the shoulders of his handlers, while Ingemar's cornermen revive him. That's Howard Cosell, far right, climbing into ring with microphone to interview Floyd for ABC-TV. (NEA)

trains like the oldtimers," Bimstein said at the time. "The oldtimers loved their work and so does this fellow."

The second Johansson-Patterson fight had the crowd of between 40,000 and 45,000 in a frenzy. In the second round, Ingo came right out and nailed Floyd high on the head. Floyd was stunned but was able to retreat and get through the round. It was the only round Ingo won. He was counted out in the fifth round. "I think it was the hardest punch I ever hit anyone," Patterson said afterward. "For the first time I feel I'm a real champion."

Patterson thus was heavyweight champion of the world for the second time—the first former heavyweight champion to regain the title.

A decision was made to go ahead with Bout No. 3. The title rematch between Floyd and Ingo drew heavy bidding. Miami Beach finally won. So did Patterson. He sent Johansson back to his heavy contracting business and fishing boat in Sweden with a sixth-round knockout, thus ending the longest playing dramatic TV series since Abie's Irish Rose.

SONNY LISTON
(1932–1971)

Sonny Liston, born into a family of 25 children, was a study in despair. Except for winning the heavyweight championship of the world from Floyd Patterson, not very much ever turned out as he expected.

His biggest fault lay in the fact that he grew up thinking that criminals were great people. As a youth, he was arrested 19 times and served two prison terms. He served his first prison term in 1952, at the Missouri State Penitentiary. He was back in again in '57. "I didn't mind prison," Sonny once said. "It was the first time in my life I got three square meals a day."

Sonny Liston was a man with two records—one inside the prize ring and the other inside prison walls. He was arrested 19 times and served two prison terms. To his credit, he never attempted to dodge his past. (Photo courtesy *Tacoma News Tribune*)

"Liston's entire background, from his childhood to the years he spent in jail, was in association with criminals," said Dr. Charles P. Larson, noted pathologist and former President of both the N.B.A. and W.B.A. "Hoodlums of the worst sort. Through his boyhood and early adult life, those associations made such an impression on him that he actually developed an adulation for the low-life criminal element. He idolized those who could beat the law. Those who made a lot of tainted money and got away with it were his heroes. His judgment of right and wrong was all distorted. When he was champion, we had a problem giving him a decent image. He was always in trouble, it seems. He drank too much, he brawled too much, he hung out with punks too much. We were forced to assign detectives to tail him and keep him in line."

On September 25, 1962, Liston demolished Patterson in the first round to win the championship. He was the first world heavyweight champion who could neither read nor write.

"He was a genuine illiterate," Dr. Larson said. "He was a poor, dumb man. I was President of the W.B.A. during his reign, and we finally sent him to Father Edward P. Murphy, S.J., in Denver, where he was taught to read and write some."

It is significant that the record books do not list Sonny's manager. Dr. Larson said he never could find out who owned Liston's contract or got his money.

"But you can be sure that whoever his silent partners were gave him the short end of the stick," Dr. Larson said. "It finally dawned on Sonny that he seldom got a fair deal from anybody. That was to be expected, of course, because the men who ran his business were nothing more than crooks themselves."

The first person to show a sincere interest in Liston was Reverend Alois Stevens, the athletic director at Missouri State Penitentiary. He sensed Sonny's angry contempt for the world and, quite naturally, channeled these energies into boxing. Liston's fists were big, he was big, and there always was that cold, menacing look in his eyes.

Born in St. Francis County, near Forest City, Arkansas, on May 8, 1932, Liston began his professional career in 1953 with a one-round K.O. of Don Smith in St. Louis. After that there was a long string of knockouts as he climbed the ladder toward the heavyweight championship. There was just too much dynamite in both hands for most fighters to handle him. Until Muhammad Ali stopped him in 1964, Sonny's only defeat in 36 fights was on points to Marty Marshall the second year after he started fighting.

Liston was given the runaround for several years, but it was inevitable that Patterson would have to fight him sooner or later. The bout was finally held in Chicago, on September 25, 1962. It took Sonny only 126 seconds to finish his night's work. In the third fastest finish in heavyweight boxing history, 2:06 of the first round, he crumpled Floyd to the canvas with two ponderous left hooks. Patterson's share of the gate was $250,250; Liston got $69,515. The closed-TV revenue brought Liston's total to $282,015.

The fighters fought a second time, on July 22, 1963, in Las Vegas. The odds favored Liston, 4–1. It was the Chicago Story all over again. A fast first-round K.O. sent the thirty-year-old Patterson to boxing's scrapheap. Liston didn't even have enough time to work up a mild sweat.

Patterson never lived down those two lopsided losses to Liston. After the second defeat, he hid behind a false beard and mustache for a month because the shame was more than the pain. He even talked about retirement. The overpowering Liston could do that to a fighter.

The Liston magic ended in Miami Beach, February 25, 1965, when he balked at coming off his stool in the seventh round and lost the title to Cassius Clay (C.C. had not yet changed his name). An attempt to win back the crown, May 25, 1965, at Lewiston, Maine, left many boxing fans pinching their noses. One of those suspecting Sonny of going into the dry tank was author Jim Bishop, who was hired by the Mutual Broadcasting System to do the between-the-rounds color story of the fight.

"The only smart people that night were the natives, who stood on a hill outside the arena," Bishop said recently. "Liston had all the character of a mongrel, but he could hit. Clay, running backwards, caught him with a faint flicking right which might, under the right circumstances, rupture a mosquito. Liston gave it a moment of consideration and fell on his face. He was four feet from my microphone. The referee lost his mind and ran to the far side of the ring to pick up the count from the timekeeper. Liston, hearing no audible sound, rolled over on his back and looked up to find out what the hell happened to the referee."

Liston's low-grade performance turned Bishop's tongue to acid. "Professional fighters are beset by fear; they are afraid to fight," Jim added. "They constitute so many pounds of mobile meat with eyeballs like $ signs. As a group—there are exceptions—they are witless slobs who are trained like dancing bears. The best? My choice would be Harry Greb. He trained on good booze and bad women. But he was a boxer and a slugger and he had an instinct, not to hurt, but to *kill*."

Liston continued to fight for five more years. He won 15 of his last 16 bouts, mostly against stiffs. He officially retired on June 29, 1970, and was found dead by his wife at their Las Vegas home, six months later. He was only thirty-eight. Cause of death was never publicly revealed.

CASSIUS CLAY (MUHAMMAD ALI)
(1942–   )

Jim Murray dropped me a note saying he had ambivalent feelings about traveling all the way to Kinshasa, Zaire, in Africa, to cover the Ali-Foreman fight for *The Los Angeles Times*. "Like, why can't they hold it in New Orleans—or Shelby, Montana?" he asked.

It was history's first 4 o'clock in the morning fight where both principals were, presumably, sober, and where neither one of them had a broken beer bottle. Foreman was billed as the home run hitter and Ali was supposed to bunt him to death. But Ali was the slugger from the start.

"It looked like an elephant being slapped around by a mouse; a butterfly chasing an eagle," wrote Murray afterward. "Ali tumbled Foreman on his ear at 2:58 of the eighth round after beating him into a lump for the first seven rounds. Foreman went down like a guy falling out of a seventh story window. He tried to get up but he didn't know which way it was. Foreman couldn't hit Ali if he was tied to a tree. He never won a round. Hell, he never won a minute. And so Muhammad Ali, God help us, is the heavyweight champion of the world again and we'll never hear the end of it."

For their 24 minutes of fighting time in the Zaire ring, Ali and Foreman earned $208,333.33 per minute, or $3,472.16 per second . . . before taxes. The promoters had guaranteed them both $5,000,000 apiece!

Ali thus became the second man in history to regain the heavyweight championship. And he wanted his detractors to eat crow. "I hope that the boxing world will finally recognize me as the professor of boxing," he said.

HEAVYWEIGHTS

At his peak, 1964–1968, Muhammad Ali deserved to be ranked among the best heavyweights in history; certainly will be remembered as one of the most controversial and complex men prizefighting has known. (Photo courtesy Madison Square Garden)

"Those know-nothing writers thought I was getting old, that my reflexes were gone. But I am the greatest heavyweight champion of all time."

"Cassius is as great as he says he is," agreed Floyd Patterson, who had predicted a Foreman victory by knockout. "I'm happy for him. Now I have to share the record with him—the record of having won back the heavyweight championship."

Cassius?

"I still call him Cassius Clay because his mother still calls him that," Patterson explained. "We're good friends, and when we're together, alone, he doesn't object to my calling him Cassius. It's only when people are around that he wants to be called by his Muslim name."

There is no telling what heights Ali might have reached had his battle with the federal government over his military draft status not lopped three and a half years off his career. At his peak, he stood 6 ft. 3 in. and weighed 210 lbs. and he moved with the grace of a ballet dancer and punched with a speed hard to follow with the naked eye.

"Ali's a heavyweight who moves on his legs, and very few heavies do that," Willie Pastrano said. When asked what exactly was Muhammad's best punch, Lou Bailey, a sparring partner, replied, "All of them." Marv Jenson, who managed Gene Fullmer, added: "Ali has the fastest hands of any heavyweight I've ever seen." Muhammad heartily agreed with all of them.

Muhammad Ali was born on January 17, 1942, the son of a Louisville, Kentucky, house painter and grandson of a slave. By the time he was twenty, he stood 6 ft. 2 in., weighed 193 lbs., had a 46-inch chest and a 32-inch waist. In 1960, at eighteen, he won the Olympic light-heavyweight title by knocking out a Belgian, a Russian, an Australian and a Pole.

"I was so proud of that Gold Medal I even wore it to bed," he said later. At the time, Ali was a pleasant, outgoing youngster who had not yet taken the blustering, bragging role of his later years.

Many professional promoters made efforts to sign Ali, but he finally put himself in the hands of 11 Louisville businessmen, headed by wealthy Billy Reynolds. The syndicate's arrangement was to pay all expenses and to give Muhammad $500 in cash each month and 50 percent of his earnings. Fifteen percent of the remainder was put into a pension fund, from which Ali could begin drawing after he reached thirty-five. He received $10,000 for signing the contract and a guarantee of $4,000 the first two years. Angelo Dundee, a leading trainer, was then hired to handle Muhammad.

Ali won his first six fights, five by K.O. and most of them before the fourth round. The more he won, the cockier he became and the louder he grew. After his knockout string reached 11, he started reciting poetry ("They all must fall/ In the round I call . . .") and naming the round in which his victims would go down. He fought ancient Archie Moore, predicted his demise in four rounds—and then stopped him in 1:35 of the fourth round. He stretched his string of victories to 19.

Now he was ready for champion Sonny Liston. But no one gave him much chance against The Bear. Liston had twice mauled Floyd Patterson in the first round. There were people who said that the strongest twin powers on Earth were Sonny's left and right hands. A 7–1 underdog, Ali dodged, pedaled and punched Liston around the ring like he owned him. When the bell rang for the seventh round, Sonny remained seated on his corner stool, refusing to come out. The former Cassius Clay was the new heavyweight champion of the world. The following morning, he told a news conference that he had formally become a Black Muslim and, henceforth, wanted to be known as Muhammad Ali.

He then married Sonji Roi, a Chicago model, whom he later divorced because she refused to abide by Muslim customs.

Ali's first defense of his title was May 25, 1965, in a return match against Liston. Still baffled by Sonny's nose-pinching performance in the first skirmish, Gene Tunney was asked to comment on this second meeting.

"The last fight was, er, ah, um, curious," expressed Gene as diplomatically as possible. "Rather, say, even, mysterious. I shall be interested to see what, er, ah, um—'arrangements' they have made for the forthcoming one. Very intriguing. Rather like those Saturday afternoon serials."

The bout was staged at Lewiston, Maine, and only 2,434 customers could be bamboozled into showing up for the proceedings—the smallest attendance in history at a world heavyweight championship fight. Perhaps it was just as well. In the first round, Ali clipped Sonny on the head with what the cynics called a "phantom punch," Sonny fell down, and the referee counted him out. Fortunately, that ended for all time the Ali-Liston series.

Ali's last title defense before boxing's governing bodies stripped him of the championship because of his draft trouble was a seventh-round K.O. of Zora Folley in New York's Madison Square Garden in 1967. In between, he stopped Patterson in 12, decisioned George Chuvalo in 15, flattened Henry Cooper in 6, demolished Brian London in 3, knocked out Karl Mildenberger in 12, Cleveland Williams in 3, and outpointed Ernie Terrell in 15.

During his banishment from boxing, Ali got married again and kept busy in television, on the stage, and lecturing at colleges. Meanwhile, Joe Frazier and Jimmy Ellis shared the heavyweight title, and Frazier had it all after stopping Ellis in New York in 1970.

Ali began his celebrated comeback on October 26, 1970, after the Supreme Court cleared him, and knocked out Jerry Quarry in three rounds in Atlanta. Next, he outdistanced Oscar Bonavena in 15. Now he was ready for a showdown with Frazier. The fight was held at Madison Square Garden, on March 8, 1971. Ali and Frazier were both guaranteed a record $2,500,000! Ali publicly predicted that "Smokin' Joe falls in six."

For the first time in his life, Ali was wrong. The match went the full distance, and one of the judges had it 11 rounds to 4 in Frazier's favor. The others voted similarly. Ali's swollen face bore testimony to Joe's right and left hands. So he lost to Joe Frazier, but he fought and lost like a champion. It marked the first time he had lost in 32 straight pro fights.

Critics disagree over the degree of greatness that should be accorded Ali. Some people fault him because he never was a disciplined fighter, was never ashamed to grab and hold. His punching power always was open to question. Even Angelo Dundee readily agreed that Muhammad was not the best instruction-follower in the world. He was inclined to play games when things looked easy. He was inclined to lose his temper.

"So he wasn't truly a great fighter, the way you measure fighters," Sportswriter Arnold

HEAVYWEIGHTS

Hano said. "Great fighters are consistently great, and Ali was nothing if not inconsistent. Didn't he have his jaw broken by a man (Ken Norton) who'd never before earned more than $8,000 for a fight? No, Ali for a decade brought something more to boxing—a semblance of art, wit, style, and guile. He created an art form in the ring all his own. He didn't fight; he *choreographed* it. He was a man of wit in a witless profession. When he beat Doug Jones in 1963, for example, the New York fans booed his performance, and threw peanuts into the ring. Ali cracked the shells, ate the peanuts, and threw the shells back at the fans. Now, *that's* style."

This was also the Muhammad Ali way: When a reporter once asked him what he thought was the most important part of training for a fight, Ali replied, "Getting sex off my mind six weeks before the match. For most athletes, two weeks ahead is enough. Not for me; it wears me down. I send my wife away. I don't like too many women around my camp, no matter who they belong to."

Summing up, Jim Rondeau, a major league referee for 33 years, who also doubles as Pres-

Ali, pictured here working out on the big bag, possessed remarkable speed. "I'm fast," agreed Muhammad. "They've timed my punches, and they say I can punch faster than you blink your eye." (Photo courtesy Madison Square Garden)

ident of the North American Boxing Federation and Chairman of the Washington State Athletic Commission, picks Ali as the "greatest actor, thespian, press agent, and public relations man in the history of prizefighting."

"No matter what your opinion of him may be," Jim said, "there was something special about Ali. At his peak, you either adored him or hated him. Which is why so many millions of dollars poured into the box office whenever he fought. Never again will anybody sell so many tickets to a fight as Ali. Imagine Ali and Foreman splitting total purse money of $10,000,000—$5 million apiece!—to fight in the Republic of Zaire, in 1974. That was the richest single sports event in the history of the world.

"That was only one side of Ali. As a boxer, he was as good as the prize ring ever has had. No heavyweight had more hand and leg speed. He must go down as the fastest big man in boxing history. He was also strong and very smart. Ironically, that's why he'll never be remembered as a great puncher. He never set long enough to get ready to throw a punch. He could knock out a man of lesser size, but preferred to go the distance with men his own size.

"By disposition, Ali was a very quiet man, as opposed to his public image. But put him in front of a camera and he turned on. His personality was multi-sided. He could be all sorts of a man to all sorts of people.

"There was always the question of his courage. I felt he had dauntless courage. He took some frightful beatings, yet stayed in there to win decisions. So don't tell me he had no guts. He had plenty of guts. The only weapon he lacked as a great fighter was the big punch."

So magic was the Muhammad Ali legend that when Henry Cooper, former British heavyweight champion who once fought him, was interviewed for a job by Lloyd's of London, he discovered that "they mostly just wanted to hear my stories about Cassius Clay."

In America, however, the public did not share this enthusiasm for the once mighty heavyweight champion. An advertisers' research poll taken in 1973 showed that of 192 leading athletes in U.S. history, Muhammad Ali ranked 192nd on personal admiration. Ex-St. Louis Cardinal outfielder Stan Musial was No. 1.

Before the 1974 Foreman fight, Ali sat down and quietly set the record straight about himself. It was a side of his personality the public seldom saw.

"My name, Cassius Marcellus Clay, was a slave name," Ali explained. "It came down to me from some great grandfather. After I won the title from Liston and joined the Muslims, it was kinda embarrassing to go on calling myself Cassius Clay, after a slave fellow. I'm a black and I felt I should have an Afro name, so I went back into the names of my ancestors and chose Muhammad Ali. At first, people resisted calling me by my new name. They refused to accept the name out of ignorance and because they were so used to calling me Clay. A lot of folks didn't want to see this name-changing trend spread. But many black people with white names are finally waking up and don't want white names anymore.

"From the age of twelve I knew I wanted to be a boxer. I'm really lucky I made up my mind so early and had direction. Life is really short and you must get started quickly. I knew I wanted to be a fighter—a fighter who stayed with his people, married within his own race, and didn't sell his people and forget them. I've seen too many blacks become successful and then look down on their own and leave them. This spirit of sticking with my black brothers and sisters was always in me. They are forever first with me.

"I was once asked about the theatrics of my career. Did I regard prizefighting as essentially show business? Well, it's kinda hard for a person to be both. I've been blessed with the ability to write poems, to predict rounds when I'd K.O. an opponent. For example, I predicted 15 times when I'd stop a man, and 11 times I was right. A funny thing happened when I fought Archie Moore, an old man at the time. I predicted round 4. In a pre-fight flash of poetry I scribbled: *When you come to the fight/ don't block the aisles/ and don't block the door/ for you all may go home after round 4.* Well, old Archie was falling and stumbling around the ring in the third round, and I grabbed him and said, 'Don't you fall now, it's not the fourth round yet.' Then I finished him in the next round.

"Outside the ring, I was called colorful,

flamboyant, outspoken—the Louisville Lip It was all part of the campaign. Like a politician stumping for votes. You do a lot of flashy things to earn attention and win. I talked a lot and was loud and sometimes obnoxious because I wanted to promote my fights. I always managed to think up a new gimmick to sell tickets—such as that floor scuffle I had with Frazier on TV before our second fight. Brainstorms like that just came and I acted upon them. It was good for business. I gave the boxing public what they wanted to hear.

"You get many versions about my troubles in 1968, when I refused to take up arms for the United States and was stripped of my title. Now listen to my side of it. In Houston, when I was asked to stand up and be sworn into the service, I thought about all the black people who'd been here for 400 years—all the lynching, raping and killing they'd suffered—and there was an Army fellow my age acting like God and telling me to go to Viet Nam and fight Asians who'd never called me Nigger, had never lynched me, had never put dogs on me—and outside I had millions of black people waiting to see what I was going to do. I said to myself, this guy in the Army suit ain't God—so when he asked me to step forward I just stayed there. I couldn't wait for him to call my name, just to say no. I couldn't take that step because I knew the war was wrong, it was against my religious beliefs, and I was willing to go to jail for those beliefs. Fortunately, the Supreme Court saw I was serious, and they gave me justice.

"Am I patriotic? My interpretation of allegiance to America is to obey the laws, as long as they don't conflict with my religious beliefs, and obeying God's laws. This, I feel, should be satisfactory to any country—no stealing, no killing, no outright misuse of people, and treat others as you, yourself, would want to be treated. So when you talk about patriotism, I don't know what *American* patri-

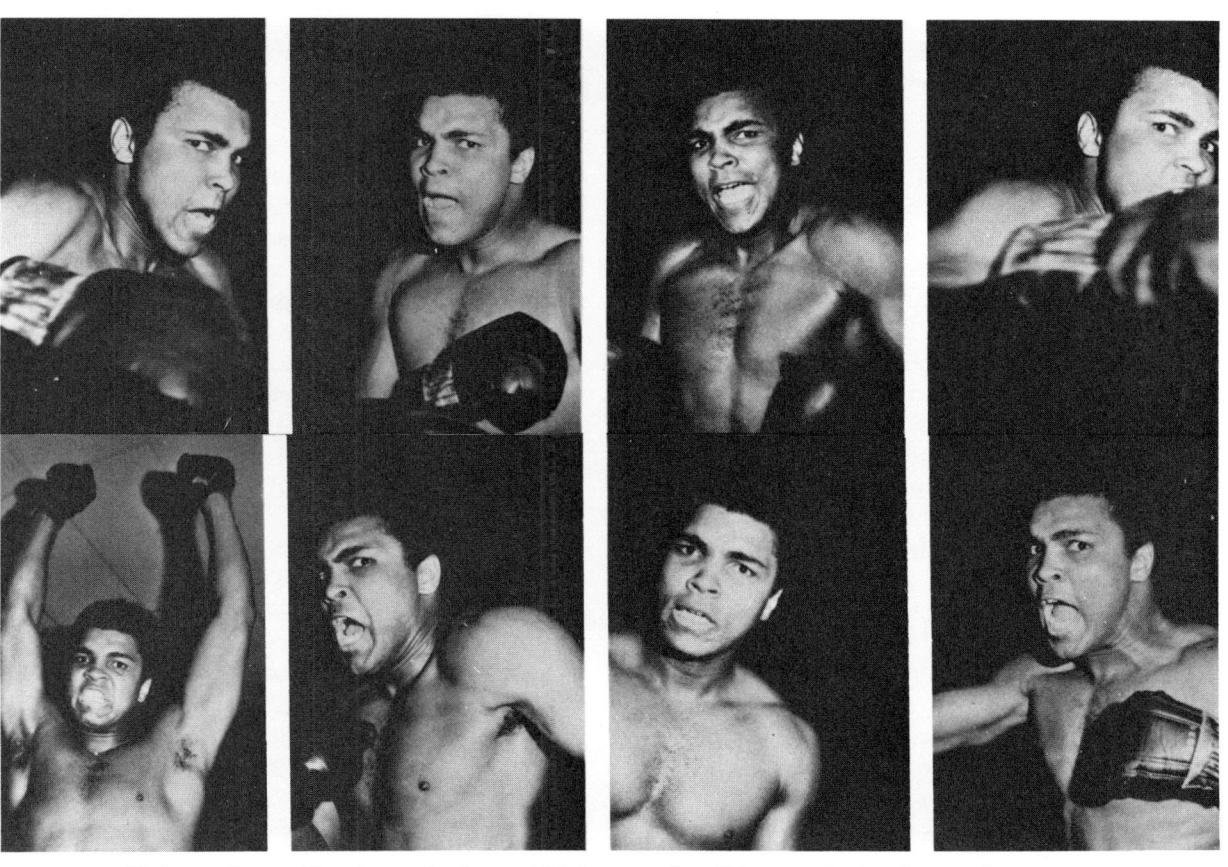

Referee Jimmy Rondeau singles out Muhammad as "the greatest actor, orator, press agent, and public relations man in the history of prizefighting." (Photos courtesy Madison Square Garden)

otism means. If they say stand up and salute the flag, I'd do that out of respect, because I live in the country—but in my heart I wouldn't say I love the flag. As a matter of fact, I don't love the American flag at all. I'd be crazy to say I love a flag of a nation that brought my people over here and kept them in slavery for so many years. It's a shame to say, but blacks have been here for four centuries, fought in all the wars, been so faithful as slaves helping to build this country, and as a people they're still hungry. So they have a right to protest so much. Freedom and independence means a lot to me. I'm as bold as you can get. I've wanted to show my people that you don't have to sell yourself cheaply to get what you want out of life. I hope some have seen this. I hope I have shown them that you don't have to crawl and kiss somebody's boots to get a fair shake.

"If I was back to twelve years old and they told me I wasn't going to make it in boxing, I don't know what I would have done with my life. Unfortunately, I didn't stay in school like I should. I wasn't enthused to read or write or work, I hate all that book work and tests and stuff. But if I'd had my choice of careers, I'd been a doctor, because I like to help people. If I see a man sick, just to know I could operate and relieve him of pain would be a big inspiration to me.

"Another thing I'd liked to have been was a policeman. I see a lot of things happening today and wish I was a policeman. I could jump out of the squad car and stop the trouble and soothe tempers. You see a nut speeding a hundred miles an hour through town where children are playing and you wish you could catch him and lock him up. So in this spirit I'd probably have been a policeman—anything where I could help people, especially *my* people."

JOE FRAZIER
(1944–   )

Because they fought and were built much alike, Joe Frazier frequently was compared to Rocky Marciano. Rocky piled up 19 K.O.'s and 2 decision victories in his first 21 professional bouts for a .905 knockout percentage. His 43 kayoes in 49 fights leads the all-time heavyweight championship list with an .878 knockout percentage.

Frazier, an inch taller and 15 to 20 pounds heavier than Marciano, tied Rocky's early pace with 19 knockouts and 2 decisions. Rocky was twenty-four years old by the book, but actually closer to twenty-six when he started fighting for money. Frazier turned pro when he was twenty-two, after winning the 1964 Olympic heavyweight title, and was twenty-four by the time he had his first 21 fights.

Marciano had 25 fights before he fought his first name fighter, Roland LaStarza, and won a close decision. At the same age, Frazier had already beaten Oscar Bonavena, Eddie Machen, Doug Jones, George Chuvalo, Buster Mathis and Manuel Ramos.

Like Marciano, Frazier came to fight. His pet expression on the way to the world championship was, "I'm comin' out smokin'." The resemblance to Rocky was striking in other ways, too. Joe was dedicated in his training just as Rocky was. Both of them trained as they fought and their gym fights were wars. They were willing to take a punch to land one of their own. Both men smashed away at the body to soften up an opponent and to open up the head defenses. "When the body dies, the head rolls," was the way oldtimers put it.

Muhammad Ali once called Frazier "a street fighter," or gutter fighter. It wasn't a nice-sounding term and wasn't meant to be one. In the generic sense Ali meant that every battle Frazier fought was a battle for survival. Jungle tactics always proved the most effective, and Frazier swarmed all over his opponents, spurred by his inborn lust for combat, and swung away viciously until the other man dropped.

Rocky Graziano was a gutter fighter. So was Jack Dempsey. Mickey Walker was one. Stanley Ketchel was another. So was Harry Greb. The list is a long one. Some of them learned boxing skill but the most important factors by far were the killer instinct and the big wallop.

The road traveled by Frazier to his multimillion-dollar showdown with Muhammad Ali in 1971 had been long and dusty. It started at Beaufort, South Carolina, where he was born on January 12, 1944. He never finished the ninth grade; a teenage dropout who drove a tractor on his father's poverty-pocket farm.

When he was seventeen, Joe went north to Philadelphia, where he was just another 230-pound guy named Joe when trainer Yank

Durham spotted him in a local gym trying to melt all that fat off his body. There were 12 brothers and sisters down home and Joe had a job slaughtering cattle in a Kosher slaughterhouse. "In those days," Frazier recalled, "my legs were so round I couldn't get my pants on. That's what I was doing in the gym, trying to slim down."

Under Durham, Frazier trimmed down to a muscular 205 pounds and won the Olympic championship—the first man ever to win both the amateur and professional heavyweight titles.

The same year Joe quit school he got married. Six years later he knocked out Woody Gross in one round in his first pro start. He had three more fights that year, 1965, and won them all. From the start, Joe's style consisted of putting pressure on an opponent. People called him "a big Henry Armstrong," because of his ability to hit and slip punches.

In 1970, after he knocked Bob Foster out in the second round, Foster complained, "My corner told me after the first round to wait for my spots, but Joe wouldn't let me wait."

Frazier's detractors said he was only a pretender who never would have been champion if Muhammad Ali hadn't had his crown taken away from him. Joe ignored the taunts and jeers. And he remained unruffled with those blacks who called him a white man's champion. "I'm no Uncle Tom," Joe once said. "I'm black . . . blacker than Clay. The next time I see him, I'm gonna ask him to show me one black spot on his brown body."

Frazier always referred to Ali as Cassius Clay. He refused to call him Muhammad Ali.

"People said Clay had a cause and I didn't," Joe said. "But what's the cause? What's it mean to be a black champion? What'd it ever mean? What'd it mean for Jack Johnson to be champ? Or Joe Louis? Did it help the black folks? Did it? I didn't need a cause to fight because I fought for my family, for myself, for my pride. Cause? Hell, my cause was *me!*"

On the night of March 8, 1971, Frazier got the chance to show his critics just how good he was as he came on with a flourish in the last five rounds to thrash Ali before a roaring crowd of 20,455 that paid $1,352,951—both indoor boxing records. The fighters received purses of $2.5 million each to decide the true heavyweight champion of the world.

From his hospital bed, through swollen jaws, Ali said, "Frazier is not a great boxer. He is just a great *street* fighter." Frazier wound up in the hospital, too, suffering from "athlete's kidney," an ailment caused by physical and psychological pressure. He was on the shelf for 10 months. He fought only twice in 1972 (kayoes over Terry Daniels and Ron Stander), and then, on January 22, 1973, George Foreman won the championship from him by knocking him out in the second round—the first time he had been K.O.'d in 31 professional fights.

It was a bad period for Smokin' Joe Frazier. In January, 1974, he lost to the man he said would never beat him—Muhammad Ali.

"I whupped him," chortled the Pied Piper of Pugilism.

Joe Frazier was the first man ever to win both the Olympic Games and the world professional heavyweight championships. (Photo courtesy Madison Square Garden)

Frazier resented the way Ali rubbed it in.

"I couldn't be his friend," Joe said. "I wouldn't want to be his friend. Our personalities are different. Clay has to be seen all the time, he says where he's going, what he's going to do, who's going to be there, what time he's going to leave. Me, I get in and out of places so quiet people don't even know I'm there. I got nothing to hide, but I got a right to be a private man. I'm not going to let anybody change me. Muslim fellow comes up to me on the street, I listen to him, but I ain't

In one of his brighter moments, Frazier pointed to wall-sized photo showing him knocking down Muhammad Ali in their March 8, 1971 fight in New York. Joe won the decision. (Photo courtesy Madison Square Garden)

going to accept him. I know just who I am. Before I was heavyweight champion of the world, I was the same man. I moved around the city, I didn't have no trouble with police, with the businessmen, with people who wanted my autograph. I ain't trying to be good to make people love me. I don't *need* to be loved. When I get out there to do my roadwork, I'm alone. When I get in the ring, I'm alone. I go where I've got to go—I'm always alone."

Win, lose or draw, Joe Frazier was his own man.

GEORGE FOREMAN
(1949–)

George Foreman is the first to tell you that he wasn't exactly an Eagle Scout when he was a teenager growing up in The Bottom, the name of the tough Houston, Texas, slum where he was one of seven children of a broken marriage.

Always big and strong for his age, "Monkey" (the family nickname for him) was drinking with older boys and getting into gang fights by the time he was thirteen.

"I admit that back there, I tried my best to be bad, tried all through my teens, only it just didn't work out," Foreman recalled. "Mosta the guys in the Fifth Ward, the black slum where we lived, would like to get around me on the street—they was smaller and older—an' they told me how big I was and what I could do; they were pimps an' like that. An' I tried. I drinked a lot, and hung around corners, and I had these ambitions to be a great thief, a great burglar, a great hijack man, an all-around hustler. But I was a complete failure. I even failed at purse-snatchin'. My buddy, Charley Miller, an' me both loved our mothers, so when we'd grab some old lady's purse, she'd holler, 'Oh, Lord, don't, oh, Jesus, help, don't take my money,' we'd think of our mothers and drop the purse. An' then Charley would say, 'Hey, man, if we leave it on the sidewalk some other dude gonna take it. Let's take it back.' An' so, we'd run all the way around the block and give it back to the lady, an' she'd cuss us out, an', well—we was thieves, but we just couldn't stand to take no one's money. That's when I knew my hustlin' days was over. An' I settled down an' got some odd jobs to help out at home."

So there George was one day, a sixteen-year-old high school dropout, his life of crime behind him, watching the TV with his mom. Mrs. Foreman, who worked both as a cafeteria cook and as a barber, had suffered a nervous breakdown but had gotten better by this time. "Suddenly," George recalled, "Jim Brown, remember him, he played football for the Cleveland Browns? And Johnny Unitas, they were *both* on the TV, giving a commercial about the Job Corps. When I heard *them* guys endorse that program, I said to mom, 'I gotta go!' An' she agreed, an' I went. I wanted to prove to her that I wasn't a total loss."

George was sent to the Job Corps Center at Grants Pass, Oregon, where he studied bricklaying and carpentry. He sent his mother $50 a month. "For the first time in my life," he said, "I felt I was someone."

Later, he was transferred to the big Job Corp Center at Pleasanton, California, to learn how to assemble transistor radios. His reputation as a brawler had preceded him. When he beat up a fellow Corpsman, there were suggestions he be sent home. But Stephen Uslan, director of the center, had another idea. "If he likes to fight so much, he may as well fight in the ring." So George was taken under the wing of "Doc" Broadus, physical education instructor and former lightweight boxer.

After it dawned on George that someone was actually interested in his future, he worked hard. He won the heavyweight boxing title at Pleasanton, then the Golden Gloves championship in San Francisco. He also finished his two-year stint, got his high-school equivalency diploma, and was runner-up in the heavyweight division of the national Golden Gloves tournament in Milwaukee.

Doc Broadus got George a job at $465 a month teaching boxing at the Pleasanton Job Corps Center. "That job just turned me around," George said. "I felt I was doing something useful." Meanwhile, he so improved his own skills that he won the National Amateur Athletic Union heavyweight crown and made the U.S. Olympic Games boxing team that went to Mexico City in 1968.

George's first opponent in the '68 Olympics was a Polish fighter named Lucjan Trela, who stood only 5 ft., 7 in. Punching down, George couldn't get his weight into his punches; punching up, the Pole could, and to this day the three rounds with the Pole stick in

George's mind as his toughest fight. But he got the decision, and from there on, the Olympics was a breeze.

In his final match, George bounced around the ring like a kid after stopping the Russian heavyweight Iones Cepulis in 2:30 of the second round. Then, for the TV cameras, he whipped out a little American flag and waved it around and became famous. Overnight, his victory and the flag-waving gesture made George a hero. Back home in Houston, the police who used to chase him provided him with a motorcycle escort. Going to Washington, he called on President Johnson at the White House. The President, under fire over the Vietnam war, looked tired and frazzled. "He looked like he was on the ropes," George remembered. George then presented LBJ with a small plaque. "This is to thank you for making the Job Corps possible," he said, "giving young Americans like me a chance for hope and dignity." There were tears in the President's eyes as he accepted the tribute.

Foreman turned professional in 1969 and won his first fight, a three-round K.O. of Don Waldheim in New York. In fact, he won all of his first 40 fights, 37 by knockout. When he took on Joe Frazier for the championship, in 1973, he was a 3–1 underdog. Yet he floored Frazier six times and knocked him out in two rounds.

In George's corner the night he became champion were Doc Broadus, Dick Sadler, his manager, and Archie Moore, who had been brought in by Sadler as consultant. Doc had played scout: "I watched Frazier training for the fight, and I looked for any secret moves. I didn't see any. In fact, he wasn't working out as well as when he was an amateur. He just led with his head, same as always, come right at you with his eyes pointed up. I told George, 'Just drop that hammer on him,' and that's what he did."

George's guarantee for the Frazier fight was $385,000. He was well on his way to becoming a multi-millionaire.

Foreman, with arms like wagon tongues and shoulders like a blacksmith, quickly earned the nickname of "Lightning Destroyer," because of his explosive punching power. In his first three heavyweight title fights in the space of 14 months, George literally shredded three opponents in the combined time of 11 minutes and 43 seconds. He took Frazier out in 4:43, Joe "King" Roman in two minutes, and Ken Norton in five.

"I don't slap people around so they can yell how they'll beat me the next time," Foreman said. "After the referee is done counting, they just want to get away."

He showed the same dispassion toward sparring partners. "Sometimes it gets awfully hard on these guys," he said, following a workout in the gym in which he flattened one mate. "Even if I tap them, it hurts. But I want to be the most destructive man in the whole world. I want to be an executioner."

Just watching George train with a heavy punching bag held stationary can be a near-terrifying experience. The rafters shake, the floor rumbles.

"It's hard to imagine anyone surviving many of those punches, much less remaining on his feet," Dick Sadler said. "George's left jab can stop a man in his tracks." Henry Clark, who was California heavyweight champion and one of George's sparring partners, calls him the strongest man he's ever worked with. Much of George's punching power originates in his heavy legs. He does not throw wild, swinging hooks. Tex Maule, of *Sports Illustrated,* compared his punches to a baseball pitcher's deliveries. "That is, you'd say he throws sliders, not curves. The punches reach their destination faster than a wider punch would—and land more heavily."

On the middle knuckle of each of Foreman's hands is a long, dark and thick callus, a memento of the many hours he devotes to bag and people-punching.

"He's like a Mack truck," Ken Norton said. "He can be far more physical than Ali. With Ali it's more of a chess game."

Well, Ali was the master chessman on October 30, 1974, in history's first heavyweight championship fight held by the dawn's early light. Before the fight, he wrote a letter to Donald Karchmer, eleven, a student at Rosewood Junior High in West Hollywood, California:

Dear Donald: I was delighted to hear from you. You may not think so but I really appreciate each and every letter I receive. I feel good now, I'm in good shape and razor sharp. In case you are a little apprehensive regarding my upcoming fight, let me inform you that this is going to be the prettiest, most masterful upset that boxing has ever seen. I guarantee this and I couldn't be more serious. Please forgive the brevity of this letter but I have much to do and must move on. I hope you achieve success in whatever you try to do. Sincerely—Muhammad Ali.

It was a strange chapter in the history of the prize ring. After the fight, Ali went around trumpeting that "Foreman has no punch. He punched like a sissy. I knew I had him before the first round when he couldn't stare at me."

During the fight, George Parnassus, seventy-eight, the Los Angeles boxing promoter, was so disgusted with Foreman's inept performance that he left the Los Angeles Forum, where he had been watching on closed-circuit television, after the seventh round and missed the knockout. "I could see it coming," George said. "Foreman fought like an amateur. There are three reasons why a fighter gives a bad performance. One, lack of condition. Two, lack of ambition. Three, lack of ability. There's no remedy for the last one. Foreman was guilty of the first two."

A failure as a hustler and thief in his youth, George Foreman succeeded as a prizefighter. Jimmy Rondeau, shown here stopping the bout after Foreman demolished Ken Norton at Caracas, Venezuela, in 1974, rates George "an even better puncher than Joe Louis." (Photo courtesy Jim Rondeau)

Many people were suspicious of the result of the Zaire affair. You heard such digs as:

"It was a dump!"

"Something fishy. No way Ali could knock Foreman out—no way!"

"Foreman didn't try! He threw it!"

But the scores of reporters who witnessed the event from ringside were astounded at such skepticism. Almost to a man, they felt it was a good fight. There was no reason for suspicion.

"I have found fighters to be atrocious actors," commented Norman Mailer, the prize-winning author who covered the bout for *Playboy* Magazine. "No fighter can feign a collapse without giving himself away. I thought it was a hell of a fight."

Prior to the fight, I talked to Jimmy Rondeau, who had refereed the Foreman-Norton bout, about George. Jimmy didn't think Ali had a chance. He was very high on Foreman.

"Foreman is probably the biggest heavyweight who's also a puncher," Rondeau said. "The only champion who compared with him in size was Carnera, and Primo was not a puncher or boxer. Ali is almost as big, but not nearly as strong. I rate Foreman an even better puncher than Louis. He can hit, he can jab, he wants to get you out of there in a hurry. He's so anxious to finish you off that he'll hit you from any direction he can. It doesn't make any difference what position you're in. It's difficult to referee a Foreman fight because of his intensity. When he trains for a fight, he's a mean S.O.B. He doesn't want to shake hands with anyone, he hates to talk, he's moody, he just wants to be left alone. His big problem is fat. He has a weight problem. He loves to eat. He says he's prettier slim but happier fat. He says if he can ever afford it, he's gonna eat all he wants and he's going to be *very* fat. He goes as high as 250, then melts down to around 215 for a fight. This means he can't eat the way he normally does. He has to eliminate a lot of dishes from the diet he loves. So when he's *lean* he's *mean*."

After Foreman lost his crown to Ali, I talked to Rondeau again. He said he had to agree with Dick Francisco, who had called me after the match and said: "We were all wrong about Foreman. He fought a very dumb fight. He was a bull in a bullring. Ali was the matador—all he needed to make the performance complete was a cape."

For George Foreman, it was an education. Dick Sadler, his manager, said he learned something, too.

"Life under Mobutu Sese Seko, the President of Kinshasa, is less than thrilling," Sadler confessed upon his return to the United States. "That's a harsh rule over there. Both fighters were virtual prisoners until after the fight. Thank God for the boat they threw my great-great-grandpappy on. I'd rather be in America with all its racism than over there in Africa."

It was an incredible statement. For the first time in more than 300 years, a black man had seen some good resulting from slavery.

LIGHT HEAVYWEIGHTS

A Chicago boxing promoter and manager named Lou Houseman is generally credited with creating the so-called cruiserweight, or light-heavyweight, division. That was back in 1903, when the No. 1 fighter in his stable, Jack Root, outgrew the middleweight class.

Root boasted an impressive record among the 160-pound combatants, but found himself in the dubious position of either retiring or challenging the 220-pound Jim Jeffries for the heavyweight championship.

To bridge the gap, Lou Houseman proposed the light-heavyweight class, and suggested a top weight of 175 pounds. He thus solved Jack Root's problem and the division has been a boon to prizefighters in the 161–175 pound range ever since.

JACK ROOT
(1876–1963)

On April 22, 1903, Jack Root started something. He started the light-heavyweight division of boxing. He also became its very first world champion.

Before his death in Los Angeles, in 1963, he told how it all happened.

"I had a sharp manager," Root said. "Lou Houseman was also sports editor of a Chicago newspaper. Since I was having trouble making the weight as a middleweight, and because Jim Jeffries, the heavyweight champion, weighed 220, Lou felt that an in-between division was needed to keep fighters like me in business. He suggested making the limit 175 pounds and the idea caught on. The upshot was I was matched with the great Kid McCoy in what was billed as history's first light-heavyweight championship of the world. We fought 10 bloody rounds, and I won."

Jack Root was a highly intelligent prizefighter, both in and outside the ring. He died a millionaire, having made it in California real estate. Inside the ropes, however, his principal meal ticket was a right-hand punch. He knocked out 24 opponents in 53 professional fights with it.

Root was born Janos Ruthaly in Austria, on May 26, 1876. He was brought to America as a youth and, taking the prize ring name of Jack Root, had his first pro bout in Chicago at the age of twenty-one. He launched his career with a four-round K.O. of Charley Upton—and continued winning until August 18, 1902, when George Gardner stopped him in 17 rounds.

From the start it was evident that Root was no geezer. When the chips were up for grabs, when the pressure was really on, he came through. There was no quit in him. He won 39 of his first 42 bouts, had two draws, and the other one was broken up by the police. Twenty-four of those victories were knockouts.

Only Gardner (twice) and Marvin Hart were able to K.O. him.

Root fought Hart at Reno, Nevada, on July 3, 1905, and was stopped in 12 rounds. The retired Jim Jeffries refereed and advertised the match as "a championship fight for my vacant heavyweight title," but Hart never won universal acclaim as heavyweight champion.

GEORGE GARDNER
(1877–1954)

George Gardner fought like a man on a mission.

It was a perpetual game of greyhound and coyote when he charged out of his corner. As the greyhound, he was strong, fast, alert, and dangerous. Opponents had to be on their toes to keep from being eaten alive.

Gardner stood nearly six-feet and weighed 165 and was a graceful, effortless fighter. Or, as Knute Rockne used to say, "he was *liquid.*"

Born at Lisdoonvarna, County Clare, Ireland, on March 17, 1877, Gardner carried precision all the way to the light-heavyweight championship of the world. He began his prize ring career at Manchester, New Hampshire, with six straight knockouts, in 1897. Six years later he was world champion. He held the title for only 144 days. In his very next bout after winning the championship from Jack Root, Gardner gave it up to Bob Fitzsimmons in 20 sizzling rounds in San Francisco.

George Gardner fought in an era when boxing was saturated with first-rate champions and challengers. He met many of them, including Jack Johnson, Peter Maher, Jim Flynn, Marvin Hart, Joe Walcott, Kid Carter, and Bob Armstrong.

At forty-one, balding Bob Fitzsimmons, right, came back from Jim Jeffries defeat to win world light-heavyweight title from George Gardner, in 1903. (UPI)

Gardner had 65 professional bouts—two of them the same night! On February 8, 1904, he battled both Fred Cooley and Jim Discoll on one boxing card in Chicago. Won them both, too.

PHILADELPHIA JACK O'BRIEN
(1878–1942)

History has not been kind to Philadelphia Jack, the first Yank to beat an English heavyweight champion. (George Chip by a K.O. at Newcastle-on-Tyne, May 20, 1901.) Stanley Ketchel left him for dead with his head in his own resin box one March night in 1909, and the public never forgot it.

This was too bad because "Spats" O'Brien met the very best, from lightweights to heavies, between 1896 and 1912, kayoed Fitzsimmons for the light-heavyweight title and performed the feat of no-decisioning Jack Johnson in six rounds.

O'Brien, 5 ft., 10½ in., and never much more than a middleweight, was born Joseph Francis Anthony Hagen in West Philadelphia, January, 1878. His father, a Londonderry man, disapproved of the manly art. But his son was a Corbett man. Hence the O'Brien. (Borrowed logically enough from a chum named O'Brien.)

The ambitious stripling patterned his style after Gentleman Jim's—jab, run, parry. He also practiced the drawing-room graces, though he must have regarded the social ladder as something you prop up against the Biddle mansion. In his heyday, O'Brien was a frequent guest and antagonist of Major Anthony I. Drexel Biddle, who encouraged a series of boxing teas, followed by three brisk rounds of polite mayhem. (A tea hound named Al Kaufman flattened his distinguished host, who later taught the Biddle System of bayoneting an opponent—slashing instead of jabbing—to the U.S. Marines.)

Biddle introduced society to the fight game and its great exponent, O'Brien. And society was charmed. Dapper Jack was ever his own best press agent—in fact, the ring's early champion—but he hired one anyway along with a secretary and valet. On the road he required 25 trunkloads of finery to clothe his ego.

Yet Jack lived up to his idol, Gentleman Jim, in one respect—he was a gentleman where it counted most. He even served a brief tenure as heavyweight champion. On December 20, 1905, he kayoed Bob Fitzsimmons in 13 rounds, then clinched the title in Los Angeles on May 8 by drubbing Tommy Burns in 20. (Before the fight, Burns startled the countryside by announcing that the fight was supposed to be a fake, but would be on the level anyway.)

Philadelphia, which has seen so many good fights and fighters, has never known another like Jack O'Brien. Over the 17 years he fought, he lost only three decisions and was knocked out only three times—by Young Peter Jackson, Stanley Ketchel and Sam Langford. Unfortunately, the thriller with Jack Johnson was sandwiched between the two Ketchel fights. Three weeks after his splendid performance against "Li'l Arthur," O'Brien and Ketchel were parties to one of boxing's all-time riddles. O'Brien stabbed Ketchel foolish for seven rounds. In the eighth, he began to tire. In the ninth, Ketchel knocked him down for nine. In the tenth and last round, with seven seconds to go, Ketchel knocked O'Brien unconscious. Jack's head landed in a square, flat box of sawdust just outside the ropes near his own corner, which he and his handlers used as a spittoon.

"Get up, old man!" yelled Major Biddle, Jack's society rooter from Philadelphia. "Get up, and the fight is yours!"

But Jack, in the sawdust, was dead to the world. The bout ended before he could be counted out. By New York boxing law at the time, it was a no-decision fight. O'Brien had clearly won it on points; just as clearly, Ketchel had knocked him out. Connoisseurs still argue the issue today. Win or lose, it was a big one for Ketchel, for O'Brien was a man with a great record, who had fought and beaten heavyweights.

Jack O'Brien later opened a physical culture emporium that enjoyed outstanding success. He lived until 1942, when he died of pneumonia.

Nobody had to give a benefit for Philadelphia Jack O'Brien.

Philadelphia Jack O'Brien was first American to beat an English heavyweight champion. (NEA)

JACK DILLON
(1891–1942)

The fact he was nicknamed "Jack the Giant Killer" tells you something about Ernest Butler Price, alias Jack Dillon. By comparison with most light-heavyweights, he was a peewee. He stood only 5 ft., 7½ in., and weighed a mere 158 pounds.

Jack Dillon was the original "carpetbag" fighter. That is, he had a different manager in every town. Typical was for him to get off a train in the A.M. and fight in the P.M. the same day. His fists were for hire. In 1912, to give you an example, he fought five times in February, five times in October, and four times in November.

"I just like to fight," explained Dillon, simply.

Jack Dillon was America's answer to England's Tom Sayers, the middleweight champion who went around beating the heavyweight greats of Europe back in the 1860s. Like his ancient counterpart, Dillon was compactly built, with finely proportioned shoulders, a cavernous muscular chest, a strong jaw and a forehead indicating deep intelligence, a head which would not disgrace a scholar. Something more subtle than mere physique matched this man: there was never a great man, nor a great fighter, without character, and Dillon had character. Handsome, affable, articulate, with clean chisel-cut features accentuated by his trademark, a crew-type haircut, Jack frequently was mistaken for a college man.

All his life he matched himself against big men. Talk about the biblical David! David met only one Goliath, *he*, Jack Dillon, fought dozens. Men like Battling Levinsky, Porky Flynn, Fireman Jim Flynn and Harry Greb. Yet he was *never* knocked out in a career spanning 14 years (1908–1923) and 240 professional fights!

James J. Corbett managed a big heavyweight in 1916 named Tom Cowler. The old heavyweight champion was touting Tom as "the best heavyweight in the world." Dillon challenged him. On February 1, a bout was arranged in New York. After a slow first round, Dillon stalked out in the next stanza and pumped a left hook squarely on Cowler's whiskers. It took them an hour to revive Tom. Gentleman Jim never did get over his humiliation.

Five months later, on Independence Day, at Dewey, Oklahoma, Giant Killer Jack engaged Jim Flynn for promoter Billy McCarney. The ring was set up outside in the old Fair Grounds in 110-degree heat. It was so hot that between rounds McCarney had to put cabbage leaves on the referee's head to stall off a stroke. Dillon felt it was too steaming to fight and in the fourth round decided to end it. He hit Fireman Jim so hard that Flynn was still sitting on the canvas when Dillon climbed out of the ring. McCarney said he was amazed that Flynn was able to stay down so long.

"Jack had to hit him pretty hard to keep him there," Professor Billy said. "No one could have stayed on that sizzling canvas for a second if he'd been conscious. No kiddin'. Flynn had a blister on his butt for a week."

Born February 2, 1891, at Frankfort, Indiana, Dillon was something of a "mail-order" champion. That is, he and his manager, Sam Marburger, went to Dan Morgan for some advice and wound up writing letters to sports writers all over America, claiming the light-heavyweight championship of the world.

But to make it official, Dillon agreed to fight Al Norton for the vacant title at Kansas City, April 28, 1914. Dillon won in 10 rounds. Jack battled Norton again a year later, this time at Memphis, Tennessee, and knocked him out in the fourth. At a post-fight party three hours later, Norton was asked how he felt. He appeared puzzled by the question.

"Did Dillon hurt you much?"

"Dillon?"

"Yes, Dillon. He knocked you out in the fourth. Don't you remember?"

"I don't even remember fighting him," replied Norton.

When Giant Killer Dillon hit 'em, they usually didn't wake up very soon. He rocked them to sleep.

On October 24, 1916, Dillon defended his title against Battling Levinsky in Boston. "It was the sixth time they'd fought," said Dan Morgan, who managed Levinsky, "Dillon having won the five others without difficulty. But Jack had been dissipating and, in this final meeting, was only a selling plater compared with my boy. Levinsky won eight out of the 12 rounds and I got myself another world's champ."

Dillon retired in 1923 with only a small portion of his earnings. He opened a sandwich shop in Florida and lived behind it until his death at Chattahoochee, August 7, 1942. Efforts were made in Indianapolis to bring the body to Indiana, its rightful resting place, but nothing came of the campaign. The underbrush has long since covered the headstone marked simply:

"Jack Dillon, 1891–1942."

BATTLING LEVINSKY
(1891–1949)

Battling Levinsky holds one of the prize ring's most unique records: On New Year's Day, 1915, he fought *three* main events in three different places! He boxed Bartley Madden in Brooklyn in the morning, Soldier Kearns in New York that afternoon, and Gunboat Smith at night in Waterbury, Connecticut.

Thirty-two rounds of fierce no-decision fighting!

Levinsky was no kin to Kingfish Levinsky, the clownish Chicago heavyweight of later years. His real name was Barney Lebrowitz and he was a genuine professional. He held the light-heavyweight championship of the world for four years.

In this modern age of dual championships, court battles, attachments of purses and closed-circuit television, it may be hard to believe that, back in Levinsky's prime, boxing titles could be and often were claimed by *mail*.

You know the Jack Dillon story. One day, in 1910, he and his manager walked into Dan Morgan's office for advice. Morgan was Levinsky's manager. Dan wound up putting two stenographers to work typing out letters to sports writers all over the country, claiming the light-heavyweight title for Dillon.

"You just announced it to the country," Morgan told me. "That's all there was to it. Not long after, a stranger walks in and says he's a fighter. I'm used to that line and before he can open his mouth I say: 'I don't want any blotters.'

" 'I'm not a salesman, Mr. Morgan,' he says, 'I'm a light-heavyweight. All I want is a chance.'

"I give him the eye and say, 'What did you say your name is?'

" 'Barney Williams.'

" 'Oh, you're the guy who's been runnin' backwards down in Philly and always goin' the limit.'

" 'That's right, Mr. Morgan.'

" 'Well,' I ask him, 'what do you do, box and mix?'

"He said, 'No, I circle and circle, move back, then rush in and tie them up a lot.'

"I said, 'Well, up here in New York all we do is *fight*. Do you think you can fight?'

"And he said, 'Yes, sir, Mr. Morgan.'

"As if by magic—fate—luck, call it what you will, but just then in rushed Jimmy Johnston, the St. Nicholas arena matchmaker. 'Dan,' he said, 'I'm stuck for a heavyweight. You gotta help me. I've got a big, soft heavy and need somebody to fight him—*tonight!*'

"I flashed Barney Williams the eye. I said, 'Will you fight him?' He beamed from ear to ear. 'Sure,' he said. 'Okay, Jimmy,' I said, 'you got your man.'

"I took Barney over to St. Nick arena and helped him lace on his gloves. Jimmy Johnston came down to the dressing room and told him to hurry. I said, 'Jimmy, who did you say we are fighting tonight?' 'Oh,' he said, 'just a bum.'

"Before going upstairs I show Barney a few moves and then usher him to the ring. I sat him down in his corner and give him his instructions. Suddenly, the crowd starts cheering and clapping. I look up and there's Porky Flynn climbing between the ropes. Porky's the guy Jimmy called a 'bum.' He's a big, tough slugger from Boston with a terrific reputation. He tops Barney by 40 pounds and has fought all the good ones, including Sam Langford and Jack Johnson. Jimmy Johnston is sitting at ringside and I glare down at him. He grins back, knowing he's put one over on me. I say nothing about this to Barney, who sits on his stool all quiet and peaceful. Obviously he knows nothing about Porky's background.

" 'Listen,' I tell him, 'this bum's a poser. When the opening bell rings, he never leaves his corner for 30 or 40 seconds. He stands over there like an ape, flexing his back muscles and trying to impress you. So as soon as he turns around to face you, hit him with the left. If he doesn't go down–run!'

"Well, Barney brought a Sunday punch up

from the floor, but missed the jaw and caught an eye. Porky's knees buckle, but he keeps his feet. His eye balloons up like a melon and he can barely see after that. Barney gets on his bicycle and keeps out of range. At the end of the round he returns to our corner and I tell him to wait until the last 10 seconds of each round and then go to work on Porky with both hands. Well, what happened after that was beautiful indeed to watch. He made pork chops out of Porky and easily wins the newspaper decision. He fought like a champ and I was proud of him. I christen him Battling Levinsky and I tell Joe Humphries, the ring announcer, to do me a favor.

"'Joe,' I say, 'announce to the folks that my new Jewish find is now named Battling Levinsky and defies any Irishman in the country to lick him.'

"Not long after, I send him against Jack Dillon, who's been dissipating too much. They fight in Boston, my boy Levinsky wins and I got myself another world's champ."

Battling Levinsky stood 5 ft., 11 in. and weighed 175. Two of his stoutest rivalries were with Dillon and Harry Greb. He fought Dillon nine times, Greb six times, the latter no-decision matches.

Up to 1920, the only one to flatten Levinsky was Jack Dempsey. "Jack Kearns duped me into thinking Dempsey was only a second-rate club fighter," Morgan said, "so I agreed to put the Battler into a six-round exhibition with him. It was the biggest boner I ever made as a fight manager. At the end of the first round, my boy said to me, 'Dan, this guy wants to kill me!' But Levinsky was no quitter and for two more rounds he walked right back in there toe to toe with Dempsey. In the sixth he got leg-weary, and when Dempsey dropped him I threw in the towel. Afterwards, I told the newspaper guys, 'Dempsey will be the next heavyweight champ.' Jack was probably the greatest rough-and-tumble fighter who ever lived. He might as well not have worn boxing gloves."

Early in Levinsky's career, Jim Corbett brought over a highly touted British Empire heavyweight champion named Tom Cowler. Corbett and his protégé were sitting in an automobile one day with the late Ted Dorgan, famous sports cartoonist and friend of Morgan. Dan happened along and Ted called him over. "Meet the next heavy champ," he said. Morgan looked Cowler over carefully and said, "Nope, he looks like a bum to me."

"The guy had a weak face," Dan said. "Not a mark on it. All great fighters, then and now, had some marks on them—a scar, a cut or a tin ear. This guy looked more like a Sunday-school teacher. I put Levinsky in with him, after Corbett got mad at my remark, and Levinsky ran Cowler right back to England where he told the rest of the British big boys we were a 'rude lot.' There's no place for pity in boxing. If he's a good fighter, the most easy-going fellow outside the ring may become the most vicious man alive once a fight starts. That's what makes boxing such a tough game for a real human being. Many fighters can't bear to hammer a helpless, bleeding opponent until he is finished. They remember him as he looked at the start, fresh, clean, strong. They don't want to *hurt* him. They *can't*.

"But look at the *great* ones. Bob Fitzsimmons used to slug it out with a pet tiger cub he had that grew into vicious maturity.

"Ketchel was an exception to the human race—a savage, bloodthirsty. Dempsey was so wild the night he fought Firpo I thought he was going to bite him. Gene Tunney could be cunning and mean, too. He liked to break your nose and cut you up. He never cared how much he cut you, he'd always take his time. In 1922, he beat my boy Levinsky on points in 12 rounds. The Battler was trying to regain the light-heavyweight title from him and Gene fought that night like his life was at stake.

"And then there was Joe Louis. Joe's best friend was supposed to be John Henry Lewis. There were stories before their fight that Joe would take it easy with John Henry, who was half blind in one eye. Then they fought. Louis beat John Henry into a helpless pulp in the first round and then knocked him out in the second round. That's the difference between great and near-great fighters."

Levinsky lost his title on October 12, 1920, at Jersey City, when Georges Carpentier knocked him out in four rounds. It was only the second time he had ever been counted out.

Battling Levinsky was a prizefighter who truly loved to fight. He was born on June 10, 1891, in Philadelphia, of Jewish-American parentage, and died on February 12, 1949.

LIGHT HEAVYWEIGHTS

Nearly half of his life was spent in the prize ring. He fought more than 400 bouts; 52 times in 1915, six matches in one week!

"Tom Jones was my first opponent in Philadelphia," Levinsky once recalled. "The match was held at Lew Bailey's old Broadway Club. Jones drove a wagon for the Jones Company and named himself after the company. Before the opening bell, Tom called referee Nick Hayes over to his corner and whispered something in his ear. Nick then announced to the male audience: 'Gentlemen, Tom Jones wants me to say that this is his first professional fight.' Then the bell rang and we came out of our corners and I crossed my right and Tom went down and was counted out. After coming to, Tom again called Nick over to his corner and whispered something in his ear. Nick then raised his hand to the audience for silence, and shouted: 'Gentlemen, Tom Jones wants me to announce that this is his *last* professional fight.'"

Dan Morgan normally gave Levinsky Wednesday nights off from fighting. So one Wednesday night the fighter arranged to take his sweetheart to a leading Broadway show. After he was gone, promoter Jimmy Johnston phoned Morgan and asked if Levinsky was available.

"I need him for the main event over at St. Nick tonight," Jimmy said. "My star has come down sick."

"He's over at the theater," Dan said.

"Get him," Jimmy said.

Morgan rushed over to the theater just as the curtain for the first act was going up. He found Levinsky and told him he was needed over at St. Nick.

"But I have no gear," Levinsky protested.

"That's all taken care of," Dan said, grabbing him by the arm.

Levinsky turned to his girl friend and said, "Honey, I'll be right back. Don't worry about a thing."

They got a cab and raced to St. Nick, where Levinsky flattened his opponent in the first minute of the second round and was back at the theater alongside his date in time to catch the second act.

"In all my ring career I never met a man who gave me so many laughs as Morgan," Levinsky recalled one time. "The old Irishman had many Irish friends in New York, none of whom thought, of course, that a Jew boy could possibly be a good fighter. One day we were strolling down Broadway and Dan met an old friend who was very deaf. 'Mike,' Dan told him, 'I want you to meet my new champion, Battling Levinsky. He's a great fighter.'

"'Please speak a little louder, Danny me boy,' Mike said. 'I didn't catch the name.'

"Dan lifted his voice. 'I said I want you to meet my latest find, Battling Levinsky, the new light-heavyweight champion of the world.'

"Mike still stared at him blankly. Morgan

Battling Levinsky truly loved to fight. In 1915, he fought three main events the same day! (UPI)

tried once more. Putting his mouth right to Mike's ear, he shouted: 'BATTLING LEVINSKY, MIKE; HE'S A GREAT FIGHTER!'

"The old man shook his head and said: 'It's no use, Danny. It sounded like *Levinsky* to me.'"

Battling Levinsky died only six months after Morgan buried another of his pets, little Knockout Brown. Dan was eighty-one years old when he told me about it.

"I can guess what Kayo said to Levinsky when they were reunited again," Morgan said. "He probably asked: 'What's keepin' Morgan?'"

GEORGES CARPENTIER
(1894–   )

Georges Carpentier captivated the public as few other fighters living or dead. In France, he became a national institution like Chevalier, Mistinguet, Colette and Bernhardt. And his popularity never waned when Jack Dempsey, the black-bearded villain, shattered the legend of his invincibility.

The Orchid Man was a dashing fellow, *un brave homme* as well as *un homme brave*. At one time in his fabulous career, he held a championship in every weight division from flyweight to heavyweight. Only one title, the light-heavyweight championship, was universal, though the rest—championships of France and Europe—were perfectly respectable.

Carpentier was the idol of every maundering maid the world o'er. He had the dark good looks and engaging charm of a fairy tale prince. Yet there was nothing superficial about him. His adroit manager, Francois Descamps, often persuaded him to play the prima donna both in and out of the ring, but it was only an act to build up the box office. In private life Georges remained unspoiled by all the excitement.

Phydias, the sculptor, could not have improved on the Carpentier figure ("the most beautiful I've ever seen," said Heywood Hale Broun). And when George Bernard Shaw had watched him kayo Joe Beckett, a British heavy, in less than two minutes of the first round, he wrote, "I was startled by a most amazing apparition. Nothing less than Charles XII, the madman of the North, striding along in a Japanese dressing gown as gallantly as if he had not been killed almost 201 years before."

Georges copped a real plum when he won the light-heavyweight championship in Jersey City's West Side Park on Columbus Day, 1920. He flattened the great Battling Levinsky in four rounds, a feat which only three other fighters were able to accomplish, and he became the first Frenchman to hold a bona fide world prize ring championship. Unfortunately, Paris had to witness his loss of the crown when Battling Siki brusquely ended his reign in the sixth round, on September 24, 1922.

Georges Carpentier at one time or another held a title for every weight division in Europe, from flyweight to heavyweight. (UPI)

Carpentier actually took a slightly cynical view of the prize ring. He came by it naturally, for he had grown up in one of the most cynical environments of modern times, the boxing industry as conducted in Europe from 1900 to 1930. When he was eleven or twelve, he was apprenticed to Descamps by his parents. Descamps ran a small gymnasium and taught Carpentier boxing, *la savate* (the popular French sport of "boxing with your feet"), acrobatics, contortionism, etc. Carpentier began to box exhibitions in Lens saloons, with Descamps passing the hat. When the boy was thirteen, Descamps took him to Paris to fight professionally. When he was only seventeen, Carpentier became welterweight champion of France, and then of Europe.

English heavyweights were the ladder by which Carpentier rose to the Dempsey bout and wealth. He finally won what was called the "heavyweight championship of Europe" by knocking out Bombardier Billy Wells in one round.

After scoring an impressive four-round KO over Battling Levinsky at Jersey City, on July 2, 1921, to win the light-heavyweight championship of the world, Carpentier was signed to fight Dempsey. As history was to record, the 168 lb. Frenchman was no match for the 188 lb. American in size or strength.

The bout was the first to be broadcast, with Graham McNamee describing the action, and it had the whole nation taking sides for or against Dempsey.

Carpentier landed in the United States several weeks before the match. He had never seen Dempsey. He was a Frenchman on a holiday, a goodwill emissary.

Dempsey trained at Atlantic City.

"As for Carpentier," recalled Grantland Rice, "I never was sure that he did train. He was never on exhibition to the press—never on a scale—about the only time we'd see him was on a rubbing table or sauntering into a restaurant. But the story of that fight—badly overplayed, but eaten up hoggishly by the public—was actually ordained days beforehand. The culmination of Carpentier's mental and physical unpreparedness was seen near his dressing room just before the fight at Boyle's Thirty Acres—not by me, but by my wife Kit and Sophie Treadwell McGeehan, W. O. McGeehan's wife and a fine reporter in her own right. Sophie was covering the color story for her paper. A lot of New York's carriage trade was there and that was part of the story. Well, it had started to rain before the bout. Sophie and Kit spotted a little exit to somewhere and they decided to get in out of the rain. They were in this little room, sitting on a rubbing table and complimenting themselves on their abode when a cop entered and said to them, 'Ladies, where do you think you are?' They told him they were out of the rain. He said, 'You've got to leave. You're in the Frenchman's dressing room!' At that moment down the corridor came Carpentier. He was dressed and was as white as a sheet—thin—and, Oh Lord, but he looked frightened. And a few steps behind, wearing trunks and a heavy red sweater, and unshaven, came Dempsey—big, tough and bristling. He dwarfed the cops guarding him. Kit looked at Sophie who, of course, was staring. Studying the contrast between the two men, she said. 'The poor French boy. Why, he'll be murdered!' They then returned to their seats and waited for the Angel of Doom to claim Carpentier."

Elmer Davis, who covered the bout for *The New York Times,* noted that Carpentier had muscles, and formidable muscles, but he said it was hard to pay attention to the muscles. "The center of attraction was his eyes—gray eyes, rather eager, rather excited, in a gray face, with blond hair brushed back above it; a face that had more than ever the curious girlish quality that would hardly be looked for in an aspirant to the heavyweight championship," Davis wrote. "Eagerness and enthusiasm were there but more than all an apparent realization that he represented France, that he represented millions of soldiers who had fought in the trenches and that this day was the climax of his whole career. His eager intensity, his fiery slightness, gave to some of the onlookers a curious sense of resemblance between Georges Carpentier and another French champion of old. He suggested Joan of Arc. And over this slender, eager, almost devout personage hovered the crafty Francois Descamps, his manager, a fat, excitable man wrapped in a gray sweater, a light brown cap on his head."

At 3 o'clock exactly Jack Dempsey came in. His entrance brought a much louder cheer than the challenger had evoked. Dempsey nodded and smiled slightly, but only for a moment. His famous scowl was on his browned unshaven face. Under black eyebrows and curling black hair he glowered stolidly, sullenly. He crossed the ring to shake hands with Carpentier, then returned to his corner.

In a moment the vigilant Descamps was in Dempsey's corner as Jack held out his hands to be wound with bandages and adhesive tape. "No, no, no!" Descamps shouted and tore the rolls of tape out of the hands of Dempsey's seconds. The belief that Dempsey's terrific pounding of Willard had been made possible in some degree by his tape-wound hands was strong in the Frenchman's camp, and Descamps was determined that only the soft gauze bandages permitted by the New Jersey Boxing Commission should be used. After a brief but bitter argument he gained his way. Meanwhile, Jack Kearns was showing no interest in Carpentier's hands, nor very much in Dempsey's.

There was an interlude while Joe Humphreys, the scarlet-faced announcer, exercised his cracked voice through the amplifier and introduced first the distinguished guests, and then the fighters. Through it all Dempsey glowered, as before, preoccupied and somber. Then the seconds tumbled out of the ring and at 3:16 P.M. the gong signaled the beginning of the fight.

"It was all over in four rounds," Grantland Rice recalled. "But had Dempsey wanted to put the slug on Carpentier, I think he could

When former welterweight champion Ted "Kid" Lewis of England stepped up in class, Carpentier, right, promptly knocked him out in the first round. Bout was fought in London, in 1922. (NEA)

have nailed him in the first round." One story going the rounds claimed that Tex Rickard asked Dempsey to carry Georges for three or four rounds to keep from turning boxing's first million-dollar gate into a million-dollar fiasco.

The bout also produced another first—the first closed-circuit broadcast of a sporting event. David Sarnoff wired up a number of arenas and lodge halls within a 700-mile radius of Jersey City, and beamed forth a radiocast of the fight that sold more than 200,000 tickets at $2.00 a ticket.

Many American sports writers felt Carpentier had no business in the same ring with Dempsey. "He was an imposter," John Lardner said. "An adequate lightheavyweight, but an imposter among heavyweight contenders. Who can ever forget when, in that fourth round against Dempsey, he lay on his right side, his legs kicking and a small trickle of blood running from his sobbing mouth? *That* was the truth of him!"

Rumors persisted afterward that the defeat had shattered Carpentier physically. However, he returned to action in reasonably good trim in 1922. After knocking out Ted (Kid) Lewis in London in May of that year, he suffered a reversal. Battling Siki, the humble Senegalese, promised to lose the bout, but Siki forgot his promise and won the light-heavyweight title from Georges. The Frenchman fought only a few more times after that. In subsequent years, he acted in plays, revues, films, and vaudeville and operated bars in Paris and on the Riviera.

In 1924, before his retirement from the ring, Carpentier and Descamps came back to America for a bout with Gene Tunney. But first he warmed up against Tommy Gibbons at Michigan City, Indiana. Carpentier looked old and drawn for a man of thirty and he lost the newspaper decision in 10 rounds. He fought the ninth round with swollen ankles, a sure sign of poor condition. His share of the purse was $70,000.

Two months later, he fought Tunney at the Polo Grounds. It ended in a welter of blood, with Tunney chopping Carpentier to shreds in 15 rounds. Carpentier showed crowd-pleasing courage, however, and tried to fight back, but the referee awarded Tunney a T.K.O.

Carpentier's charm for audiences outlived his prestige as a fighter. After he lost so badly to Tunney, a blonde leaped into the ring and tried to scratch Tunney's eyes out.

In 1926, during an attempted "comeback" in America, large crowds paid to see Carpentier fight Eddie Huffman in New York and Tommy Loughran in Philadelphia. A number of reporters met the boat when he arrived in the New York harbor for the Huffman bout. Jack Curley, agent for Carpentier in the U.S., served as interpreter for the news conference.

Carpentier's cynical view of the fight racket was plainly evident during the question-and-answer session. He had not figured on any of the newsmen knowing French, but the man from *The New York Times* did, and he filed a transcription of the dialogue, as follows:

Curley (to Carpentier): "What do you want to give the boys?"

Carpentier: "Tell them anything you want."

Curley: "Georges says he is very happy to be back in the United States and enjoys above all his association with writers."

Carpentier (to Curley): "Get rid of this gang as soon as possible. I've got a date at 7:30."

Curley: "He says he'd like to fight Paul Berlenbach for the light-heavyweight title and wishes you boys a Happy New Year."

In 1948, when Carpentier returned to America again, this time to watch Marcel Cerdan, a fellow countryman, win the middleweight championship from Tony Zale, in Jersey City, a reporter made reference to Carpentier's nickname, "the Orchid Man." When the remark was translated for Carpentier, he wrinkled his nose.

"Others called me by the name of a flower—not me," he said. "I was not so sweet."

BATTLING SIKI
(1897–1925)

The story of the simple soul corrupted and destroyed by civilization has been told in many ways *ad nauseam*. In prizefighting it is the story of Louis Phal, a stocky Senegalese tribesman who joined the French Army in World War I, wiped out a German machine gun nest single-handed, became light-heavyweight champion of the world and died of bullet wounds in a Manhattan gutter, after surviving a stabbing earlier in the same year.

Louis was born in the Senegal on September 16, 1897. Legend has it that when he was ten or twelve years old, a French actress touring the African colonies saw him in St. Louis de Senegal, was impressed by his appearance, and took him into her personal service, giving him, for reasons based on classical Greek, the name of Louis Phal. This was later Anglicized as Louis Fall. He did not become known as "Battling Siki" until 1913, when he began to box professionally at the age of fifteen.

The Senegalese have always been fiercely proud of their combat record. As well-drilled mercenaries fighting the white man's peculiar wars, these magnificent warriors are unsurpassed. They terrorized the Kaiser's lines by their courage and ferocity.

Louis Phal liked the army. He had been conscripted into the Eighth Colonial Infantry Regiment of the French Army and distinguished himself as the bravest soldier in his outfit. When his unit was pinned down by machine gun fire, he cheerfully obliterated the hornet's nest, permitting his regiment to advance. This spontaneous act of valor won him both the *Croix de Guerre* and the *Medaille Militaire*. He was only seventeen years old.

After the Armistice, Louis returned to Paris as a servant to the French actress. He grew restless. No one was interested in his wartime heroics. After all, hadn't he killed more Germans than he could count? Why, then, should he not enjoy the privileges of an honored citizen? How could a simple servant exercise his special rights as a hero of civilization?

Louis found an answer in the makeshift boxing rings of Paris. Here a man could use brute force and gain the respect of thousands. He too would become a prizefighter!

Phal was an immediate hit. He weighed 175, stood 5 ft., 11 in., was well-muscled with a leaping, bounding, lunging style from which he got slapstick effects that amused the galleries. His tremendous strength and fierce expression drew capacity crowds to the music halls and "palaces of sport." The French were fascinated, for here was Rousseau's "noble savage" come to life, his "natural" endowments pitted against the sophistries of *le boxe*. His opponents were terrified when he rolled his eyes like a rogue stallion. And from ringside to "the gods" (the French peanut gallery) the crowds roared their approval.

Louis delighted in his ring name, "Battling Siki." In the two years prior to his title match with Georges Carpentier, he compiled an impressive record of victories. He was an awkward bozo, but his long pendulous arms could fell an opponent with one clout.

When he was finally matched with Carpentier, all the forces of mythology were loosed upon the public. By the afternoon of the fight, September 24, 1922, in Paris, the billing might well have read, "Beauty vs. the Beast."

Much balderdash has been written about a Siki-Carpentier "deal" without due regard for human psychology. Certainly the ring officials were determined that Carpentier would win. But it was obvious from the opening bell that Siki had other ideas. All of the humiliations he'd experienced as a hero of the Republic goaded him on. Was a white hero better than a black hero? *Merde!* Hadn't he, Louis Phal, alias Battling Siki, killed more Germans than Carpentier had seen throughout the whole war?

When Siki answered the opening bell, he was foaming at the mouth. He missed with two haymakers, and the artful Carpentier promptly floored him with a right hook to the chin. Siki arose at six, all passion spent—at least for the moment. The idol of France scorned his advantage. Instead, he decided to toy with his fantastic black opponent before delivering the *coup de grâce*. A round or two of trifling to amuse his beloved public—what difference could it make?

For the next four rounds Carpentier put on the exhibition that the crowd of 55,000, largest in European boxing history, had paid to see. Occasionally Siki would jolt him with a desperation blow, but Georges was completely in command and enjoying himself hugely.

In the sixth round an enraged Siki carried his attack to the ribs with devastating effect. Suddenly Carpentier was in trouble. As he reeled toward the ropes, the Senegalese caught him with a left hook that ended the fight. Carpentier's leg became entangled in the ropes and he floundered to the canvas, where he lay writhing in agony.

A shocked silence fell over the spectators. The referee didn't even bother to count. Instead he announced that Siki was disqualified for tripping and throwing the champion. The reaction of the crowd was a beautiful thing to behold. "Crooks!", "Frameup!" screamed the fans with one accord. The officials went into a quick huddle around the judge's table. Yes, it was decided, the referee had been in error! He should have consulted the judge before making his decision! One has only to read the rules of the French Boxing Federation!

The French people with their innate sense of sportsmanship and fair play had delivered the verdict, and Battling Siki, ex-servant, was the new light-heavyweight champion of the world.

The story of Battling Siki is the saga of a simple soul corrupted and destroyed by modern civilization. (NEA)

It cannot be said of Louis Phal as Shakespeare said of Coriolanus that "He could not carry his honors even." Louis was a child of old Africa, where titles and trinkets are held in high regard and the height of sartorial splendor may be a pair of red pajamas and a topper.

In exercising a champion's prerogatives, Louis indulged himself to the limit. His exotic duds would have qualified him for the grand finale of *Hellzapoppin*. As a boulevardier, he resembled a vision by the surrealist poet Jean Cocteau: top hat perched rakishly on the side of his head . . . ablaze with diamonds . . . a beautiful blonde on his leash arm (the arm that guided a pair of domesticated lions) . . . and a revolver in his free hand for commanding attention and scattering pigeons in droves.

Louis had his run-ins with the Paris police. When he was drinking he could be rather nasty, and inevitably there were sidewalk scuffles. By the time he agreed to put his title on the line against Mike McTigue of County Clare, he had already dissipated a deal of his former strength.

The odds were heavily in favor of the Irishman, but Siki's manager made a fatal error in agreeing to a Dublin match to be held on St. Patrick's Day, 1923. Paris' *enfant terrible* lost on points in 20 mediocre rounds.

Bereft of his title but nothing daunted, Phal headed for New York in the autumn. In his selection of mad clothes, he stopped traffic all along Broadway. He almost always wore full dress when he roamed the streets of Manhattan at night. By day, he often appeared in a high hat, a frock coat, red ascot tie, striped trousers, spatted shoes, and a monocle. He carried a gold-headed cane with his pet monkey perched on one shoulder. On other occasions he strolled the Great White Way in a tiny alpine hat that resembled a peanut shell precariously balanced on a large chestnut burr.

Sometimes, he gave away all of his stylish clothes and went home by cab in his underwear. Other times he walked the Hell's Kitchen streets with an attendant, who carried a goatskin bag of wine on his shoulder for Siki to swig from when he felt the need. He had the reputation of being dangerous when drunk, mild and affable when sober. He was known for his favorite joke of hailing a cab, taking a ride, and then challenging the driver to fight for the fare.

When he had it, Siki was a big spender. He sometimes tipped five or ten times the amount of the check in restaurants and speakeasies. Once, having made $5,000 from a fight in New York on a Friday, he was turned out of his rooming house, broke, the following Monday. Another time, he gave away all the money in his pockets to passengers on a Lackawanna Railroad ferryboat.

Sports writers referred to him repeatedly as a "child of nature," "a natural man," and "a jungle child." The New York *World* described him as having "the mentality of a backward toad, but with the soul of a god."

M. Hellers, who'd managed him in France, admitted that Siki was "a fine lad but just a little bit crazy." True, he was illiterate, never having been to school, but Siki could make himself understood in a number of languages, including English, French, Spanish, Dutch, and German.

"Pa" Levy, his manager in America, was the only one who probably really understood the Mohammedan-born Siki. Levy loved Siki as a man loves a friendly but mischievous pet. Siki called him "Papa Bob" and often assaulted him with moist kisses much the way an Airedale slaps his master on the cheek with a sopping tongue.

Siki laughed at life as he laughed in Paul Berlenbach's face throughout their fight in the old Garden in New York, March 13, 1925. The harder Paul slugged him the more he seemed to enjoy the joke. It was no joke, though, when Berlenbach knocked him out in the 10th round.

Americans found Siki vastly entertaining. He was by turns an engaging or mischievous child and was treated as such. Laugh at him, and he would laugh back at you. Greet him with a hearty salutation, and he would hail you in return. Doff your hat, and Siki would respond with a sweeping flourish of his topper.

New York policemen adopted a paternal attitude toward Siki, who tried his own hand at directing Broadway traffic. His tribal dance, executed on busy street corners or in the middle of a traffic jam, would have taken first prize at the Savoy. Only the cab drivers, bartenders and hoodlums whom he knocked around found it hard to take him philosophically.

One of Siki's idols was Luis Angel Firpo, though his admiration was founded on envy. Someone had told him that Firpo had knocked a full-grown horse stone cold with one punch—just *one* punch, mind you, aimed at the submaxillary. At first, Siki was unimpressed. He wanted to know if Firpo had ever bitten a lion. Why, of course. Firpo had not only bitten but *eaten* lions!

This was too much for Siki. Nothing would do but that he find himself a good stout horse. Obliging wags supplied two horses: a hauler of ice and a hauler of coal. Siki approached the first brute and delivered his Sunday Special, then stepped back so that the animal wouldn't fall on him. Dobbin merely swished his tail. Siki tried to poleax the second nag with similar results. Crestfallen and as hurt as any child, Siki withdrew to his hotel to sulk.

Siki fought only six more times after the frightful hiding Berlenbach gave him. Then, on Monday, December 14, 1925, he told his wife he was going "out with the boys" and would be back early that night. At 4:15 A.M., a patrolman found his body lying in the gutter in front of 350 West 41st Street. A vest-pocket .32-caliber pistol was found nearby. Two bullets had been fired from it. An autopsy showed that these had entered Siki from *behind*. It also revealed something else: Siki had suffered from anemia.

Battling Siki was given a Christian burial. The Reverend Adam Clayton Powell, later the renowned senator, delivered the eulogy. The body was clothed in evening dress, surrounded by seven Mohammedan pallbearers in turbans.

Siki left an estimated estate of $600.

His murder was never solved.

MIKE McTIGUE
(1892–)

By fighting an Irishman in Dublin on St. Patrick's Day, 1923, Battling Siki insured his loss of the world light-heavyweight championship, in all innocence. At that, the Senegalese Slasher forced Mike McTigue to go 20 rounds to earn the title.

This is not to take anything away from McTigue, however. For 60 minutes of fierce milling, he punished Siki with a bruising body attack, played chopsticks on his chin, and left him weaving back to port.

Michael Francis McTigue was born on November 26, 1892, at County Clare. The 5 ft., 9 in., 175-pound Irishman took the long way to the championship. It took him 14 years as a professional to get there.

Whoever managed Siki in Dublin was outdone by Joe Jacobs, who managed McTigue and matched him with Young Stribling 26 weeks later at Columbus, Georgia. Young Stribling was Georgia-bred and born, king of the cane brakes and a hero throughout all of Dixie. Jacobs was aware of this and, for good measure, took along his own referee for protection.

McTigue and Stribling traded jabs, whistled murderous hooks back and forth, and at the end of 10 rounds it was pretty close. The referee gave the decision to McTigue—and jumped out of the ring. So did McTigue. So did Jacobs. Jacobs must have been a little slow. He was cut off and hemmed in by angry partisans.

"We're going to take you out of town and hang you," growled the leader of the mob. They didn't, though. Jacobs changed their minds by saying, "Hang me! Go ahead! But tomorrow my gang will be down here and they'll blow this goddamned town off the map!"

Jacobs never had a mob, of course, but the crowd didn't know that. They backed off and let him through. Then they went searching for the referee. They cornered him in his dressing room.

"Who *really* won the fight?" they asked.

What could he say? This was a lynch party.

"Stribling," he said.

An eight-rounder had been scheduled to follow the main event. One of the fighters was supposed to be Willie Phfeffer, who was McTigue's sparring partner, but Willie refused to get into the ring. The police saved Willie, Mike, Joe and the referee by escorting them to the safety of a waiting train. When the train got safely out of Columbus, Jacobs asked the referee who he thought really won the fight. Like a politician, the referee had all the right answers.

"McTigue," he said.

So that's the way it officially went into the record book, and, for the time, all was well in the McTigue camp. Then, on May 31, 1925, in New York, Mike lost the championship to Paul Berlenbach on a decision in 15 rounds. He knocked Berlenbach out in four rounds in a return match two years later, but by that time Paul was no longer the champion.

McTigue continued to fight professionally right up into the 1930s, meeting many of the good ones: Mickey Walker, Tiger Flowers, Tommy Loughran, Jack Sharkey, Tuffy Griffiths, Leo Lomski, and Jack Delaney. Yet in all his 22 years in the prize ring, he fought only once on St. Patrick's Day.

Mike was no dolt.

He wasn't going to push all that stuff about "Irish luck" too far.

PAUL BERLENBACH
(1901–   )

The bloodthirsty loved Paul Berlenbach. The "Astoria Assassin" looked like a fighter. He had a flat nose, wide shoulders, and thick, muscular arms and a nice set of pins. He also had a sizzling, bursting bomb for a right hand. He was quick, tough, and knew his way around.

Born in New York on February 18, 1901, of German-American parents, Berlenbach fashioned a peculiar career. He won the heavyweight wrestling championship at the 1920 Olympic Games, and two years later added the National A.A.U. heavyweight boxing title to his laurels.

Paul Berlenbach's first 11 pro bouts ended in K.O.'s. He won the first 10, and then, in the 11th, Jack Delaney flattened him here in the fourth round. Fight was held at Madison Square Garden, in 1924. (UPI)

That's a hot one: wrestler turns prize fighter. Nowadays it is the other way around.

Berlenbach turned professional in 1923. Though he had been fighting as a heavyweight in the amateurs, at 5 ft., 10½ in. and 170 pounds he was able to make light-heavyweight as a pro and scored 10 straight knockouts before being stopped in four by Jack Delaney.

A busy fighter—he fought 20 times in 1924—Berlenbach was not discouraged. He came back from the Delaney defeat by putting together 14 more knockouts. The string included a 10-round K.O. of Battling Siki and a decision over Young Stribling.

But Berlenbach's big hour was on the night of May 30, 1925, when he won the title from Mike McTigue.

Within the first six months after winning the world championship, Berlenbach successfully put his title on the line against Jimmy Slattery (K.O., 11) and Jack Delaney (Decision, 15). Young Stribling was the next to challenge him for the crown and went the way of Delaney (Decision, 15).

Then, on July 16, 1926, Delaney coaxed Berlenbach into a Brooklyn ring for another shot at the title and this time the French-Canadian playboy walked away with a 15-round decision and the championship. After that, it was pretty much downhill for Berlenbach. In 1927, Mike McTigue K.O.'d him in 4, ditto Delaney in 6, and Mickey Walker decisioned him in 10. On April 17, 1929, Paul Berlenbach went back to where he came from. He became a professional wrestler.

In 1971, Berlenbach was elected to Boxing's Hall of Fame.

JACK DELANEY
(1900–1948)

It was always Ladies' Night when handsome Jack Delaney donned the gloves. The 5 ft., 11½ in. French-Canadian wowed the matron and the maid like no one since Carpentier. It might be said that Delaney's Screaming Mamies formed the vanguard of today's female fight fans.

Smiling Jack lived with a carefree abandon peculiar to an age of mythology. But like so many of his fun-loving brethren, he was all business when the work gong sounded. When he was in the mood, he could be as ruthless as that old night owl, Harry Greb.

His manager, Pete Reilly, regarded Jack as a problem child. He even offered a piece of Delaney to a Connecticut clergyman if the good Doctor would be so kind as to keep this sinful young man in the paths of righteousness.

True, Delaney loved the primrose even as the laurel, but Pete was revealing a rare display of horse feathers when he imagined that the gleam in Delaney's eye could be related to the Chalice.

No one will deny that when Jack was bad, he was horrid.

On the night of April 30, 1928, he did a Leon Errol climbing through the ropes to do battle with Jack Sharkey and thus became the first fighter in history to knock himself out in the first round. (Did he ever return to that party? Who will ever know!) In his two bouts with that shadow-dancer Jimmy Slattery, Jack was way off form, but these were simply bad Delaney nights in keeping with the excesses of an age of gods and goddesses.

On the warring side, Delaney asked no quarter of any man. On the eve of his first engagement with the great Tiger Flowers, a reporter inquired as to his chances.

"Ask Flowers the same question," he replied, "and if he says he's going to beat me, tell him he's full of birdseed and that Jack Delaney is picking himself by a knockout in an early round."

Jack won by a knockout in the second, and a month and a half later he kayoed Flowers in the fourth.

This stout *courrier du bois* was born in St. Francis, Canada, March 18, 1900. His real name was Ovila Chapdelaine (no relation to the romantic creation of Louis Hemon), and this so upset a ring announcer that he settled for "Jack Delaney," and the name stuck.

Jack showed little inclination for methodical destruction in the early days of his ascendancy, so his first manager, Al Jennings, sold his contract to Reilly for $600. Delaney proceeded to gross a fortune. His Ebbets Field fight with Paul Berlenbach grossed $450,000 while the $201,613 gate he made with Jimmy Maloney in 1927 was a Garden record until Louis and Walcott topped it in 1947 by $15,000.

Tex Rickard knew that the "Rapier of the North" was box office, win, lose or draw. So he touted Jack as his lead attraction for the new Garden and signed him with Berlenbach for the opening match.

Now Jack met the "Astoria Assassin" four times in his jaunty career, and he had previously kayoed this formidable opponent in the old Garden on March 15, 1924—no mean feat when you consider that Berlenbach had previously kayoed 23 men in a row.

Therefore, the second meeting was fraught

with "meaning" to odds-makers, scribes and Delaney's female following. The bout took place on December 11, 1925, and Jack started like a house afire. In the fourth round he decked Berlenbach, who arose at "two" and then reconsidering his move, returned to one knee to await the nine count. This act of obeisance gave rise to the Great Knee Controversy, which raged in the papers for days afterward and sent the rules committee into executive session. The complaints, of course, arose from Delaney's partisans since Berlenbach had come on to win the decision in 15 torrid rounds.

When he got down to business, carefree Jack Delaney could be as ruthless as another old night owl, Harry Greb. (UPI)

Jack settled accounts with the "Assassin" in Ebbets Field on July 16, 1926. Despite a broken thumb, he won 13 of the 15 rounds and took the light-heavyweight crown. The gals nearly tore him apart.

The man from the North Woods fought all of the good ones—Tommy Loughran, Maxie Rosenbloom, Mike McTigue, Johnny Risko, Slattery, Flowers and Sharkey. His Philadelphia draw with Loughran on July 16, 1925, is regarded as one of the great exhibitions of all time—a "classic," if you will.

Jack was a born combatant who could hit with tremendous force. His judgment of distance was simply uncanny. He believed in the separation of home and office. Thus, he maintained a large camp at Lake Winnipesaukee, New Hampshire—close to the Northern Lights—but he did all his training in a musty old gym in Bridgeport, Connecticut.

This superb ringman began his fistic career in 1919. When he won the title from Berlenbach, he immediately relinquished it to campaign among the heavies. He "retired" in 1928 after knocking out Nando Tassi.

Jack made a brief comeback in 1932 before he finally quit for good. Among his *post bellum* activities he opened the famous Jack Delaney's on Sheridan Square in Greenwich Village. In 1948, he died of cancer in Katonah, New York.

TOMMY LOUGHRAN
(1902–)

On the way to his championship years (1927–1929) as a light-heavy, Tommy Loughran served a spell as chief sparring partner for Jack Dempsey. Several days before the first Tunney bout, Loughran outboxed Dempsey by a city block for three rounds in the champ's final workout.

Afterward, Dempsey asked a friend: "Well, how'd I look today?"

"Fine," the man said.

"You're crazy!" Dempsey snapped. "Tommy made me look terrible and you know it! Tunney would have murdered me today."

Tommy Loughran made a lot of sluggers look terrible. He was a master boxer. Attesting to his defensive skill, he was kayoed only twice in 227 bouts—by Jack Sharkey and Steve Hamas. He fought 14 men who held world titles at one time or another: Mike McTigue, Harry Greb, Tunney, Johnny Wilson, Jack Delaney, Georges Carpentier, Jimmy Slattery, Pete Latzo, Mickey Walker, Jim Braddock, Sharkey, Baer, Carnera, and Al McCoy.

Loughran stood 5 ft., 11 in. and weighed 175. He fought professionally for 19 years (1919–1937) and started out as a knockout specialist. The record book credits him with a lifetime total of only 18 K.O.'s. Eleven of these were scored in the first two years. "But then I broke my right hand," Tommy said. "I fought most of my career with a broken hand. Nobody knew anything about it. I could take a guy out with my left hand, but I always held back, because I knew if I hurt the left mitt I was through. So I stopped going for kayoes and concentrated on the smart stuff." Between 1926 and mid-1935, Tommy didn't score a single K.O.

With no punch to rely on, Loughran developed finesse by shadow-boxing in front of a full-length mirror to the playing of phonograph records.

"Those records gave me a perfect sense of time," Tommy said. "They ran just under three minutes, about the distance of a regulation round, and I got so I instinctively knew just when a round would end. Folks were always amazed that I was always in my own corner when a round ended. Bong! would go the bell and I'd simply step back and sit down on my stool. The other guy would have to trudge all the way back to the other side of the ring—a long way back in a 15-round fight. Because I knew when the round would end, I'd maneuver myself around the ring so I'd be in my corner when the bell rang. It gave me a big psychological advantage. It made it appear that I was in control of myself and the

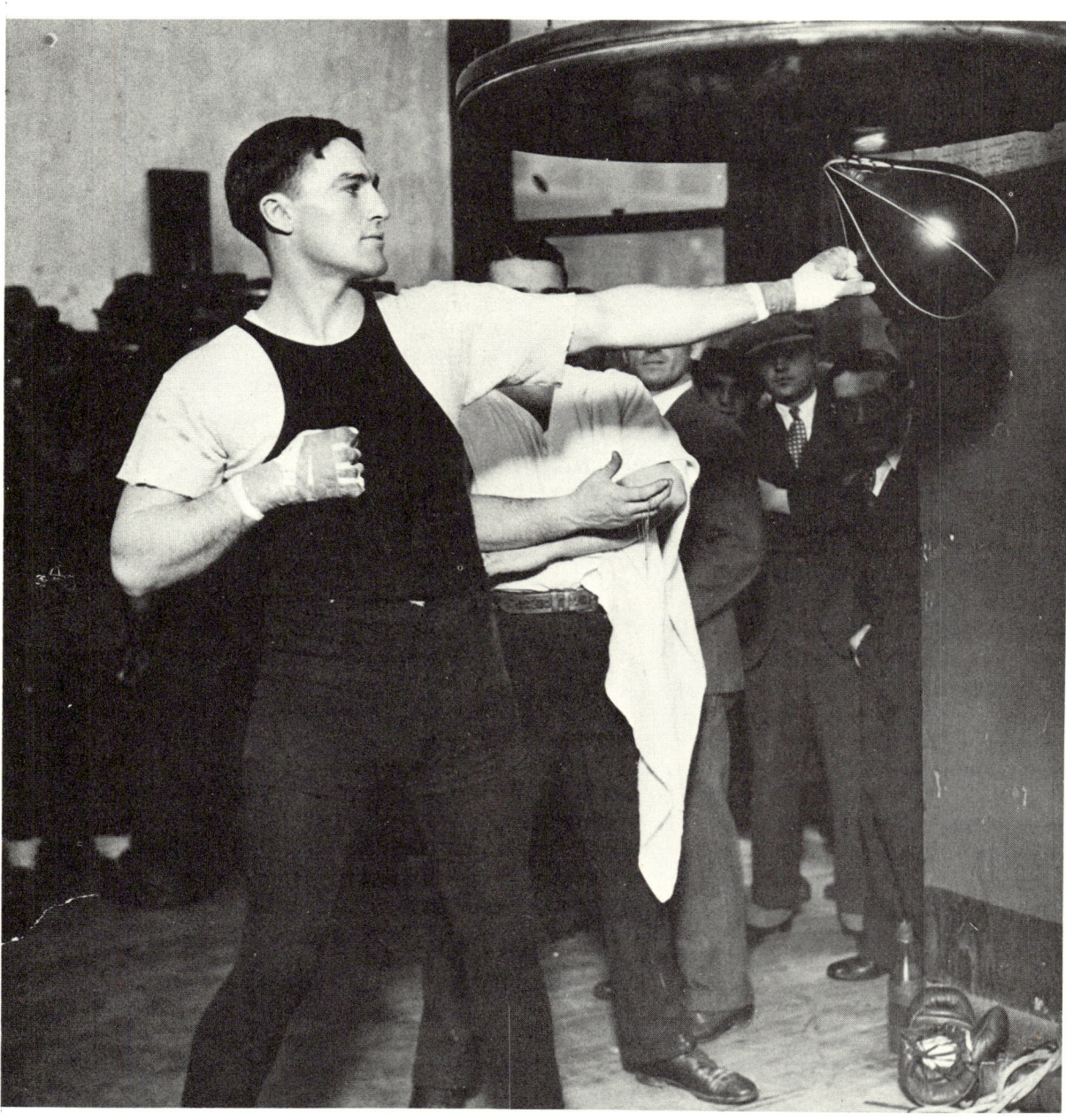

Master boxer Tommy Loughran was kayoed only twice in 227 pro fights. He fought 14 men who held world championships. (AP)

ring whenever it happened. It also saved my legs."

Loughran practiced in the basement of his home. He fixed up a small gym, complete with mirrors. He studied his movements in the reflections, the way ballet dancers work out. Tommy said, "I could watch myself punch the bag, skip rope and shadowbox. This enabled me to see how I looked to an opponent. I saw what he saw. He didn't know how *he* looked to *me*. All he saw was me. So I had an advantage. In my mind, I knew how both of us looked, and I could set him up for certain maneuvers. I could sucker him into almost anything. Jim Corbett, who was boxing's all-time master, used to come to my fights. He once told me that I did things in the ring he'd wanted to do. But he said he never got a chance to try them on an opponent because he had only 33 fights in his whole life. The

When a prizefighter wins a world championship, *Ring* Magazine, the bible of boxing, gives him an expensive belt. The ritual was originated by the late Nat Fleischer, here shown presenting a belt to Tommy Loughran in 1927 after Tommy won the vacant light-heavyweight title in bout with Mike McTigue. (AP)

average fan sitting there didn't appreciate the meticulous science behind my various moves—the footwork, the balance, the coordination, the stepping in and out to set an opponent up for a stiff shot—but Corbett could see what I was doing. He knew exactly what was going through my mind. We thought alike."

After Jack Delaney relinquished the light-heavyweight title, Loughran soundly thrashed Mike McTighe in 15 rounds at Madison Square Garden to win the world championship. That was on October 27, 1927. Two years later, he outgrew the division, retired his title undefeated, and moved on to the heavies.

Tommy was born in Philadelphia, on November 29, 1902. He was only seventeen when he started in the prize ring, and before he was twenty, he fought four world champions. Sharkey was the first to knock him out (1929), but he came back to work his way up the heavyweight ladder and a title bout with Carnera. He made a big score on February 6, 1931, when his jabs and flashy feints made a chump out of Maxie Baer to earn a 10-round decision.

Before the match, the muddled Maxie had gone around New York selling pieces of himself to eager buyers. Everybody got a chunk of him, for sums ranging from $500 to $10,000. The fun-loving Baer quickly spent the dough on broads. So after losing to Loughran, he showed up the following day to collect the purse for his end of the waltz.

"I walk into the room to get my pay," Maxie said, "and there I see nothing but the awful lookin' faces of those bums who'd bought pieces of me!"

The addlepated Maxie had sold exactly 113 percent of himself!

Baer had breakfast with Jack Dempsey the morning after losing to Loughran. Jack had refereed the bout. Maxie was feeling low. "Tommy had me lookin' at left jabs all night—lefts, lefts, lefts . . . that's all I seed," complained Maxie.

"You could've stopped him in the first round," Jack said.

"How?" Maxie asked.

"Take off your coat," Dempsey ordered. Max shucked off his coat. "Now lead with a left, just as Tommy did." Max led. "YOW!" yelped Maxie. "You broke my arm!" rubbing it painfully. Dempsey had dropped his big right fist across Baer's right biceps with paralyzing force as Max led with his left. "But that's *illegal!*" cried Maxie. "I know," grinned Dempsey, "but the ref will usually only warn you the first time."

On March 1, 1934, Loughran met Carnera for the heavyweight championship in Miami. The Preem outweighed him by 105 pounds. Though he hardly laid a glove on Tommy, Carnera's weight advantage was too much of an obstacle to overcome and Tommy, who had been fighting for 16 years and was over the hill, lost a 15-round decision. "But I didn't escape injury completely," Loughran said. "The big toe of my right foot was fractured when Primo stepped on it with his size 15's. Before the match, my manager, Joe Smith, and I had discussed strategy. I told him I was concerned about Carnera's size and what he might do to me in the clinches if he decided to put his weight on me. Joe said he had the solution to keep the big guy away from me. He then went to a drugstore and got the dammest-smelling hair grease he could find. It was so sweet-smelling it made you gag. So after Carnera and I got our instructions from the referee and went back to our corners to wait for the bell, Joe dabbed a glob of that sickening hair grease on my head. When Carnera clinched, I'd tuck my head up under his nose and he'd nearly faint. I still got pictures of him, sniffing the air in disgust, and trying to shove me off him."

Loughran was a fighting champion. He was always willing to give a worthy contender a crack at his light-heavyweight crown. He turned back such challengers as Jimmy Slattery, Leo Lomski, Peter Latzo, Mickey Walker, and Jimmy Braddock. Lomski, Jimmy Darcy, King Levinsky and Dave Maier all had him on the floor—and he bounced back each time to win.

Tommy's biggest pay day was the $60,000 he collected for fighting Sharkey. He was still rolling in sugar after he retired from the prize ring in 1937. He became a sugar broker in New York.

MAXIE ROSENBLOOM
(1904–1956)

Hollywood's Maxie Rosenbloom played the role of the dumb pug so often and so well that, frankly, you have to be alarmed. Did Rosey's Runyonesque portrayals of bouncers, trainers and punch-drunk stooges determine his final image in the public memory? This would be unfortunate since Rosey was not only an independent thinker with a rapier wit but an ex-fighter who was one of the most amazing light-heavies of all time.

Maxie explained his long success in the ring with a typical Rosenbloomer: "I didn't drink, I didn't smoke and I didn't leave dames alone." That figured in an era of fighting playboys when Harry Greb and Jimmy Slattery, among others, did most of their "training" in actual ring combat.

Maxie recalled leaving Texas Guinan's shortly before sunrise to do a little road work for the bout with Mickey Walker. "I kept my sweater and road shoes in Tex's office (anybody who says Rosenbloom never trained is a liar), and I hit the road about four-thirty in the morning," he said. "Well, I'm struttin' through Central Park in Manhattan when whom do I meet but that crazy Irishman Walker. He nods, and I nod. I could see the bum was hard as a rock and in real good shape. So Walker did all the training, and I won the fight."

In his salad days, Maxie was one of the busiest fighters in the business. For one period of four and a half years he averaged a fight every two weeks—a record rivaled only by Freddie Miller, who was in action once every 13½ days for three years and four months.

In September, 1933, Maxie worked the milk route through Texas. On the 12th he opened in Fort Worth, where he decisioned Joe Rice in 10 rounds. On the 19th in San Antonio he won another 10-rounder from Chuck Burns. On the 22nd he defeated Young Stribling in Houston, and on the 28th he walloped Rosey Rosales, another heavyweight, in 10 rounds in El Paso. Quite a month for a world's champion!

In 16 years, Maxie logged more than 300 bouts and was kayoed only twice. He put his title on the line eight times and fought 108 bouts during his four-year reign as king of the light-heavyweights. An open glove fighter, he literally slapped his opponents silly (hence the moniker "Slapsie Maxie," affectionately donated by the late Damon Runyon). And his victims included the likes of Jimmy Slattery, Dave Shade, John Henry Lewis, Jimmy Braddock, Al Gainer, Pete Latzo and Walker. As late as 1938 he was outfoxing Lou Nova and other first-rate competitors.

Rosenbloom decisioned Slattery for the 175-pound title in Jimmy's home town, Buffalo, June 25, 1930. He lost it to Bob Olin on an off-night in the Garden on November 16, 1934. Of all his many opponents, Maxie rates Jimmy the smartest of the lot and discounts the Rosenbloom anecdote that he and Slattery once bet on each other. "I just wanted to keep his name alive," he explained.

Maxie was mighty proud of his championship. He once fell for the daughter of a Canadian tycoon. When she turned him down on the excuse that her old man wanted her to marry a title, Maxie wanted to know what was wrong with the "light-heavyweight title."

As the champ, he reigned with a careless

Maxie Rosenbloom was one of the most amazing light-heavyweights of all time in an era of fighting playboys. (NEA)

benevolence that endeared him to columnists and courtiers. A veritable Potenate of the Present, he was prodigal to a fault, favoring in particular the gaming tables and his beloved "broads." Maxie estimated that he gambled away over a quarter of a million dollars and didn't care less. ("Well, I could have won a million if they'd given me credit.")

The champ bought a Rolls-Royce from Harry Richman and hired a massive Negro chauffeur, a heavyweight, to drive him around. The deal was somewhat complicated by Maxie's gambling habits. When the driver figured it was about time he got paid, Maxie said he was flat broke. Then he suggested a wonderfully zany settlement: "Why don't you get in the back seat, and I'll drive you around?" The driver, who later became one of Rosey's overpaid sparring partners, was agreeable so the champ drove him all over town until the debt was paid.

Maxie was born in the shadow of the Williamsburg Bridge, a tough neighborhood. His schooling lasted through the third grade, where he remained an extra year ("My old man was in the fourth, and I didn't want to pass him"). Following a stretch at a reform school, Maxie returned to the streets where he could always find the trouble he was looking for. Another kid, a slick little hoofer named Georgie Raft, "discovered" Maxie in a brawl in which the future champ got all the worst of it. According to one version of the story, Raft was so impressed that he advised Rosenbloom to don the gloves for eats.

Young Maxie played the tank towns and perfected his skill as a master-slapper. In three years he was ready for Jack Delaney, Tiger Flowers and any heavyweights he could get.

Some wiseacres had Maxie tagged as a dumb cluck who couldn't add up the fingers on one hand. As his manager, Frank Bachman, put it, "Sure, he's crazy, but crazy like a fox. So they laugh and call him stupid—so what? Rosey has the last laugh because he's the guy who gets paid off."

In 1937 Maxie played his first bit part in *Nothing Sacred*. He also opened Slapsie Maxie's joint and married beautiful Muriel Faider, a child psychologist.

Following his divorce in 1945, Maxie toured the globe with Max Baer in a night club routine that earned up to $5,000 a week.

The frolicsome pair suited each other like dice—in fact, they had the time of their lives just going broke. Maxie finished the first week in Las Vegas owing the club $20,000. When the owner finally calmed down, Rosenbloom transfixed him with his best Chinese stare.

"Mister," he explained. "I tried saving a long time ago. I made three big ones, and one time my roll was $150,000. I dropped $130,000 in the crash, $10,000 on the broads and the rest on a trip around the world. I decided never to save again, and I've been happy ever since."

Maxie made good his vow. He died broke in 1956—but he went out with a smile on his face.

JIMMY SLATTERY
(1904–1960)

There was nothing half-way about Jimmy Slattery. He could either box you dizzy or knock you dead. Up to the time when the Buffalo Irishman started to take on John Barleycorn at catch weights, he represented an almost perfect blend of finesse and ferocity.

At nineteen, he was stiffening bruisers like Joe Egan, outstabbing cuties like Young Stribling. He was feathery on his feet, had swift hand-action and a sense of timing so true he seldom missed a punch. If he had been as dedicated to the gloves as to gaiety he would have achieved all-time greatness.

As it was, he had to settle for the light-heavyweight championship of the world. On August 30, 1927, he out-pointed Maxie Rosenbloom to gain the title, lost it to Tommy Loughran three-and-a-half months later.

It could very well be that Slattery was the last of a distinctive Irish fighting breed that worked both sides of the street, power and polish.

James J. Corbett was once heard to deplore simultaneously the failure of Slattery to capitalize on his potentials and the growing neglect of the feint as a boxing stratagem.

"That's what makes Slattery all the more disappointing," the old heavyweight champion said. "Jimmy could feint you into a trap with either his body or his head. And he could do it as if by instinct. In fact, all of his moves seemed dictated by nature as distinguished from a practiced routine."

Slattery had two memorable fights in New

York, losing both. In 1925, a 1–5 favorite, he was stopped by Dave Shade, a relatively light hitter. It was subsequently disclosed he had done little or no training. Three years later he was outpointed by Tommy Loughran in a 15-rounder with his title on the line. But from the standpoint of sheer ring artistry it was a valid classic. The attitude of the crowd that night was what impressed the writers at ringside most. Generally, fight fans demand blood. Boxing, no matter how brilliant, leaves them cold. But that night there were cheers after each round. It was indeed one of boxing's finest hours. Though only twenty-three years old at the time, Slattery was already over the hill. Time and dissipation had caught up with him, withering his once dazzling skills, and yet for 10 rounds he was magnificent. It wasn't until he had spent his stamina that Loughran was able to take command.

Slattery died in his sleep at fifty-six, alone and probably in want. Most of the obituaries mentioned that promoter Tex Rickard once had tapped him as the one most likely to dethrone Jack Dempsey.

The moral of Jimmy Slattery's debacle is this:

The primrose path is no place for road work.

BOB OLIN
(1908–1956)

Bob Olin was the last Jewish prize fighter to win the light-heavyweight championship of the world. Coincidentally, he won it from Maxie Rosenbloom, who was also Jewish. That was at Madison Square Garden, on November 16, 1934, when Jewish fighters ruled the roost in most weight divisions.

Olin held the title for less than a year. On October 31, in 1935, John Henry Lewis took it away from him in St. Louis (Decision, 15 rounds). Olin tried to win it back a year and a half later in the same city, but this time Lewis finished him off (K.O.) in 8 rounds.

Born on Independence Day, 1908, in New York, Bob Olin began his ring career in 1929 in a flourish. He won 18 of his first 19 pro bouts, 13 by knockouts. At his best, however, he was an inconsistent fighter. His record is spotted with 26 defeats.

Olin lost to Lou Brouillard twice in 1934, and Abe Feldman held him to a draw, before he beat an aging Rosenbloom to win the world championship. While he was champion, he lost two non-title bouts to Dutch Weimer and John Henry Lewis. His second loss to Lewis was the only time he put his title on the line.

Olin was a fair boxer, fast of foot, and had a good right hand. As a matter of fact, he won more bouts by K.O. (24) than by decision (21).

The former light-heavyweight champion operated a successful restaurant in Manhattan after hanging up the gloves in 1939.

A heart attack killed him in 1956.

JOHN HENRY LEWIS
(1914–1974)

John Henry Lewis will go down in prize ring history as the poor guy who was bounced crazily off the ring ropes by Joe Louis, one of his best friends. It was a one-round knockout that made strong men turn their heads away, aghast.

What people forget is that JHL was light-heavyweight champion for four years (1935–39) and lost only 8 times in 104 prizefights. He knocked out 54 opponents. That K.O. by Louis was the only time he was ever knocked out.

John Henry, whose great-great-uncle was Tom Molineaux, first of America's super heavies, was the first black man to fight Joe Louis professionally. Except for this single mistake, he was a very intelligent man, talked like a college professor, and could do fractions.

Born in Los Angeles, May 1, 1914, but raised in Phoenix, John Henry turned pro when he was only fourteen. He won the world title from Bob Olin on a 15-round decision in 1935 and defended it successfully against Jock McAvoy, Len Harvey, Emilio Martinez, Al Gainer, and Olin. The future looked bright, but Louis quickly dimmed all that in less than three minutes. John Henry never fought again. Good ol' Joe, his friend, convinced JHL that there had to be an easier way to make a living.

MELIO BETTINA
(1916–   )

Melio Bettina was a 5 ft., 10 in., 180-lb. southpaw out of Bridgeport, Connecticut, who could be as dangerous as diphtheria when the spirit moved him, which was often.

In 15 years of prize fighting, he won 82 of 99 bouts, 36 by knockouts. Only Frank Zamoris, Gus Lesnevich and Johnny Flynn ever K.O.'d him. He gave Billy Conn two of his hardest fights in losing 15-round decisions.

Bettina was a bull in the ring. He'd stalk his opponent, pin him against the ropes, then flail away with both hands like the rat-tat-tat of a tommygun.

He turned professional in 1934, won 14 of his first 17 bouts. Between September 28, 1936, and May 15, 1939, he ran up another string of 25 out of 27 bouts, 15 of them K.O.'s.

When John Henry Lewis retired in 1939 and left the light-heavyweight championship vacant, Bettina knocked out Tiger Jack Fox in nine rounds, on February 3, and quickly claimed the world crown. Six months later, in his first defense, he lost the title to Billy Conn. Ten weeks afterward he tried to win it back and again Conn won in 15 rounds.

Melio Bettina's last shot at the light-heavyweight championship was in Cleveland, on January 13, 1941. Anton Christoforidis won on points in 15.

Bettina continued to fight through 1948. He won seven of his last eight bouts, but by then he was thirty-two and decided to retire after Johnny Flynn knocked him out in six rounds.

Bettina was managed by Jimmy Grippo, the professional hypnotist and sleight-of-hand expert. He was chiefly celebrated around Stillman's Gym, however, as the only man who ever victimized the proprietor. One day, in the course of a handshake, he lifted Stillman's wristwatch. He apologized and then relieved him of his wallet.

"What's so great about that?" Lou Stillman said afterward. "He once picked Herbert Hoover's pocket in the White House."

It seemed only logical that Bettina would have a manager who doubled as a hypnotist.

Both were good at putting people to sleep.

BILLY CONN
(1917-   )

Billy Conn was the last of the lustrous Irish fighters.

Ringworms had a saying about him: "He never went into the ring he wasn't the boss."

Conn came out of the slum sector of East Liberty, Pennsylvania, and in just five years fought his way from a 10-round victory over Fritzie Zivic at 147 pounds to his first brush with Joe Louis. Along the way he beat such competent middleweights as Babe Risko, Vince Dundee, Teddy Yarosz, Young Corbett, Solly Krieger, and Fred Apostoli, and won the light-heavyweight championship of the world from Melio Bettina.

Joe Louis confessed that Billy the Kid gave him his toughest fight. "I almost lost that first bout with him," Joe said. There's no doubt that the Brown Bomber's career might have ended then and there if Conn hadn't unwisely tried to slug with the champion in the fatal 13th round, after having had the fight won.

Joe Louis claimed that handsome Billy Conn, the last of the lustrous Irish fighters, gave him his hardest fight. (NEA)

"I had him on the hook and lost him," Conn said. "He weighed 199½ to my 174 and I guess I looked like he could break me in half. In the fifth round I thought he would. He belted me with a right-hand punch in the belly and I opened my mouth, not for air but because I was hurt. I don't think Louis knew what he'd done to me. He didn't press and I had the next couple of rounds to pull myself together. Then I got rolling. I was spearing him coming in and stepping in with one-twos. Right up into the 12th I was running the show. I thought I had him ready to pop over."

Gentleman Jim Corbett once pointed out that there comes a day in the life of every prize fighter when he is better than he ever had been or ever will be again. "I had my night against John L. Sullivan," Corbett said.

Billy Conn had his biggest hour on June 18, 1941. Never again would he reach such a peak and there would be another night, five years and one World War later, that would leave him with a bitter memory. But first, there was the Army, which used him not as a soldier but as an entertainer, boxing for the troops in the European theater.

Promoter Mike Jacobs had wanted Conn to join the Navy. "But I want to join the Army," Billy told him.

"Join the Navy," Mike insisted.

"But why should I join the Navy?" Billy said.

"Because Louis joined the Army," Mike said. "He done like I told him he should." Jacobs was a schemer. "See?" he said. "Louis in the Army, you in the Navy. It looks very good. When the war is over, maybe before, we have another fight. You get even with Louis. The champion of the Army and the champion of the Navy."

Billy the Kid was unimpressed.

"What difference does it make?" he said. "Who wants to be in the Navy? Suppose I should get seasick?"

"Join the Navy," Mike said. Mike was Billy's mealticket.

"All right," he said, finally. "Where do I go to sign up?"

Mike told him and he started for the door. Two hours later, Billy was back in Jacobs's office. "I joined the Army," he announced. Mike leaped from his chair. "What!" he shouted. "The Army! I said the Navy! Louis is in the *Army!*"

"So am I now," Billy said. Mike sat down. He closed his eyes, suppressing a strong desire to strangle Conn. Then: "Go ahead," he said, "tell me what happened."

Billy said he had carried out Mike's instructions. He went down to the Navy, there were a lot of guys milling around and he didn't know which way to go. There was an old guy there and he was hollering at everybody. He was wearing a sailor suit—well, not exactly a sailor suit, Billy said. "He's got on a uniform," Billy explained. "He's got a cap on and a lot of gold stripes on his sleeves. I go up to him and ask him which way do you go to join the Navy and he starts yelling at me."

"Get over there!" he roared at Billy. "Get in that line over there!"

Billy didn't like this big bloke roaring at him like a lion. He wanted to bust him in the mouth but he didn't because he was an old geezer. Instead, he asked, "Are you in the Navy?" The old salt was fit to be tied. Was *he* in the Navy? "All right," Billy said to him,

"on account of you're in the Navy, I am going to join the Army because I don't like bums like you and if you are my age, I will put the slug on you."

"So," Billy told Jacobs, "that's how I come to join the Army."

Uncle Mike put his face in his hands and bawled.

When Jacobs finally did get Louis and Conn back in the ring together again (Yankee Stadium, June 19, 1946), it turned out to be a dismal performance. At a pre-fight press conference, Conn said, "Louis says he hopes to knock me out this time around. Well, that's a lot of wishful thinking. I'm in great shape. If Joe doesn't watch out, he might get knocked out himself."

Once the fight started, however, Billy showed so little inclination to punch that Louis was perplexed. At the end of the first round, Bugs Baer, the Hearst humorist seated at ringside, looked up at Joe and said: "Poor old Joe looks like a guy who had a date and the other guy didn't show up."

The fight ended after 2 minutes and 19 seconds of the eighth round. After the fight, there was a cut across Conn's nose, and his eye was bruised. But he was laughing and cynical with a wit that denounced himself. He had not changed. Not even having Louis catch his jabs like puffballs thrown by a tyke could shut off his humor.

"He fixed me, didn't he?" Billy said.

"When did he hurt you?" he was asked.

"When he hit me," he replied, sneering.

"What are you going to do now?" a reporter said.

"He racked up my cue for me," Conn said.

"Are you going to fight again?"

"As lousy as I was," Conn said, "and you're asking that. I should re-enlist in the Army I was so lousy out there tonight."

The following morning, Billy said he had made up his mind to retire. "If I can't beat Louis I have to quit," he said. He did.

Conn was twenty-nine years old when he hung up his gloves. He confessed later, however, that perhaps he retired from the ring too soon.

"I wish I could have fought Louis one more time," he said. "I don't want my kids growing up thinking their old man was yellow."

Though that fight was his most successful promotion, Uncle Mike Jacobs had hoped to top Tex Rickard's high marks for the two Dempsey-Tunney tussles. His goal had been on a $3,000,000 gate. He might have made it, too, but he scared off a lot of customers by scaling ringside seats at $100 per ticket. He had to settle for a $1,925,564 gate, the record for New York City, and a crowd of 45,266.

Born October 8, 1917, on Shakespeare Street in East Liberty, Billy the Kid was only thirteen years old when he began hanging around Johnny Ray's gymnasium and pool hall. Parochial school seldom slowed him down. He got as far as the eighth grade. He was in trouble with his teachers most of the time. One day the nun said to him: "Why do you keep coming back here? You don't learn anything. Why don't you enroll in a trade school?"

So Billy signed up at a trade school. They had him making wooden spokes for automobile wheels. He said to himself: "Hey, what am I doing? They don't have wooden spokes on automobile wheels no more." That's when his formal education stopped.

Billy was sixteen, stood 5 ft., 11 in. and weighed 130, when Johnny Ray took him to Fairmont, West Virginia, to fight a boy named Dick Woodward. Billy received $2.50 "and a helluva beating" for going four rounds.

The bouts that earned Billy his first big headlines were two he had in New York a month apart with Fred Apostoli in 1939. Apostoli was the middleweight champion, but his title was not at stake because Conn was over the weight. Both were terrific fights, for here were two real brawlers who derived a savage joy from throwing and absorbing punches. Conn won both decisions in 10 and 15 rounds.

Thereafter, Conn moved up swiftly. He quickly grew into a light-heavyweight and before the end of the year won the world championship from Bettina. He successfully defended his crown in a return bout with Bettina and twice against Gus Lesnevich, and then relinquished the title to campaign among the heavyweights, although he still weighed only 175. His goal was clear: a championship match with Joe Louis. On his way to that June 18, 1941 night he hammered out victories over Bob Pastor, Al McCoy, Lee Savold, Ira Hughes, Dan Hassett, Gunnar Barlund and Buddy Knox.

A week before the Louis bout at the Polo Grounds, Billy's manager, Johnny Ray, predicted that Conn would win.

"He's convinced me by the way he's trained," Johnny explained. "Wait till you see him. He never went into a ring he wasn't the boss. He will be the master of Louis. Joe won't have to look for him when the fight starts. Billy will take charge."

Most of Joe's opponents had been visibly frightened of him, but not Conn. Billy was brimming with self-confidence. He had a very positive attitude.

The atmosphere surrounding the double-decked concrete and steel stands of the Polo Grounds was reminiscent of older and better times in boxing that night, with 54,487 wildly excited men and women sitting in rows extending back as far as the eye could reach. The gross gate was $450,000.

This great crowd saw Conn fight a battle that was true to his style, of necessity, but better than usual. And it saw Louis fight as a champion should, a champion who refused to become discouraged though he was buffeted about outlandishly at times. Billy almost exclusively boxed Louis through the first seven rounds. Having gone so far—most people had expected Joe to knock out Conn, as he had done to 15 previous challengers—Billy became overconfident in the eighth and was blasting his way past Louis in grand style. He made a target of the champion's jaw for right-hand smashes. The blows lacked steam, but the success of his sudden attack lifted his spirits.

As the fighters came out in the ninth round, Billy taunted Joe: "You got a tough fight tonight." Louis nodded. "That's right," he said, and continued shuffling into a rival who weighed 25½ pounds less than he did. Billy went right on banging him around the ring scandalously.

Repeatedly Conn drilled home with his right to the jaw in the ninth. He ripped full-arm rights to the body. Left jabs brought blood from Louis' nose. A left hook to the body hurt Joe before the bell. All the time Louis was helpless to counter the barrage.

Infuriated in the tenth, Louis pressed Billy. They traded blows, giving as good as they received. Through the eleventh Conn fought gallantly as he pounded away at Louis from all angles, beating Joe about the face and jaw with rights at long range and about the heart and body at close range. Louis winced at times, but he could do nothing about the attack.

In the twelfth, Conn, after an exchange in which one of Louis' lefts cut him under the left eye, suddenly rocked Louis on his heels with a full-arm left hook to the jaw. Staggering, Louis dived into a clinch to keep from falling while Conn fought furiously in a bid for a knockout.

Maybe this shot that went true and staggered Louis made Billy too sure of himself. At any rate, he was the pursuer instead of the pursued as the thirteenth round started and he made the mistake of getting too close to Louis too often.

Battered by Louis' powerful lefts and rights about the head, Billy emerged from close quarters flailing furiously for Louis' jaw with lefts and rights in an outburst that brought the crowd out of their seats. Suddenly Joe's right shot out on an opening with a blow that landed flush on Billy's jaw. Billy's knees buckled. He swayed backward. He was plainly hurt, and Louis knew it. And Louis thundered in with that patented savagery that was characteristic of him when he saw he had an opponent dazed. About the head and face he fired numerous rights and lefts while Billy sought to cover and backpedal. Some of the blows missed, but many of them landed, carrying force even against Billy's defense of raised gloves. Louis then shifted his attack to the body. He hurt Billy and sapped the speed from his legs. Billy was slipping about precariously when Louis drove over the fatal right-hand blow to the jaw that toppled him in defeat within two seconds of the end of the round and shattered Billy's dream of a heavyweight championship.

James P. Dawson covered the fight for *The New York Times* and he said later that Louis never came closer to losing than he did before knocking Conn out. "Billy came within the proverbial eyelash of creating one of the biggest upsets of all time," Dawson declared. "He displayed a brand of battle few people dared expect, least of all Louis. Through those first 12 rounds, Billy held Joe even in action and on rounds. Then the fight ended as it had been predicted it would end. The blow landed high, but it was a powerful one and Billy was counted out by Referee Eddie Joseph in 2 minutes and 58 seconds of the 13th round. That's the way of the ring. One second you are on top, the next you are down in despair. Billy learned this the hard way. He had come within two rounds of what was almost certain victory. It must go down as one of the greatest heavyweight battles of all time."

Thus ended the Era of Gaelic Boxing Glory.

"It will never return," Billy Conn said after his retirement in 1948. "The Irish are too rich today to risk their necks in the ring. A man has to be hungry to fight."

Recently, Conn and Louis got together again in Billy's home town of Pittsburgh at a benefit for a boys' club. The banquet room was packed with people who had paid $20 a ticket to see the film of the Louis-Conn fight. Suddenly, on the screen, it was June 18, 1941, again. When the room went dark, except for the beam of the movie projector, Louis turned his back on the screen and shambled off toward the bar. What was happening up there did not interest him. He had seen it many times before. But Conn remained in his seat, watching the film, absorbed.

Behind the closed double-doors of the bar, Louis sipped brandy. Every once in a while he stuck his head between the doors, saw Conn in the last row of folding chairs, and called, "Hey, Billy, have we got to the 13th round yet?"

"It's only the seventh," Billy told him, as he watched himself on the screen attacking with increased confidence, scoring with left hooks.

Louis went back to the bar.

In the back of the hall, at the bell for the 11th round, someone called out, "Hey, Billy, you're still ahead." Conn built up his lead in the 11th and 12th rounds; Louis was shaky. Just then Louis walked out of the bar, and Conn told him, "I'm fixin' your ass."

The 13th round began, and Louis found a seat on the aisle. No longer bored, he stared hard at the screen. Suddenly Conn got up and started for a room where a buffet was set up.

"Hey, Billy," someone wanted to know, "where yuh goin'?"

"To get some rigatoni," Conn said.

"But the fight ain't over yet."

"I already know the ending," Billy said.

ANTON CHRISTOFORIDIS
(1918–   )

Anton Christoforidis drove fight announcers nuts. By the time they finished pronouncing that last handle the program was usually over.

C-h-r-i-s-t-o-f-o-r-i-d-i-s was an import from Greece who made his American debut in 1939 with a 12-round decision over Solly Krieger, the former middleweight champion. Five weeks before that, he said goodbye to Europe by beating another ex-middleweight king, Lou Brouillard, in Paris.

With a small bag of blueprints, Chris charted a speedy course straight to the light-heavyweight championship of the world. That route carried him over Willie Pavlovich, Frank Zamoris, George Burnette, Jimmy Burns, Joey Sutka, Tony Bruno, Jimmy Reeves and Jimmy Bivins. All told, the "Golden Greek" fought only nine times in the United States before hooking up with Melio Bettina, on January 13, 1941, to win the N.B.A. light-heavyweight championship of the world. Billy Conn had vacated the title to campaign among the heavyweights.

Two fast knockouts of Italo Colonello and Johnny Romero in April of '41 led to Christoforidis putting his crown on the line against tough Gus Lesnevich a month later in New York. Lesnevich won on points in 15. Chris never fought in another championship bout.

Christoforidis was born at Messina, Greece, on May 26, 1918, and later became an American citizen. In 1942, after being held to a draw by Nate Bolden in Chicago, he joined the Army. Six months later he was discharged, returned to the prize ring and lost decisions to Jimmy Bivins and Lloyd Marshall—and then joined the *Navy!*

A fighting fool, Anton Christoforidis.

First the Army, then the Navy—the Golden Greek kept in the thick of things.

GUS LESNEVICH
(1915–1964)

You had to notice "The Russian Lion" because his presence in the prize ring demanded it. He was trim, muscular, with big-chin determination. At 5 ft., 9 in. and 174 pounds, the 19th light-heavyweight champion of the world had a look of command; there it was, like a stamp upon him: The Boss.

Grizzly Gus bossed the 175-pound class for seven years.

Born on February 22, 1915, at Cliffside, New Jersey, of Russian-American parentage, Lesnevich won the Golden Gloves sub-novice championship in 1933, turned professional the next year and won 20 of his first 22 bouts. On November 17, 1936, Lesnevich's path to the championship was suddenly jolted by world middleweight champion, Freddie Steele, in Los Angeles. It marked the first time Gus had ever been knocked out.

The first round was a nightmare for him. After several preliminary jabs, Gus moved inside. Steele, who could punch with either hand like a triphammer, peeled back half a step and unloaded a short, teeth-jarring left hook followed by an exploding right to the chin. For the rest of the three minutes Gus spent more time on his back than on his feet. Somehow, his handlers got him back to his corner. It was more of the same in the second round. Gus moved around the ring as if mesmerized, absorbing a savage fusillade of left hooks and straight rights. It was as if he had gotten his face caught in a paddle wheel. He went down a total of 11 times in less than six minutes of fighting. The referee finally stopped it.

"Many of my fans think that second-round

Gus Lesnevich was boss of the light-heavyweight division for seven years. (UPI)

kayo over Gus was my greatest fight," Steele told me recently. "I hit him with everything but the ringpost. But you have to give him credit. A less courageous fighter might have called it quits then and there. Not Lesnevich. He stuck with it—and three-and-a-half years later he was light-heavyweight champion of the world."

On his way to the crown, Lesnevich fought defending champion Billy Conn twice, in 1939 and '40, and lost them both on points. When Billy the Kid moved on to the heavyweights, Gus won the vacated title with his win over Christoforidis.

"Gus was a good champion," Steele said. "He improved with age. At his peak, he was a strong, sturdy fighter with two good hands. He was always in shape. He had a tremendous pride in wearing the crown and defended it with his life."

Lesnevich twice successfully defended his title against Tami Mauriello, did his war stint in the U.S. Coast Guard, then, at thirty-one, traveled to London and defended the championship against Freddie Mills. Wrote Gilbert Odd, the British boxing writer:

"Lesnevich found Mills easy to hit, having him on the canvas several times in the first round. But Freddie made a good recovery, split open Gus's left eye and looked like winning on the referee's intervention when the champion tossed over a great right-hand punch that was a winner all the way, the bout being stopped in the 10th round."

Four months later, Lesnevich was back in London, but failed to give weight and reach to Bruce Woodcock, the British heavyweight champion, and suffered the fourth knockout of his career. Unperturbed, Gus returned to the U.S. and knocked out Billy Fox, Bettina, Mauriello, and Fox again in 1 minute, 58 seconds.

Gus gave Mills another shot at his title in London, on July 26, 1948, and this time the Britisher won on a close points decision, then Gus fought Joey Maxim for the American title, but again lost on points. He finally retired from the ring when Ezzard Charles kayoed him in seven rounds in a heavyweight championship bout at New York in 1949.

Lesnevich was only thirty-four when he quit, but he felt like an old man; too much of his youth and his zest for fighting had been left in the resin of too many rings. He was only six days past his forty-ninth birthday when he died at Cliffside Park, New Jersey.

FREDDIE MILLS
(1919–1965)

Freddie Mills, an Englishman, never fought in the United States, yet the light-heavyweight champion of the world was closer to the American style of ringmanship than many of his New World contemporaries.

An aggressive, walk-in slugger, the former R.A.F. sergeant polished up his primitive style in the boxing booths of Merrie Olde England, in 1935. Nobody knew the Mills story better than Gilbert Odd, who covered the British prize ring scene for more than a half-century.

"Freddie's boyhood hero was Jack Dempsey," recalled author Odd. "He tried to pattern his footwork and shadowboxing after Jack while pushing a milk float through the streets of Bournemouth. On fight nights in the town, he'd climb on to the roof of the local

In 15 years of professional fighting, light-heavyweight champion Freddie Mills gave fellow Britishers plenty to cheer about. (UPI)

boxing hall and watch the fighting through the skylight. He took his holidays by attaching himself to a West Country traveling boxing booth and learned the game the hard way. Born at Parkstone in Dorset, he was wrapped up heart and soul in fist-fighting and before his seventeenth birthday had won a novices' competition. He turned pro in 1936 and couldn't get enough of it. He averaged a fight a month in his first four years. There wasn't a lot of science about his style, but there was plenty of gusto and most of his opponents caved in under such fierce and steady assault. That's how he picked up the nickname, 'Ferocious Fred.' When he felt in the mood, however, he could use a perfect straight left."

Sergeant Mills joined the R.A.F. in 1939, but was permitted to fight professionally and took on Jack London, from West Hartlepool, for the British version of the light-heavyweight championship. He was outweighed, yet hustled London around and lost only on points. It marked the first time he had ever gone 15 rounds.

Mills then spent a year in India. When he returned he looked up promoter Jack Solomons. "Can you get me a fight?" he asked. "Can I get you a fight!" cried Solomons. "You are a blessing in disguise!" Solomons had planned to put Bruce Woodcock in with Gus Lesnevich, but Bruce couldn't make it, so Mills was given the chance at Lesnevich's title. Still rusty from the long layoff, Mills was floored by some powerful rights to the jaw in the first round and hit the deck several times.

"It seemed he wouldn't last long," Gilbert Odd said, "but he staged a remarkable recovery and at the end had Lesnevich bleeding badly from a cut over his left eye. Gus had to knock him out in the 10th to win the fight."

One of those at ringside was the late Eddie Borden. Eddie later became Editor of *Boxing & Wrestling* magazine, an American monthly.

"Talk about bloodbaths," Eddie told me. "Mills and Lesnevich slugged it out for 10 solid rounds; nearly 30 minutes of steady pounding. Neither man would take a backward step. It was one of the greatest slugfests in English history."

Two years later, Mills was rematched in London with Lesnevich. This time he was the victor. Then, on June 2, 1949, he made a bid for the British Empire heavyweight championship and went 14 thunderous rounds with the bigger Woodcock, but discovered he could not give away so much poundage. He dropped more from exhaustion than a punch and was counted out.

Freddie fought for the final time on January 24, 1950. Joey Maxim knocked him out in the London ring to return the light-heavyweight championship to the United States. After the bout, Mills had to have five slivers of bone removed from his jaw. He also lost several teeth. It was the worst defeat of his career. He quit the ring to become a radio-TV personality and a boxing promoter.

Mills fought professionally 96 times in 15 years and gave the British plenty to cheer for. He loved those home crowds and resisted every offer to lure him from England. He rejected come-ons of $25,000 and $30,000 to fight Harold Johnson in Philadelphia and an $80,000 guarantee to fight Lesnevich in Cincinnati.

Freddie Mills—popular, happy-go-lucky, and generous to a fault—went out the same way as Battling Siki. On July 25, 1965, his life was snuffed out by bullets under mysterious circumstances. It happened near the night club he owned at Charing Cross Road in London. The case was never solved.

JOEY MAXIM
(1922–   )

Jack Kearns became almost legendary between the two world wars because of his ability to make money with prizefighters. After the second war, to show that he still had the magic touch, he repeated an old trick by steering still another fighter to a championship. The fighter, Joey Maxim, who became world's light-heavyweight champion under Kearns, will not shine brightly in history books.

"He is just a footnote sort of fighter—cute but pedestrian, the critics agree, and practically punchless," wrote John Lardner. The late Sports Editor of *Newsweek* remembered that Kearns one day tried to convince him that Maxim was better than Dempsey. "He don't hit quite so hard as Dempsey," Kearns said with something like boredom in his voice, "but otherwise he's better."

Since this was in the late 1940s, shortly before Maxim's bout with Olle Tandberg, the Swedish heavyweight champion, it was sus-

LIGHT HEAVYWEIGHTS

pected that Kearns was misusing Dempsey's name for advertising purposes. Doc did not really believe it, and neither did his listeners, who shifted their feet uncomfortably and withheld comment, because there was nothing polite to be said.

The best that can be said for Joey Maxim is that he was a Fred Astaire in boxing shorts. The fact that he was completely unmarked after 15 years of prize fighting was something in the way of proof that he knew how to take care of himself. He was a superb *defensive* fighter and boxed himself out of trouble every time he got into it.

Guiseppe Antonio Berardinelli (Maxim's real name) was a natural light-heavyweight.

In one of the oddest fight endings in history, Joey Maxim and the heat stopped Sugar Ray Robinson in light-heavyweight title bout in New York, in June, 1952. (UPI)

To show the world he still had the magic touch, manager Jack Kearns steered Maxim to the light-heavy championship in 1949. He is pictured here with Joey and Indiana boxing executive Arch Hindman. (Photo courtesy Arch Hindman)

Making 175 pounds was no problem for him. He was the first man to beat Floyd Patterson.

Joey stood 6 ft., 1 in. and weighed 175. He was born in Cleveland in 1922 and started prize fighting in 1941. Eight years later he beat Gus Lesnevich for the title; his K.O. of Freddie Mills in 1950 in London made it official. Ezzard Charles stopped his bid for the heavyweight championship in 1951, but Maxim extended the defending champion 15 rounds.

"Charles was the toughest man I ever fought," Maxim admitted. "Jersey Joe Walcott didn't give me much trouble, even though the record book says he won two out of three decisions from me. The referee gave me more trouble. Every time I turned Walcott around, he whacked me in the ass. Forty whacks, and the referee don't do a thing!"

Maxim was a party to one of the oddest fight-endings in ring history. This was on June 25, 1952, and Sugar Ray Robinson was punching the sawdust out of him for 12 rounds. Then suddenly Robinson collapsed from the 104-degree heat under the Yankee Stadium floodlights and couldn't come out for the 14th round. Joey was declared the winner and still light-heavyweight champion of the world on the most technical "knockout" anyone could remember. He was paid $100,224, plus $20,000 of the theater-TV rights.

The next day when Doc Kearns lifted the check with the six big numbers on it, he refused to allocate any of the credit to mother nature, lady luck—or even Maxim. "Next time *I'll* knock out Robinson even quicker," he told the press. "Now I'd like to take on that Walcott, or Marciano. I'll fight anybody in the world." Fight managers usually say "we" when boasting, but Kearns did not even allow his fighter a piece of the pronoun.

Joey trailed all the way until he knocked out Freddie Mills in the 10th. "Just like Dempsey," said Kearns. "All of today's fighters are bums. But I got the best bum of the lot."

Joey Maxim had surprisingly small, almost feminine hands. But there was nothing dainty about them once the work bell rang.

ARCHIE MOORE
(1913–   )

Archibald Lee Moore was the magnificent Mongoose of the prize ring for more than 22 years.

He was also one of the cleverest boxer-punchers in history. The old shoe is a modern version of a musty story: He will be remembered as the man whom all the heavyweight champions ducked until it was too late for him.

Archie Moore was a contender for a world championship for 16 years. The only title he won during that period was "Archie the Trouper." When he couldn't get important bouts in the U.S., he put the show on the road and traveled half-way around the world to earn eating, pleasure, and walking-around money. Flexing his muscles and looking debonair in a beret and mustache, he went to Australia, where he was his own advance man, his own press agent, doing a job build-

Ring-crafty Archie Moore (right) battered Jimmy Bivins in 1951, won fight by T.K.O. in 9th round. (UPI)

ing up Archie Moore, and he was magnificent. He fought in Melbourne and Sydney and Adelaide and Tasmania, winning seven straight fights and the middle, light-heavy, and heavyweight titles of Australia along the way. It was a great distance to go for the price of a meal, but boxing's most famous strolling player made his point. The bigger money would have to open the doors to him.

First, however, he agreed to fight for Joey Maxim's crown for practically nothing in St. Louis, on December 17, 1952. It was Archie's contention, and a lot of experts went along with him, that Gus Lesnevich and Freddie Mills dodged him when they held the light-heavyweight championship. Moore had remained a perpetual nuisance, and finally maneuvered Maxim into the ring when he made the price right. By the time Maxim finished taking his $100,000 guarantee and the expenses had been paid, Moore received only $800 for the honor of winning the world title. He was the second oldest man to rule the light-heavies. Only forty-one-year-old Bob Fitzsimmons was older. Moore, however, went on to establish another record: In 1962, he still held the championship, making him the oldest titleholder in history. While he hedged on his exact date of birth, he was somewhere between forty-five and forty-eight years old in 1962.

Boiled down to the essentials, the dossier on Archie the Gypsy runs like this: Archibald Lee Moore, born (?) at (?). Profession: prizefighter. Height, 5 ft., 11 in.; weight, 175. Fought more than 100 amateur bouts; turned professional in 1936; won 39 of first 45 pro bouts, 35 by K.O. Won light-heavyweight title from Joey Maxim, 1952, and vacated it, 1962; engaged in 12 world title bouts. Holds the all-time career record for kayoes with 136. Fought Rocky Marciano for heavyweight championship in New York, September 21, 1955, knocked out in 9; kayoed by Floyd Patterson, 5 rounds, Chicago, title bout, November 30, 1956; kayoed by Cassius Clay, Los Angeles, 4 rounds, November 15, 1962; retired in 1964 to start movie-TV career.

Archie Moore was a genuine professional. He had as formidable a slugger as Marciano down in the second round, and handed Maxim, the cutie, a sound boxing lesson. Archie was a difficult target to fight. He'd shuffle forward in a weaving crouch, looking for an opening. The crouch kept his breadbasket out of reach. Gloves and crossed forearms fenced off his chin. He took most blows on arms, shoulders and the top of his head. Not many opponents broke through that baffling defense.

Angelo Dundee, who was Clay's trainer, confessed he was a little afraid of the Moore fight.

"Moore was a master at cutting off the ring," Dundee said. "It means you keep the other man in the ring from moving around you, sliding away to one side or the other. Because Clay was so fast and nimble on his feet, part of his defense was his ability to slip away to one side or the other when an opponent thinks he has him pinned. Archie pinned him on the ropes once and hit him with his best right hand and the punch shook Cassius right down to his toenails, but he wasn't confused. He understood everything that was happening and finally he just overpowered Moore. Frank Sinatra and Dean Martin were sitting behind Moore's corner hollering for him, but that didn't bother Cassius either. He just went about his business. But Archie taught him something in that fight. When he trapped Cassius on the ropes he feinted Clay, and Clay slid away like he had against other fighters and slid right into Moore's right hand. He never made that mistake again."

A few years before fighting Clay, Moore, aged forty-four, give or take five years, still had his show on the road, an audacious defiance of the natural laws. On the eve of the 1958 Kentucky Derby, at Louisville, he busted up Willi Besmanoff, Jersey Jones's young German heavyweight. When Besmanoff was called upon for a pre-fight statement, he gave it as his considered opinion that doddering antiques like Mr. Moore ought to retire and leave the enervating business of fist-fighting to the younger generation. When Archie was asked to make a pre-battle observation, he told a group of sports writers who just happened to be in the Blue Grass country to cover the Derby: "It is very nice for all of you from far away to come to Louisville just to see me box. May I remind you that the Derby is being held here on Saturday and, since you are already here to watch me fight, you may as well stay over and see the race."

The magnificent Mongoose, fat, weary, wheezing and elderly, then clambered into the ring and made the German beat an orderly retreat for 10 rounds. Before leaving Louisville for the Pacific Coast where he had a bout scheduled in Vancouver, British Columbia, the following week, and another in San Francisco the week after that, Archie conceded that he was just fighting himself into shape against Besmanoff. In about a week, he said, he'd be down to 190 pounds and a week after that he would weigh 185 and be ready "to go either way"—down another 10 pounds to make the light-heavyweight limit, or up for another heavyweight match. His ability to make weight was as mysterious as his age.

"The process is a secret formula I picked up long ago from an Australian Aborigine," Old Archie would wink at the curious.

He was truly a remarkable fighter. On May 2, 1955, he fought Nino Valdes, a stiff puncher, at Las Vegas, Nevada, and he was so fat his belly bulged out to here. When he smiled you could hardly see his eyes. It was a 15-round bout and when he walked back to his corner at the end of the eighth round, he sat down so hard he almost broke the stool. Charlie Johnston, his co-manager, was concerned.

"Listen," he said, "you're losing. Do you think you can pick up now and go on?"

"No," Archie said, smiling.

That worried Charlie, especially when Archie lost the ninth and 10th rounds. Just before he went out for the 11th round, Charlie warned him: "You better not lose any one of these rounds because, if you do, we blow the fight."

"Stop worrying," Archie said. "Valdes is through."

What Mr. Moore did to Mr. Valdes in the next four rounds was short of murder. "All he needed," Charlie Johnston said afterward, "was those first 10 rounds to fight himself into shape."

At one time or another, Archie called San Diego, St. Louis, Miami, Toledo, Indianapolis, Cleveland, and Los Angeles "home." Home was where the money was. Now he is back in San Diego again, working with youths. In 1974, he talked most candidly about his life in the prize ring.

"I was never angry at an opponent," he said. "I was angry only for having to earn my living in this manner and for being treated as a minority. So I used my fists in the prize ring to work out my anger against social injustice. But I never felt vicious toward an opponent.

"It takes a great deal of skill to succeed in boxing, and skill comes only with practice and repetition. I was lucky to be endowed with those certain qualities needed in the ring: a quick brain, catlike reflexes, and courage. Even as a raw recruit, I sensed I had much more than the average fighter, such as naturally heavy hands, an astute mind, and fortitude. I started boxing professionally when I was nineteen. But I had had much experience before then. Actually, I had my first fight in Mississippi when I was only seven. I decided then and there I'd have to know how to fight to survive. Even then I was made aware that there was something wrong in the way blacks were treated in a white society. So the only escape, I felt, was with my fists.

After retiring from the prize ring in 1964 to begin a movie-TV career, Moore continued to work with youth and amateur boxing. He is pictured here with Dick Rall, left, three-times national intercollegiate lightweight champion from Washington State University, and coach Ike Deeter, whose W.S.U. boxing teams won the Pacific Coast championship eight times. Photo was taken at the Golden Gloves tournament in Seattle. (Photo by J. N. Johnson)

"People—sports writers—always question me about my true age. I don't deny anything. My mother gives one age and I claim the other. The boxing records say I'm fifty-eight and she says I'm sixty-one; take your pick. I'm prepared to go by what she says. I *know* my age.

"My parents divorced when I was small and I went to live with an aunt in St. Louis.

All three are still alive and I love them dearly. I still see them. My childhood in St. Louis was made happy by an understanding aunt. She did the best she could for me. But because there wasn't a man around the house—my uncle was dead—I felt it was a good time to get out and test my masculinity—and I wound up in reform school for 22 months. That experience taught me a lasting lesson. I learned to respect authority. I also learned to respect myself. In short, I learned mutual respect.

"When I got out I joined the Civilian Conservation Corps (CCC) and started planning for a career in the prize ring. But, first, I had to have the body to go along with my plan. So I began developing my muscles with excessive hard work in the CCC. I lifted bricks into trucks, I chopped down trees, I used pick and shovel. This developed my forearms and shoulder muscles for punching power. And so I became a prize fighter. It was the fastest way to get my mitts on large sums of money. I wanted money. I wanted great gobs of it. I wanted something I could *move* with. The prize ring would make up for the time I had lost in reform school. Or so I believed. As it turned out, there was no shortcut to riches for me. I had to wait sixteen years for my big chance. I'd set my goal so high I knew I was going to have a hard climb to get there. My goal was the championship of the world.

"Right in the middle of my career, in my late twenties, I became seriously ill. Right in the prime of life. I suffered from perforated ulcers and had to go to the hospital. Complications set in. I recovered, and when I walked out later the sports writers described me as looking 'a hundred years old.' I had gone down to 110 pounds. That would seem to finish my fighting career, whereas actually it was only the beginning. What did I do? I was raised in a Christian family and I prayed like I'd never prayed before. Lying there in that hospital bed, I asked the Lord: 'Lord,' I said, 'I know I am not too young to die, because sometimes I know you even take life from the womb. But, Lord, my aunty and little niece have nobody but me to look out for them. So, Lord, I have to live. I *got* to live. You must spare me my life for now.' That's the last thing I remembered before dropping off into a coma for five days. Jack Washington's mother sat at my bedside and she said that I kept repeating in my restless sleep, over and over: 'I gotta live . . . I gotta live. . . .' And then, suddenly, I was awake again. There I was—alive. It was 38 days before they let me leave the hospital.

"That was in 1941. Four years later, I found myself in the challenger's position—No. 1 contender for the light-heavyweight championship of the world. But Joey Maxim demanded a $100,000 guarantee to defend his crown. This kind of money was hard to come up with. But we finally found backers, I won the title, and my end of the purse for winning the light-heavyweight championship of the world was $800. Maxim had his $100,000 but I had the title. Now I had something to reach the world with.

"My toughest fight? I guess my fight with Yvon Durelle at Montreal in 1958 was just about the most dramatic of my career. Dramatic because he knocked me down three times in the early rounds. It appeared like curtains for me—and yet I fought back to win it in the 11th. I had to call on every human resource to beat him. I went way back in my memory to come up with the tactics which prevented him from knocking me out. That's what experience can do for you when the chips are down. My experience carried me along until my head was clear and I could set him up for the knockout. That's the way it is in life. You get knocked down again and again, but you get up and keep trying; you try another angle, you try another way, until finally the answer comes to you and you hit that main road. It's a mental attitude as well as physical.

"My last major fight was with Muhammad Ali and I was pushing fifty. Before the fight, he predicted it would be 'Moore in four,' meaning he'd K.O. me in four rounds. I knew what Ali was trying to do to me, because he learned from me. After all, when he was only a youth of nineteen I taught him. So I knew the game he was playing, and at the weigh-in when he started sounding off I wanted to slap his face.

"The fighters who influenced me the most as I grew up were Jack Johnson, Jack Dempsey, and Kid Chocolate, the featherweight. I still rate Johnson as the greatest heavyweight in history. He brought tricks into boxing he must have invented himself. He was an all-around fighter. I tried to pattern my style after

Johnson. George Foreman reminds me of him."

A remarkable man, Old Archie.
Toujours le Moore.

HAROLD JOHNSON
(1928–   )

Harold Johnson possessed all the important qualifications for prize ring greatness: superb boxing skill, a powerful kick in his gloves, fighting heart, and the finest physique of his era.

If there was a single flaw it was his lack of drive. Some said he never cared—either about winning the light-heavyweight championship or the money that went with it.

Jim Rondeau, the Seattle referee who has been working bouts for 33 years, claimed Johnson had another flaw.

"He had a weak chin," Rondeau said. "But other than that, next to Billy Conn he probably had the fastest hands of all the modern light-heavies. He was a splendid boxer, a classic example of Marquis of Queensberry fighting. Johnson was a fine defensive prizefighter and a great jabber. He was also an excellent right-hand puncher, but not as dangerous a puncher as Bob Foster. I have to fault that chin, however. Five guys knocked him out—Walcott, Moore, Billy Smith, Medeios, and Herschel Jacobs. For 14 rounds he had Archie Moore on the run and then old Archie caught up with him and doused the lights."

Strange things seemed to happen to Johnson. He did get into the damnedest situations. In 1946, he received his first paycheck for prize fighting. He knocked out 14 of his first 17 opponents. By August, 1954, he looked to be the best light-heavy in the world. He had a 48–5 record. He had stiffened 22 and only Jersey Joe Walcott had ever stopped him. Then he met Moore for the title. Harold had lost three out of four bouts to Archie but they had been close. Archie then made it four out of five.

Hard luck haunted Johnson for some time thereafter. Billy Smith, no bargain as a fighter, starched him in two. But then he stopped Paul Andrews, and his followers were again encouraged.

Came Philadelphia, May 6, 1955. Harold was matched with Julio Mederos, a Cuban who was a fifth-rater in any language. Mederos flattened him in two. Harold explained

Ring critics faulted Harold Johnson for a weak chin and lack of drive. (NEA)

later that he had eaten a poisoned orange just before ring time and thus blamed his defeat on the fruit. Folks lifted their eyebrows on that one, but with the blessings of all boxing commissions Harold resumed his life work and won his next 19 bouts. The string included a nine-round K.O. of Jesse Bowdry at Miami Beach, February 7, 1961, for the N.B.A. version of the light-heavyweight title, which Moore had vacated three months earlier. He then won a 15-round decision from Doug Jones to settle all questions for world recognition. Twelve months later Willie Pastrano took it away from him. He fought only nine more times and then retired, in 1971.

WILLIE PASTRANO
(1935–)

You can't prove it by the record book—only 14 knockouts in 84 professional prize fights—but Angelo Dundee testifies that Willie Pastrano could always hit a ton.

"He and Cassius Clay were the only two fighters I ever knew who could make the heavy bag *sing*," said the famous trainer. "Most fighters hitting the big bag, it just goes thump, thump, thump, a kind of soggy sound, but I could always tell, walking up the steps to the gym, when it was Willie or Cassius working on the big bag. They made it *sing*. You could recognize them from the sound of the punches."

Dundee was the trainer for both Pastrano and Muhammad Ali. "Willie was easier to handle," Angelo said. "For instance, I could say to Willie, 'Bend your left knee so you get more range from your left hand, and you can hit harder with it,' and he'd bend his left knee. But I couldn't be that direct with Cassius. I had to say after a workout, 'I liked the way you threw your left. You are right—if you bend your left knee, you can stick harder, and I think you ought to keep it up.' If I did that, then he would keep on bending the left knee."

Ali was always watching and learning. He studied other fighters. If you analyzed his style, you saw it was made up of a lot of mannerisms he picked up from sparring with Pastrano during the early days of his career and turned to his own use. Willie and Ali boxed in the gym for the first time in July, 1959. Willie threw his jabs fast, one right after another, pip, pip, pip, and afterward Muhammad was doing the same thing. Pip, pip, pip. He also picked up Willie's way of sliding from side to side, slipping jabs.

"They boxed one round, that first time," Dundee recalled. "And though Willie had been fighting professionally for nine years and Cassius was still an amateur, Cassius did everything right and Willie did everything wrong. I stopped it after one round and told Willie he must be going stale. 'You looked terrible, man,' I said to him. 'What's the matter with you?' And Willie said, 'This cat is a good one, Angie.' Then Cassius came over and told Willie that he was a shoo-in to beat Alonzo Johnson, his next opponent. 'I've already boxed the other guy, so I ought to know,' Cassius told him. That made Willie feel better, but I found out later that Cassius had told Johnson the same thing. For the record, Johnson beat my Willie on points."

Most light-heavyweights couldn't touch speedy Willie Pastrano with a whip. (*Tacoma News Tribune*)

Born in Miami, Florida, on November 27, 1935, Willie Pastrano began his prize ring career fighting four-round preliminaries in New Orleans in 1951. In his first 23 pro bouts, he lost only once (to Al Pellegrini). Then came the doldrums. From May 25 to November 30,

Former world middleweight champion Freddie Steele greeted Angelo Dundee, left, and Pastrano at Seattle-Tacoma International Airport when they flew west in 1956 to fight heavyweight Pat McMurtry at Tacoma's Lincoln Bowl. Bout drew 11,000 and Willie won decision. (Photo by Lyle Lathrop)

1953, he dropped decisions to Del Flanagan, Johnny Cesario, and Italo Scortichini, and was held to a draw by Elmer Beltz. The future did not appear very bright. But then he caught fire and won a total of 18 fights in 20 bouts—the other two were draws—in 1954, '55, '56, and the early part of '57.

Pastrano was being hailed now as the "dazzling" light-heavyweight "who is giving TV audiences the opportunity to watch skill at its highest peak."

"He reminds me of Gene Tunney, Tommy Loughran and Jimmy Slattery," wrote Eddie Borden. "He is headed for the championship. He looked exceptionally good in trouncing Joey Maxim. He scored big over Chuck Speiser and also drew with Willie Troy in a sensational match. He defeated crafty Bobby Dykes, and is destined to carve a niche in boxing history."

Pastrano often gave away weight to opponents and still won. He beat such touted heavyweights of the 1950s as Rex Layne, Charlie Norkus, Pat McMurtry, Willi Besmanoff and Brian London.

"I trained Pat McMurtry for his fight against Willie," said Seattle's Dick Francisco, the ex-Marine fighter pilot who won the light-heavyweight All-Service title in World War II. "The bout was fought in Tacoma and drew more than 11,000. From Pat's corner I got a very good look at Pastrano and would rate him as the second best boxer in the history of the light-heavy division. Of course, Joey Maxim ranks first. Remember, now, I said *boxer*, not puncher.

"Willie was classy, a Fancy Dan. Brian London and Jose Torres were the only two ever to knock him out. Most fighters couldn't touch him with a whip. He was superbly schooled by Angelo Dundee, the finest trainer in the business. You can't give Dundee enough credit. He's an excellent teacher and can communicate with his fighters. He has rapport, and that's the secret. His fighters believe in him. He's a clever corner man and works like a machine. Together, Angie and Willie were a tough team."

Davey Ward concurs. The old Tacoma welterweight—he won 43 of 44 pro matches before World War II closed his prize ring career—was the referee when Pastrano decisioned McMurtry in Tacoma, on August 24, 1956.

"Willie showed me that night in Lincoln Bowl he could do just about everything," Davey said. "He was polished in every phase of the game. He listened to his corner well, he boxed well—and he could take a terrific punch well. He was always in position to punch and was a good in-fighter. He had a magnificent, lightning-fast left hand.

"In the second round, McMurtry hit Willie with a murderous right hand. I saw Willie's eyes roll back as though he was out on his feet, but he went on to fight back on instinct and guts. Just before the end of the third round he started coming out of the fog. Sitting on his stool between rounds, he told Dundee: 'That bum hurt me, now I'm going to get him!' I heard Dundee say: 'No you don't. You box him, he's dangerous.' Pastrano followed orders and fought back to win on points.

"One thing about Angie working in the corner, he could spot the shots for his fighter. He knew which punch to tell the fighter to throw.

"Another thing I liked about Pastrano, he had a trick of pulling an opponent off-balance, and moving from side to side. He kept his opponents completely befuddled with that left hand and dancing in and out, bobbing and weaving. He most certainly was a great champion in the tradition of great light-heavyweight champions."

Despite 15 years in the ring, Pastrano fought in only four championship bouts. He won the crown from Harold Johnson in 1963, knocked out both Gregorio Peralta and Terry Downes defending it, and was knocked out himself by Jose Torres in 1965, his last fight.

JOSE LUIS TORRES
(1936–)

Jose Torres was nothing more than a beefed-up middleweight, but he pulled off one of the biggest surprises of the Sixties when he clobbered Willie Pastrano to win the light-heavyweight championship of the world.

Seven years out in the cold had made him awfully hungry.

An unusually intelligent man, Torres was keenly aware of the irony in his career. Like Floyd Patterson before him, he was burdened by the overcautious matchmaking of his manager, Cus D'Amato, who was boycotting the old International Boxing Club and New York's Madison Square Garden—which between them controlled most of the lucrative fights. So until he won the title, the largest purse Torres got was less than $15,000.

Persistent rumors claimed that Torres lacked the desire and skills to beat first-class fighters during this dry spell. Thus it was partly in desperation that he moved up to the light-heavyweights at the end of 1964, and in just four months he had hit the jackpot with a world championship.

"They were all shocked when I beat Pastrano," Jose said recently. "But I knew I would win the title. Nobody had to tell me I could fight. All I needed was a chance. They said I fought a lot of stiffs on my way up, but some of my opponents put up better fights than some of the headliners. My bouts with Ike White, Kid Anslem and Burke Emery were tougher than with ranked fighters like Bobo Olson, Wilbert McClure—and even Pastrano."

Ratings had a special place in Jose's life, often because he had none. For most of his years as a middleweight, he was never listed among the Top Ten—and all too frequently the numbers game dictated the big-money championship matches. Torres was paying the penalty of being a D'Amato fighter. So he got a new manager, and even then the best rating he could muster was No. 4 among the light-heavies.

The result was he was a hungry fighter. Once he had to live in a single room in Brooklyn's tough Red Hook section, and was lucky if he had a clean change of clothes hanging in the closet. Right after he won the title he went out and bought 20 suits, 20 pairs of shoes and four dozen shirts. His wife didn't have to wash his clothes by hand anymore.

Torres's long road to fame and riches started in the streets of Ponce, Puerto Rico. He was the second of seven children. He never finished high school. He joined the Army and learned all about prizefighting. Jose said it was a combination of circumstances that pushed him into boxing.

"It was a way to get out of K.P., guard duty and other such details," he said. "Besides, I loved to fight. I caught on fast. Within 18 months I'd pounded my way into the Antilles, Caribbean, Second Army, All-Army and Interservice Championships as a light middleweight. In 1956, I won the U.S. Olympic title, but Laszlo Papp, the Hungarian, outpointed me for the World Olympic crown at Melbourne."

After two and a half years in the Army, Torres was discharged, went to New York and looked up D'Amato, the manager of Floyd Patterson. Cus used Jose in sparring sessions with Patterson and Sugar Ray Robinson. Subsequently, he developed a style much like Floyd's—elbows in, gloves up in front of his face, resting on his cheeks.

"Everybody thought I picked up the peek-a-boo style from Floyd," Torres said. "They're wrong. I picked it up from Bobo Olson. Bobo was my idol. When I started fighting I copied him."

After 42 amateur bouts and beating Norman Smith in the National A.A.U. championship finals, Torres turned pro. He started fast, putting away opponents with quick, accurate barrages of seven and eight punches. He soon picked up the nickname of "Quick Hands." Everyone expected to see him follow in the footsteps of Patterson to a world championship—everyone except the sportswriters, that is. They called his fights "mismatches" and labeled the men he fought as "stiffs" and "popovers."

Then, in September 1959, Torres took on Cuban slugger Benny (Kid) Paret in his first pro appearance in his native Puerto Rico. The bout ended in a draw. Torres shrugged off the growing criticism and came back to the U.S. to beat Randy Sandy, Tony Dupas, Mel Collins and Ike White. By 1962—four years after turning pro—he was still unbeaten in 26 bouts. Torres tried to get a fight with Paul Pender, the recognized middleweight champion in New York, Massachusetts and Europe, but the deal fell through when Pender demanded a $100,000 guarantee. Bitterly disappointed, Torres went back to Puerto Rico in May, 1963, for a ten-rounder with Florentino Fernandez of Cuba. The fight ended in the fifth round, with Torres hanging helplessly on the ropes.

"It was the first fight I ever lost," Torres said. "I saw the movies of the bout and he really had me beat. It's crazy, but the only times I didn't fight well were in Puerto Rico, and each time against Cubans."

Here Torres cut loose from D'Amato and started a new campaign to capture the middleweight crown. He whipped Don Fullmer at Teaneck, New Jersey, and then in early

1964 took on Jose Gonzalez, his first fight in Madison Square Garden, and won on points in a close decision.

Now managed by Brooklyn real estate man Cain Young, he was awarded another appearance at the Garden and decisioned Wilbert (Skeeter) McClure, the highly touted 1960 Olympic champ. Then Torres moved up to the light-heavies and kayoed Bobo Olson in the first round. For his efforts, Jose went home with only $2,000, while Bobo received $10,000. But the crowd loved Jose and the sensational way he handled the balding ex-middleweight champion earned him a shot at Pastrano.

With D'Amato back as his trainer, Torres took off for Hillsdale, New Jersey, to get ready for the champion, physically as well as psychologically. "I have no respect for Willie's punch or his left hand," Jose said. "He moves good, but some time he must come close to me—and then—POW—it's all over."

On the day of the fight—March 30, 1965—Torres scaled 171¼, the heaviest of his career, while Pastrano weighed in at 174½. That night, 18,112 fans paid a Garden record of $239,956 to watch Torres batter Pastrano from the opening bell. He drew blood in the first round. In the sixth, Pastrano was smashed to the canvas for the first time in 14 years of prize fighting by a thundering left hook to the pit of the stomach. Pastrano barely got back on his feet at the count of nine. By the ninth round, referee Johnny Lobianco, noting Pastrano's battered features, stopped the fight. The world had a new light-heavyweight champion.

Torres held the title for 20 months. He thrice successfully defended it against Wayne Thornton, Eddie Cotton, and Chic Calderwood.

That brought him up to the top contender, Dick Tiger, whom he fought twice. On December 16, 1966, Tiger won the title from him, and then proved it was no fluke by beating Torres again five months later. Both bouts lasted 15 rounds. Torres fought only twice again, winning both on K.O.'s, then retired.

Jose Torres was a multi-talented young man. There was his singing career—he sang Spanish songs in a rich baritone while accompanying himself on the guitar—and he was good enough to appear on Ed Sullivan's network TV show; and also part-time jobs as a public relations man for a beer company and an airline. He also picked up tidy fees as an announcer, real estate promoter and New York newspaper columnist.

Jose Luis Torres was proof-positive that not all fist-fighters end up punch-drunk.

DICK TIGER
(1929–1971)

Dick Tiger was a very tough cat indeed.

It took the Nigerian 10 tough years of waiting for his first shot at a world title, but, once there, he kept the middleweight and light-heavy divisions jumpin'. His big chance came on October 23, 1962, in San Francisco, when

Nigeria's Dick Tiger won both the middleweight and light-heavyweight championships of the world. (UPI)

he won the middleweight crown from Gene Fullmer; then in a rematch he fought Fullmer to a draw, before beating him decisively in a third bout. Next came the fight against Joey Giardello in Atlantic City, December 7, 1963, when Tiger lost the title on a close decision. He was thirty-three years old and Giardello turned Tiger into an angry, bitter man by making him wait two years for a rematch.

"I have met a lot of people in the United States," Tiger said during that period, "and they are good people. But it is lucky I did not meet Giardello first. If I did, I would never have any respect for Americans."

Tiger finally got his chance again and regained the middleweight title from Joey, on October 21, 1965. After that, crowns rolled. Emile Griffith won the world middleweight championship from him in April, 1966, and then Tiger turned right around six months later and captured the light-heavyweight title from Jose Torres.

In 81 professional bouts, Dick Tiger was knocked out only once—by Bob Foster the night (May 24, 1968) he lost the light-heavyweight championship.

Tiger was born in the small Nigerian village of Amaigbo, Orlu, on August 14, 1929. He was twenty-six years old when he went to England, where he lost his first four pro bouts. He was supposed to be a set-up for Terry Downes, but finished off the London star in five. This was followed by a nine-round K.O. of Pat McAteer for the British Empire middleweight crown, plus a string of five more victories, and Tiger was off for America.

America suited Tiger, and once he settled down he proved to be of world class. Americans never ceased to amuse him, however. "When I first arrived," he once said, "folks over here thought Nigerians were cannibals. They even asked me if I was. They thought I grew up in the jungle surrounded by wild beasts—sort of a son of Tarzan. I never was in a jungle in my life. I don't even know if they have them in my part of Africa. I never saw a wild animal until I moved to England and visited the Liverpool Zoo. But when people start asking me silly questions about life in the wild, I make up stories about growing up with lions and tigers as pets—and how I was an elephant boy."

In a New York restaurant one time, Dick lunched with some friends. As the waiter approached, he gave them a little wink and then his expression grew stern when the waiter asked how he wanted his steak. "You fix it the way it should be," Dick said, menacingly. "I don't know anything about beef. In my country we eat *people*."

Dick Tiger's real name was Richard Ihetu. An Englishman dubbed him Tiger "because he jumps around the ring like a tiger."

He confounded everyone in 1969 by beating Nino Benvenuti. He was forty years old at the time. Eight months later he bowed out of the prize ring by dropping a 10-round decision to Emile Griffith.

Seventeen months after that he was dead—the victim of cancer.

BOB FOSTER
(1942–   )

Bob Foster was a world champion almost without opposition. The only fighters who beat him were heavyweights—Muhammad Ali, Joe Frazier, Zora Folley, Ernie Terrell, Doug Jones and Mauro Mina.

Foster was the first to chalk up an unbeaten record against light-heavyweights—48 in the pro ranks and 102 in the amateur class. As champion, he successfully defended his light-heavyweight title 14 times. That eclipsed Archie Moore's record of 11 successful title defenses in the division.

Born at Albuquerque, New Mexico, on April 27, 1942, Foster turned pro in 1961 and won all of his first seven bouts. Seven years and 27 bouts later he was meeting, and beating, Dick Tiger, defending champion, for the world light-heavyweight title in New York.

Foster's record as a professional is an all-time light-heavyweight mark of 42 knockouts. All told, he won 51 of 58 pro matches. He announced his retirement in 1974 after a hassle with the World Boxing Association and the World Boxing Council, the sanctioning bodies. A sergeant in the Bernalillo County (Albuquerque) Sheriff's department, Foster planned a career in law enforcement work.

MIDDLEWEIGHTS

Although the middleweight class was not recognized as a distinct division until 1884, there had been men fighting at that weight as early as 1867. Tom Chandler whipped Dooney Harris in a 33-round bare-knuckle slugfest in San Francisco that year and then announced to the world:

"I claim the championship of my class."

He weighed 156 pounds.

In 1884, after George Rooke and Mike Donovan had taken turns claiming the title, a boxer named George Fulljames designated the 156-lb. weight class as "the middleweight division," and challenged the world. Nonpareil Jack Dempsey answered the challenge. He suggested that each man wear heavy driving gloves. Dempsey knocked out Fulljames in the 22nd round and thus became the first middleweight champion to win the crown wearing gloves. Top weight in the class is now 160 lbs.

JACK DEMPSEY, THE NON-PAREIL
(1862–1895)

Jack Dempsey, the original, was hailed by critics as the most perfect fighter of modern times. At his peak he was without a peer, thus the tag, "The Nonpareil."

Dempsey, whose parents brought him to this country from Ireland when he was very young, was employed as a cooper in a Brooklyn barrel factory. He broke into sports as a collar and elbow wrestler at Harry Hill's famous resort in downtown New York in 1883, when he was twenty-one years old. After losing a match to Eddie Meehan in Revere Hall, Boston, he turned to boxing—not such a pronounced shift in the days of London Prize Ring rules.

Dempsey had not been fighting three years

when he was recognized as the lightweight leader. Jack McAuliffe took over when Dempsey outgrew the class.

The Nonpareil stood 5 ft., 8 in., weighed 150 pounds at his best.

Dempsey's battle with Johnny Reagan on December 13, 1887, is without parallel in ring history. It was waged in two rings. The first, pitched on a Long Island beach, became submerged in water in the fourth round. The battleground was moved 20 miles and the fight finished in the cold and snow. Dempsey won by a knockout in the 45th round.

Dempsey's fight against George LaBlanche in San Francisco in 1889 was responsible for a major change in ring rules. The Nonpareil took the bout as he would an exhibition—without special training. Outweighed 10 pounds, Dempsey gave LaBlanche an artistic clobbering for 31 rounds. Suddenly in the 32nd round, LaBlanche swung around on his heel, catching Dempsey on the jaw with the back of his hand. Dempsey dropped like an Arctic thermometer, and he was out just as cold. This led to the pivot blow and backhand hitting being barred.

Dempsey's last big fight took place with Bob Fitzsimmons in New Orleans in 1891. In the 13th round Ruby Robert pleaded with Dempsey to quit to keep from being beaten to death.

"A champion never quits," replied the Nonpareil. "You'll have to knock me out."

Fitz charitably did so in the next round.

Dempsey, who taught McAuliffe the fine points of boxing, was a good instructor and a man of great character.

"Get mad!" he used to tell pupils and sparring partners. "You can't fight unless you are mad at the other fellow."

The Nonpareil always fought that way—as though the man in the other corner was his worst enemy.

Dempsey brought polished boxing skill, sterling character and an appreciation of the finer points of ringmanship to the modern ring.

He died young—at thirty-eight—in Portland, Oregon, from tuberculosis.

TOMMY RYAN
(1870–1948)

Joseph Youngs, alias Tommy Ryan, was an outstanding boxing instructor in the Not-So-Gay Nineties who practiced what he preached. The Redwood, New York, welterweight-middleweight won the welter championship from Mysterious Billy Smith in 1894, and then claimed the middleweight crown a year later after Bob Fitzsimmons abdicated the throne to campaign among the heavies.

Rated the smartest boxer of his day, Ryan only entered the ring on his own terms, but once inside, he was a terror. He stood 5 ft., 8 in. and his weight fluctuated between 142 and 158 lbs.

Tommy Ryan taught Jim Jeffries the fine points of boxing and trained him for his title bout with Bob Fitzsimmons.

Born of French and English parentage, on

Jack Dempsey, the Nonpareil, was middleweight champion of the world during the years 1884–1891. (UPI)

March 31, 1870, Tommy went forth to do battle when he was only seventeen. He gave himself an early Christmas present on December 21, 1888, by knocking out Dick England in 33 rounds. A few months later he did the same thing to Mike Shaughnessy in 23 and 46 rounds, and then drew with Jimmy Murphy in 57 rounds. In 1890, he stopped Con Doyle in 28 rounds, and then on February 16, 1891, he went the longest distance of his prize ring career—76 rounds—before flattening Danny Needham in Minneapolis.

It was also in Minneapolis where Tommy outpointed Mysterious Billy Smith in 20 rounds to capture the welterweight championship, on July 26, 1894. When Fitz beat Corbett three years later, the enterprising Ryan simply claimed the middleweight crown and defied anyone to try and take it away from him. He wore it with dignity until he retired from the ring in 1907 to run a gymnasium in Syracuse.

Tommy Ryan was so darned clever that he frequently outfoxed himself. Such was the case when Kid McCoy pulled his famous double cross. When the Kid was a green youngster sparring in Ryan's camp, Tommy took sadistic delight in pounding him to pieces. McCoy swore revenge and bided his time until he could sucker his instructor.

A beautiful opportunity arose when Ryan of Redwood outgrew the welterweights and let his condition lapse during the winter of 1895–96. McCoy baited his trap by sending Tommy a sweet little note pleading for a chance to earn a few bucks so he could live out the winter. He skillfully implied that he was a sick man in abominable shape and that the loser's share of the purse, which naturally would be his, would help provide for badly needed medical care.

Tommy was touched and flattered, which is to say hornswoggled. He readily assented to the match and proceeded to train by getting a shave and a haircut. On the night of March 2, 1896, McCoy showed up in perfect condition. He mauled Tommy something awful before laying him out in the 15th.

STANLEY KETCHEL
(1886–1910)

If you were to list the ring record of Stanley Ketchel for a boxing fan who never saw him fight and then asked that fan to describe the kind of man who came to mind on the basis of those achievements, the fellow probably would answer:

"Well, he was built like Gargantua's twin, 7 feet tall, 450 lbs., scared you to look at him, and went around tearing New York telephone books in two."

Stanley Ketchel was the stuff of myth. He entered mythology at a younger age than most folk heroes, and he still holds stoutly to his place there.

Francis Albertanti, the late New York boxing press agent, once told me about the fight fan who was spitting beer and adulation at Mickey Walker one night in a saloon soon after the Mick had won a big fight.

"Kid," said the fan to Walker, "you're the greatest middleweight that ever came down the road. The greatest. And don't let anybody tell you different."

"What about Ketchel?" spoke up Albertanti in the background, stirring up trouble.

"*Ketchel?*" screamed the barfly, galvanized by the name. He grabbed Walker's coat. "Listen, bum!" he sneered at Mickey. "You couldn't lick one side of Steve Ketchel on the best day you ever saw!"

There are hundreds of stories about Ketchel. As befits a figure of myth, they are half truth—at best—and half lies. He was lied about in his lifetime by those who knew him best, including himself. He had a lurid pulp-fiction writer's mind. He loved the clichés of melodrama. His own story of his life is full of naive, dime-novel trimmings. These tall tales weren't necessary. The truth was strong enough. Ketchel was champion of the world, perhaps the best fist-fighter of his weight in history, a genuine wild man in private life, a legitimate all-around meteor, who needed no faking of his passport to legend.

Ketchel lived a crowded life. As a youth, he worshipped the James brothers and would rather have been a great train robber than middleweight champion of the world. Even his name had certain stature: Stanislaus Kiecal, "The Michigan Assassin." The record of his life is soaked in fable and sentiment. The bare facts are these:

Ketchel was born on September 14, 1886. His father was a native of Russia, of Polish stock. His mother, Polish-American, was fourteen when Ketchel was born. His friends called him Steve. He won the world's middle-

MIDDLEWEIGHTS

weight championship in California at the age of twenty-one. He lost it to Billy Papke by a knockout, and won it back by a knockout. He was champion when he died, by the gun. He stood 5 ft., 9 in. He had a strong, clean-cut Polish face. His hair was blondish and his eyes were blue-gray.

There was a true fiendishness in the way Ketchel fought. Like Jack Dempsey, he always gave the impression of wanting to kill his man. Philadelphia Jack O'Brien, a rhetoric-lover whom he twice knocked unconscious, called Ketchel "an example of tumultuous ferocity." He could hit powerfully with each hand, and he had the stamina to fight at full speed through 20- and 30-round fights.

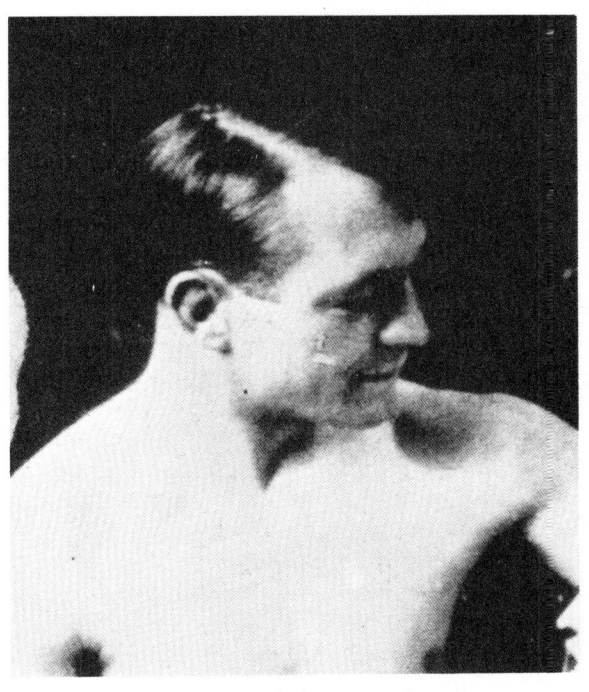

Stanley Ketchel, one of the most handsome men ever to enter a prize ring, lived a crowded life. The record of his career is soaked in fable and sentiment. (Photo courtesy the late Dumb Dan Morgan)

Ketchel had a savagery of temperament to match his strength. From a combination of ham and hot temper, and to make things tougher on the world around him, he carried a Colt .44, which was at his side when he slept and in his lap when he sat down to eat. At his training camp in the Bronx, New York, Ketchel once fired the gun through his bedroom door and shot his faithful trainer Pete the Goat Stone in the leg when Pete came to wake him up for roadwork. Ketchel then leaped into his big red Lozier car and drove Stone to the hospital for treatment. He sobbed all the way, driving with one hand and propping up Pete's head with the other.

The great moments of Ketchel's life were divided among three cities: San Francisco, New York and Butte, Montana. Each city was at its romantic best when Ketchel came upon it.

He was a kid off the road, looking for jobs or handouts, when he hit Butte in 1902, at the age of sixteen. He'd run away from Grand Rapids by freight when he was fourteen. Butte was a bona fide dime-novel town. It was made for Ketchel. Built on what they called "the richest hill in the world," it mined half the country's copper. The town looked sooty and grim by day, but it was red and beautiful by night. It had saloons, theaters, hotels, honkytonks and fight clubs by the score. Name actors and name boxers played the town.

Ketchel caught on as a bellhop at the Copper Queen, a hotel and place of amusement. One day, he licked the bouncer—and became bouncer. "He had the soul of a bouncer," said Dumb Dan Morgan, "but a bouncer who enjoyed the work." So much so that he expanded the job, fighting all comers for $20 a week for the operator of the Casino Theater, when he was not bulldogging drunks at the Copper Queen. If Butte was made for Ketchel, so was the fight game. He used to say that he had 250 fights around this time that do not show in the record book.

Ketchel began his prize ring career in little towns of the West like Butte and Miles City and Lewiston and Gregson Springs and Colma and Marysville, and nobody stood up to him for long. Certainly not Kid Tracy, who fell in one round; not Young Gilsey, who lasted only three and a half rounds; and not Kid LeRoy and Bob Merrywell and Jimmy Kelly and Kid Foley and a lot of others who went down and didn't get up. Ketchel knocked unconscious 35 of his first 40 opponents. Between 1903 and his death, he fought 61 times, piling up knockout streaks of 11 and 21 (46 in all). He lost only four bouts.

In the manner of style and ferocity of attack, Billy Roche, who refereed several of Ketchel's matches, compared him with

Dempsey. "But he was the exact opposite when it came to nerves," Billy told me once. "Unlike Dempsey, he had no nerves; at least I never saw any signs of them—and when they have them they show 'em. They can't help it."

In the dressing room before battle, Ketchel was as cool and unconcerned as if he had no thought whatsoever of the business at hand. A half hour before his historic heavyweight fight with Jack Johnson, Ketchel sat in his dressing room smoking a cigarette and telling sports writers a funny story when one of his handlers bawled through the door: "Come on, Steve, it's time to go to work!" Ketchel ignored the summons, and quietly went on finishing his story and cigarette, hurrying neither. Finally, he stood up.

"Well," he said, "let's go on out there and finish that skunk!"

"Before another important bout," Roche recalled, "he sat in his dressing room trying to memorize the words of a song called 'O'Brien Had No Place To Go.' He planned to sing it at a banquet being given in his honor after the fight. He hadn't quite finished the task when the call to the ring came. So during the fight he continued mulling the song words over in his mind, and by the final round he had the lyrics down pat. For the most part, Stanley was just a hard-punching, carefree kid who grinned as he punched and never matured."

Dan Morgan claimed that Ketchel was an exception to the human race. "He was a savage," Dan told me. "He'd pound and rip his opponent's eyes, nose and mouth in a clinch. He couldn't get *enough* blood. His nickname fit him like a glove."

Morgan was amused when he talked about the time Willie Lewis, a very fine welterweight, tangled with Ketchel at the old Pioneer A.C., in New York. The date was May 27, 1910—less than five months before Ketchel was shot to death.

"Willie had just come back from France with his manager, Dan McKetrick, and the boys were booked for a six-round no-decision match," Morgan said. "Ketchel, who was knocking out two and three heavyweights a month at the time, was doing Lewis a great favor to consent to the match. Most fans knew he would probably let Lewis last the distance and give them a good show. He couldn't lose his title in those no-decision affairs except by being knocked out.

"One afternoon, before the bout, I am riding around New York with McKetrick in his new French car when he pulls up in front of a little Italian church. He says, 'I am going in and light a candle and make a wish.' We enter the church, light candles, say our prayers and leave. You're not supposed to talk about what you wished for or how much of a contribution you left, but once we hit the sidewalk McKetrick turns to me and says, 'I dropped a quarter in the box and said a prayer that Willie knocks Ketchel out.' I just looked at him and said nothing.

"I'm in Lewis's corner at the fight. The bell rings, Ketchel comes over and misses Willie repeatedly. It's plain to see he's not trying too hard. Near the end of the round, Lewis lets go a terrific right for the chin. It misses Ketchel's chin, but lands flush on his nose, breaking it and covering Stanley with blood just at the bell. Ketchel gives Lewis one look. I don't miss it. He storms back to his corner, kicks the stool out of the ring and refuses to sit down at all. I leave Lewis's corner and call to McKetrick, 'He's all yours.' At the bell, Ketchel runs across the ring, puts a paralyzing left into Lewis's body, brings Willie's head forward, then smashes him with a right to the chin. A hook to the mouth drives the upper part of Lewis's face in on his back teeth. That was all for Willie.

"They carried Lewis to his dressing room where a doctor had to pry his jaws apart. Willie came around all right and I turned to McKetrick. 'Where the hell do you get your nerve?' I asked him. 'For a quarter you wanted the middleweight championship of the world!' He looked at me and replied: 'What do you mean? It would have been all right—only the saint didn't stand up!' "

Ketchel's fight with Philadelphia Jack O'Brien, on March 26, 1909, was something in the way of evidence that handlers count. The bout earned a place in prize ring annals as one of the best of all time. Confident and hard-hitting, O'Brien had the early rounds all to himself. He punched and battered Ketchel all around the ring. Then, at the end of the seventh round, Jimmy Johnston, Stanley's second, went to work on him.

"Look, ya bum," he began, "if you don't go after this guy in the next round we're sunk. You'll be mobbed if I can't get you away from here fast, after your lousy performance. Now, here's the idea. I've got a hack waiting right outside the door. Your clothes are in it. I've got two tickets to Boston. Try to last out the next three rounds. When they're over, you make a dive through the ropes for that hack. Your reputation is all shot anyway—you can dress on the way to Grand Central."

Convinced that if he allowed O'Brien to finish him in the ring the fight mob would probably finish him permanently, Ketchel went out swinging. For three rounds, he stood toe to toe with O'Brien and slugged it out. He smashed away to head and body while taking everything the Irishman could dish out. Seconds before the final bell, a crushing right to the chin dropped O'Brien.

"The bell saved him," Johnston recalled. "But O'Brien was unconscious for several minutes after the fight. The bout went into the record book as no-decision. I don't think Ketchel ever found out that I didn't have a hack waiting for him that night. I was just trying a little psychology. And it worked."

One of Ketchel's closest cronies in the final months of his life was Jack Kramer, who had managed him early in his career.

"Ketch used to tell me that he was sure he would die young," the late manager once recalled. "'It's going to happen, Jack,' he'd say. 'I'll die before I'm thirty. And I'll die in a fast car.' The prediction made a special impression of me on nights in San Francisco when the two of us went driving together in his Lozier, with Ketch at the wheel. He was a wild man, whipping around corners on two wheels and yelping with joy.

"One day, we were racing down Golden Gate Avenue and Ketch spotted this fruitstand on the curb, piled eight feet high with oranges, apples, grapes, pears, grapefruit and bananas. A crazy glint came into his eyes. 'Hold on, Jack,' he cried, and before I knew what hit me he plowed the Lozier into the fruitstand. Produce flew in six dozen directions. It was all just a big joke to Ketch. The owner of the stand, a little Italian, came at Ketch with blood in his eye—and a big butcher knife. Unperturbed, Ketch wrestled it away from him, and said, 'Here, old man, this should cover the damage,' and he peeled off a $100 bill from a large roll in his pocket.

"Another time, we were driving down Market Street to Robertson's Bird Store, where he stopped and went in for a bag of bird seed. Then he went next door into The Emporium, the big department store, and bounced from counter to counter showering bird seed on the pretty girl clerks. I asked him what the hell he thought he was doing. 'Just feeding the *chickies*,' he laughed. Ketch was the Peter Pan of the fight game.

"Ketch fought in my stable for a while, then joined Willus Britt. That was quite a combination. They juiced up each other's imagination. When Willus took Ketch East for the first time after leaving me, he dressed him in chaps and spurs and billed him as a cowboy. Ketch was never a cowboy, though he would have loved to have been one. He was a semiretired hobo—even after he had money, he sometimes rode the rods from choice. He spent most of his early life hobo fashion. Jim Tully, the author of books on tramp life, knew Ketch during his road days, and once told me that Ketch was the best-read man he ever knew. Jim said that in boxcars, in lodging houses, in tramp jungles, Ketch always had a book with him, and usually the book had been 'borrowed' from some small-town public library. Ketchel had a sincere love for reading and learning, though some historians have tried to pass him off as an illiterate.

"Ketchel came out to California from Montana in 1906 and was matched with George Brown in Sacramento. Brown could fight like hell, but Ketch knocked him out in three. That got him a shot at Joe Thomas. Thomas was going around the Bay Area claiming the world middleweight title. They fought at Marysville on July 4th. Sunny Jim Coffroth, the bigshot promoter, brought a party of friends from San Francisco to watch Thomas 'trim another sucker.' Sunny Jim almost dropped dead seeing Thomas barely escape with his life and a draw in 20 rounds. Ketchel's career took off like an old-fashioned Fourth of July skyrocket after that. Coffroth was so impressed with Ketchel that he quickly rematched him with Thomas in San Francisco, on September 2, 1907. It was scheduled for 45 rounds and turned into a blood bath. Both men were down for counts of nine, but Ketch finally stopped him in the 32nd round. They fought again several months later; this time Ketch finished him off in 20."

Now, there was nothing left between Ketchel and the official middleweight title but Jack Twin Sullivan. The Sullivans from Boston, Jack and Mike, were big on the Coast. Jack had as good a claim to the championship (vacated by Tommy Ryan the year before) as any middleweight in the world. But he told Ketchel, "You have to lick my brother Mike first." Ketchel knocked out Mike in one round. Then, on May 9, 1908, he became the recognized world champion by knocking brother Jack cold in the 20th round.

In June 1910, Ketchel returned to Jack Kramer (after an argument with Willus Britt) and knocked out a heavyweight, Jim Smith, in what proved to be the last fight of his life. Though he could fight, he was in bad shape, like a fine engine abused and overdriven. To get back his health, Kramer sent him to live on a ranch for a while in Conway, Missouri, in the Ozarks, not far from Springfield. His host was Colonel R. P. Dickerson, an old friend.

Ketchel ate some of his meals at the ranch's cookhouse and took a romantic interest in Goldie, the cook. Goldie was not much to look at. She was plain and dumpy. But because she was the only woman on the farm, Ketchel ignored this, as well as the fact that Walter Dipley, a new hand on the ranch, was thought to be her husband.

On the morning of October 16, as Ketchel sat at the breakfast table, Dipley shot him in the back with a .38 revolver. Ketchel was hit in the lung. He lived for only a few hours afterward.

When Wilson Mizner, the famous wit and close friend of Ketchel's, learned by telephone that Ketchel was dead, he cracked: "Start counting now, because he'll get up at nine."

Goldie, it turned out, was a wife in name only. Dipley, whose right name was Hurtz, had a police record. They were both sent to jail; Dipley, sentenced to life, did not get out on parole till 24 years later.

Ketchel's grave is in the Polish Cemetery in Grand Rapids, Michigan, where he was born.

Stanley Ketchel always had supreme confidence in himself. This led to his famous fight with Jack Johnson in 1909. It was obviously a mismatch even for Ketchel, and there were hints of an agreement on the part of Johnson to carry his smaller foe. (This never was confirmed or denied by either side.)

In the 12th and final round Ketchel went for Johnson the instant the bell sounded. Johnson greeted him with a left prod, and someone in Ketchel's corner shouted, "Now then, Stanley!" Ketchel reacted with a gigantic sweeping right fist that curved around Johnson's neck. Johnson tumbled awkwardly to the floor, a big grin on his face. He got back on his feet almost immediately and met Ketchel's assault so effectively that Ketchel impaled himself on Johson's fists. He went down with a sickening thud and lay spread out on the canvas like a martyred eagle. Johnson peered down at him anxiously as the referee tolled the count. After it was all over, Johnson tip-toed over to Ketchel's corner, where he slumbered still on his stool, and heaved a mighty sigh of relief to see him still breathing.

Later, Johnson explained: "I thought I'd killed him. See here," and he displayed one of his gloves sodden with blood—Ketchel's blood. There were several cuts on the leather. "That's where I uppercut him on the mouth."

The match attracted upwards of 10,000 paid admissions, while another 3,000 were turned away. It grossed $40,000.

Despite the ending, Ketchel won many new friends by his showing. From the time he entered the ring until he was packed back to his corner in the 12th, he was dead game to the core. Outweighed, over-reached, and in every way the physical inferior of his much bigger opponent, he fought a cool, well-planned, gritty fight. His face was puffed and he was bleeding at the nose and mouth before three rounds had passed, but he kept following Johnson around the ring undaunted. However, the correspondent for *The New York Times* reported that Jack appeared to be holding himself back much of the time.

"Three times only did it look as though Johnson went in to knock out Ketchel," wrote the *Times* man in his dispatch. "Once when Ketchel landed a clean left hook on the jaw that broke the skin and raised a lump, once when a similar blow caught him from the other side, and the last time when he ended the fight. Throughout the fight Johnson's 'golden smile' flashed out at intervals over Ketchel's shoulder in the midst of their wrestling bouts. This happened whenever he picked the smaller man off the floor and set him down again in another place. He did it frequently, and apparently without effort.

"Twice Ketchel was thrown to the floor by

the rush of Johnson's attack. Neither time did a blow land. At other times Ketchel avoided the charges by skipping nimbly to right or left or backing swiftly away. They sparred for openings for long periods and there was little real fighting through the earlier rounds. For reasons known only to himself, Johnson preferred to keep away, and when he had felt the force of Ketchel's left hook he seemed more than ever ready to go slow about his work."

In his dressing room after the fight Johnson talked about Ketchel.

"He's a good puncher and a strong man," Jack said. "I must say that he has given me a sorer chin than I ever had before. He takes a solid punch. I hit him some pretty heavy blows."

After he had recovered, Ketchel claimed it was a lucky blow that beat him. "I'm in better condition than Johnson right now," he said. "Go over and look at him; he's dazed still. But for that one blow I'd have beaten him."

Ketchel lived up to the tradition that a good man doesn't know when he's beaten.

For all his greatness, Stanley Ketchel will probably be best remembered for being the first fighter to state those famous words of the prize ring:

"Shake hands now and come out fighting."

And he said it in the ring.

On July 4, 1908, in Milwaukee, Ketchel whipped Billy Papke, although narrowly escaping defeat. As the opening bell rang, he stepped to the center of the ring and was greeted with a vicious right-hand smash to the chin. He fell to his knees as if hit by an anvil. At the count of nine, he rose, still dazed and staggering. Some of the Papke supporters claimed that referee Jack McGuigan gave Ketchel a slow count. McGuigan never refuted the accusations. Later, however, he confided to intimates that Papke's blow had all the earmarks of a foul, since Ketchel was struck as he extended his hands for the traditional first-round handshake. For the rest of the fight, Ketchel fought on by instinct and won the decision in 10 rounds, but he didn't come out of that first-blow fog for nearly an hour after he got back to his dressing room. The loss was Papke's first and a stunning one.

The pair met in the ring again later that year (September 7th) in Los Angeles. Since it was still traditional for prizefighters to tip gloves at the opening bell, Ketchel again stuck out his hands. WHAM! Papke brought another haymaker up from the floor and

Billy Papke, right, gave Ketchel his toughest fights. Here they pose for camera prior to start of their second match in which Papke won the world title. (UPI)

In third and final fight between Ketchel and Papke, Stanley got his revenge in the 11th round on a knockout at San Francisco and regained title. (UPI)

landed flush on the nose, breaking it and closing Stanley's eyes. The blow dropped him and he rolled on his back. Though he managed to get back up and tried valiantly to fight back, Ketchel couldn't fully recover from the second "sneak punch." He thus took a fearful beating before falling like a wounded dove in the 12th round.

Ketchel lost none of his confidence. The day after losing his crown, he begged Willus Britt to get him a third match with Papke. Britt astutely maneuvered Tom Jones, Papke's manager, into making one of the most foolish moves in boxing history. Jones signed his fighter for a third bout with Ketchel in San Francisco two months later. This time Ketchel was ready for Billy. As the fighters met at the center of the ring for the referee's instructions, Ketchel looked at Papke and said:

"There will be none of this handshaking business after the bell. Shake hands *now*— and come out fighting!"

They did.

And Ketchel knocked out Papke in the 11th round to get his title back.

BILLY PAPKE
(1886–1936)

William Herman Papke, the Illinois Thunderbolt from Spring Valley, Illinois, was a rugged counter-puncher with pale, pompadoured hair and great hitting power. He is remembered best for having given Stanley Ketchel his toughest championship fights.

In 1908, they fought three times. Ketchel won the first and third bouts, Papke the second.

Billy Papke was a mean, thorny German-American who hit with the force of a piledriver and could take a ton of battering. When he fetched a foe a clop on the chin, the impact made a noise like a big bass drum. Between 1905 and '19, he fought 64 times and scored 29 kayoes. He dumped his adversaries in sections: rump, shoulders, head. Ketchel was the only one to knock him out. When he warmed to his task, he lit up the ring with sparks. He possessed a killer instinct and loved to fight.

"Billy was innately cruel," said Dumb Dan Morgan. "In the gym he had no mercy on his sparring partners, and would fairly slaughter them. He would knock out a tiny flyweight if they put one in there to spar with him."

A middleweight of rare, seemingly fantastic, talents, Papke was born on September 17, 1886. He began fighting professionally 19 years later. In November 1907, he scored two kayoes in one evening, over Charley Haghly and Bartley Connolly, and eight months later flattened both Johnny Carroll and Frank Mantell on the same card.

His two historic fights with Ketchel came in '08. Earlier in the year, Ketchel had won a decision from him in Milwaukee. The first of their two big ones took place in Vernon, on the fringe of Los Angeles, on September 7. Jim Jeffries was the referee—the retired undefeated heavyweight champion, Ketchel's only rival as a national idol. Billy won the championship by that infamous "sneak" punch, a stunning left on the jaw, described in the Ketchel chapter. Stanley's eyes were shut almost tight from then on; his brain was dazed throughout the 12 rounds it took Papke to beat him down and walk away with the crown.

Friends of Ketchel used to say that to work himself into the murderous mood he wanted for every fight, Ketch would tell himself stories about his opponents: "The sonofabitch! He insulted my mother. I'll kill the bastard!" Thus no self-whipping was needed for the return title bout with Papke. The fight took place in San Francisco on November 26, eleven weeks after Papke's treacherous *coup d'etat* in Los Angeles. It lasted longer than it might have—11 rounds; but this was the result of pure sadism on Ketchel's part. Time

Referee Jim Jeffries tolls count over Stanley Ketchel on way to awarding 12th-round K.O. to Billy Papke in 1908 upset at Vernon, California. (UPI)

after time Ketchel battered the Thunderbolt to the edge of coma; time after time he let him go, for the sake of doing it over again. It was something of a miracle that Papke came out of it alive.

On July 5, 1909, at Colma, California, Billy and Stanley fought for the fourth and last time. Papke tore into Ketchel for 20 rounds, but the effort was in vain. The decision went to the defending champion.

After Ketchel was murdered, Papke again claimed the middleweight title and agreed to defend it against Johnny Thompson in Sydney, Australia, on February 11, 1911. Billy spent 23 days on an ocean liner getting there. On the same ship with him was Walter Kelly, the well-known vaudeville comedian of the period (and uncle of Princess Grace Kelly).

"Like most boxers," Walter once recalled, "Papke was lively company. During an 18-hour stopover at Honolulu, we were advised to purchase a number of cheap colored undershirts which could be exchanged later with the Fijians for valuable souvenirs. The natives considered this garment, in addition to a loin cloth, the last word in sartorial perfection, so we laid in a good supply. Then we started our nine-day journey through southern seas for the port of Suva in the Fiji group.

"At the port of Suva, where a British garrison was stationed, Papke agreed to fight an exhibition bout against a black named Emmori, the servant of the garrison captain. Emmori was a fierce-looking six-footer and he outweighed Billy plenty. The captain explained that his servant had picked up a little boxing science from the soldiers and was getting chesty. I officiated as timekeeper.

"At the sound of the opening bell, Emmori raced across the ring at Billy and let fly a right-hander which, had it landed, would have torn Papke's head off. There were about 300 natives looking on and amid their savage cries and cheers, Emmori ripped into Billy, swinging like a gate. Papke parried or ducked all blows and stalled through the round. During the minute rest period I walked over to him and said, 'You had better drop this cannibal or he may bite you.'

" 'Watch this next round,' Billy said.

"At the bell, Emmori again hit the warpath on a dead run, but Billy cleverly sidestepped and rocked him with a left punch to the breadbasket. The natives were now shrieking their war cries. Emmori stopped like a baffled bull, dazed and furious. Then, with some muttered native oath, he again rushed. This time Papke met him headon, with a righthand flush on the chin. For an instant Emmori stood as though poleaxed and then fell face downward, dead to the world. Instantly, the 300 natives in the rear of the hall started, in unison, the wierdest and most awesome song I had ever heard. They thought Emmori had been killed. It was their Death Song. But Emmori finally came to and the funeral services were abandoned. It was the strangest boxing bout I ever attended."

There was nothing strange about the way Papke lost the middleweight championship, however. Thompson just plain clobbered Billy in 20 rounds.

Seven and a half months later, the middleweight picture suddenly grew very cloudy when Thompson vacated the throne. Once more, Papke claimed the title—and promptly lost a 20-round decision to Frank Mantell, on February 22, 1912. Outside of California, however, Papke was still recognized as world champion. He made the experts look very good with victories over Billy Leitch, Marcel Moreau, Georges Carpentier and George Bernard. And then he ran into Frank Klaus. The bout was fought in Paris, on March 5, 1913. Klaus was awarded the title on a foul in the 15th round. Billy fought only three more times and then retired from the ring.

Though Papke survived Ketchel by 26 years, he died just as abruptly. In 1936, Billy killed himself and his wife at Newport, California. Philosophically, some men just aren't meant to live long lives.

FRANK KLAUS
(1887–1948)

Frank Klaus would have won no beauty contest at Atlantic Beach, but put a pair of trunks on him and stick him in a prize ring and suddenly he became the most decorative object in the house.

Klaus, 5 ft., 8 in. and 160 pounds of brawn and muscle, was a holy terror. His fists were like great legs of mutton. The mere sight of the one-time Pittsburgh millworker was enough to make stout hearts quail. One good blow and he'd drop a man like a bullock.

Frank was born in Pittsburgh of German-American stock on December 30, 1887. He began prizefighting in 1904. On the way to becoming the fifth middleweight champion of record, he tuned up on Stanley Ketchel, Harry Lewis, Billy Papke, Joe Thomas, Willie Lewis, Jack Dillon, Porky Flynn, Twin Sullivan and Knockout Brown. All were no-decision matches.

Klaus made his big score in 1912. He beat the great Jack Dillon and then went to France and mowed down Georges Carpentier, Marcel Moreau, and M. Boine. The string of triumphs earned him a shot at Papke's crown.

The title bout with Billy was staged in Paris, on March 5, 1913, and the challenger won on a foul in the 15th round. Seven months later George Chip relieved him of his championship by knocking him out in six rounds in Pittsburgh. They fought again two months later in the same ring and this time Chip stopped him in five rounds. In a total of 89 professional bouts, those were the only two times Klaus was K.O.'d. Jimmy Gardner and Hugo Kelly were the only ones ever to beat him on points.

Klaus was managed by George Engel, who also managed Harry Greb. Engel was a rough-and-tumble fighter himself and often scrapped with Klaus to keep him in line. One night, in Paris, they started battling on the second floor of their hotel, rolled down the steps, and finished the melee in the lobby. They were rewarded with a $750 bill from the management.

Boys will be boys.

GEORGE CHIP
(1888-1960)

George Chip is really nothing more than a footnote in the pages of the record book. On April 6, 1914, so-so Al McCoy knocked him out in 45 seconds, still a record for the shortest world championship fight.

Chip held the title for less than six months.

While the record of George Chipulonis (his real name) does not look very impressive on paper, he was the kind of fist-fighter that modern managers would love to get their hooks in. His record (38 victories in 155 bouts) is belying, because 97 of his matches were no-decision affairs. What's more, he did not run away from the punchers who packed rocks in their gloves. He went the distance with such old pros as Jack Dillon, Harry Greb, Jimmy Clabby, Knockout Brown, Mike and Tommy Gibbons, Eddie McGoorty and Johnny Wilson. Durable and dead game, the Scranton, Pennsylvania, Lithuanian fought from 1908 to 1922 and was knocked out only three times.

Chip was managed by oldtime manager Jimmy Dime.

With a name like Dime, George Chip should have wound up in the chips. Nowadays it wouldn't even buy him a cup of coffee.

AL McCOY
(1894-1966)

Al McCoy was not precisely the real McCoy. As a matter of fact, he was not even a McCoy. His real name was Al Rudolph, which better suited him, because inside a roped square he was about as unfriendly as Rudolph the red-nosed reindeer.

"I'd just as soon forget about him," said Dan Morgan, McCoy's last manager. "Al was the original *cheese champion*. After he beat George Chip, he hit the skids, and Ted Dorgan told me to get rid of him. Nobody wanted him so I gave him back to his old man."

McCoy's chief claim to fame was that he was the first southpaw to win a world championship. His one bright moment in an otherwise undistinguished career was when he scandalized the sports world by knocking out 4-1 favorite Chip in that record time of 45 seconds in Brooklyn.

For the next three war years he engaged in a total of 35 no-decision matches. Then, on November 14, 1917, he returned to Brooklyn to face the music. Tough Mike O'Dowd put out his lights in six rounds to win the middleweight championship.

Born at Rosenhyn, New Jersey, on October 23, 1894, McCoy began fighting professionally in 1908 and retired in 1919.

Thus ended the saga of sock for the unreal McCoy.

MIKE O'DOWD
(1895-1957)

Mike O'Dowd was proud to fight out of St. Paul, Minnesota, because that was also the home of his idol, Mike Gibbons. O'Dowd, who was born in the Twin City on April 5, 1895, was eight years younger than his illustrious protégé. And as luck would have it, he won the prize that somehow eluded Gibbons throughout his career—the middleweight championship of the world.

Mike's style—walk in and slug—was the opposite of Gibbons', but as an infighter, O'Dowd knew all the tricks. He could break a man in half, then abruptly switch his attack to the chops.

When Mike O'Dowd finished grammar school, he took a job as a telephone lineman. He boxed and played semi-pro football on the side, and by 1913 he was ready to show his stuff.

The friendly Irishman won the title from Al McCoy, the original cheese champion, by a six-round K.O. in Brooklyn's old Clermont Rink, November 14, 1917. Shortly afterward he joined the Army and became the first American prizefighter to land in France.

On May 6, 1920, Mike went to Boston and lost the title in 12 rounds to another cheese man, Johnny Wilson. Then he committed an unpardonable sin—in a New York rematch with Wilson, Mike was defeated on St. Patrick's Day, 1921.

New York State recognized Mike as world champ when he was fouled by Dave Rosenberg on December 2, 1922. Late in his career, he incurred his one and only K.O. in 116 bouts. Jock Malone was the culprit.

JOHNNY WILSON
(1893–)

Joe Nuxhall, the youngest (fifteen) ballplayer ever to pitch in the big leagues, recently was asked what made left-handers different.

"I guess it's because we're always going against the world," grinned the long-time Cincinnati southpaw. "The earth turns one way and we throw the other."

Johnny Wilson was something in the way of refutation to all those jokes about portsiders. He was a robust southpaw who thought like an orthodox fighter.

"For a left-hander, Johnny's fairly clever," conceded his manager, Frankie Marlowe.

The Harlem Italian walked the plank at a time when the middleweight division was loaded with prominent contenders: Billy Papke, Frank Klaus, George Chip, Mike O'Dowd, Harry Greb, and Tiger Flowers. A fellow could get hurt in that bunch!

Wilson was unique—a New Yorker who was actually born in New York! He changed his name from Panica to Wilson and started fighting professionally in 1911. He lost only once in his first 24 bouts, 14 ending in knockouts.

On May 6, 1920, Wilson won the middleweight title on points from O'Dowd in 12 rounds. He defended it against Chip, O'Dowd, Bryan Downey and K.O. Jeffee, and then lost it to Harry Greb in 15 rip-snortin' rounds in New York, on August 31, 1923. Johnny challenged Greb in a return title match, and the results remained the same: Greb in 15.

Between 1911 and October 1926, Wilson fought 122 times. He piled up 43 kayoes, was knocked out only twice himself.

In 16 years in the prize ring, Johnny Wilson made his point: not all southpaws who go into the battle pit are necessarily dolts.

HARRY GREB
(1894–1926)

If you have ever been on an airplane exploding in mid-air then you know the exact sensation of what it was like to stand toe-to-toe with Harry Greb and slug it out with him inside a prize ring. The object was survival. Trying to stay on your feet with him seemed like pure damn foolishness. Do this and you won a moral victory but got a black eye and lumpy nose for your trouble.

Greb could be meaner than a junkyard dog; a homicidal hooligan who beat up more bad guys than John Wayne, a kicking, goring, stomping bull of a man. He had more notches on his weapons than a frontier sheriff.

Hooligan Harry scoffed at those who felt he should train. He found that a saloon made a nifty gym.

"All I need is a shine, shave and shampoo," he'd tell his worried handlers. Between the ring and the dance floor, Greb was just too busy to follow any training regimen. "I keep in shape fighting," was how he put it.

Harry Greb was a wonder. He was only 5 ft., 8 in. and 158 lbs. when he fought Gene Tunney's ears off for the light-heavyweight championship (a lesson, incidentally, that enabled Tunney to take Dempsey). Harry was a speed demon who operated from bell to bell like the changebox in a five-and-dime. His style was as unique as the Charleston or the Turkey Trot. A "spray" hitter, he hurled more leather from more angles for more hits than possibly any glove artist in the history of the prize ring. In 1925, he creamed Pat Walsh in two rounds down in Atlantic City, after which Pat said, "I thought somebody had opened up the ceiling and dumped a carload of boxing gloves on me."

Most of the fighters of his time considered Greb the best craftsman in the ring. He used every trick known to his medium. He wore his trunks high, to create the idea that he was being fouled. From this fictitious starting point, he thumbed, he heeled, he butted. His rapid punches worked two ways, coming and going, forehand and backhand. He bit ears. He dragged the laces of his gloves over old wounds. He held and hit; a referee with a sense of critical values said after one fight, "He showed me the two best hands I ever saw—the left for holding, the right for hitting."

It was Harry's hardened philosophy that the best kind of fight is the full fight, in which everything goes. All his ill will found a focus in the referee. He didn't like the ref because the ref represented, to him, the authority that tries to hamper the full fight. Few fighters have hated referees worse than Greb did, or caused them more misery. More than once, Harry clipped, tripped or elbowed referees who were trying to break up his inside work in the clinches. Sometimes, he openly challenged officials.

Outside the ring, by natural extension, Greb was a cop hater. It's a fact, though, that most of his outside fights were with hoodlums, not cops. He feared nothing human, gun-bearing or otherwise. His only known fear, which may have come out of his growing blindness, was of going to sleep in the dark. The lights always had to be on when he turned in.

It was Kid Norfolk, a good light-heavyweight, 10 pounds bigger than Greb, who put out the light in Harry's right eye, in Pittsburgh, in 1921. Almost all the men Greb fought were bigger than he was. He liked it that way. "Big guys don't bother me," he said. "They get in their own way." Greb and Norfolk were in a clinch, when the thumb of the Kid's left glove scraped a thoughtful course across Greb's eyeball. The retina became detached. The eye was a disk of pain afterward. In a few more months, it was good for nothing.

Blind in one eye, Greb went on fighting that way for four more years, and with his left eye growing dimmer. He won the world's middleweight title—and defended it—in

It was Harry Greb's hardened philosophy that the best kind of fight was the "full fight." (UPI)

semi-darkness. Not until 1926 did he consent to an operation to save what was left of his sight. By then, he had fought more than 300 fights. He had gone up against 16 men who held, had held, or were to hold world championships—and licked them all.

"A cross between a wildcat and a hornet's nest," Grantland Rice called him.

"The fastest fighter I ever saw," Jack Dempsey said.

In point of time, Greb's career coincided with Dempsey's; but Jack Kearns never let Dempsey face Greb in a formal fight. Once, in 1920, while Greb was training for Billy Miske, he and Greb had sparred a few rounds. Greb had slapped the crouching heavyweight champion around, and bounced away before Dempsey could do more than cock a punch. Kearns ran the small man out of camp.

Greb's own weight ranged from 140 pounds to 160. He never stood taller than 5 ft., 8 in. As he met the good ones, regardless of size (George Chip, Tommy Gibbons, Mike Gibbons, Bat Levinsky, Frank Mantell, Frank Klaus, Soldier Bartfield, Jack Dillon, Jeff Smith, Mike O'Dowd, Zulu Kid, Mike McTigue), he became a consummate technician. It's probably true that no fighter of record ever fought so many of the top men of his time as Greb did. Joe Chip and Kid Graves were the only ones ever to kayo him, and the five decisions he lost went to bigger, heavier men.

On May 24, 1922, Greb won the light-heavyweight championship from a bigger man, Gene Tunney, and lost it back to him in '23. Then he won the middleweight crown from Johnny Wilson (August 31, 1923), and lost it to Tiger Flowers in '26.

Greb and Tunney fought a total of five times. Their first match stands in the records as the one and only defeat of Tunney's entire career. Grantland Rice said it was the bloodiest fight he ever covered.

"Harry handled Gene like a butcher hammering a Swiss steak," Granny recalled. "How Gene survived 15 rounds I will never know. By the third round he was literally wading in his own blood. After the fight was over Gene told me he had lost nearly two quarts of blood. That first scrap with Greb convinced me that Gene meant to stick with prizefighting. I tried to tell him that Greb was too fast for him, to go after a softer touch. But Gene was down at the boxing commission posting a $2,500 bond for a return match with Greb two days after his defeat. Then he spent nearly a year getting ready for Harry. He got his title back, too. In fact, they fought four more times and Gene won them all."

Tunney, himself, did not hesitate in naming Greb the dirtiest fighter he ever fought.

"I would say without qualification that of all the fighters I met," Tunney said, "Greb was the least interested in the rules. In our first bout, he gave me a terrible whipping. He broke my nose, maybe with a butt. He cut my eyes and ears, perhaps with his laces. But don't think he didn't hit me, either. My jaw was swollen from the right temple down the cheek, along under the chin and part way up the other side. The referee, the ring itself, was full of blood—and it happened to be mine. But it was in that first fight that I knew I had found a way to beat Greb eventually. I was fortunate, really. If boxing in those days had been afflicted with the Commission doctors we have today, who are always poking their noses into the ring and examining superficial wounds, the first fight with Harry would have been stopped before I learned how to beat him. It's possible, even probable, that if this had happened I never would have been heard of after that."

Greb was the nearest thing to perpetual motion that ever stepped into a prize ring.

"He deserved to be called The Human Windmill," Dan Morgan told me. "I've been in boxing 67 years and never saw a fighter throw more punches. He threw so many punches that the breeze from his misses gave opponents pneumonia. He tossed leather from all directions in fusillades, barrages, salvos and volleys. Naturally, being so fast and throwing so many punches, he was not a great knocker-outer (46). To shoot a real shock punch, a fighter must get more or less *set*, be more or less stationary for a second or fraction of a second. Greb was never still in the ring, so most of his knockouts were of the T.K.O. variety, brought about when the referee halted the bout to keep Greb from cutting up his opponent like mincemeat. Out of the ring was another matter, though. Harry seemed to brood about the fact that he was not a knockout artist and woe betide anyone who crossed his path when he was drinking and getting gloomy about the matter. Sometimes he would go into a speakeasy, have a few drinks, then walk up to the biggest guy in the joint—usually 50 to 75 pounds heavier than himself—announce that he could knock out any man in the world, and then flatten the poor guy. Then he'd work down to the smaller fellows . . ."

It was an invaluable lesson to those customers who were badly in need of a licking and it convinced Greb that once *set* he could hit like Dempsey. That's what Harry always liked about a nice cozy saloon—a man could enjoy a quiet drink and beat hell out of his neighbors.

Greb liked his little joke. Days before his memorable donneybrook with Mickey Walker, the welter champ, Harry was a 7–5 favorite, but on the eve of battle he scared the life out of the gamblers. At 2 A.M., Murray Lewin, the boxing writer, was standing in front of Lindy's on Broadway gabbing with the biggest group of gamblers in the country, most of whom were bearish on Greb. A cab drew up, and out stumbled their hero flanked by two skirts. Greb waved a besotted greeting to the gamblers and collapsed. The gals bundled him into the cab, and sped off.

The horrified gamesters were chattering, but they weren't talking. "So that's what we're betting on!" groaned one finally. Then they dashed to the phones and bet everything they had on Walker, whom they knew to be in the pink.

The following night at the Polo Grounds, a clear-brained, formidable-looking Greb climbed through the ropes. The gamblers were laying 3–1 against him, and he'd bet his end of the purse on himself.

"How d'ya feel?" a writer called out as the debonair Harry lounged in his corner.

Greb grinned.

"How did those dumb gamblers like that act I put on for them last night?"

In a sense, the Walker fight was the climax of Greb's ring career. He was then thirty-one. With his one good eye fading, with weight and the inroads of night sports beginning to slow him down at last, Harry brought all his guile, speed and ferocity to a head, and won his toughest match.

His fight career began in 1913, a little less than 19 years after he was born in the Garfield-Lawrenceville region of Pittsburgh. There's a legend that Greb invented his ring name by reversing the spelling of his real name, Berg. The story is wholly mythical. His father was Pius Greb, born in Germany. His mother was of Irish descent. Greb was christened Edward Henry, but took the name of Harry from a brother who had died. Harry ran away from home when he was fourteen.

From 1913 on, with time out for Navy service in the First World War, Greb learned that the assets that made him unique in the ring were speed of foot, hand and body—and stamina. Greb was a strong, faster fighter in the 10th or 15th rounds than he was in the first or second. This quality mystified strangers, for it was known that he did little training in gyms, beyond a few games of handball and some work with the light bag, when his night life left him time for such things. "I do my training in the ring," Greb said. He kept his reflexes sharp by fighting, and he fought every few days to support his night life.

When Greb found a man who could make a good fight with him, he fought him in bunches; nine bouts with Fay Keiser, eight with Whitey Wenzel, five with Soldier Bartfield, five with Tunney, six with Bob Roper, six with Jeff Smith, seven with Chuck Wiggins. There was no taint of vaudeville in these bouts—it was Greb's nature to try to cut flesh and break bones whenever he got in the ring.

"The little sonovabitch never stopped trying to ruin me," Wiggins recalled. "Seems like I lived for four years with one of his thumbs in my eye."

It's an odd truth about Greb's ring career that he was at his best as a fighter in the early years, before Kid Norfolk thumbed him—but most famous later, when half blind. He was not a national figure till 1922. Long before then, he had fought and easily whipped some of the best-known heavyweights in action: Bill Brennan, 197 pounds; Gunboat Smith, 185; Homer Smith, 190; Jack Renault, 195; Charlie Weinert, 185; Willie Meehan, 185.

Then the limelight caught Greb. In a space of four months in 1922, with one eye gone, with the reflexes and the rubbery body no longer in their prime of efficiency, he outfought and outboxed the three top light-heavyweights in the country, Tunney, Tom Gibbons and Tommy Loughran. A year later, he won the middleweight championship by slapping the ears off the left-handed spoiler and con man, Johnny Wilson.

Greb fought Loughran dirtily. He figured he had to. He proved he was faster than Tommy, who was then rated the fastest man in boxing above the lightweight class. "Hell," Dempsey said one night, "Greb is faster than Benny Leonard."

Greb's work in the Loughran title bout brought screams of hatred and anger from the crowd. Losing bettors tried to lynch him. Greb supporters fought back. Fights broke out in the ringside and galleries. It was always that way when Greb fought.

"After a Greb fight," said Jack Lawrence, a sports reporter who covered them all in New York, "it was a relief to watch a normal fight. When Greb worked, the emotion in the crowd and the ring was so high that it wore you out."

Greb was king of the alley fighters. His conception of happiness was a strong and single-minded one. And he knew only one way to realize it: by fighting wherever he could, whenever he could, as hard as he could, for whatever he could get. He seldom haggled over terms for a fight. If the proceeds tended to be slim, he swelled them by betting on himself in nearly every start he made that went to a legal decision. Damon Runyon once wrote about his betting: "Greb would send it in like no other fighter that ever lived."

Only two things mattered to Greb—fighting and making love—and the little dude was a champ at both. In his work clothes, he looked like a drugstore masher. His black hair was plastered back in a pompadour, his gray face was lightly coated with powder, and he always wore a vanilla-colored dressing gown into the ring. Only his nose, flattened and shapeless, was out of key with the rest of him. On a dude in a different line of work, it might have suggested that he had once stayed a little too long in somebody's wife's bedroom.

Women warmed and stimulated Greb. Women and fighting were the only things in life that made sense to him—women for pure pleasure, fighting for money and for pride of performance. He was a man who liked two girls at once. One night in 1925, when Greb was driving with several girl friends, five thugs stopped his car and waved the party out into the street. "I'm Harry Greb, pal," Greb said to the leading heister. "That's nice," said the leader, and hit Greb in the jaw, while his companions began stripping jewelry off the women. In the battle that followed, Greb laid out three of the stickup men, acquiring a slight knife wound in one ear in the process. The other two ran off, with a diamond ring and a lady's purse. Greb and the girls, when the police had carried the three losers away, continued on to the party for which they'd been headed.

Greb drank sparingly, he had no use for good food (hot dogs and ice cream were his notion of high *cuisine*), he disliked cards and other games, he read nothing except the prose of a few Pittsburgh sports writers. Once, Gene Tunney told him about a book he'd been reading. "Do you read books?" Greb asked. Tunney said yes. Greb stared at him curiously. "Gene," he said, "you're crazy." As for women, Greb's sister, Ida Edwards, once made the point that Harry did not become a celebrated chaser till after the death of his young wife, Mildred, in 1923.

Two weeks after Tunney shook up the fight fans by beating Dempsey in 1926, Greb was badly hurt in an automobile smashup. He had spells of dizziness in the days that followed. His head ached steadily. On October 22, he went to Atlantic City to be operated on by Dr. Charles S. McGivern, his long-time physician. The operation was intended to help Greb's breathing. He had been gasping since the auto accident because a bone between the bridge of the nose and the base of the skull had been fractured. As to what happened after Greb went under the anesthetic, only Dr. McGivern could guess. He said he suspected that Harry's heart had been tired out—and he died on the operating table of cardiac trouble. He was only thirty-two. His estate was estimated to be $75,000.

In 1955, Dr. McGivern decided to tell the truth publicly that Greb had been blind in one eye. "Before that," the doctor said, "I kept quiet to avoid hurting his career. I'm talking now because I want to show what kind of man Harry Greb was. For five years, he fought half blind."

An eye for an eye? Then Harry Greb was the only blind man among the ring immortals. He might well have amended his training credo to read: "All I need to win is a shoeshine, shave, shampoo—and *one* eye."

THEO (TIGER) FLOWERS
(1895–1927)

Tiger Flowers, the first Negro to win the world middleweight title, was a champion with a punch and a prayer. The Georgian Deacon was the original Praying Puncher. An ordained minister, he carried the Bible into the ring with him—and opponents usually got the message.

The Tiger was a quaint character. An earnest Christian, he admitted that he had a tussle with his conscience when reaching a decision to make pugilism a career. The 114th Psalm convinced The Deacon that it was not anti-Christian to fight:

"Blessed be the Lord my strength which teacheth my hands to war, and my fingers to fight."

Flowers always prayed before he went into the ring.

The Tiger won a 15-round decision from Harry Greb, February 26, 1926, to become champion. He also beat Greb in a return match five-and-a-half months later.

To Greb, his first loss to Flowers was sickening. Admittedly, Tiger was a man of some ability—cute, shifty, and hard to fight, though a grabber and a clutcher. But Greb could not respect him. The action was close that night he lost the title to The Deacon. In fact, some reporters at ringside thought Greb won. So did the referee, Gunboat Smith. However, knowing nothing of his near blindness, they could not fail to see that much was gone from the speed and fury that had made Greb great. Greb himself refused to think so.

They fought again in July of the same year. It was a replay of Greb's new frustrations. Again, the fight was close. Again, the referee voted for Greb. Again, the two judges favored Flowers. The working press had trouble collecting its own votes and thoughts. At a late stage of the bout, one of Greb's girl friends, a vision of beauty and grace from Broadway, had swept into the press rows and began throwing punches at men who had been unkind to Greb in print.

Greb, in Pittsburgh after the fight, showed the weight of the gloom and depression that were on him now. "Flowers is okay," he said, wretchedly, "but he's not a champion. He's not a champion."

"Did you take a bath on the fight?" Greb was asked.

"What do you think?" Greb said. "I bet my end of the purse. I lose."

Two months later, Greb was dead.

Flowers wore the middleweight crown only nine months. Mickey Walker took the title from him in 10 in Chicago, December 3. The Georgia Deacon never quite forgave the Lord for losing to the Toy Bulldog. He sat in his dressing room late after the bout, poring over his Bible to find, if he could, how he had failed Him—while the new champ caroused the early-morning hours away with champagne.

"I haven't lost faith," Flowers said later, "but I'm puzzled and hurt as to how the Lord could have let me down."

Tiger was not a dynamic puncher, but he was amazingly clever, fast and had courage. He never ducked a fight, gave all the good ones of the day a shot at him. He fought 150 bouts in nine-and-a-half years, scored 49 knockouts. Among his victims were Greb (twice), Maxie Rosenbloom (twice), Pete Latzo and Eddie Huffman, all by decisions. Flowers earned nearly a half-million dollars in the ring.

Flowers was a losing party to one of the weirdest decisions of modern times. On December 23, 1925, he fought Mike McTigue, former light-heavyweight champion, on a charity card which also featured Tony Canzoneri and Fidel La Barba.

McTigue won a 10-round decision, but many of the experts had Flowers winning by as much as seven rounds to three. One veteran writer, Frank F. O'Neil, called it a foul fight. "Both fighters were guilty," O'Neil said. "I thought Mike landed more below-the-belt blows, but Tiger didn't complain. He just kept plowing in, flailing away, causing McTigue to revert to pier six tactics, such as holding on to Flowers and uppercutting him. I had Flowers winning big."

Long after the crowd had gone home, Eddie Purdy walked back to the Garden ringside. Flowers was with him.

"I'm looking for my sweater," Purdy explained.

"An' Ah'm lookin' for that decision what they say Ah done lost," Tiger said.

Born at Camille, Georgia, August 5, 1895, Flowers started his professional fighting career in 1918. He stood 5 ft., 10 in., weighed 160 at his best. The son of a railroad porter, Tiger knocked out heavyweight Leo Gates in four rounds, November 12, 1927, at the Garden in New York. He died four days later after an operation. Strangely, Tiger won his last fight in the same ring where he made his New York debut. He left his family $100,000.

MICKEY WALKER
(1901–)

The devil must have dropped his hat into the ring when stub-nosed Edward Patrick Walker was born. The Magnificent Mick was one of the last of a wild breed who loved to brawl for the hell of it, drunk or sober, regardless of the time, place or circumstance. He fought every class from featherweights to heavies, and he won titles in two of them. He married seven times, and drank enough to keep six bootleggers busy. "Mickey will best be remembered as the middleweight who had the best left hook and the biggest thirst in the business," etched the *Los Angeles Times'* Jim Murray in one of his comic masterpieces. "If it hadn't been for the one, the thirst, the other, the hook, might have made him the only 155-pound heavyweight champion in modern history."

"Sober or stiff," Mickey agreed once, "I belted the guts out of the best of them."

Walker always had a smirk on his Irish kisser when he climbed through the ropes, and it took some doing to wipe it off. Some boxers box; some sluggers slug; Mickey wanted total war with no holds barred, and many of his fights resembled one-man riots. He simply thrived on punishment, soaking up punches like the imperturbable Bat Nelson or hooking for dear life as long as he or his opponent could stand. Mickey loved a bloodbath, preferably his own and his opponent's mixed. And when heads began to butt and elbows flail, sure he was the happiest man alive!

Though he made his earliest fights as a featherweight and a lightweight, the Mick never did have the frail, wispy look of the typical "little" fighter. His arms, jaws, and shoulders were those of a heavyweight, if a miniature heavyweight. The late Francis Albertanti, sports writer and press agent, nicknamed him the "Toy Bulldog." He even looked like a bulldog. He had a puggish retrousse nose, and the more it got punched,

the more it retroussed. The scar tissue that dropped around his eyes increased the canine effect. So the nickname fitted Mickey's looks and ring manner very well. He could hurt a man with head punches, especially with his left. But his favorite style was the style of attrition. He bored in behind a shield of elbows and shoulders, and then stayed in, jolting the body with bruising, bone-hurting punches till he'd built a bonfire in the victim's ribs, and the latter's hands came down to stop the torture, leaving his chin exposed.

It was never the way he looked that made Mickey special, however. It was the fact that he feared nothing and no one—and that once he started something, a fight, a career, or a night on the town, he didn't know how to quit. In size, he was never more than a well-fed middleweight. But no 165-pounder since Bob Fitzsimmons covered more ground and asked fewer questions.

The Mick was magnificent as a fighter, a playboy, and a big spender. He used to boast that he earned and redistributed $4 million between the end of one World War and the beginning of the next. He was also romantically remarkable, with a total of seven marriages to a total of four women.

"Mickey not only fought return prizefights, he fought return *weddings*," cracked John Lardner.

Unorthodoxy always was the breath of life to Mickey Walker. He was born at Elizabeth, New Jersey, for instance, with a bang, not a whimper—an obstetrician, fighting to bring him into the world, on July 13, 1901, gave Mick a black eye in the process.

He was eighteen when he fought his first professional fight at the Foresters Club in Elizabeth, for $10. The program was enlivened when his mother, a stalwart woman, fell into the audience throught a skylight in the roof of the club. Women had not been admitted to boxing shows, and she'd been trying to see the fight through the skylight when her own heft sent her crashing. She thus arrived, feet first, in a ringside seat just in time to see her son get a draw with a youth named Don Orsini. Mrs. Walker was a fight fan. Her husband, a bricklayer, was not. He wanted an intellectual career for the boy.

Mr. Walker got Mickey a job in an architect's office in New York. Mick was only fourteen and a target for the office jokesters. One

In size, Mickey Walker was never more than a well-fed middleweight, but no 165-pounder since Bob Fitzsimmons covered more ground and asked fewer questions. (NEA)

day a draftsman named Weinberg played a trick on Mickey and Mickey hit Weinberg with a left to the body and a right to the jaw and was fired the same afternoon.

Mickey then successfully resisted a short course in architecture at Columbia University. By the end of the First World War he was working, and fighting, in the Jersey shipyards. His dock fights earned him extra booze money—and the reputation of a happy brawler—and his path led straight to glory.

Mickey was twenty-one on the night of 1922 when he won the world welterweight championship from Jack Britton in 15 rounds at the old Madison Square Garden. He kept on top of Britton and smothered the champion's classic moves. He brought his youth and his zest to bear, wilting the old master's strength with body punches and numbing Jack's muscles with every blow that was blocked.

Jack Bulger, Mickey's manager, died in 1923. A few months later, at the suggestion of Damon Runyon, the firm of Walker & Kearns was born. A coolness had developed between Kearns and Jack Dempsey, primary source of income for him, so Doc tied his star to the Toy Bulldog. They made a natural team. Each stimulated the imagination of the other.

When Doc took over, he was well aware of the law of prizefight economics: the higher the weight, the bigger the purses. Neither he nor Mickey was much disturbed when they let the welterweight title get away from them in 1926 (through the careless gesture of boxing Pete Latzo in Pete's home town). Six months later, moving upward instead of backward, Mickey went after Tiger Flowers's mid-

At the suggestion of Damon Runyon, Doc Kearns, right, tied his star to the Toy Bulldog in 1923. As playboys and big spenders, they made a natural team. (UPI)

dleweight championship, and won it. Walker confessed later that Kearns had kept his water bottle laced with gin, to guarantee dramatic results, and that Scarface Al Capone had personally mixed his evening's gin ration. Mickey won the championship with a blazing finish.

Walker and Kearns took a trip to Paris to celebrate. They blew a big bankroll in less than two months. To get a new roll started, they returned home, where Mickey fought Mike McTigue, Paul Berlenbach and Ace Hudkins. Mickey stiffened the wily McTigue in one round. He whipped the powerful Berlenbach in 10.

The Mick now buckled down to business. Some of his greatest feats still lay ahead. Kearns hungered for triumph among the heavyweights. Having lost Dempsey, he dreamed of grabbing the big title back with his Toy Bulldog. Walker lent himself to the crusade from sheer, happy love of a fight.

"I'm short, and I ain't too tricky, so I can't step around these big guys like Greb or Tunney could," he said once. "But when I get in where I can slam their guts, they feel just the same to me as the little fellows." To make his point, he then went out and punched the whey out of such bigger men as Johnny Risko, Paulino Uzcudun, K.O. Christner, and Kingfish Levinsky. All ranking heavyweights.

Mickey Walker suddenly stood near the summit of the fight world. Jack Sharkey, though he'd blown the title to Schmeling on a foul the year before, was probably the most skillful heavyweight alive when he fought Mickey at Ebbets Field, in Brooklyn, in 1931. Mickey had officially given up his middleweight title to get the match. He spotted Sharkey 29 pounds and five inches in height. More than 35,000 people paid a quarter of a million dollars to see the fight, and most of them yelled for Walker as he carried the fight to Sharkey, crowding him backward. When it was over, the Mick had come as close to winning as a man can do without making it. It went down in the book as a draw.

One year and a thousand highballs later, Walker went against Schmeling. That was in 1932, when Max was at his peak, and he punched Mickey almost senseless. Walker later said that the sharpshooting German nailed him early and then slowly and patiently broke him apart. In the eighth round, with Mickey glassy-eyed and slack-kneed, Kearns signaled to the referee to stop the fight.

"I guess this was one we couldn't win, Mick," Doc said earnestly, when the fighter had pulled his brains together. Mickey gave him a bleary stare. "Speak for yourself, Kearns," he snorted, spitting blood on the floor. "You're the one who threw in the sponge, not me."

That was the end of the line for Walker, going up. He had fought the two best heavyweights in the world. He had gone as far as 170 pounds of nerve and courage could take him. The last fight came in New York, in 1935. Erich Seelig, an ordinary middleweight, mauled and chopped the Bulldog's flabby, aging flesh to pulp—and there was nothing Mickey could do about it.

After that, Walker did the natural, traditional thing: he opened a bar. His first saloon, on Eighth Avenue and 49th Street, across from Madison Square Garden, lost $20,000 in its first year. "I was my own best customer," Mickey said. As he lounged around the place, hand-shaking the fans who remembered him, it occurred to Mick that he'd suddenly become a typical ex-pug. Mickey could never stand being an average guy in the average world. Thus began the reincarnation of Mickey Walker the "special guy." He strolled over from the saloon one day and walked into an artists' supplies store on Broadway and bought himself $200 worth of paints, brushes, canvases and easel. A few days after that, he bought himself a beret and a smock. The rest is history. The Walker of 1961 was a man who, without having taken a lesson in his life, could get his paintings shown in one-man exhibits. Critics noticed his work. The reviewer for the *New Yorker* called him "a primitive."

"Twenty-five years ago, if somebody had called me that, I'd a knocked him on his can," Mickey said at the time. "But all he meant was that I got something special. He can't figure out what it is, but it's special."

Mickey was once asked to pick his toughest fight, and without hesitation he said, "My second fight with Greb. I think I won that one." The record book shows they fought in the ring only once, Greb winning by a gory but unanimous decision. So what was this business about a *second* match?

As Walker told it, he met Greb by chance, after midnight following their 15-round scrap, at Billy LaHiff's Tavern, just off Broadway. They went from there to the Silver Slipper, lovingly—except that as they got out of the cab in front of the Slipper, Walker turned to Greb and said, "I just want you to know, you Dutch rat, that you wouldn't have won tonight if you hadn't given me the thumb."

"Why, you Irish sonofabitch," Greb growled, "I could lick you on the best night you ever saw! Matter of fact, I think I'll whip you again right now!"

Greb made one mistake—he started to take off his coat. Walker waited until it was halfway off and then let him have it. The punch would have flattened anyone but Greb, who slammed his head against a cab as he rolled on the sidewalk. But he was up at the count of three and the second free-style gutter brawl of the night was on.

Customers burst out of the Slipper to watch. Cabs stopped, and delighted hack drivers began placing bets. It was an old-fashioned alley fight as the willing contestants backhanded, kicked, gouged, thumbed, elbowed and belted away.

Finally, Pat Casey, a burly cop, shoved his way through the crowd and grabbed the two grown delinquents. "Why, I'm ashamed of yez, I am," he chided boxing's dead-end kids. "Fightin' like a couple of school boys is it, and in a respectable neighborhood! Fightin' fer nuthin' whin ye might be gettin' paid fer it like hard-workin' decent citizens!"

Casey then bumped their heads together and hustled Greb and Walker into separate cabs.

For years thereafter, Walker kept the story alive, at banquets, and on radio, with no fear of successful contradiction from the deceased Greb. But Greb's friends, spitting with rage, denied that the second fight ever happened; in their book, Greb, "the quickest, trickiest man in a brawl that ever lived," could never have lost a street fight. Besides, they said, one Greb pal or another was with him most of the evening, and none of the mob saw a fight. Granted, Harry did see Mickey briefly at the Slipper, but both of them had other things to think about—a couple of girls with unusual chest expansions. Street fighting was farthest from their minds.

It's a lovely story, that second bout, but not many boxing people believed it ever happened. It probably belongs to mythology.

Mickey Walker was a little man who fought them all, large and small, in a golden age of prizefighting. In 1955, he was voted into the Boxing Hall of Fame, along with Greb, Tunney, and Benny Leonard. Mickey drew the highest vote.

Unfortunately, the Walker story does not end on a high note. On April 18, 1974, the wire services reported that Mickey was found by police in Brooklyn in predawn hours, lying on a street corner, ailing, broke, unconscious. Investigation revealed that he had been living in a rooming house in Elizabeth, New Jersey. His only income was from Social Security and from oldtime boxing fans. Walker's explanation had that old familiar ring.

"My managers got a lot of my money," Mickey told investigators, after regaining consciousness. "So did all my wives. They all got a lot of it except me."

All his life, the Mick had been driven by an inner need to be somebody "special," a guy who was noticed, a man of distinction. He could not face the thought of existence as a typical used-up, ear-bending, run-of-the-mill ex-pug. After three managers, two careers, seven wives, and $4,000,000, it was a helluva way to bow out.

GORILLA JONES
(1906–   )

There were fighters in the hungry Thirties who wanted no part of Mr. William Jones, the 5 ft., 6 in. Memphis middleweight with the strength of a gorilla. Those who contracted to wage war with him did so with grave misgivings.

Gorilla Jones was a damaging fighter who scored 53 knockouts and 44 decisions in 141 professional bouts. He was never knocked out.

Jones was born in Memphis on August 25, 1906. He took up boxing in 1924. When champion Mickey Walker vacated the middleweight division to campaign among the light-heavyweights, Jones decisioned Tiger Thomas in Milwaukee, on August 25, 1931, in an elimination bout to claim the crown. After beating Oddone Piazzo and Young Terry in title matches, Jones lost his championship in Paris in '32, when he fouled Marcel Thil in the 11th round.

Gorilla Jones is scarcely remembered now by most sports fans, except as a part of the agate type in boxing record books. He has been retired from the prize ring for 35 years, but Freddie Steele remembers him still.

"I rate Jones the cleverest fighter I ever fought," Steele told me. Freddie held the middleweight crown during the years 1936–38. He drew with Gorilla in '34 and later pounded two decisions out of him. "In the first fight in Seattle, Jones stabbed me with his left and then kept dropping his arm. I let fly with a right hand—just what he'd been waiting for—and he pulled back and countered me with a right of his own, almost tearing my head off. I fought him again later in Milwaukee and pulled the same trick on him. He grabbed on to me and said in the clinch, 'Boy, you sure remember!' "

Though born in Memphis, Gorilla appeared in the prize ring there only once in a career spanning 17 years. He fought the bulk of his matches in the Midwest and on the Pacific Coast.

Gorilla Jones stayed with the fight game until 1940. Then he took a job as Mae West's bodyguard and cultivated an antic disposition—that is, sporting a lion cub on a leash, duding up in garish garb, etc.

BEN JEBY
(1907–   )

Morris Jebaltowski resembled a spirited club fighter who liked to mix it up. The New Yorker had plenty of nerve and a good body attack. However, his acquisition of the middleweight crown was indeed fortuitous.

The 5 ft., 8 in., 157-pound Jeby was really bearish in 1932. He kayoed Al Delmont, Babe Marshall, My Sullivan, Billy Kohut, Leo Larrivee, Nick Palmer and Paul Pirrone. When Gorilla Jones left the middleweight title up for grabs, Ben met Chick Devlin in a "playoff" held in Madison Square Garden, November 21, 1932. Ben won the decision in 15 rounds, and claimed the New York version of the crown.

Ben fell from his perch eight and a half months later on August 9, 1933. Lou Brouillard, who also liked a good scrap, stopped Jeby in seven rounds in New York City.

Ben had a bad year in 1934, sat out 1935 and quit the ring in 1936 after victories over Al Cocozza and Jackie Aldare.

Jeby was born on November 21, 1907 and began his ring career in 1928. He won 54 of 73 contests, lost 12 by decision and was kayoed twice.

MARCEL THIL
(1904–1968)

It's too bad that Marcel Thil paid his one and only visit to the States when he was already thirty-three and past his prime. France's first middleweight campion arrived in 1937 to meet Freddy Apostoli in the Carnival of Champions on September 23, 1937. Thil, who resembled a toy tank, held his own against the young Californian for eight rounds before age, a bad gash over one eye, and Arthur Donovan ended the fight in the tenth. The old master immediately returned to France and hung up the gloves for good.

Thil, son of a chainmaker, was born in St. Dizier on May 4, 1904. During the First War, American soldiers stationed at Bettaincourt-Roche took a shine to the kid and taught him how to handle himself. Young Marcel purchased his first pair of gloves in exchange for three dozen eggs.

When he was eighteen, Thil took a job as a coalhauler in Reims and boxed at the amateur club, Wonderland Remois. In 1923, he joined the Navy and the following year won the middleweight service title.

Marcel was always seasick so he asked for a discharge at the end of his three-year hitch. He turned pro in 1926, losing his first fight to Kid Nitram, the best middleweight in Marseille, on August 8. In 1927 he went to work for the Citroen plant in Paris and met his manager, Alex Taitard, who later became his brother-in-law.

In Paris, Marcel quickly established himself in the prize ring as a superb craftsman. Following a string of wins, he was engaged by Jeff Dickson, the American manager of the Salle Wagram and Palais des Sports. The payoff came on June 11, 1932, when he beat Gorilla Jones in Paris for the world championship. Though Jones was disqualified in the 11th round, Thil really earned the belt.

The years rolled by, and the hairy little man continued to defend his crown, usually by decision. Len Harvey, Kid Tunero, Ignacio Ara and Gustave Roth failed to dislodge the indomitable Marcel. As a matter of fact, only age could defeat him.

VINCE DUNDEE
(1904–1949)

Vince Dundee was a paradox. He had the build and mannerisms of a club fighter, but the record of a scientific boxer.

Born Vincent Lazzaro in Italy in 1904, he was the younger half of the fighting Dundees, both world champions. Joe Dundee, winner of the welter crown, was two years older.

Vince bunched 150 pro bouts in 14 years; 85 ended in wins by decision, 27 by K.O.

One of Vince Dundee's biggest assets was his composure in the heat of battle. He never lost his head. He could take a punch. In fact, he usually fought his best when he was hurt.

"He's one of the toughest, gamest fighters in the history of the middleweight class," said his manager, Max Waxman, in 1935. In 142 fights, he had never been knocked out. "Not only is he dead game and rugged," Waxman pointed out, "but he is clever and resourceful. He knows all the tricks of the game."

Dundee began fighting on September 19, 1923, and did not lose until October 15, 1926, when Andy DiVodi won a decision over him. He fought for nearly 11 years before he was awarded a shot at Ben Jeby's middleweight title. The March 17, 1933, bout settled nothing. It ended in a 15-round draw. Then Jeby lost the championship to Lou Brouillard, who, in turn, lost it to Dundee, on October 30, 1933. Dundee lost three of nine matches in 1934. Young Stuhley and Tommy Rios beat him on points in non-title bouts, and then he put his crown on the line against Teddy Yarosz in Pittsburgh, on September 11, 1934, and lost a 15-round decision.

Dundee was knocked out only once in his career. It happened in Seattle, on July 30, 1935. He had been offered a substantial guarantee to step 10 rounds with sensational Freddie Steele, who had been restoring the breath of life in the middleweight division. The Tacoma star was the hottest attraction in the Pacific Northwest since Jimmy McLarnin came out of Vancouver, British Columbia. More than 90 percent of Steele's opponents had been on the canvas. Dundee was even money to stop him, however, after recent victories over Paul Pirrone and Babe Risko. Dundee was twenty-seven, Steel twenty-two. Dundee had a four-pound advantage over Steele, but the latter was two inches taller and outreached him, 72½ to 71½. The second largest crowd in Puget Sound boxing history, nearly 10,000, stormed the ice arena in Seattle. Only Jack Dempsey, on an exhibition barnstorming tour, topped the gate of $17,527, which was considered large in those Depression years.

On the eve of the fight, Waxman asked the Washington State Athletic Commission to instruct the referee not to stop the bout under any condition because of cuts, fouls or for any other reason.

"Prizefighters must take chances and are paid to fight," Waxman said at the time. "They must expect grief every now and then. I tell my boxers to keep fighting. I have never had a fighter win or lose a bout on a foul or

In 150 professional bouts, the only man ever to knock out Vince Dundee, above, was Tacoma's Freddie Steele. (NEA)

because of injury. Just let 'em go and settle the argument."

What followed was pure massacre. Steele floored Dundee 11 times in two and a half rounds of fighting. Referee Tommy McCarthy finally stopped it. Dundee wound up in Seattle's Providence hospital with a broken jaw.

"It was a right-hand smash to the jaw, the last blow I dealt," Steele said afterwards. "It knocked Dundee down. I heard the bone crack. It nauseated me. I'm glad the referee stopped it. It's cruel, all right, but so is life in so many ways."

Dundee fought only seven more times after the Steele match. He never was quite the same again.

Steele was right. Life can be cruel.

Vince Dundee died of amatrophic lateral sclerosis at Glendale, California, on July 27, 1949.

He was only forty-seven.

TEDDY YAROSZ
(1910–1974)

Jab—right cross . . . jab—right cross. That was Teddy Yarosz, who herded his opponents all over the ring, never giving them a chance to get set. The clever, fast-moving middleweight, 5 ft., 10 in., 158 lbs., took pains to study the opposition with scientific thoroughness. His rewards added up to 90 victories on points and 16 knockouts in 127 bouts.

Thaddeus Yarosz was born on Pittsburgh's north side, June 24, 1910, of Polish-American parents. He was the second oldest in a family of five brothers and three sisters. His older brother, Ed, and Ted fought in the amateur ranks at the same time. Three times they came up to the finals in the welterweight division of the same tournament—and three times brother Ed defaulted to Ted. Teddy lost only two decisions in 39 amateur fights.

Ted's father died when Ted was only a sixteen-year-old high school sophomore. Both he and Ed quit school and went to work as family breadwinners. Later, Ted took part of his ring earnings and hired a private tutor to help him study for a high school diploma. In 1933, he talked about entering Geneva College.

When he broke into the fight business in 1929, Yarosz won 55 in a row before Eddie Wolfe held him to a 10-round draw in New York, October 7, 1932.

Teddy was managed by Ray Foutts, an East Liverpool, Ohio, promoter. The day after Yarosz turned twenty-one, they signed a 10-year contract.

"How long do you think my boxing career will last, Ray?" Ted wanted to know.

"Oh, about six or seven years," Foutts replied.

"Make the contract for 10 years," Ted said.

Which was how Ray Foutts wound up with a middleweight champion of the world.

Teddy Yarosz won the N.B.A. version of the middleweight title by decisioning Vince Dundee in 15 rounds in Pittsburgh, on September 11, 1934. It was his third victory over Dundee. Ted then whipped Johnny Phagan and Kid Leonard before he incurred his one and only defeat by a K.O. In a non-title match at Scranton, tough Babe Risko broke through the vaunted Yarosz defense and finished Teddy in seven.

The knockout earned Risko a shot at the title, and Teddy lost by a close 15-round decision in Pittsburgh, on September 19, 1935. The pride of the Steel City continued to win on points until the old legs began to go. When he lost four of his last six bouts, all by decision, he wisely withdrew from the ring in 1942. He was 63 when cancer claimed him in 1974.

EDDIE (BABE) RISKO
(1911–1957)

Babe Risko was an enigma.

The Syracuse middleweight got the most out of his credentials. The official records show that he won only 27 of 51 prize fights, scored a mere 7 knockouts, while suffering 9 kayoes himself. And yet 18 months after he started his career, in 1934, he was meeting—and beating—defending world champion Teddy Yarosz.

A lot of people called Risko a lucky stiff, because Yarosz turned an ankle and finished their match on a swollen pin.

"Risko was an underrated fighter," testified Freddie Steele, who won the crown from Babe in Seattle, on July 11, 1936. "He was big, husky, and dead game. He never gave up. He battled you from gong to gong. He was a better than average fighter."

After losing to Steele, Risko's career continued to slide downhill. He finally retired in

Freddie Steele, right, smelled blood—and the world middleweight championship—as he pounded out a 15-round decision over Babe Risko at Seattle, July 11, 1936. (Photo courtesy Freddie Steele)

1939. Eight of his last 11 opponents knocked him out.

Risko, at 5 ft., 10 in. and 160 lbs., was managed by Gabe Genovese. He was the first prizefighter who was publicly identified with Frankie Carbo, the underworld character who wound up serving a long term in the federal penitentiary at McNeil Island, near Tacoma, Washington. For years, rumors persisted that Carbo allegedly told some of the middleweights what to do. In 1967, I was invited by officials at McNeil to lecture to a class of about 25 prisoners. Much to my surprise, Carbo was among them. After the hour I talked to Frankie separately about his connection with boxing in New York in the old days. He would neither confirm nor deny the role he once played in the championship picture.

When I was ready to leave, I asked him: "Frankie, how are you getting along over here?"

"I ain't doin' *hard* time," he said. "They treat me okay."

"I'm going back to New York soon," I told him. "Anything you want me to tell the fight guys there?"

"Jus' tell 'em I'm doin' jus' great. Jus' great. Dis is a great life."

The last I saw of Frankie Carbo, a guard was escorting him back to his cell. It wasn't my idea of a "great" life!

If Carbo cut in on the boxers' purses, Freddie Steele didn't know about it. In 1956 Steele admitted to Sports Editor Dan Walton, of *The Tacoma News Tribune*, that there was a possibility that his managers, Dave and Eddie Miller, may have had some deal with Carbo. This was at a time when Carbo was prominently mentioned during a boxing probe in New York as the underworld figure who was virtually dictator of big-time prizefighting.

"Sure, I knew Carbo," Steele told Walton. "I first met him when I went to New York in 1937 to fight Risko, and later he was in Seattle for a couple of my title fights. I didn't give it much thought at the time as Carbo wasn't as well known as he is now. We never had a contract, other than those required by the commissions, but the deal I had with Dave and later with Eddie was that they took one-third of the purses for the non-title fights after all the expenses had been taken off the top. For the championship matches Dave or Eddie took a 50 percent cut but the manager paid all expenses. I always got my half, but it's possible that Frankie Carbo cut in on the manager share. I don't know. Dave or Eddie never told me. I never had any reason not to trust either of them and I figured that if there was anything I needed to know they would tell me."

Babe Risko's real name, incidentally, was Henry Pylkowski. He took his fighting name from Johnny Risko, the fine old heavyweight. The similarity ended there, however.

FREDDIE STEELE
(1912–   )

Freddie Steele, chisel-chinned, handsome, was a beautiful thing to see in boxing trunks. Ducking, weaving, moving all the time. Smothering punches with flurries of punches. Hitting with blinding speed. Landing four or five times for one. Blotting out the attack with counterattack. He could Fancy Dan with the best, and blast your head off with either hand. Give him six inches and the lights went out.

Mickey Walker called him "the hardest short-puncher in history." Gorilla Jones picked him as "the best all-around fighter I ever fought." Fred Apostoli said the same thing. "He heaved his bombs in all directions," Apostoli recalled. Gus Paine, one of Steele's cornermen, said the tip-off was in those eyes. "When they shaded over, watch out," Gus said. "You knew somebody was about to tumble."

Steele walloped seven men who previously or subsequently held world championships. He was the only one to K.O. Ken Overlin, for example—and Ken went on to win the middleweight crown. He knocked out Ceferino Garcia twice—and Garcia went on to capture the championship. He floored Gus Lesnevich 11 times before the referee stopped the bout in the second round—and Lesnevich went on to win the light-heavyweight title. Bill Miller, the Los Angeles sports writer, said he never saw a man take such a licking as Steele dished out to Lesnevich on November 17, 1936.

Dan Walton, now retired, was Sports Editor of the *Tacoma News Tribune* and covered the Steele years. "Freddie was versatile," Danny told me. "He could kill you with either that left hook or the right hand. He could adapt his style to different fighters. He had incredible speed. The late Dave Miller, his manager, always said that Steele's biggest asset was his ability to recover his stamina. For a fairly tall (5 ft., 11 in.) skinny kid, he could really take a punch. His footwork was superb, and he was deadly on the inside. He knocked out Garcia with body punches.

Steele came along 15 years too soon. What a TV attraction he'd have been. Exposure on the network tube would have let Easterners see him at his peak. As it was, they saw him in Madison Square Garden only at his poorest. He did not fight well back there. When Dave Miller died, Steele lost all desire to go on. He never did recover from the shock."

Steele found his niche in life on the first try, going almost directly from swaddling clothes to a man's world in the prize ring without intermediate stops. He was thirteen years old when he started fistfighting professionally.

Dick Francisco still remembers the first time he saw Steele fight: "It was at the Coopville (Washington) Indian Water Festival, a carnival. Freddie's end of the purse was $2.50."

Steele was already a pro when he enrolled at Bellarmine High School, in Tacoma. He played fullback on the Lions' football team under the name of "Johnson." Gus Paine was a teammate. "That was in 1928," Gus recalled, "and Steele took the assumed name because he didn't want Dave Miller to know he was playing football. Freddie lived a double life."

The road to the middleweight championship thereafter was a wavering, jerky line such as might have been drawn on the fistic map by an old, unsteady hand. From bottom to pinnacle, the line took nine years to complete.

If you lived in Tacoma in the 1930s, he had to be your hero. Everybody in town (pop. 150,000) loved him. When he won the championship from Babe Risko, the conservative *Tacoma News Tribune* ran a picture of him in his war togs that covered the whole front page, banishing the German and Japanese war-scare news to the inside pages. And for the next two years, during his reign, Steele became *our* man. Down on Clay Huntington's block, the kids battled each other to decide which of them would call himself "Freddie Steele" when they squared off in neighborhood smokers. The name Steele made the town on Commencement Bay one of the hottest fight towns in the Far West. His brand of boxing packed the old Coliseum arena to the rafters month after month. He had to be your hero, if you were from Tacoma.

Time marches on....

He stood there at the bar, this man of the past, and talked about yesterday as though the clocks hadn't moved. Suddenly he was young again and strong while memory transported him to another day.

"I was born in Seattle on December 18, 1912, but lived most of my life in Tacoma," Steele told me. "By the time I was thirteen I already had had nine professional fights. I weighed 95 pounds wringing wet. I guess you would have called me a fleaweight. I won

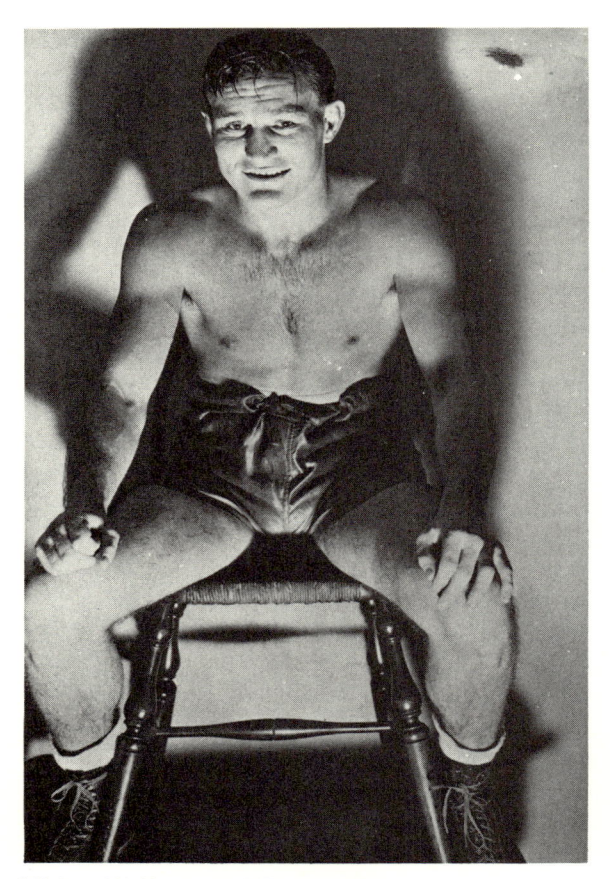

Mickey Walker rated Freddie Steele as the hardest short puncher in boxing history. Steele walloped seven men who previously or subsequently won world championships. (Photo courtesy Freddie Steele)

eight of them and got a draw in the other. I fought under the name of Freddie Steele even then. I was paid $5 apiece for the first three bouts; the next three earned me $7.50 each; and the three matches after that paid me $12.50. I was rich!

"I remember one time in Cleveland. This was in 1938, when I boxed Carmen Barth. My title was at stake. He was a fine fighter, too, but I had a real good night and knocked him out in the 7th. We fought there for a priest who was staging a benefit. It was in February and was cold. I did my roadwork on a road circling Lake Erie and it was so cold I nearly caught pneumonia. On the night of the match, a real blizzard hit Cleveland. We rode to the arena in a taxicab and when we got out of the cab at the curb we couldn't even see the building, it was snowing so hard. Nobody could get to the fight, but we fought anyway. I ended up fighting for nothing more than meal money—and I was the middleweight champion of the world!

"How did Dave Miller and I get together? Well, I was thirteen years old and boxing four-round prelims up in Bellingham. Dave had another fighter in the main event. I knew my family was going to move down to Tacoma, so after my bout I walked over to Dave, who was from Tacoma, and said, 'Mr. Miller, I'm moving to Tacoma. May I come over and work out in your gym?' I still weighed only 95 and he glared down at me and said, 'Oh, sure, sure.' He really wasn't paying much attention to me. But the day after I arrived in Tacoma I took my little bag and went over to his gym—and he kicked me out. I was persistent, and kept going back. And he kept kicking me out. So finally I got a job as delivery boy in a drugstore a block away from the gym. On deliveries I'd stop off at the gym and pester Dave. He kept telling me to leave.

"Finally, he agreed to get me a fight. He figured I'd lose and he'd be rid of me. But I won, and after that he had to let me stay.

"Unlike a lot of prizefighters, I loved to train. I worked hard at it. I knew dedication was a shortcut to the top. Corny but true. I guess I was a born fighter. Gus Paine says I was cold-blooded. I liked seeing guys fall. Before a fight I was seldom nervous. I often heard that Rocky Marciano could take a snooze before a big fight. I was the same way. I guess Jack Dempsey was the worst when it came to nerves. They told me you didn't even dare to speak to him the day of a fight, he was so wound up.

"My relationship with Dave Miller was like that of Jimmy McLarnin and Pop Foster. We had a father-son respect for each other. Didn't even bother to have a signed contract together; didn't need one. Dave was this sort of a fellow: Some years before I joined his stable, he had a fighter booked for a bout down in Chehalis. On the afternoon of the match, he gave the kid a $5 bill and told him to go get himself something to eat. 'Meet me back at the arena at 6 o'clock,' Dave told him. That's the last Dave saw of him. He never returned. Since a purse of $50 was involved—and those being hungry days for Dave—he climbed into his fighter's work togs and went through with the bout himself! He won, too.

"My best fighting weight was about 152. I still weigh only 178. The night I fought Babe Risko the first time in a non-title match—I had to beat him in a non-championship bout first before they'd give me a shot at his crown—I agreed to come in over 160 pounds. So on the morning of the fight I rose and had a big plate of scrambled eggs, toast and three cups of tea. Then we drove over to Seattle for the weigh-in. On the way, we stopped off at this restaurant, where I drank two tall glasses of water and picked up 10 silver dollars in exchange for a $10 bill (there was lots of silver around in those days). When we finally arrived at the doctor's office for the weigh-in, I stripped off everything but my shoes. In each shoe was hidden five silver dollars! I got on the scales—and the arrow pointed to exactly 160¼ pounds. With the stuff they're minting our coins with these days, I'd never have made weight for Risko!"

Steele won a 10-round decision from Risko the first time, and then lifted the crown from him three and a half months later in Seattle in 15 rounds. Ed Honeywell, the long-time Tacoma sports writer, was at ringside and remembers the details.

"Risko could be a durable fighter when he wanted to fight," Honeywell said. "Freddie did not knock him down, but was satisfied to fight a conservative fight. He won a clear-cut, no-argument decision. Risko fought well, but Steele was intent on winning the champion-

THE ENCYCLOPEDIA OF WORLD BOXING CHAMPIONS

ship, so he took no chances or risks, played it close to the vest, and didn't give Babe an opportunity to win by a lucky punch. He followed his pre-fight plan perfectly and did just what he went out to do. He won the middleweight championship of the world."

Steele thinks he reached his peak the night he floored Vince Dundee 11 times, before referee Tommy McCarthy stopped it. "I begged McCarthy to stop it at the end of the second round," Steele said. "Dundee was out on his feet, but Max Waxman, Dundee's manager, had an agreement that the referee couldn't stop it. Tommy finally did, however.

"I think the hardest punch I ever took was from Tommy Fielding, a little-known Victoria, British Columbia featherweight in 1931 in Tacoma. You remember those numbers they had for the rounds above the middle of the ring at the old Coliseum in Tacoma? Well, Fielding hit me with a right in the third round and the next thing I remembered was looking up at the round and it was No. 6. I'd been out on my feet for three rounds and fighting instinctively."

Steele started as a welterweight and fought some of his greatest battles in that class. Later, however, he grew into a full-fledged middleweight and knocked out fat guys, long guys, tough guys, bums. He went to war at

In 1939, Steele went to Hollywood and started a second career as an actor. He is pictured here on the studio set of "Anything Goes," in 1936, with, left, Bing Crosby, Ethel Merman, and Dave Miller, who managed Freddie when he was middleweight champion. (Photo courtesy Freddie Steele)

least once, sometimes two and three times a month. The record book lists 38 K.O.'s in 95 bouts. "That's short of the actual count," Steele told me. "On my eighteenth birthday I had had 45 pro fights already. After that, they started keeping a record of my career. Actually, I had 138 bouts and lost 5. I was only twenty-five when I quit permanently. After losing my title to Hostak, I figured if the other guys could hit like that, I was in the wrong business."

Davey Ward, the referee from Tacoma, was one of Steele's chief sparring partners for the Hostak fight. He told me that the truth behind Steele's defeat has never been known.

"Freddie was not in the best of shape for Hostak," Ward said. "Earlier in the year, he'd broken his breastbone in the Apostoli scrap in New York. Then, two weeks before he fought Hostak, there was the Solly Krieger match in Seattle, and while we were tuning up for that I rebroke the bone in Freddie's chest. But he told no one about it and fought Krieger anyway. Just before he fought Hostak, he admitted to me in a gym workout that the cracked bone still hurt. I wanted him to postpone the bout, but he insisted on going ahead with it. He told me to keep quiet. Later, people who saw him lose to Hostak accused Freddie of coming out against Al with his hands down. What they didn't understand was that the chest injury prevented him from lifting his gloves where they belonged. So Hostak finished him off in the first round, flooring him four times, and bye-bye championship."

Dan Walton was very close to Steele, and he felt Freddie's decline as a top fighter started with the death of Dave Miller almost two years before losing the title.

"Dave had managed Steele ever since he was a featherweight," Walton said. "They were very close. Steele leaned heavily on Dave. Without Miller in his corner Steele seemed to lose some of his dynamic skill."

"When Miller died," Davey Ward said, "Steele died. He lost all incentive to go on. After Dave's funeral, I remember, Freddie asked me what I was going to do with my money. I told him I was going to buy some new boxing equipment—shoes, togs, punching bag. Freddie said, 'Keep your money. You can have my stuff. I'm not going to have any more use for it. With Dave gone from the corner, I can't fight anymore.'"

In 1939, Steele gave Ward all of his gear and went to Hollywood to start a second career as an actor. Urged on by Bing Crosby, a native of Tacoma who'd been one of Steele's biggest fans, Freddie started out in movies as a stunt man and double for Errol Flynn. He worked his way up to featured roles in "Hail the Conquering Hero," "The Miracle of Morgan's Creek," and "G.I. Joe," the story of Ernie Pyle, with Robert Mitchum in the starring role. Steele won critical acclaim as the bewhiskered sergeant who cracked under the strain of foxhole life.

"In the Pyle picture," Steele recalled, "they wanted me to chew tobacco in all my scenes. I couldn't stand the stuff, so I chewed Blackjack gum instead. As an ex-fighter, I guess you could say I went from pug to plug."

FRED APOSTOLI
(1913–1973)

This was in San Francisco several years ago and Fred Apostoli pointed to a big photo of himself when he was champion, and said, "The more that happens, the more you've got to love the whole country. Me—sent to an orphanage when I was five and middleweight champ of the world at twenty-five. I mean, anybody who dies a nobody in America does it on his own. Because this is the easiest place in the history of the whole world to walk out and be a big shot. It's beautiful. All you need is a little nerve."

The cold, unvarnished facts were these:

Fred Apostoli, Italian-American, born (1913) and died (1973) in San Francisco; Golden Gloves and National A.A.U. middleweight champion, 1934; fought 72 pro bouts, 1935–1948, winning 61 (31 by K.O.); held New York State version of world middleweight title, 1938–39, lost it to Ceferino Garcia, 7th-round K.O.; fought 11 men who previously or subsequently won world championships.

Apostoli, 5 ft., 7 in., 154 pounds, knocked out Freddie Steele and decisioned Glen Lee twice within three months in 1938 at Madison Square Garden to claim the middleweight title. But he made his biggest splash in classics against light-heavyweights Billy Conn and Melio Bettina in '39 and '40.

Apostoli was part of one of the most unusual promotions in prize ring history. On September 23, 1937, at the Polo Grounds,

Mike Jacobs staged *four* 15-round title bouts. Apostoli knocked out Marcel Thil in the 10th round to gain recognition by the New York State Commission as world champion; Barney Ross retained his welterweight title against Garcia; Lou Ambers beat Pedro Montanez to keep his lightweight crown; and Sixto Escobar lost his bantamweight championship to Harry Jeffra.

As a child, Apostoli spent six years in a Catholic orphanage after his mother died. There were four children in the family and his father couldn't raise them all, so Fred was turned over to the Sisters. It was the policy of the nuns to let the boys settle arguments with boxing gloves. "I had a lot of fights, never lost a one," Fred remembered. "When I was nine, the Sisters asked all of us what we wanted to be when we grew up. I said I wanted to be a fighter. I was twenty years old when I won the A.A.U. Nationals at St. Louis in 1934. I fought five times in three nights to win the middleweight crown. Joe Louis rocked three guys to sleep in three nights in the same tournament to win the light-heavyweight championship."

The record book lists Freddie Steele as Apostoli's first professional opponent. Apostoli said the book is wrong.

"Actually, I had six pro bouts before Steele, and won them all," Apostoli said. "*Then* came Steele, up in Seattle. Freddie was my *seventh* pro fight; the first time I ever went 10 rounds. He knocked me out in the last round. I went into the match confident I could beat him. He was an established headliner and the incentive was there. I started out fast, and unloaded everything I had in an effort to deck him. But Freddie could take a punch. He took my best shots for six rounds, and then turned it around and really cleaned my clock in the last 12 minutes. He banged me to the canvas three, four times in that last round. But I was back on my feet when the referee stopped it with only a minute left. I was terribly tired, bloody, badly beaten. Steele was about the toughest man I ever fought. I'd caught him at a bad time, while he was on the way up. Thirteen and a half months later he was the champ."

Marv Tommervik remembers that Apostoli brooded over that defeat for three years. Tommervik was a great All-American football player at little Pacific Lutheran University, located at Tacoma, and served in the Navy with Apostoli at Norfolk, Virginia, in 1942.

"I'd signed up with Gene Tunney's physical fitness program during the war and Apostoli was our instructor," Tommervik recalled. "When he learned I was from Steele's hometown, he opened up one night and talked about how he had planned his strategy for the second bout with Freddie. He told me, 'I knew that to beat him I'd have to overcome my short arms. So I figured to get inside and wear him down with body punches. And that's what I did. I plowed into him, stayed on top of him, and kept away from his left. I was really a wild man that night. It'd taken three years to get a rematch with him, and when the referee stopped the bout in the 9th after Steele had been down, I was so elated I cried. God, I was so happy I beat him because I'd been thinking about him all those years.' Apostoli was built like Popeye, with short, powerful arms. He was always in shape. Even in the Navy he worked us hard. He was strong, durable, a miniature Rocky

Though he won the middleweight championship, in 1938, Fred Apostoli also campaigned among light-heavies and gave Billy Conn one of his toughest fights. (NEA)

Marciano. Steele, he said, was just about the greatest puncher he ever fought."

Apostoli gave Billy Conn two of his hardest bouts.

"He was the toughest fellow I ever fought," Conn testified. "He busted me up like kindling in the second match and put me in the hospital for five days."

Mike Jacobs thought Apostoli would win the second Conn fight. Before the match, he called Fred into his office and said, "How much can you weigh?" Fred knew what the wily old promoter was thinking. He was thinking that if Fred got past Conn, he would be the logical contender to fight Joe Louis.

"I know what you're thinking, Mr. Jacobs," Fred Apostoli said. *Not a chance!*"

In his first fight with Bettina, Apostoli took a terrific beating through the early rounds. Returning to his corner after an especially bad three minutes, Apostoli sat down and began to cry like a baby. "What's the matter with me?" he demanded of Whitey Bimstein, his handler. "I can't fight a lick."

Bimstein worked over Apostoli for a few moments. Then, just before the bell, he hauled Apostoli to his feet and smacked him a clout on the jaw. "Now get in there and fight!" he screamed. At the end of the round, Apostoli looked fresher than he had all night. "Do that again," he said, "I can beat this guy."

Bimstein was at a loss to explain how it worked.

"Fred didn't get mad at Bettina for socking him, and he didn't get mad at me for socking him," Bimstein said later. "But every time I hit him he got so mad at Bettina that he won the fight."

AL HOSTAK
(1916–)

In the first round at Seattle's old Civic Stadium Al Hostak smashed a straight left hand stiff to the chin of Freddie Steele, knocking the world champion from neighboring Tacoma halfway across the ring, but when Steele got back up to retaliate, he found a fighter there with both hands working.

That was the pattern in one of the briefest middleweight championship bouts in history. Hostak would send Steele to the floor, dropping him cleanly, while the referee tolled the numbers off. When Steele went down, he would get up, trying to clear the cobwebs from his head. He looked inept and even foolish against the challenger's devastating attack. In less than two minutes under the severest punishment, Steele went down and never got up.

Thirty-seven years should be long enough for memories to forget, but the picture of Hostak hovering over Steele won't turn off. Puget Sound ringworms still talk about the fight—debate, argue, get mad.

Steele, himself, has no excuses, however.

"Al was a good puncher," Freddie told me. "If he could get to you and hit you in the first two or three rounds, you were in trouble. He hit me in the first round and suddenly everything fogged up. I couldn't get going. You take a punch much better after you get warmed up. It often took me several rounds to untrack and open up."

And Hostak?

"I was just fortunate I never fought Steele at his peak," Al confessed. "I caught him at the proper time, when he was on the way down and all the incentive had gone out of him."

Davey Ward wants to clear up several points about that July 26, 1938, title fight.

"It has been written that Hostak won the crown from Steele with a *lucky* punch. That just isn't true. I trained with Steele and a week before the bout I told him: 'Freddie, you're taking Hostak too lightly. He's a terrific puncher.' But Steele regarded the match as just another fight. He had been looking ahead to a trip to London, where he was going to fight Jock McAvoy, the British middleweight champion. I was to go with him. So he was looking past Hostak to McAvoy.

"I felt Steele should have come out boxing Hostak more. Instead, he decided to punch. So Hostak tore into him with a good left hook, shaking him up. Steele started retaliating with a right hand. He started throwing it straight but couldn't raise the elbow. He got it up just this high, when Hostak threw a short left hook, no more than six inches, and hit Steele on the chin. Down Steele went. That was the beginning of the end. Steele went down twice more and was pulling himself up by the ropes for the final time when Jack Dempsey, the referee, counted him out.

"Right after the fight, Steele disappeared. I found him in one of the booths in the dress-

Al Hostak trained hard for his 1938 title bout against champion Freddie Steele. It paid off. The Seattle challenger kayoed the Tacoman in the first round to win world middleweight crown. (*Tacoma News Tribune*)

ing room, alone, bawling. He looked up at me with tears streaming down his cheeks, and said, 'How could this happen to me? How could I let a bum like that beat me?' It was a very emotional scene.

"Hostak, of course, was no bum. Except for his brittle hands, which finally drove him out of the racket, he was a very good fighter. Look at the great fights he gave Tony Zale and Solly Krieger. He busted both hands on Solly's jaw and still fought 11 rounds before being stopped. On the night Al won the title from Steele—a bout that grossed upwards of $85,000—Hostak's share of the purse was little more than $800! That sort of arithmetic would take the heart out of any pro fighter. And yet Hostak never complained. He refused to knock the fight business."

Clay Huntington, originator of the Washington State Sports Hall of Fame, remembers that two Tacoma sports announcers, Jerry Geehan and Harry Jordan, were denied permission by the promoter to hook up their radio lines inside the ball park to broadcast the Steele-Hostak match back to Tacoma. 'So on the night of the fight," Clay said, "Jerry and Harry crawled up this telephone pole outside Civic Stadium and, with the aid of binoculars, called the blow-by-blow description from there. That's the first time I ever heard of anyone broadcasting a world championship fight from atop a telephone pole!"

There were rumors that the fight was fixed. Dan Walton discounts this.

"Steele opened at 3–1," Walton said, "but a flood of small bets—$2, $5, $10—came in on Hostak. This money was traced to the radio fans, who had heard Hostak score all those knockouts over their radio sets. They thought he was great. The odds went to even money and Hostak even went into the ring as a slight favorite, 10–9. The rumors that the fight was a fake were carefully checked and all found to be totally false. The actual fact is, Steele plain got clobbered. You must also remember that Steele had been boxing professionally for almost a dozen years. The wear and tear of the ring and the years had begun to show on him, although few noticed it at the time."

It was the first world championship fight ever held in the Pacific Northwest; it drew 30,102 fans who paid $85,031.25—both figures state records up to that time.

Hostak won his shot at the title by scoring 15 straight knockouts, some of them over opponents who had gone the distance with Steele. Al had tremendous potential, but eventually became susceptible to cracked knuckles and swollen fingers. Those brittle hands proved a permanent handicap. He was such a powerful puncher (47 kayoes) that he was forever on the mend. In the years 1937–39, he fought a total of 19 times. All but one fell at the feet of Hostak—but that one, Solly Krieger, stood up for 15 rounds and won Al's title.

"It was not one of his better fights," recalled Ed Honeywell, who covered the bout. "Little Eddie Marino was working in Hostak's corner and called Al every name he could think of. He called him yellow, cowardly, gutless, a cheese champion—those were his words. And the way Hostak fought that night with his title at stake, I was inclined to agree."

Hostak redeemed himself on June 27, 1939. He won the championship back by stopping Krieger in the fourth round.

Then came three murderous contests with Tony Zale. They battled in Chicago, Seattle, Chicago, in that order. Zale won the first, a non-title match, by a 10-round decision. This earned him a crack at the title in Seattle, July 19, 1940. Rejuvenated by the hometown partisans, Hostak piled up an early lead only to wilt in the stretch. He went down in the 13th and never could regain his former stature. Zale gave him a chance to get the title back, on May 28, 1941, but this time Al went out in two.

Hostak, whose parents were of Czech descent, was born in Minneapolis on January 7, 1916. He fought professionally from 1934 to 1949, then retired to private business in Seattle, where he was raised.

Two Seattle prizefight experts, Jim Rondeau and Dick Francisco, were asked to make a final assessment of Hostak. I put the question to them in 1974. They had had 25 years to think about Al's proper niche in boxing history.

"Hostak was a helluva puncher," Rondeau said. "He was a *winger*. If he could hit you on the chin he could kill you. Unfortunately, that's all I can say about his ringmanship. He was never a boxer. He needed a stationary target. In my judgment, he caught up with Steele and won the title after Freddie was all through. Steele had only recently come off of that terrific non-title beating by Apostoli and I don't believe he had anything left for Hostak. If he did, he didn't have a chance to show it."

"Hostak had bombs in both hands," Francisco added. "I don't rate him a bad boxer. He was more of a defensive puncher, really. And he could take a punch. I remember the second Steve Belloise fight in Seattle (August 26, 1947) at the end of Al's career. Belloise hit him with everything but the ringpost, yet Al didn't go down. As a matter of fact, he battled back and won the decision.

"His big weakness was those brittle hands—and thin wrists. He also had trouble with good scientific boxers and Fancy Dans. With punchers, however, he could really go, because he could catch them with that swift right hand. He knocked Steele out with one of the hardest punches I ever saw. They could have counted to a thousand and Freddie never would have gotten all the way up. He caught a helluva punch. And remember, Steele had a reputation for being able to take a punch. He had endurance. Davey Ward points out that Freddie possessed a very, very slow heartbeat, right around 56–58, meaning he was plenty strong. But that didn't help him the night he met Hostak.

"When we're discussing middleweights of the 1930s and 1940s, keep in mind that the division was exceptionally tough. We had at least 30 or 40 middleweights who were top-rank during that period, and you really had to be something extra special even to get a shot at the world championship. Only the heavyweight division was more popular."

Recently, I asked Dr. Charles P. Larson, the internationally renowned Tacoma forensic pathologist and former President of the World Boxing Association, if he saw the Steele-Hostak fight.

"I was there," Dr. Larson said.

"Then you saw the fight," I said.

"No," he said.

"But you were there," I insisted.

"I know," he said, "but I was late getting seated. When I finally settled and turned back to look at the fight—it was all over. *I never saw a thing!*"

SOLLY KRIEGER
(1909–   )

Solly Krieger was a blunt, stolid fighter, a physical man whose abiding love was knocking other men down. He sprayed rights and lefts with a motion so compact and so fluid that it appeared as natural as a politician's smile.

Freddie Steele told me that Krieger was the toughest opponent he ever fought. "He could take a punch and could throw a punch," Steele said. "Solly was very hard to nail as he fought out of a shell and in a crouch. Always dangerous, he was the one-punch-and-out type of slugger and could turn the tables on you damn fast. We fought in Seattle, in 1938, and I was forced to go 10 rounds to beat him. The fact that I was still champion didn't intimidate him one bit."

Krieger was born in New York on March 28, 1909, of Jewish-American parents. He began his prizefighting career in 1928. His path to the middleweight championship was cluttered with thorns. In the first trough of the Depression, he scratched out a living fighting four- and six-round preliminaries in and around New York. Along the way, guys with names like LaGray and Aldare and Rossi and Berglund and Terry and Rankins and Quaill beat him. His last bout of the year in '31 was a knockout by Vince Dundee.

In mid-1935, Solly began to find himself. He fought a total of 46 bouts over the next three years, winning 35, including 29 knockouts. One of these victories was a 12-round decision over the future light-heavyweight champion, Billy Conn (though Billy later came back to decision Solly twice).

Krieger was twenty-nine years old when he won the middlweight crown from Al Hostak, a 7–1 favorite. He was a middle-aged man as prizefighters go. "Have you ever been tired and cold, and had a cup of hot coffee laced with brandy?" Krieger asked. "Remember how the stiffness and soreness seeped out of you, and a warm glow spread through your insides? Well, that's the way I felt the night I upset Hostak."

Solly's reign lasted less than eight months, however, for on June 27, 1939, Hostak knocked him out in four rounds to regain the title. Krieger fought on for two more years, losing 6 of 13 bouts. He finally hung up the gloves after Lee Savold beat him, on July 22, 1941. He started out as a middleweight, but added weight (175 lbs.) and wound up fighting light-heavies and heavies. All told, Krieger engaged in 111 bouts, scored 53 K.O.'s, won 27 by decision, was knocked out

3 times, lost 21 decisions, and fought 7 draws.

CEFERINO GARCIA
(1912-   )

Ceferino Garcia, 24th middleweight champion of the world, was the biggest (5 ft., 6 in., 145 pounds) Filipino ever to scale the ring heights. He was also the first prize fighter to popularize the "bolo punch." Garcia was born in the Philippine Islands in 1912 and spent his boyhood toiling in the sugar cane fields. He developed his famed punch by wielding a bolo knife in the cane fields—sort of a combination right uppercut and half hook. He began his career in 1927, and after two unsuccessful attempts to win the welterweight title, against Barney Ross in 1937 and Henry Armstrong in 1938, he moved up to the middleweight division and K.O.'d Fred Apostoli in seven rounds to win the championship, October 2, 1939. On March 1, 1940, he held Armstrong to a draw in defense of his crown, but lost it to Ken Overlin in New York the following May 23. Garcia was not much of a boxer-type, but could hit like a muleskinner. Of his lifetime total of 71 victories, 52 were scored by knockouts! There was no bull about his bolo.

KEN OVERLIN
(1910-1969)

Easy—nothing to it! At least that was the impression conveyed by Ken Overlin when he sashayed around the ring with such natural grace and poise. Poise—that was the word! Overlin had it in abundance.

The 5 ft., 8 in, 160-pound Irishman from Decatur, Illinois, had all the answers. He won 125 of 146 bouts. He was knocked out once but it took a champion to do it—Tacoma's Freddie Steele.

Ken was born in Decatur in 1910. He began his ring career in 1932, won 33 of his first 34 fights. The lone defeat during the streak was a questionable decision to Vince Dundee.

This sort of showing placed Ken squarely in line for a title bout, and on May 23, 1940, in New York City, he decisioned Ceferino Garcia for the New York State Commission's version of the middleweight crown. This particular source of recognition was considered "universal" at the time.

Overlin lost the New York edition of the title to Billy Soose in New York City on May 9, 1941. He continued to pile up points until he quit the ring in 1942 to join the Navy. His last prize ring appearance was on June 26, 1942, a 10-round draw with Freddie Apostoli at Norfolk.

BILLY SOOSE
(1917-   )

Billy Soose, out of Farrell, Pennsylvania and Penn State College, is one of the few college guys ever to win a championship. He gained recognition as middleweight champion of the world in New York State in May of 1941 by winning a decision from Ken Overlin. At the time, Tony Zale was champion in the eyes of the National Boxing Association, but as Soose had beaten Zale in an over-the-weight match, he generally was regarded the world over as top man in the division. The two never met again, for in November of 1941, Soose relinquished the title to fight as a light-heavyweight. He joined the Navy in January, 1941, was later commissioned as a lieutenant. Billy was a fighter before he knew the halls of learning. He fought on the so-called "bootleg amateur" circuit as a high school kid and had about 200 fights. He enrolled at Penn State in 1936, where he was a man among boys on the boxing team. Opponents refused to fight him. He became a professional in 1938. Billy made Paul Moss, a Penn State alumnus and Hollywood writer, his manager. Moss said he didn't know anything about prize fighting; nevertheless, Soose said he was his manager. The fight mob regarded them as a quaint pair—a college fighter with an amateur manager. But they weren't funny any more when Billy beat Overlin for the title. Billy Soose was indeed a college man who learned his boxing lessons well.

TONY ZALE
(1913-   )

and ROCKY GRAZIANO
(1922-   )

Never in the annals of licensed brutality was there a private war like Zale vs. Graziano! Not one of their three title bouts went six full rounds, yet they provided more fireworks than most fans had seen in a generation of mayhem.

Prior to their first meeting, neither fighter

could be classed as a world-beater, and once separated, each quickly vanished from middleweight prominence. But together they were great. How come?

Certainly the pairing had all the dramatic ingredients you could want: old champion vs. young challenger . . . solid citizen vs. irresponsible brat . . . Chicago (via Gary, Indiana) vs. New York (courtesy of Brooklyn). But even more important than these assets were the motivating conditions—(1) Tony and Rocky realized that if they didn't murder each other, their fighting days were numbered, (2) neither had any intention of going 15 rounds, and (3) each was sufficiently untutored to resort to desperate measures. Thus was born one of the great rivalries of the modern era, a feud comparable to Nelson vs. Gans, Ketchel vs. Papke, and Jack Britton vs. Ted Kid Lewis.

Their first death-defying feat took place in Yankee Stadium on Spetember 27, 1946. Gary's "Man of Steel" was thirty-two, a veteran of twelve years in the ring and a champion who hadn't defended his title in five years. Anthony Florian Zaleski had served out the war as a petty officer first class. In Puerto Rico, where he was stationed for the most part, he'd kept in pretty good shape putting sailors through their paces. Following his discharge in December of '45, he'd set out along the tune-up circuit and had six knockouts in a row behind him when he climbed in against Graziano.

Rocco Barbella, Brooklyn's favorite juvenile delinquent, was twenty-four, a Marciano in miniature with a brawling style and a runaway right hand. A great crowd-pleaser, Rocky was also that rare phenomenon, a fight fan's fighter. In his five short years of campaigning he'd racked up 32 kayos in 54 bouts, losing 6 fights by decision.

Graziano was lousy with good health and local color; Zale had just recovered from a severe case of pneumonia. In the chill night air, the excitement crackled like sparks on a trolley wire.

Zale, an excavator, went right to work on the Graziano midsection, and in less than a minute Rocky was rolling around on the canvas like a kid with a stomach ache. But he bounced back wielding Indian clubs. Why, these two guys wanted to kill each other!

Near the end of the second round Graziano's vaunted right hand caught Zale on the chops, and dropping an odd curtsey, the champ keeled over. Rocky was so fired up for the kill that referee Ruby Goldstein had to drag him away, but the bell saved Tony at the count of four.

The next three rounds were strictly from ancient Rome. Graziano went berserk, hurling knockout blows in wild, looping trajectories. Zale lurched and spun—a reveler on a queerly lit street. It seemed impossible that he could survive. His right thumb was broken, his knees pointed every which way. But

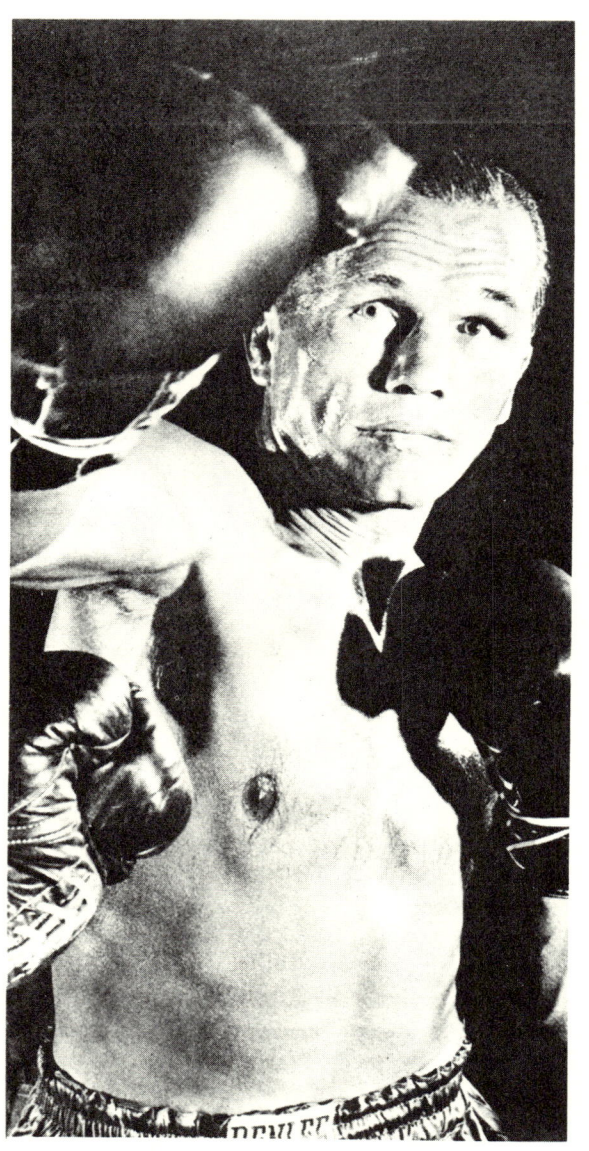

The name Tony Zale is permanently notched in history books. In 1958, he was elected to the Boxing Hall of Fame. (UPI)

Rocky was wild enough to bungle the job, and Tony stayed alive.

The Stadium was in an uproar as the sixth round began. Graziano huffed and puffed, and then he paused for breath. Zale did not hesitate. This was it—"the moment of truth," as the aficionados would say. The man from Gary slammed his broken right hand into Graziano's breadbasket and followed with a stunning left hook that brought down his tormentor and the house.

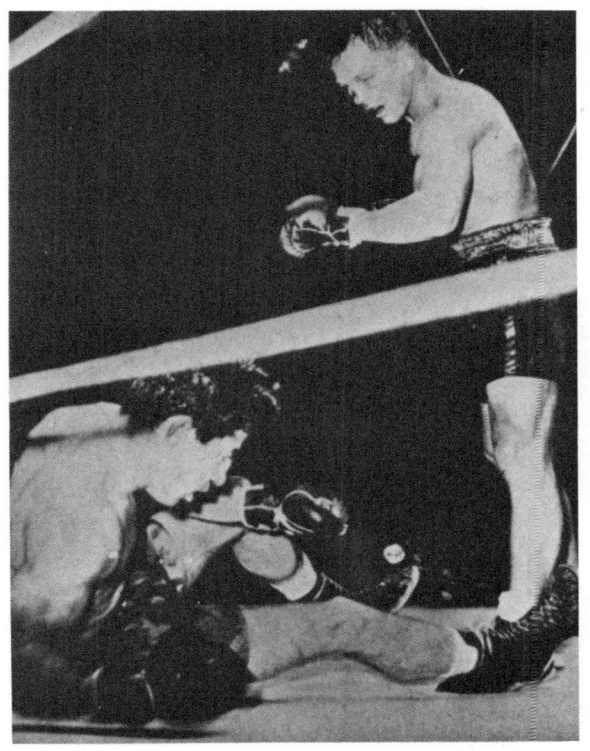

In blood-spattered bout at Yankee Stadium in 1946, Zale rocked Graziano to sleep in 6th round. (INS)

It was all over. In less than six rounds two desperate men had given the fight game back to the fans. The gross gate was $342,497. Each fighter received $78,892.82—a record payday for a middleweight bout.

"We really earned the dough," Graziano recalled. "He hurt me plenty. I got a terrific pasting around the body from a great fighter. I urinated blood for several weeks. For a couple of days after the fight I was still dazed."

On his table in the dressing room Zale looked like a man who'd been beaten up by a gang of hoodlums. His face was haggard with pain; he was speechless from exhaustion. But the writers had their story: Tony Zale, the "retread" champion, the "pug" who'd lost to Billy Soose, had gone and got himself one helluva win!

If the first bout resembled a benefit for Murder, Inc., the return match was a two-man riot. Tear gas couldn't have torn these vicious rivals apart.

The fight took place in Chicago's sweltering indoor Stadium, on July 16, 1947.

"Tony was the only fighter who'd ever knocked me out," Graziano said. "And I was in there for revenge. It was no boxing match. It was a private war, and if there hadn't been a referee, one of us would've wound up dead. The fight lasted only 18 minutes, but I still get nightmares thinking about it!"

Once again Zale took charge at the opening gong. He punched an eye-filling hole above Graziano's right orb.

"It was like he hit me with a gun butt," Rocky recollected. "He ripped it wider in the second and really went to work on me in the third."

Tony floored Rocky with a right to the jaw. As usual, Graziano bounced back without waiting for the count and ran into a murderous barrage that would have reduced most fighters to selling pencils on street corners.

Rocky was in bad shape when the round ended, and the referee wanted to stop it. The challenger pleaded for time. Okay, one more round, the referee warned, and if the carnage continued . . .

Rocky was virtually blind in his right eye. The swelling had closed it shut. Frank Percoco, his cut man, took a quarter out of his pocket and used the hard edge to open the swelling.

"How's that, Rocky?" Percoco asked.

"Better," Rocky grunted. "The vision's back."

In the dramatic reversal that followed, Graziano was completely oblivious of the crowd, the referee, the frantic ministrations of his seconds. Zale was only a blur still in his right eye, but the ex-street fighter waded in with mawkish brutality, slobbering curses and hurling wild roundhouse punches.

The thermometer showed 105 degrees in the fetid enclosure and worse under the ring lights. The bug-eyed fans, dripping wet in their shirtsleeves, had paid to see a repeat of the first scrap, and that was exactly what they were getting. It was, in polite parlance, a "revolting spectacle"—a cruel, bloody roughhouse that couldn't possibly last the distance. The two sluggers simply beat each other to a pulp until one of them, Zale, could no longer raise his leaden arms. Then, in the sixth, the referee stepped in and shielded Tony from Rocky's bull-like charges. Maybe you saw the picture in the papers afterward. Tony was hanging over the middle strand of the ropes, his gloves nearly touching the canvas, and Rocky was right behind him slamming his right hand into Tony's back. Tony took 11 or 12 of those punches on the back before the referee pulled Rocky away and let them take Tony out of the heat.

Graziano, still off his nut with rage and blood lust, began pummeling Whitey Bimstein, his trainer. And as the crowd roared, Whitey kept slapping him in the face and croaking, "Rocky, snap out of it! Hey—Rocky! You're the world's champeen!"

A radio announcer thrust a microphone at the besotted champ. "Hey, Ma!" Rocky bawled. "Your bad boy done it!"

"The ref shouldn't have stopped it," Zale said in the dressing room. "I wasn't down."

"You would have been killed," he was told.

"I'm a champion," Tony said. "The only way a champion is supposed to lose is to get knocked dead on the floor."

The slugfest drew $422,920, a new indoor record.

After the fight, Rocky went back to the hotel and with his wife went into the bedroom to wake their little daughter Audrey and tell her that her father was the middleweight

Rocky Graziano, right, evened the score by stopping Zale in the 6th round at Chicago, in 1947, to become middleweight champion. (INS)

champion of the world. Audrey was three then, and when they woke her she stood up in the crib and looked at her father and saw the bandages over one eye and the other eye swollen and closed and the welts on his face.

"What happened, Daddy?" Audrey asked sleepily.

"You see what I said?" Rocky said, bending over and pointing his finger at Audrey. "Now stay outta the gutter."

Years later, Bill Heinz bumped into Frank Percoco at Stillman's Gym. In the big, quiet room of the main gym two lightweights were sparring under the two naked light bulbs over one of the rings. Percoco was standing behind the empty rows of chairs, watching, when Bill came in.

"Have you still got that quarter from Chicago?" Bill asked him.

"Sure," Frank said. "You don't think I'd let go of that, do you?"

And Bill said, "I never knew of twenty-five cents that paid off at such a price."

Eleven months after Rocky stopped Zale in Chicago, the third and last of their Sweet Tickets was on again, this time in Newark, New Jersey, June 10, 1948. Tony regained the middleweight truss by a knockout in the third, but the rubber match was another slam-bang affair in the tradition of the Dempsey-Firpo fight.

Following their great series, the old pro, now thirty-five, and the brash youngster, still only twenty-six, rapidly lost ground. On September 21, 1948, in Jersey City, the great Marcel Cerdan took Zale's title and retired him from the prize ring forever. The Frenchman clobbered the goat-browed ex-gob for 11 rounds before referee Paul Cavalier counted him out on his stool.

Meanwhile, Graziano continued to kayo minor opponents. Then he challenged Ray Robinson for the championship in Chicago, April 16, 1952. To earn a shot at Robinson, Rocky had to come from behind and knock out Tony Janiro in Detroit, with only 25 seconds left in the fight. "I remember walking back to my corner at the end of the 9th round and my manager saying to me, 'Rocky, you're going to lose the fight. You're behind, you gotta knock him out to win,'" Graziano recalled recently. "But in that last round, it was obvious that Tony had slowed up. Luckily, I spotted an opening and smashed him with one good shot and he went down on his back and was counted out. But Tony was a good, tough kid, a very good fighter, and he nearly ended my career that night."

Robinson versus Graziano was a classic match. It pitted brawler against a master boxer. White against black. Brooklyn opposing Harlem. Rocky went into the fight with 52 knockouts; only Zale (twice) had ever been able to stop him. As for Sugar Ray, he had the amazing career record of 130 wins, only two losses—once to Randy Turpin and once to Jake LaMotta—and he avenged both defeats by walloping Jake and stopping Randy. Thus, the match for which America had been waiting seven years was set. A near-record crowd of 22,264 jammed the Chicago Stadium.

Robinson, a 4–1 favorite, weighed 157¼ lbs. for the fight; Rocky came in at 159½.

Fighting out of a half-crouch, similar to Rocky Marciano, Graziano kept crowding Sugar Ray in the first round, waiting for an opening, hoping the champ would make a mistake. Neither man gave ground. Robinson showed respect for Rocky, keeping him off with his left hand and smart combination punching. Sugar Ray had a slight edge in points at the end of the round. Rocky, with a reputation as a slugger, surprised many with his boxing skill. Don Dunphy, who broadcast the fight, said: "You can't tell from the first round how the fight is going to go, it is that close."

Both men were much more deliberate in the second round. Rocky continued to stalk Ray, forcing him against the ropes, cutting off escape routes, trying to set him up for a right hand. The action was fast, but neither man was hurt.

"So far," Dunphy told his audience, "it's a very close match, with Robinson barely ahead on points. Rocky . . . stalking, stalking, stalking; Robinson, counterpunching with that left jab." All of the action came in the third round.

Suddenly, Rocky exploded with his right and Robinson went down. It was a genuine knockdown. There was no mandatory eight count, however, and Robinson was back on his feet instantly. A minute to go, and the champion got on his horse and backpedaled. Rocky let him get away. He had had Robinson in real trouble, but when the fog cleared, it was the same old Robinson once more, moving around the ring, first to the left and then to the right, both hands pumping. Then, without warning, the guillotine fell. Ray drove home a right-hand smash to the jaw and Rocky was counted out.

Looking back on the bout today, Graziano says: "The only pre-fight strategy I had was to go in there and punch. That's all I could do, punch. I really thought I could knock him out. But Ray doublecrossed me and knocked me out instead."

"My main thought was to keep from being hit with that hard right fist of his," Sugar Ray adds. "Fortunately, that punch Rocky hit me with in the third round was a little high; good thing he didn't hit me on the chin, or probably they'd still be counting over me. It was a clean knockdown, no fluke. When you fight a guy like Rocky, you're either C-sharp or B-flat—you must be in tune or end up in the meat wagon."

"I didn't really hit him good," Graziano recalls. "But when he went down and then got up, I figured to rush him and finish the job. But Sugar Ray was a beautiful boxer, his legs were still nimble, and I couldn't catch up with him."

Graziano fought his last professional fight five months after the Robinson defeat. It was against the college kid from Michigan State, Chuck Davey, and Rocky lost the decision in 10. That was all for the pug from Brooklyn.

Tony Zale reached the top the hard way. After 95 amateur bouts (50 K.O.'s, 37 decisions, 8 losses), Tony spent two Depression years trying to convince himself that getting messed up—and occasionally messing up other guys—was more profitable than working in Gary steel mills. He might have returned to the mills permanently if Sam Pian and Art Winch hadn't discovered him at the late age of twenty-four. They made him an inside fighter, matched him with the right opponents and masterminded a shot at the N.B.A. championship.

In his two fights with the recognized world champ Al Hostak, Tony came from behind to establish himself as the guttiest of the gutty. He came in over the weight for their first (non-title) bout in Chicago. Hostak beat him to shreds in five rounds before Zale came roaring back to win going away. The victory earned him a shot at the world championship in Al's home town, Seattle, where Zale withstood another barrage, then destroyed the defending champion in the 13th round.

When Billy Soose vacated the New York State title, the N.B.A. proposed that Zale fight George Abrams for the undisputed world crown. They met in Madison Square Garden on November 28, 1941, and Tony won on points after butting Abrams' left eye early in the match.

After stepping up to the light-heavyweight division and losing a 12-round decision to Billy Conn, Zale said goodbye to boxing for the duration. He joined the Navy. Tony remained in it so long that few could say, off-hand, who the champion of the middleweight division was.

On a night in Toots Shor's during the war some of the mob were sitting around talking about the current champions and comparing them to those who had gone before them, which is one of the oldest subjects of saloon discussions. They did all right with Joe Louis, who was in the Army, and Gus Lesnevich, who was in the Coast Guard, but when they got to the middleweight champion there was an embarrassed silence.

"I give up," one of them said. "Who is he?"

After a pause, another said:

"I can't think of his name but I can see him. He is that flat-faced, blue-eyed Pole out of Gary, Indiana."

Then:

"I got him. Tony Zale."

When Zale was discharged after four years he went right back to Gary, picked up his championship belt and defended it nobly. The fight mob remembered who he was, all right, that night in 1946 at Yankee Stadium when he rocked Graziano to sleep.

History did not forget Tony Zale again.

In 1958, he was elected to the Boxing Hall of Fame.

Rocky Graziano's first big splash came in 1945. He was only twenty-three at the time, a hard-bitten, big-mouthed alley fighter off the streets of New York's rough East Side, where you learned to fight before you could walk. He talked tough and acted tough, and from the day Irving Cohen, fight manager, took him over, had demanded fights with the best in the country. "Get me Robinson," he roared for a week. This despite the fact that in his last five fights he had fought two small-club draws and then clumsily lost a pair of 10-round Garden decisions to Harold Green.

Cohen did not get him Robinson, but he did get him Billy Arnold, who was nineteen and being hailed as the new Joe Louis.

"I'll knock his brains out," Rocky said. "He's mine. I'll give him to ya for a present when I'm through."

Despite his youth, Arnold hit with the authority of a thirty-year-old veteran and had lost only one of his last 33 fights. He had scored 28 knockouts. Graziano had compiled a good record, too, piling up 25 K.O.'s in 46 bouts, but he had been held even and beaten by guys who didn't approach Arnold's class. The oddsmakers in New York firmly established Arnold as a huge choice. You couldn't find a guy who gave Rocky a chance. He was regarded just as a small-club fighter being thrown in with a polished comer who was likely to stiffen him in one round.

But you couldn't tell that to Rocky. He kept telling his mob, "Bet me. The odds are terrific. Bet me and I'll make a lot of cabbage for ya." Arnold was anywhere from 5–1 to 12–1 and there were no takes—except one. Rocky put down a flat bet on himself. Because of Arnold's age, the bout was limited to eight rounds. There was a crowd of 14,037 in Madison Square Garden that night.

Everybody was surprised in the first round as Rocky went out, pressed his man and made Billy look bad. Arnold had scored 14 first-round knockouts, but now Graziano was on top of him, throwing right hands to the midsection and causing trouble. But Arnold settled down in the second round and shook Rocky from head to heels with a wicked left hook over his low-slung right. Rocky rocked, and then came on, catching a whistling straight right hand. For the next three minutes Arnold battered Rocky all over the ring while the crowd roared. That was what they had come to see. It didn't seem possible Rocky could stand up. Time after time right hands set him on his heels.

In the corner, Cohen leaned over to Whitey Bimstein, the trainer. "We better stop it," he said. "We'll lose not only the fight, but the fighter, too, if this keeps going."

The career of Graziano was in the balance. At the bell his handlers rushed up the steps. They were intent on stopping the fight in the corner and it would mean the third straight Garden loss for Rocky, and almost certain elimination from boxing's big time.

"How are ya, Rocky?" Bimstein rasped as he bent over the fighter.

"Fine," Rocky replied.

"Do you know who this is talkin' to ya?"

"Whitey," Rocky said, "I'm surprised at ya. The bum hit me some pretty good shots but you oughta know I take better than that. I got this guy openin' up now. I'm goin' out there and knock his head off, right in this round."

The bell for the third round rang and Rocky went out after his man. As Billy pulled back to throw a left hook, Rocky got his first big punch in. It was a looping right hand—the punch which was to send him to the middleweight championship two years later. The right caught Arnold on the chin and it was all over. Arnold was badly hurt and Graziano leaped in like a tiger. If there was one thing Rocky could do with his hands, it was to finish off a man who was hurt. He had the killer instinct and now it was working overtime. He connected with another solid right and this time Billy went down. Somehow, he got up, just beating the count. Graziano raced after him again and once more Billy went down. This time he pulled himself up and staggered along the ropes to his feet at the count of six. He was dazed but his eyes were clear. The referee allowed the fight to continue and Rocky tore in. He grabbed Arnold by the throat with his left hand and began to hammer right hands into the helpless Billy's face. Billy sagged into a neutral corner for the count of seven, got up again and was caught with one wicked right before the referee decided it was over at 1:54.

After the fight, Graziano was roaring. "I tole ya I'd do it. What'd I tell ya? The bum never hurt me. I just wanted him to open up."

Over in the loser's dressing room, Arnold looked around his room, then asked reporters, "What hit me?" The fight left its mark on him, too. He never was able to make another good fight. In 7 minutes and 54 seconds of fighting, a champion was born—and a great prospect killed off.

After that, Graziano, the former inmate of Riker's Island and Fort Leavenworth, enjoyed huge success as the Bad Boy Who Made Good. Upon retirement from the ring, his round pizza smile was everywhere in evidence as a "guest" of Show Biz and various schools, where he lectured the youngsters on citizenship. Hollywood films even gave his life story the full treatment, complete with message.

Red Smith once recalled the afternoon that "Professor" Rocky was asked to address a dancing school for children in Manhattan on physical culture. Rocky's little daughter was a member of the class. The place was crawling with moppets and mommas and photographers. He wore slacks and a gleaming white shirt with the cuffs turned back and a small rust-colored bow tie.

Hips-deep in small fry, Rocky did a little tap dance for the benefit of the photographers. His feet went slappety-slappety, slippety-slap. He was pretty good at it. The picture-taking went on for a solid hour. When all the cameras were gone, the children squatted tailor-fashion on the floor and Rocky stood facing them, flexing his arms.

"Now, children," he began, "I'd like to see you quiet."

They chattered on rapturously.

"Quiet!" the lady instructor commanded. "Mr. Graziano is going to speak to you."

They subsided slightly.

"Now, dancing," Rocky told them, "is very good for you, especially for boys. When I was real young, I t'ought dancing might make a sissy out of ya, but it's very, very good for youse. If youse is good little boys and girls maybe someday youse'll be movie stars."

His audience squealed.

"Youse don't wanna be movie stars?" Rocky said. "Who wanna be movie stars?"

There was a babble of voices.

"Well," Rocky, said, "ya got any questions for me?"

Nobody had.

"My last fight," Rocky volunteered, "went 10 rounds."

The response was confused.

"Well," he said, "that's all I can tell 'em. What else can I tell 'em?"

He turned back to the tots and said, "God bless ya, and be good citizens."

Dick Schaap, author and editor of *Sport* magazine, said he would never forget the first meeting with Rocky. They met in the office of Rocky's agent to discuss collaborating on an

A triumphant Rocky Graziano dramatically stands over slumbering Johnny Greco. Rocky won by a 3rd-round K.O. in the 1951 match at Montreal. (INS)

article together. Rocky had quit boxing, and he was into the acting bit.

"Do you still work out?" Schaap asked him.

"Oh, yeah," he said, "I wukk out uppa Gottam."

Rocky's agent translated for Dick: "He said he works out at the Gotham Health Club."

"What do you do there?" Schaap asked.

"Uh, I wukk out," Rocky said, "uh, with Paul Newman, Ben Gazzara, Tony Franciosa . . ."

"That's terrific," Schaap said. "With friends like that, do you ever go to the Actors Studio?"

At that time, the Actors Studio was the hottest thing in acting. There they stressed barechested, plain-spoken method acting.

"Oh, yeah," Rocky said. "Funny ting ya should ask that. I was up dere jus the udder day. I walk up the stairs, I go inside and dere's four guys standin' in a corner learnin' how to be actors. And ya know what?"

"No, what?" Schaap said.

"Dey're all trin' tuh talk like me."

MARCEL CERDAN
(1916–1949)

One of the most tragic events in boxing history was the death of former middleweight champion Marcel Cerdan in a plane crash in the Azores on October 27, 1949. Cerdan, the greatest of all French champions, was enroute to the States to take back the title that Jake LaMotta had snitched from him. But this was incidental. The world grieved because Marcel had succeeded where de Gaulle had failed—he had revived the pride and prestige of a battered nation.

The only precedent for Cerdan's immense popularity on both sides of the Atlantic was the adulation of the French war hero, Georges Carpentier, during the Twenties. But Cerdan was more than a match for his American competitors. On September 21, 1948, in Jersey City, the Frenchman won the title by reducing tough Tony Zale to a helpless wreck in 11 rounds. He lost the title in Detroit on June 10, 1949, to the unpopular LaMotta. Though hopelessly handicapped by an injury to his left arm in the first round, Marcel survived ten rounds against an opponent he would otherwise have mauled.

Born in Sidi-bel-Abbes, Algeria, of French-Spanish parentage, Cerdan was raised in a family "stable" with three fighting brothers and their manager, Cerdan pere, a benign butcher. During the invasion of France he served briefly in the coast artillery before the Germans relieved him of his duties and sent him back to Casablanca.

Marcel and Lucien Roupp, the manager appointed by Papa Cerdan, journeyed to France in 1942 to meet the Spanish champion, Jose Ferrer, for the European title. Cerdan flattened the Spaniard in Paris in 83 seconds, but the Germans pronounced Ferrer the winner when Cerdan passed up a banquet in his honor and hurried home to Casablanca. He did not collect his share of the purse—a million francs—until 1945.

The handsome middleweight disposed of Gustave Humery, European welterweight champ, in a mere 21 seconds and, discounting a few disqualifications, won all his fights, prior to his great showing in the States.

In his debut against Georgie Abrams in the Garden on December 6, 1946, the rugged Cerdan immediately endeared himself to the crowd. Abrams was lucky to survive the ten rounder.

Then Marcel kayoed Harold Green in two heats, and thereby hangs a tale. On his last day of heavy work before the fight, the Frenchman broke his right hand sparring a light-heavyweight. Roupp, who was acting as his trainer, co-managers Sammy Richman and Jo Longman, and Lew Burston, who had brought Cerdan to the States, argued and pleaded with the young man to cancel the match. Cerdan was adamant! He'd never withdrawn from a fight—*jamais!*—the show must go on! . . . *c'est une question d'honneur!* . . . of course, he would fight!

On the eve of the Garden engagement on March 28, 1947, the bookmakers found out about that bum hand, and the 14–5 odds on Cerdan fell to even money. Green was no pushover—he'd beaten Rocky Graziano two out of three fights—and an upset win would have placed him in contention for the title.

Cerdan knew that Green's weakness was a right to the forehead. In the second round he saw an opening and caught Green above the brow with a one-shot right that floored his opponent. Neither Green nor the 19,000 howling customers knew what that blow had cost Cerdan. He made certain of that when Green got up and came after him again. Marcel used his right once more to block a left hook and then countered with a brutal left to the gut.

Marcel Cerdan's last fight. Jake LaMotta, facing camera, won Cerdan's title, June 16, 1949, in Detroit, when the Frenchman could no longer continue because of injured hand. (UPI)

Green went down, and referee Eddie Joseph ended the proceedings at 2:19.

Forty-eight people died in the plane crash in 1949, including Ginette Neveu, the violinist, and Boutet de Monvel, the well-known portrait painter. But it was the name of Marcel Cerdan that spoke for all the rest in headlines throughout the world. When Lew Burston heard the news, his hair turned grey. Even Jake LaMotta wept and lit a candle.

In recognition of Cerdan's courage, gallantry and sportsmanship, the French government awarded him the posthumous title of a *chevalier* in the Legion of Honor.

JAKE LaMOTTA
(1921–)

Jake LaMotta, the Bronx misanthrope, parlayed a jail record into the middleweight championship of the world. Jake, by his own admission, began stealing at the age of ten—little things like hub caps, copper wiring and typewriters. Once it was a violin. Caught in a burglary, he threw a hatchet at a cop. While awaiting sentence for that, he waylaid a shop owner and hit him over the head so hard with an iron pipe that he didn't find out till he got out of jail that the man had lived. "He was paler . . . grayer and weak-lookin', but alive," said Jake without emotion.

When he became a famous fighter, Jake repaid his loyal fans by throwing a fight to a Blinky Palermo fighter named Billy Fox. When he quit fighting, he left his faithful wife and three kids, opened a saloon in Miami and ran it until he got picked up and sent to jail again for contributing to the delinquency of a fourteen-year-old girl.

LaMotta was one of the most unpopular champions of all time, and therein lay the secret of his perverse appeal. Fans by the thousands turned out to "hate Jake" and see the little monster brought to heel by some clean young middleweight *sans peur et sans reproche*. In return, Jake cordially detested most people. The late Jimmy Cannon recalled a typical LaMotta incident that happened in a New York spaghetti joint. Rocky Graziano and LaMotta were eating up a storm when an old man walked over to pay his respects.

"Sit down," said Rocky, good-naturedly.

"No!" LaMotta snarled. "Don't sit down! I don't want no part of you!"

Bewildered and offended, the old man left.

"Whaddya wanna act that way for?" Rocky demanded.

"Because I don't want no friends," LaMotta snapped back.

One can only imagine the mean little world of Jake LaMotta, a world of hostile shadows where night comes early. In Jake's book, everyone was a "bum" and only nice guys finish last. Jake seldom finished last, and only one fighter had his number—Sugar Ray Robinson. The dancing man beat him five times, though in their second meeting, in Detroit, February 5, 1943, Jake won the decision to become the first fighter to beat Robinson in a professional contest.

The barrel-shaped LaMotta became the foremost authority on Robinson.

"He fought only in spurts," Jake said, describing Ray at his peak. "When he hit, he used short punches in lightning combinations. He aimed at a specific target, and he could knock you out with a punch. He made a fighter fight his fight. He could be the aggressor and lay back and counter. Weight didn't mean a thing to him. He was too fast for the ordinary fighter and socked like a heavyweight because of his speed and timing. Strength doesn't make power. It's coordination, balance and leverage."

Robinson treated 30 million viewers—14,802 on the scene and the rest clustered around television sets in 39 states—to one of the goriest spectacles in recent years when he seized LaMotta's middleweight crown in Chicago Stadium on St. Valentine's Day, 1951. Though a 7-2 underdog, Jake forced the fight. He trudged forward, swinging from a low crouch. He brought blood from Robinson's nose. LaMotta was ahead as the 9th round began, but Robinson had shrewdly paced himself. After being pinned against the ropes for 20 dramatic seconds in the 11th round, Robinson counterattacked. By the 12th round LaMotta was all but defenseless. He was too groggy even to keep his guard up. "I kept swinging," said Robinson afterwards, "and he kept standing." Ray used every combination in his vast repertoire in a vain effort to knock Jake off his feet. Jake was a mess, but he would not go down.

In 2 minutes and 4 seconds of the 13th round, a ringside statistician computed that LaMotta was hit 56 times before the referee mercifully stopped the fight. For days afterward, in elevators and lunchrooms, on trains and street corners, Americans everywhere discussed it with the excitement of people who had seen a prizefight that had everything—an underdog who went out ahead, a sudden turn in the tide, an unbelievable display of gameness and a great fighter winning a championship.

Five months later Irish Bob Murphy, a redheaded dock-walloper, mauled Jake something awful, and this time LaMotta called it quits after seven rounds. No "bum" was going to floor Jake LaMotta.

This amoeba in boxing gloves—this personification of a Bronx Cheer—was likewise unorthodox in his training habits. Harry Stickevers, the veteran manager, told me that Jake was beyond understanding. "Once before a fight I saw him sit down and drink a bottle of wine and eat a couple of plates of spaghetti," Harry said. "He did everything to the hilt—eat, work, play, fight. He worked hard in the gym. He burned up sparring partners in relays. He'd go 15 rounds of continuous sparring daily."

The squat (5 ft., 8 in.) LaMotta was endowed with a pair of arms that seemed to move like tentacles, constantly weaving, flailing, striking from all angles. His left hook was deadly, and his sneak overhand right a constant peril. He liked to return punch for punch, and on the inside, he could break an opponent wide open. No one could hold him. Basically he fought in a style that seemed natural to him. He kept coming at an opponent. They hit him and he kept coming. They hit him harder and still he came. He took their best shots and didn't go down and they realized, with the beginnings of terror, that Jake, who didn't seem to mind pain or shock, sooner or later was going to knock them silly. He could take a beating that would knock another man senseless. Even when he dumped to the powerful light-heavyweight, Billy Fox, in 1947, Jake stayed on his feet. He took a terrible beating that night. He had been paid to take a beating. But his pride was such that he refused to go down and finally the referee had to stop the fight in the fourth. LaMotta lost as arranged, but stayed true to his conscience, such as it was.

LaMotta was extremely dangerous in the clutch. "Take the night LaMotta beat Laurent Dauthuille," said Randy Turpin, recalling the 1950 title bout in Detroit. "The announcer kept saying Jake was through, out on his feet. Yet what did he do? He knocked out the Frenchman in the 15th round—the last 13 seconds of the fight. Just one punch!"

LaMotta was born in New York City on July 10, 1921. He turned pro in 1941, and in Detroit eight years later, on June 10, 1949, he kayoed Marcel Cerdan in the 10th round for the world championship. After the fight, Jack Dempsey was asked for his appraisal of Jake.

"In action," Dempsey said, "LaMotta violates nearly all the fundamentals of punching and defense that oldtime trainers taught. If he'd been given the right instruction early in his career, there's no telling how far he'd gone. As it is, he just won the championship."

Cerdan, who had ruined his hand in the first round, was signed for a rematch four months later. The Frenchman was en route to America for this return bout when he died in a plane crash in the Azores, October 27, 1949.

LaMotta held the middleweight crown for 20 months and successfully defended it twice against Tiberio Mitri and Dauthuille before Robinson caught up with him. On April 14, 1954, Billy Kilgore won a 10-round decision from Jake at Miami Beach, and soon after Jake formally announced his withdrawal from the fight racket. No one was sorry to see him go. The feeling was mutual.

"I'm not trying to whitewash myself," LaMotta said later. "I was a thief, I threw a fight, I did two terms in jail and I'm lucky I wasn't a murderer. But those rats who run boxing made me look like Little Lord Fauntleroy by comparison."

Jake finally took his revenge upon all society under the most unlikely circumstances. For some opaque reason he was drawn to the stage and landed a role in *Clutterbuck*. He was given a 12-line curtain speech, which he "memorized" and promptly forgot. When his big moment arrived, Jake couldn't hear the prompter.

"Louder!" Jake yelled.

Then turning to the tittering audience, he bellowed:

"I HADDA HUNNERD FIGHTS! HOW MANY YOU HAD?"

SUGAR RAY ROBINSON
(1920–)

Sugar Ray Robinson is the only prizefighter in history ever to win the same world championship *five* times.

That's a record for instability that may last for a thousand years.

The Harlem Hotshot also owned another record: With the exception of Carmen Basilio, he knocked out every middleweight champion he ever fought.

The one-time undefeated welterweight champion and five-times middleweight titleholder scaled heights never achieved by any other fighter of any era. He has been called "the greatest fighter of his time."

He slugged the rugged Jake LaMotta to win the title for the first time. He stopped Randy Turpin after leaving the title in England on temporary lend-lease. He twice stiffened Bobo Olson, who had borrowed the crown while Ray was away dancing in a night club act. He demolished Gene Fullmer, his conqueror of an earlier match, with a single punch only two days before his thirty-seventh birthday.

In a career spanning 18 years, Robinson, 5 ft., 11 in., hammered out 181 professional victories, including 109 knockouts. A fast and clever fighter, he beat everything they could throw in with him. He could box, maneuver and punch exceptionally well. His box office magnetism was all that kept boxing in the big league for a long time.

Sugar Ray wasn't especially strong, yet he packed a punch like the kick of a misanthropic mule. The secret of his special stiffener, he said, lay in perfect coordination and the speed with which he unloaded on his befuddled victims. He knocked out 9 of his first 10 opponents, 6 in the first heat, as an amateur.

His knockout record after turning professional was incredible. He belted out 20 of the first 25 combatants he met, 9 before they heard the second bell.

"I started hitting better after I turned pro because I slowed down," Robinson told me. "In the amateurs a boy fights only three rounds and he has to go at top speed all the way. He's not balanced right to let go a punch. But in the pros, the fights are longer and he has more time to work and size up his opponent. He can maneuver a guy and set himself to get all his power into it."

Born in Detroit, May 3, 1920, Robinson was more interested in making his feet, not his hands, behave when he was twelve and his parents separated. He moved from Detroit to New York with his mother and he had nothing on his mind but dancing. Watching his fancy footwork in the ring later, it wasn't difficult to envision him as a first-rate hoofer. To stretch his mother's income as a laundress, the boy hustled errands in a grocery store, shined shoes, danced for pennies on Broadway and Lindy-hopped like crazy at rent parties in Harlem. He just did manage to squeeze in three years at the De Witt Clinton High School.

When Ray was sixteen, he wandered into the Salem-Crescent Club and joined George Gainford's boxing class. Gainford belonged to the old school which believes a boy learns to fight by fighting. So he put Robinson to work jabbing and jolting at every grubby club which offered a watch or a few bucks under the bridge at midnight. Ray's amateur record showed 89 bouts, but the truer number was closer to 125—all wins.

Those were the days when the bootleg amateur circuit was flourishing. Robinson said a gent whose name, spelled by ear, came out "Zavalavavitch," gave him a worse licking than any professional he was ever to meet later.

"He never had me on the floor," Ray said, "but he did everything but slug me with a ball bat. I knew nobody could hurt me after I got out of the ring alive."

Robinson picked up his nickname on the bootleg wheel. He beat a Canadian champion something awful one night at Watertown, New York.

"Max Kase, of the old New York *Journal-American,* was at ringside," Sugar Ray recalled. "I was climbing out of the ring after just scoring one of my first few knockouts as an amateur—I never kayoed many opponents in those early years—and Max said to my manager, George Gainford, 'That's a sweet-lookin' kid ya got.' An' a lady in the front row overheard him and piped up, 'Yeah, he's *sweet as sugar!*' Max put it all together and later I changed my name legally from Walker Smith to Sugar Ray Robinson. Robinson? I once borrowed the name from a Harlem barkeeper and never bothered to give it back."

When Ray told that story to Graziano, Rocky was reminded of how he picked up his fighting name.

"My real name was Rocco Barbella," Rocky said. "But I got into trouble with the law when I was a kid and the boxing commission wouldn't give me a license to fight. So I went to this guy named Rocco Graziano and told him to loan me his birth certificate so I could get a license to fight. He said, sure, and I used his name to get the license. Later, I found out that the original Rocco Graziano had a bigger police record than me!"

Sugar Ray turned professional on October 4, 1940, knocking out Joe Echeverria in two in New York. Nine months later, after winning 19 more bouts, 16 by knockouts, he beat Sammy Angott, the lightweight ruler, in Philadelphia's Shilo Park, playing an *allegro con brio* with his hands on Angott's face for 10 furious rounds.

Four months later Robinson, having outgrown the lightweight class, moved up to the welterweights. The man he drew this time was tough Fritzie Zivic, the flat-nosed, pulp-eared veteran of more than 100 scraps, clearly established as the king of the division.

Zivic was a mean bloke. He had learned the fundamentals of his brutal trade as a small boy in his father's saloon in Pittsburgh. When the entire Zivic brood, including Pop and four older brothers, became embroiled with spirited neighbors in spirits, young Fritzi helped defend the family honor and property by crawling along the bar rail biting alien legs.

Robinson had to give away six and a half pounds and a lifetime of experience to Zivic. He was meeting a cutie who knew every trick in the book. Again the wise guys were skeptical that the undefeated Sugar Ray could retain his status and his health. They weren't too sure he could take care of himself in the clinches and didn't know how he would react to a stiff poke in the puss or whether he was gaited to go 10 swift rounds with a good and resourceful puncher.

All the questions were answered and punctuated emphatically by Robinson's cutting and slashing gloves. He really won the fight by out-roughing and out-smarting and out-punching Zivic in the clinches. The wise old gaffer fetched Robinson a soulful clop on the chop and staggered him in the seventh round, but Ray bounced back like an election repeater in the eighth and cooled off Zivic for the remainder of the exercises.

Two months later Robinson made the victory stick by knocking out Zivic in the 10th round.

If Robinson had a fault in those early days, it was a strong tendency to go haywire and ignore Gainford's instructions from the corner. Before the opening bell in the first Zivic match, Gainford shouted in his ear:

"Go out and hit him on the chin with the first punch. Take a chance and whomp him a good one, ya hear?"

Robinson proceeded to box Zivic dizzy. He didn't toss a good one until the third round. Going into the last round it was obvious he had the decision pretty well wrapped up. Gainford issued another order:

"Stay away from him! Don't slug with him!

THE ENCYCLOPEDIA OF WORLD BOXING CHAMPIONS

Just stick and slide! Keep away from him, and you is home free!"

So Robinson knocked, and not boxed, Zivic's ears off in an all-out effort for a knockout.

In spite of this fault, Robinson always had unusual poise, even in the twilight of his career when the holes began to show. After Angott nailed him with a crushing left hook and drove him to the ropes, Robinson drifted back to his corner and laughed off his handlers' anxious frowns.

"The guy's a sucker for throwing that left hook," he said. "The next time he does it I'm going to slap him silly with a right cross."

He did.

From the beginning, Robinson had one characteristic which is the hallmark of a good fighter: He would fight back like a fiend when the situation looked darkest for him. In one of his early pro bouts he and Oliver White each landed a bomb simultaneously on the other's chin, and both hit the canvas at the same precise instant. Robinson got up and knocked out White with the next punch.

Sugar Ray won 40 straight professional fights before Jake LaMotta beat him in 10 rounds in Detroit, February 5, 1943. After Marty Servo abdicated the welterweight crown in 1946, Robinson beat Tommy Bell to claim the title. Then, on February 14, 1951, he picked up the middleweight champion-

Bobo Olson ducked the glove of Sugar Ray Robinson but lost a close decision in 1952 middleweight title bout in San Francisco. All told, Robinson won the middleweight crown five times. (UPI)

ship by knocking out LaMotta in 13 rounds in Chicago, a title he was to handle as if he were playing a game of musical chairs.

In sequence, here it is again. After winning the middleweight title from LaMotta (1951), he lost it to Turpin (July, '51), won it back from Turpin (September, '51), retired, then regained the crown from Bobo Olson (1955), lost it to Gene Fullmer (January, 1957), regained it from Fullmer (May, '57), lost it to Carmen Basilio (September, '57), and regained it from Basilio for a final time (March 25, 1958).

On the way to his comeback against Olson, Ray dropped a decision to Tiger Jones, a good but not spectacular campaigner. This was the second bout of a comeback from two-and-a-half years of retirement following a light-heavyweight title match with Joey Maxim. When he lost to Jones, the scholars wrote off the comeback as a failure. But Ray claimed that the Jones defeat actually did him some good.

"When I retired," Ray explained, "I was recognized as a good fighter, the best around at the weight. If it had been just win, win, win when I came back, it wouldn't be anything new. They'd just say, 'Well, there he is; there's still nobody around good enough.' When I lost to Jones, though, it made it a bigger thing I was trying to do. Even my own crowd quit on me. Nobody thought I could do it, and when I did it was a bigger thing. That's how the Jones fight was good for me."

In 1943, Ray whipped a man of championship caliber named Henry Armstrong. In the following 15 years, he met 11 good enough to hold world titles—Sammy Angott, Marty Servo, Fritzie Zivic, Kid Gavilan, LaMotta, Rocky Graziano, Olson, Turpin, Fullmer, Maxim and Basilio.

Joey Maxim was the only one on the list he did not defeat. Their June 25, 1952, title bout was fought in 104 degrees under Yankee Stadium lights and stands as the most bizarre championship fight of our time. Robinson, thirty-one, collapsed on his stool in the corner and could not come out for the 14th round when he had an unbeatable lead over Maxim and a third world title virtually in his grasp. Some scorecards had Sugar Ray winning by as much as 10–3 when the end came.

Robinson could not beat both the hottest June 25th night in New York history and the 15½ pounds he gave away. It went into the record book as a knockout for Maxim, the first knockout, such as it was, ever scored against Robinson in 202 professional fights.

For the first time in the history of championship prizefights, a referee was also knocked out. Referee Ruby Goldstein collapsed from the heat and had to be replaced by substitute Ray Miller in the 11th round.

A crowd of 47,983 paid more than $400,000 at the gate. This, plus $100,000 from theater TV, created a new receipts record for a light-heavyweight title bout, topping the $461,789 that the Paul Berlenback-Jack Delaney match drew 26 years before.

"I'm getting to be an old man," wheezed Robinson after the bout. "I can't laugh about it. Every time I get into a ring and lay it on the line, I get it proved to me. A punch lands on my jaw that shouldn't have. Or a punch of my own, that maybe should have ended the fight, doesn't land at all. I get hurt where I didn't used to get hurt. Try and laugh that off."

A swan song? Not in the least. In March of 1958 he was still climbing into the battle pit—and coming away with the world's championship!

"Why do you do it? Why do you continue to fight?" Ray was asked before beating Basilio in 15 rounds in the return title bout in Chicago.

"It's my ego," Ray said. "They say I'm cocky, they say this and that. Well, I *am* cocky. Show me any good fighter and he's got to be a cocky guy. Got to believe he can whip anybody. Yes, what's big to me is the honor. Little kids just want to reach out and touch you. That means more to me than the money."

Looking back over his career in the ring, Robinson identified Fritzie Zivic as the wiliest fighter he ever fought.

"He had all the answers," Ray said. "He was boxing's dictionary."

Robinson credits Artie Levine with hitting him the hardest.

"We met in Cleveland in 1946 and early in the match he hit me a shot I thought would bust my head," Ray said. "The first thing I remembered was the referee counting 5, and I thought to myself, gee, the ref's starting off with 5—what happened to 1, 2, 3 and 4? I was several rounds clearing the fog out of my head."

Out of the ring, Robinson was a friendly man. He was more handsome and more intelligent than most professional pugs, and he laughed easily. But once the bell rang, he underwent a startling metamorphosis. His kinky hair, smeared with stickum, actually stood on end. The red rubber mouthpiece distorted his face in a malevolent leer. His eyes were cold, angry.

Don Dunphy, the man Curt Gowdy calls "the greatest fight announcer who ever lived," believes that if you took every possible ingredient that goes to make a great prizefighter, Ray Robinson had them.

"He could box, he could punch (109 K.O.'s), he could take a punch (kayoed only once in 202 bouts), he was as game as they come (went 12 or more rounds 17 times), he had plenty of heart, and above all, he had great desire," Dunphy pointed out. "Any ingredient that any champion ever had—and I think Ray Robinson had them all."

Sugar Ray had three vices. He dreamed up break-neck dance routines (Bojangles Robinson was his idol), he loved to sing with a quartet which imitated the Ink Spots, and he bet furiously on himself. If that last one was a vice, then the First National Bank is a den of iniquity.

RANDY TURPIN
(1928–1966)

One of the biggest recommendations for boxing immortality you can give Randy Turpin is that Sugar Ray Robinson, the best fighter of his generation, would have nothing more to do with him after fighting him twice.

The Englishman was a first-class fighting man. Tremendously strong, the unorthodox British and European middleweight champion's greatest claim to fame was his victory over Ray Robinson for the world championship in 1951, only to have Sugar Ray stop him with a neck-saving rally in the 10th round and win the title back two months later.

Turpin, 5 ft., 11 in. and 159 pounds, was a dangerous and thoroughly unpredictable slugger. He was a good boxer but did not hesitate to throw a naked right-hand sneak punch. It was this bolt from the blue that defeated Robinson in their first fight.

Because of past injuries to his right hand, Turpin developed his left to a point where he could deliver a knockout punch with either one.

A friendly, smiling man outside the ring, Turpin was all business once he started fighting. "No fighter can have any friends when he's in the ring," Randy said. "You're on your own then. Sometimes, though, I'd like to have my friends in there with me, just so they'd know what it's like. You don't get the same thrill outside the ring."

Randy Turpin, one eye closed, waits for referee Ruby Goldstein's count to reach 9 before rising to resume second bout against Sugar Ray Robinson. Fight was stopped in 10th round and Robinson declared the winner. (UPI)

Turpin had a dry sense of humor. One night, his manager, George Middleton, said to him in the corner between rounds: "Randolph, I took every punch for you in that last round," and Randy said to George, "Then you get in here for the next round, and I'll take the punches for you."

Turpin was asked what was the first thing he noticed about Ray Robinson in the first round of their first fight. He said he went back to his corner after those first three minutes and told his handlers, "It's not so bad." He said it was difficult to tell much about an opponent in just one round unless he was the sort who could start fighting straightaway and kept throwing punches. Of Robinson he said, "I think Ray wants a bit of time." When did he know he had the Robinson fight won? "When the bell rang ending the last round" Randy said.

Randolph Adolphus Turpin was born at Leamington Spa, England, on June 7, 1928. His father was black, his mother white. He was the third son in a fighting family. His brother Dick, the eldest, was the first colored fighter to win a British title. Randy, a cook in the Royal Navy during the war, began boxing professionally in 1946, after winning five British amateur titles.

When brother Dick lost the British middleweight crown to Albert Finch, Randy redeemed the Turpin honor by stopping Finch in five rounds. Four months later, Randy added the European title to his string of growing laurels by knocking out Holland's Luc van Dam in 48 seconds. Then five months after that—the world middleweight championship.

Randy had an unorthodox English style. He got way up on his toes, sometimes even left them and threw his entire body at an opponent behind a punch. Red Smith suspected he had always been a club fighter, from his boyhood days in the carnival booths of England to the night in Madison Square Garden in 1953 when he tried to recapture the middleweight championship (vacated by Robinson) in a 15-round loss to Bobo Olson.

A lot of experts crossed Turpin off as all worn out at the ripe old age of twenty-five. He fooled them. Turning his attention to the light-heavies, Randy flattened Don Cockell to win the British and European championship. To this he added the Empire middleweight crown with a victory over South Africa's George Angelo. He later vacated the light-heavyweight title to fight Olson for the world middleweight crown, and when that failed he returned home and beat Arthur Howard to win the British light-heavy championship for the third time.

Turpin fought only twice again after being knocked out by Yolande Pompey in 1958. He finished his career with K.O.'s over Eddie Marcano and Charles Seguna. Having invested his money well, the future appeared bright for Turpin, but like so many ex-boxing champs down the years, the final chapter had a tragic ending—he committed suicide in 1966.

CARL (BOBO) OLSON
(1928–   )

For five rounds Bobo Olson outboxed Doug Jones in the Chicago Stadium but in the sixth Jones hit Bobo on the chin and Bobo hit the deck. He fell in sections, made a half-hearted try to regain his feet, then snuggled on the canvas as the count reached 9. At 10, his handlers got him upright, placed a towel over his head and led him from the ring.

That was on August 31, 1960. Watching the fight, I was reminded of another night in 1955 in the same arena when Bobo fell in the second round under a lusty punch by Ray Robinson. Joe DiMaggio, seated just back of the press rows, stared at the reposing Bobo and when the referee had gone through the numbers, he said: "This fellow just doesn't get up, does he?" Joe, you see, had been in the Polo Grounds in New York, six months before, when Archie Moore took Bobo out with a single punch in the third round. So Bobo was completely in character when he succumbed to the first punch of any consequence landed by Doug Jones.

The pity of it was that Bobo Olson was once a very good fighter. He never could beat Robinson, although he tried it four times, but at one period he could beat every other middleweight just below Sugar Ray's level and in 1953, while Robinson was off in Europe "getting Paris in my legs," he won recognition as a champion of the world in that class by mauling Randy Turpin (October 21, 1953) in New York. He defended his crown five times before giving it back to Robinson, who had vacated it in the first place.

Off the mean streets of Honolulu, where he was born, July 11, 1928, the son of a federal narcotics inspector, Olson fought his first pro bout at the age of fifteen and quickly earned a reputation as a brawler. He became a postwar hero in the islands and climbed rapidly through the ranks on the mainland even after Robinson had kayoed him in 12 rounds in Philadelphia in his first appearance in the East (October 26, 1950). Until Robinson's return to the prize ring, Bobo so completely dominated the middleweights that, still growing in poundage and skill, he was matched to fight Moore for the light-heavyweight title.

There were many who were surprised at the ease with which Moore disposed of Bobo. One of them was Rocky Marciano.

"I hate to admit it," Rocky said later, "but I picked Olson to beat Moore. As a matter of fact, I bet fifty dollars on him—and I never made a bet on a fight before."

"How did that come about?" he was asked.

"Well," Rocky said, "Al Weill is the best judge of fighters I ever knew and when he told me he was going to bet a lot of money on Olson, I told him to bet fifty bucks for me. But I didn't take only Al's word for it. Remember when I was training in Calistoga, California, for my fight with Don Cockell?"

"What happened there?"

"Didn't you hear it?" Rocky asked.

"Hear what?"

"The crowd at the workouts every day. No? Well, all I could hear when I was in the ring or coming out of it, was guys yelling: 'Bobo Olson will take care of you, you bum!' Or: 'You can lick the Englishman, but stay away from Bobo!' I'd never seen Olson, but I figured he must be a very tough guy and maybe too young and strong for Archie and when Al told me he was betting on Bobo I thought I shouldn't pass up a chance like that to get in on a good thing."

Olson was managed by Sid Flaherty, the 6 ft., 2 in., 215-pound Irishman who operates one of the largest boxing stables in the country. Sid expected Bobo to train hard. He insisted upon rigid conditioning. Bobo did not balk at the discipline. He usually arose at 6:30 A.M. for daily jogs of four miles along Ocean Beach. Even when he wasn't in training, Olson still churned through the sand several times a week. For his second fight with Robinson, he ran 522 miles by pedometer count. To toughen up his jaw, he pulled up a 35-pound cement block with his lower teeth several hundred times a day.

At his peak, nobody ever mistook Bobo Olson for anything but what he really was: a rough dock walloper who fought like a man with only one life to give—and it didn't belong to his opponent. There was a fierceness in his thick black chest hair and the huge tattoos high on each arm. When he had something to fight for, he was a tireless puncher; not a crushing puncher, but a strong and solid middleweight who made a lot of guys awfully sick.

Bobo figured the turning point in his career came in the second Robinson fight (March 13, 1952).

"Before then I just didn't seem to be going

For all his slightly fragile appearance, Bobo Olson took a punch exceptionally well and could dish it out. (NEA)

On way to winning decision, Olson floored challenger Rocky Castellani in 12th round in title bout in San Francisco, August 20, 1954, to retain his middleweight crown. (NEA)

anywhere," Bobo said. "I liked to fight but I had no championship ambitions. Then, near the tailend of the second match against Sugar Ray, I suddenly felt I had it. The first time we fought he'd knocked me kicking, the only K.O. against me then, but I wasn't ready for him at that time. I still had too much to learn. I was in over my head against a great fighter. He didn't hurt me, though; he didn't cut me up any. The punch that flattened me caught the side of my head and left me a little dizzy but I was okay a day later. So in the second fight, I was being careful. I moved ahead but I was cautious when backing out of clinches. Then it dawned on me along about the 13th round. I mean, this new feeling. Robinson, I recognized, was the best fighter ever in the 160-pound class and there he was all tuckered out. As for myself, I honestly felt as good as I did at the start. I knew, in my heart, I was stronger than him at the finish. Even though the judges gave him the decision, I'd proven something to myself: that if I could outlast him there was no reason why I couldn't someday be champion."

Recently, I talked to Danny Rodriguez about Bobo. Danny was Olson's trainer. He said Bobo's looks were deceiving.

"He fooled you," Danny told me. "That is, he appeared to be on the defense all the time, with his arms and gloves and hunched shoulders protecting him, yet he was far more aggressive than he was credited. Bobo was a big middleweight, a hurtful body puncher. He ruined a lot of good fighters, guys who were never the same afterward. A counter-puncher, he looked best against aggressive, busy fighters. He liked his opponents to come to him. A combination fighter, he worked particularly well from inside and zeroed in on the belly. His most effective stance was to rest his head on his rival's shoulder while he drilled holes into the midsection, just like a buzzsaw. He was tireless. He punched from bell to bell."

Bobo retired from the prize ring in 1966

after losing a decision to Don Fullmer. Today, he works as a public relations man for the Teamsters. He weighs over 200 pounds but still runs several miles a day and has fixed up his garage in Santa Rosa, California, like a gym.

One afternoon, this big guy walked into Bobo's gym and said he wanted to be a prizefighter. Bobo slipped the big gloves on him and sparred a couple rounds with him. The kid was game but it was evident he would never be another Marciano.

"Look," Bobo told him, after wiping off the blood-stained face, "I've been in the fight racket since I was nine. It's a vicious business. So take my advice and try some other sport, like football or baseball."

Bobo didn't see the young man for five years. Then, one day, he was tapped on the shoulder.

"Hey, remember me?" asked this big kid. "I'm the guy you told to pick another sport."

The guy's name?

Daryle Lamonica—quarterback of the Oakland Raiders!

GENE FULLMER
(1931–)

If you want to know what it is like to be a brawler, to be badly battered, to be cut up from ear to ear, all you have to do is look at an old picture of Gene Fullmer after a fight. He bore all the marks of the trade: welts over his eyes, the flat nose, swollen ears, the toothless grin—it was all there, splashed all over his homely kisser.

Few oldtimers confused the West Jordan, Utah, middleweight with Stanley Ketchel, although Fullmer did have several qualities to recommend him. Along with strength and bottomless courage, he brought brutality to the 1950s. His primary instinct in a ring was for brawling. Quick and punishing, he could pick a man apart as he stalked him. Put somebody reasonably stationary in front of him and he would hit him, again and again and again. Now and then things would get out of hand, and then the event would hang on the precipice of manslaughter. That's when the adrenalin flowed.

It was said of Fullmer that he went to the hunt with loaded 16-inch guns. After turning professional in 1951, 19 men were counted out at his feet as he ran up a streak of 29 victories in a row. Gil Turner, stylish and fast, was the first to beat him. They met twice again within a year and Fullmer won them both.

Gene decisioned Charley Humez in 1956 to become the No. 1 contender for Sugar Ray Robinson's title, but the dancing man made him wait six months before giving him a chance to wear the crown. Despite Ray's awesome reputation, Fullmer was confident he could beat the thirty-six-year-old champion. "I never was one of those who rated Robinson the greatest fighter, pound for pound, of all time," Fullmer said. "At least, not so far as Gene Fullmer was concerned. My fights with him were not the toughest of my career. In four bouts with him, I won two, drew once, and was knocked out once by him. But my style gave him plenty of trouble."

Gene Fullmer bore all the marks of the prize ring: welts over his eyes, flat nose, outsized ears. He brought brutality to boxing in the 1950s. (NEA)

The night Fullmer won the middleweight title from Robinson (January 2, 1957) he felt he was in charge. "Ray kept clinching and I kept slugging him on the back of the head, rabbit-punching," Fullmer admitted. "He complained about that. The rabbit punches, I mean. Well, he didn't like the decision after 45 minutes of milling, either. I cut the ring off and put pressure on him. I never gave him much room to roam and hit me from long-range. When the decision was finally announced it was the biggest sensation of my life. I mean, Robinson figured to walk all over me—he had little respect for me—and there I was, the worst fighter he ever fought, walking off with his crown. That had to be my biggest night, because I was not exactly Robinson's No. 1 cheerleader."

The limelight was wonderful while it lasted—which was only four months! On May Day, 1957, the bitter rivals met in Chicago, and Robinson knocked the crown off Gene's head in only five rounds. Few world champions had come up and gone out so fast. Within months Fullmer was all but forgotten.

Time marched on, however, and gradually Fullmer inched his way back up the ladder, leaving wreckage behind with names like Tiger Jones, Chico Vejar, Neal Rivers, Milo Savage, Jimmy Hegerle, Spider Webb, Joe Miceli, Savage again, and Wilf Greaves. This earned him another chance at the middleweight championship (since vacated by Robinson), and he knocked out Carmen Basilio to claim the N.B.A. version of the title.

Fullmer held the crown for two years the second time around. His six title defenses included a draw with Joey Giardello, a 12-round K.O. of Basilio, a 15-round draw with Ray Robinson, a 15-round decision over Robinson, a 15-round decision over Florentino Fernandez, and a K.O. of Benny Paret, the welterweight champion who died a couple of weeks later after being knocked out by Emile Griffith.

Gene's championship reign ended on October 23, 1963, when he lost a 15-round decision to Dick Tiger. He fought Tiger twice again trying to get the title back, but lost another decision in the second bout and was knocked out in seven rounds in the other match. It was only the second time in 64 pro bouts that Fullmer was ever counted out. Robinson was the only other to scorch his britches. Three straight losses to Tiger convinced Fullmer it was all over, and he retired in 1963.

After Sugar Ray leveled him, Fullmer went to Robinson's dressing room and congratulated him as soon as the smelling salts took hold.

"I sure got the message, Ray," Mormon Fullmer said. Here was a fist-fighter swallowing his chagrin gamely.

Born at West Jordan, on July 21, 1931, Gene Fullmer came out of the same Utah copper mines from which Jack Dempsey arose, but was named Gene after Gene Tunney, Dempsey's conqueror. Marv Jenson was his manager.

Fullmer began his ring career in the amateurs. Dick Francisco, Chairman of A.A.U. Boxing in the Pacific Northwest, remembers how green Gene was the first time he saw him. Dick handled both Fullmer and Rex Layne when they fought in the National A.A.U. Boxing Championships in Boston.

"Gene arrived in Boston without even a pair of boxing shoes," Francisco recollected. "He won the Nationals in a pair of borrowed shoes."

Something borrowed, something new.

Gene Fullmer wound up owning his own mink ranch back in Utah.

CARMEN BASILIO
(1927–   )

The first thing to establish about Carmen Basilio is that there really was one.

Gnarled and craggy-faced, he stood 5 ft., 6½ in., weighed 156, had two arms and two legs,

Challenger Gene Fullmer ducked Sugar Ray Robinson's best shots and scored enough points with his piston-like body punches to go on and win middleweight title in New York, January 2, 1957. Fullmer called it "the biggest night of my career." (UPI)

both eyes, a flat nose, most of his hair and teeth, and he was good to his mother. In other words, he was quite mortal except when he got paid to crack heads and bust bones on fight nights.

Basilio belied the book. There were days in the gym when he could not have scared a midget. He'd have won no prizes as a bag-puncher, and he was no threat to Fred Astaire skipping rope. "Nothing more than a glorified club fighter with plenty of heart," chorused his critics. Then how did they explain the fact that he won the welterweight title twice, and then busted up Sugar Ray Robinson to become only the second welter champion to dethrone a middleweight champion under Queensberry rules? (Robinson was the other.)

"Basilio was just about the toughest man I ever fought," Sugar Ray said. "You couldn't afford to be discouraged by him. You had to keep him off you. You had to keep fighting him. Trying to stop him was like trying to stop a freight train. I felt like 10 guys jumped me."

Basilio fought like Tony Zale. His scars told you what his profession was. There was a bald streak in his right eyebrow. The lines of old cuts made the world see what a bloody dollar he made. Until Gene Fullmer did it at the tailend of his career, Carmen was never knocked down by a blow, and nobody ever licked him twice.

Basilio and Robinson met twice, once in New York and the other in Chicago. Their fights were described by New Yorkers as the greatest matchup since the old Brooklyn Dodgers quit playing the Yankees. The first bout was fought in Yankee Stadium, on September 23, 1957. A crowd of 38,000 paid $560,000, the second largest non-heavyweight draw in prize ring history. Sugar Ray, thirty-seven, was seven years older than Basilio, but carried a seven-pound weight advantage and was five inches taller.

Up to the evening of the fight, there was a notion among seasoned observers that Robinson could accomplish anything he set out to do, because he always had accomplished it. He was the choice of many handicappers. The reasoning behind the selection went something like this: Since he abandoned his career as a song-and-dance man to return to prizefighting, Robinson scored one-punch knockouts against two champions—Bobo Olson and Gene Fullmer. Basilio had always been hit, always would be hit. Robinson would hit him, and it was not reasonable to expect that Carmen, a welterweight, could survive the punches that left two middleweight champions for dead.

But Robinson didn't follow this line of reasoning. He got licked. The score on many cards was nine rounds for Basilio, six for Sugar Ray. As viewed through most bifocals, Robinson did succeed in nailing Carmen with the same solid shots that had disposed of Olson and Fullmer. Throughout the fight, Basilio never fired a single shot that did as much damage as Robinson's best blows.

However, Robinson was a one-punch fighter. At no time was he able to put together the remorseless combinations that once were automatic for him. Basilio hit and hurt, would drop into a weaving crouch, hide there until the fog had cleared from his brain, then come clambering in to swat his man with implacable resolution. Never did Robinson turn on the sort of storm which had, years before, destroyed the almost indestructible Jake LaMotta.

The only reasonable conclusion seemed to be that the years had blunted Robinson's reflexes, that never again would he overwhelm an opponent as tough and determined as Basilio, who had fought like a small-scale Rocky Marciano.

"He was five inches taller, so I worked on his midsection a lot, and made him work the whole fight," Basilio said after the fight. "When the bell rang ending the fight, I walked back to my corner sure I'd won. I did, too. Judges Artie Aidala and Bill Recht had me the winner, and referee Al Berl voted for Robinson. A poll of 34 boxing writers at ringside showed 19 for me, 8 for Robinson, and 7 even. But there was agreement on one point: it was a helluva fight! When I got back to my dressing room I locked myself in an office and wouldn't see anyone. Robinson's left jab and quick hooks had done quite a job on my face and I didn't want anybody to see what a bloody mess I was."

To win, Basilio had slammed Robinson's body. Outwardly, Robinson seemed fine and unmarked in his dressing room but they had to help him get dressed and it was not until a long time after everybody in the ball park had gone home that Jackie Barrett, the matchmaker for the I.B.C., left. "I had to wait," he explained, "until Robinson was ready to go home. He was hurt a lot worse than anybody knows. He took a terrible body licking."

The fight had been brutal. Basilio, standing too erect, caught a frightening amount of punches in the early rounds. Then he got down low and came on in the middle rounds and in the 11th seemed to have Robinson nearly out. But Robinson made a remarkable comeback and almost pulled it out with a last-gasp rally in the 13th and 14th rounds. That was the broad pattern. But mostly, the event revolved around this kind of viciousness: Robinson hit Carmen low in one of the rounds and, patronizingly, he asked, "Hurt you, Carmen?"

"No, do it again and see what happens," Basilio snapped.

Basilio never pretended a liking for Robinson. A year before their first fight, Carmen, in Ray's eyes, was just another broken-nosed pug. Why, Ray couldn't even remember his name. Several times on the street and in gyms he snubbed him. Basilio never forgot. "He got to know me pretty well in that first fight," Carmen said. That he did. Robinson grew to know him as a rough and tumble fighter who slugged from a crouch, rushed like a good football guard, and didn't get discouraged

Carmen Basilio, the welterweight champion, lands with right hand on jaw of middleweight champion Sugar Ray Robinson in 4th round, then went on to pile up enough points to win decision and Robinson's title in 1957 match in New York. Basilio was thirty years old, Sugar Ray thirty-seven. (UPI)

when he was tagged. "I might have looked a little clumsy," admitted Basilio, "but I didn't get hit too often. It wasn't as bad as it seemed. I rode most of those blows and escaped their full power. The record book shows I was K.O.'d twice, but they were T.K.O.'s, both by Fullmer. No one ever counted 10 over me."

Basilio's style of fighting was deceptive. "I watched him box in Miami once and thought I had a good line on him," spoke one of his sparring partners, "but after I'd worked with him I realized that you had to be in the ring with him to appreciate just what he does. From the outside he looks easy to hit, but when you are in there with him he looks a lot different."

Return matches rarely live up to the first fight, but Basilio and Robinson hardly could have been dull when placed in the ring together. If a racing secretary were handicapping the pair with the idea of bringing them to the wire in a photo finish, the handicaps would have been exactly what they were. Basilio got seven years in age, and Robinson seven pounds, five inches in height and five-and-a-half inches in reach. That brought them so closely together that they battered each other into a state of exhaustion each time they fought. There wasn't a knockdown in 30 rounds.

Basilio and Robinson met again in Chicago six months and two days after the first bout in what was afterward called "The Battle of the Shuttered Eye." Basilio fought the last 11 rounds with one eye closed. Little Cyclops fought and fought, until the end found him a huddled, bruised figure in a strange heap, praying on one knee in his ring corner while the judges added up their scores. He was the image of grotesquery, his face resembled a dish of borscht and his ghastly left eye was black and shut firm as if stapled.

"I could have gone another 15 rounds," Basilio insisted.

"The only place you're going," Harry Grayson said, "is Bellevue. If you have many more fights you'll be knocking on the bughouse door."

Robinson, hearing of Basilio's remark, mumbled ungrammatically, "Well, maybe he could have went another 15, but he wouldn't have went them with me."

Sugar Ray won the split decision, but he was quick to admit it was the toughest of his 181 victories.

"I kept catching his right uppercut all night and he scored a lot of points with it," Basilio said. "This time it was the referee who voted for me, and the two judges gave it to Ray. After that, Robinson refused to fight me again. Too bad. A third fight—the rubber match—would have made us both rich."

The second Robinson bout made Basilio think that Chicago was a jinx city for him. He simply could not win there. Four times he fought in Chicago, and four times he lost. Chuck Davey and Billy Graham beat him there in 1952, Johnny Saxton in 1956, and Robinson in 1958.

Saxton won Basilio's welterweight title from him on points in 15 rounds. Carmen didn't think he lost. "He ran like a deer most of the night and wouldn't fight," Basilio said. "Yet he got the decision. But I got even the following September. It took me only nine rounds to knock him out. I banged him good. That made it a win apiece. In a third match, five months later, I settled all arguments and knocked him out in two rounds."

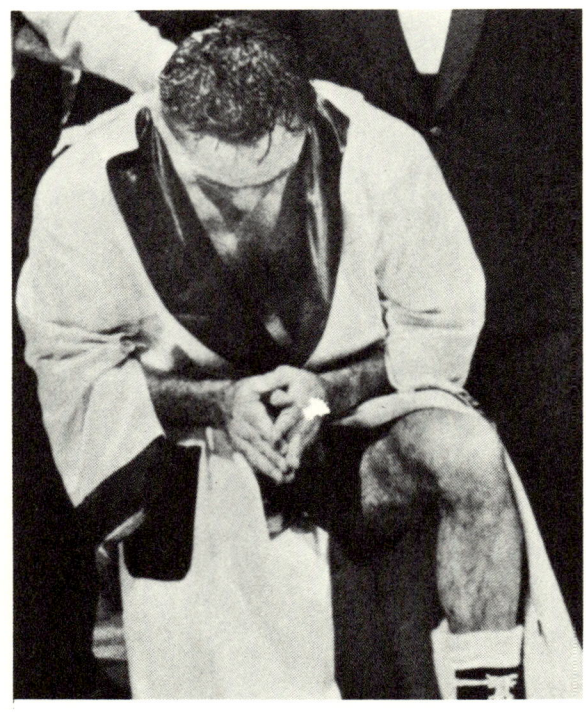

In the flush of victory over Robinson, Basilio knelt in Yankee Stadium ring and offered a prayer of thanks for winning the middleweight championship. (AP)

Born on April 2, 1927, at Canastota, New York, Italiano Basilio won 11 of 14 amateur matches before turning pro in 1948. He won 18 of his first 22 prizefights. Then, in 1950, he beat former lightweight champion Lew Jenkins, the first time he had ever gone 10 rounds. Three years later he beat another ex-champ, Ike Williams, and then lost, won and fought a draw with slick Billy Graham.

On September 18, 1953, Basilio lost a 15-round decision to welterweight champion Kid Gavilan in Syracuse. In the second round, he floored Gavilan, the first time the Cuban ever had been knocked down. "I thought I won," Basilio said. "But the judges gave it to Gavilan. The decision caused quite a stink. A lot of TV fans thought I won."

Two years later, Basilio knocked out Tony DeMarco, by now the champion, to win the world welterweight crown. He lost it to Saxton nine months later, won it back, and then went after Robinson's title. He had to vacate his welterweight crown when he beat Ray, however, because there was a rule stating a fighter could not hold more than one world championship at a time.

Unlike Robinson, Basilio hated crowds and bright lights. He enjoyed training alone. He admitted that he worked three times harder when he was shielded from the public. The crowds didn't seem to bother him the night he won the middleweight title, though. He fought the fight of his life. One of his fans, who was sitting at ringside, pulled out all the stops in his loyalty to the one-time onion farmer. "You don't have to hit him, Onion Eater," the man shouted. "Just breathe in his face!"

TERRY DOWNES
(1936–   )

Irony ringed Terry Downes's life in the prize ring. An Englishman who adopted an American style, he appeared without much acclaim in London in 1957, determined and fearless, and quickly became the class of the British middleweight division. Within two years he won, lost, and won back the British championship—and 18 months later, lost, won, and lost back the world middleweight crown to Paul Pender. Then, after only 37 months of actual fighting stretched over eight years (1957–1964), he lost to Willie Pastrano in an attempt to annex the light-heavyweight title, and suddenly quit the prize ring in disgust. He was only twenty-eight.

Gilbert Odd, the British boxing historian, recalled the details.

"No one loved to fight more than Terry," Odd said. "Born at Paddington, he sharpened his tools in a North London amateur club. Then he went to the United States with his parents when his sister was hospitalized in a car accident. Terry stayed on, joined the U.S. Marines, and earned a spot on the 1956 Olympic Team. But when it was discovered that Terry was born in England he was disqualified from competing in Melbourne. When the Downeses moved back to Paddington, Terry resumed his amateur career. Finally, in 1957, he turned pro and his whirlwind, non-stop, hard-punching style quickly made him top boxoffice in London.

"Terry's biggest problem was cuts. Damage around his eyes and nose cost him some bouts he should have won, but he put middleweight champion Pat McAteer out of business and then knocked out Phil Edwards to claim the British title. He lost it to Scotland's John McCormack on a foul, then stopped him in a return match. He whipped Edwards again to win the Lonsdale Belt outright, and then never defended his British title again. After that he won a decision over Joey Giardello.

"Downes then went to Boston and challenged Paul Pender for the world title and was stopped in seven rounds. A return match at Wembley Arena in London, on July 11, 1961, saw Terry forcing Pender to quit in the ninth round with a nasty eye wound. The rubber match was fought in Boston, with Pender winning on points in 15.

"After turning in a fine performance to beat Ray Robinson at Wembley, Terry begged his manager to get him a shot at Willie Pastrano. They fought at Manchester's Belle Vue. Terry looked like the winner all the way, until Pastrano pulled a beautifully timed right to the chin to stop him in the 11th. Terry tore off his gloves in disgust and never fought again."

PAUL PENDER
(1930–   )

By reputation, Paul Pender was never a great champion. As a fighter, he had been clever, game, a spoiler, but never an outstanding puncher, because of brittle hands. At one period, he broke his mitts six times in six bouts. Those tender knuckles sidetracked him three different times early in his career.

"I always had trouble with my hands," Pender said. "They never felt good. I never broke them again after 1958, but they were always a question mark."

Pender was twenty-eight and on the Brookline, Massachusetts, Fire Department, his home town, when he began the third of his boxing comebacks, in 1958. He won nine fights in a row and then talked Boston promoter Sam Silverman into getting him a title fight with Ray Robinson, who by this time owned the world championship for the fifth time. Sugar Ray agreed to the match, figuring Pender was going to be a soft touch.

"Ray thought I was a nothing," Pender recalled. "I got 25 percent of the purse."

The bout was fought in Boston, on January 22, 1960. Robinson was pushing forty, his legs were spent, and all he had left were memories. Pender whacked him around the ring for 15 rounds and when the 45 minutes were used up, Massachusettes had a new champion. Robinson tried to get the title back six months later, but again the points were all in Pender's favor.

"In 30 rounds of fighting him, Robinson landed only one punch that hurt me," Pender said. "That was in the second round of the first bout. He caught me right behind the ear, a very vulnerable spot, just after the bell. Ray was old when I beat him. My strategy was to wear him down and then break him down. Actually, I was no youngster myself. I was thirty—and how many guys fight for a world title at thirty? There was no question in the second fight. No one disagreed that I beat Robinson the second time."

Born at Brookline, in 1930, Pender stuck close to home. Except for two trips to Brooklyn and one to fight Terry Downes in London, all of his fighting took place in New England rings. As a matter of fact, the record shows he fought a total of only six times in the last three years of his career—and all were world title bouts!

In 1961, he beat Downes (K.O., 7) and Carmen Basilio (Decision, 15), and then lost the crown to Downes (K.O., 9). He fought only once in 1962, when he outpointed Downes in 15 to regain the championship. That was on April 7. He never fought again. Seven months later, the various world boxing associations stripped him of his title for inactivity.

JOEY GIARDELLO
(1930-   )

The role of "often a bridesmaid but never a bride" was played by Joey Giardello for seven years (1953–1960). He considered himself the No. 1 contender for the middleweight championship, but nobody would give him a crack at the crown. "They treated me as if I were a communicable disease," he lamented. "Robinson, for example, purposely avoided me. For 15–16 fights in a row they told me I'd get a title fight and nothing happened. The only guys who'd fight me were guys like Bobby Boyd and Willie Troy—guys who were also trying to be top contenders."

The first time Joey ever went 15 rounds was when he fought to a draw with Gene Fullmer for the N.B.A. championship in the Montana State College fieldhouse at Bozeman, on April 20, 1960. Fullmer was a 3–1 favorite. Joey had a reputation for tiring in the middle rounds, but he went full out that night and a lot of people who saw it thought Joey was the winner. It was the only time—in or out of the ring—that Giardello ever felt vindictive, because he knew that Fullmer would dodge him after that.

"He's too damned yellow to fight me again," Joey said after the bout. "He's a dirty fighter, the only crumb I ever really hated. He's a crybaby, too. Whenever I gave him a little of his dirty stuff back, he'd whine to the referee. But when he did it to me, he'd say, 'Excuse me, just an accident.' Accident hell! He kept butting me all night. So I gave it right back to him and he yelled bloody murder to Harry Kessler, the ref. Fullmer can't take his own medicine. They called it a draw. But no way was it a draw. I won at least nine rounds, but we were fightin' out in his part of the country and no way were they going to take his title away from him."

Fullmer took the opposite view, of course.

"Joey was not the cleanest fighter I ever met," Gene said. "He purposely butted me on the head several times. That's how he cut his eye. I didn't do it, he did it to himself. One of his butts fractured my skull. I asked him why the dirty stuff and he said he wanted my championship. He was the first guy ever to bang and butt me intentionally. Sure, I was accused of being a dirty fighter by fans, but no fighter (except Joey) ever accused me of it. I might have had a *crude* style, but I never fought dirty. If Giardello said I was dirty, then he lied."

The Fullmer match settled nothing for Giardello's championship aspirations. His only hope was that Dick Tiger would win the crown from Fullmer. "And then he'll give me another crack at the title," Joey reasoned. "Tiger will fight anybody." It seemed like a slim hope at the time.

But then Tiger *did* win the title from Fullmer and in December, 1963, at the age of thirty-three, Joey Giardello became middleweight champion of the world when he outboxed and outpunched Tiger in 15 rounds in Atlantic City. To Joey, it was like reaching the light at the end of the tunnel. Up to that night, he was just another contender. But suddenly everything fit together as easily as the last piece in a jigsaw puzzle, and he looked like a professional killer in there. Every so often he pinched his checkbook to see if it was all real.

"It took me 16 years and more than a hundred fights to get there," Joey recalled. "Years of frustration, years of punishment, years of disgrace. There were days when I asked myself if the price was worth it. I mean, it would have been terrible to fight all those years and spill all that blood and not win the title. Thank god, it wasn't wasted. It was more than the money. It was the honor of calling yourself *champeen!*"

Giardello's career spanned both the golden days of postwar boxing, the greedy television era, and then the bleak depression period. His manager for most of his career was Anthony Ferrante. But in 1962, Ferrante sold Joey's contract to a man in the storm-window business for $7,500. After Joey beat Tiger to win the title, he spent most of his $12,500 purse to buy back his freedom. He wound up as his own manager, putting his financial affairs in the hands of a couple of Philadelphia lawyers, Michael J. DelCollo and Don D'Agui. "Lawyers make the best managers," Joey said. "They don't take such a big cut. A lawyer looks out for *you*, a manager looks out for *himself.*"

Joey has some definite ideas about what has happened to boxing. "It was more glamorous in the old days," he said. "There were better fighters around then, too. I could hardly get into the first 10 in those days. I didn't get rated till 1952 or '53, right around the time I fought Billy Graham in Madison Square Garden. He was a great fighter. Now, there are maybe one or two good ones in the ratings. The rest are flashes in the pan. Kids are rushed too fast now. If I had a fighter, I'd make him wait 20 fights before I'd let him go eight rounds. Then his body is ready to go eight rounds. I won 35 bucks my first fight. I started fighting in October of 1948. But if I'd won the title when I was younger, I wouldn't have any more money today. I used to gamble and spent a lot."

With prizefighters, that last had a familiar ring.

Joey Giardello fought a total of 133 professional bouts. And yet, upon retirement in 1967, his face was remarkably clear of scar tissue. It tells you what a skillful defensive boxer he was.

STILL ACTIVE

EMILE GRIFFITH
(1938–   )

In his first 17 years in the prize ring, Emile Griffith held the world welterweight championship twice and the middleweight crown three times.

Born on February 3, 1938, in the Virgin Islands, his version of the game of musical chairs went as follows: He won the welterweight title on a K.O. over Gaspar Ortega in 12 rounds, June 3, 1961; lost it to Benny Paret via 15-round decision, September 30, 1961; won it back from Benny on a fatal 12-round knockout, March 24, 1962, after which Paret died from head injuries. In 1963, Emile lost and regained the welter wreath in a pair of bouts with Luis Rodriguez.

Having proven himself among welters, Griffith moved up to middleweight and won the world championship on a 15-round decision over defending champion Dick Tiger, April 25, 1966; then lost it a year later to Nino Benvenuti, 15-round decision; won it back from Nino, on points, September 29, 1967; lost it again to the Italian, decision, March 4, 1968.

NINO BENVENUTI
(1938–)

Born at Trieste, Italy, on April 26, 1938, Nino Benvenuti began his ring career in 1961 and won his first 65 bouts in a row. In 1967, he won and lost the world middleweight championship in decisions with Emile Griffith; he won the title for a second time, a 15-round decision over Griffith, in New York, March 4, 1968; then lost his crown for a final time, November 7, 1970, on a third-round K.O. by Carlos Monzon.

Benvenuti's last recorded fight was in May 1971, yet he has never officially declared his retirement.

CARLOS MONZON
(1942–)

Born at Santa Fe, Argentina, Carlos Monzon became a professional prizefighter in 1963, won 16 out of his first 18 bouts. The former meatpacking house worker scored 58 knockouts in his first 98 pro matches, including a 12-round kayo over Nino Benvenuti of Italy in 1970 to win the world middleweight championship. Through 1974, he successfully defended his crown 10 times, 7 by K.O. From October 28, 1964, through '74, Monzon registered 76 fights without defeat (9 draws included). In his first 11 years of prizefighting, he dropped only 3 decisions in 98 matches.

Italy's Nino Benvenuti, right, came off the floor to win the middleweight title in 1967 here from Emile Griffith. (UPI)

WELTERWEIGHTS

In 1892, Mysterious Billy Smith, a tough, mean 145-pounder from New England, punched Danny Needham into defeat and the welterweight division had its first recognized world champion.

Until then, the welters were unofficial.

The term "welters" is an English horseracing expression, and as far back as 1792 some small British fighters started battling among themselves and designating themselves as *welters*. They weighed in at 145 pounds or less and the class gradually gained prominence. Since the days of Smith the class has produced a list of champions reading like a Boxing Blue Book.

MYSTERIOUS BILLY SMITH
(1871–1937)

Captain Cooke, editor of that fine old Boston paper, the *Police News,* had a visitor one day in 1890. Fellow named Smith—Amos Smith of Eastport, Maine. Mean lookin' kid. Part Irish. Chip on his shoulder big as a railroad tie. Welterweight, he said. Didn't look it. 'Bout five feet eight or nine, the Captain reckoned. But hungry, *real* hungry.

The Captain found him a couple of fights in which Amos Smith failed to distinguish himself. And then he vanished as suddenly as he had appeared.

Months went by before reports reached the Hub of the far-ranging exploits of one Billy Smith of Boston. No one could recall the name so Captain Cooke gave it a handle— "Mysterious Billy Smith."

Yep, it was Amos, all right, and he was doing pretty well for a mean kid not yet twenty. Out on the West Coast he beat Spider Kelly in five rounds. In 1892, he kayoed Billy Armstrong in 13, and then on December 14th of the same year, he won the United States welterweight crown by halting Danny Needham in 14 rounds in San Francisco. Four months later, on April 17, 1893, at Coney Island, young Smith flattened Tom Williams of Australia for the world championship.

Billy Roche always said that Mysterious Billy Smith was as rough a character as

189

Elbows McFadden. Roche was in a position to know—he managed both.

"They were two of the roughest and toughest fighters I ever saw," Roche told me. "I learned all the tricks from them. I've always said that Billy was the toughest fighter I ever saw, but I'm drawing a line as fine as a silkworm's thread, for Elbows McFadden could also dish it out in large quantities.

"Smith was the only fighter who had Joe Walcott's number. They fought half a dozen times, and, while record books may not agree to the letter, Smith had the better of 15-, 20- and 25-round battles. I recall Walcott showing up for one match with a long pistol in his backpocket, and Smith saying that even if he used that it wouldn't do him any good.

"Take Smith's fight with Eddie Butler in the Illinois mining town of Spring Valley. Billy and Eddie were about to tangle for the gate receipts when rugged miners began climbing through the windows. Billy appealed to the management, but the crowd gave him the horse laugh. So Billy worked his way around the room socking every gate crasher who appeared in a window until he'd shamed the promoter into action of a sort. Billy was out to give the crowd a run for the money—$750—but when they began beaning him with lumps of coal, he finished off Butler in a hurry. Then came the grand finale, a good old-fashioned riot with Billy the center of attraction as he flailed about him busily with two water bottles."

Mysterious Billy Smith drew twice in six rounds with Tommy Ryan before the two played it for keeps in a 20-rounder in Minneapolis, on July 26, 1894. Joe Choynski, a pal of Ryan's, refereed and gave Tommy the decision.

Then followed the first of Smith's battles with Joe Walcott, and it was a corker. In the clinches, charming Billy bit Joe on the scalp while the stocky West Indian hit low and kicked Smith in the slats. The referee left them to their fun and called it a draw in 15 rounds. Next time they fought, Smith won in 20 rounds.

Following his retirement, in 1920, Mysterious Billy settled down in Tacoma, Washington, and operated a hotel and Turkish bath. After that, he moved to Portland, Oregon and ran a saloon. When he died, on October 16, 1937, he joined Jack Dempsey the Nonpareil as an immortal Oregonian—by choice and not by proxy.

KID McCOY
(1873–1940)

Norman Selby, alias Charles (Kid) McCoy, lived by violence, by trickery, and by women. A born scrapper, he trained for the prize ring by slugging brakemen and railroad detectives from coast to coast, inventing new punches in the process. Professionally, he fought 200 fights, and was beaten in only six of them. He married eight women—one of them three times—and shot another to death. For the murder, he went to San Quentin for seven years.

Kid McCoy was a complex personality. There was vanity in him, and guile, wit, cruelty. There was also some larceny, and a great capacity for enjoying himself.

It's possible that for his weight, which ranged from 145 pounds to 170, McCoy was the finest fighter in the world, when he was at his best. Jim Corbett called him "a marvel, a genius of scientific fighting." Philadelphia Jack O'Brien said of him: "Vicious, fast, and almost impossible to beat."

It was a strange fact about McCoy that he did not need his tricks to be great. He cheated because he loved to cheat. Fighting on the level, he would still have been the real McCoy.

Once, while McCoy was running a New York gym, he said to a new pupil one day, as the boy came in the door, "Who's that with you?" The pupil turned to look. McCoy hauled off and knocked him down. "That's your first lesson," he said, "never turn your head on an opponent. Five dollars, please."

McCoy got a lifelong pleasure out of teaching this lesson. In Philadelphia, in 1904, he fought a big, promising Hollander named Plaacke. Early in the fight he began to point frantically at Plaacke's waistband. "Your pants are slipping!" he muttered. "Pull 'em up!" Plaacke started to reach for his pants with both gloves. McCoy smacked him on the chin, and knocked him down. "Stay down," snarled McCoy, "or I'll tear your head off!" The Dutchman, terrified by the Kid's sudden savagery and by the cruelty that transfigured his impish face, stayed down for the count. He went back to Holland on the next cattle boat.

The phrase which keeps McCoy's name famous was born in San Francisco, in 1899. At least, McCoy always said so, and while he was one of the most fertile and tireless liars of his time, there's a strong chance he was telling the truth. He said he went to the Coast that spring to fight Joe Choynski. Earlier, in San Francisco, a Joe McAuliffe had easily whipped a man named Peter McCoy. Kid McCoy, following this low-class act with a better one, gave Choynski a savage beating in 20 rounds, flooring him 16 times. The press hailed him with gratitude: "Choynski is beaten," a headline said, "by the Real McCoy."

As to how Norman Selby got the name of McCoy to begin with, he said he ran away from home in Indianapolis with two other boys when he was fourteen or fifteen. They rode the train to Cincinnati. Cops met them at the Cincinnati station, alerted by the boys' fathers. "Are you Norman Selby?" a cop asked Norman. "I'm Charlie McCoy," he said. The night before, through the train window, he had seen a sign, "McCoy Station." So when he made his first prizefight it was under the name of Charlie (Kid) McCoy.

True or not, there's no doubt that he began fighting early in life as Kid McCoy. Some say his first bout, for $5 or $10, was against Charleston Yalla. Some say it was against Pete Jenkins, in St. Paul, in 1891. He beat Jenkins in four rounds.

McCoy quickly gained an awesome reputation, sailing along unbeaten until stopped by Billy Steffers in Clevelend, in 1894. The Kid had marvelous speed and elusiveness, besides his tricks and the cruel, cutting power of his punches. By practising endlessly, he was able to run sideways, or backward, nearly as fast as the average man can run forward. "In a backward race, in fact, I could probably beat any man in the world," he said once. He improved the use of his left hand by eating, writing, and throwing a ball lefthanded. From every good fighter he fought or watched he learned something.

At home one day, McCoy studied a kitten toying with a cloth ball. He noticed the cat's paw came toward the ball at an angle instead of in a straight line. McCoy wondered what the results would be if he used the same stroke, with a quick, sharp twist, similar to the spin given a bullet by the rifling in the barrel. He practiced the punch on a sack of cement. It hurt his knuckles but he could make powder out of dry cement. Then he tried the punch in the ring, cutting his opponent to shreds, and—POW!—McCoy's famous "corkscrew punch" was born.

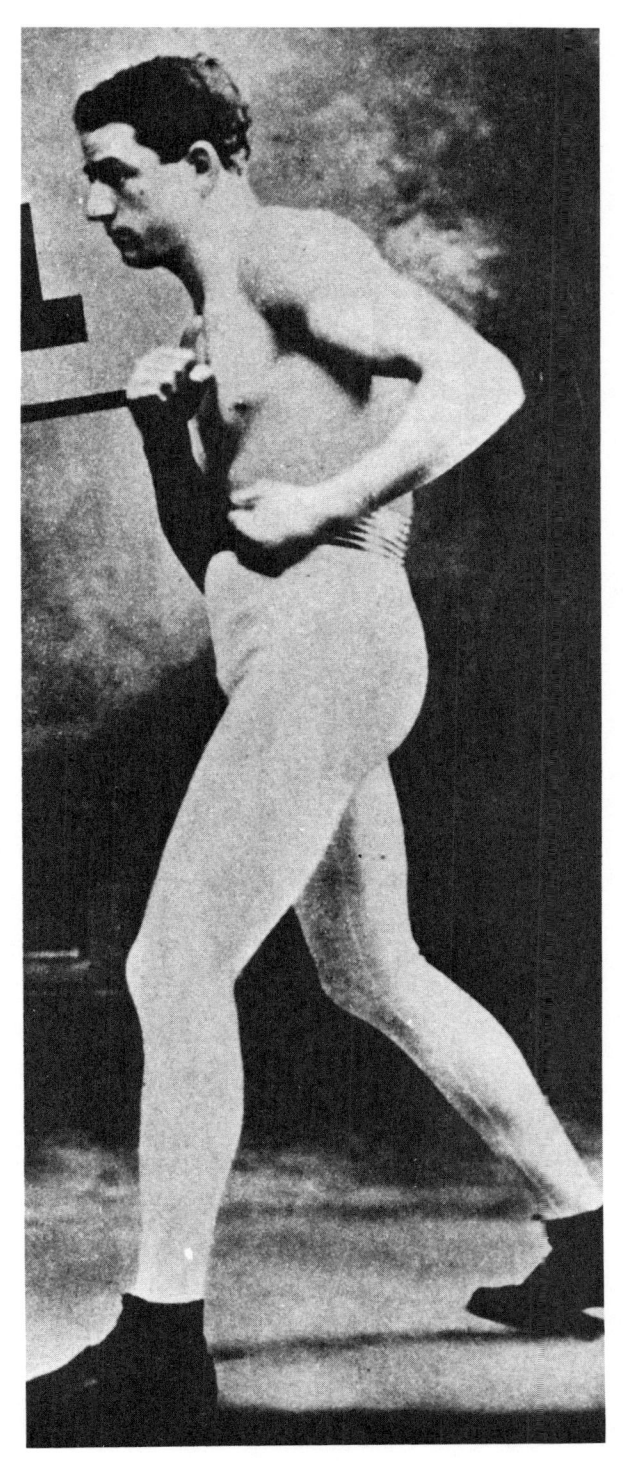

The "Real McCoy"—a complex personality. (UPI)

McCoy was twenty-three years old when he was matched with champion Tommy Ryan, thought by many to be the most skillful boxer extant, for the welterweight title in Maspeth, Long Island, on March 2, 1896. It was a match Ryan had no worries about. McCoy had sparred with him several years earlier, and McCoy had deliberately made a poor impression—chiefly by a sort of cringing timidity. In one of the workouts, he had asked Ryan not to hit him around the heart. "It makes me sick, Mr. Ryan," he had said. "And it gives me a sharp pain that frightens me. If I didn't need the money I wouldn't even be a fighter."

In their title fight, Ryan did his best to hit McCoy around the heart. But few of his blows found the mark, and in the 12th round, growing impatient and frustrated, Ryan suddenly exposed his own chin. McCoy saw the opening and let fly with a stinging straight right. It caught Ryan flush on the button, and left him drained of all his strength and science. McCoy then slashed and mauled the helpless champion until the 15th when he knocked him out.

McCoy worked day and night to add to his own legend. He could not help swindling—it was in South Africa, at Bullawayo, that he fought a 250-pound black called the "King of the Kaffirs." In the first round, McCoy, running backward, lured the giant into his, McCoy's, corner. The King, in sudden pain and confusion, looked down at his bare feet, and McCoy, at the same moment, brought up his right hand and knocked the Kaffir senseless. As it happened, just before the fight began, McCoy's seconds had sprinkled the floor with *tacks*.

But there was far more than deceit in McCoy; there was also courage and ferocity. Against odds, he could fight like a tiger. Playwright Maurice Maeterlinck had seen the Kid fight in Europe, and he once described him as "the handsomest human on earth."

McCoy outgrew the welterweight class and gave up the title; also outgrew a brief claim to the middleweight crown, and was fighting them as big as they came when he announced his retirement in 1916. He served several years in the U.S. Army during World War I, and when his enlistment was up, he headed for California. He got a few bit parts in Hollywood movies, but this career died quickly. In 1922, he became an official bankrupt—assets: two suits of clothes. One way and another, he took the busy, hot town for a dollar here and a dollar there, and hung on.

In 1924, McCoy found his way into the life of Theresa Weinstein Mors, a goodlooker who divorced her wealthy husband to move in with the Kid. They lived together under the names of Mr. and Mrs. N. Shields. The Kid wanted marriage in more than name, however. Mrs. Mors did not. They quarreled. Neighbors heard a single gunshot. The next morning, the janitor found Theresa lying dead on the floor of the bedroom she had shared with McCoy. She had been shot once, in the left temple. A .32 pistol lay nearby.

The police caught up with McCoy as he was running amok a few blocks away through Westlake Park. He later told the prosecutor, "I had to kill that woman." It took the jury 78 hours to convict him. He was given a sentence totalling 24 years, but he was paroled in 1932 for good behavior. He got a job as watchman in one of the Ford Motor Company's public gardens in Detroit.

On a trip to Rushville, Indiana, near the place of his birth, McCoy took unto himself an eighth wife, Mrs. Sue Cobb Cowley, a cousin of Irvin S. Cobb, the humorist. His marriage went well. His job with Ford was for life. One day he was asked if he ever saw his former wives.

"You won't believe it," McCoy lied smugly, "but I see them all, regularly. Every year I give a party, and every woman I've ever been married to comes to Detroit to see me again."

In everything he did, as his days wound down to the final, strange hours, the Kid's mind and his sixty-six-year-old body worked smoothly and well. And then, on an April night in 1940, he checked in alone at Detroit's Tuller Hotel. He wasn't sick, or broke. Registering with the night clerk, he left a call for 10 the next morning. It was when he failed to answer the call that the manager went up with a passkey, and found him dead. An overdose of sleeping pills had put him out, and away. Nobody but Kid McCoy knew what special sin in his life had been too big for him to live with any longer—and he wasn't talking.

MATTY MATTHEWS
(1873–1948)

Handsome Matty Matthews was famous for his long aquiline nose. The welterweight champ dropped a dozen in his day, but the

Matthews beak retired unscathed—a fair indication of his boxing prowess.

When Jack Dempsey had his nose remodeled, Matty told Dan Morgen, "Jack wants a schnozz like mine, and I would have been grateful for a turnip like he had. That was a real fighter's nose."

Matty defended the honor of his nose at 5 ft., 7½ in. and 138 pounds, fighting trim. He wrested the welterweight crown from Rube Ferns on October 16, 1900, though he always maintained that he earned it when he kayoed Mysterious Billy Smith (Ferns had won the title from Smith on a foul). Anyway, Rube won it back from Matty by belting him out in the 10th.

Matthews was born in New York, July 13, 1873. He quit public school early and went to work for a tea warehouse, hustling cases by the truck load. Now there were an awful lot of tea parties around the turn of the century, and the more tea the ladies drank, the stronger Matty became until he attracted the notice of Old Eagle Eye Charlie White.

Charley arranged a tryout with a local battler, Johnny Bennis, in the basement of the old Clinton A.C. Matty kayoed Bennis in the 18th. The fight was really mad too—Bennis spent four months in the hospital while for three weeks Matty couldn't have swung a tea bag to his shoulder. That's the way they fought in those days.

"I earned $100,000," Matty recalls with a long pull on his faithful pipe. "But I took my share of physical punishment—unlike some of our present day fighters. You know, when I was a kid, boxing was good for boys. Now it's only good for promoters. They ought to give the game back to the boys."

When the going got rough, Matty worked at a variety of jobs. At one time he rode a diving horse into a tank at the Hippodrome. Later he took a job at the Brooklyn Navy Yard.

RUBE FERNS
(1874–1952)

Jim "Rube" Ferns had to win the welterweight title twice to prove he deserved it. The first time, it fell in his lap as that mean hombre, Mysterious Billy Smith, fouled out in 21 rounds in Buffalo, January 15, 1900. Rube lost the crown to Matty Matthews, the ring's Cyrano, by a 15-round decision in Detroit the following October 16th. Then he regained it by a 10th-round knockout over Matty in Toronto, May 24, 1901.

Joe Walcott ended Rube's second reign the 18th of December of that year at Fort Erie. It took Walcott only five rounds to dispose of the world's second welterweight champ.

Rube was born in Pittsburg, Kansas, on January 20, 1874. The 5 ft., 8½ in., 145-pound country boy took up fighting in 1896 and scored six knockouts in a row. In those days of the long haul (40 rounds or more) and a sixty percent purse for the winner, Rube won 39 of 50 bouts. He could take a man out with either hand and did so 31 times.

The rugged Kansan left the ring in 1906. He died on June 11, 1952, in the city where he was born.

JOE WALCOTT
(1873–1935)

Among the candidates for a niche in the Old Timers' section of boxing's Hall of Fame is welterweight champion Joe Walcott, whose name kindles a lot of memories from the graybeards who once thrilled to his masterful style and always have regarded the West Indian Negro as the original Giant Killer.

Walcott remains one of the very few men to

The original Joe Walcott fought anyone from welters to heavies and is down in history as one of the few prizefighters to remain active for more than 20 years. (NEA)

campaign professionally for more than a score years. He started in 1890, retired in 1911. In between that period, an awful lot of leather was thrown. Seldom weighing more than 145 pounds and standing only 5 ft., 2 in., he fought and defeated not only welterweights, among whom he belonged, but middleweights and light-heavyweights as well. He fought Kid Lavigne and Mysterious Billy Smith and Kid McPartland and George Gardner and Rube Ferns and Philadelphia Jack O'Brien and Joe Gans and Sam Langford, among other leading lights of his era.

Born in Barbados, West Indies, in 1872, he had no background as an alley brawler, yet he plainly was made for fighting and became a professional when he was eighteen years old. His very first bout, on February 29, 1890, was something of a harbinger—he knocked out Tom Powers in two rounds in Boston.

In 1901, Walcott scored a five-round K.O. over Rube Ferns at Fort Erie to win the championship, lost it to Dixie Kid on a disputed foul in the 20th round in San Francisco in 1904. However, Dixie Kid outgrew the welterweight division and Walcott was again recognized as champ. He lost the title permanently in 1906 to Honey Mellody.

Walcott was something of a physical freak. Despite his size, he had the stamina of a bull. He beat light-heavyweight George Gardner in 30 rounds, went 25 rounds against Billy Smith, held the great Sam Langford to a draw in 10 rounds. He engaged in battles of 20 rounds 13 times. The little man simply loved to fight.

It was Walcott who, in a way, was responsible for putting the immortal Battling Nelson in the important money. Joe was unable to keep a date to fight Martin Canole for promoter Alex Greggains in San Francisco in 1904. Billy Roche had seen Nelson flatten Spider Welsh in 16 rounds in Salt Lake City and suggested to Alex that he substitute Bat for Walcott. Nelson took the bout for $750 and knocked out Canole in the 18th round. Nelson went on to put the lighter men in the big money for the next five years.

DIXIE KID
(1883–1935)

Aaron L. Brown (alias Dixie Kid) is best remembered as the kid who beat the great Joe Walcott, a 15-year veteran, for the welterweight championship of the world.

Strangely enough, some record books hardly note the feat. But Dixie Kid, 5 ft., 8 in., 145 pounds, was a true champion. Born December 23, 1883, at Fulton, Missouri, he began prize fighting at the age of sixteen, scoring 18 knockouts in his first 20 professional bouts.

On April 30, 1904, Dixie Kid and Walcott were matched for the championship in San Francisco. It was Youth vs. Age and in the 20th round Old Father Time caused the thirty-two-year-old Walcott to get careless as he fetched a low blow. Dixie Kid was awarded the title on a foul.

The rivals met again two weeks later in the same ring. This time it ended in a 20-round draw.

Shortly thereafter Dixie Kid outgrew the class and Walcott claimed the vacated title.

American prize rings saw nothing of the Missouri Negro after March of 1911. Dixie Kid went to Europe and campaigned extensively in France, England, Ireland and Scotland. He retired from the ring after knocking out Billy Bristowe in two rounds, March 30, 1914.

Dixie Kid died on April 13, 1936.

BILLY (HONEY) MELLODY
(1884–1919)

Honey Mellody was aptly nicknamed. The Irish American from Charlestown, Massachusetts, was indeed a honey of a welterweight. He was clever and durable, packed a powerful punch, and was totally unafraid.

Starting in 1901, he won his first 10 bouts by knockouts. On October 16, 1906, he beat the original Joe Walcott in 15 rounds at Chelsea and claimed the welterweight championship of the world. He also defeated Walcott in a return match the following month.

Mellody's claim to the crown was violently disputed by Joe Thomas, who had K.O.'d Honey at Chelsea six weeks before he whipped Walcott. The pair were matched again on March 6, 1907, in Philadelphia, but the dispute was not solved as it was a six-round no-decision affair. Mike (Twin) Sullivan settled the issue a month-and-a-half later by taking the title from Mellody in 20 rounds in Los Angeles. Honey fought for another six years, mostly no-decision matches in and around New England, and finally retired after beating Dave Powers on January 30, 1913.

The former welterweight champion of the

world was a wholesome chap, clean-living, popular. In or out of the battle pit, Honey Mellody, 5 ft., 7 in., 145 pounds, lived up to his last name and then some—he was always on key.

MIKE (TWIN) SULLIVAN
(1878–1937)

Fighters thought they were seeing double when they climbed into the ring against Mike Sullivan.

You couldn't blame them.

The Cambridge, Massachusetts, Irishman had a twin brother named Jack (also a boxer) and the pair were so identical they kept opponents, ringworms and record-book compilers befuddled right to the end. More than once, during their amateur days, Mike weighed in and the slightly heavier Jack did the fighting.

Mike was a welterweight, Jack a middleweight. Both could hit like mules, but only Mike won a championship. He whipped Honey Mellody in twenty rounds in Los Angeles, April 23, 1907, to win the welter wreath.

Joe Gans and Stanley Ketchel were the only ones able to K.O. Mike.

The Sullivan twins were prematurely balding. This added to the general mix-up. Each also had a crossed and floating left eye, which disconcerted foes even more. Fighters watched the other fellow's eyes and feet in those days. Each Sullivan had a slightly-hooked nose. While they were born in Cambridge, they spoke with an Irish brogue thick enough to be fresh from the Auld Sod. Each had a fine sense of humor. They sang and danced well enough to appear in vaudeville, but disliked show business.

The twins tackled the most formidable warriors of their time, but because Jack was always the heavier their lists of foes are almost entirely different. There was, however, the celebrated case of Jack attempting to avenge Mike's first-round knockout by the fabulous Stanley Ketchel at Colma, California, in 1908. Jack gave it all he had three months later but went out like a third strike in the 20th.

Mike met such as Elbows McFadden, Jack Blackburn, Joe Gans, Honey Mellody, Jimmy Clabby and Jack Dillon. Jack squared off with renowned warriors like Philadelphia Jack O'Brien, Kid McCoy, Tommy Burns, Fireman Jim Flynn, Joe Thomas, Marvin Hart, Frank Mantell, Frank Klaus, Billy Papke, Joe Jeannette, Dillon, Gunboat Smith and Battling Levinsky.

A thick book easily could be written about the Sullivans. Their father rented horses and carts to contractors in Cambridge, and the boys wound up in that business, sticking with it until it was thoroughly outmoded. They kept busy, earned top money of the day, and were careful with it. Mike was quite religious. They were total abstainers while in competition, but Jack kicked around a little in later years. Mike quit fighting at thirty-five to look after the father's business. Jack remained in the thick of things until he was forty-four. As a tribute to their skill, both left the ring almost totally unmarked. No other pair of twins went as far in any line of athletics, and theirs was the toughest of all.

JACK BRITTON
(1885–1962)
and TED (KID) LEWIS
(1894–1970)

Jack Britton and Ted (Kid) Lewis were the lusty parties to the longest rivalry the prize ring has ever known.

The Irish-American and the Englishman fought 20 times in six years. From August 31, 1915, to February 7, 1921, they outclassed just about every leading welter and middleweight from Seattle to London.

Of the two-score times they fought, Britton won 4, Lewis 3, there was 1 draw, and 12 were listed as no-decision affairs.

The Englishman knocked Britton down more times (6) than any other fistfighter in history. In June, 1917, they fought *three* times. The first two were no-decision matches, but in the third, on June 25th, Lewis carved out a bloody 20-round decision to win the undisputed world welterweight championship.

Ted (Kid) Lewis was the first Englishman in history to cross the seas from his native land and win a world's boxing championship. He started as a featherweight, went on to box in six weight divisions in 20 years, and in 1913 became the first to use a mouthpiece in a prize fight. He twice held the welter title of the world.

Gershon Mendeloff—his real name—was born in the tough Petticoat Lane section of London's teeming East End, the English equivalent of New York's lower East Side, on October 14, 1894. He had his first professional fight at the age of fourteen and received sixpence and a cup of tea as his end of the purse. His next victory earned him a silver cup, which promptly melted overnight on the mantelpiece at home. After that, life got better. He won the British featherweight title at seventeen, added the European crown, then the world welterweight championship, to go on to take his place alongside immortals Freddy Welsh, Jimmy Wilde, Jem Driscoll, Owen Moran and Jack (Kid) Berg as the greatest of British champions. In a total of 253 pro bouts, Lewis won 155, had 9 draws, and 65 went into the record book as no-decision.

Lewis, 5 ft., 5½ in. and 147 lbs. at his best, was a cruel, vicious, cunning, combination boxer-fighter with a swift left hook. The killer instinct of the jungle was definitely there. When he had an opponent hurt he gave him no mercy. Jack Britton hated him. All of their bouts were grudge fights.

Britton was managed by colorful Dan Morgan and, together, they established a record that will stand forever: the 20-bout feud with Lewis. At the time, Lewis was the British welterweight champion. When he arrived in America, in 1914, his manager, Jimmy Johnston, pulled Morgan's own trick on Dan and promptly *claimed* the world's 147-pound title. Morgan protested, so he and Johnston put their heads together and decided to match their pair and settle all arguments. It was the start of the greatest series of return bouts in history.

This was in the era when bouts were won not so much in the ring as in the telegraph office, by the fighter whose manager could get there first and flash his version of the match to the out-of-town newspapers. The sports editors simply took the manager's word for it as to which man won the fight. So whenever Britton and Lewis fought, it was as much a battle between Morgan and Johnston as it was between their fighters.

One night while this famous road show was appearing in Cincinnati, Morgan and Johnston agreed beforehand that they would telegraph the newspapers a draw. But in the sixth round Morgan looked over in Lewis's corner and Johnston was not in sight. Morgan grabbed his chief second and said, "You take care of Britton but don't tell him how to fight. He already knows how to fight." Then Morgan lammed out, hailed a hack, and raced for the telegraph office. Johnston was there ahead of him, of course, but he hadn't yet had time to get any wires off to the papers and they shook hands again and made it a draw.

"Another time," Morgan told me, "Johnston returned to New York after a Britton-Lewis fight squawking. Seems there weren't any

Of all the fighters managed by Dumb Dan Morgan, Jack Britton was the most remarkable. He fought for 26 years and was still a champion at thirty-seven. (Photo courtesy the late Dan Morgan)

In 253 recorded bouts, Ted (Kid) Lewis was kayoed only four times; this was one of those times, when Georges Carpentier stopped him in the first round, in London, 1922. (UPI)

wires in the fight club and he couldn't get the word to the press. And he couldn't phone his message in because I'd hired me a half-dozen guys and planted them in all the phone booths in the neighborhood until they got the signal from me, along about the seventh round, that my man was the winner."

Morgan and Johnston had Britton and Lewis in another town fighting in a little ball park and Jimmy brought a "cousin" along with him who claimed he was a newspaperman. Jimmy and his "cousin" had wired the park, with wires running from under the ring and out beneath the grandstand so that they could beat Morgan getting the word back to the papers. But the scheme didn't stop Morgan. Dan found out about it and went down to the telegraph manager in the town and told him that he, Morgan, owned $500 worth of stock in the company. Johnston hadn't thought of that. Then Dan got two telegraph linemen from the manager and hid them under the stands. When Dan flashed them the signal, they went clip-clip with their wirecutters. When Johnston discovered his private pipeline cut he screamed bloody murder, but Morgan was already on his way downtown to Western Union. Johnston got there, too, after a while, and the following day Sid Mercer, who was a sports editor back in New York, printed both telegrams.

"Johnston's wire was sent in the fifth round and Morgan's in the ninth," Sid wrote. "But Morgan had a headstart and beat Johnston by half an hour."

Along the way, Ted (Kid) Lewis won British and European titles at three different weights—the feather, welter and middleweight.

One of his oddest fights was against the French war hero, Georges Carpentier, May 11, 1922, in London. Lewis was outweighed by 35 pounds, but he challenged the French heavyweight in an attempt to win back international prestige for the British. Carpentier had stiffened all the good English heavies. The ending—for Lewis—was sudden, if not confusing. Early in the first round, Carpentier jolted Lewis with a solid smash on the beltline. Lewis thought the blow was low and turned his head to complain to the referee, charging a foul. While his head was turned, Carpentier knocked him out.

Lewis fought until he was thirty-five and then became a haberdashery salesman in Piccadilly. Right up to his death he was still revered by the British as though he'd just won the world championship the day before yesterday.

It is doubted if the prize ring ever knew a more assiduous trouper than Jack Britton. Of all the fighters managed by Dan Morgan, he was the most remarkable. He was active in the ring for 26 years and was still a champion at thirty-seven. He fought the best men of several succeeding eras, a record eclipsed in point of time only by Bob Fitzsimmons. So far as the number of bouts is concerned, Jack outscored Fitz by more than five to one.

Dan Morgan booked his welterweight all over. The tank towns saw as much of him as

Madison Square Garden. He fought 10 times in Canton, Ohio, for example, and Savannah, Georgia, featured him five times in a row.

Britton was a master craftsman. He could make a punk fighter look good, a one-sided fight look breathlessly close. Did you ever hear of such sensational welterweight contenders as Jake Barada, Bat Kopen, Goats Doig, Dave Palttz, Izzy Tanner and Arturo Shekels? They all went the limit with Britton, the fans saw exciting shows, and the promoters made a little money.

Jack, a good-looking, brainy Irishman, stood 5 ft., 8 in. and weighed 144. He was born at Clinton, New York, on October 14, 1885. He broke in as a prize fighter in 1905. From then until he called it a career he tackled the finest lightweights and welters, among them Benny Leonard, Packey McFarland, Ted Kid Lewis, Mike O'Dowd and Mickey Walker. At forty-three, he was still beating some of the top fighters around.

"Before Britton came to me, he was getting nowhere fast," recalled Morgan. "He'd been fighting about eight years when a West Side Irishman, who'd given up on him, brought him to me. I'd seen Jack fight and saw his potential. His only fault was that he refused to train. So when he came to me, I said: 'All you guys from Philly are alike. You fight your six rounds and then go hang out in some pub. Well, you've got to live regular hours, if you fight for me.' Jack agreed to change his ways. I started him off in Boston and he walloped out Eddie Murphy, a terrific puncher, in the 10th round. After that, the purses grew—$5,000 here and $10,000 there. We went on to split more than $400,000. The last year he fought for me—in 1922—he earned $150,000.

"Britton was always ready to defend his title. We scheduled a match with a youngster in the Midwest one time who was knocking everybody dead. This was late in Jack's career and his age was showing. Despite his cleverness, he was getting floored quite frequently. When we came into this town the local press was predicting that the hometown phee-nom would knock my old man out and win the championship.

"'Listen,' I told the writers, 'so you think your kid can stop my old man, do you? Well, I'll tell you what I will do. I'll let you count him out. Bring some stopwatches to ringside and if Britton gets knocked down you time the counting. If he's down for 10 all you do is yell *out* and the referee will take your word for it.'

"On the night of the fight, the sports writers all came armed with stopwatches. And all around the ring and throughout the arena, even way up in the gallery, the fans carried watches and clocks of all descriptions. Stopwatches, alarm clocks, grandfather clocks . . . all kinds. The tick-tock, tick-tock almost drove me deaf."

Morgan suddenly stopped in the middle of his story and chuckled.

I asked, "Well, how did the fight come out?"

"Oh," he said, "that kid ain't hit my old man yet."

Britton's real name was William J. Breslin. Despite his flawless generalship, he sported elaborate cauliflower ears. They looked like big leather buttons. He used his left ear to keen advantage. He called it his cushion. Rolling with them, he could take punches on it all day and not feel them.

Good boxers acquire tin ears as well as sluggers. The slugger comes straight in, gets bashed on the beezer or above the eyes. The boxer rolls with punches or they graze his ears. Anyway, the ears get it. Jem Driscoll, for example, had a pair of cauliflower ears the size of porkchops.

Once, while Britton was touring the country fighting local wonders, his opponent's manager took one look at Jack's tin ear and told his fighter to keep pounding it. While the kid socked the ear, Britton concentrated on the midriff. In the ninth round, the kid had punched himself out and Britton put over the sleeper. Jack won many a fight using that left ear as a decoy. He also had a peculiar left-hand punch. He'd bring it up to an opponent's chin while pulling away from a counter blow. It was a very annoying habit and made him exceedingly hard to hit.

Dan Morgan was a total abstainer and expected the same from Britton. During the wild Twenties, however, they were constantly called on by big shots of the social, financial and racket worlds for "complimentary tickets" for their fights or the procuring of choice seats. The beneficiaries of their good nature invariably returned their courtesy by shipping them cases of the best whisky and brandy.

"I always figured booze did much more

good on the outside than on the inside," explained Dan, "so I used the stuff to rub Britton down. He had the best rubbing alcohol in the world. Brandy cost $1.25 a shot those days. *Nothing* was too good for *my* boy."

Britton first laid claim to the welterweight title after winning a 12-round decision from Mike Glover in Boston, on June 22, 1915, three months after he and Lewis fought for the first time, a no-decision affair. Lewis then won a decision from Britton, on September 27th—and the Morgan-Johnston argument was on.

"After that," Morgan said, "the world welterweight title bounced back and forth like a shuttlecock. In all their fights, my man and Lewis never shook hands once. Jack refused to participate in the traditional act at the beginning of their bouts because he hated Lewis, feeling he was a dirty fighter. Each succeeding fight was better than the last one. Britton beat Lewis in 20 rounds to claim the crown in 1916 at New Orleans, lost it back to him at Dayton in 1917, and then regained it again at Canton in 1919. That was the greatest day in Irish history. My Irishman knocked out an Englishman (ninth round) on *St. Patrick's Day!* The pace was fierce. Blood flowed out of both men. Britton had Lewis down three times in the sixth; he was so arm-weary I ordered him to ease up in the next two rounds to catch his breath. His recuperative powers were amazing. By the ninth round he was ready to go back to work. I told him, 'Just think of your Irish ancestors and go out there and stiffen this Englishman!' Jack did as he was told and knocked Lewis kicking."

That was Morgan's cue.

He rushed down to the nearest Western Union office and dispatched 350 telegrams and cables. They read:

"An Irishman, Billy Breslin, alias Jack Britton, knocked out Ted (Kid) Lewis, the English welterweight champion, on this St. Patrick's Day. Long live Ireland. Thank you."

Dan's list was most impressive.

"The big shots I sent cables to included the Kaiser, then taking it on the lam in Holland," he said. "I also sent one to the King of Siam, another to Australia, and even one to King George. How do you like that Englishman? He and the rest of his tea drinkers didn't even bother to reply. But the King of Siam replied—in *Siamese!*"

Britton was an old man of thirty-seven when he lost his title to young Mickey Walker in 1922. Jack didn't particularly want to fight Mickey but agreed to the match when Morgan told him that their cut of the gate amounted to 55 percent. This meant that Walker was fighting for slightly more than expenses. There was so much talk that the fight wasn't on the level that William Muldoon, Chairman of the New York Boxing Commission, declared all bets off. It was later learned that the only reason for all the gossip was that Walker had agreed not to knock out the aging Britton. It turned out to be a whale of a fight, Mickey winning on points in 15.

The quiet and well-mannered Britton retired from the prize ring in 1930, lost a fortune when the Florida real estate bubble busted. He became boxing instructor at the Downtown Athletic and Catholic Youths' Clubs in New York, where he taught boys clean living and self-defense.

Britton and Morgan went on seeing a lot of each other. They both liked football. One Saturday, they traveled up to the Yale Bowl to watch the Bulldogs play Princeton. They were amazed at the ferocity and tenacity and ruggedness of the college kids.

"Some of those lads ought to make good heavyweights," Dan told Jack. "They're big and fast and game, and they have brains."

Britton did some calculating.

"Dan," he said, "let's talk to some of them and teach them to box. We might find a champion and make ourselves rich again."

They placed an advertisement in the New York and New Jersey papers: "All college boys interested in making lots of money as prize fighters report to Dan Morgan and Jack Britton at Grupp's Gym."

Sixty college boys showed up at Grupp's the first day. Three weeks later half of the aspirants had decided that fighting was not for them. After another week there were only 10 left. Then there were but three. At last, all but one had disappeared.

"But this last one was something to get excited about," Morgan told me. "Britton and I affectionately called him the Princeton Tiger. He was tall, fast and clever. He flashed a rapier left and Britton taught him all the moves. He was a tiger, all right. I envisioned a stack of greenbacks a mile high.

"One day, it happened there was no one around Grupp's to spar with our tiger. Suddenly, a solid, bull-necked, flashy-eyed guy in a leather jacket walked in asking for me. He said he wanted to be a fighter and was told I could fix him up. I gave him the once-over.

"I asked him, 'Have you done any fighting?'

"'Oh, sure,' he said.

"'Who'd you ever lick?'

"'I stiffened nine cab drivers last week.'

"I was impressed. Cab drivers at that time were a rugged type of citizen. So I led him to a big punching bag and told him to punch. He almost tore the rafters down. He swung wide and had no idea how to hit. But he could blast. Then I got him some trunks and shoes and told him to put them on. I sent word down to Britton that I had a sparring partner for our tiger.

"When I started lacing gloves on the stranger, he protested. 'I can't fight with them things on,' he hollered. 'I always fight with bare fists. I don't need no gloves.' I explained to him that gloves were obligatory. I said, 'We might all be thrown in jail if gloves are not worn.' He reluctantly let me slip them on him.

"So we got the pair into the ring and I told the stranger that he should drop his head a bit and tear in at the other fellow. 'He'll hit you with a jab or two,' I told him, 'but as soon as you get in close give him all you've got with both hands.'

"Britton noticed that the stranger knew nothing about the art of boxing. He was plainly worried. He felt we were taking too much of a chance. 'My tiger will kill this poor guy,' Jack whispered to me. 'We'll see,' I said.

"I rang the bell. The Tiger bounced off his stool and wasted no time landing a looping left to the body. He drove a right to the chin, a left and right to the body. But the stranger shook off these blows and bored in. He let fly with both hands, smashing the Tiger's nose, ripping a gash under one eye and doubling him up with body punches. Then he flattened the Tiger with a vicious right uppercut to the jaw. As Britton dragged our lifeless Tiger back to his corner, the stranger turned to me and said, 'Well, Mr. Morgan, I gotta loaded truck waitin' for me at the corner and I gotta make some deliveries. Maybe I'll see you tomorrow.' Then he put on his pants and shoes and socks and leather jacket and cap and beat it. A few minutes later the Tiger was dressed and beat it, too. We never saw hide or hair of either of them ever again.

"That's life. You have to be philosophical about those experiences. But, as I've always said, college boys don't belong in the prize ring. They get hit on the head and then go out and phone mother."

PETE LATZO
(1902–1968)

Pete Latzo was just another tough kid from the Pennsylvania coal mines when he ran across Paddy Mullins, the fight manager. Pete's brother Steve had already established himself as a damn good welterweight, and the way Paddy figured. . . .

"It wouldn't do to have two Latzos in the welters," Paddy said. "So we'll give you a new name. Young Clancy."

Well, Pete went along. As "Young Clancy" he won some here, and dropped some there. He acquired a reputation as a first-rate club fighter, but obviously that was a hell of a way to make a living. So he got busy and beat guys with names like Frankie Schoell and Wally Hinkle and Georgie Ward and Harry Galfund and K.O. Phil Kaplan and Patsy Haley and Mannie Owens and Italian Joe Gans and Morrie Schlaifer. The apprenticeship lasted for seven years and took him to such places as Buffalo and New York and Wilkes-Barre and Boston and Omaha and Brooklyn and Oakland and Hollywood. Then, on May 20, 1926, he was given an opportunity that comes to few club fighters—a crack at Mickey Walker's welterweight crown. The bout took place in fabled Scranton, in Pete's home state. Among those covering the fight for the big city newspapers was Damon Runyon, who was amazed by the carnival spirit in the streets of Scranton. Latzo was not the least overcome by all the commotion. After all, he had fought in Scranton exactly 25 times since March, 1922, and had always given the folks their money's worth. He was their hero.

"Nearly all of the show windows of the city are decorated in some manner suggesting the battle tomorrow night, as Boston and New Haven and Philadelphia and other cities decorate for a football game, or as Louisville decorates for its Derby," Runyon wrote on the eve of battle. "All the talk around here is of the fight. People are coming in from the surrounding towns for miles around. The hotels are jammed. Not all of the visitors can hope to see the fight, as it is to be held in an armory that seats only about 9,000. A lot of them are here just to get a touch of the general excitement."

That was the kind of electric drama generated when Latzo clashed with Walker for the world championship. The highly partisan crowd went berserk as Pete won the 10-round decision.

The hard-bitten Slav, who was born at Coloraine, Pennsylvania, on August 1, 1902, lost his title to Joe Dundee a year later in New York (Decision, 15 rounds). Then he put on weight and tackled the bigger boys, seasoned pros like Maxie Rosenbloom, Jimmy Braddock, Jimmy Slattery, Tommy Loughran, and Leo Lomski.

Pete ended his 15-year career on a dying fall. He lost 11 bouts in a row. Teddy Yarosz, who was just three months away from winning the middleweight crown, pushed him through the trapdoor for the last time. He knocked him out in the fourth round. Only one other opponent—Morrie Schlaifer—had ever done that to him in 150 bouts.

That's the way it was for Pete Latzo on June 5, 1934.

He never fought again.

JOE DUNDEE
(1902-   )

Joe Dundee was the first of the Fighting Dundees and one of the few champions in history to lose his title on a foul.

The mishap occurred in Detroit, on July 25, 1929. Dundee was matched with Jackie Fields, who held the N.B.A. version of the welterweight championship. Dundee was recognized in New York State as world titleholder. The bout was thus a showdown for the undisputed crown.

While it is still a dim horror story to Dundee, Fields remembers the details: "Joe did not particularly have a good night. He was slow getting off the dime. I started fast, red-hot. I wanted that undisputed title. I floored him a couple of times in the first round, and several more in the second. The last time I knocked him down he started to crawl on his hands and knees, grabbed the rope, wheeled around and slugged me below the beltline. All I was wearing was one of those old-fashioned aluminum safety cups, and when he hit me I thought I was going to die. I guess I passed out because the next thing I knew Willie Rooney, my manager, was leaning over me in the dressing room and saying I'd won the fight and the world championship on a foul. I thought he was kidding, but it was true. Dundee was disqualified in the second round for hitting low and I was the champion."

The Dundee camp was guaranteed $50,000 to fight Fields, and it bet the entire purse on Dundee. However, all bets were off in the event of a foul, so they didn't have to pay. Fields had been a 2-1 favorite.

Dundee had the physical equipment to be an outstanding welterweight. He stood 5 ft., 7 in. and weighed 145. One opponent said he looked tough enough "to go bear hunting with a switch." He had ridges of muscle above the beltline, legs like tree stumps, hamlike fists, and a flat nose.

He was born in Italy in 1902. His Christian name was Samuel Lazzaro. He started prize-fighting in 1921, and won the New York portion of the world title in 1927 with a 15-round decision over Pete Latzo. His reign as champion was tarnished by *four* non-title defeats. Johnny Indrisano beat him, Young Jack Thompson knocked him out, Jimmy Finley held him to a draw, and Al Mello trounced him twice.

On the positive side, Joe Dundee was a wear-'em-down type of mauler, relentless, stalking his prey like an animal, with his left hand held high, and the right cocked and ready to sink off his chest to the other guy's body. He piled up many of his points in the late rounds, when he had an opponent all tuckered out. He won 62 of 123 matches in this fashion.

YOUNG JACK THOMPSON
(1904-1946)

Cecil Lewis Thompson was the first of the welterweight champions to finish his career without a knockout against him. Since his retirement in 1932, only Barney Ross, Kid Gavilan and Carmen Basilio could make that statement.

Young Jack Thompson was a good all-around fighter. Testifying to his punching power were 31 K.O.'s in 66 pro bouts. "Thompson made a lot of old men out of opponents," said Ray Alvis, who managed him. "He was shifty, fast, and could whack your head off. He started off in 1928 winning 29 of 35 bouts. Twenty of his victims were knockouts."

Thompson's 36th fight was an N.B.A. title

match against Jackie Fields, who decisioned him in 10 rounds, in 1929 in Chicago. Less than a year later they fought again in Detroit, this time 15 rounds, and Thompson won the title. Fields was so disgusted with himself he announced his retirement. "I was overtrained," Jackie said. "I couldn't get my hands up. He licked me and won the decision."

On September 5, 1930, Thompson put his crown on the line against Tommy Freeman, who nine months before won a 10-round decision over him. Freeman made it two in a row as he won a 15-round decision and the championship.

On April 14, 1931, Thompson joined the select circle of ex-champions who have regained their titles. He kayoed Freeman in the 12th round in Cleveland.

Six months later he was an ex-champion once more. Lou Brouillard permanently relieved him of royal status by punching out a 15-round decision.

Young Jack Thompson was born in San Francisco in 1904. At his fighting peak, the California black stood 5 ft., 8 in. and weighed 145. His prize ring career lasted only seven years (1926–1932), and he was only forty-two when he died. A short span by today's standards—but long enough to rule the welters twice!

LOU BROUILLARD
(1911–)

Lou Brouillard, squat and southpaw, had the strength of a bucking horse. The French-Canadian hit like a bloke gone beserk. He won 60 of his first 64 professional bouts, 44 by knockouts, and was stopped himself only once (by Tiger Jack Fox) in a career total of 140 fights.

You might say that Brouillard held one-and-a-half world championships. That is, he beat Young Jack Thompson in 1931 for the welterweight crown, and two years later flattened Ben Jeby to earn recognition in New York as middleweight champion. His claim to the latter was not universally accepted, however.

In 1932, Lou lost his welter title to Jackie Fields, and in '33 Vince Dundee won the middleweight championship, American edition, from him in 15 rounds.

Brouillard was a losing party in Paris to a strange title series. Twice, in 1936 and '37, he challenged Marcel Thil for the middleweight crown—and twice French officials disqualified him for fouling. The first match went four rounds, the second was stopped after six.

Lou retired from the ring in 1940 to join the U.S. Army, and then settled down at South Hanson, Massachusetts to raise canine retrievers. Something of a canine himself in the ring, he was right at home working with the breed.

JACKIE FIELDS
(1907–)

Jackie Fields was a mastodon of distinction in The Game for nearly a decade. Among other prizes, he won a Gold Medal for beating Joe Salas in the featherweight finals of the 1924 Olympic Games, and later, as a pro, he *twice* captured the welterweight championship of the world.

Jackie was a master of his craft. He blocked punches well, blunted opponents' speed by crowding them into corners, bludgeoned their heads and bodies, and excused a lot of them from the night's exercises early in a bout. He kayoed 28 and was himself knocked out only once—by the great Jimmy McLarnin in 1925.

Fields had had only nine pro bouts when he fought McLarnin. Except for a six-round draw with Johnny Lamar, he'd won them all. "The only reason I agreed to fight McLarnin is that the promoter said he'd give me $5,000. Well, I was buying a home for my mother and that was a lot of money. So I took the fight and Jimmy flattened me in the second round and broke my jaw. He floored me four or five times and my corner threw the towel in. I felt terrible afterward and told my manager, Gig Rooney, I wasn't going to fight anymore. I had more than ten grand saved up and my Jewish mother said no more fighting. You know how Jewish mothers are. I promised her I'd quit, but Rooney came back and talked me back into the ring. He conned me good. He said I lacked guts and that I owed it to myself to go back in there and prove to the world I was a real champion. So I moved up to the welterweights and the rest is history."

Jacob Finkelstein (his real name), the son of a Chicago butcher, was born on February 9, 1907, and moved to Los Angeles when he was thirteen. He learned how to fight in the streets of L.A., and later at the Los Angeles Athletic Club, where he sparred in the gym with Fidel LaBarba, the flyweight amateur champion. Fields won 51 of 54 amateur bouts, including the Olympic title, and then turned pro in September of 1924. His first victory as a professional was over Joe Salas, whom he defeated in the Olympic finals. "It just broke Joe's heart," Jackie recalled. "He refused to speak to me again after that fight."

Five years later, Jackie won the N.B.A. welterweight championship from Young Jack Thompson in 10 rounds in Chicago. Thompson won the crown back 10 months later in Detroit. On January 28, 1932, Jackie became welter champ for the second time with a decision over Lou Brouillard in Chicago. On February 22, 1933, he lost the title to Young Corbett III in San Francisco.

Fields had only one more fight. On May 2, 1933, he whipped Young Peter Jackson in Los Angeles and then suddenly announced his retirement. He was only twenty-six years old. Jackie had suffered an eye injury in a 1932 auto accident in Hammond, Indiana, and lost the vision in it. Unlike Harry Greb, he needed *both* his eyes to get the job done in the ring.

TOMMY FREEMAN
(1904–   )

No one ever accused Tommy Freeman of being a recluse. Between January 9th and March 1, 1931, the Arkansas Razorback defended his welterweight title *five times*— against Pete August, Eddie Murdock, Duke Trammel, Kid Kober and Alfredo Gaona.

He put up his title once too often that Spring, however, and on April 14th, Young Jack Thompson came along and kayoed him in the 12th round to take the crown away from him. For Freeman, it was his seventh fight in four months!

Freeman was a perfect combination of boxer and club fighter. A great crowd-pleaser, the Irishman was a solid infighter who stuck to his last. Over a 17-year period, he won 144 of 185 matches, including 69 K.O.'s.

Tommy was born at Hot Springs, Arkansas, on January 22, 1904. He took up prizefighting in 1921, and really caught fire between mid-1923 and mid-February 1926, when he put it all together and won 39 bouts in a row. He waited nine years for a chance at the world championship, and on September 5, 1930, his time finally arrived via a 15-round decision over Thompson, who seven months later taught him never to play musical chairs with the championship!

YOUNG CORBETT III
(1905–   )

Ralph Capabianca Giordano fought and conquered the best welters with a shuffling southpaw style that bordered almost on magic. He gave boxing lessons to such solid headliners as Sam Langford, Young Jack Thompson, Jack Zivic, Jackie Fields, Ceferino Garcia, Mickey Walker, Gus Lesnevich, Billy Conn and Fred Apostoli.

Fighting under the alias of Young Corbett III, he won the welterweight championship

Young Corbett III was still fighting main events 21 years after he turned professional. (AP)

from Fields on February 22, 1933 (a *dozen* years after he began) and lost it to Jimmy McLarnin 97 days later.

The 5 ft., 7 in., 147-pound Italiano was born in Naples on May 27, 1905, came to America and started boxing in 1919. He was still fighting main events 21 years and 166 bouts later. He lost only 12 fights, was kayoed only three times (by Eddie Morris, McLarnin and Apostoli). He never lost a match in 1940, his final year in the ring.

Corbett joined the Fresno, California, police force after bowing out. It was a most logical move. After all, he had been keeping law and order in the prize ring for 22 years.

JIMMY McLARNIN
(1907–)

Jimmy McLarnin, with the face of a baby but the punch of a man, was a promoter's dream.

Flacks—those dream-up, steam-up guys—built him up as part lion, part tiger, and part John L. Sullivan, Jr.

Jimmy held the welterweight championship of the world in an era when the lighter divisions enjoyed spectacular ascendancy. On his way to the title, the popular little man from Vancouver, British Columbia (by way of Belfast, Ireland) knocked out Sergeant Baker in a round, Al Singer in three, Ruby Goldstein in two, and Sid Terris in one. This mad dash for the world crown culminated in a first-round K.O. of Young Corbett III, in Los Angeles, on May 29, 1933, only seven-and-a-half months after knocking out the great Benny Leonard in six rounds to end Benny's comeback.

Then came Ross—Barney Ross. They fought three times in exactly one year. The series began on May 28, 1934, and ended on May 28, 1935. The title popped back and forth like a tennis ball. Barney won the first bout, lost the second, and then won the crown back again. Each match went the full 15 rounds. The last one was the best.

The late Henry McLemore reported it this way:

"For 15 rounds at the Polo Grounds last night McLarnin, once again the baby-faced bomber, threw every punch he had, executed every wile learned in years and years of fighting the best of 'em. But it wasn't enough.

"As proof that condition alone didn't win for Ross, McLarnin won the 15th and final round; won it with as gallant a last stand as any champion ever made. For three full minutes he stood toe to toe, chin to chin, with Barney, and fired his last round of ammunition. He didn't save a bullet. When the bell rang he didn't have a left hook or an uppercut or a right cross left in his body. If he had to lose—and he did—he certainly chose the magnificent way. He went down swinging.

Jimmy McLarnin was all smiles raising his hand in triumph after knocking out Young Corbett III for welterweight title in Los Angeles, in 1933. (Photo courtesy Jimmy McLarnin)

"When the boys came out for the 12th it was anybody's fight, and you knew that the title, and the gold and the glory that goes with it, rested on what happened from there out. Ross, despite breaking a bone in his left hand in the sixth round, went out for it. He took the 12th with a left to the stomach that popped McLarnin's mouth open and bent him double.

"Ross took the 13th by a mile. He was all over Jimmy from the bell and at the finish McLarnin was spreading his legs after the manner of a man in a tug-of-war, to keep upright. McLarnin started bravely in the 14th, shaking Ross from top to bottom with a one-two a second after the start, but Ross, never so vicious as when stung, launched a counter-offensive that forced his man to dig in."

In the scoring, the Associated Press had it

10-4-1 Ross. Referee Jack Dempsey scored it 5-3-7 Ross.

Immediately after the fight, Pop Foster, Jimmy's manager, told the press that McLarnin was through with the fight game. When Ross heard this he said that Jimmy was foolish to hang up his gloves.

"He's got a hundred winning fights left in him," Barney said. "He was hell tonight. Plenty hell. And don't let my managers, Art and Sam, tell you it was an easy fight. I was in there doing the fighting, and I know. I'll never have a tougher one."

More than 31,000 spectators paid $144,080 Depression dollars to see the third fight, as compared with $138,000 for the first bout and $197,000 for the second.

Actually, McLarnin fought three more times before calling it quits. He wound it up with 10-round decisions over Tony Canzoneri and Lou Ambers in 1936.

All told, Hall of Famer McLarnin defeated 13 men who at one time or another held world championships. One of boxing's biggest attractions in the late 1920s and 1930s, his bouts with Goldstein, Terris, Sammy Mandell and Billy Petrolle drew a combined audience of more than 600,000. Few prize fighters of any era have been more idolized and lionized.

"I was very lucky," Jimmy told me. "I made close to half a million dollars in the ring and saved most of it. In my last fight I beat the lightweight champion of the world, and when I retired at twenty-nine the only mark on me was a big ridge of bone across the back of my right hand, the result of hitting too many other fighters too hard. I wound up with a fine tile business in Los Angeles, a wonderful wife and four healthy children."

For years after he quit the prize ring, people kept coming up to him and asking, "Don't you miss the ring, Jimmy?"

Jimmy tried to give them an honest answer.

"No," he told them.

"Quit kidding," they insisted. "You loved every minute of it."

"No," Jimmy said, shaking his head, "I didn't love it at all. I didn't even like it. It was strictly business."

Jimmy told me that it was the first hundred seconds of a fight that were the hardest for him. "You're cold physically," he explained. "Your muscles are a little stiff and your reactions are a little slow. You're unsettled mentally. There was always a moment, just before the opening bell, when I'd stare through the floodlights hanging above the ring and try to pick out the people who were for me and the people who were against me. On some faces I saw more hostility than was called for. Then I'd look back across the ring at the man I was going to be fighting and try to remember how I was going to fight him and how I'd figured he was going to fight me. For an instant, I'd draw nothing but a blank. I'd be nervous and a little scared, and the feeling didn't usually pass until the fight started and somebody had been hit.

"This business of learning is never finished. I knew fighters who might have been world champions but who ended up punch-drunk simply because they stopped working on their weaknesses. Most fighters who got that way were managed by characters too lazy or incompetent to make them keep learning. Some of them thought they could learn by experience what they hadn't learned in the gym. They forgot, or never knew, that boxing is one business in which too much experience can be disastrous. Getting hit doesn't teach you how not to get hit. Getting hit too much slows your reflexes. The more you get hit, the easier you become to hit, and the easier you become to hit the more often you get hit."

In his entire career of 77 professional fights, Jimmy McLarnin was knocked out only once, by Ray Miller in 1928. Miller picked that night out as the greatest achievement of his career.

"But I paid the price for it," Ray grinned. "My Irish friends wouldn't speak to me. Wherever I went people glared at me for having knocked out their hero."

Miller later became a liquor salesman. One day he walked into an Irish saloon in Manhattan hoping to make a sale. The saloonkeeper, a little bit of a guy, gave Ray stiff sales resistance. To soften him up, Miller pointed to a large picture of McLarnin hanging on the wall back of the bar.

"A pretty good fighter," Miller commented.

"*Pretty* good!" snapped the saloonkeeper. "He was only the greatest fighter, pound for pound, who ever lived!"

"Well," Miller said, "if that's so, I couldn't have been so bad myself. I'm the only man who ever knocked him out."

McLarnin wrapped up his prize ring career here in victory in 1936 as he out-punched Lou Ambers in New York. (Photo courtesy Jimmy McLarnin)

"YOU?" cried the proprietor. "You knocked Jimmy out? What's your name? Miller, is it? Nobody by that name or any other name ever knocked McLarnin out!"

There was a record book under the bar and he hauled it out. He quickly turned to McLarnin's record.

"Oh, here you are," the owner said. "I knew you weren't telling the truth. It's right here he beat you in 10 rounds—March 22, 1929."

"So he did," Miller said. "But that was the second fight. We fought twice. Now look here." Ray pointed to the agate type: "Nov. 30, 1928, Detroit . . . KO by Ray Miller 8th round."

When the saloonkeeper saw that Miller was telling the truth, his face suddenly reddened. "You ought to be ashamed of yourself!" he stormed. "I wouldn't have your booze in my place for nothing! GET OUTTA HERE!"

The story had a happy ending, however. Miller cooled him off and finally made a sale and eventually a regular customer out of him.

"But every once in a while he'd look at me kind of funny-like," Ray Miller said, "and I was sure he'd never really forgiven me."

Jimmy McLarnin was born in Belfast, Ireland, on December 19, 1907, emigrated as a small boy with his family to Vancouver, British Columbia, where he developed a fondness for boxing. He built himself a makeshift gym in the basement of his father's store, and spent all of his spare time learning all he could about the "sweet science." At fourteen, he met Pop Foster, a World War I veteran who was recuperating from wounds at Vancouver Army Hospital. Pop was a graduate of London's boxing booths. He knew a prospect when he saw one. He encouraged Jimmy to be a prize fighter.

After cleaning up everything available around the Pacific Northwest, Pop Foster took Jimmy to California to campaign among the toughest flyweights, bantams and feathers; stars like Pancho Villa, Fidel LaBarba, Pal Moore and Bud Taylor. McLarnin tore into them all, head to head. He feinted, blocked, counter-punched. He made opponents swing at the air in frustrating misses. All the while he kept up a sharp, staccato one-two, slashing, beating their faces, and punching the stamina out of their legs and bodies. He stayed right in there, too—straight left, right cross, left hook, right uppercut, left jab, right jab . . . he threw every punch in the book at them. Pop Foster had schooled him well.

Strange thing about Pop. He was the champion pinchpenny. He guarded his savings with his life. Most managers take the standard 33 percent of their fighter's earnings. Not Pop. He took 50 percent of Jimmy's.

"But wait a minute," Jimmy told me. "Get it right. Pop was the grandest manager and friend a fighter ever had. Do you know that he actually refused to touch a penny of my purses until I had $25,000 in the bank? He was on the level. I wasn't like some of the less fortunate who had gangsters for managers. In 1934, I remember, I put $100,000 in the bank. Only $7,000 of that went to the government. Imagine what I'd pay now."

The late Scoop Conlon, oldtime Hollywood press agent for the stars, knew the Pop Foster personality well.

"He was tight-fisted by nature," Scoop said. "He'd been raised in poverty and never forgot the hungry days. Pop never spent a cent more than he had to. The first time he took Jimmy to New York for a bout he dug up four sparring partners. He made sure they were still amateurs. Jimmy sharpened up on them for several weeks and when it came time to break training camp, Pop called together the four sparring mates. 'You did a good job,' he told them. 'When Jimmy fights in New York again, I'll get in touch with you.' Then he handed each boy a cheap blue necktie. One of the kids had the audacity to ask Pop for pay. Pop waved him off with a shrug: 'I don't want to ruin your amateur standing.' "

McLarnin took up golf after retiring from the ring and teamed up with Conlon in tournament competition. After playing 18 holes at Lakeside Golf Club in North Hollywood one day, Jimmy told Scoop he had a dinner date with Pop at the Biltmore in Los Angeles. He went to the clubhouse to confirm the appointment by phone.

"Pop," Jimmy said, "I'll meet you at 6. I'm bringing along the missus. Okay?"

"Sure, Jim," Pop replied, "but you'll have to pay for her dinner. I only invited *you*."

Pop Foster adored Mrs. McLarnin, too, but Jimmy paid.

Now here's the punchline: Pop lived until he was eighty-three, and when he died he left his entire fortune—$240,000—to his boy, Jimmy McLarnin.

Miserly old skinflint, did you say?

BARNEY ROSS
(1909–1967)

It was difficult to take your eyes off Barney Ross, standing in his corner before a fight, the way he was when the bright floodlights were shining down, when his robe was off and there was just the red gloves strapped on his hands, ready to go to work. It rather annoyed him to think that an opponent felt he could beat him. His indignation was usually valid. Very few could. Barney lost only 4 fights in 78 professional bouts. He was *never* knocked out. He was never even knocked down. Barney, you see, was a genuine pro. A strange pride carried him to the heights.

Barnet Rosofsky (his real name) remains history's only Jewish prizefighter to win two different world championships. He was born in the asphalt jungle of New York City's lower East side on December 23, 1909. His family moved to Chicago during his boyhood and he began boxing as an amateur in and around the Windy City in 1926. He signed for his initial professional bout three years later, beat one Virgin Tobin, and went right on belting a lot of meatballs for eating and walking-around money. Three-and-a-half years later Barney was the lightweight and junior welterweight champion of the world. The speed with which he rose from obscurity to international prominence made a lot of Depression-sick Americans believe in miracles and Santa Claus again. The art of fiction was not dead after all.

What special tools, if any, did Barney Ross have? Well, he was fast, very fast, and deft and extraordinarily skillful. He was also blessed with rapid reflexes and a keen sense of timing. He had a practiced left hand and a fair right and when he chose to throw punches he could deliver them in swift and accurate combinations. No one could take a punch better. You could almost see the little wheels spinning around in his head as he sized an opponent up. He'd take it easy for a few rounds, readying his strategy, and suddenly he would open fire with all the guns, like houses falling down. You had to wonder where he got the juice inside his arms.

Ross fought at a time when the lighter divisions enjoyed tremendous ascendancy. He didn't win his championships from punks, meatheads with gunmen for managers and a string of fake fights behind them. He beat such able men as Billy Petrolle and Ray Miller and Battling Battalino and Sammy Fuller and Ceferino Garcia. More important, he beat Tony Canzoneri in 10 rounds in Chicago, on June 23, 1933, to win TWO titles in one night—the lightweight and junior welterweight championships of the world. Eleven months later, he won a decision over the great Jimmy McLarnin in New York to add the welter wreath to his growing store of laurels.

The Ross-McLarnin series was one of the most exciting in history. They fought three times. Baby Face Jimmy regained the crown from Barney in their second meeting (September 17, 1934), and the following Spring Ross won it right back again. All their bouts went the distance.

When the Irishman and the Jew tangled,

In a lifetime total of 78 pro bouts, Barney Ross never once was knocked down. (UPI)

sparks flew. It was like watching a pair of young bull elephants tussling. Both boys were as far from the run-away-and-come-again type as you could imagine. They would stand toe to toe and trade punches savagely, making xylophones of one another's short ribs. You could hear the flop, flap, flop of leather bruising human flesh way up in the balcony.

In New York, McLarnin was a villain. He had made a practice of beating Jewish fighters. He drew more Jews to the fights than most Hebrew ringmen. They flocked to see the Irishman take his lumps, but Jimmy flattened such Jewish idols as Kid Kaplan, Jackie Fields, Sid Terris, Joe Glick, Ruby Goldstein, Al Singer, and even the great Benny Leonard, when he was in the twilight of his career. So it was that Ross's two wins over McLarnin were greeted with extra loud rejoicing by the country's Jewish population, and they made Barney their new hero, an Olympian figure lifted aloft.

Ross put his welterweight title on the block against Izzy Jannazzo in 1936, and against Garcia in 1937, winning both. Like his matches with McLarnin, these, too, went the distance. Come to think of it, Barney traveled the entire route 45 times in a lifetime total of 78 professional bouts. Obviously he loved to fight! He was no head-hunter, but when the spirit moved him he could crank up his Sunday punch and go home early. He scored a total of 20 knockouts. When he connected, the ring lights swam like a river of gold. His punches came so rapidly foes had little chance to brace for them. They would reach for him, but Barney wasn't there. His hands were there, but never Barney.

Barney Ross discovered on the night of

Three of the greatest welterweight title bouts in history were between Ross and Jimmy McLarnin. Here Barney outpoints Jimmy in their third match in 1935 in New York. (AP)

May 31, 1938, at Long Island City Bowl, that he was over the hill. He was fighting Henry Armstrong, his crown was at stake, and he realized it was the end of the line when Hammerin' Hank hit him with a right hand in the seventh round.

"I had my left raised to strike and I saw the punch coming," Barney related, "and he hit me. Right away he hit me again with the same punch and then he caught me with a hook. I knew then. I knew that if Armstrong could hit me that punch, then I was through. There was nothing left for me."

Barney took a dreadful hiding from Armstrong for 15 rounds. The coils and springs and nuts and bolts in the once finely oiled little fighting machine were all worn out, but he wouldn't go down. Poor Barney. There he stood, in the middle of the ring, a pathetic figure, half blind, blood-spattered and dazed, stumbling, groping for his brown opponent, whose round head was bobbing like a cobra, as he struck again and again. The merciless mauling fogged Barney's brain. Instinct kept him reaching out his glove, probing the empty air for Armstrong as a man fumbles along a wall in the dark. Then with the pleas of thousands booming out of the murk beyond the gleam of the ring lights, many crying, "Stop it! For God's sake, stop it!" Armstrong let go a volley of assorted lefts and rights in the fourteenth round. Barney's legs bent like reels suddenly hit by a heavy breeze—but he didn't go down. He rocked and swayed but stayed upon his feet. What held him up? He could hardly move his legs, they were like stones, but he could brace upon them. Somehow, he withstood the terrible battering until the final bell, and at the end he was only a shell of his former self, a stumbling, mumbling pulp of a bloody mess. But he was on his feet, wasn't he? However rockily upon them. *That* was one distinction they couldn't take away from him. *No* one ever floored Barney Ross!

In his dressing room afterwards, Barney sat hunched on the rubbing table, solemn-faced and wordless, his face puffed out and bruised, and listened while Mike Jacobs told him how much money he could make in another fight. Finally, Barney said, "No, thank you, Mike. This was the last time. I'm quitting." For some months after that Uncle Mike would ask, "Barney, do you need any money?"

And Barney would reply, "Not the way you mean it, Mike."

After a year had passed, Mike told Barney how glad he was that the former champion had not tried a comeback. Barney confided later that he was certain it was his third bout with Garcia in New York, on September 23, 1937, when he had to go all-out for 15 rounds to keep his welterweight title, that took it all out of him. He broke his left hand and had to finish with just his right hand—and Barney never was a particularly strong right-hand puncher.

On visit to Seattle before his death in 1967, Barney Ross chatted with old friend, referee Jim Rondeau. (Photo courtesy Jim Rondeau)

Ross rested for six months, then tried out the mended mitt against Henry Schaft and Bobby Venner in April of 1938, knocking out them both. Convinced he was sharp again, he put his crown up for grabs the next month and Armstrong grabbed it.

"When you start to slide in this racket," Barney conceded, "nobody can stop it. There's only one way to go—down. You might as well face it. I told myself I'd take only but one bad beating. That'd be the day I quit."

Henry Armstrong gave him that one beating.

He was only twenty-nine years old when he announced his retirement.

On January 18, 1967, Barney Ross lost his last fight. He died of throat cancer in Chicago.

HENRY ARMSTRONG
(1912–)

Henry Armstrong was the little man who introduced the word "simultaneously" into the lexicon of prizefighting. Little Perpetual Motion is the only one ever to hold three world titles—featherweight, welterweight and lightweight, in that order—at the same time (August to December, 1938).

Henry Armstrong is the only prizefighter ever to hold three world championships simultaneously. (Photo courtesy Henry Armstrong)

In the life of Armstrong, Horatio Alger never had it so good. Through the early 1930s, Hank fought to stay off the breadlines, engaging in some 62 "benefits" and bootleg amateurs before he ever saw a decent payday. He was the dupe of some of the most vicious rascals who ever threw a preliminary boy into three fights on the same card. He entered his first pro ring with two broken ribs, sick from lack of food, and was knocked out in three rounds. The first big-time manager he approached for help in the gym told him, "I don't handle Niggers." Over one stretch—1931—when he won 85 straight fights, 66 by K.O., young Hank lived in flophouses and never was paid more than $2 a fight.

Through nearly two decades, Armstrong was a classic study of struggle, tragedy, success and disillusionment. In Mexico, he was robbed of his first good purse—$1,500—by an absconding promoter; at his peak in 1937–38, he was signed for 16 matches in six months with skilled fighters like Benny Bass, Bill Beauhuld, Alf Blatch, Petey Sarron and Chalky Wright and wound up in a sanitarium with a nervous breakdown. He was used, abused and confused by a succession of tinhorn handlers. In 15 years and 261 fights his slashing windmill style earned him more than $1,000,000—but he retired broke.

Even the manager who took him to greatness, Eddie Mead, let him down. When Mead dropped dead of a heart attack shortly after Henry lost the last of his Triple Crowns, most of the fortune had vanished. Investments he never understood and wild gambling had cleaned him out. When he was winging in the punches faster than the eye could follow, no ball park or stadium could contain the crowds he could draw. But Broadway and Harlem, too, forgot in a hurry.

The Armstrongs of Columbus, Mississippi, were a study in poverty; virtually slaves as they worked as sharecroppers on a cotton plantation. Their 11th of 15 children was born Henry Jackson, Jr., on December 12, 1912. The mother, America Jackson, was mostly Cherokee Indian, the father of Negro-Irish mixture. When Henry was five, the Jacksons sought survival elsewhere, in St. Louis.

"I never understood why we should be the beaten-down race," Henry said later. "Certainly, Jesus has said that all men are created in his likeness. But I didn't know much about the Bible as a boy. All I knew was that I had to fight back, or surrender my pride. Boxing, I decided, was the thing."

Through boxing history few more homicidally inclined fighters have been turned loose between the ropes. Henry learned to fight—to survive—in White-vs.-Negro gang wars in East St. Louis. Finesse escaped him. His method was to herd an opponent along the ropes or pin him in the corner and let fly with a fusillade of hooks to the body and head until he fell down. Defense meant nothing. He simply smothered you with blows and took what he had to take with his bullet head bowed on a 16-inch neck. When he floored Lou Ambers twice in August 1938 to win his third title (lightweight), he was rushed to surgery from ringside. He had swallowed at least a quart of his own blood; his mouth was ripped until his lower lip hung over his chin.

They called Armstrong's most chilling punch "blackout"—a peculiar looping right which was neither hook nor jab nor swing, but a high, flicking-fast blow to the chin. "It moved in a circular path, but only about 10 inches," Henry said, "a terrible thing to do to anybody. Most of them never saw it coming."

Barney Ross didn't see it the night of May 31, 1938, at Madison Square Bowl on Long Island. Henry, then the featherweight kingpin and a 5–2 underdog, staggered Ross, the welterweight champion, with "blackout" in the first minute of the fight. Henry never let Barney get set again. It's doubtful that any champion ever stood up under more awful punishment than Ross through 15 blood-flecked rounds. Twice Henry gestured to the referee to stop it. Barney had nothing left for a face. In the last two rounds, he continued to take a frightful beating.

"On that night Henry won the welterweight title from me," Ross recalled later, "he was as great a fighter at his weight as ever lived. I was in the hospital a week. I never fought in the ring again."

The third Armstrong crown, actually the first of the three he swept in a period of 11 months, came with his long-delayed chopping down of Petey Sarron in October 1937 in the featherweight division. Sarron was lightning fast, but in the sixth round, Henry, who had taken a fearful beating earlier, went crazy. He rushed Petey to the ropes and smashed him with 14 straight punches until the titleholder slid to the floor and was counted out in a sitting position.

In March 1940, Armstrong came within a hair of winning his *fourth* world championship—did win it, in fact, according to many oldtimers. At Los Angeles, they put Henry, weighing 139, in with Ceferino Garcia, the middleweight champion at 152 pounds, and confidently expected Garcia to handle him with ease. On the basis of the weights, people called it a mismatch. Yet Armstrong swarmed all over Garcia, rocked him and was rocked in turn. Most writers gave Henry a slight edge in the gory affair. But the judges called it a 10-round draw.

This, then, was a fantastic fighter, with resources of vitality known to few men who have lived by their fists. When he ran down, he did so very slowly and by an agonizing process. The featherweight championship went first, when he no longer could make weight. He abdicated. Ambers regained his lightweight honors in 1939 when, in a wild brawl, Henry hit low in five rounds and lost on points by that margin. In October 1940, Fritzi Zivic decisioned a weary, lackluster Armstrong to take away his last title. The death of Mead put the period to the story, unless you count Henry's comeback attempts through 1945. He had kept so little of his fortune that, at thirty-three years of age, he tried to make his legs carry him to the impossible.

Much of Henry's ring earnings were spent by "Fat Eddie" Mead, whose total disregard for money and a fixation that he could read a scratch sheet better than any horse-track price-setter should have landed him in jail.

Where to place Armstrong as a fighter is a matter of wide dispute. But many rate him with Joe Gans, Bat Nelson and Benny Leonard, and two generally overlooked measures of his greatness are on record. In the year 1937 he scored 26 knockouts in 27 bouts, the longest string of K.O.'s against competent opposition in the history of the prize ring. If a man stayed six rounds with Henry, he was on borrowed time.

Little Perpetual Motion was always moving. He bobbed, weaved, danced and swung all over his foes in a continuous whirl. Even in his corner, while slipping on his gloves before a fight, he continued to shift around nervously and throw shadow punches.

Barney Ross once recalled that when he and Henry walked out to get instructions from the referee for their title fight, Barney was surprised to note that the brown-skinned challenger was wringing wet. Sweat ran down his chest; he panted. In the dressing room, it developed, Henry had stepped 10 fast shadowboxing rounds—with a 15-round world title battle yet to fight!

Armstrong's heart was a medical marvel. Doctors found it one-third larger than the average central organ of the vascular system, with the lowest beat ever discovered in an athlete. He could slug and keep slugging from bell to bell and never tire.

Time marches on. It has been 30 years since Henry Armstrong fought his last prizefight. There is no bitterness evident in him. Looking back on his career, he remembers the late Barney Ross for his courage and ring craftsmanship; Baby Arizmendi for his ability to absorb punches.

Fritzie Zivic, however, brought out the jungle in Armstrong. "He thought it was fun to win fights by cutting opponents up instead of knocking them out," Henry said. "So I gave him the same treatment."

But the quality of mercy was in him, too. Bummy Davis was scared stiff the night he fought Armstrong. "When I walked out to shake hands with him, he was shaking and he was chilled," Henry recalled. "I wanted to give him the confidence to fight me. I went back to my corner and said a short prayer for him. 'Lord,' I said, 'don't let Bummy crack up.' Well, the Lord must not have heard, because I walloped poor ol' Bummy from ring post to ring post, and finally signaled to the referee to stop the fight. I wanted to get it over as fast as possible, because I didn't want to humble Bummy, he was so chilly and shaky."

Today, Reverend Armstrong is a Baptist minister in St. Louis—a humble preacher who is devoting the rest of his life toward converting the weak and the wicked to his church. "I've found love of mankind," he says. Reverend Armstrong had a midnight "vision" 26 years ago which turned him to the ministry. The voice woke him out of a sound sleep, and said, *You shall preach.*

Evangelist Henry Armstrong has been extolling the virtues of the Good Book ever since. "Do no evil to others, and no evil shall lay hold of thee," he tells more than 500,000 revival listeners annually.

Irony seldom was better served than with the spiritual rebirth of Reverend Armstrong, ex-prizefighter. Certainly no man of God ever endured a more rugged training course.

FRITZIE ZIVIC
(1913–   )

Fritzie Zivic, who came from Harry Greb's neighborhood, grew up in the hardened Greb philosophy that the best kind of fight is the full fight, in which everything goes.

It is still a toss-up as to which man was the dirtiest—Greb or Zivic.

"Greb was before my time," Ray Robinson once said, "but when it came to the dirty stuff, Zivic gets my vote as all-time king. He taught me more in 20 rounds of fighting than

Armstrong was a fantastic fighter, with resources of vitality known to few men. His heart was a medical marvel. (UPI)

anybody. Why, he even taught me how you can make a man butt open his own eye!"

Sugar Ray and Zivic fought twice within two-and-a-half months in 1941–42. Robinson won the first bout by a decision, and the second on a K.O. in the 10th round.

They labeled Fritzie a one-man assassination squad. They said he considered a fistfight as just another excuse for guerilla warfare. They accused him of being hot-headed and harum-scarum.

"I hadda fight dirty," Fritzie said. "Boxing was my business—a *dirty* business, inside as well as outside the ring—and to survive 19 years and 230 bouts in it I hadda use every trick I knew. If I hadn't fought dirty I never could have won the welterweight title from Hank Armstrong, who knew just as many tricks as I did. I tell ya, the only trouble with boxing today is that there aren't enough good, dirty fighters around."

What I like about Zivic is that he doesn't take back any of it. He doesn't try to cover up the stories about his dirty tactics and how he wishes that he, and not Greb or Tony Galento or some other, could be remembered as the all-time champ of the street brawlers, and about all the crude, gross and vicious things he did. It was the way he fought, and he admits it.

Zivic's three heroes were Jack Johnson, Dempsey and Greb. "All terrific dirty fighters," Fritzie said. "And to them you can add Marciano, one of the best after-the-bell punchers I ever saw; Archie Moore, a cutie; and alley-fighter Sandy Saddler. They called Dempsey's right hand Iron Mike but Jack once told me his best weapon was his double left—a left to the groin followed by a left to the head. That's what he flattened Jack Sharkey with—and I got the movies to prove it."

Zivic forgot Tony Galento. A lot of people think *he* was the dirtiest fighter of all time. He sure gave the spectators a lot to talk about. He was the participant in some of the bloodiest and foulest fights since the days of bareknuckle bruising. Tony still feels his only mistake was not fouling Joe Louis. The only thing Galento was scared of was a 550-pound Russian bear—the only trained boxing bear in the world. He must have done 50 carnival shows with that bear, boxing three two-minute rounds. Tony once was asked if he ever levelled on the bear, to see if he could flatten him.

"Hell, no," Tony said. "That bear was a mean sonovabitch. If you belted him good he'd liable to *eat* you."

In Zivic's mind, one of his greatest hours in dishing out the dirty stuff was the night he battled Bummy Davis. The referee allowed both fighters to completely express themselves in the ring. Bummy had a reputation of being a disreputable hoodlum. Giving Fritzie the business was second nature to Bummy. He belted Zivic low maybe 30 times, kicked him, thumbed him, gouged him. Finally, Fritzie started giving it right back to Bummy with his thumbs and his laces and walked around the referee and whacked Davis. A lot of guys who fought Zivic used to take it or maybe beefed to the referee, but Bummy didn't know how to do that.

Before it was over, the arena was in an uproar, with the crowd yelling and people throwing things and the cops were in the ring. The upshot was that Zivic got off Scotfree and Bummy was fined $2,500 and suspended for life in New York State.

While no one was better qualified at the unholy tactics than Fritzie, he is quick to point out that he never lost a fight on a foul in his life. "I'd give 'em the head, choke 'em, hit 'em low, but never in my life used my thumb," Zivic says. "I was fightin' for my life, it was no Maypole dance."

Dick Francisco, a Marine captain and fighter pilot in World War II, testifies what it was like to be in the ring with Zivic. Dick, a National A.A.U. boxing official and Seattle businessman today, won the All-Service Light-Heavyweight championship during the war. He fought Zivic in a three-round exhibition in Texas while he was a flying cadet trainee at Corpus Christi. Fritzie was stationed at San Antonio in the Army Air Corps.

"I could still make middleweight in '44," Francisco recalled. "But the weight advantage didn't help me a bit. Fritzie roughed me around the ring like I was a sack of beans. He did everything but bite my head off. Spun me, thumbed me, heeled me. He gouged, cuffed, kicked. He cut my eye and rubbed it with the laces. He hit me low, butted, choked, gave me the elbow. He banged me in the groin, said, 'Pardon me.' He whacked me low again, said, 'Sorry.' He'd show me the left hand—and then hit me with a right. He called it the *Fritzie Zivic lefthand-to-the-side-and-hit-'em-with-the-right* punch. Yes, sir, anytime you were in there with Mr. Zivic you could forget about Queensberry Rules."

Zivic, born on May 8, 1913, grew up in the tough Lawrenceville section of Pittsburgh, where he fought his way to and from school every day. When he ran out of raw meat on the hoof to buff around, he fought with his own brothers, Pete and Jack, just to keep his hand in. Both brothers later were members of the U.S. Olympic Boxing Team. Jack won a Gold Medal at the Olympics in Belgium in 1920. Their parents were Croatian, from the old country.

Fritzie had his first professional fight in 1931, won some, lost some, and then in 1936 he was paid $2,500 to fight Billy Conn in Pittsburgh. This first good payday convinced him that he wanted to be a prizefighter, even though the judges awarded Conn a split decision.

Four years after the Conn fight, Zivic was matched with Henry Armstrong for the welterweight championship of the world. Fritzie shocked the boxing world by outlasting Hammerin' Hank in what was afterward called "the bloodiest battle seen in New York in years." Zivic's end of the purse was $3,400.

Only Ray Arcel's patchwork on Armstrong kept Arthur Donovan, the referee, from stopping the bout. "Henry was bleeding so freely there wasn't much I could do," Arcel said. "But he didn't go out easily. Fritzie cut him up so terribly I had to use adrenalin and a venom solution to stop the flow of blood. After that, all I could do was pray for Armstrong."

In the 15th round, Zivic had Henry down for a count of four, but he got up and finished the match. It was the first time Fritzie ever went 15 rounds. He felt like he could have gone 40.

"Ever since I was a kid," Zivic recalled, "I'd wanted a Cadillac. So the day I fought Armstrong for the title in New York, I went in and looked at the biggest Cadillac I could find. Well, that night Henry gave it to me pretty good early in the fight and I could see that Cadillac rollin' farther and farther away from me. Henry gave me the elbows and the shoulders and the top of the head. I could give that stuff back pretty good, too, but I didn't dare or maybe they'd toss me out of the ring. Well, in the seventh round I gave him the head a couple of times and choked him a couple of times and used the elbow some, and the referee said: 'If you guys want to fight that way, it's okay with me.' 'Hot damn!' I told my manager, Luke Carney, in my corner. 'Watch me go now.' And from there out I saw that Cadillac turn around and come rollin' back."

Zivic bunched together a total of 232 pro bouts between 1931 and 1949. Eighty of his 157 victories were kayoes. When Fritzie's big guns found the range, his opponent's shoulderblades smote the ringboards like a salami thrown at the wall. Ironically, no champion in history lost more decisions, 61. But win or lose, they knew they'd been in a street brawl. "Fritzie was the only guy I ever knew who could start a fight in an empty room," cracked Lew Jenkins.

Zivic licked such champions as Sammy Angott, Red Cochrane, Jake LaMotta and Jenkins, and also fought Billy Conn, Ray Robinson, Beau Jack and Bob Montgomery. "Sugar Ray was a great fighter," Zivic said. "He could take it as well as dish it out. He could really move. I fought him twice. His hands pumped like pistons. They looked like they went off automatically. He was always dangerous, even when badly hurt. You could never take chances with him."

Fritzie fought LaMotta four times. Each bout was decided by a split decision. The night Fritz copped a 15-round decision off him (July 12, 1943), Zivic bet $1,000 against $2,500 on himself!

Red Cochrane finally took the title away from Zivic, on July 29, 1941. Zivic contested the decision. "I never lost that fight," he said. "The referee gave Cochrane the fight. Everybody knows I won."

Fritzie Zivic's brawling style attracted fight fans in droves. His second bout with Armstrong (January 17, 1941) set a Madison Square Garden attendance record (23,190), and he kayoed Henry in the 12th round. His pay this time was $25,000—and he got his Cadillac.

FREDDIE COCHRANE
(1915–   )

The smart set along cauliflower lane called Red Cochrane a club fighter, a second-rater with no future in the game. They should have remembered that Red hailed from Mickey Walker's home town, Elizabeth, New Jersey, where he was born on May 6, 1915.

Red hung on like a bulldog for eight hard

years, and on July 29, 1941, right next door in Newark he decisioned Fritzie Zivic for the welterweight crown. Cochrane, a 10–1 underdog, outboxed and outfoxed the brawling Zivic in what was regarded as a major upset.

The Irishman never got around to defending his title once before joining the Navy in 1942. Upon his discharge in 1945, he scored six knockouts and was twice flattened in the 10th round by Rocky Graziano. Red gave Marty Servo a crack at his title in Madison Square Garden, February 1, 1946, and was stopped in the fourth round. He didn't need glasses to read the handwriting on the wall.

MARTY SERVO
(1919–1969)

Schenectady's own Marty Servo never got a red cent for winning the welterweight crown from Freddie Cochrane in Madison Square Garden, February 1, 1946. Al Weill, Marty's manager, had guaranteed Cochrane $50,000 for defending the title, but the gate was only $42,000. So Marty kayoed Cochrane in the fourth, and Al still had to kick in $8,000.

Servo was still the champ when he was forced to leave the ring in 1947 as a result of a busted nose. Rocky Graziano did the job in a one-sided, over-the-weight affair that lasted only two rounds. The nose never did mend properly, and after a few exhibition bouts, Marty realized the jig was up. So in August of 1946, five months after the Graziano nose job, Marty retired—without once defending his crown.

The upstater won 91 of 95 amateur fights before turning pro in 1938. In 56 fights for the money he was beaten only four times, twice by a knockout.

JOHNNY BRATTON
(1927–)

No sooner did Johnny Bratton become welterweight champion of the world in 1951 than he hit the skids and vanished from the fight scene. Only the psychiatrists who finally caught up with him could explain what happened—and they weren't talking.

At midnight of March 14, 1951, the Chicago black was sitting on top of the world. He'd just decisioned Charley Fusari for the N.B.A. version of the crown at Chicago's indoor stadium, and the future looked very bright indeed. Sixty-five days later, Bratton was a very unhappy young man. Kid Gavilan snatched his title away from him unceremoniously in 15 rounds, in New York, and suddenly the road ahead was so dark he could hardly see the left jabs and bolo punches in front of his face. Five months afterward, Johnny started out along the comeback trail, but the old zip was gone. There were "moments"—the victories over the two Frenchmen, Pierre Langlois and Laurent Dauthille—but for the most part it was all downhill. When Del Flanagan stopped Johnny in nine rounds in 1955, Bratton tossed in the towel. It marked four defeats in a row for him. He was tired, confused and broke, having dissipated the $300,000 he'd earned in the ring. After a siege of despondency, Johnny entered the Cook County Psychopathic Hospital.

Bratton was born in Little Rock, Arkansas, on September 9, 1927. He began his ring career in 1944, won 59 of 86 bouts. After he left the psychopathic ward, he got back on his feet and held a full-time job in Chicago.

KID GAVILAN
(1926–)

Kid Gavilan parlayed a windmill attack and a bolo punch into the welterweight championship of the world. He was the first Cuban ever to win a world boxing title. (Kid Chocolate's featherweight crown, 20 years before, was recognized only in New York State).

The Kid's real name was Gerardo Gonzales. Some experts ranked him ahead of all other fighters of his day for sheer all-around class. He defended his title four times within 13 months (1952–1953), knocking out Chuck Davey, and beating Billy Graham, Carmen Basilio and Johnny Bratton on 15-round decisions. "He's a lot tougher than I expected," Davey said, after hitting the deck. "His style is confusing and hard to figure out." Davey was Gavilan's 26th victim in 27 bouts (the other was a draw with Bratton).

What Gavilan lacked in brute strength he more than compensated in ring craft, guileful strategy and subtle surprise moves. When he suddenly switched to southpaw for two rounds against Davey, it completely confused the popular southpaw from Michigan State. Chuck hadn't lost a match in 40 pro bouts. Asked why the change in tactics, the one-time Camaguey sugarcane fieldhand grinned. "I just wanted to show him I could fight southpaw, too," he said. One never knew when Gavilan was playing possum. He stalked his quarry as a jaguar shadowed its prey. He feigned grogginess only to ambush an unsuspecting foe with a lethal punch to the wind or the jaw. He let his opponents set the pace. He was a whimsical mixture of sentimental softness and flinty hardness, gentle with those he didn't particularly have anything against, vindictive as an Apache Indian when stalking those he hated.

Gavilan could box and punch with both hands, he could dance away and slip punches, he could beat his way in close and fist-whip at an accelerated speed or he could stay off and feint and jab, feint and jab, then deliver the goods. He could withstand punishment, too. His record proved that. In his lifetime of fighting—he started when he was twelve and had 143 bouts as a pro—Gavilan was never kayoed. Only one man ever put him on the floor, Ike Williams in 1948.

The Kid resembled Kid Chocolate in many ways—open-handed, light-hearted, quick-tempered. He sometimes failed to remember that boxing is a dead-serious business. The first of his four fights with Billy Graham came practically during the Cuban's honeymoon and after less than a week of training. He lost, of course. Six months earlier he'd been stabbed in the back of the neck during an altercation, post-midnight, with three men, thereby forcing a postponement of his Chicago match with Beau Jack. The only time he seemed to encounter trouble was when he engaged in non-title bouts with no significance attached to them. Then he was inclined to let up, training listlessly and acting a little too much the playboy. That was how a tyro like Bang Bang Womber could outpoint him in 1953.

Gavilan won the title in 1951, decisioning Johnny Bratton in 15 rounds, and after defending it six times, lost it the same way to Johnny Saxton in 1954.

He fought them all. He fought the tough ones several times. He went 15 rounds with Sugar Ray Robinson in a losing effort for the title in 1949, a year after he'd dropped a 10-round nod to Robby. "Only three men ever hurt me—Sugar Ray in our second fight, Tommy Bell and Walter Cartier," Gavilan said. "I think Cartier was the toughest puncher I ever fought."

Kid Gavilan was the only fighter named after a saloon. Most Cuban fighters traditionally have used ring names and when Fernando Balido, Gavilan's manager, turned little Gerardo Gonzalez over to Manolo Fernandez, his trainer, Fernandez suggested shaving off the boy's hair and calling him Kid Cocito. Manager Balido balked. Then someone else suggested that they name Master Gonzalez after Balido's own saloon, El Gavilan (the Hawk), and that was it.

Television did well by Gavilan and his handlers. The company of Gavilan, Balido, Medina & Lopez gave TV fans a wide selection of bolo punches, rumba rhythms and sibilant Spanish curses instead of half-gainers into a dry tank. Senor Medina was a trainer who composed Latin-American music and sang it at the drop of a castanet. For a brief period the group dispensed with Senor Medina's ser-

Kid Gavilan unleashes his famous bolo punch to earn decision in Cleveland here over Aldo Minelli, in 1953. (NEA)

218 THE ENCYCLOPEDIA OF WORLD BOXING CHAMPIONS

vices and employed little Charley Goldman as trainer, but it soon developed that poor old Charley couldn't tell the difference between a samba and a right hook, and Senor Medina got his water bottle back. Senor Lopez was a wholesale importer of Cuban fighters and a retailer of rumba bands, which he presented in a Manhattan deadfall called the Chateau Madrid. One of the liveliest acts on Channel 4 was the performance of Gavilan's board of directors in the corner between rounds. They gathered in an angry circle around their tiger and flung violent adjectives into one another's face, often ignoring The Keed who just sat quietly on his stool with an expression of complete boredom. What went on in Gavilan's corner frequently was far more entertaining than what took place in the center of the ring, and far more dangerous to life and limb.

Kid Gavilan was born on January 6, 1926, at Camaguey, Cuba. He ran out of competition

Billy Graham delivers a right to Gavilan's jaw in their controversial 1951 battle for the title in New York. Gavilan was awarded the decision, but a lot of people felt Billy won. (UPI)

in the welterweight division and campaigned among the middleweights in 1954. He tried for Bobo Olson's crown, but dropped a 15-round decision. Then, in his very next ring appearance, on October 20th, he lost his welterweight title to Bratton in Philadelphia.

Gavilan was a most picturesque character, his barrel chest fastened to pipestem legs and weighing only 151 lbs., yet he hit like the hammer of Thor. Rivals learned he could take it, too. They saw him shake off punches that should have leveled him for keeps, but he'd come back fighting, arms poised for a retaliatory knockdown.

On July 7, 1952, Gavilan whipped Gil Turner in Philadelphia to win the welter title vacated by Ray Robinson. The victory guaranteed him some sort of financial security for life. The Cuban government, you see, had a standing offer of $200 a month retirement pay to any native son who won a world's boxing crown.

JOHNNY SAXTON
(1930-   )

Johnny Saxton learned early in life that you can't win them all. There's the big dream and the little dreams, and you may get the big one and some of the little ones, or never the big one at all.

That's a part of prize fighting.

The big dream, Johnny Saxton got twice.

Born on Independence Day, 1930, in Newark, New Jersey, the black welterweight crowded plenty of fireworks into a dozen years of boxing (two as an amateur). After cleaning up all 147-pounders in Golden Gloves and National A.A.U. competition, he turned pro in 1949 and won 37 straight bouts in the first four years. On October 20, 1954, he whipped Kid Gavilan in 15 rounds in Philadelphia to win the welterweight title.

Saxton was just getting used to wearing the crown when Tony DeMarco knocked it off his head in the 14th round in Boston. This happened on April Fool's Day, 1955—but there was no joke about it for Johnny. A year later, opportunity came banging at his door again, when he decisioned Carmen Basilio, victor over DeMarco, to become champion for a second time. His reign didn't last for long, however, as Basilio, in a return title match six months later, snuffed him out of the welterweight picture permanently. In the ninth round, they had to scrape Saxton off the ring apron and lug him back to his dressing room.

Saxton fought only five more times, losing four of them, three by knockouts. As the man said, you can't win them all.

TONY DeMARCO
(1932-   )

Tony DeMarco was not a polished puncher, but the Boston Bomber was a busy little man, a mauler, a steady worker going for the crusher.

His attack was crude. Tony's special weapon was a left hook, and he'd take a terrific hiding while waiting for an opening to get off one good shot.

He was a sucker for the clever stuff.

Leonardo Liotta (his real name) stood 5 ft., 5 in. and weighed 147 pounds. He started fighting professionally in 1948, won his first seven bouts, six by K.O. Between January 14, 1949, and May 15, 1952, he fought 31 times, winning 26. But along the way he was kayoed by Art Suffolatta and Chick Boucher, and dropped decisions to Eddie White, Bryan Kelly and Gene Poirer. DeMarco finally quit the prize ring in disgust in mid-1952, but was coaxed out of retirement a year later and ran up an impressive string of victories over such stalwarts as Paddy DeMarco, Teddy Davis, Johnny Cesario, George Araujo and Chris Christensen. When the streak reached 15, including 10 kayoes, he was matched with the old pro, Jimmy Carter. The bout ended in a draw.

A title match with champion Jimmy Saxton was inevitable. So on April 1, 1955, before a partisan hometown Boston crowd, DeMarco upset the oddsmakers by knocking out Saxton in the 14th round to win the welterweight championship.

The glory of DeMarco was short-lived. He lost the title two months later in Syracuse, when Carmen Basilio flattened him in the 12th round. On November 30, 1955, he made an attempt to regain the crown, but the plot had the same ending—Basilio, K.O., 12th round.

DeMarco fought only 16 more times in the next 7 years, and of his 11 victories, 3 were over men who formerly held world championships: Wallace (Bud) Smith, Kid Gavilan, and

Don Jordan. His last bout was a victory over Stefan Redl, on February 6, 1962.

VIRGIL AKINS
(1928–)

Virgil Akins was the first fighter from St. Louis to earn the title "world boxing champion," and it took him 11 years after turning pro to do it.

Until he stopped Vince Martinez in four rounds in St. Louis, on June 7, 1958, to gain undisputed claim to the welterweight crown, Akins had a reputation for inconsistency. The charitable looked at his so-so record of 47 wins and 17 defeats and put him away as an in-and-outer.

But after watching him dispose of Tony DeMarco, Isaac Logart and finally Martinez, whom he floored eight times, one was goaded into wondering how on earth he ever lost to such as Charley Baxter, Art Persley, Nelson Levering, Joe Fisher, Gene Parker, Joe Brown, Luther Rawlings, Johnny Saxton, Johnny Gonsalves, Andy Brown, Charlie Sawyer, Franz Szuzina and Gil Turner. It was left to Jimmy Cannon to ask the obvious: "What miracle of chemistry turned Akins, at thirty, a fighter's middle age, into such a harmful puncher?"

Actually, Akins, who turned professional in 1948 after winning 14 out of 15 amateur bouts, did most of his losing as a youth. Few top-seeded welters beat him after he convinced himself he could fight. His kayo of Martinez was his 28th knockout among a total of 48 victories. Virgil battered the Paterson, New Jersey, cutie around the ring as if he was a mere rag doll.

Fighting Akins was like trying to fondle a garland of boa constrictors. His win over Martinez represented the last leg of an elimination tournament framed by the world championship committee after Carmen Basilio tossed the crown into public domain when he advanced to the middleweight division.

DON JORDAN
(1934–)

Don Jordan was the product of a childhood so bleak that it was almost no childhood at all. By circumstances, he was forced to overcome more obstacles, possibly, than any modern prizefighter since Jack Dempsey's hobo days.

Born in the slums of the Dominican Republic, on June 22, 1934, the 14th child in a family of 11 boys and 8 girls, Jordan came up the ladder swinging to survive, and that was why he happened to spend time in several reform schools, including the Preston School of Industry at Ione, California.

"Do you want the truth?" Jordan asked Peter Heller. "Before moving up to Los Angeles to live, I was a professional assassin. That's right. I got paid to murder people. Down in the Dominican, it was a way of life. I was killing people for pay when I was only ten years old. One month, I guess I musta killed 25 or 30 people. Blew their brains out with bamboa, poison dart. Straight in the neck. Just for the money. The police didn't care. First time I killed a person, I went off and puked; second time, no feeling. So when I came to America I staked a man to the ground and burned him. I got three years in prison for that. I was fourteen years old."

In reform school, young Jordan joined a boxing program. He mopped up everything in the Golden Gloves, fought his way to the Olympics in Helsinki, where he was disqualified. He returned to Los Angeles and turned pro, in 1953, and won 19 of his first 21 bouts. Within two years after becoming a professional, he was fighting such headliners as Lauro Salas, Art Aragon, Joe Miceli, Paddy DeMarco and Jimmy Carter. On October 4, 1954, he decisioned Art Ramponi in 12 rounds in Los Angeles to win the California welterweight crown.

Just when his future seemed brightest, the doors suddenly closed against him. He was the victim of a squeeze play. The "mob" decided to take him over—the rough way. By sheer starvation. He couldn't get a fight. Many months later he was back in business again after a state investigation broke up the mob.

Don Jordan's long climb to the top finally ended happily for him on the night of December 5, 1958, when he pulverized Virgil Akins for 15 rounds in L.A. It earned him $13,447, his biggest payday. Small pickin's as championship purses go, but for Jordan it was the pot o' gold at the end of the rainbow.

Jordan held the welterweight crown for 18 months, then lost it to Benny Paret in 15 rounds in Las Vegas, on May 27, 1960. After that, he hit the skids, losing eight straight bouts in one streak. He finally retired in 1962 and wound up employed as a machinist at Douglas Aircraft.

BENNY (KID) PARET
(1937–1962)

Shortly before his May 27, 1960, title match with Benny (Kid) Paret, Don Jordan was asked to talk about the little Cuban's free-wheeling style of fighting.

The champion pondered the question.

"I don't know how I'll fight him because I don't know nuttin' about him," he said, finally. "Nobody seems to know nuttin' about him."

So Jordan carried only skimpy knowledge of Paret into the Las Vegas prize ring with him and lost on points in 15 rounds. Before the night ended, he was just another ex-champion. Benny Paret was the new welterweight champion of the world.

Nothing much changed in the life of twenty-three-year-old Paret, after that. Nobody still knew "nuttin'" about him. He talked very little and knew no English, and he greeted the New York press with a confused wrinkle on his scarred brow. He didn't know what to make of all the hoopla and fuss over his winning the world championship. Unpretentious Benny was simply a misfit in Bigtown.

Once he got into a taxi to go to a luncheon being staged in his honor at Madison Square Garden and ended up in Brooklyn charged with an enormous fare. He didn't know what to tell the driver. So he went back to the Bronx where he lived and everybody at the luncheon was left waiting. Manuel Alfaro, his manager, told him to stay out of taxicabs. "You shouldn't be riding around in them, Benny," he said. "It's too much trouble for you to try to tell the driver where to go."

Born on March 14, 1937, at Santa Clara, Las Villas, Cuba, Bernardo Paret won 28 out of 29 amateur bouts before he was eighteen, then turned pro in 1955 and won his first 13 matches. His record after five years was 31-7-3. The total included two losses (decisions) to Luis Rodriguez, a loss to Gaspar Ortega, draws with Jose Torres and Federico Thompson, and two wins over tough Charley Scott.

Paret was a helter-skelter puncher with more footwork than knockout power. In 50 pro fights, he scored only 10 kayoes. But Benny proved in the Thompson bout he could take a punch. Federico, champion of South America, bombed him all over the ring, yet Benny stood his ground and fought back to earn a draw. The performance won him the chance to fight Jordan for the championship.

After losing a non-title match to Ortega, Paret lost his crown to Emile Griffith in Miami Beach, on April 1, 1961. Griffith belted him out in the 13th round. Benny won it right back six months later, however, via a 15-round decision in New York. Then he attempted to win the middleweight crown from Gene Fullmer, but was kayoed in the 10th.

Three-and-a-half months later, Benny Paret was dead.

In his final—and fatal—ring appearance, Paret fought Griffith for the third time in less than a year. This one ended as the first bout had—by a K.O.—only now Benny didn't get up after being counted out in the 12th. That was March 24, 1962, and Griffith had more incentive that night than just winning back the title. Paret had grossly insulted him at the weigh-in and Emile hungered for a full measure of revenge. He got it in the 12th round, when he unleashed a fearful volley of hooks and uppercuts before Paret, who was propped up in a corner of the ring, fell slowly to the canvas.

The punches burst some blood vessels inside Benny's head. Clots formed and put pressure on his brain. He was rushed to the hospital, where doctors poked holes in his skull to relieve the pressure. But it was too late. Benny died 10 days later without having regained consciousness.

Griffith vowed he would quit the prize ring. The ghost of Paret followed him everywhere. It was several years before the memory dimmed and his gun-shyness left him.

As for Benny Paret, he became another of Boxing's grim statistics: one of the 20 men who died annually in the prize ring!

LUIS RODRIGUEZ
(1937–   )

Luis Rodriguez seemed miscast as a fist-fighter, not by virtue of skills but of personality and inclination. He was as natural and uncomplicated a creature as Snoopy. He approached life with humor, not rancor. His spidery fingers and pipestem wrists did not seem to equip him to be welterweight champion of the world and neither did his outlook. He was born to make people laugh instead of bleed. He had a charm and gentleness about him seldom seen in a prizefighter. The false pride was totally absent.

To Luis, prizefighting was a simple business proposition, nothing more. They told you to unload your bombs, and you unloaded your bombs. They told you to knock your opponent out, and you knocked him out. When he fought Emile Griffith, a peevish young man who had killed in the ring and whose pride was fierce, Luis explained in a pre-fight interview: "I know Emile a good fighter and a good person. I think I am good fighter and good person. Is all right. We have to fight. After fight, we continue. I, good person, he, good. Fight has nothing to do with this."

Griffith was Luis' nemesis. Luis lost only four fights in the first 10 years of his career, and three of them were to Emile, each time on a disputed decision. "We were both such good fighters that both of us deserved to be champion," Griffith said later. "It's just too bad we came along at the same time."

Born in the canebreaks of Cuba on June 17, of either 1937, 1938, or 1939 (he was never clear about the exact year), raised in the teeming streets of Havana, the adored brother of four sisters, Luis began fighting as a lightweight in 1956 and won 35 fights in a row before dropping a split decision to Griffith in December 1966.

A natural 147-pounder who stood only 5 ft., 8 in. on skinny legs, Rodriguez devoured a steady diet of bigger middleweights when other welters hid from him. No welterweight since the early days of Sugar Ray Robinson fought so often in the heavier division. Twice in 1965, Luis went where even devils feared to tread—into the ring against Rubin Carter, rated as the hardest-hitting middleweight in the business at the time. Carter threw bombs like a heavyweight. In their first bout, Rubin landed a big right hand on Luis' jaw, and Luis, who had never been knocked out, got up and boxed rings around Carter the rest of the way for the decision.

The second fight was even easier. Carter was so frustrated and discouraged in the late rounds after failing to land a single good punch that Luis got bold and threw some right hands of his own.

In 1962, Rodriguez moved into the No. 1 contender's spot for Griffith's crown. His big moment came in March of 1963 at Los Angeles, where he won his only decision over Griffith and claimed the welterweight title. But in a June rematch 79 days later in New York, Emile got his title back. Griffith made his point a year later by winning another split decision from Rodriguez at Las Vegas.

The flashy Rodriguez also had trouble with Curtis Cokes. In 1961 they split decisions in two bouts, before Cokes kayoed Luis in the 15th round five years later. Luis blamed an unscheduled flight to Havana for his first defeat by Cokes. He'd been on a plane going from Miami, where he now lived, to Texas to fight Cokes. He had not been back to Cuba in five years. Suddenly, the plane was highjacked in midair and detoured to Havana, where a sour-looking Castro soldier poked a submachinegun in Luis' ribs and threatened to detain him. Luis was so shaken by the experience he was in no emotional condition to fight Cokes, and he lost. He then demanded an immediate rematch, got it and won decisively.

Rodriguez was back fighting middleweights in 1969. Even fought Nino Benvenuti for the world championship, but was knocked out in the 11th.

In 121 official pro bouts, Luis Rodriguez won 107, with 49 of them kayoes. He was knocked out only three times.

STILL ACTIVE

CURTIS COKES
(1937–)

Born June 15, 1937, Cokes' home town is Dallas, Texas. He began his pro ring career in 1958 and won 21 of his first 23 matches. On August 24, 1966, he earned the W.B.A. version of the welterweight crown with a 15-round decision over Manuel Gonzalez, in New Orleans. Then he decisioned Jean Josselin in 15 rounds to gain full world recognition on November 28, 1966, and successfully defended his world championship four times. Cokes finally lost his title to Jose Napoles, by a K.O. in 13 rounds in Los Angeles, April 18, 1969.

JOSE NAPOLES
(1940–)

Born on April 13, 1940, at Santiago de Cuba, Oriente, Jose Napoles started his prize ring career in 1958. He won 72 of his first 78 bouts, 52 by kayo, including a 13-round knockout of Curtis Cokes in Los Angeles to win the world welterweight championship. In 1970–71, he lost and recaptured the world crown in two fights with Billy Backus. Napoles successfully defended his title nine times.

BILLY BACKUS
(Birthdate Unknown)

The Syracuse, New York, welterweight started fighting professionally in 1962. He won 36 of his first 56 pro bouts, half by K.O. He knocked out Jose Napoles in the fourth round to win the world welter title in Syracuse, December 3, 1970, and lost it the same way (K.O., fourth round) in Los Angeles to Napoles, June 4, 1971. Backus had a bad year in 1973, dropping three of four bouts.

LIGHTWEIGHTS

The history of the lightweight division in America dates back to 1868, when Abe Hicken defeated Pete McGuire and proclaimed himself "cham-peen of the lightweights."

He weighed 130 pounds.

However, it wasn't until an Englishman, Arthur Chambers, who had aided the Marquis of Queensberry in framing the Queensberry rules, came to the United States, in 1879, that a world lightweight champion was officially crowned.

The 133-pound Chambers was so recognized after defeating Johnny Clark at Chippewa Falls, Canada, in a bloody bout lasting 2 hours, 23 minutes. Clark was finally counted out in the 136th round! Since then, the lightweight division has produced some of the finest strategists in boxing history.

ARTHUR CHAMBERS
(1847–1925)

Arthur Chambers, the lightweight division's first recognized world champion, was a party to one of the most savage fights on record.

On March 27, 1879, the 5 ft., 4½ in., 120-pound Englishman sailed 136 rounds (2 hours, 23 minutes) with John Clark in the snow at Chippewa Falls, Canada. This was a bareknuckle brawl, too! By the 94th round, the snow's color had changed from vanilla to strawberry. Chambers had ripped off Clark's ear and John's handlers couldn't stop the bleeding. He fought on anyway. The gore soon froze to his face, and he tore back into the champion viciously, ripping the pink flesh into slices, like strips of bacon. But the end came when Clark couldn't get off his stool for the 137th round. Loss of blood had taken all his strength. Chambers, too, paid dearly for the victory—he never fought again.

Born on December 3, 1847, at Salford, Lancashire, England, Chambers fought from 1864 to March 1879. During that period he compiled a total of only 14 bouts, but all of them were iron-man ding-dongers. He battled 64 rounds with Fred Finch, 105 with Dick Goodwin, 56 with George Fletcher, 63 with Jem

Brady, 44 with Ned Evans, 43 with Bob Mullins, and 40 with Tom Scattergood. And there was no TV bonus to cut up in those days, either!

Top pay for Arthur was the $2,000 he won on a sidebet he made with Billy Edwards, another Englishman, in 1872. They fought on a Friday at Squirrel Island, Canada. The crowd, mostly rawhide loggers and backwoodsmen, cried for blood. Billy gave it to them. He bit Arthur on the ear. Arthur complained to the referee to make Billy stop feasting on him. In the 26th round, after repeated warnings to Edwards, the ref stopped the match and awarded Chambers a victory on a foul.

Billy loudly denied biting Arthur.

"After all," he protested in his defense, "I'm a Catholic and ain't supposed to eat meat on Friday!"

Good try, Billy.

JACK McAULIFFE
(1866–1937)

Two other greats of Sullivan's era were Jack McAuliffe and Jack (the Nonpareil) Dempsey. The triumvirate made up one of boxing's most legendary combinations—the Three Jacks.

Jack McAuliffe, the "fashionplate pubilist," was the only champion before Rocky Marciano who never lost a fight. He was the Dapper Dan of the ring, the most colorful and popular boxing champion that ever held a title in a lighter division. For twelve years, McAuliffe reigned as king of the lightweights and ruled with a regal air. He had the mien of a Richard Mansfield and would wax theatrical in the ring. There was something lordly in his manner as he threw off his robe and acknowledged the plaudits of the crowd.

McAuliffe was born in Cork, Ireland in 1866. He spent his childhood days in Bangor, Maine. He lived a rugged life in a waterfront neighborhood which offered little in the way of amusement except a lively fight now and then. Jack joined in these with lusty enjoyment.

The McAuliffes moved to the Williamsburg section of Brooklyn and young Jack went to work in a cooperage. Jack Dempsey, the Nonpareil, and Jack Skelly, another promising fistic star, were fellow workers. Dempsey taught McAuliffe the finer points of boxing.

McAuliffe fought his first fight in New York in 1884, defeating Bob Mace in three rounds. He entered Billy Mulden's boxing tournament and won the featherweight and lightweight amateur championships.

In 1885, McAuliffe challenged Jimmy Mitchell for the professional championship. He became recognized as champion when Mitchell declined the issue.

After knocking out Jack Hopper in 17 rounds, McAuliffe stopped Billy Frasier in 21 rounds in 1886 for the title. Jack clinched his claim by knocking out Harry Gilmore in Lawrence, Massachusetts in 1887 in 28 rounds.

McAuliffe fought his memorable bout with Billy Myer in 1889 at North Judson, Illinois. Despite an arm broken early in the fight, Jack held the Streator Cyclone to a 64-round draw!

Three years later McAuliffe and Myer met in a rematch in the three-day "Carnival of the Three Jacks" in New Orleans which was climaxed by James J. Corbett's defeat of John L. Sullivan. This time McAuliffe knocked out Myer in 15 rounds.

McAuliffe's most controversial fight was against Jem Carney of England at Revere Beach, Massachusetts, in 1887. The men had fought 74 bitter rounds when spectators broke into the ring. Referee Frank Stevenson promptly declared the fight a draw. Carney's backers contended that gamblers who had bet on McAuliffe broke up the fight to save their bets.

McAuliffe was a master boxer, largely thanks to Dempsey the Nonpareil, and a terrific hitter. When Young Griffo, the phenomenal Australian whom many regard as the fastest man ever in the ring, came to the United States, McAuliffe outpointed him in 10 rounds.

After boxing a six-round exhibition with Kid Lavigne in 1896, McAuliffe retired undefeated. He had fought 62 times without a loss—winning 50, drawing 9 times, fighting 2 no-decision bouts and the one exhibition with Lavigne. In 1914—at the age of forty-eight—he fought a three-round exhibition with Dick Burge in London.

McAuliffe made a fortune with his fists, but couldn't hold it. Always an inveterate gambler, he went broke and finally returned to the cooper shop in Williamsburg from whence he had come to set the fistic world aflutter with his brilliance.

"Fashionplate" Jack McAuliffe ruled the lightweight division for 12 years. (NEA)

Jack soon tired of making barrels and went into vaudeville making monologues. He was successful at this, but couldn't keep away from the race tracks. He finally wound up working at the tracks for a bookmaker.

McAuliffe died in 1937. To his dying day he remained the Beau Brummel of the sports world, conspicuous in his Bond Street bowler and well-tailored clothes.

Jack McAuliffe gave the modern prize ring an elegance it hadn't had before.

He took the game out of the turtle neck sweater and put it into custom tailored clothes and white collars.

GEORGE LAVIGNE
(1869–1928)

George Lavigne, slim, flaxen-haired and babyfaced, looked more like a boy soprano in a choir than a prizefighter. In real life, however, he made Swipes the Newsboy keep a civil tongue in his head.

Kid Lavigne was the lightweight champion of the world from 1896 to 1899.

The Saginaw Kid lacked a singing voice but packed two fists that hammered out victories over the toughest opponents of the Nineties, and cleared himself a path to the lightweight title. Shortly after his six-round exhibition with Jack McAuliffe in New York, March 11, 1896, Jack retired and Lavigne claimed the title. The Saginaw Kid, who had begun his career with a string of six quick knockouts in 1885, had mowed down all contenders in America.

Lavigne sailed for England to fight Dick Burge, the British champion. They met in London, June 1, 1896, and in a slashing battle Lavigne flattened the Englishman in 17 rounds.

The epic was fought at the National Sporting Club, and the Earl of Lonsdale, President of the club, figured the cherubic little Lavigne was no match for Burge. He bet the Kid a "hundred" he wouldn't last 10 rounds. Lavigne gladly accepted the wager, instructed his manager, Sam Fitzpatrick, to bet his entire purse at the prevailing 6–10 odds. Sam did. Both were flabbergasted when they were paid in pounds—one pound approximately equal to $4 at the time. If the Kid had lost, he never would have been able to pay off.

Lavigne had a turbulent ring career. Two years before his London fight, he had battered Andy Bowen, a principal in the longest glove fight on record (a 110-round draw with Jack Burke in 1893, lasting 7 hours, 10 minutes), into unconsciousness in 18 rounds in New Orleans. Bowen's head struck the floor of the ring and he died of a concussion of the brain. Lavigne was arrested, then absolved.

Kid Lavigne twice fought Giant Killer Joe Walcott, winning both times.

Their first battle was a handicap match, the condition being that Lavigne was to be declared winner if he was on his feet at the end of 15 rounds. The bout was held at Maspeth, Long Island, December 2, 1895. It was one of the bloodiest and most savage battles ever seen.

In the 12th round, Walcott wanted to quit but his manager, Tom O'Rourke, threatened to shoot him if he did, backing up his threat by poking a big, black pistol into Joe's back. So Joe went back to work and suffered the shellacking of his life.

In their second meeting in San Francisco, October 29, 1897, Walcott gave up in the 12th round.

Lavigne fought a 20-round draw with Frank Erne at Coney Island, September 28, 1898, but the following year, on July 3, Erne outpointed the Kid for the title.

The Kid fought sporadically after that, but the old fire and stamina were gone.

Lavigne was born of French-American parentage at Bay City, Michigan, December 6, 1869. Like McAuliffe and Dempsey, the Nonpareil, he worked in a cooperage.

After his retirement, he got a job in the Ford factory in Detroit, where he worked until his death, April 6, 1936.

FRANK ERNE
(1875–1954)

Frank Erne was one of the most modest and gentlemanly lightweight champions in history. Suave, polite, handsome, well-groomed, he looked more like a dashing young Wall Street executive than a bruising prizefighter. Yet he was involved in some of the goriest, most savage contests the lightweight class has ever witnessed.

Erne was born in Zurich, Switzerland, on January 9, 1875, but, when very young, was brought to this country when his father, a brewmaster of considerable fame, was induced to emigrate to Buffalo.

Frank must have been a gentle child, for he grew to be a gentle man, but he learned to fight in self-defense when his playmates taunted him because of his—to them—strange dress and equally strange dialect.

"Every time I went out on the street," he once said with a smile, "they made fun of me and slapped my face and pushed me around. I had to do something about that, for I couldn't stay in the house all the time."

Erne became so skilled with his fists as he grew older that he caught the eye of a Buffalo promoter. The promoter liked Frank's natural speed and cleverness, suggested the boy turn professional. He was matched against a rugged chap bearing the formidable name of John L. Sullivan, Jr. The bout was fought January 7, 1894, the day before Frank's nineteenth birthday. He accepted the engagement because he wanted money to buy himself a birthday present.

"Junior" Sullivan was a miniature of his illustrious namesake. He was bull-necked, muscular, pugnacious. Erne was more of the Jim Corbett type in build and cleverness. The battle itself, however, hardly resembled the famous Sullivan-Corbett fight two years previous—except that in both instances it was a bad day for the Sullivans.

There was nothing in Erne's style that resembled the chary strategy of Corbett. He slashed and cut young John L. viciously, knocked him out 15 seconds before the bell ending the second round. Four months later Erne fought his second ring battle, against George Siddons, one of the best of the day in his class. Frank won in six rounds, but the fight was so pleasing that they were rematched a month later and battled to a draw. A draw with Solly Smith, another topnotcher, followed and young Erne decided to devote all his efforts to boxing.

Through the next six years, he fought the greatest lightweights, including George Dixon, Martin Flaherty, Jack Downey and Kid Lavigne. He battled the great Lavigne, then champion, to a draw at Coney Island. His showing delighted William A. Brady, matchmaker of the Coney Island A.C., who offered him a return match with Lavigne for the title. Erne accepted immediately, but Lavigne declined.

"Go get yourself a reputation," he told Erne.

Frank obliged by knocking out Dal Hawkins in San Francisco in seven rounds and outpointing the "Spoiler," Elbows McFadden, in 25. McFadden had knocked out Joe Gans in 23 a month before.

There was positively no escape for Lavigne. The Saginaw Kid lost his title to Erne in 20 sizzling rounds in Buffalo, July 3, 1899.

Erne defended the title twice, being held to a draw in 25 rounds by "New York" Jack O'Brien and stopping Gans in the 12th round.

"It was the only time Gans ever quit," Frank said, "and I didn't blame him. I cut him so deeply across the upper lid of his left eye that he thought the eye was coming out and asked the referee to stop the fight."

That was in the Spring of 1900. In July he met Terry McGovern in New York and was knocked out in the third round of a non-title fight.

"This," he said later, "is not an excuse. No one ever needed an excuse for being beaten by Terry. This is an explanation. Since he was a featherweight, I had to make 128 pounds for him. It was a terribly hot Summer in New York and I chose to train in town because I thought it would be easier for me to take off weight there than it would be in the country. I took off five pounds of what seemed to me at the time was flesh and blood and, in return, got ulcers. And was knocked out. Maybe, if I could have come in at 133 . . . but maybe not. Terry was a great fighter, as everybody knows."

Erne never was the same again.

In May of 1902, this time at Fort Erie, he fought Gans again and was knocked out in the first round.

Frank went to London right after the second Gans bout and knocked out one Jim Maloney in seven rounds and, from London, went to Paris. There was no one in Paris for him to fight. A form of boxing, called *la savate*, in which not only punching but kicking with padded shoes was permitted, long popular with the French, slowly was giving way to boxing. Erne, by tutoring the rising generation in the art of boxing, hastened the transition that, in time, was to produce Georges Carpentier, Eugene Criqui, Andre Routis, Ray Famechon and Marcel Cerdan. For this, he is known today as the Father of Boxing in France.

Erne, 5 ft., 5½ in. and 133 pounds at his peak, held George Dixon, the wonderful Little Chocolate and then featherweight champion, to a 10-round draw in his 10th pro fight. A year later, he lost a 25-round decision to Dixon, but by that time he was having trouble making the 122-pound limit and moved up to fight as a lightweight.

All told, he had 115 fights from 1892 to 1908.

On September 17, 1954, he died. He was seventy-nine.

Eight years before, on December 14, 1946, Erne had been reported killed in an auto crash in San Bernardino, California. Frank lived to deny the reports, however, pointing out that the victim was not Erne, but a man named Frank Ellsworth, one of his many admirers. Ellsworth was such a fan, as a matter of fact, that when police examined the body they found old newspaper clippings telling of the real Frank Erne.

Frank Erne, indeed, added great prestige to the lightweight division, and is recognized as one of the most competent combatants the class has ever had.

JOE GANS
(1874–1910)

Joe Gans was truly "The Old Master."

His skill and deftness in the prize ring earned him undisputed claim to that title.

At 5 ft., 6 in. and 133 pounds, the Philadelphia black put a unique leaf in the story book by knocking out Spike Robson, the English lightweight champion, with a right-hand smash to the right hand.

Robson was aware of the great Gans' punching power and fought with left shoulder high and his gloved right fist held protectively in front of his jaw. Gans bided his time, waiting until the Englishman's right was in just the correct position, then shot a jolting smash to Robson's right fist, causing him to knock himself out!

Gans belongs in boxing's Hall of Fame not only because he had tremendous natural ability, but because he *studied* his business (a practice too seldom followed anymore). To Joe, fighting wasn't a haphazard profession. He studied it as diligently as any lawyer ever delved into Blackstone, and he graduated *cum laude.*

The Old Master was so good he had a tough time getting matches unless he "did business" with the opposition.

Gans and Battling Nelson took part in what many oldtimers believed was the greatest lightweight championship rivalry in history. They first fought at Goldfield, Nevada, on September 3, 1906, for Tex Rickard. The weight limit for the lightweight class in those days was 133 pounds, *at ringside.* (Today they weigh in at noon on the day of the bout). Billy Nolan, who was Nelson's crafty manager, insisted that Gans weigh in with all his

Joe Gans was so good he had trouble finding opponents who would fight him. (NEA)

It was the end of the trail for Gans as he sat on his pants taking the count after being floored by Battling Nelson, July 4, 1908, in San Francisco. (UPI)

boxing togs on, including gloves. He demanded that the weigh-in be held in the ring just before the opening bell. Consequently, Gans entered the ring very thin, drawn and ill from meeting the unreasonable demands.

Oddly enough, Bat wanted to cancel the match because he was suffering from a severe chest cold, but he went ahead with the bout when Nolan told him that Gans couldn't make the weight. That was, indeed, one for the book: two sick men fighting for the lightweight championship of the world! Ironically, the bout remains the longest world title fight on record under Queensberry Rules. In the 42nd round, Bat hit Gans low, and Joe was awarded the match on a foul.

Gans never recovered from that weight-making ordeal. He contracted tuberculosis and two years later Nelson caught up with him again and knocked him out in the 17th round to win the title.

Starting in 1891, Gans fought for 19 years. He took part in 20 bouts of more than 20 rounds. He frequently climbed into the ring "handcuffed" by orders from his manager, Al Hereford, to "take it easy."

His stance gave Gans a perfect defense. He stood erect, hands held at chin level, ready to block and counter. He moved sparingly and his trip-hammer punches traveled only a few inches. He was a past master of feinting but couldn't be feinted.

Gans won the lightweight title by knocking out Frank Erne in one round at Fort Erie, on May 12, 1902. He then hung on to the crown for six years. His biggest purse was the $11,000 he earned from the first Nelson bout at Goldfield. That was $12,000 less than the Durable Dane received. Win, lose or draw, Gans had agreed before the match to let Bat have the fattest part of the purse.

Born in Philadelphia, on November 25,

1874, Gans died in Baltimore, on August 10, 1910, only 15 months after his final fight.

Historians often compare Benny Leonard favorably with Gans as the greatest of lightweights.

That figures.

Benny always said he modeled his style after The Old Master.

BATTLING NELSON
(1882–1954)

Battling Nelson was a slightly built, scrawny-looking little man, with sunken cheeks, haunted, deep-set eyes, and a slender, almost fragile body, a consumptive pallor, and hands too big for the rest of him. You wouldn't have turned in the street to look at him unless you had been told that he was one of the most durable prizefighters who ever lived.

Bat was a smoldering volcano of suppressed emotions. In boxing's savage body contact—that atavistic throwback to the bludgeoning battles of the Stone Age—he found emotional release. Shy, introspective, and not too brainy outside the ring, he was the calm of a Summer evening before a storm. Once that work bell rang, the Dr. Jekyll in his nature was metamorphosed into the Mr. Hyde of combat. It was as "Mr. Hyde" that his unhappy rivals knew him. They couldn't understand how such a skinny little guy could have stunned them without using brass knuckles.

One of the late John Lardner's favorite stories about Bat was of the time he took a bath in the lemonade concession on the eve of the Dempsey-Willard fight in Toledo. Lardner remembered that it was one of the first Toledo stories he had ever heard.

Nelson, financially unsound at times, and somewhat eccentric from punches, happened to have a job in Toledo. He was "covering" the fight for the Chicago *Daily News*. His influence over his ghost writer was not sufficient to make the latter spell "Battling" with one "t" in the by-line, as Nelson preferred it. His salary brought him food, but not shelter. He slept on the ground outside the wooden arena. On the eve of the fight, the July heat drove him to appropriate the bathing suit of Jack Kearns, Dempsey's manager, and take a splash in Lake Erie. Kearns flew into a rage when he heard of it. He had Nelson evicted from the camp, and the bathing suit burned.

"Still looking for relief," said Lardner, "Nelson wandered about in the twilight until he came upon six galvanized tubs standing in a tent near the arena. Each contained a mixture of lemon syrup and melting ice. The Battler took a lengthy bath in one of them in his underwear; the garment had to be torn from him in strips by friendly hands after the concessionaire found him and pulled him out of the tub."

Professor Billy McCarney, the educated boxing strategist, and Thomas V. Bodkin, a theatrical business manager, conflicted on the amount of damage Nelson's impromptu dip did to the sale of lemonade the next day. Bodkin was inclined to disparage the effect.

"People drank the stuff," he said. "They'd heard about Nelson, but they were too hot and thirsty to care."

On the other hand, McCarney said that the news of Nelson's bath spread like wildfire about the grounds on the day of the fight.

Battling Nelson. (UPI)

"Did it hurt the sale?" Lardner wanted to know.

"Did it hurt sales?" Billy asked. "My good man, did you ever see the Battler?"

Always beaten up, but seldom beaten, Battling Nelson was regarded as a physical oddity not quite of this world. Jack London called him "The Abysmal Brute." The scrawny-necked "Durable Dane" never blinked his little gray eyes as he moved relentlessly through a barrage of leather to wear down an opponent. Jimmy Britt, who fought Nelson four times, said that the Bat's eyes were always wide open, staring and absolutely expressionless.

"It got on a guy's nerves," Jimmy confessed. "After a while you began to wonder if he was human."

Probably no one will ever know what very real pain Nelson endured. He once fractured his left arm in the middle of a 15-round bout. He later confided that the injury "tended to make me somewhat cautious and possibly kept me from winning by a knockout."

Oscar Matthew Nelson would have been right at home among the bareknuckle boys of the gaslight era. A lightweight champion of fabulous endurance, the eerie Dane plodded through round after round of brutal adversity to reach his goal. Certainly no fighter since the Heeney-Sullivan days was such a glutton for punishment.

Nelson was great because neither he nor his opponents knew when to quit. Joe Gans and Jimmy Britt collapsed from sheer exhaustion trying to batter Bat into submission. And when he was over the hill at twenty-seven and there was no right side left to his face after 40 grueling rounds with Ad Wolgast, he could still spit through the blood and snarl, "What do you think of that dumb referee? Stopping it when I would have had him in another round!"

Never a great slugger, Bat beat the greatest sluggers of the day: Young Corbett, Herrera, Hyland, Hanlon. His 12-second knockout of Billy Rossler was a record for 26 years, and his feat of flooring Christy Williams 42 times in 17 rounds before knocking him out still stands as a record. Never a particularly gifted boxer, he kayoed the top craftsmen: Canole, Spider Welsh, Britt, Gans. He held the masterful Abe Attell to a 15-round draw.

Bat was born in Copenhagen, Denmark, on June 5, 1882, and grew up in Hegewisch, Illinois, with six brothers and a sister. The lusty Danes and Swedes of Hegewisch were still fighting the ancient wars of old Scandinavia so Bat learned to use his dukes early. At thirteen, he quit school to work for 15¢ a day as an ice cutter on Lake Michigan. The hard work inured him to hardship and toughened his slender frame until he had stored up enough endurance to last him a lifetime. At his peak he stood 5 ft., 7½ in. and never weighed more than 133.

In 1896, Nelson was working as a meat-cutter when Wallace's Circus came to town. A come-on gimmick featured a rugged "champion," billed as "The World Renowned Unknown," who challenged the Scandinavian population for miles around. One dollar was the bait for anyone who thought he could last three rounds with the pug. Bat figured he could use the buck to see the circus, so he climbed into the ring as the band played "Down Went McGinty." The "unknown" lived up to his billing as Bat finished him off in two minutes of the first round.

After he beat Ole Olsen for the championship of Hegewisch, Bat's father forebade him ever to fight again. Bat rebelled, and on June 15, 1896, he ran away from home to become a professional prizefighter. In a note to his mother, he wrote: "Going away, Ma, to seek my fortune." He didn't return for four years.

For six lean years Bat roamed the Midwest in search of loose change. He worked for a while at "Old Ironsides," inevitably named for the "Blue plate special"—a tough 15¢ steak. Then Teddy Murphy found him and took him all the way West. Bat got the break he was looking for in San Francisco. When Joe Walcott was unable to keep a fight date with Martin Canole, for promoter Alex Greggains, Billy Roche suggested Bat. Billy had seen Nelson kayo Spider Welsh in the 16th round at Salt Lake City, in 1904, so Bat did the same for Canole in the 18th round and picked up $760. This was the start of five lucrative years during which he led the lighter men into the big money. He was the first little man to fight for shares of $20,000 and $30,000 purses.

Sunny Jim Coffroth, the California promoter, was anxious to get as much mileage as possible from the $20,000 he was willing to put up for a Nelson-Britt rematch, so he asked

Billy Roche how far he felt the boys could go. "I don't think two such battlers can last more than 45 rounds," Billy told him. Which was how the first of Coffroth's famous 45-round marathons began.

Nelson and Britt fought at Colma, California, on September 9, 1905. Bat had already dropped a couple of shorter bouts to his rival, including a recent 20-rounder in San Francisco, on December 20, 1904. But at Colma the longer distance was too much for Britt. Knowing full well he couldn't go 45, Britt tried to finish Nelson and found it so exhausting that he fell on his face in the 18th round.

On September 3, 1906, Bat, who was under the management of tight-fisted Billy Nolan, fought another classic for the world championship with Joe Gans at Goldfield. Billy Roche was there and always maintained that Bat would have beaten Gans if he hadn't fouled him in the 42nd round.

Nelson had 150 fights and cleaned up more than $250,000 in his 20 years of prize fighting. When Wolgast nearly clubbed him to death at Port Richmond, on February 22, 1909, he was moving forward, not back.

He was a shy brute and slow to make friends. His likes and dislikes were either black or white, but personal feeling never interfered with his ring work. To him, boxing was strictly a money proposition and he knew how to knuckle down to business. He was incorruptible, and behind that bleak stare, a sensitive human being marched blindly into fame.

Battling Nelson held the lightweight title from July 4, 1908, until February 22, 1910. He died in Chicago on February 7, 1954. His only contribution to the science of the prize ring was a short left hook to the liver, delivered with the thumb and forefinger side of the glove, but his aggressiveness, punching power and ability to absorb punishment made him one of the all-time greats.

The generation that knew Battling Nelson faded out long ago. Boxing fans of today—if they think of Bat at all—think of him as a musty legend rather than as a man of flesh and blood. But when the moon comes up over the local cemetery, casting ghoulish shadows across the tombstones, I like to think that the ghost of old Bat slithers from marker to marker looking for some phantom opponent to go 40 rounds with.

I can see him now, a slight, ungainly figure in blood-stained battle trunks, an odd little wool cap perched astride his shock of light hair—all eyes, all nerves, all fight.

AD WOLGAST
(1888–1955)

Poor Ad Wolgast was the archetype of the punch-drunk prizefighter. The "Michigan Wildcat" was a tragic example of what can happen to a man whose brain has been exposed to too many years of murderous pounding. Virtually to the day of his death in 1955, he continued to train in California for a return match with Bat Nelson, whom he defeated for the lightweight title 45 years before and who died in 1954.

Wolgast lived out his life in a phantom world populated by old prize ring ghosts. His mind failed him shortly after he lost his title and he labored under the hallucination that he was to go back and fight Nelson, the man who gave him his toughest battle, one more time. Jack Doyle, a Los Angeles promoter, took pity on him and assumed full charge of him. Doyle provided Wolgast with a little gymnasium, where Ad did his training. He seldom missed a morning workout, convinced he must be in condition for Bat.

W. O. McGeehan, who was the founder of the "Aw nuts" school of American sports writing, picked the Wolgast vs. Nelson title match as the most savage fight he ever saw.

"In the 40th round Nelson was pressing feebly forward while Wolgast's gloves were hurling crimson splashes around the ring every time they struck the battered face," McGeehan said. "Nelson would not yield an inch, but it became so cruel that the most hardened ringsiders were calling upon the referee to stop it. Finally Eddie Smith stepped between the men and pushed Nelson to his corner. Nelson snarled at him in protest, but his seconds caught him and pushed him onto the stool in the corner. The referee then raised Wolgast's hand—the new lightweight champion of the world."

Wolgast and Nelson might have spelled each other with profit. Both were durable diehards who could make the long-long fight. And like Bat, Wolgast was the beau ideal of sluggers, hotheads, and the hen-pecked of the species. He was a professional to his cuticles. So was his manager, Tom Jones, the spiffy

Kankakee barber who resembled a western con man. Together, they looked like a couple of characters from a Ring Lardner yarn.

Funny thing about Ad, he was as brittle as a pretzel, always breaking an arm or fracturing a rib, usually on the eve of battle. Following his marathon with Nelson, he busted an arm in a scrap with Jack Redmond in Milwaukee, on June 10, 1910. Only July 4, 1913, he broke his left hand fighting the original Mexican Joe Rivers. The year after that his right arm was "kayoed" in the eighth round of his scrap with Freddie Welsh in New York City.

Life for Ad was just as dangerous inside as out. While training for Welsh at Vernon, California, in 1911, Wolgast was stricken with appendicitis, a setback that gave Willie Ritchie his big break. And no sooner had he recovered than he contracted pneumonia.

They called Wolgast the "Dutchman," which is to say that he was born of German-American parents on February 8, 1888, in Cadillac, Michigan. Ad, a converted southpaw, stood 5 ft., 4½ in. when he broke into the fight racket at eighteen, and he could make all kinds of weight under 133.

"He was one of the greatest fighters I ever knew," declared Tom Jones. "It was a pleasure to manage him. He would fight anybody. Once I decided to have a bit of fun with him. I rang up his hotel room and told him I'd just signed him up as a substitute boxer for several matches that night. I told him he had to be ready to go in three hours. 'All right,' he said. 'Wake me up in a few hours, and I'll get ready to go with you.' I said, 'But, Ad, you haven't even asked who it is that you're going to fight.' And he said, 'No, and I don't care. Just wake me up so that I won't be late getting into the ring.' He was that way all the time. He'd say, 'Get me anybody for any time, and I'll fight him any time you say.' He did, too."

Wolgast and Joe Rivers collaborated with the referee in a ring classic of a strange sort altogether. After 12 furious rounds it was all even. In the 13th both fighters connected at the same time, and two bodies hit the deck with one resounding thud. Everyone figured they were both out cold. But referee Jack Welsh caused a near riot when he pulled Wolgast to his feet and counted out Rivers.

Ad was the perpetrator of one of the prize ring's classic remarks. It happened during his six-round bout with Dan Morgan's spunky little K. O. Brown in Philadelphia, in 1911. Brown was as cross-eyed as Ben Turpin, and it was almost impossible for an opponent to tell which way he was looking. Wolgast was thoroughly baffled, then disgusted. When K. O. staggered him with a terrific left hook in the fourth, Ad fell into a clinch and snarled, "Why don'cha hit where you're lookin'?"

Wolgast was a quiet sort outside the ring, though supremely confident. At one time he hocked the family jewels to bet on himself.

Ad was lightweight champion of the world from 1910 to 1912. When he lost his title to Willie Ritchie, he started out the bout as though he would walk all over Ritchie. Then Ritchie suddenly landed a wild swing flush on Ad's jaw. Wolgast dropped to his knees, all but out. As he was about to collapse he drove two foul punches into Ritchie's groin. Even when badly hurt, he had the rattlesnake's instinct to strike back. Jim Griffin, the referee, ruled Ritchie the winner on a foul in the 16th round.

Wolgast was 67 when he died in a Cam-

A converted southpaw, Ad Wolgast was so supremely confident in his ability that he once hocked the family jewels to bet on himself. (NEA)

arillo, California, sanitarium, still believing that he would someday fight Bat Nelson again. Nelson had passed away the year before. He didn't like Bat. He didn't like the ham in the little Dane. In their last fight, Bat had enlisted the services of Abdul the Turk, who carried him on his shoulder down the aisle.

"Looka dat! Jus' looka dat!!" growled Wolgast.

In the 23rd round Nelson felled Ad for what he believed was a K. O. Turning to the newsreel cameras, he threw up his arms and shouted, "Twenty-three skidoo!", a popular rallying cry of the day. But the next moment his jaw dropped a foot: the battered Wolgast had seized him by the legs and was pulling himself upright hand over hand. That was the turning point. The dead-game Ad came from behind and kept coming. So did Bat, but Ad had the range.

Wolgast wanted just one more shot at Bat. He was still going to the gym and getting in his daily licks almost to the very end. He was still doing roadwork. Liquor and tobacco were out because he wanted to be in top shape for the Bat.

Ad Wolgast, you see, was one fighter who never knew when he was licked.

WILLIE RITCHIE
(1891–)

Gerhardt Steffen, alias Willie Ritchie, was the second lightweight champion in history to win the title on a foul. Yet no lightweight in the annals of the division was more deserving to wear the crown. Dogged little Willie worked overtime to become a bona fide challenger, had Ad Wolgast beaten when the champ from Cadillac fouled out, and defended the title with daring and tenacity.

Willie Ritchie was born in San Francisco on February 13, 1891. When he was sixteen, he was fighting his heart out in four-rounders at local gyms. After every lightweight bout, he would climb into the ring and challenge the winner—a standing joke with the spectators who jeered him.

Packey McFarland proved to be Ritchie's special angel. When Wolgast was stricken with appendicitis on the eve of his match with Freddie Welsh in Los Angeles, McFarland recommended his sparring partner, Willie. On November 30, 1911, Willie gave

Ad Wolgast, left, tears into Willie Ritchie in 1912 world lightweight title match at Daly City, California. Ritchie won crown from Wolgast on foul in 16th round. (Photo courtesy the late Dan Morgan)

the scholarly Welshman a whale of a fight over 20 rounds. Though he lost the decision, he had suddenly become a top contender.

Three months later in Philadelphia, it was Willie in for McFarland against Young Erne, whom he held to a no-decision in six. This respectable showing paved the way for a title shot against the Cadillac Wildcat.

You have to go back to September 4, 1872, to finger the first lightweight championship won by a foul. On that occasion Billy Edwards lost to Art Chambers at Squirrel Island, Canada. Forty years later at Daly City, California, on Thanksgiving Day, a reeling Wolgast hit low in the 16th. But it was Willie who was robbed since he had his man on the verge of a K.O.

Ritchie made the title pay rich dividends. He began with the toughest contender in sight, Mexican Joe Rivers, whom he flattened in 11 rounds on the Glorious Fourth, 1913. Then came Leach Cross, Harlem Tommy Murphy and Charley White, another "near" champion. And still Willie was king. He wanted Welsh again but made the mistake of signing for a London bout. Willie was the aggressor all the way, but Welsh's superb boxing skill earned him the British decision and the title.

The Pride of Pontypridd refused to give Ritchie a return match, the war broke and the San Franciscan became boxing instructor at Camp Lewis, Washington. He returned to the prize ring to fight Benny Leonard in Newark, New Jersey, April 28, 1919. The match was scheduled for eight rounds, but Leonard gave Ritchie such a shellacking that a second threw in the towel 20 seconds before the final bell.

Willie Ritchie retired from the ring in 1927 and the next year was appointed boxing inspector in California. When he discovered that the game was rotten with politics, he demanded a full investigation. In 1937, he was named Chief Inspector, a job he held until retirement in 1961.

FREDDIE WELSH
(1886–1927)

Freddie Welsh combined cleverness with deceptive speed, hit harder than he appeared to and was in a class by himself when it came to ring generalship. He brought brains to the fist-fight business when such a commodity was looked upon askance.

The "Pride of Pontypridd" was the most intellectual and resourceful of champions.

Welsh, 5 ft., 7 in. and 133 lbs., was born Frederick Hall Thomas on March 5, 1886, at Pontypridd, South Wales, the town that gave Jimmy Wilde to the prize ring. But Freddie was purely an American boxing product. He picked up his fighting nickname along with the fundamentals of prizefighting while acting as porter, general handyman and occasional sparring partner in Dr. Kneip's gymnasium in downtown New York. The clients called him "Welsh" because of his nationality.

Freddie Welsh learned his fighting the hard way, but thoroughly. He was a vegetarian and made a study of scientific training and diet. He figured a man never fought more than three minutes in a round and that one-quarter of the time was spent resting on his stool. So he trained for a sprint rather than a mile, giving his legs the same attention as his hands and arms. He was therefore faster with his fists and feet than any man he ever fought, including Jem Driscoll and Abe Attell.

Welsh won the lightweight championship

Freddie Welsh, the "Pride of Pontypridd," brought brains to boxing in an era when candle power was looked upon askance. (NEA)

of the world in his 10th year of boxing by beating Willie Ritchie in 20 rounds in London, on July 7, 1914, held it for three years and then lost it to Benny Leonard, May 28, 1917.

Boxing was dead in New York in 1905, so Welsh went to Philadelphia, where the sport flourished. After trouncing preliminary boys, he met Tim Callahan, a veteran once managed by Billy Roche. Callahan made Welsh look like a sucker. Instead of being angry, Freddie thanked Tim.

"You showed me the value of a left jab," he said.

Welsh painted a white dot on a punching bag. He learned not only to lead but to plant the impact blow squarely on the dot. He developed a sensational left jab. He also developed leg work, such as feinting, wheeling, sidestepping and stopping suddenly.

Freddie's highly original training methods amused spectators but the wisdom of his approach proved itself.

Welsh fought three great battles with Packey McFarland, losing the first, a 10-rounder, and then drawing in 25 and 20 rounds.

He beat the great Ad Wolgast twice. And he had the better of Ad, Bat Nelson and Benny Leonard in no-decision affairs.

Welsh was a physical culture enthusiast. He retired from the prize ring after Leonard defeated him, became a captain in the Sanitary Corps of the Army during World War I and did admirable reclamation work as director of physical education at Walter Reed Hospital.

Following his retirement from boxing in 1922, Welsh opened a health farm at Summit, New Jersey. His open-handed generosity sapped his wealth and shortly before his death, on July 29, 1927, the property went to satisfy a mortgage.

Freddie Welsh, an avid reader of good books and intimate friend of Elbert Hubbard, was a regular little gentleman. And he could fight like blazes, too—as testified by the fact that Benny Leonard was the only one able to knock him out in 167 fights!

BENNY LEONARD
(1896–1947)

Heywood Hale Broun called Benny Leonard "the white hope of the orthodox." The famous essayist believed that no performer in any art was ever more correct than this Jewish-American from New York City.

"Benny follows closely all the best traditions of the past," Broun commented in 1922. "His left-hand jab could stand without revision in any textbook. The manner in which he feints, ducks, sidesteps and hooks is unimpeachable. The crouch contributed by some of the modernists is not in the repertoire of Leonard. He stands up straight like a gentleman and a champion and is always ready to hit with either hand."

Always the perfectionist, Benny's proud boast was that he'd never had his hair ruffled in a prizefight, which was a fact. He wore his hair plastered back, oiled so that it had the smooth shine of a patent leather shoe—and it stayed that way through each fight. To get Benny's goat, the moment they met in the middle of the ring Leo Johnson reached over with his long left arm, glove open, and deliberately rumpled Benny's hair. This annoyed Benny, and he tore wildly into Leo with both arms pumping. He never stopped banging away until Leo was flat on his back, counted out in the first round.

Harry Hershfield, the raconteur, once visited Benny's training camp in New Jersey. That night, they ate at a big kosher restaurant in nearby Lakewood. Benny's appearance provoked a hum of excitement by everyone but an old rabbi.

"Who's that?" the rabbi asked the head waiter, pointing to Benny.

"Why, that's Benny Leonard!"

"Who is he, an actor?"

"No, no, he's a pugilist!"

"He's a pu—a WOT?"

"He's a pugilist," explained the head waiter. *"He hits people."*

Benny, indeed, hit people. No fighter in ring history could shift his attack from the head to the body and then back to the head again quite like the lightweight champion. The Leonard "book" might well be titled, "The Complete Master Guide to Boxing." With every bout, no matter what the competition, he learned something new. And in the gym he practiced what he learned. He slipped and blocked punches, he improved his head weave, he polished that left jab that had the wallop of a right-hand smash, and he rehearsed the jab to the face followed instantly by a hook to the jaw.

He made his sparring partners tear into

him. If he could duck under the blows and land a couple of hooks, he felt he was getting somewhere.

"That's what a training camp is for," he'd explain. "You gotta get used to fighting so you can work on weaknesses."

His sparring crew loved Benny.

"Boy, oh, Boy," one of them chuckled after a go-round with the Professor. "I got the greatest job in the world. I get fifteen bucks a day for beatin' hell out of my boss."

Benjamin Leiner was born on Manhattan's lower East Side on April 7, 1896. He did a lot of things when he was fourteen. "I was the champ of Sixth Street and Mickey Fogarty was the champ over on Eighth Street," Benny recalled. "His neighborhood wasn't big enough so he thought he'd move in on my territory. It was some fight. We squared off in Fatty Smith's backyard. You might have thought we were in the Garden. There must have been 200 kids to watch, and half of them wanted to be managers and handlers. We fought barefisted and for three rounds Fogarty and I flailed away. We were so bloody we could barely stay on our feet. It was no better between rounds. We both had too many handlers, and in their eagerness to help out they nearly murdered us. I finally flattened Mickey in the fourth round and was called the winner, but it really wasn't a fair fight. It was just a case of Mickey having *rougher handlers* than I."

Always the perfectionist, Benny Leonard brought all the best traditions of the past to the prize ring. (NEA)

Benny survived two discouraging knockouts before he was seventeen and went on to really cut his teeth on Irish fighters. Those were the days when the neighborhood clubs were loaded with talent, and feuding between Irish and Jewish partisans often led to riots. When the Leons and the McGoverns tangled, you could expect "cracked crowns and bloody noses," and many of those intramural bouts were settled by police decisions.

One night in 1916, Leonard took on Frankie Conifrey in the Star A.C. in Harlem. Frankie was getting the worst of it so his brother tried to stop the fight. The Harlem Irish had a bundle of dough riding on Conifrey and the beer bottles immediately started to fly. Benny's loyal supporters answered the challenge, and by the time the bluecoats arrived, everybody was ready to be sewed up.

One of Benny's first idols was the great Leach Cross, who popularized boxing in the Jewish communities of New York and was the first prize fighter to be written up in the *Jewish Forward*. Cross was a tremendous competitor and a great teacher, as Leonard was after him.

Benny came by his ring name early in his career through the usual announcer's booboo. Peter Prunty didn't quite catch the name Benjamin Leiner.

George Engle was credited with teaching Benny how to sacrifice some of his amazing speed for punching power. Benny then proceeded to knock out every contender and name fighter in the lightweight division with the exception of southpaw Lew Tendler. Among his K.O. victims were Willie Ritchie, Charley White, Joe Mandot, Johnny Kilbane, Ever Hammer, Richie and Pinky Mitchell, Joe Welling, and Rocky Kansas.

In the seventh round of the Mandot fight, held in New York's St. Nicholas Rink, December 17, 1915, Engle told Leonard to grip the canvas with his toes so he could get leverage for his right hand. Leonard tried it and left Mandot for dead.

Until Leonard came along, the leading contender for Freddie Welsh's crown was Johnny Dundee. Dundee and Leonard engaged in eight no-decision matches, all of them humdingers.

"It was like sparks flying," Dundee told me. "You could see our brains working overtime. Sometimes my radiator boiled over. You had to move, move all the time to keep Benny from catching up with you and knocking you out."

Leonard got his first crack at Welsh's title on May 28, 1917, in New York. When Freddie was counted out in the ninth round, he was suspended upright on the ropes.

Benny liked to weigh in at between 130–133 pounds. Always in fighting trim, he never lost a *decision* in 209 bouts, though he was knocked out on three occasions late in his career. Leonard was so good that he could carry a first-rate opponent without the latter even suspecting it.

The champion had some narrow escapes. On July 5, 1920, in Benton Harbor, Michigan, Charley White came within an ace of lifting the crown. In the fourth round, White battered and shoved Benny clear out of the ring. Fortunately for Leonard, White was a bit slow on the uptake, and the champion was able to bluff him out of his advantage.

Leonard was something of a psychologist. In the preliminary huddle he would usually drop a remark or two well calculated to disconcert or infuriate an opponent. "Don't forget, Joe, when I knock you down, take the full count," he'd say, or, "I can't carry you tonight—friend of mine is betting ten grand on me."

In his first bout with Lew Tendler at Boyle's Thirty Acres, on July 27, 1922, Benny was badly hurt but talked his way out of a serious jam. "Come on now, Lew, let's make it look good," he encouraged the amazed Philadelphian, who hesitated just long enough to permit Benny to recover.

For weeks in advance of the fight, stories had been circulated about the ill-feeling that existed between Benny and Lew. This ill-feeling was evident throughout the battle. Benny repeatedly appealed to the referee about Tendler's blows being low and several times Harry Ertle warned Lew to be more careful. Tendler only snorted.

Before the match the heavy bettors favored Leonard. Tendler was chiefly a slugger, they felt. He had a wicked left hand. The bout proved that the estimation of Tendler was correct, but his peculiar southpaw style prevented Leonard from displaying any of the brilliant cleverness of hands and feet that usually spotlighted his work. Instead he was compelled to change his style and fight Lew's style. He was forced to slug, and slug he did. He literally slugged his way to victory.

The first five rounds were all Tendler's, but in the sixth Benny showed the first flash of the form that made him champion. In the seventh it was the Leonard of old once more, but in the eighth Tendler crashed a vicious left to the jaw causing Benny's knees to sag, and for a moment it appeared to be curtains for him. But that was the last flash in the pan for Lew.

Starting in the ninth round and through the tenth, eleventh and twelfth, Benny treated Tendler to a severe drubbing. At the end of the bout both men were bleeding freely. Benny's left eye was swollen and cut. He had lost a tooth in the fifth round and blood spurted from his mouth. He had a lump alongside of his right eye. He had been compelled to expend every ounce of energy in his perfectly trained body.

As for Tendler, his nose was bleeding and tiny crimson streams trickled from the corners of his mouth—mute but convincing attestations that Leonard's bombs had reached the target.

"Benny met a tartar," wrote one newsman. "Never before as champion has he absorbed so much punishment. The easy romp that he may have expected developed into a beehive of boxing gloves. He was forced to unleash an attack he has seldom before been forced to display. He fought with a viciousness that almost amounted to desperation."

There were no knockdowns. Oldtimers called it one of the best lightweight championship battles in history. The majority of the rounds saw Benny and Lew standing toe to toe and slugging it out.

Leonard's victory was by the scantest of margins; so close, in fact, that, had it not been for his whirlwind finish in the twelfth and final round, Tendler might have been awarded the championship. Many scorecards had it six rounds apiece.

The bout was one of the biggest money producers in the history of the prize ring, drawing gross receipts of $327,565. Of this Benny got $121,755, while Tendler received $62,500. Promoter Tex Rickard netted an estimated $90,653. The match drew 50,000 people.

A Leonard fight was always top box office. He fought Tendler again a year later, this time at the Polo Grounds, and it drew $452,648. Benny won a decisive 15-round decision the second time around. He had had time to think about Tendler.

Perhaps the wildest of all of Benny's bouts was the sensational brawl with Richie Mitchell at Stanford White's old emporium, on January 4, 1921. Ann Morgan promoted the match to raise money for her Devastated France fund, and Society turned out in formal attire. According to Whitey Bimstein, the great trainer, Benny had placed bets ranging from $1,000 to $10,000 that he would finish Mitchell in the first round. But Richie upset the dope by coming up for the third time and decking Benny with a jolting left to the stomach. Benny stared at his corner bemusedly as he pictured loose greenbacks scattering in the wind. "Don't worry, fellas," he told his handlers, "I'm getting up."

He did and managed to hang on until the bell. The next three rounds saw more of the same excitement, with both fighters banging away for dear life. In the sixth, Benny poured it on, flooring Richie three more times. The third knockdown of the round finished him.

There has never been a more obliging fellow outside the prize ring than Benny Leonard. Once several sports writers from Washington, D.C., came to him with a rather unusual request. They knew of a promising young featherweight whose manager didn't know beans about prizefighting. If they could steal this kid from under his manager's nose for a few hours, maybe Benny could give him a few pointers.

"Is he a nice boy?" was all Benny wanted to know.

The writers assured him the kid was okay, and Benny took him on free.

"We learned more about boxing in two hours than we had been able to pick up in ten years," testified one of the reporters. "Benny taught the boy things it had taken him years to learn. The kid went on pretty far in pro boxing, but if he had had Benny around to teach him regularly he would have become a champion."

Leonard was a boxing instructor in the Army during World War I. He eventually tried his hand at welterweights. In a title match with Jack Britton in New York, in 1922, he lost his head for the first and only time in 15 years. Jack was down on one knee when Benny fouled him in the 13th round. The foul cost Benny the fight.

In 1925, Leonard retired for the first time.

He returned to the ring as a thirty-six-year-old welterweight in 1931. He was fat in the middle and thin on top, but he boxed his way to a big match with Jimmy McLarnin. The bout was fought in the Garden on October 7, 1932, and Benny dropped Jimmy in the first round. McLarnin came charging back and took control. You should have heard Benny yak when referee Arthur Donovan stopped the bout in the sixth. "Hell!" cried Benny, "I'm still on my feet!"

Ned Brown always claimed you'd have to match Leonard with Joe Gans to determine the all-time lightweight champion of champions.

"As a matter of fact, Benny insisted that Gans *did* give him his toughest fight," Ned told me. Ned was sports director of the old *New York World* and was close to Benny.

"How's that again?" I asked Brown. "Why, Benny was only fourteen years old and fighting Mickey Fogarty when Gans died."

"I know that," Ned said, "but Benny still claimed he once fought Gans. He said the fight took place in the winter of 1919. . ."

Leonard was training for a four-round match with Willie Ritchie in San Francisco at the time, according to Ned, and the night before the fight, Billy Gibson, who managed Benny, arranged for the lightweight champion to sleep at Moose Taussig's training camp. Moose ushered Benny into a long dormitory. All the beds were empty. There didn't seem to be any other fighters staying at Moose's camp that night. Moose told Benny to take any bed he wanted.

"You'll find them all comfortable," he told Benny. "Bat Nelson used to like that one over there. Jimmy Britt preferred the one near the window. Young Corbett played the field. Terry McGovern liked that one. And this one? Oh, you picked a good one. That's the one Joe Gans slept in." Then Moose left the room.

The dormitory looked kind of eerie by candlelight. Benny was tired, but when he snuffed out the candle and slipped into bed, he couldn't sleep. He tossed around restlessly and thought of all the great fighters who had passed through old Taussig's place. Suddenly a chill ran up his spine, as he sensed there was someone in the adjoining bed. He felt somewhat panicky, and sat up in bed, feeling around on the night table for some matches to light the candle.

Immediately the fellow in the next cot shot out of bed and came at Benny. "Hey, fallas," he shouted. "Pipe the new punk in Joe's bed!"

Benny couldn't imagine how all those others got in there. They must have been hiding under the covers, he supposed. But there they were, and they weren't friendly.

"Let's get him outta there, Terry!"

"Sure, Jimmy, let's do that!"

They were about to close in on Benny when a slim black man walked softly into the dorm.

"Hey, Joe, here's a bum in your bed!" they shouted. Benny knew it was Joe Gans without even looking.

"Who are you, boy?" Gans asked.

"Benny Leonard," Benny replied, and then feeling like a dope, added, "the lightweight champion of the world."

Everyone laughed at Benny, but Gans held up his hand and quieted them.

"Just a moment," he said. "Step out here, boy, and let's see what you can do. Don't be afraid. I ain't gonna hurt you. Just put up your hands and let's go."

They started to box, Benny and Gans. There was no referee They fought and fought, the two of them, all through the night.

"It was a terrific battle," Benny insisted. "But all through it I had the feeling that Gans could have taken me whenever he wanted. Suddenly he raised his hand again. 'That will do, boy,' he told me. 'Now you get back to bed—in *my* bed.' And then he vanished.

"When Billy Gibson came around the next morning, he looked at me sort of funny and said, 'What's the matter, Benny? Couldn't you sleep?'

"'No,' I told him. 'I was too busy fighting.'

"Billy frowned. 'First time I ever knew of a four-round no-decision bout to worry you so you couldn't sleep.'

"I didn't dare tell him about my *fight* with Gans. He probably wouldn't have believed me anyway. Just a dream? Yes, I suppose it was, but I'll tell you this. As long as I live that *sparring match* with Gans was the biggest thrill of my career."

Benny Leonard served as a lieutenant in the Merchant Marine during World War II. In 1947, he died in the prize ring while refereeing a bout.

It was the way the old champion would have wanted to go.

JIMMY GOODRICH
(1900–)

The name of Jimmy Goodrich frequently crops up in the conversation when boxing men are talking, because fight guys have been trying for years to figure out how one man could lose so many bouts and go so far.

Consider his record: of 101 matches, he lost 30 decisions, was held to a draw 14 times, and scored only 6 K.O.'s. Not exactly an awe-inspiring performance. Yet the record book lists the Scranton, Pennsylvania, Irish-German as the eleventh lightweight champion of the world.

Fortunately, Goodrich reached his peak in 1925, the year Benny Leonard retired as undefeated lightweight champion. On July 13, in New York, Jimmy knocked out Stan Loayza in two rounds in an elimination tournament to win recognition by the New York State Commission as champion. This was only the third K.O. of his career—and it couldn't have been more timely!

Five months later, in Buffalo, Rocky Kansas, a genuine pro, won the title from Goodrich via a 15-round decision.

Jimmy slid fast after that, hitting bottom in 1930, his final year, by losing seven of his last eight bouts (the other was a draw).

James Edward Moran, his legal name, was born at Scranton on July 30, 1900. He began fighting in 1919. In the years that followed he proved that you should never underestimate courage and endurance. They carried him all the way to the title.

ROCKY KANSAS
(1895–1954)

Unorthodox Rocky Kansas was unpredictable. He did nothing according to rule. Heywood Hale Broun described his fighting style as being as formless as the prose of Gertrude Stein.

Broun found a delightful impromptu quality in Rocky's boxing. "Most of the blows which he tries are experimental," the famous essayist observed. "There is no particular target. Like the young poet who shot an arrow into the air, Rocky tosses off a right-hand swing every once and so often and hopes it will land on somebody's jaw."

In 165 bouts, that right-hand bludgeon kayoed 32 opponents, the same number he won by decision. He was beaten only 13 times. The other 81 bouts were recorded as no-decision bouts.

Rocky Kansas is remembered best for giving Benny Leonard one of his hardest matches. That was on February 10, 1922, the title was on the line, and Rocky was a rhinoceros. For 15 rounds, he kept crowding Benny, tearing into him from gong to gong. In the first clinch Benny's hair was rumpled and his nose bled. Here were two young fighters in the ring and one was quite correct in everything he did and the other was all wrong. And the wrong one was winning. But style prevailed, and in the 11th round Rocky dropped his guard and Leonard hooked a powerful short right hand to the chin and down went Rocky for the count of nine. Pat Haley, the veteran fighter and referee, said that never had he seen a short right hand as perfectly executed as that one. From then on, Benny had the fight under control.

Leonard won the decision. Years afterward, Rocky said he felt he should have been awarded the championship that night. "But those New York guys couldn't see anybody but Leonard," he complained. Later that year, on July 4th, they were paired again. This time Leonard won by a T.K.O. when Rocky suffered a broken arm in the eighth round and couldn't continue.

Rocky Kansas won the lightweight title 15 years after he started. The former Buffalo newsboy was far past his prime when he outfought defending champion Jimmy Goodrich, on December 7, 1925, in 15 rounds. Along the way to the championship he fought all the good fighters of the day: Johnny Dundee, Ad Wolgast, Johnny Kilbane, Lew Tendler, Freddie Welsh, Frankie Britt, Richie Mitchell, Charley White, Willie Jackson, and Leonard. On February 18, 1921, Rocky knocked out Mitchell in one round soon after Richie's sensational battle with Leonard in New York, where Mitchell knocked Benny out of the ring.

Rocky held the world championship from December 7, 1925 to July 3, 1926. Sammy Mandell won it away from him with a 10-round decision. After the fight, Kansas announced his retirement, then made a final comeback attempt in 1932. His "comeback" opened and closed the same night, after Joe Trippe kayoed him in the sixth round.

Christened Rocco Tozzo, Rocky was born on April 21, 1895, in Buffalo. He was paid $1 for his first four-round bout in 1911. He earned considerably more ($50,000) the night he lost the title to Mandell. Rocky invested his money in stocks, and when the great Wall Street crash of '29 toppled the country, he lost more than $200,000. To earn a living, he worked on construction jobs and as a city employee in Buffalo. Cancer claimed him in 1954.

SAMMY MANDELL
(1904–1973)

Sammy Mandell scored his highest marks in ring history when he whipped Jimmy McLarnin and Tony Canzoneri in defense of his lightweight championship.

He beat McLarnin in 15 rounds (May 21, 1928, New York), and Canzoneri in 10 rounds (August 2, 1929, Chicago).

Slammin' Sammy, standing 5 ft., 5½ in. and weighing 135, was an aggressive, take-charge fighter who could adapt his defense to any attack. He slugged with the sluggers, boxed with the boxers, and mauled with the maulers. On his way up and at his peak he dodged no one. He met such diversified styles as Johnny Dundee, Sid Terris, Jimmy Goodrich, Jackie Fields, Billy Petrolle and Al Singer.

Mandell's real name was Samuel Mandella. He was born at Rockford, Illinois, on February 5, 1904, of Italian-Albanian parentage. He started fighting professionally in 1920, lost only one bout in the first four-and-a-half years. He won the lightweight title from Rocky Kansas, July 3, 1926, and lost it to Al Singer (K.O., first round), on July 17, 1930.

In 15 years of fighting (1920–1934), Sammy lost only 17 of 168 bouts and was kayoed only 5 times, while scoring 28 knockouts himself. Sixty of his total ended with no decisions.

Romanticists dubbed handsome Sammy the "Rockford Sheik," but there was nothing romantic about him once the work bell rang.

AL SINGER
(1909–1961)

Al Singer was a born star....

"Literally," the old lightweight champion once explained, and he pulled open his shirt and there, where his finger pointed, was a perfect five-cornered star directly over his heart. "It was just a speck when I was born," Al said, "and as I fought my way closer and closer toward the title, it got bigger every day. Whether or not there was any omen about the birth mark, I don't know. I wasn't superstitious about such things. As a matter of fact, on my way to the weigh-in for my title fight with Sammy Mandell, I deliberately walked under two ladders and picked up a black cat and petted it. I was never finicky about lucky ring corners, either. I'd just as soon go into one used by a string of losers as one known as 'the winners' corner. It was all the same to me."

Back in the golden days of boxing, Old New York produced many outstanding fighters of the Jewish faith: Abe Attell, Leach Cross, Izzy Schwartz, Maxie Rosenbloom, Benny Leonard, Ruby Goldstein, just to name several. Al Singer was no exception.

Mild and thoughtful outside the ring, Al was outrageously confident once inside the work pit. He packed a tremendous wallop (24 kayoes), and he could box; for a lightweight he fell very, very hard. In 70 pro bouts, he lost only 8.

Al was a big attraction in New York. He fought 64 of his 70 fights there. That's where the big money was. On his way to the world championship, his eldest brother died.

"He took care of me all my life," Al remembered, "and his death broke me up. He was only twenty-nine and left a young wife and two little girls. I vowed to take care of them as long as I lived. I'll never forget when Harry died. I was scheduled to fight my first big fight in the Garden. You know what that means to a young fighter. Harry died on Monday, was buried on Wednesday, and I had to go through with the bout on Friday. A solemn practice among the Jewish people is a period of seven days of staying indoors to Shiva in what is regarded as mourning the dead. I figured the best thing to do was to accept my first big chance and go through the period later. And I did."

Two-and-a-half years later he bagged the lightweight crown. On July 17, 1930, he disposed of Mandell in one round in New York. Four months later, November 11, in the Garden, Tony Canzoneri finished Al with a couple of left hooks in only 66 seconds.

Nothing deterred, the ex-champ took on welterweight Jimmy McLarnin in an overweight match, September 11. Al was going great guns in the third when McLarnin pinpointed a straight right to the jaw. It looked like black curtains for Al, but he was up at nine just as Jimmy was completing one of his famous victory handsprings. Immediately Singer rushed in wielding a king-size haymaker which missed by a shadow. McLarnin countered with a left to the jaw that dropped Al for the full count.

After losing his championship to Canzoneri, Singer fought only nine more times, winning eight of them. He joined the Army in 1942 and never returned to the prize ring again.

TONY CANZONERI
(1908–1959)

The first time Tony Canzoneri met the New York fight mob he was decked out in short pants, lace collar and patent leather shoes. It was asking too much of licensed fortune-tellers to foretell that one day young Tony would step up and take rank with Joe Gans and Benny Leonard as one of the three greatest lightweights in history.

When Canzoneri rode the crest—in that splashy span between the time he won the featherweight title from Benny Bass and the lightweight crown from Al Singer, until he hammered Lou Ambers to recapture the lightweight championship in 1936—he was a baleful, brutal, clever combatant. He had a stunning right-hand punch, with the courage and stamina of a bull. When he was still only seventeen, he battered down the veteran Johnny Dundee, reduced Jackie (Kid) Berg, the Britisher who held the junior welterweight title, to a pulp, boxed the ears off tough Billy Petrolle, and sent the great Kid Chocolate to the showers in two rounds.

Tony fought Berg twice within six months in 1931. He kayoed the Englishman in the third round to win the junior welter title, and then pummeled him for 15 fierce rounds and won on points in defense of his lightweight crown. This last one was fought in New York on September 10, 1931. In Berg's corner that night was Ray Arcel, the great trainer. Jackie was a special favorite of Ray's. His pet name for him was Yitzel, after his Jewish faith.

Crouching in Berg's corner, Ray winced and shuddered in vicarious pain as Canzoneri poured lefts and rights into Jackie's middle. Sometimes the whistling gloves seemed to disappear altogether, bringing a gasp from Berg and a groan from Arcel. Still up and fighting back at the final bell, Jackie did an about-face and marched back to his corner.

"Yitzel!" Arcel said shakily, "how do you feel?"

"Fine, thank you," Jackie Berg said. "And you?"

While Tony Canzoneri was lightweight champion he had a court jester named Beezy Thomas, a diminutive escapee from the Congo who had jumped ship in New York. He also shined shoes at Stillman's Gym, where Tony worked out. One of Beezy's buddies was Battling Norfolk, a former heavyweight who made a living by rubbing down fighters after their workouts. Norfolk was the house patsy around Stillman's.

One day, some of the pranksters set up a tiger rug, head and all, in Lou Stillman's office, and then got Beezy to call in Norfolk.

"I weren't scared," Norfolk said. "It just make me sick in my stomach."

Another time, they called Norfolk on one of the phones at the gym and then put a rabbit in the booth with him and held the door shut. When Norfolk came out, his eyes were as large as saucers, and he said, "They put me in there with a *monster*. That make me sick to my stomach, too."

As the son of a grocery store owner in the Italian section of New Orleans when he was growing up, Canzoneri was a bootblack. Later, he limited his working hours to blacking eyes. Six years after starting his boxing career, on November 14, 1930, he stopped Al Singer in 1:06 of the first round to win the lightweight championship. It was the second fastest K.O. on record for a title bout.

Canzoneri fought in 20 world championship matches in 15 years. On February 10, 1928, he won the featherweight title from Bass, kayoed Singer two years later to become lightweight champion, knocked out Berg in 1931 to win the now defunct junior welter crown, lost the lightweight title to Barney Ross in '33, and regained it by whipping Lou Ambers.

There was no quit in Tony. "No geezer," as they say around the fight camps. He would never give up, never took the easy way out.

Born on November 6, 1908, at Slidell, Louisiana, Canzoneri grew up in New Orleans, only three blocks from where Pete Herman, the great bantamweight champion, lived. On weekdays, Tony, eleven, worked out in the gym and fought in the streets. His papa went around boasting to friends: "My li'l Tony . . . hee-za gonna be cham-peen." Mama Canzoneri had other plans for her little Tony. He was going to be a *gentleman*. On Sundays, she dressed him up in patent leather shoes, knee-length pants, lace collar, and sent him off to Mass.

Holder of three world titles—featherweight, lightweight and junior welterweight—Tony Canzoneri was one of boxing's most idolized fighters. (NEA)

There was nothing sissy about the way young Tony handled his dukes, however. After his family moved to Brooklyn, and Tony took up prizefighting seriously, he won his first 14 professional fights, 7 K.O.'s in a row.

On December 23, 1925, a year after leaving New Orleans, Tony knocked out Danny Terris in four rounds; the very first K.O. of record at the then brand new Madison Square Garden. That was one of 44 kayoes Tony scored in a total of 181 fights. On the other hand, he was knocked out only once, by Al (Bummy) Davis, in the last fight of his career. That took place on November 1, 1939, and Tony was over the hill by then, but the fans still loved him. So when Bummy knocked him out they booed Bummy and hated him for it.

Canzoneri was only nineteen years old when he won the featherweight title from Bass. During the following years that he ruled the roost, Tony was one of the game's most idolized fighters. He gave the fans their money's worth. They turned out in droves to watch him belt around such respected professionals as Joe Rivers, Tommy Ryan, Andre Routis, Bobby Garcia, Joe Glick, Eddie Zivic and Jimmy McLarnin. He won 139 of his 181 total bouts.

At his peak, Canzoneri stood 5 ft., 4 in. and scaled 126. He fought anyone they wanted to match him with, he brimmed with self-confidence, and he wasn't worried in the least over what could happen to him in the ring.

On May 8, 1936, Tony fought Jimmy McLarnin in the wind-up in the old Garden in New York. Before the action started, they met in the middle of the ring for instructions from the referee, and when Tony started back to his corner he walked into the hanging microphone. It took 12 stitches to close the cut but there wasn't time then. They mopped up the blood with a towel and shoved Tony out for the first round. He was groggy and he lost the round. It was the last one he lost that night.

LOU AMBERS
(1913–   )

Lou Ambers was a first-rate fighter and a genuine champion in an era when there were a lot of lofty lighties. He won the lightweight championship from Tony Canzoneri, for whom he once had been a sparring partner, split in two title fights with Henry Armstrong, and then finally dropped the crown to Lew Jenkins.

The road to the top was perilous.

"All right, you want to be a fighter," his father told him, when he left home to hit the road in 1932. "Don't come home with a black eye."

Luigi D'Ambrosio (his real name) had scored a few minor triumphs around Herkimer, New York, his home town, and the big money of Manhattan beckoned. But nobody was interested in an unknown lightweight. Unable to afford to train in Stillman's Gym or any of the other prizefighting hangouts, and rejected by one matchmaker after another and with his funds dwindling to the barest eating money, Lou walked the streets, slept in Central Park, the subways and Grand Central Station until he got a break.

Lou hung around the smaller gyms. One day, he met a man who said he was a manager and could get him some fights on a bootleg "amateur" circuit which was then thriving in central New York and small towns across the Pennsylvania border.

Their first stop in the manager's rattletrap old car was Kingston, New York. They were told that the local boxing card had already been filled but that one of the featured fighters named Otis Paradise had failed to show up. The promoter told them that if at ring time Otis still was missing, then Lou could fight in his place. Otis never showed up.

Nobody informed the ring announcer of the change in the program. He introduced Lou as "Otis Paradise." So the imposter from Herkimer climbed into the battle pit and walloped out his opponent in the first round. The crowd liked that and Lou, still fighting under the alias, was asked to fight again the following week. He soon grew into a popular attraction on the bootleg circuit and earned regular eating money. The record book shows that Lou Ambers fought a total of 102 pro bouts in nine years. What is missing from the official statistics is that he had some 80 more bouts under the name of "Otis Paradise."

Among the prizefighters he whacked around on the bootleg wheel was Frankie Wallace; the same Frankie Wallace who shortly thereafter beat Freddy Miller, the featherweight champion, in an over-the-weight match. Lou told himself: "If I'm good enough to beat the guy who beats the featherweight champion, what am I doing fighting for peanuts?" He went back to Manhattan. By now everyone around the gyms knew who "Otis Paradise" was and it wasn't hard for Lou to get fights in the smaller clubs around New York.

Lou's big break came the night Al Weill happened to stroll into the Coney Island Velodrome. Lou was engaged in a hot battle with Tony Scarpati. Weill needed only one look to convince him that Lou was a prospect. Making a few discreet inquiries, he learned that Ambers was being managed by a Filipino postal clerk so, after asking himself whether he should do it, Al consented to take over the management of Lou. Ambers never did find out whatever became of the original Otis Paradise, though he suspected Otis must have gone around boasting about all the bums he knocked out on the bootleg circuit.

Weill knew he had the makings of a real champion the night Fritzie Zivic broke Lou's jaw in Pittsburgh. Though blood gushed from Lou's mouth like ketchup from an upturned bottle when he came to his corner after the seventh round, Weill didn't have it in him to disregard Amber's plea that he be permitted to finish the fight. The bout went on, and for the last three rounds not only did Ambers avoid being hit but he scored enough points himself to win the decision.

On the train back to New York after the fight, Weill discovered that Lou's jaw was fractured. He had fought the last part of the bout suffering from excruciating pain. That accident laid Lou up for six months. It would have ruined almost any other fighter, but Ambers went on to win the world championship.

Lou won the lightweight title from Tony Canzoneri, a great fighter, and lost it to another, Henry Armstrong. The championship fights were all 15-rounders.

Whitey Bimstein, Lou's trainer, said he'd never forget when Lou won the crown from Canzoneri. Lou told Whitey before the match that if he won he was going to get drunk afterward.

"So he won the championship," Whitey said, "and then he had one beer and he was drunk."

Lou's loss to Armstrong (August 18, 1938) drew 20,000 fans into Madison Square Garden. Sports writers called it "one of the fastest, most furious and savage bouts ever fought in New York."

Ambers made a stouthearted, courageous fight out of it, but he couldn't stop the doughty little black man from California. Armstrong had extra incentive going for him: He was out to become the first man in history to hold *three* world boxing titles simultaneously—featherweight, welterweight, and lightweight.

Hammerin' Hank had Lou down in the fifth round with a crushing right to the jaw, but the knockdown, with Lou plainly hurt, happened just a flash before the bell rang and, at the count of one, Ambers was saved.

In the sixth, Ambers went down again, and again was visibly hurt and on the way to a K.O., under a barrage of stunning punches. This time he stayed down until the count of eight. He got back up with his head still awhirl, but in a remarkable demonstration of ring generalship fended off Armstrong's heated bid for a knockout. Under this forced pressure for a K.O., Henry grew wild and ineffective. The more he stepped up the tempo, the more furious he became with himself. Meanwhile, Ambers, emboldened to counterfire, upset Henry's fight plan.

In the ten rounds he won Armstrong did everthing but knock out Ambers. He had Lou so weary at times that it seemed Lou could not possibly go on. But Lou did survive, and, more, he came storming back. He came back gloriously, desperately, and in the thirteenth round nearly turned the tables on Armstrong with a fury of stinging lefts and rights. But that effort took a lot out of him. He was practically out on his feet in the last two rounds when he again rallied, only to be brought up short by Armstrong.

At the end of the final round, Armstrong looked the vanquished instead of the victor. He finished the bout on wobbly legs. His lips and mouth were bruised and bleeding, and there was a gash an inch long on the lid of his left eye. Ambers didn't look much better after about the toughest battering he or any other lightweight had absorbed in the history of this ring title.

Armstrong weighed 134 pounds to Ambers' 134½. The bout officials, to the derisive shouts of noisy protests ringing in their ears, voted 2–1 in favor of Armstrong. Referee Billy Cavanagh and judge George Lecron felt Armstrong won, and judge Marty Monroe voted for Ambers.

Lou Ambers was the ideal fighter. He gave his last trainer, little Charley Goldman, very little trouble. Lou was dedicated, worked faithfully, stayed in shape between fights, and was considerate of those around him.

Ambers won back the lightweight championship from Armstrong in New York a year later. Finally he lost the crown to Lew Jenkins, one who might have been a great prizefighter had he taken the profession more seriously. Jenkins knocked Ambers out in the third round to win the title, on May 10, 1940. They fought again nine months later, and this time Ambers went out in seven.

Lou's contract with Al Weill still had a few years to run, but Weill made him retire.

"I'm not going to see you abused," Weill told him. "I won't let you fight again. I have you tied up so you can't fight for nobody else."

Lou stormed and shouted all over the place, but Weill stubbornly held his ground. He wouldn't change his mind.

"Listen, Lou," he said, "you've got money in annuities. You're not going to starve. You're my boy, my baby. I'm not going to let you get abused."

So Lou Ambers quit the prize ring and joined a much bigger fight. He enlisted in the U.S. Coast Guard to serve in World War II.

LEW JENKINS
(1916–)

The story of Lew Jenkins is the story of a fighting man—a fist-fighter, a booze-fighter, and a gun-fighter in two wars.

His credentials were most impressive.

Writing of him as a fist-fighter the day after he dismantled Pete Lello in Madison Square Garden, the late Dan Parker testified: "Jenkins looked like a great champion. Certainly no lightweight within the memory of this present generation of fans could hit like this bag of bones."

Speaking of him as an infantryman decorated with the Silver Star in Korea, his general said: "He's a great combat soldier. He's famous up and down the front."

Speaking of himself as a booze-fighter comparable with the homicidal Harry Greb, Lew said: "People who knew Greb say he was a junior compared to me."

You might say Lew was ambidextrous. That is, he was able to be at the same time a world champion in the ring and a champion bum outside it. According to the various laws and standards of conduct of the place in which he lived, which was the earth, he was a guy who, when he was lightweight champion, didn't live or behave like one. He was an irresponsible whack, a good puncher and a good guy, but wild and not very dependable.

It was Lew's pleasure to while away the weeks between bouts by sparring with Haig & Haig, or, crouched astride the motorcycle he loved so much, jousting with trucks in Broadway traffic. Two or three days before an important match that Mike Jacobs had made for him, the skinflint promoter was walking to lunch just as a motorcycle came screeching out of Fiftieth Street and roared into the Manhattan traffic on smoking tires. Jacobs, shuddering, turned white in the face when he recognized the rider.

"Hey, Mike!" Jenkins shouted happily. "Look, no hands!"

You had to like the nutsy Lew. His love affair with the motorcycle began with him asking, "How d'yuh turn the damn thing *on?*", and ending with, "How d'yuh turn it *off?*" When he took up the banjo, he explained his interest with, "I hear fellas get a lot of dough for writing songs. I'm gonna write some." And after Henry Armstrong creamed him in Portland, Oregon, he told his manager: "You're nuts, I wasn't knocked out! Uh, where am I?"

It was an effort to understand Lew Jenkins. There was the story of his match with Armstrong, for example, when Lew trained faithfully every night until 4 A.M., employing methods not recommended by Emily Post, wherefore Henry knocked him down seven times. "How'm I doing?" Lew kept asking in the dressing room afterward, unaware that the referee had stopped the fight.

There was the one about his Philadelphia fight with Bob Montgomery which had to be postponed when Lew got word his mother was dying and rushed home to Texas. Returning for that one he rolled off a mountain in his car, got bunged up so badly he couldn't have trained even if he'd ever been sober enough to train. That time he got off the floor and whipped Montgomery in the fiercest fight Philadelphia had seen in a generation.

There were so many other tales that were as true as they were difficult to believe—of his draw with Fritzie Zivic when Lew was late for the weigh-in because he was fried; of the second time he stopped Lou Ambers after a training course that included two auto accidents; of the evening when he stopped Tippy Larkin and said mournfully, "That man was the most convinced knocked-out man I ever knocked out."

There was also the time he got beat up by Red Cochrane and everybody called Lew a disgrace to boxing. There was no way of knowing what they'd have called him if they'd known about the three vertebrae in his neck that he had broken three weeks earlier by riding that blamed motorcycle of his into a traffic circle at 3 o'clock in the morning.

Lew Jenkins was born Verlin Jenks on December 4, 1916, at Milburn, Texas. He began prizefighting when he was eighteen. After that, he lost 38 of 109 bouts. He won the world championship from Lou Ambers in 1940 and lost it to Sammy Angott 12 days after Pearl Harbor. A lot of other guys whipped him on the way out of the business and then he and his banjo and his motorcycle disappeared from the prizefight scene in New York.

Nobody seemed to know what had happened to Lew. Then one day, during the Allied invasion of Normandy, a couple of American war correspondents found themselves off the French coast on an LST that was tied up to another LST attached to the Coast Guard.

"Hey," said one of them, "know who's aboard that other tub? Lew Jenkins, the fighter."

"The old lightweight champion?"

"The same."

They hadn't known Jenkins before the war, but they'd heard about him in the war zone. One story going the rounds told about the time Lew was stationed on this post and a big mess cook picked on him. The cook stood 6 ft., 2 in. and weighed 240 and Lew stood only 5 ft., 7 in. and scaled about 135. Lew put his right hand in his back pocket and he kept it there. He cut the big lug to ribbons and knocked him down six times just with left hooks before the big guy quit.

"After that," Lew said, "he didn't pick on me no more."

One of the war correspondents on the LST was Bill Heinz, one of the finest fight writers ever to cover the New York scene. So he stepped across to the other LST and looked Lew up and they sat on the deck shooting the breeze. They got talking about fighting, not in the ring but G.I. style. Lew wore dirty blue jeans and a faded blue shirt and a smudged white cap stuck on the back of a wild bush of hair. There he sat, a bony little guy with the heavy brows of a fighter and those pale, sunken eyes and that gaunt face, and he'd been back of the Japanese lines, landing men and supplies in Burma. He'd also taken part in the landings in Sicily and Salerno, and he'd been decorated by the British and had a number of citations from the U.S. government. At Normandy, on D-Day, he had been up and down many beaches in the small boats, bombed and strafed and shelled and with G.I.'s getting killed all around him.

"Lew," Bill asked him, "how's the Coast Guard?"

"I guess it's all right," Lew said, in that Texas drawl. "But I don't like it."

"Why?" Bill said.

"Because," Lew said, "we don't fight."

His admiration for the foot soldier was something close to worship.

"There's nothing like the infantry," Lew said. "A soldier is the most wonderful thing in the world. Oh, sure, the Navy and the Coast Guard get guys killed, too. But we take the soldiers into a beach and then we go away and leave 'em there. When this war is over, every guy here ought to get a good house to live in and a good job. He's earned it. If he don't get that, he's being cheated. If I had a house, I'd want a soldier living in it."

The words were spoken with pure reverence.

After he got out of the Coast Guard, Lew came back and enrolled in a school of bricklaying in Philadelphia, but gave that up. He tried a comeback in the ring. He beat some obscure guys and lost to some and got knocked out by some. They had to feed him whiskey from the water bottle to keep him from coming off a drunk in the middle of a round and falling on his face on the canvas. They made him a bum in the papers. The comeback wasn't particularly successful.

Lew Jenkins appeared happiest when he was fighting G.I. style. After 14 years in the prize ring and three in World War II, he signed up for a hitch with the Army in Korea here and won the Silver Star for gallantry. (UPI)

Then, one day, somebody at Stillman's said he'd heard that Lew Jenkins had gone and enlisted in the Army. What was it? A gag? Between 14 years in the prize ring and 3 years in World War II, hadn't he seen enough fighting? It would have been hard to explain why Lew had to join the Army. It might have sounded maudlin to say that in the Army, surrounded by death, Lew at last had found life with a meaning. In Korea, he finally got what he wanted—a foxhole on Bloody Ridge with the gol' darned infantry. Got the Silver Star for gallantry, too. Only the very best soldiers got that.

G. I. Lew.

Few men ever came off the sports pages and stood up in war like he did.

SAMMY ANGOTT
(1915–   )

Sammy Angott considered himself about the luckiest stiff in the world. The lightweight division's eighteenth champion was paid handsomely for doing what he did best. Which was one of the principal reasons why the Italian from Washington, Pennsylvania, fought so well for so many years.

Angott was a first-class fighting man for 15 years (1936–1950). He wasn't made to be a doormat. When the blue chips were down, he showed the courage of a catamount, beating such seasoned campaigners as Petey Sarron and Davey Day and Baby Arizmendi and Bob Montgomery and Lew Jenkins and Allie Stolz and Willie Pep and Ike Williams and Johnny Bratton. The great little Beau Jack was the only one in 114 bouts able to stop him.

When Charlie Jones, his manager, first saw him, he said the only thing that could keep Sammy from the title was being struck by lightning, or a truck. Lew Jenkins, the irresponsible whack, was neither, though he could sock like a ten-ton moving van, and on December 19, 1941, Angott out-speared him for 15 rounds at Madison Square Garden and won the title.

After reaching the summit, Sammy retired and "unretired" three different times. He was as unpredictable as a woman motorist at an

Angott was one Sammy who never ran. (NEA)

intersection. Angott retired as champion in 1942, returned the following year to regain the crown from Slugger White, then lost it again to Juan Zurita in 1944. *This* Sammy was never one to run!

BEAU JACK
(1921-)

No fighter belonged so completely to prizefighting as the little black man they called Beau Jack.

Beau made the cycle: from shoeshine boy, to lightweight champion of the world (New York State version), and back to shoeshine boy again.

As a main-eventer in 20 bouts in old Madison Square Garden he brought in $1,578,069. Yet he wound up like so many prizefighters, dead broke. Those close to Beau charged that the illiterate shoeshine boy from Augusta was city-slicked out of his ring earnings by unscrupulous handlers. Whatever the truth, Beau was not precisely the investment-broker type himself. He lived recklessly, spent foolishly, and was an easy young man with his money while he had it.

"With him money is secondary," Chick Wergeles, who managed him, said in 1945. "He says money is for givin' away. How about that? He loves to fight. He says, 'Just so I keep on fightin' somewheres, I love to fight.' If he didn't get no pay for it, he'd still wanta fight just to relieve the monopoly."

The broad, flat-faced li'l champ had a dedication and stomach for fighting seldom matched. No one trained harder. He'd be at Stillman's Gym when it opened and he would be there when it closed. When he was not bag-punching or rope-skipping or boxing, his eyes would be fixed on those who were. After a fight, win or lose, he always would have the same question. "Were it a good fight?" he would ask. "Did the people like it?"

Beau Jack didn't have a particularly big punch, but he knocked out 40 of his 111 opponents during his career. He stopped them by wearing them down to a frazzle and then belting them out.

"I understand," Bill Heinz once said to him, "that you pray before every fight."

"Tha's right," Beau said, grinning.

"For what do you pray?"

"I pray that nobody get hurt. Then I pray it be a good fight."

"Don't you ever pray to win?"

"No," Beau said, shaking his head. "I would never do that."

"Why not?"

"Suppose I pray to win," Beau explained. "And supposin' the other boy, he pray to win, too. Then what God gonna do?"

There used to be a question about Beau's true age. Wergeles, in 1946, tried to pass him off to the press as twenty-three.

"Twenty-five," Beau corrected him.

"No," Wergeles said, "you got it wrong again. You was nineteen when you started fightin' and you been fightin' four years. Twenty-three."

"Look," Beau said stubbornly. He lifted an index finger and ticked it off as though counting. "I was born in Augusta, Jojah, on April the first, 1921. That makes me twenty-five."

"Okay," Wergeles said, "twenty-five."

Two years in the Army had improved Beau's education. Now he could read and write some, and count numbers.

"He reads his own letters himself," Wergeles said. "He amazes me how he improved 100 percent reading and writing in the Army. He reads his own newspaper stories by hisself now."

"I just boxed only once in the Army," Beau said. "At Benning in Jojah. They've five hundred paratroopers going overseas wants me to box, so I boxed for 'em and afterwards after they got over there I kep' gettin' letters from 'em how they always remember what I done."

Beau Jack might have been an April Fool's Day baby, but he was nobody's fool when it came to fighting. It took him only three years after he turned pro in 1940 to work his way up to a title shot. On December 18, 1942, he kayoed Tippy Larkin in the third round in New York to win the New York State version of the world lightweight championship. Five months later he lost it in 15 rounds to Bob Montgomery, but shortly before he went into the Army he won it back from Montgomery. Then, in a rubber match, on March 3, 1944, Montgomery outpointed him to take the title back for the second time.

In his prime, Beau fought most of the top lightweights and welterweights around, including triumphs over Fritzie Zivic (twice), Henry Armstrong, Sammy Angott and Juan Zurita. The record shows he won 83 of his

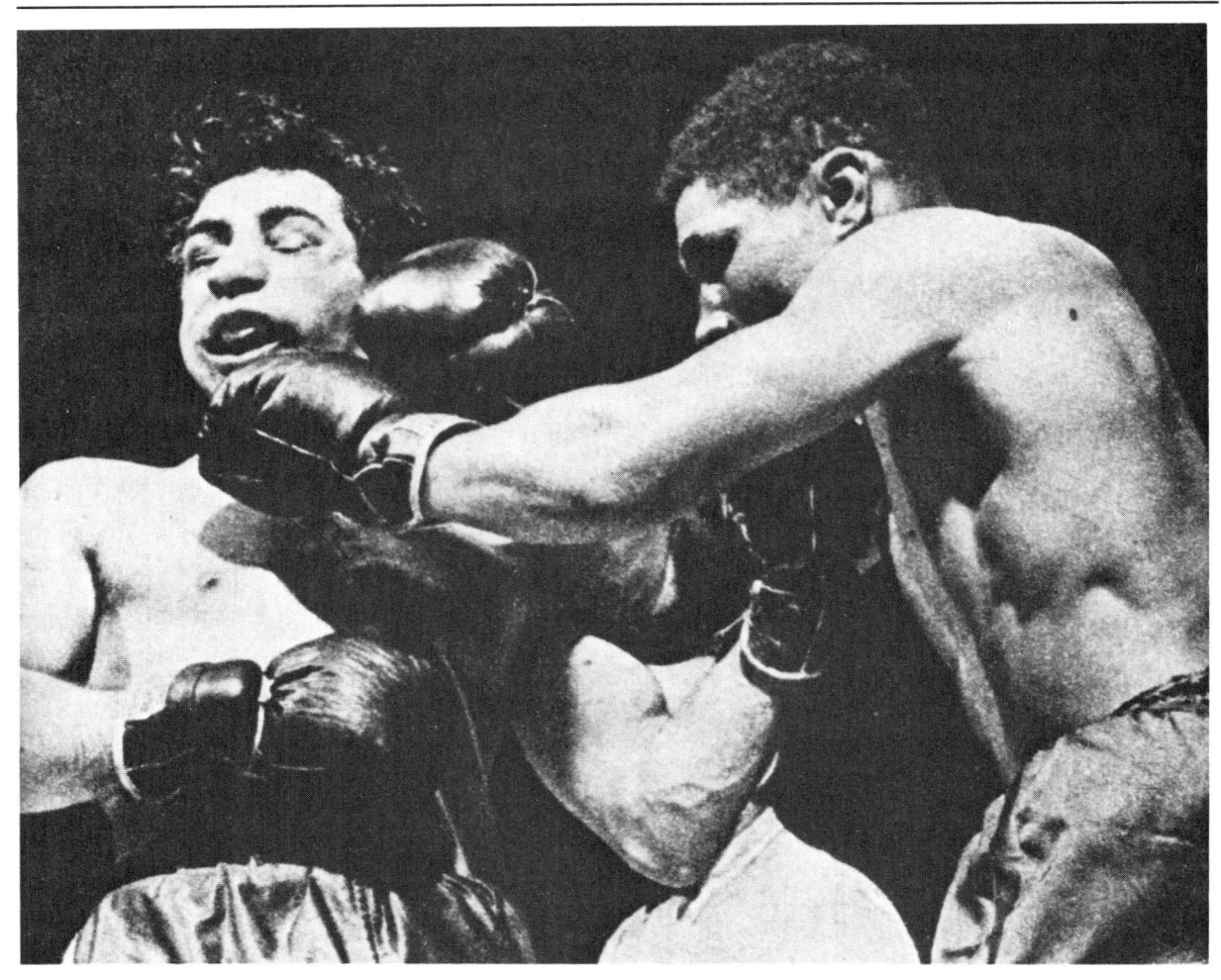

Little Beau Jack, right, lands a right here to the jaw of Johnny Greco. In a match fought in New York, in 1946, Beau won the 10-round decision. (UPI)

111 pro bouts. He fought 5 draws, was kayoed only 3 times. He retired in 1955 and went back to shining shoes again, at a Florida hotel. The cycle was completed. He started as a bootblack and now he was a bootblack once more.

"Only now I get twenty dollahs foh a shine," drawled Beau Jack. "These bigshots with the monay wan a former world's champ to shine their shoes, so they ask for me."

BOB MONTGOMERY
(1919-   )

Bob Montgomery was one of the few fighters to regain a championship from the man to whom he lost it.

Bob was no hulking bruiser, but he did have courage and knew all the tricks for survival. He also had durability and strength, as testified by the fact that 51 of his lifetime total of 97 pro bouts lasted 10 or more rounds. In 11 years, he was stopped by only three men—Al Davis (1944), Wes Mouzon ('46) and Ike Williams ('47). His 75 victories were virtually evenly divided between decisions (38) and knockouts (37).

One of Montgomery's biggest assets was that he was fast enough to storm at opponents with a volley of punches, smash four or five blows off their heads and bodies, and be out of range before they could land a single answering punch.

Bob Montgomery was born on February 10, 1919, at Sumter, South Carolina. He began his career in 1937 in the amateurs, winning 22 out of 24 matches. The following year, he turned pro, and mowed down 24 straight foes like tin soldiers, 17 by K.O.

On May 21, 1943, Montgomery decisioned Beau Jack in 15 rounds and won recognition by the New York Commission as lightweight champion of the world. They fought three more times, twice with the title at stake. On November 19th of the same year, Beau got the crown back (Decision, 15 rounds).

Montgomery began a campaign for a return title match. In January, 1944, he battered Joey Peralta and Ike Williams, and then, on February 18th, he went in against Bummy Davis at the Garden in New York and woke up the next morning sure it was all a bad dream. For Bummy, a 1–10 underdog, stiffened the ex-champion in 63 seconds of the first round. When the bell rang, Davis, the "Brownsville Bum," walked right out and threw his right and missed around the head. Montgomery grabbed the arm and turned Bummy around, and when he did Bummy threw the hook and Bob went down. When he got up Bummy hit him again. And that's all there was to it.

For winning, Bummy was paid $15,000 —considerably more than he got for selling produce off a pushcart on Blake Avenue in Flatbush when he was younger. "I could sell anything," Bummy said. "I was the best tomato salesman in the world." So after he beat Montgomery the sports writers went into Bummy's dressing room and all he wanted to talk about was how good he could sell tomatoes.

The third and final title meeting between Montgomery and Beau Jack was held at the Garden only three weeks after Bob lost to Davis. This time Montgomery stood up for the full 15 rounds and regained the championship.

On August 4, 1944, in Bob's last fight before going into the Army, they fought again. No title was at stake. Beau Jack won on points in 10 rounds.

When Montgomery returned from service seven months later, the old form was missing. Between mid-1945 and February 7, 1947, he lost non-title matches to Nick Moran (Decision, 10), Mouzon (K.O., 2) and Tony Pellone (Decision, 10).

The Pellone defeat was particularly galling to Bob, because Tony, a welterweight, was not overly gifted. Montgomery had whipped Pellone in an earlier fight at the Garden in what Tony said was the biggest purse he ever got.

"I got $8,513 for my end," Tony said. "Whatever money I made I always took home to my old man, because I had 10 brothers and 2 sisters. So I took the money home and I gave it to my old man, and he said to me in Italian: 'How you fixed?' and I said, 'I'm broke.' He said, 'All right, here.' He gave me the $13. I said, 'Hey, Pop, 13 is unlucky. Give me $14 instead.' Then my old man said, 'No, give me one dollar back. That makes 12.'"

In 1947, Montgomery and Ike Williams were on a collision course. There was some difference of opinion as to which was world lightweight champion. The N.B.A. picked Williams, while New York Commissioners chose Montgomery. On August 4, 1947, in Philadelphia, Ike settled the issue by blasting Bob out in the sixth round.

Montgomery never won another fight. After losing seven in a row in 1950, he gave up the ghost. The magic was all gone from his once golden gloves.

JUAN ZURITA
(Birthdate unrecorded)

Juan Zurita had most of the championship equipment. The engineering consisted of a swift right hand, a rock jaw, speed, courage and strength. He also wore the unmistakable mark of the professional pugilist—an ear mangled by frequent blows until it was finally dried up into a blob of flesh and cartilage, a grand old "tin" ear.

The Guadalajara, Mexico lightweight began his career in 1933, starting out sensationally with 13 victories in succession. At this rate, estimated his fans, Juan would be a champion in no time. The facts, pure and simple, however, are that Zurita didn't get his gloves on the title for *11* years. On March 8, 1944, he decisioned Sammy Angott in 15 rounds in Hollywood, California, to win the N.B.A. edition of the world's lightweight championship. A year later, in Mexico City, Ike Williams took the crown away from him by knocking him out in two rounds. That was Zurita's last fight.

Juan stood 5 ft., 3 in., weighed 122. Williams and Henry Armstrong (twice) were the only fighters ever to K.O. him. He won 70 (22 by K.O.) of 83 professional bouts. There was nothing synthetic about Juan Zurita. He was the real thing.

IKE WILLIAMS
(1923–)

The call of the wild was strong in Ike Williams. His speed and punching power completely bewildered opponents. Sixty of his 153 adversaries wound up with their britches in the resin, gnarled forms lolling on the ring apron scarcely cognizant of the ref's arithmetic as he tolled off the inexorable tally of the count.

Not a few authorities called Williams the finest all-around lightweight since Tony Canzoneri. "Ike was cruel and relentless, and he had finesse," testified the late Eddie Borden. "He could have played piano with boxing gloves on."

Williams was born in Brunswick, Georgia, on August 2, 1923. He left school at the age of sixteen to help support his family and settled in Trenton, New Jersey, where he sharpened up his fist-fighting tools by defending the "corner rights" of his newspaper stand. Developing into a good boxer and hard puncher, he started as a pro on March 15, 1940. Almost exactly five years later, on April 18, 1945, he won the N.B.A. version of the lightweight title by knocking out Juan Zurita in Mexico City. On August 4, 1947, he kayoed Bob Montgomery in six rounds in Philadelphia to earn full recognition by all as world champion.

Before Jimmy Carter stopped him in the 14th round in New York, on May 25, 1951, to win the title from him, Williams successfully defended his crown seven times in six years.

Ike Williams stood 5 ft., 9½ in. and weighed 135 at his peak. In 16 years of fighting, he won 124 (60 kayoes, 64 decisions) in 153 pro bouts. He was counted out only 6 times.

Ike was an all-around athlete in high school, excelling in the sprints, a trait he carried into the prize ring with him. Once he heard the referee utter those words "Shake hands now, and come out fighting," Ike Williams gave chase to many a foe.

JIMMY CARTER
(1923–   )

James W. Carter was the first world boxing champion to win and lose the same title *three* times.

Between May 25, 1951, and June 29, 1955, he won the lightweight crown from Ike Williams (K.O., 14th round), lost it to Lauro Salas (Decision, 15 rounds), regained it from Salas (Decision, 15 rounds), lost it to Paddy DeMarco (Decision, 15 rounds), rewon it from DeMarco (K.O., 15th round), and lost it to Wallace (Bud) Smith (Decision, 15 rounds).

Jimmy received only $1,377, plus $2,250 from TV, when he flattened Williams to win the championship for the first time. Because of his in-and-out title record, the skeptics asserted that Carter was a victim of "Carbonization," that is, he was supposed to have taken his orders from Frankie Carbo, the underworld character who for years allegedly "owned" the lightweight division. (The charges were never proven.)

Consequently, it took people a long time to recognize Jimmy Carter's boxing ability. After stopping Williams, it wasn't for two years, in two title bouts, that Jimmy finally became recognized for what he was—a fine all-around prizefighter. The two bouts in mention were the Tommy Collins match in which Carter floored the brash Bostonian 10 times before the referee stopped it, and the George Araujo affair, in which Carter met a legitimate lightweight title contender and proved to the public that he was the master.

Carter was a solid workman. He didn't

Ike Williams, right, bowed before Kid Gavilan's flailing fists in two 1949 bouts. (UPI)

Jimmy Carter drops Ike Williams in 1951 lightweight title bout. Carter won world championship on a T.K.O. in 14th round. (UPI)

blow you down with a punch—he was not that rugged a socker—but he would stalk you and flick the jabs in your face and try to double you up or wear you down to the point where you were ready to be taken.

At his peak, he was a solid champion.

Carter was born at Aiken, South Carolina, on December 15, 1923. He began prizefighting in 1946, retired in 1961. He stood 5 ft., 7 in., weighed 135 lbs. He won 80 of 120 pro bouts, fought 9 draws, was kayoed only 3 times.

JOE BROWN
(1926-   )

Joe Brown won the lightweight championship of the world the hard way and the long way around. Old Bones was thirty years old (middle-aged by a prizefighter's yardstick) and had been fighting as a pro for 10 years, but it wasn't until August 24, 1956, that he was able to catch up with the crown, winning it on a decision from Wallace (Bud) Smith in 15 rounds.

Before then, he had won fights and he had lost them. He knocked out many of his opponents and he was knocked out. But he kept learning to fight until he became a true professional.

Born in New Orleans, on May 18, 1926, Brown defended his title four times during the first 16 months he held it—all knockouts. The challengers were Smith, Orlando Zulueta, Joe Lopes, and Ralph Dupas.

Did you see him on television, May 7, 1958, when he stopped Ralph Dupas in the eighth round in Houston? It was Houston's first world's championship fight and attracted an all-time Texas record gate (11,000 fans paid $68,740). Brown's share of gate and TV receipts was $48,000.

If you saw the fight, you saw a man working expertly at his trade. Brown wore the elusive Dupas down by stalking him and hitting him in the body when he caught up with him. By the sixth round, Dupas was Joe's, almost for the asking. Dupas had a curious habit of leading with his right hand, which was all right against suckers—but against a pro, it was fatal.

Brown baited him by letting him do it a few times, then, in the eighth round, hit him hard in the belly . . . and backed off . . . and waited for the right-hand lead . . . and when Dupas started it, Brown dropped him with a left hook to the chin and that, really, was the fight. Dupas had the benefit of a long count because Brown, like Dempsey against Tunney in 1927, couldn't wait in a neutral corner. But by now Dupas was doomed and when he got up, Brown was taking him apart and, after one more knockdown, the referee stopped the fight.

Joe Brown's small, delicate, almost ladylike hands belied his socking power. He won 30 of his first 60 bouts by kayoes. He finished with a total of 48 knockouts in 160 pro bouts. In five-and-a-half years, he defended his title 12 times, losing it finally to Carlos Ortiz in 1962.

Brown fought for 25 years (1946–1970).

Old Bones Joe was one Brown who truly did it up brown.

LAURO SALAS
(1927-   )

Lauro Salas's boyhood dream was to become a great bullfighter, but a funny thing happened to the little Mexican on his way to the bull ring. He became instead history's first undisputed world boxing champion from Mexico.

Little Lauro was a colorful clubfighter with a rock jaw, a free-swinging style and a habit of putting on whirlwind finishes. Whenever he fought at the Olympic or the Hollywood Legion Stadium in Los Angeles, the management played *Virgen de la Macarena* over the loudspeaker—the bullfighter's song—as he jogged down the aisle to the ring. And as he bounced into the ring, head bowed and right hand raised in semi-salute, he'd bow to the four corners of the arena in the same manner as the *matador*.

Salas was a natural 126-pounder, a tough little guy who looked like a 20th-century version of Alley Oop. Born at Monterrey, in 1927, the fourth son in a family of seven boys and four girls, he ran away from home at the age of eight to become a bullfighter. His papa gave him a sound licking.

"Later, I sold papers and shined shoes at the boxing arena in Monterrey," Lauro said. "I got to know the matchmaker real well. One night a fighter does not show up and the matchmaker ask me do I want to fight. I say sure and I knock the guy out in three rounds. I got one peso—and another beating from my father. He get mad when he find out my opponent was my own brother, Santos! After that, I fight only strangers."

When he was nineteen, Salas got the price of bus fare and moved to Los Angeles. Starting with a four-round decision over Bobby Dykes in 1946, he won 14 of his first 17 pro bouts in America. On his way to the California featherweight title, he lost to Harold Dade, Carlos Ortiz and twice to Sandy Saddler. His big year was 1952, when, as a 10–1 underdog, he won the lightweight title by a split decision over Jimmy Carter, but lost it back to him in a rematch at Chicago Stadium five months later.

Salas carried the fight a good deal of the way but didn't have enough experience to pile up the necessary points to win. He showed a flurry of his old form in the 11th and 12th rounds, but Carter came on to win. Salas never fought in another world title bout.

Managed by Jimmy Fitten, he retired in 1961 after being knocked out by Sebastio Nascimento and Bunny Grant.

A great champion, Lauro Salas? Hardly. He lost 52 of 148 pro bouts. The best thing you can say about him is that he *persevered*.

Years of fierce pounding left Little Lauro's cheeks heavily scarred, his eyebrows obliterated by tiers of intricate flesh. Perhaps the best part of his bloody story was of his comeback after his palmier days. He saved his money. Back down home in Monterrey, he bought a supermarket for his parents, a nice house for them, several more small houses to rent, a drugstore for his sister to run. Lauro

Lauro Salas became Mexico's first undisputed world champion in 1952 when he upset lightweight Jimmy Carter in Los Angeles. (UPI)

put her through medical school and a brother through law school.

"I invested my ring earnings in my family," he said.

PADDY DeMARCO
(1928–)

They called Paddy DeMarco "Billygoat" because of the way he butted, bulled and manhandled his opponents.

The boy from Brooklyn was not precisely the Emily Post type. Minus great natural ability, he rose to the lightweight championship by using his head for more than keeping his ears apart. He made what physical equipment he had go a long ways.

Billygoat Paddy had the kind of punch that if he swatted a fly you'd have laid 6–5 on the insect getting up and swatting back. You think I'm kidding? The record shows he knocked out only 8 men in a lifetime total of 104 pro bouts!

When DeMarco fought Sandy Saddler at the Garden in New York, on October 28, 1949, Jack Dempsey was at ringside to analyze his style. "Paddy's swinging left slap leaves him so wide open that Saddler was able to nail him repeatedly with left shovel-hooks to the breadbasket and score big points," Dempsey said afterward. "Paddy violates a prime boxing rule—always land punches with three outer knuckles of your fist."

The result was that Saddler gashed De-Marco's face so badly that Paddy was forced to retire from the fight in the ninth round.

Born on February 10, 1928, Paddy was raised in Brooklyn and later trained in Trinity Gym, the oldest gym in New York. His ring idol was Eddie "Cannonball" Martin, who came from the same neighborhood. DeMarco was managed by Jimmy Dixon and scored upsets over Terry Young and Billy Graham on his way to the lightweight title. He became world champion on March 5, 1954, by busting up Jimmy Carter in 15 rounds at Madison Square Garden and lost the crown back to Carter eight months later in San Francisco.

Originally, DeMarco, whose record for 1952–53 showed six defeats by opponents of distinction, was matched with Carter for the title as a "nothing" opponent, but from nothing he became something. A lot of people felt that his possession of the title, as short as it was, merely demeaned the division because he was a fighter past his prime of mediocre talent.

Despite his detractors, the Brooklyn Billygoat can say to himself forever more:

"I was the world's champion."

It's a line that can last a lifetime.

WALLACE (BUD) SMITH
(1929–1973)

Wallace (Bud) Smith was the modern generation's number one in-and-outer. That is to say, when he was hot, he sizzled. When he was cold, he was as frigid as an arctic snowdrift.

Smith's amateur record—he won the 1948 National A.A.U. lightweight title—promised great things to come. He won a dozen of his initial 13 professional bouts and his potential appeared limitless. Suddenly and mysteriously he turned spotty, losing and winning, losing and winning; very much like a bloke who had turned robot and somebody was tampering with the mechanism.

In 1953, however, the engineering apparently got a good oiling and Mr. Smith caught fire again. He boffed out five straight opponents with his special embalmer, lost and won a few more, and then was matched with champion Jimmy Carter in Boston, on June 29, 1955. Smith showed flashes of his former promise that night and won the nod and title in 15 rounds.

Success seemingly went to the Cincinnati Negro's head. After whipping Carter again in a return title bout, Smith dropped three straight non-title matches to Larry Boardman, Tony DeMarco and Joe Brown. The latter was signed for a championship fight against Smith in New Orleans, August 24, 1956, and Brown came out of the smoke with a 15-round decision and the crown.

After that, Mr. Smith went all to pieces, being hammered into a twilight state in his next six fights. Curiously, success just doesn't agree with some people.

Bud Smith was only forty-four when he died.

CARLOS ORTIZ
(1936–)

Carlos Ortiz twice won the lightweight championship of the world to prove his class.

He first won it from Joe Brown (April 21, 1962) and then lost and won it back from Ismael Laguna within seven months in 1965.

The Puerto Rican-born New Yorker had earlier held the junior welterweight crown, winning it from Kenny Lane (1959) and losing it to Duilio Loi (1960).

Born at Ponce, Puerto Rico, on September 9, 1936, the 5 ft., 7 in. Ortiz began fighting professionally in 1955, was undefeated in his first 26 bouts before Johnny Busso decisioned him in 1958. In his last 32 matches before retirement in 1972, Carlos had a won-draw-lost record of 28-1-3. The string included 17 kayoes. All told, he defended the lightweight championship 11 times. In his last defense, Carlos (Teo) Cruz won the crown from him via a 15-round decision at Santo Domingo, on June 29, 1968. In 70 pro bouts, Ken Buchanan was the only man ever to K.O. him—in his last fight (September 20, 1972).

CARLOS (TEO) CRUZ
(1937–1970)

One of the greatest little fighters ever to come out of the Dominican Republic, Carlos (Teo) Cruz was late in finding himself after an inauspicious start.

He was twenty-two before he turned pro, lost 7 of his first 13 bouts, then was undefeated in his next 10 matches. Just as it seemed he was picking up a full head of steam, he lost 4 out of 6 more fights.

Born on November 4, 1937, Cruz was thirty years old when he whipped Carlos Ortiz in 15 rounds (June 29, 1968) in Santo Domingo to win the lightweight title. Eight months later he lost it to Mando Ramos in Los Angeles on an 11-round K.O. It was only his second defeat in his previous 26 bouts.

Carlos Cruz was back on the winning trail with four straight victories when tragedy struck. On February 15, 1970, he and his family were killed in a plane crash off the Dominican coast. He was only thirty-two.

ARMANDO (MANDO) RAMOS
(1948–   )

Armando Ramos was a young man in a hurry. He turned pro two days after his seventeenth birthday and was only twenty when he got his first shot at a world championship.

Born on November 15, 1948, in Los Angeles, Ramos won his first 17 bouts, 11 by kayo. On his way to winning the lightweight championship from Carlos Cruz (February 18, 1969) in L.A. he lost only to Kang Suh II, Frankie Crawford and to Cruz (the latter his first attempt to win the title). In a rematch, Ramos knocked out Cruz in the 11th round. He stopped Yoshiaki Numata in six rounds in Los Angeles, on October 4, 1969, and then in his very next defense lost it on a nine-round K.O. to Ismael Laguna, on March 3, 1970.

In 1972, Ramos won the World Boxing Congress version of the lightweight title from Pedro Carrasco, on February 19th, and lost it to Chango Carmona (K.O., eighth round) in Los Angeles, on September 15th. Eleven months later, he retired from the ring after suffering a kayo by Arturo Pineda.

In nine years as a professional, Armando Ramos fought only 40 times.

He hardly got his feet wet—yet that's all he required to win two versions of the world lightweight title!

ISMAEL LAGUNA
(1943–   )

Ismael Laguna twice won the world's lightweight title to take rank with Panama Al Brown (bantamweight champ, 1929–35) as one of the two biggest sports idols in the history of Panama.

Laguna was born in little Colon, 40 miles from Panama City, on June 28, 1943, one of 18 brothers and one sister. He was a flyweight when he turned pro at eighteen in 1961. At 5 ft., 10 in., he was described as a tall Willie Pep.

Skinny Laguna won his first 27 pro bouts before losing a decision to Antonio Herrera in Bogota, Colombia. Ismael later K.O.'d him in a rematch. Before winning the lightweight title of the world, Laguna won the Panama and South American featherweight crowns.

Laguna was managed by Isaac Kresch, a Jewish Panamanian saloonkeeper, and owned by Alfred Aleman, the mayor of Panama City and director of a brewery. It was no coincidence that Laguna wound up making TV beer commercials after winning the championship.

When Davey Moore offered to give Laguna a shot at his featherweight crown a couple of years earlier, Kresch turned him down on the grounds his boy was not ready. Laguna, displaying fits of temper, walked into Kresch's bar and belted him. All was forgiven, however, when Ismael won the lightweight title from Carlos Ortiz, on April 10, 1965, in Panama City. Laguna handled Ortiz perfectly. He parried the champ's bull-like rushes neatly, busted him up and won a close, but undisputed, split decision. "He doesn't hit too hard, but he was too fast for me to hit," Ortiz said. "He's a great fighter."

Laguna had the advantage of a long reach to go with his blazing natural speed. He was very shifty, jabbed hard and defended cleverly. He was also surprisingly strong and could take a punch. Most of his opponents said he didn't hit hard, but that he was a sharp, cutting puncher. In winning 40 of his first 42 pro bouts, he was never cut but had drawn blood from 38 foes and stopped 25. No one ever knocked him out in a lifetime total of 74 bouts.

The first time he won the crown, Laguna was champion for only seven months before Ortiz bounced back to beat him in a return match. They fought for the title again two years later, and again Ortiz outpointed him in 15 rounds.

Laguna, twenty-six, worked his way up the championship ladder by winning 12 out of his next 13 matches. By this time, Mando Ramos was the champ and Laguna kayoed him in the ninth round in Los Angeles, on March 3, 1970, to regain the title. Six-and-a-half months later, he lost it for the final time as Scotland's Ken Buchanan beat him on points in 15 rounds in New York. A year later, Laguna tried winning the crown back from Buchanan, lost again, and then retired from the ring.

STILL ACTIVE
KEN BUCHANAN
(1945-)

Ken Buchanan was born on June 28, 1945, in Edinburgh, Scotland. He turned pro in 1965 and won his first 33 bouts, losing only twice in his first 51 professional fights. He won the British lightweight title in 1968, then announced his retirement from the ring the following year at the age of twenty-four, reconsidered his decision, and resumed his career a month later. Buchanan became the first Britisher in 56 years to win the world lightweight championship with a controversial, wafer-thin decision over Ismael Laguna, in 1970. In a return match, on September 13, 1971, Buchanan repeated his victory over Laguna and received a $100,000 guarantee, the largest sum ever paid a lightweight champion. It was the first lightweight title fight ever held in the new Madison Square Garden. Buchanan was a Fancy Dan boxer with a beautiful left jab and classic boxing style. His main problem was gaining weight. To make 135 lbs. for the second Laguna fight, he feasted on 12 lbs. of rich Catskill cuisine at Grossinger's, in upstate New York, and did not gain an ounce. On June 26, 1972, Buchanan was savagely mauled by Roberto Duran, of Panama, and lost his title by a K.O. in the 13th round. The Scot claimed he was fouled by a low blow after the bell by Duran's street-fighting tactics, but the verdict stood.

ROBERTO DURAN
(1951-)

Roberto Duran was born on June 16, 1951, at Panama City. Beginning in 1967, he won 36 of his first 37 pro matches, 29 by K.O. He won the world lightweight championship from Ken Buchanan, then put his title on the line three times in '73—and kayoed Jimmy Robertson, Hector Thompson and Ishimatsu Suzuki.

FEATHERWEIGHTS

OTED for dazzling speed and lethal punching, the featherweight class provides a thrilling chapter in prize ring history. The division originally had a top weight of 118 pounds, but it was set up to 122 pounds, and finally to the present limit of 126 pounds.

Irishman Ike Weir, in 1889, was the first fighter actually to be designated world champion of the featherweights, although Dal Hawkins for a time claimed recognition.

IKE WEIR
(1867–1908)

Looking at skinny little Ike O'Neil Weir, you'd have suspected that the featherweight champion from Belfast, Ireland, had nothing in his gloves but hope and heart.

Ike Weir's construction was belying. He was a tough little acorn, abnormally intelligent. The first featherweight champion of the world made up for a light punch with skill, speed, and lightning-like reflexes. He wore down opponents to their stockings, lost only 3 of 41 bouts in 10 years of fighting.

Weir was born on February 5, 1867, at Lurgan, near Belfast, and began boxing in 1885. On March 31, 1889, he sailed 80 rounds with Frank Murphy at Kouts, Indiana, for the vacant featherweight title. The match was declared a draw, but Weir later claimed the title. The following January, Billy Murphy K.O.'d him in 14 rounds to replace him on the throne.

Weir was another of those "carpetbag" fighters. He traveled all over the world to earn a payday. He went 61 rounds with Jack Havlin, 36 with Jack Williams, 21 with Willie Clark, and 20 with Tommy Warren.

In and out of the ring, Ike Weir, 5 ft., 5½ in., 118 pounds, covered plenty of distance.

TORPEDO BILLY MURPHY
(1863–1939)
and YOUNG GRIFFO
(1871–1927)

Thomas W. Murphy, styled along the lines of that fine old Bamboozler, Young Griffo, was one of the first Iron Men of the modern prize ring.

Distance meant nothing to the old featherweight ruler. He battled Johnny Murphy for 40 rounds, went 30 and 29 rounds with Jim Burge, 32 and 20 with Tommy White, 27 with Frank Murphy, and 22 and 15 with Young Griffo.

Torpedo Billy, born at Auckland, New Zealand, in 1863, stood 5 ft., 6½ in. and owned an astonishing 69½-in. reach when he began fighting in the 1880s. It was evident from the first that he had plenty of the devil in him. Uninhibited, he swung his powerhouse right like a club and basted the liver out of many of the muttonheads he fought. Twenty-five of his lifetime total of 49 victories were scored by knockouts. One night he won *two* bouts—both kayoes!

On January 13, 1890, Murphy flattened Ike Weir in 14 rounds to win the featherweight championship and a purse of $2,250, a fortune in those days. The following September, in Sydney, he lost a 15-round decision to Young Griffo in a match advertised by the promoters as for "the featherweight title of Australia." Torpedo Billy fought desperately for his life, even taking off his gloves and wading in at Griff barefisted. Afterward, Griff claimed the championship of the world.

Despite his caveman tactics and his granite physique, Torpedo Billy Murphy holds one dubious record: he was knocked out more times (nine) than any other man ever to rule the featherweight roost.

As for Albert "Young Griffo" Griffith, who will deny that the wacky Australian was the cleverest boxer who ever lived? Griffo was the prize ring's original vanishing man. Throughout his career, he lost only one American decision—and that through a referee's boo-boo. When he wasn't drifting from one gin mill to another, he was ducking his opponents silly.

Young Griffo was born in Miller's Point, Sydney, New South Wales, in 1871. Never defeated as a featherweight, he took the measure of Billy Murphy to stamp his niche indelibly on the championship, in 1890, and then successfully defended the crown against Murphy the following year. In 1893, boxing was banned in Sydney because of several deaths resulting from combat. So Griffo began looking around for new worlds to conquer.

When he skipped ashore on our Pacific Coast in the summer of '93, the pickings were so lean that he moved east. In Chicago, he whipped Solly Smith and George Lavigne. His manager, Hughey Behan, then matched him against a great Boston favorite, Ike Weir. Griffo clobbered Weir so badly that the Loop police were called in to end the fight.

When Weir returned to Boston, his tales of Griffo's prowess aroused tremendous interest. A bout was arranged with Johnny Griffin, the Braintree lad, and Bostonians flocked to the old Cyclorama building on Tremont Street to see what Griffo was all about.

The match was scheduled for eight rounds with the understanding that if both men were still on their feet at the end, it would be declared a draw. Griffo was delighted to find Billy Murphy in Griffin's corner. He didn't give bloody-all for his compatriot, whom he'd polished off back home.

Griffo was a physiological wonder. He

Oldtimers picked Australian Young Griffo as the cleverest boxer of all time. When boxing was banned in his homeland, he came to America for new worlds to conquer. (Photo from author's collection)

trained on the finest neutral grain spirits without the slightest visible effect on his speed and reflexes (the record does not indicate how many opponents he kayoed with his breath). He was also what you might call a character who beat a verbal tatoo on Murphy while playing around with Griffin.

" 'Ow I'd like to 'ave you in 'ere!" Griffo would remark to Murphy as he belted Griffin around the ring. "This is wot I'd do to ye!"

Zow! Wham! Bang!

Griffo's witty, sarcastic exchanges with Murphy and his total disregard for the pride of Braintree kept the crowd roaring with laughter. But they were also won over by his phenomenal defensive work—a subtle movement of the head, a new dance step, a feint with the eyes. Griffo was nowhere and everywhere, and in the third round he actually challenged Murphy while annihilating Griffin.

Shortly after the contest, the real Griffo appeared in the dining room of the old Hotel Clarendon to claim his modest reward. Approaching his manager, he held out an old derby.

" 'Ughey, gimme some pelf so's H'i kin toike the lads out for a good time."

Behan proceeded to fill the headpiece with loose greenbacks of small denomination. Thereupon Griffo went to the bar, dumped out the money and invited everyone to drink until the " 'atful of pelf" was gone.

One " 'atful" followed another until Griffo and his cronies were well advanced in their cups.

Murphy accepted that third-round challenge, and the bout was scheduled for two weeks later. Griffo went on a week-long drunk to ready himself for the encounter before Behan had him arrested, fined and thrown in the clink for safe keeping. An hour before ring time, the manager secured a bail commissioner, put up bond for Griffo and conducted him from the Charles Street Jail to the clubhouse. A dash of water in the face, and he was indeed "ready" for Murphy, whom he walloped something fierce.

The next outing with "Little Chocolate," the fabulous George Dixon, was a 20-rounder for the championship. Griffo again slipped away for a week at a time, but Behan appeared to be the only one who wasn't worrying.

"When I want him, I know where to lay my hands on him," Hughey explained. "And when he gets in the ring, he'll be ready."

But just to be on the safe side, he again had Griffo jailed a week before the fight, bailing him out in time to get to the clubhouse. That contest is officially listed as a draw for the distance, though actually the Sydney phantom showed Dixon more boxing than he'd ever seen before.

Griffo drifted into obscurity after the Dixon match. That free citizen served a year's sentence in a Brooklyn jail, and on the day of his release he appeared in the same ring with Joe Gans and ran circles around him!

Jack McAuliffe, the lightweight champ, was awarded the only American decision over Griffo, though Jack later admitted that he'd been beaten in the Coney Island set-to. Maxey Moore, a great amateur referee, counted the points with a "counter" in each hand—one for McAuliffe and the other for the Griff. But Moore got all fouled up and did his scoring on the McAuliffe counter.

Griffo kept vanishing and revanishing until he finally landed in an insane asylum in Chicago. When he was discharged several years later, friends raised his passage money for a one-way ticket to Australia. Young Griffo scattered this "pelf" around the pubs before dropping completely out of sight. Three years later he was seen panhandling along the Great White Way, and in 1927 he died and Tex Rickard paid for his burial. It was later discovered that Griffo had left an estate of $3,000 made up of "pickings" and the generosity of Broadway cronies.

The tales about Griffo are legend. Once when he was standing at the bar in Young Mitchell's saloon in San Francisco, a guy who had threatened to punch him barged through the door.

"Here he is now, Griff—that fellow who was looking for you," Mitchell warned. Griffo didn't bother to turn around. He looked up at the big mirror behind the bar, and when the hothead began swinging, Griffo followed the attack in the mirror and moved his head accordingly.

The fellow soon tired of fanning the air, and spinning Griffo around by the shoulders, he declared, "You win, Griffo! I was going to knock your block off, but you haven't got one. I'm licked!"

Griffo was fond of using his great speed to win barroom wagers or (better yet) drinks. One of his favorite tricks was to spread a small handkerchief on the floor, step on it and challenge anyone in the house to hit him while he stood rooted to the hanky with his hands clasped behind his back. No one so much as touched him either!

Flycatching was his greatest forte. He could swoop up a fly off the bar, release it in mid-air and catch it again between thumb and index finger. But his pet joke was to remove his shoes and get his feet shined by a bootblack.

Jack Grace, the globetrotter, probably knew more about Griffo than anyone else. Grace used psychology to persuade Griffo to train for a dove named Johnny Burns.

"Now, Griff, you're going to meet a man-eater this fight," Jack warned. "I wouldn't have matched you with him if I'd known who he was."

Young Griffo cocked his head like a toucan and regarded Grace in astonishment.

"A man-eater, sez yer?" his tongue wobbled. "Blime, old chap, who ez'e? The devil with 'im! I'll knock 'im silly, I will!"

Grace decided to really lay it on.

"You know, Griffo, that Burns lad went 198 rounds with a bloke and could have gone 100 more. Burns knocked him out. I tell you, you've got to get him early or he'll keep you up all night!"

Burns, of course, was a greenhorn, but the Aussie frowned at the inconvenience of the task before him.

"Went 198 rounds, did 'ee?" Griffo snapped. "Man-eater, eh?"

And Griffo settled down, trained like a beaver and never touched a drop before the Springfield, Illinois, encounter. On fight night he was in better shape than he'd ever been before. When the bell rang, he went after the startled Burns like a kangaroo run amuck. In the second round the riot squad had to halt the massacre.

"Man, what a beating you gave him!" Grace congratulated him after the fight.

"Beat 'im up?" Griffo snorted. "Owye should rawther say so! I took no chance of that bleedin' duck going 198 rounds with me!"

When Jack revealed his masterful deception, Griffo hit the roof.

"Just think of it!" he howled. "Me givin' up me drink to train for a raw 'un! The pleasure I gave up and the fun I lost training for the loikes of 'im!"

Griffo fought his last bout in 1904, a four-round draw with George Memsic.

GEORGE DIXON
(1870–1909)

Generally conceded to have been the finest bantam and featherweight in history, George Dixon was the first black to win a world championship. He fought in more championship prizefights than any other man in ring annals—33, six more than runnerup Joe Louis. Little Chocolate, 5 ft., 3½ in. and 118 pounds, was truly a fighting champion and is always placed among the all-time greats. He was a sprinter who could go the distance.

Long-armed and skinny-legged, swift of hand and foot, Little Chocolate boxed like a phantom, slugged like a diminutive long-

George Dixon, the first black to win a world boxing championship. (NEA)

shoreman. He possessed the ideal fighting temperament. Distance meant nothing. He could pick up speed and last all the way.

Dixon always conceded weight.

Little Chocolate held both the bantam and featherweight titles. He stopped Nunc Wallace in 18 rounds in London, June 27, 1890, to become bantam king, knocked out Abe Willis of Australia in five in San Francisco the following year to win the feather crown.

Dixon originated several training practices that are widely in use today. He was the first to shadow box.

Tom O'Rourke managed Dixon and one day Little Chocolate showed up with a squatty young Negro in tow. He assured the boss that his friend could also fight. The new member of the stable was Joe Walcott, the Barbadoes Demon.

Born July 28, 1870, in Halifax, young Dixon was a quadroon, his grandfather having been white. He worked as a photographer's apprentice until he was sixteen, when he turned to professional fighting.

Early in his career, February 7, 1890, Dixon met Cal McCarthy in a finish fight with two-ounce gloves. The men disliked each other violently. At the end of the 70th round of a terrific battle, Referee Al Smith declared it a draw. Dixon was eager to continue, but the referee was too tired and McCarthy was all in.

When George Dixon died, in 1909, Tom O'Rourke instructed the cemetery management to make up a tombstone with the engraved words:

"Here rests the gamest pugilist who ever lived."

Indeed, a most fitting epitaph.

SOLLY SMITH
(1871–1929)

and DAVE SULLIVAN
(1877– ?)

Solly Smith and Dave Sullivan are little more than footnotes in boxing records.

Smith was born in Los Angeles, in 1871, and had the strange habit of fighting draws. Seventeen of his 45 pro bouts ended with no winner. He scored only six kayoes, was knocked out himself but once, by George Dixon in 1893. He held such stalwarts as Young Griffo, George Lavigne and Frank Erne to draws, and beat such good ones as Dal Hawkins, Torpedo Billy Smith, Johnny Griffin—and Little Chocolate Dixon, the latter with the title on the line.

Four years after Dixon knocked him out, Solly came back to outpoint the great black in 20 rounds in San Francisco to claim the featherweight crown. Less than a year later, at Coney Island, he lost it to Dave Sullivan, when he broke his arm in the fifth round and had to quit.

Dave Sullivan was born at County Cork, Ireland, on May 19, 1877. He began fighting professionally in 1894, retired in 1905. During those 12 years, he fought 59 times, won only 28. Like Solly, many (16) of his bouts ended in draws.

Few champions have lost their titles under more peculiar circumstances than Sullivan. Forty-seven days after winning the crown from Smith, he met the challenge of Dixon and was disqualified in the 10th round when one of his seconds jumped into the ring. Thus, Little Chocolate got his title back. You might say that Dave Sullivan was just holding it for him while he caught his breath.

YOUNG CORBETT II
(1880–1927)

and TERRY McGOVERN
(1880–1918)

"Hurry up, Terry!" Young Corbett shouted, pounding on the door of the flyweight champ's dressing room. "Come out and get your licking!"

The challenge, which echoed all over the Hartford (Connecticut) Valley that night of November 28, 1901, is now a ring classic, etched in brass. But only because the kid from Denver added injury to insult by knocking out the great McGovern in the second round.

It was a stunning upset. Until fate came knocking at the door in the person of young William H. Rothwell, alias Young Corbett, Terrible Terry had been invincible. Opponents cringed before his violent assaults. There wasn't an insurance man in Hartford who wouldn't have underwritten those 1–5 odds on the favorite. Corbett was strictly unknown, an upstart and the underdog. But he was a cool one, and he knew what his well-calculated dare would do to the hot-tempered

McGovern. Terry was so mad when he entered the ring that he was completely vulnerable, and the cocky Corbett simply took him apart. Sixteen months later he poured more salt in Terry's wounds by flattening him in 11.

There was no reasoning with McGovern after that initial loss. They had fought at 126 pounds instead of the accepted 122, so Terry snarled at Corbett, "You ain't the champion anyway. You didn't make the weight."

"That's okay by me, Terry," his cheerful tormentor replied. "You keep the title. I'm just satisfied to be known as the guy who knocked out Terry McGovern."

That's the way it was with those two—the one all fire, the other like dry ice. Had they been born Siamese twins, they could have licked a battalion. But they belonged in the same ring, if only to serve as an example of what blind rage and overnight success can do to a fighter. After their two lulus, Young Corbett began losing repeatedly, while McGovern was never the same boy, though he beat some good ones before he retired and kayoed Harlem Tommy Murphy in one round.

The Denverite was not only the cockiest fighter ever to win a title, but once he had it, he couldn't have cared less. Prosperity was more than he could handle, and his fame and fortune were quickly dissipated.

Corbett stood 5 ft., 2½ in. and weighed 126 at his fighting peak. Whatever he did was done for broke. In the ring he fought as though his life depended on it. He opened wine with both hands. Stepping the primrose path, he updated Casanova. And no stakes were too high for this inveterate gambler.

It was the gambling that did it, along with defeats by such heavier men as Bat Nelson and Jimmy Britt. The late Jack Doyle, the "Sage of Broadway," once met Corbett in a Saratoga gambling house. The kid was broke and asked Jack to stake him a half buck. Doyle offered more, but Corbett declined.

An hour later, strolling past a roulette wheel, Doyle encountered him surrounded by an admiring crowd with a stack of chips in front of him.

"How much you got there?" Jack asked.

"About $6,000," the kid replied.

"Better cash in and git," Doyle suggested.

Corbett laughed and went on playing.

A few hours later Doyle was finishing a goodnight cigar on the veranda of his hotel when he heard someone coming down the street whistling cheerfully. It was Young Corbett.

"How'd you make out?" Doyle hailed him.

"Oh!" Corbett replied, laughing carelessly, "I lost the half buck."

The only thing Terry McGovern ever lost was his head. His terrible temper proved the difference between mere greatness and recognition as a national hero. Terry was great. He loved to fight, was a tremendous hitter, especially with his right, and was as feared in his time as Dempsey was later. In fact, Dempsey was a king-sized McGovern, to reverse the usual comparison.

Joseph Terrence McGovern was born in Johnstown, Pennsylvania, March 9, 1880, only seven months before Young Corbett saw daylight. His parents moved to Brooklyn when he was six months old, and when his father died, the scrawny little kid 5 ft., 4 in., 122 pounds) went to work to help support the family.

Terry became a professional fighter through a baseball argument. While working in a Williamsburg lumber yard managed by Charley Mayhood, Terry captained the yard's ball club. A dispute arose during a game with a rival team captained by Charley Mallay, and it was agreed that the captains should settle the issue with their fists. McGovern won, and Mayhood was so impressed that he prepared him for a ring career. He remained as Terry's trainer when Sam Harris assumed the managership.

McGovern's temper cost him a fight before he met Young Corbett. He was murdering Tim Callahan in a Brooklyn ring, July 23, 1898, when Callahan's seconds told their boy to call Terry an S.O.B. in the next clinch. Tim communicated this supreme insult as instructed and Terry blew up. He hit on the break and was disqualified in the 11th round.

In two years, Terrible Terry defeated world champions in three divisions. He kayoed Pedlar Palmer, British pretender to the bantamweight throne, in one sizzling round at Tuckahoe, New York, on September 12, 1899. He knocked out George Dixon in eight rounds for the featherweight title in New York, on January 9, 1900. And he stopped Frank Erne, lightweight champ, in three rounds in New York, on July 16, 1900. (Erne weighed 128 so the title was not transferable.)

Five months later, McGovern kayoed Joe Gans in two rounds in Chicago, but there was a distinct halitosis about this one. The rumor that Gans took a dive killed boxing in the Loop for many years.

Was Terrible Terry really as good as they say? Robert Edgren, syndicated columnist of the era, testified that he was.

"I know that had I never seen McGovern fight I couldn't possibly picture him being as great as he was," Edgren once said. "Some fighters owed their fame to being knocked out by Terry. Patsy Haley, I know, owed part of his reputation to the fact that in 1899 he lasted 18 rounds before McGovern stopped him. It would take a list this long just to name the famous little fighters McGovern finished in a few rounds.

"McGovern had a fighting style all his own, with his tremendous burst of fighting energy, lightning speed, tireless aggressiveness and terrific punching power. Trimly built with sloping shoulders, thick forearms and heavy fists, small waist, deep chest, and with the legs of an acrobat, McGovern was designed for the business. His eyebrows grew straight across, with no division above the nose, and his forehead had the classic fighting slope. He had a thick but long neck, and a long chin. They said that his chin was too long and he wouldn't be able to take a punch if anyone ever hit him there, but McGovern could take a punch and fight twice as hard afterward.

"It isn't hard to picture McGovern. In his corner waiting the first bell he was just like Jack Dempsey, quivering with the fidgety effort of waiting for the scuffle to begin. At the bell he always leaped out and was half across the ring and diving into the first attack almost before you could follow his movements. He never tried to guard or cover. One or two lightning feints to get an opening, and he was tearing into his man with a swirling flurry of blows that nothing could block and that no one could escape. His ring fury was unmatched. It was the suddenness of his attack that earned him the name Terrible Terry. The finest boxing skill was no defense against his attack. Harry Forbes, the cleverest of all bantams, learned that in Terry's second fighting year, when Terry knocked him out in 15 rounds. Tim Callahan was a ghost to other fighters, but he couldn't keep away from Terry. As for the sluggers, he outslugged most of them with ease.

"Oscar Gardner was the first to make any impression on McGovern. He hit Terry a terrific punch on the chin and knocked him down. Dazed, but driven by his fighting instinct, Terry climbed up Gardner's legs as Gardner stood over him, clung to Gardner until he recovered and fought with such fury that he knocked out Oscar in the third.

"A curious thing about Terry. He never had the slightest mark on him, for all his desperate fights. I once asked him why. He just laughed. 'Listen,' he told me, 'I fought so fast they didn't have time to hit me.'"

Frank Graham, a star columnist for the *New York Sun* and *Journal-American* for many years, used to tell a story about Jimmy Johnston, a bantamweight, that somewhat revealed just how deadly McGovern was as a puncher. One night, Jimmy was watching the fights at the old Polo A.C. when the matchmaker walked over to him and said, "We've got to make a substitution because a fellow

In the years 1899–1900, Terrible Terry McGovern whipped world champions in three different weight divisions. A hot temper earned him his nickname. (NEA)

didn't show up. Will you fight in his place?"

"Against who?" Johnston asked.

"Terry McGovern."

"Not me," Jimmy said.

Charlie Roden was sitting next to Johnston, and he offered to accept the challenge.

"You can have him," Johnston muttered.

So Charlie slipped on his fighting duds and went in against McGovern. Roden stood only about 5 ft., 4 in., and, as Frank Graham told it, "McGovern hit him so hard on top of the head that he never grew another inch!"

Young Corbett and Terrible Terry McGovern. . . .

Corbett died broke in Denver on April 10, 1927. McGovern died of pneumonia, contracted while refereeing doughboy bouts at Camp Upton in World War I. Corbett gambled, but who can say that he lost? He had more fun than anybody, and that was that. McGovern died respected and was mourned throughout the boxing world.

ABE ATTELL
(1884–1970)

Abe Attell belongs to that elite group of champions who deserve special recognition as the greatest fighters of all time. This classless fraternity, boxing's unofficial Skull and Bones, includes the likes of Gans and Greb, Dixon and Dempsey, among several others. Nice company, though Charley Harvey, who managed Jem Driscoll and Owen Moran, would prefer that Abe be tabbed simply as the best fighter in ring history, pound for pound. "It isn't even debatable," Harvey grudgingly admitted, yielding to the force of his conviction.

As a messenger boy in San Francisco, Abe began delivering his own messages with both fists. Gentleman Jim Corbett and George Dixon inspired him to become a boxer instead of a slugger. "I watched them block, slip, duck and sidestep with ease and grace and realized a fellow could be a fighter and not get hurt—if he were clever enough."

Abe was a featherweight at the old limit of 122 pounds, but he bullied the class of the light-, welter- and middleweights. Starting in 1900 at the age of sixteen, the feather duster flattened 15 of his first 16 opponents. After Young Corbett kayoed Terry McGovern in two rounds at Hartford in 1901, neither was able to make 122 pounds again and the title was claimed by Attell, who was only 17 years, 251 days old!

In October of that year, Abe made it official. He and George Dixon fought twice within eight days. The first bout ended in a 20-round draw, the second with Attell being declared the winner and champion after 15 rounds.

Abe ran out of featherweight competition after that and turned giant killer. At 5 ft., 4 in. he gave away all kinds of weight to such bigger men as Bat Nelson, Freddie Welsh, Owen Moran, Ad Wolgast, Harlem Tommy Murphy, Aurelio Herrera, Kid Broad and the original Kid Herman. You could have knocked them over with a feather! And little Abe was no more particular about referees. When he had any doubts as to the officiating, he would quickly decide the issue for himself.

Between 1900 and 1913, Abe racked up nearly 200 fights. But his lack of weight cost him dearly on two occasions. Following a six-round, no-decision bout with Bat Nelson in Philadelphia, they met again three years later (1908) in San Francisco in a merciless no-decision affair that was one of the toughest fights a fight crowd ever saw. And Abe's 20-round epic with Harlem Tommy Murphy at Daly City near San Francisco was one of the goriest bouts in ring history.

The two had already met in three no-decision matches, and both were nearing the end of their careers. Abe had weathered 12 years of fighting, Murphy nine. Sump'n had to give, and as it turned out, both men were dead on their feet at the finish. By the 17th round, the smaller, lighter Attell was so tired that he sat on the middle rope and boxed a hurricane for the last minute of the round. Harlem Tommy rallied in the final stanzas to win the decision, but you couldn't tell 'em apart for the gore.

Another night, in New York, Attell fought Knockout Brown, Dan Morgan's awkward little southpaw. It was a 10-round bout and, the law around New York being what it was in those days, decisions were not permitted except in the newspapers. K.O won the decision, which must have surprised those who didn't see the fight, because even if Abe by then was almost at the end of his remarkable years as a fighter, he still figured to box rings around Brown.

The outcome of the fight, as a matter of fact,

also surprised those who saw it, including the members of the boxing commission. The result was an inquest, or hearing, at which Attell was asked to tell his side of the story. Abe said he had a broken thumb going into the ring and a doctor had shot it full of novocain.

"My whole blame arm was numb," Abe explained, "and that's why I hadn't been able to do better."

The commissioners raised their eyebrows at that one, but they couldn't prove Abe was lying and had to let him go. But the high point of the inquest had come a little before Attell got on the stand, when K.O., a very little eral young man, was being examined. The line of questioning went something like this:

"Your name?"
"Valentine Brown."
"You are a professional boxer?"
"Yes sir."
"And you box under the name of Knockout Brown. Is that correct?"
"Yes, sir."
"On the night of January 18th, did you box Mr. Attell?"
"Yes, sir."
"Did you see Mr. Attell before going to the club, except at the weighing-in?"
"No, sir."
"Now, when you entered the ring, was Mr. Attell already in his corner?"
"No, sir, he came in a couple of minutes later."
"Did you speak to him?"
"No, sir."
"Did he speak to you?"
"Yes, sir."
"Oh, he did, did he? And what did he say?"
"He said: 'Hello, you silly looking bum!'"
That almost broke up the meeting.

On February 22, 1912, at Vernon, California, Attell lost the featherweight title on a highly questionable decision to Johnny Kilbane in 20 rounds. It was Abe's twenty-eighth birthday, he'd worn the crown for 10 years and he'll never forgive Johnny—never!

Years later, a friend, noting Abe's crooked nose splashed all over his face, asked him: "If you were so clever when you were fighting, how come you got that jagged nose?"

"Stanley Ketchel gave it to me," Abe confessed.

"But the record book doesn't show that you and Ketchel ever fought," it was pointed out.

"I know," Abe explained. "He did it with a brick. He was throwing it at a sparring partner and I walked into the line of fire."

Them wuz the days.

JOHNNY KILBANE
(1889–1957)

Senator John Patrick Kilbane of Ohio held the featherweight championship of the world for 11 years, longer than any other incumbent, and was doubtlessly its most reluctant defender.

Johnny Kilbane, who hailed from Cleve-

Abe Attell started out as a messenger boy in San Francisco, and wound up delivering messages with his fists. He lost only 10 in nearly 200 fights. (NEA)

land, settled comfortably into politics after 16 years of in-and-out, hot-and-cold prizefighting.

Inside a boxing ring, he was something of an enigma. On any given night he was just as good as he cared to be. When he was proud, he was magnificent. Such as the night (February 22, 1912) he lifted the featherweight crown from Abe Attell in 20 rounds at Vernon, California. Then there were those other times—like June 2, 1923, when Eugene Criqui stopped him in the sixth round at the Polo Grounds and took the title back to France. Criqui held the championship only 55 days.

Kilbane was always classified as a boxer. A puncher must take chances and Johnny left few openings for reprisals. "The guy's just yellow enough to be a great fighter," remarked Benny Leonard in a backhanded compliment. Benny and Criqui were the only ones to knock Kilbane out in 140 pro bouts. What he meant about the Clevelander being yellow was that Kilbane would punch with you only when he was certain no risk was involved. The fact that 81 of his total matches were no-decision affairs, tells you something about him. There was little to choose between his knockout (22) and won-by-decision (23) records.

Kilbane's old one-two combination could be obliterating when he took the notion to go home early. A stiff jab followed instantly by a right cross to the chin dropped both George Chaney and Danny Frush in their tracks.

Kilbane met and used about every style you can think of. He could box, slug, brawl or stall. When he needed the groceries, he could

Johnny Kilbane, shown here on the right working out with the big gloves, held the world featherweight crown for 11 years. (UPI)

make you look silly. He gave Kid Williams, the bantam champ, a boxing lesson for six rounds, and he belted out such maulers as Joe Rivers and Patsy Cline.

Standing 5 ft., 5 in. and weighing 126, Johnny always maintained that his toughest fight took place in his first year as a pro against Tommy Kilbane (no relative) of Cleveland, a boyhood pal. The bloody battle lasted 25 rounds, and say what you will about hometown loyalty, Johnny Kilbane never fought 25 rounds again.

Johnny was born in Cleveland, on April 18, 1889. In 1907, he got fed up with clerking in a railroad office and put on the gloves. The era demanded skill even from a raw apprentice, so Kilbane learned his boxing lessons fast. After winning the title, he exercised a champion's prerogative in those days of carrying young fighters in their home towns as long as they minded their ring manners.

Johnny Kilbane had many rabid supporters. His popularity with fight fans helped get him elected state senator in 1941. He also served as a state representative in the Ohio Legislature.

At the time of his death, on June 1, 1957 he was clerk of the courts in Cleveland.

EUGENE CRIQUI
(1893–)

Eugene Criqui, twenty-nine, the idol of France, flung his 122 pounds out of his corner and rocked Johnny Kilbane, the defending champion, with a barrage of punches that hung the American rubber-legged on the ropes.

"Stop zee fight! Stop zee fight before he keels heem!" cried the Frenchman's frenzied fans.

In his prime, Kilbane would have taken out Criqui as he had taken out Abe Attell and Joe Rivers, but this night he was thirty-four and his age was showing. Criqui, no kid himself, continued the assault. He threw so many punches so fast that Kilbane might as well have been tilting with a windmill. A savage uppercut separated Johnny from his teeth with such force that ringsiders caught the spray. Even when he was completely off balance, Criqui almost removed Johnny from his haircut with a pair of left hooks and a right uppercut delivered in split-second succession. Halfway through the sixth round Kilbane hit the floor and couldn't get up and the featherweight division had a new champion.

The date of June 2, 1923, in New York, was Eugene Criqui's finest hour in America. As a matter of fact, he fought only twice on the U.S. side of the Atlantic—both times within eight weeks—and when he returned, Johnny Dundee was waiting for him. The result was a 15-round decision in favor of Dundee.

Thus, Criqui's name went into the records as the shortest reign of any division in history. He had held the featherweight title for only 55 days.

Born on August 15, 1893, near Paris, Eugene Criqui turned pro at seventeen and fought for eighteen years. During the span he engaged in 115 bouts, won 94, lost 13. He scored 40 kayoes, was knocked out only twice himself, by Pal Moore and Danny Frush. At his peak, Criqui had winning streaks of 25 and 23.

JOHNNY DUNDEE
(1893–1965)

Johnny Dundee was thirty and in his 14th year as a prizefighter—an old man by ring standards—when he won the featherweight championship of the world.

During his crowded career, he fought seven world champions. He tackled more and tougher lightweights than any lightie of modern times.

Little Joseph Carrora (Johnny's real name) stood 5 ft., 4½ in. and weighed 124 lbs. at his best. He fought 321 times in 20 years. Dundee slid up and down the weight scale like a circus calliope, taking on all comers from bantams to welters. He was a marvel at making weight rapidly. While active, he melted off some two tons of flesh without apparently sacrificing speed or stamina.

Ten years before beating Eugene Criqui at the Polo Grounds for the featherweight title, Johnny fought a 20-round draw in 1913 with champion Johnny Kilbane. A lot of people thought Dundee won. Johnny blamed the draw on five sticks of chewing gum.

"It's a crazy alibi, I know," Johnny later explained. "But that wad of gum cost me the title against Kilbane. The day before the match I was taking a stroll in downtown Los Angeles. I noticed my shoes needed shining

Eugene Criqui sent Johnny Dundee reeling into referee Jack O'Sullivan in sixth round of 1923 title bout in New York, but Dundee fought back to pound out a 15-round decision to win the world featherweight championship. (UPI)

and I stepped into a shine parlor. I had a mouthful of gum—five sticks—and while stepping up into the shoeshine chair I stumbled and accidentally gulped down the wad of gum. That load felt like a lump of lead in the pit of my stomach. Within 10 minutes I was sick and all during the fight the next night I thought I'd throw up. It took me a week to get over it. So I suppose you could say a package of spearmint cost me the featherweight crown that first time around."

The result was that Dundee had to wait until Criqui knocked out Kilbane before he could get another shot at the title. The Frenchman wore the crown less than two months.

Billy Roche said that Dundee was the squarest and most sportsmanlike little fighter he ever knew.

"I refereed many of his battles," Roche said, "and not once did I have to caution him for holding or transgressing any of the rules."

Dundee had a highly original style which no other fighter could emulate. He fought on his toes, was dazzlingly fast on his feet. He perfected the stunt of rebounding off the ropes and hitting as he came. Johnny was not a knockerout, but this trick added momentum to his wallop.

It was while performing his pet stunt that he literally bumped into his first knockout—at the fists of lightweight Willie Jackson, a terrific thumper, in Philadelphia, January 15, 1917. They fought 10 times thereafter.

Benny Leonard and Dundee built their grueling series to eight.

Dundee was born at Shaikai, Italy, November 22, 1893. He was brought to the United States when only an infant. The family settled down in New York City's middle West 40's—Hell's Kitchen—where the parents operated a fish market. As a boy Johnny delivered fish and fought in the streets.

Scotty Montieth, a fight manager, found him and gave him the name under which he was to become rich and famous.

Montieth proved anything but a Scotsman when it came to Dundee's services, matching him with bounteous liberality against anyone who could draw anything.

Horse Player Montieth introduced his tiger to racing, and Dundee sank most of his ring earnings in a stable of not too thorough thoroughbreds.

Johnny hung on for some time after he should have called it quits. He finally retired after Ignacio Ara knocked him out in one round in Havana, February 28, 1931—Dundee's first start following a 14-month layoff.

Johnny Dundee always will be remembered as the man who brought a new and unique style to boxing.

LOUIS (KID) KAPLAN
(1902–   )

They called Kid Kaplan "Little Napoleon" and the hard-hitting Connecticut Yankee lived up to his war-like moniker by ruling the featherweights in the mid-Twenties.

Li'l Lou blew in with the Roaring Twenties. He packed a home run punch as potent as Babe Ruth's. In 1925, he won the featherweight championship and held it until '27. A human buzzsaw, his favorite stiffener was a twisting left hook. "I start off in left field," he would explain in animation. "Then I swerve towards center, and cut around first base."

In the language of the baseball crowd, fighters generally felt they'd been struck by a ball bat when The Kid whacked them. He went for the Grand Slam.

A short, stockily built fighter, Kaplan relied on strength, ruggedness, seemingly unlimited stamina, and a two-fisted attack. He kept on top of opponents, never gave them breathing room.

Born in Russia in 1902, Kaplan, 5 ft., 4 in., 126 pounds, came to the States as a youth. He was introduced to the prize ring in 1919, sweated at the Staten Island featherweight Willie Curry's punching bag, and started boxing professionally under the name of "Benny Miller." He made Newark, New Jersey, his headquarters. When Jack Dempsey made a chopping block of Jess Willard in their famous battle at Toledo, July 4, 1919, Kaplan and Curry put on an unusual exhibition at Staten Island. As the blow by blow account of the Dempsey-Willard blood bath clacked off the Western Union ticker, Kaplan and Curry pantomimed the fight for the eastern fans. Kaplan was "Dempsey" and Curry was "Willard." It was an omen of things to come, for Little Napoleon, in his prime, certainly emulated The Tiger Man.

The Kid made a bid for the featherweight title when Johnny Dundee, the champion, could no longer make the weight and relinquished the crown. An elimination tournament was instituted and Kaplan thundered through contenders with the speed of the

In a career spanning 20 years and 321 fights, Johnny Dundee battled more and tougher lightweights than any lightie of modern times. (NEA)

Super Express. "When I beat Garcia, then Joe Lombardo, I knew I had it made," Kaplan said. "Only Danny Kramer stood between me and the championship, and when we finally fought, I knocked him out in the ninth."

The Kramer bout was fought in New York, January 2, 1925; Kaplan defended his title only three times, twice against Babe Herman and once against Bobby Garcia. The first Herman defense was staged at Waterbury, Connecticut, August 27, 1925, and ended in a 15-round draw. The match attracted 20,000 spectators, grossed $59,180, which still stands as an all-time Connecticut record. Kaplan received $19,685 as his end, Herman $9,892.

The pair slugged it out for another 15 rounds in New York a few months later, December 18. This time Kaplan won the decision.

When it became apparent that The Kid, who often soared as high as 150 pounds, had outgrown the division, he gave up the title and campaigned among the lightweights. When Sammy Mandell, Al Singer and Tony Canzoneri refused to give him shots at the lightweight crown, sports writers called him "the uncrowned lightweight champ." Kaplan later whipped Mandell—after Sammy had lost the championship.

Kaplan fought such greats as Jackie Fields, Bruce Flowers, Joe Glick, Jimmy McLarnin, Bat Battalino, and Mandell. He was knocked out only three times in 13 years, by McLarnin, Billy Wallace and Eddie Ran.

The Kid's last fight was on February 20, 1933, at New Haven, when Cocoa Kid thrashed him in 10. Kaplan knew it was time to hang 'em up when an eye specialist examined him and discovered that he had vision in only one eye. But, then, Kid Kaplan was so good that he usually only needed one eye to win.

BENNY BASS
(1904–)

Benny Bass, 5 ft., 3½ in., 130, a veritable bullmoose of the ring's featherweight and junior lightweight divisions, was thick-necked, compact, and powerful. He punched like a heavyweight. He was, as someone said, the smallest heavyweight in the world.

A perpetual puncher, one who stayed on top of his enemy every second of every round, Bass was active in the ring for 17 years (1923–1940) and he met and defeated the best. When he beat Red Chapman in 10 rounds in 1927, the Russian Jew became known as "the first Philadelphian to win a world boxing title."

Tony Canzoneri took the crown from Benny in 1928, Bass fighting the final five rounds of the 15-rounder with his collarbone broken in five places.

Bass K.O.'d Ted Morgan in 1929 to win the junior lightweight championship.

ANDRE ROUTIS
(1900–1969)

That oft-defeated champion Andre Routis compiled one of the oddest records in boxing: he participated in 16 contests in which the outcome was determined by a foul.

The Frenchman won 11 fights on fouls. Seven of his first 19 pro victories were won in this manner. Only Philadelphia Jack O'Brien approaches this record with six W.F.'s. Routis himself fouled out in five bouts.

Andre was a gay, happy-go-lucky sort outside the ring. But once inside, he was a great competitor. His skimpy total of six K.O.'s is deceiving. The little featherweight could dish it out and take it without batting an eye.

Routis was born in Bordeaux on July 16, 1900. He began fighting professionally in 1919, won the French bantamweight crown from Charley Ledoux and lost it the following year to Kid Francis.

The amiable Andre arrived in New York in 1926. He decisioned Tony Canzoneri for the featherweight title in the Garden, September 28, 1928. The following year, on September 23, Bat Battalino dethroned him in 15 rounds in Hartford, Connecticut. Halfway through the fight, Andre's manager, Pete Reilly, deserted him and went to Battalino's corner. (For more on Reilly, see the run-down on Max Schmeling).

Routis was one of the ring's losingest champs. Following his knockout over Buster Brown in defense of his title, he lost the next eight fights. He finally quit the ring in 1929 after losing to Davey Abad in St. Louis, and returned to Paris to operate a bar.

CHRISTOPHER (BAT) BATTALINO
(1908–)

The "Bat" wore the badge of the street-fighter—a long, jagged and ugly scar across the bridge of his nose, compliments of Billy Petrolle. A Garrison finisher, his little caveman arms and fists served as gnarled clubs.

Bat was a strange mixture of contradictory emotions. He was one of the most fearless of fighters in the ring and yet shrank from a surgeon's knife. For example, when he had to have a blood sample taken he begged the doctor not to cut him with a knife. The doctor finally took a drop from the lobe of his ear.

You never could tell about him. He'd be losing big and the bettors, their dough riding the other way, were dreaming of what they were going to do with their windfall, when—BAM!—Bat would suddenly hear the call of the wild and knock the other fellow out. He sent many foolhardy bookies to the poor house crying the blues. Bat could absorb frightful punishment. Blows bounced off of him as though his body was made of rubber. But he always had enough in him to battle back and make a fight out of it.

Born at Hartford, Connecticut, on February 18, 1908, Bat launched his boxing career in 1927, when he flattened four other state champions on the same night to win the National A.A.U. Championship at Boston Garden. Two years later, at the age of twenty-one, he fought 15 furious rounds with Andre Routis to become featherweight champion of the world (in only his 24th pro bout).

Bat successfully defended his crown against Kid Chocolate, Fidel LaBarba, Irish Bobby Brady, Freddie Miller and Earl Mastro. Then, in his sixth defense, he was disqualified after three rounds in a return bout with Miller and vacated the title to campaign among the lightweights, when he could no longer make 126 pounds.

In a match billed as "Madman vs. Triphammer," Bat met Petrolle at the Garden in New York, on March 24, 1932. Oldtimers compared it to the greatest lightweight battles in history. The ring canvas was spattered with blood. Reporters at the ringside held up newspapers to shield themselves. The referee had to wipe blood from his hands between rounds. But still the awkward, stooping little Bat advanced, his gloves at his head for relief from the hammering it was getting. His nose, freshly broken, bubbled redly as he choked for breath. His head rocked as Petrolle punch

Ringside reporters had to hold up newspapers to protect themselves from bloody drenching as Bat Battalino, left, and Billy Petrolle stood toe to toe and slugged it out in 1932 bout in New York. Petrolle won on a K.O. in 12th round. (UPI)

after Petrolle punch landed on it. But on and on Bat went, crowding, slamming, tearing in like a madman trying to whip a triphammer. The huge Garden crowd thundered with bloodthirsty applause and excitement.

Though outweighed by five pounds and an 8–5 underdog, Bat had insisted on a 12-round match instead of 10, because he thought he had the edge for stamina. He gathered himself for a last effort in the final round, and, at the gong, sprang across the ring. But wise old Billy, the "Fargo Express," measured him as he came and connected with stinging lefts and rights on the chin, mouth and body. For the first time in the fight, Bat retreated. Billy followed him, still firing punches. Bat fell dizzily into the ropes and bounced away reeling, his eyes clouded. Before Billy could finish the job, Referee Gunboat Smith stepped between them and saved Bat from going down unconscious.

Petrolle wrapped himself in the Indian blanket which he wore instead of a bathrobe and said: "He's the gamest guy I ever fought."

It stands as the only K.O. suffered by Bat Battalino in a total of 88 recorded fights.

KID CHOCOLATE
(1910–   )

Eligio (Kid Chocolate) Sardinias earned his reputation as a "picture boxer" by watching movies of famous fighters.

It was the idea of Luis Gutierrez, his manager.

"When the Keed first came to me," Gutierrez said, "neither he nor myself knew anything much about boxing. We figured the best thing to do was to study the methods of the masters. I had read that Joe Gans had a great left hand. We lived in Havana and one day pictures of the Gans-Nelson fight were shown at a local movie house. So we watched those films every day for as long as they were in town. We studied how Gans used his left hand. Then the Keed would go to the gym and practice throwing his left hand exactly as Gans did. Study pictures of both Gans and the Keed and you'll see that Chocolate's left hand was just like Gans's.

"Then we saw movies of the Jeffries-Johnson fight and studied how Johnson tied up Jeff so easily in the clinches; tied him up so he couldn't move. We studied that and worked on it until Chocolate had the trick perfect. If you saw him tie up Al Singer inside you saw him do the same thing that Johnson did with Jeffries.

"Next, we saw the movies of the Leonard-Tendler match, and in that one we studied how the great Leonard used his right hand and blocked and feinted and moved around. Chocolate got so he could do them as Benny did. All told, he spent eight years learning from those fight films."

Kid Chocolate began his featherweight career sensationally. As an amateur in Cuba, he strung together 100 straight wins, including 86 knockouts. He turned pro in 1928 and compiled another 21 kayoes in a row. Then he went to New York in August of '28 and extended his unbroken record of victories by 13, 8 by K.O.

There are those who rate Chocolate above Young Griffo and Willie Pep. Chocolate stood 5 ft., 6 in. and weighed 126 when he kayoed Benny Bass in the seventh round to win the junior lightweight title in Philadelphia, on July 15, 1931. Then he downed Lew Feldman in 12 rounds and moved into position to challenge Fidel LaBarba for the world featherweight crown. When he decisioned the great Fidel in New York, on December 9, 1932, the New York Boxing Commission recognized him as world champion. Thus, at twenty-six, Kid Chocolate became the first Cuban to hold a world title.

Chocolate wore his junior lightweight crown until December 26, 1933, when Frankie Klick knocked him out in the seventh round in Philadelphia. Freddie Miller claimed the world featherweight title in '33 after beating Tommy Paul. But Chocolate continued to dazzle boxing fans until his retirement in 1938.

Kid Chocolate was born on January 6, 1910. In his 10 years in the prize ring he won 145 of 161 bouts and scored 64 knockouts, one of the outstanding records in featherweight history. He was counted out only twice.

FREDDIE MILLER
(1911–1962)

Freddie Miller was truly a remarkable little fighter. Sound, erect physically, quick and austere mentally, the 15th featherweight champion of the world won more than 200 fights.

Always in command of the situation, he battered opponents about as though they were gunny sacks stuffed with last week's papers.

The German-American southpaw, born in Cincinnati on April 3, 1911, started prize fighting in 1927. He won his first 27 matches, dropped a decision, then tore off on another streak of 50 consecutive victories. This second splash included four triumphs over Jimmy Harris, the only man to beat Miller in his first 77 bouts!

Miller, 5 ft., 5 in., 126 lbs., won the featherweight title with a 10-round decision over Tommy Paul in Chicago, January 13, 1933. He defended it successfully nine times during the following four-and-a-half years.

In 1934 and '35, Freddie campaigned in Europe. He was, as a matter of fact, one of the first Americans to fight extensively throughout the Old World. There were spells when he fought every week in England. The Britishers simply couldn't understand how a human could answer the work bell so frequently.

Petey Sarron, whom he had beaten in a title defense two months previously, finally won the championship from Miller via a 15-round decision in Washington, D.C., May 11, 1936.

Freddie retired from the ring in 1940 after Herschel Joiner stopped him in eight rounds in Cincinnati on April Fool's Day. That was the only time in 237 bouts anybody ever knocked out Miller. The date was significant—for few were the times that anyone made a fool out of Freddie Miller.

PETEY SARRON
(1908–)

The "S" in Petey Sarron's last name also stood for speed—with a capital S. Classy, yet rugged, he was difficult to tag. Bombing him was like trying to hit a moving target with an air rifle. He was stopped only 3 times in a total of 88 professional fights. Petey was an artful dodger.

Born in Birmingham, Alabama, in 1908, Sarron began fighting in the amateurs in his early teens, culminating this phase of his ring career in the 1924 Olympic Games in Paris.

He broke a hand shortly after he turned professional in 1926, laid out for two years, coming back just before the Great Depression. He won the featherweight championship *nine* years after making his comeback.

He outpointed clever Freddy Miller in Washington, D.C., on May 11, 1936, to win the title. He was replaced at the head of the class a year later by Henry Armstrong.

Petey was fast, but not fast enough to escape Hammerin' Henry's murderous rights and lefts. Armstrong finished the job in six rounds.

Sarron went on to win 11 bouts in succession before losing to Sammy Angott in 10 rounds in Pittsburgh, July 17, 1939. For Petey, that was the last stop. That's where he got off. But it wasn't the end of his fighting days. In 1941, he put on a soldier suit and went away to war.

JOEY ARCHIBALD
(1915–)

"It's all a matter of steadyin' a fighter's style," Al Weill said when asked how he had been so successful with Joey Archibald, a mediocre boxer who nevertheless won the featherweight title under Weill's guidance.

"You steady his style," repeated Weill, "and after you've steadied him long enough, you know which style will beat which and why."

Weill's contributions to pugilism, great as they were, did not begin to compare with his gifts to the mother tongue. It was Al who invented the present-past tense. In Weill's lexicon it was not "Joey won the fight" or "Joey lost it," but "he win the duke" and "he lose a close one."

It was Weill, also, who matched the editorial "we" of journalism with the managerial "I" of pugilism. To listen to Weill talking, you'd have thought he did all the fighting, not Joey. Talking about one of Joey's opponents one time, Weill's verbatim monologue went like this: "That bum? I licked him once but I'll fight him again if he wants me. This time I'll take 40 percent, though. He says he knocked me out two years ago but the thief is lyin'. I broke me arm in the thoid and the referee stopped it. It was only a typical knockout."

Other fight managers modestly cut their fighters in on some of the credit, but Weill figured all the credit belonged to him, so, singularly enough, he stuck to the first person. Once, after Joey won a semifinal bout in Providence, Rhode Island, his home town, and Weill was asked how he thought Joey would

Henry Armstrong, right, connects with hard uppercut in 6th round and stops Petey Sarron to win featherweight title in New York in 1937. (UPI)

fare in the main event, ungrammatical Al reflected a moment and replied: "Well, if the last bout was any *critation*, I'll win the next one, too!"

Joey Archibald was one of the handful of college men to win a world boxing championship. A medical student at Providence University, he dished out strong medicine, 28 of his opponents going down for the long count.

At his peak, Joey stood 5 ft., 4 in. and weighed 126 lbs. He first won a piece of the featherweight crown in 1938 with a 15-round decision over Mike Belloise, holder of the New York Athletic Commission's version of the world title. Six months later, on April 18, 1939, he won undisputed claim to the world championship by outpointing Leo Rodak in 15 at Providence.

Then followed three sizzling title bouts with Harry Jeffra. All went 15 rounds. Joey won the first match, lost the title to Harry in the second, and won it back in the third meeting. On September 11, 1941, four months after regaining the crown, Joey dropped it again when Chalky Wright stopped him in the 11th round in Washington, D.C.

After losing his last 12 fights, Joey retired from the ring in 1943 to join the Navy.

HARRY JEFFRA
(1914-   )

Lightsome Harry Jeffra became the fifth Baltimorean to win a world title—*two* world titles, to be precise. Harry decisioned the formidable Sixto Escobar for the bantamweight crown at the Polo Grounds September 23, 1937. Then on May 20, 1940, in his home town, he decisioned Joey Archibald for the featherweight title.

In the title scrap with Escobar, the Puerto Rican informed Harry in a clinch, "Well, I guess I knock you out now."

"You couldn't hit me with a handful of peas!" Harry snorted, and he was almost right. After 15 gruelling rounds, he was unmarked except for a swollen lip.

Though Jeffra yielded the crown to Escobar five months later in San Juan, he defeated the Islander four times . . . a remarkable achievement. Archibald also regained his title in 15 rounds from Jeffra on May 12, 1941, in Washington D.C. Harry Jeffra fought six championship matches during his career.

Jeffra, whose legal name was Ignacius Pasquali Guiffi, was a caddy before he entered the ring. The wiry, brown-haired mite was counted out but twice in 118 fights. His great footwork and snaky left were his main assets.

ALBERT (CHALKY) WRIGHT
(1912-   )

When Chalky Wright was twenty-five he was working in a Los Angeles car wash. That same year, 1937, he walked into a Tacoma gym where Freddie Steele, the middleweight champion, was training and asked him for a $75 loan.

"What do you want the money for?" Steele wanted to know.

"To get to New York," Chalky told him. "I'm going back there and win the featherweight championship of the world."

Steele gave him the $75—and four years later Chalky knocked out Joey Archibald to win the crown.

"Chalky loved to fight," Steele recalled recently. "He fought anyone from feathers to middleweights. I fought him myself (three-round exhibition, Seattle, August 7, 1937). He was carefree, good-natured, and had a good temperament for the ring. He spent the early part of his career in and around Los Angeles; his first bout in New York was in 1938, when he knocked out Al Reid in four rounds."

Chalky was born at Durango, Mexico, in 1912, and was only sixteen when he entered the prize ring and started getting cuffed around by hardened professionals. He lost to such old hands as Ramon Montoyo and Newsboy Brown and Eddie Shea and Mose Butch and Pablo Dano.

Five years after he began, Henry Armstrong took him out in three rounds in Los Angeles.

"Judging from his early record," Steele said, "Chalky hardly seemed a promising candidate for anything, except oblivion. But he had plenty of heart, was confident in himself."

Starting with an impressive two-round K.O. of Joe DeJesus at Madison Square Garden, in 1939, Chalky began putting it all together, like a mathematician working on a jigsaw puzzle. The victories piled up in monotonous consistency. He won 34 out of 38 bouts, 20 of them knockouts, and finally earned a crack at Archibald's featherweight crown, on September 11, 1941. After Joey was counted out in the 11th round, Chalky remembered his old debt to Freddie Steele. With the $75 he attached a note: "Thanks for the loan. I told you I'd win the featherweight championship."

As world champion, Chalky took on fighters like Bobby Ruffin, Richie Lemos, Harry Jeffra, Lulu Constantino, Phil Terranova and Al Brown. He also fought Willie Pep, which was a mistake. They met in the ring four times, and Pep won them all, including Chalky's title.

Chalky finished the way he began, on the downhill side. He dropped 9 of his last 10 matches.

"Even I knew it was time to quit after Ernie Hunick flattened me in three rounds at Salt Lake City in 1948," Chalky said. "I got the message."

When Chalky was champion, Harry Markson was doing p.r. work for Madison Square Garden. In one of his weekly press releases he mentioned that Chalky was a lover of classical music. This news brought a lady reporter from *Etude* magazine to Chalky's training quarters for an interview.

"Mr. Wright," she said, "what is your opinion of Mozart?"

"Well," Chalky replied, "I find him a bit heavy."

"Is that so, Mr. Wright? That's very interesting, because you're probably the only person in the world who ever found Mozart heavy. What about Bach?"

"A very clever boy," Chalky told her. "Can't miss."

"And Beethoven?"

"Dynamite."

And so it went. Afterward, Chalky went back to Markson's office. "You got me in a mess of trouble," he told Harry. "Please, let's stick to boxin'."

Dumb Dan Morgan could have told Harry that music and boxing don't mix.

"There was once this pug I knew who took up music on the theory it helped a fighter," Dan said. "When the pug was still a kid, his old lady always made him take harp lessons. He was a tough kid and hated the harp, and always run away from his maw when she called him to practice. The running did wonders for his wind. Later, the kid got wise, and he began to practice his harp a couple of hours a day. He got so good he could even play it with boxing gloves on. He claimed his musical ability helped him in the ring. In his first match, he noticed the bell was an eighth of a note off, and he started yelling at the ref he couldn't fight with an off-key bell. That brought his opponent into the argument, and when the lug wasn't looking, this kid put the slug on him and knocked him out. From then on, the kid was made. He never outpointed his opponents—he *counterpointed* them. We got to calling him The Kid With The Pizzicato Left. When he flattened a bum, he'd sing Brahm's Lullaby. All in all, music was somehow good for him, except in his final bout. He was fighting a bum that was tone deaf. It upset our hero. He'd been humming Tschaikovsky's Fifth, and the opponent looked blank at him. So our hero threw caution to the winds and forgot himself. He got reckless. The other bum almost killed him. No musical soul, that boy . . . simply no musical soul."

Good old Dan Morgan.

PETEY SCALZO
(1917-   )

One of the most familiar starting-points of boxing's Great American Success Story is the Lower East Side of New York City. From it have come such gigantic prize ring figures as Mike Jacobs, Benny Leonard, Barney Ross—and, later, Petey Scalzo.

The little Italian-American was born there on August 1, 1917. He started his boxing career in 1936, quickly becoming the New Deal for bored fans of the featherweight division. He won 38 of his first 40 professional bouts, the two being draws. Twenty-one of those were knockouts. His first defeat was an eight-round decision to Mike Belloise—three years after breaking in! Though the title wasn't on the line, he K.O.'d champion Joey Archibald in two rounds, on December 5, 1938, in Madison Square Garden. Afterward, however, the N.B.A. vacated Archibald's featherweight title and declared Scalzo the champion.

Petey held the crown until July 1, 1941, losing it to Richie Lemos in Los Angeles via a five-round K.O.

Scalzo joined the Army in 1942, engaged in three bouts the following year, and then retired from the professional ring.

What were his qualifications as a fighter? Well, he was sharp-brained, battle-poised, and he was beautiful to watch. Fast, a good puncher, alert, clever and confident, Petey advanced upon his antagonists with all the surefootedness of a lion coming up to take a trap full of zebras. The way he piled up the points, the scorekeepers could well have used an adding machine.

PHIL TERRANOVA
(1919-   )

Phil Terranova started his prize ring career at twenty-one and was N.B.A. featherweight champion at twenty-four.

Born in New York City, September 4, 1919, Terranova turned pro in 1941, six months after Pearl Harbor, and fought two and three times a month, four-, six-, and eight-rounders. He reached his peak during the years 1945–1947, when he piled up a 22–1–1 record, including a 10-round decision over Sandy Saddler. He forced Willie Pep to the limit in a 1945 title bout before losing on points in 15.

The New York Italian kayoed Jackie Callura in eight rounds in New Orleans, August 16, 1943, to earn the N.B.A. version of the featherweight championship, but lost it to Sal Bartolo, 15-round decision, the following March, in Boston.

In 99 pro bouts, Terranova won 67, fought 11 draws, and was knocked out by Chalky Wright and twice by Charley Riley. His own knockout record totaled 29.

Phil Terranova retired from the ring in 1949, after dropping 6 of his last 12 matches.

SAL BARTOLO
(1917-   )

There was nothing fancy about Sal Bartolo, but when the Boston Italian unleashed his Sunday punch it almost separated you from your haircut.

Fancy Dans like Willie Pep and Maxie Shapiro gave Sockin' Sal nightmares, but he would slug to sleep brawler-types who dared to stand toe-to-toe with him. He won 74 of 97 pro matches and was knocked out only twice in a career spanning 13 years, 1937–49.

Bartolo decisioned Phil Terranova in 15 rounds in 1944 to win the N.B.A. edition of the world championship, and lost it two years later when Willie Pep kayoed him in the 12th round in Boston. Far from washed up—he won 13 of his last 14 bouts—Bartolo retired in January 1949 after scoring victories over Bobby English and Paulie Jackson within eight days.

WILLIE PEP
(1922-   )

For Willie Pep, the game of boxing was a cat-and-mouse game. And he was the mouse. It was a most fascinating show, like watching a man stave off a starving catamount with a penknife.

"Hitting Willie is like trying to step on a flame," spoke a Mexican named Kid Campeche.

Chalky Wright told of the frustration wrought by Willie the Wisp.

"I'd like," he said, "for Mr. Pep to stand still for just one second and let me get a shot at him. I'd like just once to feel what it's like to nail him."

In his prime, the best never nailed Willie. He took Chalky in two title fights. He was not celebrated primarily as a puncher, yet the record shows he had 65 kayoes, and broke Sal Bartolo's jaw in three places. He also made a mess of Allie Stolz, knocked out Jack Leslie, Humberto Sierra, Eddie Compo, all in championship matches. If you look up the 241 fights he had in 22 active years, you will find he knocked out one of every four men he took on; and Pep took on anyone who weighed within 10 pounds of his 137.

Ray Robinson once called Willie the greatest fighter of his contemporaries. Abe Attell said the same thing. "Willie," Abe said, and from him, this was the last word in praise, "is the greatest featherweight since Attell." That he was, although there was many a featherweight who came between them to rise, to shine for a while, then to fall and be forgotten. Nobody forgot Attell and Pep. Willie had it all: the dazzling footwork, the perfect timing and the fastest pair of hands this side of a Broadway pickpocket. When he finally hung up his gloves in 1966, with a total of 229 victories, he had earned more than half a million dollars.

The Wisp of a Man from Hartford, Connecticut was all solid skill and inventiveness and the master of the unexpected. He knew all the tricks.

"I'm not a strong guy," he once said. "I got to live on my wits." The wits were sometimes laces and thumbs, a foot on the toes, a butt in a clinch. And always that speed. "I'd rather outbox a man than knock him out," perverse Willie said. "It's a matter of pride, I guess, to win the whole fight and not just a piece of it. Maybe it's not always popular with the fight crowd, but think of all the boxing you can enjoy."

Willie was perverse in other ways, too, as he demonstrated in his ding-dong series with Sandy Saddler. In their second cockfight, Pep fought what the historians regard as his all-time masterpiece. Pep always had the big heart, but in this frightful ordeal it almost burst.

In the last Pep-Saddler affair Willie undid all the good work of that second spectacular. He played it Sandy's way and ended up in a wrestling match that was a disgrace to boxing. New York State revoked his license.

It little mattered who started the rough stuff. Other fighters have run into dirty weather and still fought cleanly to win.

Then there was Willie's habit of "resigning" a fight when he felt he'd lost. He did this twice against Saddler. The first time he claimed an arm injury, which may have been a legit. The second time he simply stated he couldn't fight any more. Perfectly okay in some socialist countries, but great fighters don't do this in a benevolent republic. They fight until they drop, and then they get up at nine.

The temperamental Pep flouted his own high reputation, and on those rare occasions when he decided to coast, it was all downhill. Yet he was probably the greatest craftsman pound for pound since the Golden Age of the Twenties.

"Pep's as good as George Dixon, Johnny Dundee or Tony Canzoneri," said ex-featherweight champ Abe Attell before the first Pep-Saddler bout on October 29, 1948. So Saddler won, by a K.O. in four, and Abe had to buy a new hat. But four months later, on February 11, 1949, Abe was vindicated as Pep regained the title in one of the greatest fights of all time.

The action raced by like an old Mack Sennett comedy in high gear.

It was a savage, cruel business in which Pep made the perfect fight and Sandy repeatedly lost his temper and scrapped like an amateur. And when it was all over, after 15 rounds, Saddler appeared relatively unscathed while the victorious Pep was cut up like a ten-cent pie in a hobo camp.

In the tenth round and more than once thereafter, Willie the Weaver was out on his feet. Only a champion's instinct kept him alive as he used every trick he had learned in a hundred fights and more. It seemed incredible that he could escape when Saddler nearly garrotted him on the ropes, but time and again he would slip away, leaving his opponent tangled in the rigging.

You wouldn't have given Pep a chance before the 11th, and yet that was the round in which he won the fight. When the bell rang, he swarmed all over his tormentor, keeping him on the defensive until two-thirds of the round was over, and he was again in charge of the action.

With four rounds left to go, Willie stabbed and smothered, struck and ran, hauled and twisted, feinted and contrived. There was plenty of wrestling too, but so skillfully did Pep employ the dirty tricks he knew that Saddler was often admonished for fouling when Willie was actually to blame.

In the 14th, the hero of Hartford was once more in desperate trouble. Blood clouded his vision. His thin body heaved with exhaustion. The 15th was another nightmare, but by that time Sandy too was all in. Dog tired and dripping blood, Willie was still moving, still slipping and dodging Saddler's punches at the final bell.

This was the fight for which the gallant little fellow will always be remembered by the mob. Willie's ability to carry the fight when he was badly hurt determined the outcome. Most certainly he ran—like a package thief—non-stop through the first three or four rounds and many times thereafter. But his offensive bursts completely bewildered Saddler. And when he chose to play hide-and-seek, Sandy would lose him so completely that he must have wondered if Pep had vaulted over the ropes.

Willie was born in Middletown, Connecticut, on September 19, 1922. When he was fifteen, he made his first amateur card by lying about his age, a year under the minimum. He gave away 15 pounds at 109 and won in a waltz.

He was an obscure nobody when he went through a couple of four rounders at Madison Square Garden in 1942. Then one night he made the steady customers sit up and take notice. In the first round of a semi-windup, Pep murdered a kid named Frankie Franconeri, and when he climbed out of the ring, the Garden was sold.

Chalky Wright was the featherweight champ, and promoter Mike Jacobs was eager to find him a classy opponent. Uncle Mike was in a quandry until Eddie Walker, Chalky's manager, dropped by his office one day.

"I got the right guy for you," said Eddie.

"Who?"

"Willie Pep."

Mike shook his head.

"Nah, he wouldn't draw a nickel."

"Ask Nat Rogers," Eddie suggested. Rogers was the matchmaker so Mike called him in.

"What do you think of Willie Pep?" he asked.

"He's the hottest news in Connecticut," Nat vouched. "They'll go to see him wherever he fights."

Walker weighed in with some details. When he'd taken Chalky to Hartford and New Haven a while ago, all they ever heard about was Pep, Pep, Pep. "They think he can beat my Chalky," Eddie remarked. "I don't, but if they're going to lay it on the line to watch him try, he's for me."

That was it. Uncle Mike could hear the ancient and pleasing sound of turnstiles popping.

When Willie Pep came down out of the Hartford Valley, he pulled half of Connecticut with him. Oldtimers at the Garden that night of November 20, 1942, remembered a couple of other Hartford featherweights, Louis Kid Kaplan and Bat Battalino. But they were champs and solid little guys, and this here Pep looked like something the cat brought in.

Pep beat Wright to become champion at twenty (only Abe Attell and Tony Canzoneri were younger when they won the featherweight title). The fact that he won on the lam didn't bother his native state nor was there any letdown at the gate in subsequent appearances. Willie ran, but he got there first.

Pep had to wait six or seven more years before he received national recognition as one of the finest boxers of our time. Long before the fight crowd truckled to him, he was rescuing the Twentieth Century Sporting Club from recurrent depressions. Other fighters drew $25,000; Pep drew $50,000. And in most cases he doubled the usual take. Pep and Saddler drew $80,000 in their second title go, and it could have been $100,000 if the price scale had been higher. The fight was broadcast and televised, and it was still a sellout.

Willie put together 62 straight wins before Sammy Angott outhassled him, then another long run of victories, interrupted by a draw with Jimmy McAllister, whom he later kayoed.

Then came a shattering reversal outside the ring—a set-back that would have ended the ring careers of most fighters. In the fall of '46, Pep was almost killed when his Miami-to-New York flight crashed in southern New Jersey. Several passengers died; others were permanently crippled. Willie broke his left leg just above the ankle and incurred two fractured vertebrae and various internal injuries.

A day or two after the crack-up no one imagined he could ever fight again.

"I'm through," Willie announced in the hospital. "Through with night flying." As for fighting, he had no doubts. "I'll fight again—wait and see!"

Several months later Willie went home to Hartford, his left leg in a cast, his body swathed in bandages, his back bent forward from the fractured vertebrae. Before long he was getting around on crutches so naturally he began dropping in on his old haunts, including the Charter Oak gym. He even took in the fights in New York.

Four months after the accident Willie was burning with impatience.

"When will I ever get started?" he complained to his manager, large Lou Viscusi.

"I tell you what," Lou said to humor him, "come to the gym in two weeks and start loosening up."

Two weeks to the minute Willie walked into the gym minus the crutches.

"This is it!" he informed Lou as he stripped down, humming with joy. He tried a little shadowboxing, then some back exercises. Not an ache between Hartford and New York!

A month later Willie started on the comeback trail by defeating a so-so club fighter, Vic Flores. And that summer of '47, he risked the featherweight title against Jock Leslie in the challenger's home town of Flint, Michigan. Willie kayoed Leslie in the 12th before a gross gate of $50,000. He put his title on the line again the following February, and K.O.'d Humberto Sierra in 10. Then followed the two Saddler fights, title matches against Eddie Compo and Charley Riley and the third meeting with Saddler, in which Pep lost the crown for the second time.

Pep's comeback drive covered some 100 bouts, including eight championship matches. In the mid-1950s he was definitely heading into the sunset. On September 20, 1958, Hogan (Kid) Bassey kayoed him in the ninth round in Boston, and after that, Pep had one more fight, losing a decision to Sonny Leon in Caracas. "I retired," he said, "after losing a fight in Venezuela to a fighter who can't fight; that convinced me."

Willie went to work as a beer salesman for a New England brewery. He also had an interest in a Manhattan saloon and, later, in a Tampa girlie joint. But Willie was a flop in business, and after blowing every dollar of the small fortune he had earned as a boxer, was forced to return to the prize ring in 1965 to get himself out of hock. He had a dozen fights, including two exhibitions, and won 9 out of the 10 regulation matches. The comeback ended in 1966.

There used to be a sign in the Charter Oak gym in Hartford, where Willie trained, that read "Don't Lose Your Head." You might say that this homely sentiment became Willie's motto. And you *might* say he was fanatical in the observance—maybe even a little bit mad on the subject.

SANDY SADDLER
(1926–)

The freakishly-built Sandy Saddler—unusually tall for a featherweight, stretching his 127 pounds over a skinny, 5 ft., 8 in. frame—was one of the best boxers to campaign in a long while, just as Pep was. He could stick and move and tie an opponent up without resorting to wrestling grips. Or he could move in and knock your brains out. He was as tough for lightweights to fight as he was for featherweights, although Paddy DeMarco beat him in two over-the-weight matches hand-running.

Sandy's chief assets were his long arms and powerful shoulder muscles, which made him one of the heaviest hitters among the little fellows. His preference for slugging it out won him notable knockouts over Willie Pep (twice), Lauro Salas (twice) and DeMarco (in the first of their three fights).

Born as Joseph Saddler, on June 25, 1926, in Boston, the son of a merchant-ship cook from the British West Indies, Sandy lived most of his early and adult life in New York City. He was first spotted fighting in the amateurs in 1942 by Jimmy Johnston, one of the great managers of the era. Jimmy got Sandy to turn pro and then went about teaching him everything he knew. But Jimmy knew that ex-

The 1950 Saddler-Pep battle found Willie ahead in the early rounds. But the wobbly Sandy fought back to score a T.K.O. in the eighth. (UPI)

perience is the best teacher and put his boy into the ring against a long line of pugs, ranging from feathers to welters. Sandy took them all on without complaint. One day, Jimmy was heard to remark: "My Sandy's going to be a real fine fighter one of these days. Wait and see." Unfortunately, Jimmy couldn't wait. His ticker gave out before Sandy made the grade, and Sandy became the property of Charlie Johnston, brother of Jimmy.

Charlie did a good job with Sandy. When there was no action for him around New York, Charlie took him elsewhere; to Havana . . . to Mexico City . . . to Caracas . . . to Jamaica . . . and a lot of places in the Caribbean no one but geographers and travel agents ever heard of, bringing him back to the States when there was a spot open for Sandy and the money was right. Meantime, Sandy gained valuable experience against all types of fighters and all sizes. He saw, for him, new corners of the world, and he collected, if not a small fortune, at least a fairish number of American dollars.

Of his four title matches against Pep, some may recall Sandy as a cross between a boxer and wrestler, but in those catch-as-can combats he was merely adapting his tactics to meet the requirements of a situation posed by an aging and desperate Willie.

The Pep-Saddler series wound up in the record book thusly:

October 29, 1948:   Saddler won title, K.O. fourth round, Madison Square Garden.

February 11, 1949:   Pep regained title, decision 15 rounds, Madison Square Garden.

September 8, 1950:   Saddler won title back, K.O. eighth round, New York.

September 26, 1951: Saddler successfully defended title, K.O. ninth round, New York.

The last two matches were bloody, miniature massacres. Forced by Pep to resort to streetfighting, each time Sandy managed to come up with the better strangle holds, headlocks, airplane spins and drop kicks.

In his boxing career, Saddler won 144 fights, 103 of them by knockouts, lost only 16 times. He was kayoed only once, by Jock Leslie, in Sandy's second pro fight.

Charlie Johnston made only one mistake with Saddler. He could have had a crack at the lightweight championship when Ike Williams held it but he waited a little too long for Ike to grow old. Ike grew old overnight and Jimmy Carter moved into the vacancy that Johnston had planned for Sandy.

But it didn't turn out too badly. Sandy still had the featherweight title as late as January 1957. There's no telling how long he would have kept it had he not decided to retire from the ring due to failing vision caused by an eye injury in an auto accident.

HOGAN (KID) BASSEY
(1932–   )

Few fighters did so much for the tiny man in recent years as Hogan (Kid) Bassey. Born as Okon Bassey Asuque, on June 3, 1932, at Calabar, Nigeria, the compact (5 ft., 3 in., 124 lbs.) little featherweight with the Oxford-accented speech lost but seldom on a nine-year road from obscurity to the world championship.

Bassey won the title by knocking out rugged Cherif Hamia, a most impressive little man, in 1957, after Sandy Saddler retired.

Hogan (an Anglicized version of his first name Okon) had a pair of ebony fists that were among the swiftest weapons in the ring. He also possessed typical British aplomb and a habit of understatement. Defending his title in Los Angeles, in '58, against the idol of Mexico, Ricardo ("Pajarito") Moreno, Hogan was battered ruthlessly in the first round. Moreno had caught him off guard and off balance, for Hogan was accustomed to a somewhat more leisurely and polite opening. It was all Bassey could do to survive the initial three minutes. He was bloody and hanging on for dear life at the bell.

Bassey returned to his corner, fell on his stool, looked up at his seconds and made just one remark.

"Blimey!" he said.

Bassey proved that night that he fought best when he was hurt. Moreno, who punched hard enough to knock out welterweights, hit him between the eyes with a blockbuster early in the second round. It hurt Hogan, but it was the beginning of the end for Moreno.

In the third and last round, Hogan pounded the muscular Mexican so savagely that spectators out in the third row had to duck the spray. He threw so many punches so fast that it was a wonder Moreno never caught cold by the breeze. The fight grossed $215,047 and Bassey celebrated his big payday by sending Moreno home in a blanket.

How did a boy from Calabar, Nigeria reach the featherweight championship?

"I really started to box in Lagos," Bassey explained. "That is where I won many amateur bouts and also where I became Nigerian and West African bantamweight champion after I had become a professional."

He spoke precisely, as a boy might who had been taught in an English private school.

"When I was fourteen," he said, "my mother and father sent me to an aunt and uncle in Lagos to continue my education because, at that time, the schools in Calabar were not very good. In Lagos, there were clubs for boys, where they are encouraged to play football and to box and to engage in other sports. Why am I called Hogan? That is my name. Okon Bassey Asuque. Anyone who is named Okon is entitled to call himself Hogan, if he wishes to. There were many Hogans in Nigeria. The boys there take the names of many famous fighters. There are Joe Louises and Ezzard Charleses and Archie Moores and Ray Robinsons all over the country.

"And how did I get to England?" Bassey was living in Liverpool during his spell as world champion. His manager was George Biddles, a pub keeper in Leicester. "Well," Hogan said, "a chief police constable came out from England, and he was also a coach of boxing for the English police. He saw me and suggested that I go to England and, as I had run out of opponents, I took his advice. In Nigeria, I had many fights that do not show in the record book. They were not important enough for anyone to put down. Actually, my fight with Moreno was my 88th, or 26 more than the record book shows."

Kid Bassey started to see the handwriting on the wall in March 1959, when Davey Moore stopped him in the 13th round to relieve him of the featherweight crown in Los Angeles. Five months later, they were rematched; this time Moore finished the exercises in 11 rounds. That was enough for little Hogan. After 11 years in the ring, he hung up the gloves. In 1963, Nigeria named him Director of Physical Education.

DAVEY MOORE
(1933–1963)

Davey Moore, a good, game fighter, was another of boxing's tragic figures who lived and died by the sword.

Born on November 1, 1933, at Lexington, Kentucky, and raised in Springfield, Ohio, Davey had the tools: natural aptitude, instinctive skill, plenty of punch, and courage. He was a member of the U.S. Olympic Team as a bamtamweight at the 1952 Games in Helsinki, where he was eliminated* in his third fight by Ho King of Korea.

Moore turned professional in 1953, won 16 of his first 19 matches, including 10 kayoes. Between 1957 and 1963, he piled up strings of 18 and 19 wins in a row. On March 18, 1959, he scored a 13-round knockout over Kid Bassey to win the world featherweight championship in Los Angeles. During his reign as champion (1959–63), he had 14 "non-title" fights and officially defended his crown five times.

A lovely little fellow, cheerful, Davey had five kids named after movie stars and other celebrities. "My wife loves movies," he explained one time. Between fights, he took a job parking cars at a Santa Monica hotel. The fight mob thought it was undignified, but Davey didn't think so. The extra job kept his kids in shoes.

Born too small, Moore could not be the football player he wanted to be, nor the baseball player. His only way out of poverty was on horseback or in boxing gloves. He chose boxing.

Davey had 67 fights. He did not survive his last one, March 21, 1963. Matched with Sugar Ramos for the championship, he went down in the 10th round and did not get up. He had suffered a terrific beating around the head.

"It just wasn't my night," Davey said afterward in his dressing room at Dodger Stadium in Los Angeles. "But I can't take anything away from Ramos."

His eyes were still blurry. He had trouble trying to focus them. "I know I can fight much better than I did tonight," he almost whispered. His brain was bleeding slowly as he talked. The slow leak soon became a burst.

An hour later, Jim Murray went back to Davey's dressing room. He was surprised to find the door tightly shut. He pushed it open. Willie Ketchum and Eddie Foy III, Davey's handlers, were stripping the fighting togs off the ex-champion. As they saw Jim, they put fingers to their lips. Jim closed the door softly. He thought Davey was under sedation.

"He was," Murray said later, "God's sedation."

Davey Moore was dead.

"There are excuses," Jim Murray said. "There always are. Davey is a puncher. He always approached every fight as if his opponent were a punching bag. He worried about the other fellow's head and let his own take care of itself. He fought Sugar Ramos as if the fellow owed him money. A ringsider pointed out it was not a fight, it was Russian roulette with six-ounce gloves."

SUGAR RAMOS
(1941-   )

No one ever had to teach Sugar Ramos how to box. He was the ultimate natural.

Abruptly, this Cuban featherweight was the wonder of Havana prize rings from the start. The fans recognized it and so did matchmakers.

This is what he did:

Born at Matanzas, Cuba, five days before Pearl Harbor was bombed, Sugar was only sixteen when he fought his first prizefight in 1957 and clicked off 32 straight bouts without a defeat; 24 of his opponents were counted out. All told, he knocked out 39 of his first 65 rivals, lost only 7.

The Ramos championship years were bunched between March 1963 and September 1964. He kayoed Davey Moore in Los Angeles to win the featherweight crown, and lost it by a 12-round knockout at the hands of Vicente Saldivar in Mexico City.

Ramos was inactive in 1973.

JOHNNY FAMECHON
(1945-   )

How could Johnny Famechon miss? His father was lightweight champion of France; Uncle Emile held the flyweight title; and Uncle Raymond made it a hat trick with the French featherweight crown.

The youngest of the famous Fighting Famechons did not begin his prize ring career in his native France, however. It began in Melbourne, Australia, where Andre Famechon had taken his family to live when Johnny was five. Despite his dad's protestations, Johnny fought his first pro bout when he was only sixteen. The senior Famechon felt his son was too scrawny to be a fighter, but changed his mind after Johnny won the Australian featherweight title at the age of nineteen and after only 21 fights.

Johnny Famechon lacked a powerful punch, but made up for it with speed, guile and clever footwork. He knew all the moves and perfected a left jab that he could land with effect while on the move.

After taking out Johnny O'Brien (K.O., 11) and Billy McGrandle (K.O., 12) in winning and defending the British Empire featherweight championship, Famechon challenged world champion Jose Legra, the Spanish-based Cuban. The match was fought in London. Described by one British writer as "one of the fastest 15-rounders every fought anywhere," Famechon won on points, 74½ to 73¼, and returned to Australia a national hero.

On July 28, 1969, only six months after becoming champion, the twenty-four-year-old Famechon put his title on the line against Fighting Harada, ex-world fly and bantam champ from Japan. Harada gave Johnny the fight of his life before losing by a full point in 15 rounds. This called for a return match, and Johnny obliged by knocking out the Nip in 14 in Tokyo.

At twenty-five, something went out of Johnny. He lost a close decision to Mexican Vicente Saldivar, in Rome, and instead of asking for a rematch, he called a press conference a day after losing his title and announced his retirement from the ring.

STILL ACTIVE
VINCENTE SALDIVAR
(1943-   )

When Vincente Saldivar stopped Sugar Ramos in the 12th round, September 26, 1964, he became the first undisputed Mexican featherweight champion and the 12th left-handed titleholder in history. A dedicated and resourceful fighter, not gifted with any great natural skills but always trying to do everything he can to improve himself, Saldivar is a mechanical fighter, very strong, very well-conditioned and very patient. He does not fluster easily. He won 36 of his first 39 pro bouts by applying relentless pressure. A southpaw, he holds his hands high, jabs long with his left and hooks hard with his right. He is a punishing puncher, but not an explosive one. His greatest asset is fast hands and effective counter-punching.

Born May 3, 1943, the son of a Mexico City businessman, Vincente is one of eight children. He turned pro in 1961. On his way to the world crown he kayoed 25 opponents. He defended the title in eight straight bouts, winning five by K.O.: Salvidar announced his retirement in October 1967, then made a comeback in '69 and regained the championship (May 9, 1970) from Johnny Famechon, a 15-round decision. He lost the title to Kuniaki Shibata (K.O., 13 rounds), December 11, 1970.

KUNIAKI SHIBATA
(1947–)

Born on March 29, 1947, in Tokyo, Japan, Kuniaki Shibata won 41 of his first 49 prizefights, plus three draws, after starting his career in 1965. He won the world featherweight title on a 13-round knockout of Vincente Saldivar, in 1970, then lost the championship two years later when Clemente Sanchez stopped him in the third round. In 1973, he quit the featherweight division and became world junior lightweight champion.

CLEMENTE SANCHEZ
(1947–)

Born at Monterrey, Mexico, July 9, 1947, Clemente Sanchez won the 1972 Golden Gloves featherweight title and then turned professional the following year. He won 39 of his first 51 bouts, fought three draws, was kayoed only once. Between May 3, 1968, and May 19, 1972, he scored 26 K.O.'s in 28 bouts, including a three-round knockout of Kuniaki Shibata to win the world championship. On December 16, 1972, Sanchez vacated his title when he had more and more difficulty making 126 lbs.

BANTAMWEIGHTS

The bantamweight division was fairly well established around 1885, when the smallest fighters, scaling approximately 105 pounds, were called "bantams," or "little chickens." There wasn't too much activity in the division until the late Eighties, about the time that Tom Kelly and George Dixon were buzzing around claiming the championship. The two men fought a nine-round draw, then Kelly retired from boxing, and Dixon was left alone with the world title. When he outgrew the class, Jimmy Barry took over the crown.

Top weight for bantams today is 118 pounds.

JIMMY BARRY
(1870–1943)

Jimmy Barry looked as if he belonged in a horse race, not a prize ring. If he'd been any tinier he'd been invisible. He looked as if he had to get up on a chair to turn off the light switch. You couldn't have picked him out of a crowd of Singer Midgets.

The Chicago banty rooster stood 5 ft., 2 in. and weighed 107 lbs. Despite his cut-rate size, he never lost a fight in a career stretching from 1891 to 1900. Packing a trip-hammer punch, 39 of his 59 pro wins ended in a knockout.

Born in Chicago of Irish-American parents, on March 7, 1870, Jimmy began fighting professionally at twenty and knocked out his first 11 opponents. On September 15, 1894, at Lamont, Illinois, he sailed 28 furious rounds with Casper Leon, knocking him out, and claimed the world bantam championship. In the second official defense of his title, three years later, he hit Englishman Walter Croot so hard in the 20th round that Croot later died in a London hospital of brain damage. Barry was haunted by the tragedy for the rest of his life.

HARRY HARRIS
(1880–1959)

The third official world bantamweight champion was unusually tall for his class—a "towering" 5 ft., 7 in. Harry Harris was an amazingly clever boxer. He knew all the tricks. His left jab was a pippin, and he could glide around the ring like a man on ice skates.

Harry was defeated twice by decision in 52 fights. He won the bantamweight title via 15-round decision from Pedlar Palmer in London, England, March 18, 1901, and retired undefeated in 1907 after beating Harlem Tommy Murphy.

Harry was born in Chicago on November 18, 1880. He began fighting professionally in 1895. When he withdrew from the ring 12 years later, he became a successful Wall Street broker.

HARRY FORBES
(1879-1946)

Harry Forbes hit the deck nine times—a record for a bantamweight champ—but he won the world title, by gum, at a time when the division was at its peak. The 5 ft., 4 in. Irishman from Rockford, Illinois, depended almost entirely on speed and skill.

Forbes first challenged Terry McGovern for the crown in New York City, December 22, 1899, and Terry obliged by stopping him in two rounds. When the Hartford terror outgrew the bantams, Harry won the vacant title by a 15-round decision over Casper Leon in Memphis, April 2, 1901.

The new champ successfully defended his prize on three occasions and overcame Abe Attell and Frankie Neil in non-title smokers. He agreed to a return match with Neil for the title, and in San Francisco on August 13, 1903, Frankie ended Harry's two-year reign in the second round.

Forbes was born in Rockford on May 13, 1879 and began his professional career in 1897. In the course of his 128 fights, he fought 23 draws—second only to George Dixon for little men.

He quit the ring in 1912. Harry died December 19, 1946, in Chicago.

FRANKIE NEIL
(1883-1970)

On the average, a fight manager is a human harpy who squeezes all he can out of the blood and bones of husky and courageous young fellows and then tosses them callously aside when they are battered hulks of no more financial advantage to him.

But there are exceptions.

Just a few.

Francis James Neil, out of San Francisco, drew one of the exceptions—his Pappy. Jim Neil, who owned a racing stable in California, considered prizefighting a sideline. He managed his son because no one else could handle him.

Son Frankie was a pugnacious son o' a gun—in and out of the ring—who didn't scare worth a dime. He just plodded in and messed up opponents, swinging his murderous left hand like a pitchfork. He wore a gargoyle grimace and a fierce snarl and he was as mean-tempered as a bulldog.

The records show that Frankie won only *one* decision—whereas 24 victims fell to the canvas after he unleashed the power in that muscular left arm.

Frankie Neil came crashing down the pike in 1900, winning 14 of his first 17 bouts by knockouts. Three years after he started prize fighting he K.O.'d Harry Forbes in San Francisco in two rounds to win the bantamweight championship of the world. He lost it to Joe Bowker in London in 20 rounds, October 17, 1904.

Neil was born in San Francisco on July 25, 1883, stood 5 ft., 5½ in. and tipped the scales at 118 at his peak, and fought until October of 1909. It was logical that Frankie should have been managed by a horse man. He always fought like a bloke racing to the wire.

JOE BOWKER
(1883-   )

Tiny Joe Bowker was a giant in his own small world of pugilism. Born Tommy Mahon at Salford, England, on July 20, 1883, he virtually dominated the bantamweight division from 1902 to '06, winning 17 bouts in a row. On October 17, 1904, he shellacked Frank Neil in 20 rounds in London to win the world bantam championship.

Bowker outgrew the division in 1905 and campaigned among the featherweights. He twice defeated the great Pedlar Palmer in March of that year to be designated British featherweight champion.

Curiously, the 5 ft., 3½ in., 122-pound Bowker fought only two times in the United States, both losing efforts. Al Delmont defeated him in 12 rounds in Boston, on March 16, 1909, and four days later, in Philadelphia, Tommy O'Toole stopped him in the second round.

At thirty-six, Bowker retired from the ring in 1919.

JIMMY WALSH
(1886–   )

You look at the record book and it says that in 120 bouts Jimmy Walsh, a bantam from Newton, Massachusetts, won 52, engaged in 18 draws and 41 no decisions, and lost only 9 times. What the record book doesn't tell you is that Jimmy was responsible for bringing the world bantamweight championship back to America.

After Joe Bowker vacated the title, Walsh met Digger Stanley, who had beaten him before, and pounded out a 15-round decision in an elimination contest in England to earn the world crown. Jimmy kept the title from October 20, 1905 to December 7, 1906, then, like Bowker before him, gave up the championship to become a featherweight.

Walsh was a clever fighter, quick of both hand and feet, and could take a punch. He was knocked out only once, by the great Abe Attell, who stopped him in the eighth round in their world featherweight title match at Los Angeles, December 7, 1906.

Jimmy's weapons included a perfect jab and a taunting right hand that didn't necessarily hurt but scored points. On May 21, 1912, this attack nearly won him his second world championship, but he had to settle for a 12-round draw with Johnny Kilbane, the defending featherweight champion.

Jimmy Walsh fought for 15 years, finally retired in 1915.

JOHNNY COULON
(1889–1973)

Johnny Coulon was a little bit of a guy, no bigger than a pepper box, but he was champion of the world before he was twenty. The tiny (5 ft., 118 lbs.) Canadian claimed the bantamweight title in 1909 after Jimmy Walsh outgrew the division, and held it until Kid Williams stopped him six years later.

He defended the title 12 times.

In 1908, he put his crown on the chopping block twice within three weeks. Two years later he defended it three times within four-and-a-half weeks! And in 1912, he defended against Frankie Conley on February 3, and against Frankie Burns 15 days later—both 20-rounders. Little Johnny put real meaning in the expression "fighting champion."

Coulon was born on February 12, 1889, in Toronto, of Irish-French parentage. He made Chicago his home early in life and stayed there the rest of his life.

Johnny began fighting professionally in 1905, retired in 1920. He later operated a gymnasium in Chicago.

KID WILLIAMS
(1893–1963)

Kid Williams had the body of a midget and the punch of a giant.

The tiny (5 ft., 118 lbs.) Dane from Copenhagen, whose christened name was John Gutenko, charmed ring audiences from coast to coast in this country.

Ruggedly handsome, The Kid with the turned-up nose knocked out Johnny Coulon in three rounds at Vernon, California, to win the bantamweight championship of the world. That was in June of 1914, only four years after he started fighting professionally.

The Dandy Little Dane held the crown for three years, until Pete Herman beat him in 20 rounds in New Orleans on January 9, 1917.

Williams was knocked out only once in 175 bouts. He K.O.'d 43. The Kid made a small fortune with his fists, but he spent it as fast as he got it.

In 1956, the Baltimore police brought a short, bull-necked, square-rigged little man into court on the charge of breaking up a saloon during a scuffle. The judge asked him what his name was.

"John Gutenko," he replied, adding that he was sixty-three.

"You look like a fighter I used to watch many years ago," the magistrate said.

"I haven't boxed in 20 years," the little man explained, "but you probably did see me fight. My ring name was Kid Williams, bantamweight champ from 1914 to 1917."

The judge asked him if he had any money and a job. Johnny Gutenko nodded.

"Good," the magistrate said. "I fine you 10 dollars plus costs. Sentence suspended. And I don't want to see you in here again."

"You won't," promised the old champ. And he didn't.

PETE HERMAN
(1896–1973)

So fantastically fast, tiny Pete Herman. His punches were timed to the beat of a hummingbird's wing. Only 5 ft., 2 in. and 116 pounds, he won the world bantamweight championship twice before his eyesight failed and he was forced to quit the ring at twenty-five.

Pete first took the title in 1917 from Kid Williams in 20 gurgling rounds. That was in New Orleans, where he was born (February 12, 1896). He defended his crown for nearly four years, lost it finally to rangy Joe Lynch in New York, on December 22, 1920, and then immediately set sail for London to fight the fabulous Jimmy Wilde. Herman, one of the

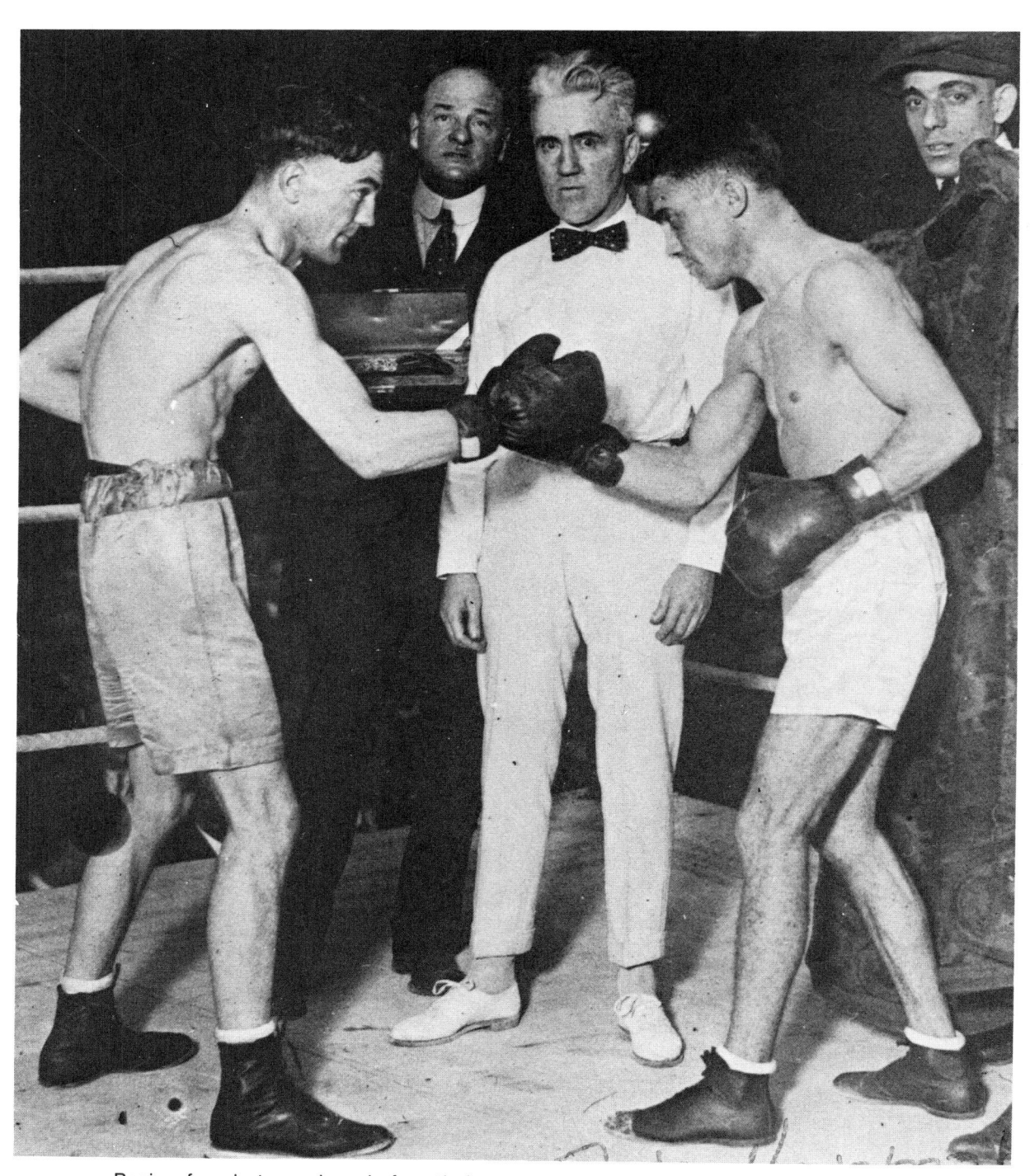

Posing for photographers before their second meeting in Brooklyn, July 25, 1921, Pete Herman, right, and Joe Lynch touch gloves. Herman had lost his title to Lynch in first fight, but in this one came back to regain it. (UPI)

game's greatest infighters, kayoed the little Britisher in the 17th round.

Back in the U.S., Herman ran into some tough opposition. He dropped two close decisions to Young Montreal before regaining the bantam title from Lynch in 15 rounds in Brooklyn, July 25, 1921. And then suddenly he was fighting in the dark.

Plucky little Pete went back to New Orleans, where he walloped Charley Ledoux in 10 rounds. Eighteen days later, he returned to New York (September 23, 1921) and lost the crown for the second time in nine months. Johnny Buff beat a blind man in 15 rounds. Instead of Buff, Petey should have been playing blind man's bluff!

Herman groped his way through five more fights, hitting and ducking on instinct alone. The record book says he won four of them. Pete was well fixed when he and his manager, Sammy Goldman, called off their partnership in 1922. Pete returned to New Orleans, completely blind. Friends helped him open a night club in the French Quarter. Pete entertained customers by going through a patented routine in which he ran his hands over the body of a prizefighter and then told him if he was of championship material or not. Sort of fortune telling by feel, you might say. Primo Carnera visited the club one day and Petey gave him the touch treatment and then told him, "You're nothing but a big muscle-bound oaf!"

One of those closest to Pete Herman was Emile Bruneau, Chairman of the Louisiana State Athletic Commision. Herman was Vice-Chairman of the Commission.

"I have been in boxing for 55 years at all levels and finally President of the World Boxing Association for two years," Emile Bruneau told me. "When you talk about world champions, Pete must be placed right up there with the all-time great bantams. Many experts think he was the greatest. We served together on the Commission for over 20 years. Even though boxing cost him his eyesight, he always insisted that prizefighting had been good to him and that if he had to do it all over again, he'd take the same path."

Pete Herman, who died in 1973, was not one to forget an old friend. In 1925, he sent Sammy Goldman, his former manager, a young fighter by the name of Tony Canzoneri.

JOE LYNCH
(1898–1965)

Like a Rembrandt painting, Joe Lynch had class written all over him. He was unforgettable. Abnormally tall (5 ft., 8 in.) for 118 lbs., he was a fine stand-up boxer who could knock your head off with a right-hand punch. He lost only 13 of 134 fights, was never knocked out.

Lynch reigned the bantams in an era when the little fellows enjoyed their greatest fame in America. He was so frail, so skinny, he looked like a moving xylophone. But once the house lights dimmed and Joe stepped from his corner, left fist high above his head, up on his toes, eyes flashing, square chin stuck out defiantly, he captured the spectators without throwing a punch.

Born in New York, on November 30, 1898, Joe started his prizefight career at Brown's Gym in a series of four-round matches. He graduated into six-rounders, and finally the longer distances. He had a dozen fights be-

Emile Bruneau, above, former President of World Boxing Association, places Pete Herman among the top bantams of all time. (Photo courtesy Emile Bruneau)

fore he fought Terry Martin, in 1916, his first pro bout, a no-decision affair. After that, he took them on as they came, and fought several times a month.

On December 11, 1918, Private Lynch was a member of the A.E.F. team when he dropped a debatable four-round decision to Jimmy Wilde. Still in mufti, he remained in London to defeat Tommy Noble in 20 rounds and lose another close decision to Wilde, this time after 15 rounds.

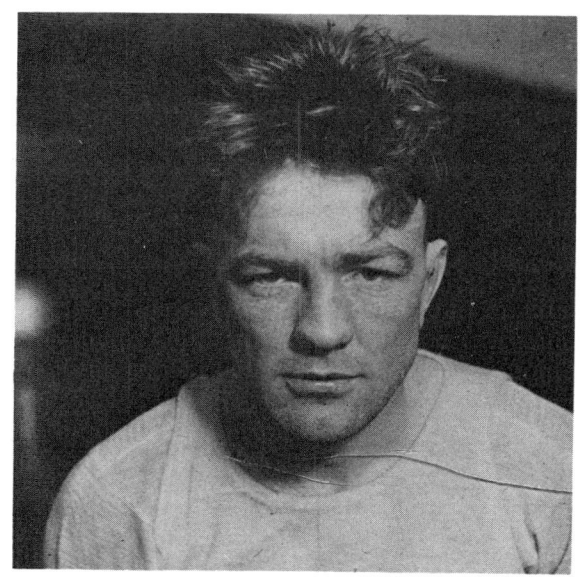

Uncombed Joe Lynch had the looks of a street brawler, but he was actually a class guy who twice won the bantamweight championship. (NEA)

Lynch struck his swiftest stride toward the tailend of 1920, knocking out Abe Goldstein in 11 rounds, Little Jack Sharkey in 15, and then winning the 118-pound championship with a 15-round decision over Pete Herman, three days before Christmas. Six months later, in Brooklyn, Herman turned the tables on Lynch in 15 grueling rounds. Some were critical enough to hint that Pete had merely left his crown with Lynch for safekeeping, while he, Herman, went off to London to dispose of Jimmy Wilde in 17 rounds.

Herman later relinquished the world title to Johnny Buff, and then Lynch stiffened the former sailor in 14 rounds (July 10, 1922) to reclaim the bantamweight championship.

Lynch had to take a Turkish bath to get down to 118 pounds for Abe Goldstein, on March 21, 1924, when he lost the title for the second time. It was time for him to retire, but Joe boxed for two more years, and was still perfectly able to take care of himself when he finally quit in 1926.

Personable Joe Lynch became postmaster of New City, New York. He retired from the ring with plenty of money and all his marbles.

Like so many fighters, Lynch died a tragic death. On August 1, 1965, he drowned while swimming at Sheepshead Bay, New York.

JOHNNY BUFF
(1888–1955)

Johnny Buff never ran from a fight in his life. Totally unafraid, game and tireless, he would have taken a trial ride on a bomb if the price had been right.

Johnny won the world bantamweight championship at a time when the division overflowed with talent. He whipped such little giants as Little Jack Sharkey and Jabez White and Abe Goldstein and Young Zulu Kid and Pete Herman. He won the title from Herman in 1921 and lost it to Joe Lynch nine-and-a-half months later in New York.

John Lesky (his real name) was born of Polish-American parentage, on June 12, 1888, at Perth Amboy, New Jersey. During World War I, he served in the Navy and fought in inter-service boxing tournaments. He turned pro in 1918, battled for nine years.

On January 14, 1955, he died in the East Orange, New Jersey, Veterans Hospital.

ABE GOLDSTEIN
(1900–   )

Abe Attell Goldstein did, indeed, borrow his first and middle names from the one and only Abe Attell. In the great tradition of New York's Jewish fighters, this Abe toughened up in the club shows that fomented so many neighborhood brawls and rivalries.

Handsome little Goldstein stood 5 ft., 5 in. and weighed 118 lbs. On his way to world renown, his manager, Willie Lewis, matched him against such high-class contenders as Kid Williams, Pancho Villa, Frank Genaro, Eddie Shea and Bud Taylor. Yet he lost only 13 times.

Born in New York City, in 1900, Goldstein fought for 11 years (1916–1927). He won the world bantamweight championship on March 21, 1924, from Joe Lynch in 15 rounds in New York, and lost it nine months later to Eddie "Cannonball" Martin in 15 rounds in the same ring.

EDDIE (CANNONBALL) MARTIN
(1903–1966)

Edward Vittorio Martino, a tough little article about the size of a nickle cee-gar, changed his Italian name to Eddie Cannonball Martin and in three action-filled years slugged his way to the world championship.

Born in Brooklyn on March 3, 1903, Eddie turned pro in 1922. During the first 20 months of his career, he fought 45 times, lost only 2 of them. He won 58 of his first 60 bouts, 22 by K.O.

Jewish fighters surrounded Cannonball's title years like bookends. He won the bantamweight title from Goldstein (December 19, 1924), the first time he had ever fought a 15-rounder, and lost it to Rosenberg (March 20, 1925).

Martin went on fighting for another six years, winning 14 and losing 8. He finally retired from the ring in 1932 after dropping a decision to Al Dunbar in Brooklyn.

CHARLEY ROSENBERG
(1902–   )

Charley Phil Rosenberg is the only prize fighter in history to have lost a championship by default. On February 4, 1927, at Madison Square Garden, Rosenberg was unable to make 118 pounds against Bushy Graham and the New York Commission declared the bantamweight title vacant. Despite the pre-fight ruling, Rosenberg went through with the bout and decisioned Graham in 15 rounds. Here was a rare case of a pugilist winning a scheduled championship match and losing his crown!

Charley, a Jewish-American, was born in New York on August 15, 1902. He started fighting in 1921 and retired after winning a 10-round decision from aging Johnny Dundee on January 4, 1929.

He was never knocked out in a lifetime total of 64 bouts.

Rosenberg had won the title from Eddie Cannonball Martin via a 15-round decision on March 20, 1925.

BUD TAYLOR
(1903–1962)

The late Nat Fleischer rated Bud Taylor above such bantamweight stars of yesteryear as Johnny Coulon, Pal Moore and Frankie Burns. No argument from this corner. After all, Taylor beat such great little men as Tony Canzoneri, Jimmy McLarnin, Abe Goldstein and Bat Battalino.

Bud took all comers. He fought no-decision bouts with Pancho Villa, Midget Smith, Pal Moore and Frankie Genaro and was equally at home among the featherweights.

The 5 ft., 6 in. Hoosier won the bantamweight crown from Canzoneri in an elimination match in Chicago on June 24, 1927.

He vacated the title in August of the following year in order to campaign among the featherweights.

Bud was born in Terre Haute on July 5, 1903. He fought 156 professional bouts (second only to Kid Williams in his class).

In 1931 he became a manager and promoter.

BUSHY GRAHAM
(1903–   )

Bushy Graham was really Angelo Geraci, who was born in Italy on June 18, 1903. Immigrants to our shores have always had a profound faith in the American Dream, and Angelo was not disappointed. He became the 16th bantamweight champion of the world.

When Bud Taylor vacated the title, Bushy decisioned Corporal Izzy Schwartz in a Garden playoff, May 23, 1928.

In the 14 years he fought, Graham met the cream of the crop . . . Tony Canzoneri, Joe Lynch, Bat Battalino, Kid Chocolate, Fidel LaBarba, Frankie Genaro, Abe Goldstein, Tommy Ryan, Charley Rosenberg. In 1931 he outgrew the division, gave up his title and seemingly retired. But in '35 he made a comeback, winning 12 of 13 before finally quitting the ring in '36.

At fighting trim, Graham stood 5 ft., 5 in., weighed 126.

PANAMA AL BROWN
(1902–1951)

Alphonse Theo Brown, a tall splinter of ebony, fought for 23 years all over America and Europe and was one of the greatest bantamweights the ring has ever known.

He sat on the bantam throne for seven years.

The Panamanian Negro, 5 ft., 11 in., only 118 pounds, had an incredible 76-inch reach and speared opponents silly. He also had great blasting hands and reshaped heads like a cruller.

Fifty-six of his 119 victories were K.O.'s.

Brown won the crown from Vidal Gregorio in 1929 and lost it to Baltazar Sangchilli in 1935. The remarkable stringbean earned more than $350,000 with his fists, yet was destitute and a patient in Bellevue's charity ward, paralyzed and suffering from consumption when the end came. It was a tragic curtain for the man who spoke six languages and was known from Panama to Paris to Broadway as one of the ring's gayest blades.

Few had loved life more.

BALTAZAR SANGCHILLI
(1911-   )

Baltazar Belenguer Hevoas brought the style of the bullfights to the prize ring. "Matador" Sangchilli did it with leather prongs instead of a cape.

Born at Valencia, Spain, on October 15, 1911, Baltazar began his fighting career in 1929. He won 22 bouts in a row, 11 by knockouts, in 1930 and '31.

On June 1, 1935, he coaxed Panama Al Brown into the Valencia ring with him and won the bantamweight championship of the world in 15 rounds. The next year, in New York, Tony Marino knocked out Sangchilli in 14 rounds to gain the title and go down in history as the only man ever to stop the 5 ft., 3 in., 118-pound Spaniard.

Baltazar and Tony fought again in October of 1936 and the foreigner outpointed Marino in 10 rounds. No title was at stake, however, as Sixto Escobar had come along in the meantime and won the crown from Marino. So the bantams were fighting only for the gate and the exercise.

Sangchilli quit the ring in 1939 after losing five straight bouts. 'Twas time for the little bull to be put out to pasture.

TONY MARINO
(1912-1937)

Like Hippolytus, or Hamlet, Tony Marino, too, had his tragic frailty; and against him, as against them, the stars seemed to be set in their courses.

The Pittsburgh bantamweight, 5 ft., 3 in., 118 pounds, held the world championship for only 64 days. He stopped Baltazar Sangchilli in 14 rounds in New York, June 29, 1936, and was kayoed by Sixto Escobar in New York in 13 rounds, August 31. Five months and six bouts later he was dead, victim of a cerebral hemorrhage.

On January 30, 1937, Indian Quintana battered Marino viciously around the head en route to an eight-round upset victory—and hours later Tony was on his deathbed.

Born in Pittsburgh in 1912, Marino started his career in 1931. He fought only 41 times, winning 27, only 7 by K.O. Tony was regarded on the ordinary side, but he had a good left hand and was well-managed by Charley Cook, a popular pilot of the period. Not even Charley could defy the astrologers, however. The stars seemed to be set against his tiger from the beginning.

SIXTO ESCOBAR
(1913-   )

Sixto Escobar, greatest of all Puerto Rican fighters, was a brawler who could club a man senseless. His blows resounded as though he were thumping on a big bass drum. Sixto weighed 118 pounds, but in his sparring sessions he would floor lightweights with the "big" gloves.

Escobar was one up on Pete Herman and Joe Lynch: he *twice* regained a lost throne. Lou Salica first won the title from him in 15 rounds in New York City, August 26, 1935. Six weeks later, on November 15, Sixto took it back from Lou in 15 rounds in New York. Then Harry Jeffra decisioned Escobar in 15 rounds in New York, September 23, 1937. And Sixto again recaptured the bantamweight title by routing Jeffra in San Juan on February 20, 1938.

The fierce little islander earned the N.B.A. title when he knocked out Baby Casanova in the ninth round in Montreal, June 26, 1934. World recognition followed when he downed Tony Marino in the 13th at New York, August 31, 1936.

Escobar fought 64 times and was never knocked out. He vacated the throne in 1939 when he could no longer make the required 118.

LOU SALICA
(1913-   )

Fight fans grew to admire Lou Salica. He learned as he went along. As he grew older he picked up savvy. He learned to pace him-

Sixto Escobar is regarded by some as the greatest of all Puerto Rican fighters. Like Pete Herman and Joe Lynch, he held the bantamweight crown twice. (NEA)

self, and he developed a wicked jab and many of the in-fighting tricks. His footwork improved, his canniness increased. He became one of the very best bantamweights of his day.

The Italian-American was born in New York on July 26, 1913, started fighting in the amateurs in 1931, where he won the Golden Gloves.

He turned pro in 1933, won 15 and drew once in his first 16 bouts. He beat the great Sixto Escobar in New York to win the bantamweight championship on August 26, 1935—this only two-and-a-half years after drawing his first paycheck as a fighter.

Escobar won the title right back six weeks later, however.

Salica got another chance at the crown on January 13, 1941, in Philadelphia, this time beating Tommy Forte to settle the championship issue.

On August 7, 1942, Manuel Ortiz relieved the two-time champion of his crown in a 12-round go in Hollywood, California. Salica and Ortiz were matched again in Oakland the next year and Manuel stopped Lou in the 11th round.

No one had ever flattened him before.

The handwriting was on the wall, felt Salica. He had reached the end of the line after 10 years and 90 professional fights. He announced his retirement.

The once golden gloves had dissolved to sand.

GEORGE PACE
(1916–   )

The amateur mythmakers, composed largely of his followers, would have you believe that George Pace was all instinct. Well, he wasn't. By championship standards, the Cleveland Negro was only ordinary, something of a club fighter type. He came by the title unspectacularly and methodically.

Pace stood in boxing's starlight only briefly; only six years, to be strictly correct. He fought but 42 times. After Sixto Escobar outgrew the class, the N.B.A. matched Pace, who was claiming the crown, with Lou Salica in Toronto, March 4, 1940, to determine a new bantamweight champion. The bout ended in a draw. Pace still claimed the world's title, so the pair were matched again. They met in September of 1940 and this time Salica won the nod.

Pace, born in Cleveland, Ohio, on February 2, 1916, quit the ring to join the Army in 1942.

HAROLD DADE
(1924–1962)

Harold Dade, out of Chicago, was a chocolate shred of muscle with a dented nose who established some sort of speed record in 1947 for winning and losing the bantamweight championship.

Dade won the title from Manuel Ortiz in San Francisco, on January 6, and then lost it right back to him in Los Angeles two months afterward.

Standing 5 ft., 5 in., Dade began his professional career in 1942, and lost only once on his way to the world crown. After losing to Ortiz, however, something went out of

Harold Dade established some sort of record as a bantamweight champion: In 1947, he won and then lost the crown within two months. (NEA)

Harold's gloves. In his last 27 matches, the best he could do was four wins and two draws. On March 29, 1955, after Paul Jorgensen stopped him in the fourth round in Houston, no one had to tell Dade it was time to retire.

Harold Dade died in 1962 in Los Angeles. He was only thirty-eight years old.

MANUEL ORTIZ
(1916–1970)

The bantamweights were in a slump when California's Manuel Ortiz happened along. Evidently, fight fans didn't believe in elves and leprechauns. Manuel changed all that when he beat Lou Salica for the title in a 12-round match in Hollywood, August 7, 1942.

Thereafter, Ortiz really packed 'em in. He had everything—phenomenal speed, endurance and a knockout punch in either hand. He rang up 41 kayoes, including an 11th round job against Salica in Oakland in 1943—the only K.O. Lou incurred in his entire career. Ortiz himself was never knocked out in 117 bouts.

The El Centro flash tied Henry Armstrong in defending his crown 20 times (only George Dixon and Joe Louis defended more often). He held on to the title on seven occasions in 1943, defended four more times in 1944. Fol-

Two-times world champion Manuel Ortiz was the last American to hold bantamweight title. His championship years were 1942–1950. (NEA)

lowing a tour of duty in the Army, Manuel successfully guarded the throne three times in 1946. Harold Dade finally lifted it in San Francisco, January 8, 1947, but Ortiz took it back in Los Angeles, March 11, of that year. After four more title defenses, Vic Toweel captured the crown in 15 rounds in Johannesburg, May 31, 1950. Ortiz never regained it after that.

The Mexican-American got off to a sensational start as an amateur in 1937 when he knocked down one Bobby Hager 17 times before flooring him for the count in the fourth round. A week later he dumped Hager 20 times.

VIC TOWEEL
(1929–)

Vic Toweel stuck around the fight racket hardly long enough to work up a good sweat. He fought only 32 bouts as a professional before he quit the ring completely bushed at twenty-five. He won the bantamweight crown when he outboxed Manuel Ortiz in 15 rounds in Johannesburg, on May 31, 1950.

Vic was a member of the Toweels of South Africa. Papa Mike was his trainer and brother Maurice his manager. Another brother, Willie, once held the British Empire lightweight championship.

Vic suffered only two knockouts in his career—both times at the hands of Jimmy Carruthers, of Australia. The Paddington Puncher obliterated Vic in one round at Johannesburg, on November 15, 1952, to capture the bantam crown. In a return match at the same site four months later, Toweel ran out of gas halfway through the fight and was flattened in the 10th round.

Toweel fought only once in the United States, dropping a decision to Carmelo Costa in Brooklyn in 1954. Three months later he retired from the ring after stopping Harry Walker.

Short as his career was, Vic Toweel stuck around long enough to establish the record for most knockdowns in a world title bout,

Jimmy Carruthers has Vic Toweel tilting like a windmill as he knocks him out in the 1st round to win bantamweight title in 1952 at Johannesburg. (AP)

when he floored Danny O'Sullivan of London 14 times in 10 rounds at Johannesburg, in 1950.

JIMMY CARRUTHERS
(1929–   )

While some fighters toil for years in the rosin of countless rings, suffering the bruises of defeat, never reaching the pinnacle, others have become champions almost overnight. One straight hand, if it finds the mark, might do the trick.

Such a fighter was Australia's Jimmy Carruthers, who, in only his 15th fight, knocked out Vic Toweel in the first round at Johannesburg to become world bantam champion, on November 15, 1952. Four bouts later he suddenly announced his retirement from the ring—after only 19 professional fights—to open a pub. He was twenty-four years old.

For the seven years, Carruthers held rank with Jack McAuliffe, Jimmy Barry and Rocky Marciano as history's only world champions to complete their ring careers undefeated. But unlike Gene Tunney, who felt it was a smart man who hung up the gloves while he was still ahead, Carruthers attempted a comeback in 1961. The long layoff had taken its toll and Jimmy conceded it was a mistake to go on fighting after losing four of six bouts. He quit in 1962.

ROBERT COHEN
(1930–   )

Robert Cohen, his little arms pumping like pistons, turned a prize ring into an eye of a hurricane. With a sledgehammer for a right fist, he was a thimble with a thump.

Standing 5 ft., 3 in. and weighing 117 lbs., the tiny Jew from Bone, North Africa whittled down opponents to the size of midgets. With audacious confidence, he hung up 13 of 37 opponents like a crumpled bit of old laundry on his way to the world title.

Cohen's home base was Paris, and French arenas overflowed like a bathtub occupied by a whale when little Robert headlined the bill. He was a crowd-pleaser, his movements oiled with the sweat of knowing effort.

After Jimmy Carruthers vacated the bantamweight championship, Cohen, with only one early defeat and two draws marring an otherwise perfect record, defeated Chamrern Songkitrat in an elimination match at Bangkok (September 19, 1954) to earn the world title. Two years later, in Rome, Mario D'Agata of Italy stopped him in six to take the title away from him.

MARIO D'AGATA
(1926–   )

Mario D'Agata, a deaf mute, substituted boxing science for silence. The tiny bantam from Arezzo, Italy struck with ruthless precision. His fists packed the force of hammers.

Mario didn't start prizefighting until he was twenty. To win the world title, he went plumb through hell. In 1954, he nearly lost his life in a barroom shooting brawl, but managed to recover enough to go back to the prize ring. He capped the comeback by knocking out Robert Cohen in six rounds in Rome, on July 29, 1956, to become the first deaf mute in boxing history to capture a world's championship. A year later, tough Alphonse Halimi took the crown away from him.

Mario was born on May 29, 1926, was one of three deaf mutes in his family, and likewise married a deaf mute. A bantamweight all his career (1950–1962), the 5 ft., 6 in. Italian let his gloves do all the talking for him. In a lifetime total of 67 pro bouts, he was kayoed only once.

ALPHONSE HALIMI
(1932–   )

Alphonse Halimi, a tailor by trade, went from needles to knuckles. Inside a prize ring, he gave them the pitch instead of the stitch.

Few fighters ascended boxing heights as rapidly as the little French-Algerian. Defending champion Mario D'Agata must have thought somebody was pulling an April Fool's prank on him when Halimi popped up in Paris, on April 1, 1957, and outpointed him in 15 rounds to claim the bantam title. The upset victory was only Halimi's 19th professional fight. He'd turned pro only 18 months before, after 189 amateur bouts; he was amateur bantam champ of France in 1953–55.

Born in Constantine, on February 18, 1932, Halimi's chief tools of body and assault were lightning reflexes, piston-sharp combinations, and courage. He was knocked out only three times, twice by Jose Becerra with the title at stake. Alphonse lost the title to Becerra in Los Angeles, on July 8, 1959—10 bouts after he had won the crown from D'Agata. Seven months later, he tried to take the title back from Becerra, but was again kayoed.

Between the period October 25, 1960, and October 20, 1962, Halimi twice won and lost the European version of the world bantam championship. He finally retired in 1964 after dropping his last two decisions.

JOSE BECERRA
(1936–)

It is one small truth of the prize ring that a lean and hungry boxer will fight like hell. At the outset, in 1953, little Jose Becerra, out of Guadalajara, Mexico, sized up the class of the world's bantamweight crop and decided that's the way he'd fight to reach the top.

He was only seventeen when he turned professional. He won 18 fights in a row before dropping a close decision to L. Ibarra. Then he bunched together another 12 straight victories. He was undefeated in the years 1958–59, won the world bantamweight crown from Alphonse Halimi along the way. Until beating Halimi, Becerra fought outside Mexico only five times (once in San Francisco, four times in Los Angeles).

Jose Becerra was awarded a trophy almost as big as he after outpointing Kenji Yonekura in Tokyo, in 1960. Three months later he retired from boxing, leaving the bantamweight championship vacant. (AP)

After becoming champion, Becerra won his next seven matches, including victories over Halimi and Kenji Yonekura in defense of the crown, before losing on an eight-round K.O. to Eloy Sanchez, in Juarez, in a non-title bout. Despite the fact that he was still world champion and had run up an impressive unbeaten string of 23 bouts (18 K.O.'s, 5 decisions), dating back to January 1958, Becerra suddenly announced his retirement right after he lost to Sanchez (August 30, 1960). The record says Becerra fought best when hungry. It took him six years and 69 pro bouts to win the title—and he fought only eight more times after becoming champion.

Masahiko (Fighting) Harada, world flyweight and bantam champion, and best fighter ever to come out of Japan. (UPI)

MASAHIKO (FIGHTING) HARADA
(1943–)

Fighting Harada was regarded as the greatest Japanese export since transistor radio.

He was the finest prizefighter ever to come out of Japan. Born in Tokyo, on April 5, 1943, Harada was only sixteen when he began his prize ring career in February 1960. He won 24 of his first 25 pro bouts.

Harada missed by a hair of winning three world championships. He won (1962) and lost (1963) the flyweight title, won (1965) and lost (1968) the bantamweight championship, and came within a point of winning Johnny Famechon's featherweight crown (July 28, 1969).

The son of a gardener, Harada won (K.O., 11 rounds) and lost (15-round decision) the flyweight title against Pone Kingpetch; decisioned the great Eder Jofre to win the bantam belt, and lost it to Lionel Rose.

Harada's final bout was on January 6, 1970, in Tokyo, where Famechon stopped him in the 14th round. The next day, Harada announced his permanent retirement from the ring.

STILL ACTIVE
EDER JOFRE
(1936–)

Born in Sao Paulo, Brazil, Jofre began his pro ring career in 1957. Losing only twice in his first 71 bouts, he kayoed 47. On his way to the bantamweight title, he stopped 27 of 40 opponents, winning the world championship with a 10-round K.O. of Piero Rollo, March 25, 1961. Jofre successfully defended his crown seven times, all knockouts, but he lost the title to Fighting Harada, a 15-round decision, on May 17, 1965. He went into retirement, 1967–68, then came back as a featherweight in 1969, winning 15 bouts in a row. On May 5, 1973, he won the World Boxing Congress version of the featherweight crown via a 15-round decision over Jose Legra.

LIONEL ROSE

Rose began his pro ring career in 1964 in Melbourne, Australia. He won the bantam

Between 1961 and 1965, bantamweight king Eder Jofre knocked out seven challengers in defense of his crown, including this 3rd-round K.O. of Katsutoshi Aoki in Tokyo, in 1963. (AP)

title from Fighting Harada in Tokyo, on February 26, 1968, decision, 15 rounds, and lost it to Ruben Olivares, K.O. 5 rounds, at Inglewood, California, August 22, 1969. Rose won 40 of his first 47 pro matches.

CHUCHO CASTILLO
(1944–   )

Born in Mexico, Castillo started fighting professionally in 1962, and won the world bantamweight title from Ruben Olivares, a K.O. in 14 rounds in Los Angeles, October 16, 1970. Castillo lost the title back to Olivares, a 15-round decision, in Los Angeles, April 3, 1971.

RUBEN OLIVARES
(1947–)

Olivares, born in Mexico City, started his pro career in 1965, scoring 22 straight knockouts. He kayoed 64 of his first 76 opponents, including a 5-round K.O. of Lionel Rose to win the world bantamweight championship, August 22, 1969. Olivares lost the title to Chucho Castillo (by K.O. in 14th) in Los Angeles, October 16, 1970, and won the crown back from Castillo five-and-a-half months later. He lost it again, on March 19, 1972, to Rafael Herrera by an 8-round kayo in Mexico City.

RAFAEL HERRERA

From Mexico City, he had his first pro bout in 1963 and won 50 of his first 57 professional matches. He won the world bantamweight championship in his 10th year of fighting—an 8-round K.O. over Ruben Olivares. Herrera lost the crown to Enrique Pinder, a 15-round decision, at Panama City, July 30, 1972.

ENRIQUE PINDER
(1947–)

Born in Panama, Pinder began his career in 1966, winning 36 of his first 43 bouts (two draws), including a 15-round decision over Rafael Herrera in Panama City to win the world bantam title, July 30, 1972. Pinder lost his crown to Romero Anaya, K.O. 3rd round, at Panama City, on January 20, 1973.

ROMERO ANAYA

Born in Mexico, Anaya turned pro in 1968, scoring 28 kayoes in his first 40 bouts, while losing only four fights himself—all by knockouts. He won the bantam title from Enrique Pinder (1973), lost it to Arnold Taylor (1973) on a K.O. in the 14th round.

ARNOLD TAYLOR

Taylor began fighting in 1967, won South Africa's bantam and featherweight titles, and lost only four of his first 34 pro matches, including a tough 10-round decision to former champion Johnny Famechon. Taylor kayoed Romero Anaya in the 14th round at Johannesburg to win the world bantamweight crown, November 3, 1973.

FLYWEIGHTS

PRIOR to 1910, the lightest recognized weight in prize fighting was the bantam division at 118 pounds. Then the 112-pound flyweight class was created. It is popularly believed that the division was made specifically for the great little Jimmy Wilde of Wales.

Wilde did not get his first honest-to-George professional fight until 1913. The governing boxing body of England didn't know Jimmy from Adam and simply established the flyweight class to whip up interest in small men. It was a splendid idea in principle and a hollow bust in practice.

Even then flyweights had as much popular appeal as a process server. The last fight for the world flyweight championship held in the United States was in New York, on December 26, 1930, between Frankie Genaro and Midget Wolgast. The American title has not been disputed in the ring since Wolgast and Small Montana met at Oakland, California, in 1935.

Harry Markson, former managing director of the old International Boxing Club, spent nearly 40 years in the business and never saw a flyweight fight, not even in a preliminary.

"The reason is obvious," Harry said. "Flyweights don't draw flies, if you'll pardon the pun. Fans want to see guys who can hit hard enough to score a knockout. The only flyweight in history who gave the customers the big bang they wanted was Wilde, and it was only during his regime that there was intense interest in the division. A crowd of 40,000 paid to see Jimmy fight Pancho Villa at the Polo Grounds in 1923. You couldn't give away that many free tickets to a flyweight fight today. That little Welshman must've been a wonder."

Wilde knocked out Johnny Rosner of the United States, in 1916, to become the first recognized world flyweight champion. He held the crown until 1923. Jimmy showed the world that nothing can compare with the little fellows when it comes to sheer speed, but interest in them all but vanished in the United States after Wilde retired and efforts to revive them failed. However, in Europe and Asia they still enjoy a large following.

JIMMY WILDE
(1892–1969)

Jimmy Wilde was a most remarkable runt by any measuring stick. The tiny Welsh wraith was the smallest of the genuine giants of sports. He was 5 ft., 2¼ in. tall, never topped 108 pounds for a fight, and was—pound for pound—the most devastating puncher ever seen in the prize ring.

Nobody had to tell him that big men fell harder. In exhibitions he knocked out men who outweighed him by 70 pounds and in formal fights repeatedly gave away 20 pounds to the ranking professionals. As closely as anyone can estimate he had 864 bouts and lost only 4. The total includes hundreds of bouts fought in the boxing booths of Britain.

The Jimmy Wilde facts are these: James Wilde, son of a poverty-stricken coal miner, born on May 15, 1892, at Pontypridd, Wales, the cradle of champions. Freddie Welsh, Jem Driscoll and Bob Fitzsimmons also came from the same section. Jimmy spent his boyhood as a pit boy in the mines. He began to fight for a living at Tylorstown, in 1908, when he was sixteen years old. He weighed 74 pounds. In a boxing booth tournament, he took on all comers and toppled fellows almost twice his size. Yet long after he had made an imposing reputation around the boxing booths, promoters and the public wanted no part of him. They felt he was a sideshow freak making a travesty of the sport.

Jimmy had about the worst physique ever owned by a man. He resembled a walking xylophone, his ribs stuck out so. His arms and legs were so scrawny that, small as he was, he seemed 10 pounds lighter than his announced 93 pounds. Fight fans nicknamed him "The Mighty Atom." In Nat Fleischer's *All-Time Ring Record Book*, the bible of boxing, a typographical error gave Wilde's height as 2½ inches. "It's a mistake, all right," Fleischer admitted, "but it's easy to understand how it happened. He didn't look any bigger."

Jem Driscoll, friend and teacher of Wilde, tried to induce the late Charley Harvey to bring Jimmy to America in 1912. Harvey took one look at the frail-looking youngster and exclaimed, "The only thing we could use him for is a watch charm."

Jimmy's appearance was belying, for he punched harder, with incredible speed and accuracy, than most lightweights. He was not at all intimidated by bigger men. Before he fought Joe Lynch at the National Sporting Club in London, on March 1, 1919, the Prince of Wales got into the ring and shook his hand and wished him luck. Jimmy then gave Lynch a 15-round shellacking. Lynch later won the bantamweight title of the world from Pete Herman.

Wilde was a sensational draw at the box office when he came to the United States in 1920, but he drove sports reporters crazy because he rarely opened his mouth.

"The runt acted more like an office boy than the world champion," said Dan Morgan. "I've seen a lot of odd characters in this racket in my time. Guys who looked like choir boys and could tear the tail out of a live tiger with their bare hands. Guys who looked

Standing only 5 ft., 2½ in. and weighing a mere 108 lbs., Jimmy Wilde had about the poorest physique ever owned by a prizefighter, yet he was a devastating puncher. (NEA)

tough enough to scare an executioner and couldn't lick me. Wilde is the only fighter I've seen, though, who made me think of going back to honest work for a living, God forbid I wanted to call the cops and have them lock up every no-good bum who had anything to do with letting such a weak, helpless little sucker put on a pair of gloves."

Wilde's punch was as phenomenal as it was improbable. The source of his terrific power fascinated scientists, who subjected him to numerous tests. Doctors gravely prodded his anemic body, peered at him through fancy instruments, timed his motor reflexes and reported that Wilde was a thoroughly normal specimen for his size. Nobody, including the doctors, knew what the tests were supposed to prove. An illiterate towel-swinger could have told them that Wilde's secret to his punching prowess was the combination of faultless, intuitive timing and coordination.

Despite Wilde's awesome reputation as a puncher, there was no dearth of amateurs who wanted to have a go at him in 1916 after he won the world flyweight title and returned one night to the boxing booths in Britain to pick up a few extra quid. He knocked out 19 blokes of assorted sizes in three and a half hours, called a brief intermission for a dish of tea, then went back and upended four more oafs in a half hour before he finally cooled off the ardor of volunteers.

Wilde made good use of all those who clamored for a crack at him in those impromptu matches. They were the only trial horses available for developing his punch and technique. Even after he turned professional, the smallest men in the business were so much heavier that they would not work out with him for fear of getting tossed into the clink by the police.

Jimmy finally proved his age, at least, by marrying when he was eighteen. You don't have to believe this, but he actually used his

The Jimmy Wilde of 1918 does his roadwork here, with his wife as pacemaker. The tiny British star often used his missus as a sparring partner. (AP London)

wife as a sparring partner. Mrs. Wilde wore a tin breastplate and hopped around their bedroom throwing haymakers like crazy while Jimmy perfected his footwork and defensive moves.

"Elizabeth Ann was fast and nimble enough to be quite useful in that role," Jimmy recalled later. "And she saved the cost of sparring partners."

Wilde flouted the axiom of the prize ring that a good big man can beat a good little man. Some of the men he fought were twice his size—once he knocked out a challenger weighing 182 pounds. Other opponents were so tall that he could not reach their chins for a clean swipe. It made little difference. He belted them out by hitting them in the belly.

Although he was only twenty-eight, Jimmy was past his prime when he fought Pete Herman, a rough-and-tumble mauler, at London's Albert Hall, on January 13, 1921. Thirteen years of fighting bigger men had taken its toll of his meager physical equipment and the percentages were catching up with him rapidly. Herman had just lost the world bantam title to Lynch. He put Jimmy on the toboggan in what turned out to be Wilde's last fight in London.

A frightful row preceded the match. The contract called for Herman to weigh no more than 118, the bantam limit, but he came in at 121. Wilde scaled 108. Ted Lewis, Jimmy's manager, refused to let his man go on at first. Wilde finally ended the confusion by agreeing to fight on condition the referee would announce from the ring that all bets were off. He wanted to protect his British fans in the event Herman's weight proved too much.

Herman used his 13-pound advantage to wear Jimmy down. It wasn't even a contest after the third round, but Jimmy absorbed a savage licking until he collapsed from sheer exhaustion in the 17th round. The referee, Jack Smith, had to pick him up and carry him to his corner. "Sorry, Jimmy," Smith told the protesting Wilde, "I had to pick you up because you don't know how to lie down."

Until Herman stopped him, Wilde lost only twice in 10 years. Tancy Lee beat him in 17 rounds, Pal Moore in 3. In return bouts, he knocked out Lee in 11 rounds and battered Moore in 20.

Wilde's loss to Herman was his only match in 1921. He remained idle in '22. In March of '23, he fought a three-round exhibition with Pedlar Palmer in England, then traveled to New York to defend his flyweight crown against Pancho Villa, on June 18th. The rust was showing, yet the old magic of Jimmy's name drew a crowd of 40,000 to the Polo Grounds. It was the only magic left. Jimmy showed occasional flashes of his old form until Villa hit him with a terrific right after the bell ended the second round. Wilde later confessed that he remembered nothing after that punch. The incident aroused a good deal of hard feeling in England, but Villa would have won the title under any circumstances. The Filipino was too young, strong and fast. He was superior in every department but one—gameness. Although Jimmy was hit practically at will by Villa, he never was counted out. "I want to keep going till I go out," he told Referee Patsy Haley when Haley stopped the slaughter in the seventh.

That was the end. The sports writers played taps for Wilde. The brutal beatings he had taken from Herman and Villa laid him up for eight months.

With the exception of the late Benny Leonard, no fighter has ever dominated his class as completely as did Wilde. Fight nuts get into a lather arguing the relative merits of champions in the other divisions, but among the all-time flyweights the issue is clear-cut: Jimmy Wilde is the only man ever mentioned.

Perhaps Gene Tunney's perspective was most accurate of all when he learned of Wilde's death in 1969 at Cardiff, Wales. "Jimmy," he said, "was the greatest fighter I ever saw."

PANCHO VILLA
(1901–1925)

"Whom the gods love they destroy early." It happened to Stanley Ketchel while he was middleweight champion and again to Pancho Villa, flyweight titlist, who died of blood poisoning at the age of twenty-four.

In his short, happy life, the 5 ft., 1 in., 109-pound Filipino compiled the enviable record of only 5 bouts lost in 102 professional fights. Only Jimmy Wilde had a better lost record (3) in the division, but whereas Jimmy was kayoed twice, the lusty Villa was indestructible. As a matter of fact, Pancho the Puncho kayoed Jimmy in the seventh round for the title at the Polo Grounds, June 18, 1923.

Muscular little Pancho Villa. "The bigger they are, the harder they fall," was little Pancho Villa's credo. Shown here training with a heavyweight, the Filipino fought all the way from flyweights to welters. (NEA)

Villa, a miniature Sandow, could go like blazes for round after round without a letup. He combined the stamina and vitality of Henry Armstrong with a set of hooks that were as effective as ice tongs.

The explosive little fellow was born in Iloilo on the Island of Panay in the Philippines, August 1, 1901. When he was eighteen, Francisco Guilledo (his real name) borrowed the fighting handle of the Mexican bandit chieftain and set out to terrorize the Philippines. In no time he captured the flyweight and bantamweight titles.

Frank Churchill brought Villa to America in 1922. Frank used to tell a story illustrating the importance of New York on the boxing scene. Pancho battled Frankie Genaro 10 furious rounds to no decision in Jersey City. The bout got scant attention in the New York newspapers. "Then Pancho went into the old Madison Square Garden and won an easy decision in a semi-windup over little-known Johnny Hepburn," Churchill recalled. "The next morning, the New York writers and photographers roused Villa and me from our sleep to get stories and pictures of him. After that, Villa was a big star."

Between July 6 and September 14, Pancho fought *seven* times in and around New York. This hectic schedule was culminated by Villa's 11th-round K.O. of Johnny Buff for the American flyweight championship.

Although he yielded the American title to Frankie Genaro on a 15-round decision, March 1, 1923, Pancho continued to bowl over the opposition on his way to a world title match with Jimmy Wilde. Following his win over Wilde, Pancho then went after bantams, featherweights, and lightweights. His swan song was his loss to Jimmy McLarnin in Oakland, California, on July 4, 1925.

Shortly before the McLarnin fight, Villa had a wisdom tooth extracted, and complications developed. So when he climbed in against Jimmy, he was a very sick little man. As soon as McLarnin was awarded the decision, Pancho returned to the dentist's chair. More teeth were pulled out, and he was told to return the next day. Instead, he threw a wild party that lasted several days. Friends tried to persuade him to enter a hospital, but when he finally complied, it was too late. Pancho Villa died on the operating table on July 14, 1925, three weeks after the infection had set in.

FRANKIE GENARO
(1901–1966)

Frankie Genaro was no bigger than a jockey. As a matter of fact, the tiny New York Italian, 5 ft., 2½ in., 112 pounds, once harbored an ambition to sit in the saddle, even got a job as a stable boy. He soon discovered, however, that the prize ring—and not the exercise ring—was his oyster.

Starting in the amateurs when he was sixteen, Fearless Frankie went on to become one of the few Olympic champions to graduate to the professionals and win a world's title. He won the Olympic gold medal in 1920, was on the same American team as Sam Mossberg and Eddie Eagen. He turned pro after returning from the Olympic Games at Antwerp, ran up a spectacular string of victories, and then, on August 22, 1922, he beat the great Pancho Villa in 10 rounds. To prove it was no fluke, he beat Villa again, this time for the American flyweight title. Genaro lost the American edition of the crown to Fidel LaBarba two years later.

LaBarba announced his retirement in 1927 to enter college, and Genaro beat Frenchie Belanger in 10 rounds at Toronto, in 1928, to earn the N.B.A. world's flyweight championship.

He put the crown on the line five times, losing in his last defense to Young Perez in Paris via a two-round K.O., on October 27, 1931.

Genaro was born in New York on August 26, 1901. He retired from the ring in 1934.

It is interesting to note that the third flyweight champion of the world was involved in seven bouts that were decided by fouls—five of them he won. But there was nothing foul about Frankie Genaro. He was a genuine champion.

EMILE PLADNER
(1906–   )

Emile Pladner's reign as world champion didn't last much longer than a coffee break—47 days to be exact. He won the flyweight title from Frankie Genaro on a one-round K.O. in Paris, March 2, 1929, and lost it back to him on a foul in the fifth round, April 18th. If nothing else, this brief splash in the limelight earned him a footnote in the *Guinness Sports Record Book*. Those 47 days tied him with featherweight Dave Sullivan for shortest reign as a world champion.

Born on September 2, 1906, at Clermont-Ferrand, France, Spider Pladner started his career in 1926, was unbeaten in his first 28 matches. He was only twenty-two when he beat Genaro. In 1931, he moved up in weight and whipped Francis Beron for the bantamweight championship of France, a title he held for several years before retiring in 1935.

Pladner fought 122 bouts in 10 years, lost only 16 (2 on fouls), was kayoed but 3 times, while scoring 34 himself.

FIDEL LaBARBA
(1905–   )

Every now and then a college man comes along who shows enough signs of being a good fighter in the making to excite those who do not know anything about the game. There are, of course, exceptions to every rule. Fidel LaBarba was one.

After winning the flyweight championship at the Olympic Games in 1924, LaBarba turned professional and won the flyweight title of the world in 1927. Seven months later he retired to enter Stanford University. Less than a year after that, he was back in the ring and, although grown heavier, he failed to win the featherweight crown.

LaBarba was born in New York City on September 29, 1905, but moved to California when he was just a kid. He was a sensation as an amateur, even better as a pro. Though he stood only 5 ft., 3 in. and weighed but 112 pounds, he had a 66-in. reach and developed a very good left hook. He held Jimmy McLarnin to a draw and beat a lot of good fighters, including Kid Chocolate and Bushy Graham and Bud Taylor.

Fidel quit the ring in 1933, went back and got his degree from Stanford, and turned to journalism. A logical profession. He always had been good copy while he was fighting.

ALBERT BELANGER
(1906–   )

Frenchie Belanger and Spider Pladner must have thought they were seeing double in title fights with Frankie Genaro. Both won and lost the flyweight championship against him.

Born on May 17, 1906, in Toronto, Canada, Belanger turned pro in 1925, won 23 and lost 4 in the first year and a half. In 1927, after outpointing Newsboy Brown and knocking out Ray Shauers, he won the vacant flyweight crown on a decision over Genaro in 10 rounds. While his reign was brief enough, Belanger did hold on to his title 23 days longer than Pladner, for it was 70 days before Genaro took it back from him in Toronto.

The Belanger Story was mostly downhill after losing to Genaro. Frenchie lost 11 of his last 22 fights. He retired in 1932 following a kayo at the hands of Frankie Wolfram.

IZZY SCHWARTZ
(1902–   )

Skitting around a ring like a gnat, Corporal Izzy Schwartz was kayoed only once in 117 professional fights. Kid Durand was the culprit. Izzy stood 5 ft., 1 in. and was a boxer all the way and behaved as one. Boxers are always on the move, seldom take time to set for the big punch; consequently, Izzy knocked out only seven opponents in his career. He concentrated on points instead. Fifty-one of his victories were by decisions.

Born in New York City on October 23, 1902, the tiny Jewish-American decisioned

Always on the move, tiny Izzy Schwartz was a master boxer all the way. (NEA)

Newsboy Brown, on December 16, 1927, to claim the flyweight championship at a time when the crown was in dispute. Stepping up in class, Izzy was matched against world bantamweight champion Bushy Graham the following May 23rd in Brooklyn and dropped a tough decision.

On November 4, 1929, Izzy's stock as flyweight champion slipped faster than the Wall Street market. He gave up the crown after losing four straight non-title decisions and fought only once more before retiring from the ring.

VICTOR (YOUNG) PEREZ
(1911–1942)

Young Perez had a brashness beyond the normal human quota. The eighth modern flyweight champion was a plodder scarred by punches who fought suspiciously like a carnival roustabout. At full throttle, the Tunis Terror could take your block off.

In a career spanning nearly 11 years, and 132 bouts, Perez walloped 26 opponents askew and decisioned 63 others. But here's one for the book: he engaged in 16 matches ending in draws—more stalemates than any man ever to hold the flyweight diadem! Win, lose or draw, the rugged little gamecock fought every minute of every round.

Born at Tunis on October 18, 1911, Perez began his pro career in 1928, quit in 1938. He won the flyweight championship in Paris on October 26, 1931, with a two-round kayo over Frankie Genaro, who was on his way down.

Perez held the crown 370 days, losing it to Jackie Brown at Manchester, England via a 13-round knockout. Young Perez' death remains a mystery. He reportedly died in a German prison camp in 1942, but the rumors were never confirmed.

MIDGET WOLGAST
(1910–1955)

Midget Wolgast was a flyweight with the punch and the pace of a mosquito. He stepped around the ring a mile a minute, his little arms pumping like pistons, but he didn't have enough juice up his gloves to break an egg.

To the untutored eye, Joseph Robert Loscalzo (his real name) must have looked both undignified and ungallant. His defensive thinking and strategy appeared a little like a preliminary boy who has had his first good crack at the lug and is skating around in the hopes that the ropes will miraculously open and let him out. But this retreat was all part of Midget's brilliant pattern. He petered many a bloke out this way, then suddenly lashed back and piled up points after he had their tongues dragging.

Born in Philadelphia on July 18, 1910, of Italian-American parentage, Wolgast started fighting as a pro in 1927. He won 22 of his first 25 matches, including recognition by the New York Commission as flyweight champion of the world on the strength of a 15-round victory over Black Bill in New York, March 21, 1930. The title had been vacated by Corporal Izzy Schwartz' retirement in 1929.

While New York State recognized Wolgast, the N.B.A. designated Frankie Genaro as champion. Nothing was settled when Wolgast and Genaro fought in New York to clear up the dispute because the bout ended in a draw. Genaro then went to Europe, lost to Young Perez, while Wolgast was dropping a decision to Small Montana in Oakland, California. That ended Midget's championship claims.

Wolgast fought 142 times, winning 81 matches by decisions. He scored only 11 knockouts. Powderpuff puncher you say?

JACKIE BROWN
(1909–1971)

England boasts three flyweight champions of the world—Jackie Brown, Peter Kane and Terry Allen. Of the three, Brown was perhaps the most typically English in his combat. He was far more concerned with skill than mayhem, although 36 of his lifetime total of 97 victories in 129 fights ended in knockouts.

Jackie made his big bid for world glory while the flyweight championship was still in dispute. Frankie Genaro, Young Perez and Midget Wolgast were all claiming to be No. 1, but Brown settled the argument on October 31, 1932, in Manchester, England, by stepping in and scoring a 13-round knockout over Perez.

Born in the Ancoats district of "Cottonopolis," in 1909, Jackie was boxing professionally at sixteen, mostly boothfighting. After winning the world flyweight title, he defended it five times. On September 8, 1935, Scotland's Benny Lynch floored him 10 times in two rounds to strip the crown from him.

Jackie's fighting years were 1926–1939. He was still a main-eventer at thirty, when he joined the British Army. At 5 ft., 5 in. and 112 lbs., little Brown generally did it up brown when it came to fighting.

BENNY LYNCH
(1913–1946)

Many Britishers rank Benny Lynch, the first world boxing champion from Scotland, next to Jimmy Wilde as the greatest of flyweights.

Squaring off against sawed-off Benny (5 ft., 5 in., 112 lbs.) offered about as much solace to body and soul as facing an angry lynch mob on a deadend street. I mean, what choice did it leave you? Caged inside the tiny Scot there lurked a tiger. In a total of 72 recorded bouts, he left 27 opponents crawling around the ring on their hands and knees looking for their lost dignity. He was defeated only 6 times in 8 years; extended one unbeaten string to 50, including 7 draws.

A calculating boxer on attack, Benny also was a superb defensive fighter, getting his gloves up and rolling and ducking and bending away from the blows, weaving around the ring like a cobra dancing to a flute. The result was that he was kayoed only once, by Aurel Toma, in his last fight.

Lynch was born in the poor Gorbals section of Scotland, on April 2, 1913. He started as a boothfighter, won 35 of 37 amateur bouts, then turned pro in 1931. Four-and-a-half years later, he kayoed Jackie Brown in two rounds in what the promoters ballyhooed as a "British, European and world's flyweight title match," but it was not until Benny won a 15-round decision from Small Montana, on January 19, 1937, in London, that Lynch won universal acclaim as champion of the world.

After twice successfully defending his crown against Peter Kane (by K.O. and draw), Lynch failed to make weight for his title defense against Jackie Jurich and abandoned the crown. The fight was fought anyway, Lynch stopped Jurich in the 12th round, and then announced his retirement from the ring after Toma bombed him out in three, on October 3, 1938. He was only twenty-five, but the old motor had simply run out of petrol. Benny became an alcoholic and was dead at thirty-three.

SMALL MONTANA
(1913–   )

Benjamin Gan ran away from home to become a prizefighter. He changed his name to Small Montana, which translated meant "little mountain," and after that, he made opponents run.

No bigger than a flyspeck, the tiny Filipino clubbed his way to the American flyweight championship by twice defeating Midget Wolgast in 1935. He also claimed the world title, an honor he lost to Benny Lynch 17 months later in London in 15 rounds.

The son of a chief of police, Small Montana kept law and order inside a prize ring. (NEA)

Small Montana was born at Negros, Philippine Islands, on February 24, 1913. His father was chief of police. Montana hero-worshipped the great Pancho Villa and carried a photo of the champion at all times.

At 5 ft., 4 in. and 112 lbs., Montana began fighting professionally in 1931 and retired in 1941. All told, he won 79 of 110 pro bouts. The fact that he knocked out only 10 opponents tells you something about his punching power, but he more than made up for the shortcoming with speed and cleverness.

Benjy (Small Montana) Gan might have been only a li'l feller, but there was nothing small about his courage.

PETER KANE
(1918–   )

Peter Kane, to quote one British writer, "could hit like the hammer of Thor." The Englishman rolled up one of the superior knockout records (51) in flyweight history. Only Jimmy Wilde, with 77, scored more.

Kane raised cain from the start. Beginning his prize ring career in 1934, he quickly catapulted out in front of the flyweight pack to become one of the division's most adulated stars. He won 41 matches in a row; 33 of them left opponents lying in the glare of arclights like stacks of ripe fish rotting in the sun. This phenomenal K.O. performance earned him a championship match with Benny Lynch, on October 13, 1937, in Glasgow. The bout drew 40,000 admissions and Lynch sent the home crowd away happy with his 13th-round K.O. victory.

After Lynch vacated the flyweight throne room, Kane fought Jackie Jurich in Liverpool, on September 22, 1938, to decide a successor to the championship. Peter won on points in 15 rounds. He held the title until June 19, 1943, when Jackie Paterson took it away from him on a first-round K.O.

Peter Kane was born at Lancaster, England, on February 28, 1918. He was sixteen years old when he started his ring career, thirty when he retired. In 95 pro bouts, he lost only 7.

JACKIE PATERSON
(1920–1966)

The basic propulsion to explain how Jackie Paterson ever won the world flyweight championship (and held it) is strong. Consider his crazy-quilt record: In a total of 90 professional bouts, he lost 25—losing 10 times while he still held the crown! No flyweight titleholder ever was knocked out more (10 times). Yet, the Swattin' Scot's own total of 41 kayoes places him third best among the little giants who have ruled the division.

Make no bones about it, Jackie could hit—and be hit. There was no compromise in his streetfighting style. It was club or be clubbed. Li'l Jackie had the castiron stomach for brawling and fans knew they would always get their ticket's worth when he was on the bill.

Born on September 5, 1920, at Springfield, Ayrshire, Scotland, Paterson began his ring career in 1938. Five years later, on June 19, 1943, he ponderously stopped Peter Kane in one round to claim the world title. He held the crown until March 23, 1948, when Rinty Monaghan flattened him in the seventh round at Belfast. Jackie thus won and lost the championship the same way—by knockout. That figured, for there was never anything halfway about him. A man of violence, he died that way—by gunshot wounds, in 1966.

RINTY MONAGHAN
(1920–   )

John Joseph Monaghan stands as Ireland's one and only world flyweight champion. It's a pity that Rinty never fought in the United States. As a matter of fact, he never once ventured outside the British Isles to do his thing. Monaghan, you see, was a song and dance man on the side, and win, lose or draw he'd serenade the boxing fans after each of his bouts. He gave the public something besides a set of cabbage ears.

Rinty Monaghan would have been perfect for those old Friday Night Fights in America. He could have done the TV commercials between rounds.

Though the record book shows a total of only 51 pro bouts, Monaghan actually fought in nearly 200 contests. He lost only eight, one on a foul. He was kayoed but once, by Jackie Paterson early in his career.

Born in Belfast, on August 21, 1920, Rinty Monaghan stood 5 ft., 3 in. and weighed 112 lbs. at his peak. He began fighting in 1935. Because he campaigned largely around home, it wasn't until 1948 that he was able to lure a flyweight champion to his lair. The result was a seven-round K.O. of Paterson.

FLYWEIGHTS

Rinty left the prize ring in 1950, giving up the world title when he could no longer make the weight.

TERRY ALLEN
(1925–   )

Edward Goveir, alias Terry Allen, was about as big as three small apples without their tails. Despite his watchcharm size—5 ft., 3 in., 111 lbs.—he was all man, and he could fight and punch and take it, too. He won 62 of 76 pro bouts, 18 by K.O.

Terry Allen was born at Islington, England, on August 11, 1925. Between September 3, 1942, when he had his first pro match, and May 20, 1946, he never lost a fight. The string included 12 knockouts and 20 decisions.

In 1949, Allen's record of 58 wins and 4 defeats earned him a shot at Rinty Monaghan's world crown in Belfast. Monaghan had knocked out Allen in London in the first round, two-and-a-half years before. This time the bout ended in a 15-round draw.

After Monaghan's retirement, on April 25, 1950, Allen won an elimination tournament to determine a new world flyweight champion, culminating his campaign with a 15-round decision over Honore Pratesi. Four months later, it was ex-champion in front of Allen's name, after dropping a decision to Dado Marino in 15 rounds in Honolulu. Terry fought for the world title twice more, losing both on decisions to Marino and Yoshio Shirai. He finally retired in 1954.

DADO MARINO
(1916–   )

Dado Marino, in one respect, was a unique specimen among world boxing champions—he retired from the prize ring a grandfather at the age of thirty-six.

Born in Honolulu of Philippine descent, on August 26, 1916, Dado didn't begin his pro career until he was nearly twenty-five. Not precisely a globetrotter, he fought his first 40 bouts in Honolulu, won 35 of them, and it was six years before he ventured outside the Islands.

Marino lost a 15-round decision to Rinty Monaghan in an attempt to win the N.B.A. version of the flyweight title, October 20, 1947. Sixteen months later, he lost on points to Manuel Ortiz in a bid for the world bantamweight crown.

Dado finally struck gold on the night of August 1, 1950, in Honolulu, when he outpointed Terry Allen in 15 rounds to capture the world flyweight championship, a victory he repeated over Allen in 1951. Then came three straight losses to Japan's Yoshio Shirai, the last two with the title at stake. After Shirai defeated him the third time, Marino retired from the ring.

YOSHIO SHIRAI
(1923–   )

Yoshio Shirai, the first Japanese fighter to win a world championship, got his biggest impetus from Dr. A. R. Cahn, an American botany professor from the University of Illinois who was stationed in Tokyo as an Army civilian in 1947.

The botany influence paid off. Shirai put many a flower in the hands of opponents.

Cahn coached Shirai in the manly art, and though Yoshio, 5 ft., 6 in. and 112 pounds, fought only a handful of matches as a professional before the war, he was ready for top-flight competition in 1948. He won 19 of his first 20 post-war bouts, including the Japanese flyweight and bantamweight titles.

On May 19, 1952, Tokyo went wild as Shirai won the world flyweight championship from Dado Marino (decision, 15 rounds). Shirai could hit like a bullwhip. He successfully defended his crown four times before losing it to Pascual Perez, the tiny tearaway Argentinian who floored him in the 12th round and went on to win a unanimous decision, on November 26, 1954. They fought again in May 1955; this time Shirai was counted out in the fifth round. Several days later, he retired from the ring.

Born in the Oji district of Tokyo, on November 23, 1923, Yoshio Shirai was thirty-two when he hung up his gloves.

PASCUAL PEREZ
(1926–   )

If ever a fist hit hard enough and a heart was stout enough, Pascual Perez most richly deserved to be a world's champion.

In Mendoza, Argentina, where he was born, March 4, 1926, the citizens didn't regard Pascual as a mere prizefighter. He was a myth, a legend, a dream, a visitation from outer space. He answered all the questions. He was an all-

Yoshio Shirai, the first Japanese fighter to win a world title, smashed Dado Marino to the canvas and then went on to win the flyweight championship on points, in 1952, in Tokyo. (AP)

Yoshio is married to former Japanese Olympic swimming star. The couple was photographed here in Tokyo with President Petronella of the N.B.A. in 1952. (Photo courtesy Dan Petronella)

around fighter: on defense, guileful as a pheasant; on attack, more dangerous than a mother lion with baby cubs. His lifetime total of 56 knockouts in 91 professional fights tells you something about his punching power.

Perez won the Gold Medal in the flyweight division at the 1948 Olympic Games in London. Four years later he turned pro. Twenty-two of his first 23 victories ended in knockouts. His 24th prizefight was a draw with champion Yoshio Shirai in Buenos Aires (July 24, 1954). They fought again four months later in Tokyo, Perez winning the championship by decision. In a third match with Shirai, May

30, 1955, again in Tokyo, Perez stopped him in five.

Perez was undefeated for seven years. When Sadao Yaoita decisioned him in a non-title bout in Tokyo, on January 16, 1959, it marked his first loss. The next time they fought, 10 months later in Osaka, the title was on the line and Perez knocked Yaoita out in the 13th round.

In his very next title match, against Pone Kingpetch, on April 16, 1960, at Bangkok, Perez was defeated on points. The following September 22, they fought again—and again Kingpetch was the victor (K.O., eighth round). Though Perez won his next 27 bouts in a row, 18 by knockouts, he never got another chance at the world championship. He finally retired after being belted out in his last two fights, in 1963.

No relation to Young Perez, Pascual was built along the lines of Pancho Villa. He never fought in the United States because there was no one here for him to fight. Most of his fighting was done in South America.

Pascual Perez came from a family of nine. In his youth, he worked as a janitor to help swell the income at home. To add to his pay, he became a prizefighter. He never went back to his broom and scrub bucket again. He confined his mopping up exercises to the prize ring.

HIROYUKI EBIHARA
(1940–   )

Hiroyuki Ebihara was born in Tokyo, March 26, 1940; he became a professional fighter at nineteen, retired at twenty-nine. Through his first five years he ran up a 38–1–1 record, including a one-round kayo of Pone Kingpetch to win world flyweight title, September 18, 1963. Ebihara lost it back to Kingpetch in his very next match four months later, a 15-round decision. He won the W.B.A. version of the flyweight crown in 1969 with a decision over Jose Severino, and lost it on points to Bernabe Villacampo, October 20, 1969, in the last fight of his career. Ebihara won 63 of a total of 69 pro bouts, 34 by K.O., was never kayoed himself.

PONE KINGPETCH
(1936–   )

Pone Kingpetch, born at Hua Hin, a seaport province of North Thailand, on February 12,

Pone Kingpetch, at 5 ft., 7 in., was tall for a world flyweight champion. (UPI)

1936, is the only man ever to win the 112-pound championship *three* times. He first won it from Pascual Perez in 1960 and lost it to Fighting Harada in 1962. He won it back from Harada in 1936, lost it to Hiroyuki Ebihara in '63, and won it back from him in '64. He lost the title for a final time to Salvatore Burruni in '65.

One of seven children, Kingpetch's real name was Nana Seadoaghob. His mother wanted him to be a Buddhist priest. Tall for a flyweight at 5 ft., 7 in., Pone began his boxing career in classic Thailander style—using the feet as weapons; he learned conventional prizefighting by reading a book written by an American. Turning pro at eighteen, Kingpetch proved an excellent long-range boxer and used his clever footwork to keep himself away from infighting. He was thirty years old when he retired in 1966.

SALVATORE BURRUNI
(1933–   )

Salvatore Burruni, born at Alghero, Italy, on April 11, 1933, was the first fighter from Italy to win the world flyweight championship. A member of the 1956 Italian Olympic Games boxing team, he began his pro ring career in

FLYWEIGHTS

After the brawl was over! From the looks of European flyweight champ Salvatore Burrini, of Italy, shown here getting a lift from Walter McGowan, the wrong man won. Actually, the points went against the Scotsman, but the crowd of 15,000 in Rome cheered him for his sportsmanship. (AP)

1957, rolling up a 76–3–1 record on his way to winning the world title from Pone Kingpetch, April 23, 1965, in Rome. Burruni lost his crown to Walter McGowan, in London, June 14, 1966. He won the European bantamweight championship in 1968 with a 15-round decision over Mimun ben Ali, and kept his bantam title until retirement in 1969. He lost only 9 bouts in a total of 109 pro matches.

WALTER McGOWAN
(1942–   )

The first Britisher to hold the world flyweight title since Terry Allen, Walter McGowan won 122 of 124 amateur fights on his way to turning professional in 1961. He was taught to box by his father, who had fought under the name of Joe Gans (his idol). Except for a tendency to cut easily around his eyes, McGowan was the complete boxer: he had punching power, cleverness, a cool temperament, and was a smart left jabber, a crisp right-hand hitter, and a sound combination puncher. On June 14, 1966, he became world champion by a brilliant victory over tough Salvatore Burruni at Wembley Arena, despite a ravaged right eye. He lost the title to Chartchai Chionoi, on December 30, '66, when forced to retire with a broken nose in the ninth round. McGowan won the British Empire bantamweight crown in 1966, beating Alan Rudkin, and lost it to Rudkin in 1968. McGowan retired in '69 with a record of 32-7-1.

ALACRAN (EFREN) TORRES
(Date of birth unknown)

Alacran (Efren) Torres, a native of Guadalajara, Mexico, won the world flyweight title with an eight-round K.O. of Chartchai Chionoi, in Mexico City, on February 23, 1969, and lost it back to Chionoi the following March 20th. Torres' early pro record is unknown; however, available statistics show he won 48 of 58 bouts, 31 by kayo.

CHARTCHAI CHIONOI
(1942-)

Born in Bangkok, Thailand, October 10, 1942, Chionoi began his pro career in 1959. An in-and-outer, he lost 11 of his first 37 fights, found himself in 1965, and won the next 14 of 15 matches (11 by K.O.), including a nine-round knockout of Walter McGowan to win the world flyweight title, December 30, 1966. Chionoi lost the crown to Efren Torres, an eight-round K.O., February 23, 1969, and regained the world championship from Torres, a 15-round decision, March 20, 1970. He lost it for a second time on a two-round K.O. by Erbito Salvarria, December 7, 1970. Chionoi won the W.B.A. version of world flyweight title with a five-round knockout of Fritz Chervet, May 17, 1973.

ERBITO SALVARRIA
(1946-)

Born on January 20, 1946, in the Philippines, Erbito Salvarria began his pro ring career in 1963 with a flourish, winning 14 of 16 bouts. He was kayoed only once in his first 44 fights. He won the world flyweight championship from Chartchai Chionoi with a two-round K.O., on December 7, 1970, and lost the crown to Venice Borkorsor, a 15-round decision, February 2, 1973.

VENICE BORKORSOR
(Date of birth unknown)

Born in Thailand, Venice Borkorsor began fighting professionally in 1970, winning 30 of his first 32 bouts, 27 by K.O. He won the world flyweight championship from Erbito Salvarria, a 15-round decision, February 2, 1973—after only 12 prizefights; he gave up his title after only five months to campaign as a bantamweight.

APPENDICES

BOXING HALL OF FAME

The Hall of Fame was started by the late Nat Fleischer, in 1954. Listed below are those electees who won world championships since the advent of the glove era.

Elected in 1954:
- John L. Sullivan
- Jack Johnson
- James J. Jeffries
- James J. Corbett
- Bob Fitzsimmons
- Stanley Ketchel
- Joe Gans
- Jack McAuliffe
- Jack Dempsey, the Nonpareil
- Young Griffo
- Arthur Chambers
- Jack Dempsey
- Joe Louis
- Henry Armstrong

Elected in 1955:
- Terry McGovern
- Abe Attell
- Joe Walcott, the Original
- Harry Greb
- Gene Tunney
- Benny Leonard
- Mickey Walker

Elected in 1956:
- George Dixon
- Jem Driscoll
- Tony Canzoneri
- Jimmy McLarnin
- Barney Ross
- Tommy Loughran

Elected in 1957:
- Kid McCoy
- Battling Nelson
- Johnny Dundee

Elected in 1958:
- Tommy Ryan
- Ad Wolgast
- Tony Zale

Elected in 1959:
- Jimmy Wilde
- Jack Dillon
- Pete Herman
- George (Kid) Lavigne
- Kid Chocolate
- Rocky Marciano

Elected in 1960:
- Johnny Kilbane
- Freddy Welsh
- Tommy Burns
- Jack Britton

Elected in 1961:
  Pancho Villa

Elected in 1962:
  Willie Ritchie
  Marcel Cerdan

Elected in 1963:
  Willie Pep

Elected in 1964:
  Georges Carpentier
  Ted (Kid) Lewis
  Lou Ambers
  James J. Braddock

Elected in 1965:
  Johnny Coulon
  Young Corbett II
  Billy Conn

Elected in 1966:
  Battling Levinsky
  Kid Gavilan
  Archie Moore

Elected in 1967:
  Ray Robinson

Elected in 1968:
  Philadelphia Jack O'Brien
  Max Baer

Elected in 1969:
  Jersey Joe Walcott
  Carmen Basilio

Elected in 1970:
  Kid Williams
  Max Schmeling
  Ezzard Charles

Elected in 1971:
  Tiger Flowers
  Paul Berlenbach
  Rocky Graziano
  Sandy Saddler

Elected in 1972:
  Billy Papke
  Fidel LaBarba
  Maxie Rosenbloom
  Beau Jack
  Fritzi Zivic

Elected in 1973:
  Jack Delaney
  Frankie Genaro
  Gus Lesnevich
  Sammy Angott

STATES IN U.S. PRODUCING MOST WORLD CHAMPIONS

(Note: Tabulation is based on where the champions were *born*, not necessarily where they later settled down. It covers only the glove era; bareknuckle champions are not included.)

State	Total	State	Total
New York	36	Kentucky	2
Pennsylvania	17	Mississippi	2
California	13	Colorado	2
Massachusetts	10	Minnesota	2
Illinois	8	Missouri	2
New Jersey	7	Maryland	2
Ohio	5	Washington	1
Texas	4	Florida	1
Michigan	4	North Carolina	1
Georgia	4	New Mexico	1
Arkansas	4	Maine	1
Indiana	4	Rhode Island	1
Connecticut	3	Utah	1
South Carolina	3	Tennessee	1
Louisiana	3	Hawaii	1
Kansas	2	Nebraska	1
Alabama	2		

RATING THE ALL-TIME CHAMPIONS
(Based on Survey of Oldtimers)

Heavyweights
1. James J. Jeffries
2. Jack Johnson
3. Bob Fitzsimmons
4. James J. Corbett
5. Jack Dempsey

Light-Heavyweights
1. Kid McCoy
2. Tommy Loughran
3. Jack Dillon
4. Philadelphia Jack O'Brien
5. Archie Moore

Middleweights
1. Stanley Ketchel
2. Harry Greb
3. Mickey Walker
4. Ray Robinson
5. Tony Zale

APPENDICES

Heavyweights
6. John L. Sullivan
7. Gene Tunney
8. Joe Louis
9. Rocky Marciano
10. Muhammad Ali

Welterweights
1. Mickey Walker
2. Henry Armstrong
3. Barney Ross
4. Joe Walcott
5. Jimmy McLarnin
6. Ray Robinson
7. Jack Britton
8. Ted Kid Lewis
9. Dixie Kid
10. Carmen Basilio

Light-Heavyweights
6. Battling Levinsky
7. Georges Carpentier
8. Jack Delaney
9. Billy Conn
10. Paul Berlenbach

Lightweights
1. Joe Gans
2. Benny Leonard
3. Tony Canzoneri
4. Henry Armstrong
5. Battling Nelson
6. Ad Wolgast
7. Lew Ambers
8. Joe Brown
9. Freddie Welsh
10. Beau Jack

Middleweights
6. Tommy Ryan
7. Frank Klaus
8. Billy Papke
9. Freddie Steele
10. Rocky Graziano

Featherweights
1. Terry McGovern
2. Abe Attell
3. George Dixon
4. Johnny Dundee
5. Kid Chocolate
6. Johnny Kilbane
7. Henry Armstrong
8. Willie Pep
9. Young Griffo
10. Sandy Saddler

Bantamweights
1. George Dixon
2. Pete Herman
3. Kid Williams
4. Joe Lynch
5. Bud Taylor
6. Johnny Coulon
7. Panama Al Brown
8. Jimmy Carruthers
9. Sixto Escobar
10. Manuel Ortiz

Flyweights
1. Jimmy Wilde
2. Pancho Villa
3. Frankie Genaro
4. Fidel LaBarba
5. Benny Lynch
6. Midget Wolgast
7. Young Perez
8. Rinty Monaghan
9. Peter Kane
10. Jackie Brown

HEAVYWEIGHT CHAMPIONSHIP BOUTS
(Asterisk indicates title changed hands.)

1889—July 8—John L. Sullivan beat Jake Kilrain, 75 rounds. Richburg, Miss. (Last championship bareknuckle bout.)

*1892—Sept. 7—James J. Corbett defeated John L. Sullivan, 21 rounds, New Orleans (used big gloves.)

1894—Jan. 25—James J. Corbett knocked out Charley Mitchell, 3 rounds, Jacksonville, Fla.

*1897—March 17—Bob Fitzsimmons defeated James J. Corbett, 14 rounds, Carson City, Nev.

*1899—June 9—James J. Jeffries beat Bob Fitzsimmons, 11 rounds, Coney Island, N.Y.

1899—Nov. 3—James J. Jeffries beat Tom Sharkey, 25 rounds, Coney Island, N.Y.

1900—May 11—James J. Jeffries knocked out James J. Corbett, 23 rounds, Coney Island, N.Y.

1902—July 25—James J. Jeffries knocked out Bob Fitzsimmons, 8 rounds, San Francisco

1903—Aug. 14—James J. Jeffries knocked out James J. Corbett, 10 rounds, San Francisco.

1904—Aug. 26—James J. Jeffries knocked out Jack Munroe, 2 rounds, San Francisco.

*1905—James J. Jeffries retired. July 3—Marvin Hart knocked out Jack Root, 12 rounds, Reno, Nev. Jeffries refereed and presented the title to the victor. Jack O'Brien also claimed the title.

*1906—Feb. 23—Tommy Burns defeated Marvin Hart 20 rounds, Los Angeles.

1906—Nov. 28—Jack O'Brien and Tommy Burns, 20 rounds, draw, Los Angeles.

1907—May 8—Tommy Burns defeated Jack O'Brien, 20 rounds, Los Angeles.

1907—July 4—Tommy Burns knocked out Bill Squires, 1 round, Colma, Cal.

1907—Dec. 2—Tommy Burns knocked out Gunner Moir, 10 rounds, London.

1908—Feb. 10—Tommy Burns knocked out Jack Palmer, 4 rounds, London.

1908—March 17—Tommy Burns knocked out Jem Roche, 1 round, Dublin.

1908—April 18—Tommy Burns knocked out Jewey Smith, 5 rounds, Paris.

1908—June 13—Tommy Burns knocked out Bill Squires, 8 rounds, Paris.

1908—Aug. 24—Tommy Burns knocked out Bill Squires, 13 rounds, Sydney, New South Wales.

1908—Sept. 2—Tommy Burns knocked out Bill Lang, 2 rounds, Melbourne, Australia.

*1908—Dec. 26—Jack Johnson stopped Tommy Burns, 14 rounds, Sydney, Australia. Police halted contest.

1909—May 19—Jack Johnson and Jack O'Brien, 6 rounds, draw, Philadelphia.

1909—June 30—Jack Johnson and Tony Ross, 6 rounds, draw, Pittsburgh.

1909—Sept. 9—Jack Johnson and Al Kaufman, 10 rounds, no decision, San Francisco.

1909—Oct. 16—Jack Johnson knocked out Stanley Ketchel, 12 rounds, Colma, Cal.

1910—July 4—Jack Johnson knocked out Jim Jeffries, 15 rounds, Reno, Nev. (Jeffries came back from retirement.)

1912—July 4—Jack Johnson won on points from Jim Flynn, 9 rounds, Las Vegas, N.M. (contest stopped by police.)

1913—Nov. 28—Jack Johnson knocked out Andre Spaul, 2 rounds, Paris.

1913—Dec. 9—Jack Johnson and Jim Johnson, 10 rounds, draw, Paris.

1914—June 27—Jack Johnson won from Frank Moran, 20 rounds, Paris.
*1915—April 5—Jess Willard knocked out Jack Johnson, 26 rounds, Havana, Cuba.
1916—March 25—Jess Willard and Frank Moran, 10 rounds (no decision), New York City.
*1919—July 4—Jack Dempsey knocked out Jess Willard, Toledo, O. (Willard failed to answer bell for fourth round.)
1920—Sept. 6—Jack Dempsey knocked out Billy Miske, 3 rounds, Benton Harbor, Mich.
1920—Dec. 14—Jack Dempsey knocked out Bill Brennan, 12 rounds, New York City.
1921—July 2—Jack Dempsey knocked out Georges Carpentier, 4 rounds, Boyle's Thirty Acres, Jersey City, N.J.
1923—July 4—Jack Dempsey won on points from Tom Gibbons, 15 rounds, Shelby, Mont.
1923—Sept. 14—Jack Dempsey knocked out Luis Firpo, 2 rounds, New York City.
*1926—Sept. 23—Gene Tunney beat Jack Dempsey, 10 rounds, decision, Philadelphia.
1927—Sept. 22—Gene Tunney beat Jack Dempsey, 10 rounds, decision, Chicago.
1928—July 26—Gene Tunney knocked out Tom Heeney, 11 rounds, Yankee Stadium, New York; soon afterward he announced his retirement.
*1930—June 12—Max Schmeling of Germany defeated Jack Sharkey in fourth round when Sharkey fouled Schmeling in a bout which was generally considered to have resulted in the election of a successor to Gene Tunney, New York City.
1931—July 3—Max Schmeling knocked out W. L. Stribling, another contender for the title, in 15 rounds in Cleveland.
*1932—June 21—Jack Sharkey defeated Max Schmeling, 15 rounds, decision, New York City.
*1933—June 29—Primo Carnera knocked out Jack Sharkey, six rounds, New York City.
1933—Oct. 22—Primo Carnera defeated Paulino Uzcudun, heavyweight challenger, 15 rounds, in Rome.
1934—March 1—Primo Carnera defeated Tommy Loughran in 15 rounds in Miami.
*1934—June 14—Max Baer knocked out Primo Carnera, 11 rounds, New York City.
*1935—June 13—James J. Braddock defeated Max Baer, 15 rounds, New York City (judges' decision.)
*1937—June 22—Joe Louis knocked out James J. Braddock, 8 rounds, Chicago.
1937—Aug. 30—Joe Louis defeated Tommy Farr, 15 rounds, decision, New York City.
1938—Feb. 23—Joe Louis knocked out Nathan Mann, 3 rounds, New York City.
1938—April 1—Joe Louis knocked out Harry Thomas, 5 rounds, New York City.
1938—June 22—Joe Louis knocked out Max Schmeling, 1 round, New York City.
1939—Jan. 25—Joe Louis knocked out John H. Lewis, 1 round, New York City.
1939—April 17—Joe Louis knocked out Jack Roper, 1 round, Los Angeles.
1939—June 28—Joe Louis knocked out Tony Galento, 4 rounds, New York City.
1939—Sept. 20—Joe Louis knocked out Bob Pastor, 11 rounds, Detroit.
1940—Feb. 9—Joe Louis defeated Arturo Godoy, 15 rounds, decision, New York City.
1940—March 29—Joe Louis knocked out Johnny Paychek, 2 rounds, New York City.
1940—June 20—Joe Louis knocked out Arturo Godoy, 8 rounds, New York City.
1940—Dec. 16—Joe Louis knocked out Al McCoy, 6 rounds, Boston.
1941—Jan. 31—Joe Louis knocked out Red Burman, 5 rounds, New York City.
1941—Feb. 17—Joe Louis knocked out Gus Dorazio, 2 rounds, Philadelphia.
1941—March 21—Joe Louis knocked out Abe Simon, 13 rounds, Detroit.
1941—April 8—Joe Louis knocked out Tony Musto, 9 rounds, St. Louis.
1941—May 23—Joe Louis beat Buddy Baer, 7 rounds, Washington, D.C., on a disqualification.
1941—June 18—Joe Louis knocked out Billy Conn, 13 rounds, New York City.
1941—Sept. 29—Joe Louis knocked out Lou Nova, 6 rounds, New York City.
1942—Jan. 9—Joe Louis knocked out Buddy Baer, 1 round, New York City.
1942—March 27—Joe Louis knocked out Abe Simon, 6 rounds, New York City.
1946—June 19—Joe Louis knocked out Billy Conn, 8 rounds, New York City.
1946—Sept. 18—Joe Louis knocked out Tami Mauriello, 1 round, New York City.
1947—Dec. 5—Joe Louis defeated Joe Walcott in a 15-round bout by a split decision, New York City.
1948—June 25—Joe Louis knocked out Joe Walcott, 11 rounds, New York City.
*1949—June 22—Following Joe Louis' retirement Ezzard Charles defeated Joe Walcott by a unanimous decision, 15 rounds, Chicago. (N.B.A. recognition only.)
1950—Sept. 27—Ezzard Charles defeated Joe Louis in latter's attempted comeback, 15 rounds, New York City (universal recognition).
1950—Dec. 5—Ezzard Charles knocked out Nick Barone, 11 rounds, Cincinnati.
1951—Jan. 12—Ezzard Charles knocked out Lee Oma, 10 rounds, New York City.
1951—March 7—Ezzard Charles outpointed Joe Walcott, 15 rounds, Detroit.
1951—May 30—Ezzard Charles outpointed Joey Maxim, light-heavyweight champion and challenger for heavyweight title, 15 rounds, Chicago.
*1951—July 18—Joe Walcott knocked out Ezzard Charles, 7 rounds, Pittsburgh.
1952—June 5—Joe Walcott outpointed Ezzard Charles, 15 rounds, Philadelphia.

APPENDICES

*1952—Sept. 23—Rocky Marciano knocked out Joe Walcott, 13 rounds, Philadelphia.
1953—May 15—Rocky Marciano knocked out Joe Walcott, 1 round, Chicago.
1953—Sept. 24—Rocky Marciano knocked out Roland LaStarza, 11 rounds, Polo Grounds, New York.
1954—June 17—Rocky Marciano outpointed Ezzard Charles, 15 rounds, Yankee Stadium, New York.
1954—Sept. 17—Rocky Marciano knocked out Ezzard Charles, 8 rounds, Yankee Stadium, New York.
1955—May 16—Rocky Marciano knocked out Don Cockell, 9 rounds, Kezar Stadium, San Francisco.
1955—Sept. 21—Rocky Marciano knocked out Archie Moore, 9 rounds, Yankee Stadium, New York. Marciano retired undefeated, Apr. 27, 1956.
*1956—Nov. 30—Floyd Patterson, a contender, knocked out Archie Moore, 5 rounds, Chicago, gaining the championship.
1957—July 29—Floyd Patterson knocked out Hurricane Jackson, 10 rounds, Polo Grounds, New York.
1957—Aug. 22—Floyd Patterson knocked out Pete Rademacher, 6 rounds, Seattle.
1958—Aug. 18—Floyd Patterson knocked out Roy Harris, 12 rounds, Los Angeles.
1959—May 1—Floyd Patterson knocked out Brian London, 11 rounds, Indianapolis, Indiana.
*1959—June 26—Ingemar Johansson, Sweden, knocked out Floyd Patterson, 3 rounds, Yankee Stadium, New York.
*1960—June 20—Floyd Patterson knocked out Ingemar Johansson, 5 rounds, to become first man to regain heavyweight title, New York.
1961—March 13—Floyd Patterson knocked out Ingemar Johansson, 6 rounds, Miami Beach.
1961—Dec. 4—Floyd Patterson knocked out Tom McNeeley, 4 rounds, Toronto, Canada.
*1962—Sept. 25—Sonny Liston knocked out Floyd Patterson, 1 round, in Chicago to become new champion.
1963—July 22—Sonny Liston knocked out Floyd Patterson, Las Vegas, Nev., for second 1st-round K.O. in a row.
*1964—Feb. 25—Cassius Clay became new champion with T.K.O., 7 rounds, over Sonny Liston at Miami Beach.
1965—May 26—In return title match, Cassius Clay K.O.'d Sonny Liston, 1 round, Lewiston, Maine.
1965—Nov. 11—Cassius Clay T.K.O.'d Floyd Patterson, 12 rounds, Las Vegas, Nev.
1966—March 29—Cassius Clay decisioned George Chuvalo, 15 rounds, Toronto.
1966—May 21—Cassius Clay stopped Henry Cooper, 6 rounds, London.
1966—Aug. 6—Cassius Clay knocked out Brian London, 3 rounds, London.
1966—Sept. 10—Cassius Clay knocked out Karl Mildenberger, 12 rounds, Frankfurt, Germany.
1966—Nov. 14—Cassius Clay K.O.'d Cleveland Williams, 3 rounds, Houston.
1967—Feb. 6—Cassius Clay decisioned Ernie Terrell, 15 rounds, Philadelphia.
1967—March 22—Cassius Clay knocked out Zora Folley, 7 rounds, New York City.
1967—May 9—Cassius Clay kayoed by World Boxing Association. Title taken away from him for refusing to accept Army draft. Clay was banned in all of U.S. and heavyweight title was vacated, thus opening way for elimination tournament to determine successor.
*1970—Feb. 16—Joe Frazier knocked out Jimmy Ellis, 5 rounds, to win the vacant title, New York City.
1970—Nov. 18—Joe Frazier knocked out Bob Foster, 2 rounds, Detroit.
1971—March 8—Joe Frazier decisioned Cassius Clay, 15 rounds, in New York as Cassius tried to become second heavyweight in history to regain crown.
1972—Jan. 15—Joe Frazier knocked out Terry Daniels, 4 rounds, New Orleans.
1972—May 25—Joe Frazier stopped Ron Stander, 5 rounds, Omaha, Neb.
*1973—Jan. 22—George Foreman, a 3½–1 underdog, scored a sensational 2nd-round KO over defending champion Joe Frazier, at Kingston, Jamaica.
1973—Sept. 1—George Foreman knocked out Joe "King" Roman at the two-minute mark of the first round in what referee Jay Edson called a "one hundred percent mismatch." The bout was held in Tokyo and was Foreman's first defense of the crown. His end of the purse was $1 million.
1974—March 26—George Foreman knocked Ken Norton down three times and out in 2 minutes of 2nd round at Caracas, Venezuela, totally dominating the fight.
*1974—Oct. 30—Cassius Clay K.O.'d George Foreman at 2:58 of the eighth round at Kinshasa, Zaire.
1975—March 24—Muhammad Ali (Cassius Clay) climbed back to his feet after a 9th round knockdown to stop Chuck Wepner in the 15th round at Cleveland.
1975—May 16—A lethargic Muhammad Ali, 220 lbs., came from behind to knock out Ron Lyle in the 11th round to retain his title. Ali was guaranteed $1 million for the fight.
1975—June 30—Muhammad Ali decisioned Joe Bugnes, of England, in 15 drab rounds in first heavyweight title bout ever fought in Malaysia.

FIGHT RECORDS OF THE CHAMPIONS

Heavyweight Champions

Name	Nationality	Fighting years	Total bouts	Knock-outs	Won on decision	Lost on decision	Draws	Won on foul	Lost on foul	No. of times knocked out	No-decision bouts	No contest	Year born	Year died
John L. Sullivan	USA	1878–05	75	16	15	0	3	0	0	1	40	0	1858	1918
James J. Corbett	USA	1886–03	33	9	11	1	6	0	1	3	2	0	1866	1933
Bob Fitzsimmons	Eng.	1889–14	41	23	5	0	1	0	1	6	5	0	1862	1917
Jim Jeffries	USA	1896–10	23	16	4	0	2	0	0	1	0	0	1875	1953
Tommy Burns	Can.	1900–20	60	36	10	4	8	0	0	1	1	0	1881	1955
Jack Johnson	USA	1897–28	113	44	30	1	14	4	1	5	14	0	1878	1946
Jess Willard	USA	1911–23	36	20	4	8	1	0	1	2	5	0	1881	1968
Jack Dempsey	USA	1914–40	81	49	10	6	8	1	0	1	6	0	1895	—
Gene Tunney	USA	1915–28	76	41	14	1	1	1	0	0	17	1	1898	—
Max Schmeling	Ger.	1924–48	71	39	14	5	5	3	0	5	0	0	1905	—
Jack Sharkey	USA	1924–36	55	15	20	8	3	3	1	4	1	0	1902	—
Primo Carnera	Italy	1928–45	99	66	18	5	0	2	1	6	0	1	1906	1967
Max Baer	USA	1929–41	79	50	15	9	0	0	1	3	1	0	1909	1959
Jim Braddock	USA	1926–38	85	26	25	20	3	0	0	2	7	2	1905	1974
Joe Louis	USA	1934–51	71	54	13	1	0	1	0	2	0	0	1914	—
Ezzard Charles	USA	1937–59	122	58	38	17	1	0	1	7	0	0	1921	1975
Jersey Joe Walcott	USA	1930–53	67	30	18	11	1	1	0	6	0	0	1914	—
Rocky Marciano	USA	1947–55	49	43	6	0	0	0	0	0	0	0	1923	1969
Floyd Patterson	USA	1952–72	64	40	15	3	1	0	0	5	0	0	1935	—
Ingemar Johansson	Swed.	1952–63	28	17	8	0	0	1	0	2	0	0	1932	—
Sonny Liston	USA	1953–70	54	39	11	1	0	0	0	3	0	0	1932	1971
Cassius Clay	USA	1960–					(still fighting)						1942	—
Joe Frazier	USA	1965–					(still fighting)						1944	—
George Foreman	USA	1969–					(still fighting)						1949	—

Note: Records do not include exhibition bouts.

Light-Heavyweight Champions

Name	Total Recorded Bouts	Total Wins	K.O.'s	Won On Decision	Lost On Decision	Times K.O.'d	Draws	No Decision
Jack Root	53	44	24	20	0	3	5	1
George Gardner	65	41	19	22	6	5	10	3
Jack O'Brien	181	101	36	65	3	4	16	57
Jack Dillon	240	91	60	31	6	0	15	128
Battling Levinsky	272	66	25	41	15	4	13	174
Georges Carpentier	106	85	51	34	7	8	5	1
Battling Siki	74	54	29	25	11	1	1	7
Mike McTigue	145	81	57	24	12	10	6	36
Paul Berlenbach	49	37	30	7	4	3	3	2
Jack Delaney	86	70	42	28	7	3	3	3
Tommy Loughran	172	86	18	78	21	2	8	45
Maxie Rosenbloom	289	210	18	192	33	2	23	21
Jimmy Slattery	128	109	45	64	9	5	1	4
Bob Olin	85	53	25	28	23	4	5	0
John Henry Lewis	104	91	54	37	7	1	5	0
Melio Bettina	99	82	36	46	10	3	3	1
Billy Conn	74	64	14	50	8	2	0	0
Anton Christoforidis	74	51	14	37	12	3	8	0
Gus Lesnevich	76	57	21	36	9	5	5	0
Freddie Mills	96	73	52	21	11	6	6	0
Joey Maxim	115	82	21	61	28	1	4	0
Archie Moore	228	193	140	53	19	7	8	1
Harold Johnson	88	77	33	44	6	5	0	0
Willie Pastrano	84	63	14	49	11	2	8	0
Jose Luis Torres	45	41	29	12	2	1	1	0
Dick Tiger	81	61	26	35	16	1	3	0
Bob Foster	58	51	42	10	2	4	0	0

Middleweight Champions

Name	Total Recorded Bouts	Total Wins	K.O.'s	Won On Decision	Lost On Decision	Times K.O.'d	Draws	No Decision
Nonpareil J. Dempsey	68	50	8	42	1	2	12	3
Tommy Ryan	109	86	48	38	1	1	9	11
Stanley Ketchel	61	49	46	3	2	2	4	4
Billy Papke	64	39	29	10	8	1	7	9
Frank Klaus	89	49	25	24	2	2	2	34
George Chip	155	38	34	4	13	3	3	98
Al McCoy	146	50	28	22	3	2	8	83
Mike O'Dowd	115	52	35	17	7	1	3	52
Johnny Wilson	122	64	43	21	19	2	2	35
Harry Greb	290	111	46	65	5	2	3	168
Tiger Flowers	149	115	49	66	5	8	6	15
Mickey Walker	148	93	58	35	13	5	4	33
Gorilla Jones	141	97	53	44	23	0	13	8
Ben Jeby	73	54	22	32	12	2	4	1
Marcel Thil	96	78	34	44	12	2	4	0
Vince Dundee	150	112	27	85	18	1	13	6
Teddy Yarosz	127	106	16	90	17	1	3	0
Babe Risko	51	27	7	20	9	9	6	0
Freddie Steele	95	84	38	46	2	3	5	1
Fred Apostoli	72	61	31	30	6	4	1	0
Al Hostak	83	65	47	21	6	3	6	0
Solly Krieger	111	80	53	27	21	3	7	0
Ceferino Garcia	116	81	57	24	21	5	9	0
Ken Overlin	147	125	23	103	12	1	7	1
Billy Soose	41	34	13	21	6	0	1	0
Tony Zale	88	70	46	24	12	4	2	0
Rocky Graziano	83	67	52	15	7	3	6	0
Marcel Cerdan	113	109	66	43	3	1	0	0
Jake LaMotta	106	83	30	53	15	4	4	0
Ray Robinson	202	175	109	66	18	1	6	2
Randy Turpin	75	66	45	21	3	5	1	0
Bobo Olson	109	91	42	49	9	7	2	0
Gene Fullmer	64	55	24	31	4	2	3	0
Carmen Basilio	79	56	27	29	14	2	7	0
Terry Downes	43	34	27	7	3	6	0	0
Paul Pender	48	40	20	20	3	3	2	0

Middleweight Champions

Name	Total Recorded Bouts	Total Wins	K.O.'s	Won On Decision	Lost On Decision	Times K.O.'d	Draws	No Decision
Joey Giardello	133	100	32	68	21	4	7	1
Emile Griffith				(still fighting)				
Nino Benvenuti	90	82	35	47	4	3	1	0
Carlos Monzon				(still fighting)				

Welterweight Champions

Name	Total Recorded Bouts	Total Wins	K.O.'s	Won On Decision	Lost On Decision	Times K.O.'d	Draws	No Decision
Billy Smith	82	30	13	17	14	4	28	6
Kid McCoy	105	81	35	46	2	4	9	9
Matty Matthews	84	47	14	33	12	1	17	7
Rube Ferns	53	41	31	10	8	3	1	0
Joe Walcott	150	81	34	47	20	4	30	15
Dixie Kid	126	78	63	15	15	3	6	24
Honey Mellody	95	56	36	20	7	6	13	13
Twin Sullivan	69	35	18	17	3	4	14	13
Jack Britton	325	99	21	78	27	1	20	178
Ted (Kid) Lewis	253	155	68	87	20	4	9	65
Pete Latzo	150	65	25	40	29	2	3	51
Joe Dundee	123	86	23	63	15	5	11	6
Young Jack Thompson	66	46	31	15	16	0	3	1
Lou Brouillard	140	110	66	44	26	1	3	0
Jackie Fields	84	70	28	42	8	1	2	3
Tommy Freeman	185	144	69	75	13	3	17	8
Young Corbett III	166	132	36	96	9	3	15	7
Jimmy McLarnin	77	63	20	43	10	1	3	0
Barney Ross	82	74	24	50	4	0	3	1
Henry Armstrong	175	144	97	47	20	2	8	1
Fritzie Zivic	230	155	80	75	61	4	10	0
Freddie Cochrane	116	72	26	46	30	5	9	0
Marty Servo	56	49	15	34	2	2	2	1
Johnny Bratton	86	59	32	27	21	3	3	0
Kid Gavilan	143	106	27	79	30	0	6	1
Johnny Saxton	66	55	21	34	4	5	2	0
Tony DeMarco	71	58	33	25	5	7	1	0
Virgil Akins	92	59	34	25	29	2	2	0
Don Jordan	75	50	17	33	20	3	1	1
Benny Paret	50	35	10	25	8	4	3	0
Luis Rodriguez	121	107	49	58	10	3	0	1
Curtis Cokes	79	61	30	31	11	3	4	0
Jose Napoles	78	72	52	20	4	2	0	0
Billy Backus	56	36	18	18	14	2	4	0

Lightweight Champions

Name	Total Recorded Bouts	Total Wins	K.O.'s	Won On Decision	Lost On Decision	Times K.O.'d	Draws	No Decision
Arthur Chambers	14	11	9	2	0	1	2	0
Jack McAuliffe	52	41	9	32	0	0	9	2
George Lavigne	55	35	16	19	3	2	8	7
Frank Erne	40	22	10	12	2	4	12	0
Joe Gans	156	120	55	65	3	5	10	18
Battling Nelson	132	59	38	21	17	2	19	35
Ad Wolgast	135	60	38	22	10	2	14	49
Willie Ritchie	71	36	8	28	8	1	4	22
Freddie Welsh	167	77	24	53	3	1	7	79
Benny Leonard	209	88	68	20	1	4	1	115
Jimmy Goodrich	110	44	6	38	32	1	15	18
Rocky Kansas	165	64	32	32	10	3	7	81
Sammy Mandell	168	82	28	54	12	5	8	61
Al Singer	70	60	24	36	4	4	2	0
Tony Canzoneri	181	138	44	94	28	1	11	3
Lou Ambers	102	88	29	59	6	2	6	0

APPENDICES

Name	Total Recorded Bouts	Total Wins	K.O.'s	Won On Decision	Lost On Decision	Times K.O.'d	Draws	No Decision
Lew Jenkins	109	66	47	19	26	12	5	0
Sammy Angott	125	94	22	72	22	1	8	0
Beau Jack	111	83	40	43	20	3	5	0
Bob Montgomery	97	75	37	38	16	3	3	0
Juan Zurita	85	72	22	50	9	3	1	0
Ike Williams	153	124	60	64	18	6	5	0
Jimmy Carter	120	80	31	49	28	3	9	0
Lauro Salas	148	83	39	44	45	7	12	1
Paddy DeMarco	104	75	8	67	19	7	3	0
Bud Smith	60	32	18	14	15	7	6	0
Joe Brown	160	104	48	56	33	9	12	2
Carlos Ortiz	70	61	29	32	6	1	1	1
Carlos Cruz	57	42	13	29	11	2	2	0
Armando Ramos	40	33	20	13	4	3	0	0
Ismael Laguna	74	64	36	28	9	0	1	0
Ken Buchanan				(still fighting)				
Roberto Duran				(still fighting)				

Featherweight Champions

Name	Total Recorded Bouts	Total Wins	K.O.'s	Won On Decision	Lost On Decision	Times K.O.'d	Draws	No Decision
Ike Weir	41	29	12	17	2	1	8	1
Billy Murphy	90	49	25	24	15	9	14	3
Young Griffo	107	49	5	42	6	3	37	12
George Dixon	150	78	30	48	22	4	37	9
Solly Smith	45	20	6	14	5	1	17	2
Dave Sullivan	59	28	10	18	11	2	16	2
Terry McGovern	77	59	34	25	1	2	4	10
Young Corbett	104	53	34	19	6	8	12	25
Abe Attell	168	91	47	44	7	3	17	50
Johnny Kilbane	140	46	22	24	2	2	8	82
Eugene Criqui	115	94	40	54	11	2	8	0
Johnny Dundee	321	113	19	94	29	2	18	159
Kid Kaplan	131	101	17	84	10	3	10	7
Benny Bass	197	140	59	81	26	2	6	23
Andre Routis	86	54	10	44	23	2	7	0
Bat Battalino	88	58	24	34	25	1	3	1
Kid Chocolate	161	145	64	81	8	2	6	0
Freddie Miller	237	201	43	158	25	1	5	5
Petey Sarron	103	75	18	57	18	1	8	1
Joey Archibald	106	60	28	32	33	8	5	0
Harry Jeffra	120	93	27	66	17	2	7	1
Chalky Wright	140	102	57	45	27	5	5	1
Petey Scalzo	111	89	46	43	12	3	6	1
Phil Terranova	99	67	29	38	18	3	11	0
Sal Bartolo	97	74	16	58	16	2	5	0
Willie Pep	241	229	65	164	5	6	1	0
Sandy Saddler	162	144	103	41	15	1	2	0
Hogan Bassey	68	55	20	35	8	4	1	0
Davey Moore	67	59	30	29	5	2	1	0
Sugar Ramos				(still fighting)				
Johnny Famechon				(still fighting)				
Vicente Saldivar				(still fighting)				
Kuniaki Shibata				(still fighting)				
Clemente Sanchez				(still fighting)				

Bantamweight Champions

Name	Total Recorded Bouts	Total Wins	K.O.'s	Won On Decision	Lost On Decision	Times K.O.'d	Draws	No Decision
Jimmy Barry	70	59	39	20	0	0	9	2
Harry Harris	54	40	15	25	2	0	7	5
Harry Forbes	130	80	30	50	4	11	23	12
Frankie Neil	56	26	24	2	9	4	4	13
Joe Bowker	51	40	8	32	4	4	1	2

Bantamweight Champions

Name	Total Recorded Bouts	Total Wins	K.O.'s	Won On Decision	Lost On Decision	Times K.O.'d	Draws	No Decision
Jimmy Walsh	120	52	12	40	8	1	18	41
Johnny Coulon	96	56	24	32	2	2	4	32
Kid Williams	204	107	48	59	14	3	7	73
Pete Herman	148	71	19	52	11	1	8	57
Joe Lynch	134	42	29	13	13	0	15	64
Johnny Buff	94	28	13	15	9	7	4	46
Abe Goldstein	129	89	30	59	9	4	5	22
Eddie Martin	90	72	27	45	8	3	3	4
Charley Rosenberg	64	36	7	29	15	0	6	7
Bud Taylor	159	70	35	35	19	4	6	60
Bushy Graham	127	101	37	64	12	2	6	6
Panama Al Brown	154	122	58	64	17	1	12	2
B. Sangchilli	77	59	24	35	12	1	5	0
Tony Marino	40	26	7	19	10	2	2	0
Sixto Escobar	64	42	21	21	18	0	4	0
Lou Salica	90	62	13	49	16	1	11	0
George Pace	42	33	15	18	5	1	2	1
Harold Dade	77	41	9	32	25	5	6	0
Manuel Ortiz	122	92	45	47	26	1	3	0
Vic Toweel	32	28	14	14	1	2	1	0
Jimmy Carruthers	25	21	13	8	3	1	0	0
Robert Cohen	43	36	14	22	2	2	3	0
Mario D'Agata	67	54	23	31	9	1	3	0
Alphonse Halimi	50	41	21	20	5	3	1	0
Jose Becerra	78	71	42	29	3	2	2	0
Fighting Harada	63	55	22	33	5	2	1	0
Eder Jofre				(still fighting)				
Lionel Rose				(still fighting)				
Chucho Castillo				(still fighting)				
Ruben Olivares				(still fighting)				
Rafael Herrera				(still fighting)				
Enrique Pinder				(still fighting)				
Romero Anaya				(still fighting)				
Arnold Taylor				(still fighting)				

Flyweight Champions

Name	Total Recorded Bouts	Total Wins	K.O.'s	Won On Decision	Lost On Decision	Times K.O.'d	Draws	No Decision
Jimmy Wilde	140	126	77	49	1	3	2	8
Pancho Villa	103	71	22	49	5	0	4	23
Frankie Genaro	129	83	19	64	18	4	9	15
Emile Pladner	122	96	34	62	13	3	10	0
Fidel LaBarba	97	72	15	57	15	0	8	2
Al Belanger	62	37	13	24	16	2	7	0
Izzy Schwartz	117	59	7	51	27	1	12	18
Young Perez	131	89	26	63	19	7	16	0
Midget Wolgast	147	96	11	85	29	6	15	1
Jackie Brown	129	97	36	61	21	4	7	0
Benny Lynch	72	57	27	30	5	1	9	0
Small Montana	111	80	10	70	19	3	9	0
Peter Kane	95	85	51	34	3	4	2	1
Jackie Paterson	90	62	41	21	15	10	3	0
Rinty Monaghan	51	42	19	23	7	1	1	0
Terry Allen	76	62	18	44	10	3	1	0
Dado Marino	74	57	21	36	11	3	3	0
Yoshio Shirai	42	35	15	20	4	2	1	0
Pascual Perez	91	83	56	27	4	3	1	0
H. Ebihara	69	63	34	29	5	0	1	0
Pone Kingpetch	40	32	11	21	5	3	0	0
Sal Burruni	109	99	31	68	7	2	1	0
Walter McGowan	40	32	14	18	3	4	1	0
Efren Torres				(still fighting)				
C. Chionoi				(still fighting)				
E. Salvarria				(still fighting)				
Venice Borkorsor				(still fighting)				

APPENDICES

PRINCIPAL RULES OF THE PRIZE RING

Weighing

Contestants shall be weighed in the presence of each other and an official of the Commission at such time prior to the bout as may be designated by the Commission.

Contestants shall appear at the time designated for weighing in unless properly excused from so appearing.

Weights and Classes

Flyweight .... 112 pounds
Bantamweight .... over 112 to 118 pounds
Featherweight .... over 118 to 126 pounds
Lightweight .... over 126 to 135 pounds
Welterweight .... over 135 to 147 pounds
Middleweight .... over 147 to 160 pounds
Light-heavyweight ...... over 160 to 175 pounds
Heavyweight .... all over 175 pounds

No contest shall be permitted when there is a difference in weight of more than twelve pounds when the lighter of the two contestants weighs between 160 and 175 pounds; or 10 pounds in weight when the lighter of the two weighs between 135 and 160 pounds; or six pounds in weight when the lighter of the two contestants weighs under 135 pounds.

Length of Rounds

Rounds for professional contests shall be of three minutes duration with one minute rest between rounds.

When a round has been completed and the bout halted, either by the respective corners or by the referee, it shall count as a knockout scored in the round scheduled to come out.

Knockdown Timekeeper

The timekeeper shall be assisted by the knockdown timekeeper. As soon as a contestant is floored the timekeeper shall strike the floor of the ring with a hammer or mallet at one second intervals as long as the contestant is on the floor. This count shall not necessarily be limited to ten seconds but shall be for the purpose of a correct count by seconds. Should the referee encounter difficulty in keeping the contestant scoring the knockdown in the farthest corner, thus interrupting the referee's count, the knockdown timekeeper shall continue to strike the floor, and the referee, when resuming his count shall again pick up the count with the beat of the timekeeper's hammer or mallet.

The knockdown timekeeper's count may, therefore, continue beyond ten (10) seconds. His count is a "guide" for the referee. The referee's count is the official count.

A contestant when knocked down shall be required to take a count of "8," whether or not he has regained his feet before "8" is reached.

Judges

(Where judges are provided by law.)

Two judges, licensed by the Commission, shall assist the referee in rendering a decision at the termination of each contest.

Licensed referees, members of the Commission, or designated officials of the Commission, may, in an emergency, act as judges.

Powers of the Referee

After a contest starts the referee has power to declare a bout "no contest" and to enforce discipline and the regulations pertaining to the conduct and behavior of contestants and seconds. The referee may stop a contest if, in his opinion, one of the contestants is badly outclassed or injured; or the referee may temporarily stop a contest and consult with the examining physician on the advisability of stopping the contest in case a contestant appears injured. The referee, with or without warning, may declare a bout "no contest."

The referee may disqualify a contestant for fouling.

Duties of Referee

The chief official of contests shall be the referee, who shall have general supervision over bouts and take his place in the ring.

The referee shall, before starting a contest, ascertain from each contestant the name of his chief second, and shall hold said chief second responsible for the conduct of his assistant seconds during the progress of the contest.

The referee shall call contestants together in the ring before each bout for final instructions, at which time each contestant shall be accompanied by his chief second only. The principals after receiving instructions shall shake hands and retire to their corners. They shall not again shake hands until the beginning of the last round.

In case of a knockdown the referee shall require the fallen contestant to take a count of "8." The mandatory 8 count shall not be waived for *any* contest. In the case of a cut eye or similar facial lacerations the referee shall consult with the ringside physician. Such consultation shall take place upon the conclusion of a round or with "time out," in an emergency, may take place during the progress of the round. The termination of the bout shall be governed by the examining physician's decision.

Mid-Ring Instructions

The referee shall, in mid-ring, instruct as follows:

"You two men are to box ... rounds, under the rules of the State of ....

"Do not hold behind the neck and punch with one hand, like this.

"Do not strike a rabbit punch, like this.

"Do not strike a kidney punch, like this.

"Do not strike with the open glove.

"Do not use backhand blows.

"Do not hit on the break away at any time. Step back cleanly.

"Break when I tell you to do so. Do not make me maul you apart.

"In case of a knockdown I want the man scoring it to retire immediately to the corner farthest removed from the knockdown and remain there until I motion him back, or I will stop counting. When knocked down you must take a count of "8." The knockdown counts as such regardless of how long you were on the floor.

"Heavy penalties are scored in case of fouls. In case you lose on a deliberate foul your purse will be forfeited. Two points are deducted from the score for each major foul committed, one point for each minor foul.

"Shake hands now and come up boxing. Do not shake again until the beginning of the last round."

"Down" Without Being Struck

A contestant who goes down without being struck, for the purpose of avoiding a blow, may be disqualified.

Should a contestant leave the ring during the one minute period between rounds and fail to be in the ring when the gong rings the signal to resume boxing, or should a contestant fail to rise from his chair at the beginning of a round, the referee shall start counting immediately, and unless the contestant is on his feet in the ring at the end of ten seconds shall declare him counted out.

Should a contestant who is "down" arise before the count of "ten" is reached, and go down again immediately without being struck, except for the purpose of avoiding a blow, the referee shall resume the count.

Counting

When a contestant is knocked down the referee shall order the opponent to retire to the corner farthest removed from the fallen contestant, pointing to the corner, and immediately begin the count over the contestant who is down. He shall audibly announce the passing of the seconds, accompanying the count with motions of his arm, the downward motion indicating the end of each second.

Should the opponent fail to stay in the farthest corner the referee shall cease counting until he has returned to it, and then go on with the count from the point at which it was interrupted.

If the contestant who is down arises during the count the referee shall continue to count to "8" and assure himself that the contestant just arisen is in fit condition to continue. If so assured he shall without loss of time order both contestants to go on with the contest. During such intervention by the referee the striking of a blow by either contestant may be ruled "foul."

If the contestant taking the count is still down when the referee calls the count of "ten" the referee shall wave both arms to indicate that he has been knocked out, and shall raise the right hand of the opponent as the winner. The referee's count is the official count.

If the round ends during the count, the timekeeper shall sound the gong once, thus indicating the termination of the round and that the contestant who is down has not been counted out.

Official K. O. Rule

When a contestant fails to answer the bell for a round "coming up" his opponent shall be credited with a "T.K.O." in the round that is "coming up," and not in the preceding round which has been fought. It is advisable to actually ring the bell for the ensuing round and actually count out the contestant who doesn't answer the bell.

Facial Lacerations

When a bout is terminated due to facial laceration or similar injury brought about by an accidental butt, and less than one half of the scheduled bout has taken place, the bout shall be called a draw.

When a bout is terminated by such an accidental butt, incurred after the bout is more than one half over, the decision shall be awarded to the contestant who is ahead.

Deliberate butting is penalized as a foul. This rule does not apply to cut eyes and similar lacerations brought about by blows.

Out of Ring

A contestant who has been knocked or has fallen through the ropes and over the edge of the ring platform during a contest shall not be helped back by his manager or his seconds. The referee shall begin to count as soon as the contestant leaves the inside of the ring ropes. If the contestant fails to return by the count of "10" he is technically knocked out. The same procedure shall apply to a contestant who leaves the ring during the progress of the bout under any circumstances.

When one contestant has fallen through the ropes the other shall retire to the farthest corner and remain there until the count is completed or his opponent is on his feet in the ring.

A contestant who deliberately wrestles or throws his opponent from the ring, or who hits him when he is partly out of the ring and prevented by the ropes from assuming a position of defense, shall be disqualified.

In case of serious injury to a contestant the referee shall be automatically under suspension until investigation by the Commission establishes whether the injury was the result of negligence or incompetence on the part of the referee or of circumstances not reasonably within his control.

A Contestant Is "Down"

A contestant is down when any part of his body but his feet is on the floor or when he is hanging helplessly over the ropes and the referee has begun to count over him. (A referee may count a contestant out either on the ropes, on the floor, in his chair, or when rising from a "down" position.)

Fouls

1. Hitting below the belt.
2. Hitting an opponent who is down or rising after being down.
3. Holding an opponent with one hand and hitting with the other.

4. Holding or deliberately maintaining a clinch.
5. Wrestling or roughing at the ropes.
6. Pushing an opponent about the ring or into the ropes, or striking an opponent who is helpless as a result of blows and so supported by the ropes that he does not fall.
7. Butting with the head or shoulder or using the knee or elbow.
8. Hitting with the open glove, or with the butt or inside of the hand, the elbow, the wrist, and all back-hand blows.
9. Purposely going down without being hit or to avoid a blow.
10. Striking deliberately at that part of the body over the kidneys.
11. The use of the pivot blow or the rabbit punch.
12. Jabbing opponent's eyes with the thumb of the glove.
13. The use of abusive language in ring.
14. Any unsportsmanlike trick or action causing injury to an opponent.

Foul Tactics

Holding with one hand and hitting with the other, which is an unfair method of landing a blow and may have decisive effect because the contestant struck is unable to avoid or move with the blow to break its force, is classed as a major foul.

The kidney punch, which is an illegal blow landing on that part of the back near the spine and over the kidneys, is strictly barred because it may produce permanent injury.

A rabbit punch is any blow struck at the back of the neck near the base of the skull, and is barred as dangerous. A blow landed on the head behind the ear, or on the side of the neck, as the opponent turns his head to avoid it, is not a rabbit punch. Any deliberate attempt to use the rabbit punch shall be penalized.

Butting with the top or side of the head is likely to cause cuts over opponent's eyebrows and other injuries affecting the outcome of the contest, and shall not be allowed. A boxer who goes in head down and leans against an opponent with his head while infighting is butting.

"Thumbing," or jabbing of the glove, has frequently caused serious injuries to the eyes, and referees must watch for this trick and, if it is deliberately used, penalize it by disqualification.

If a contestant is helpless on the ropes the referee shall instantly intervene, declare the helpless boxer "down" and proceed with the count.

In cases of minor fouls, such as hitting or flicking with open glove, clinching and prolonging contest after warning has been given, the referee shall punish persistent disregard of the rule with disqualification.

The referee may disqualify a contestant for fouling with or without warning.

Penalties for Fouling

Any contestant losing on a foul shall be automatically suspended for a period of thirty days, in addition to such other penalties as the Commission may impose.

No contestant shall commit a deliberate foul. In addition to any penalty which may be imposed for so doing, the purse of such contestant committing a deliberate foul shall, when ordered by the Commission, be forfeited and paid over to the Commission for disposition.

If a bout is stopped because of accidental fouling the referee shall determine whether the boxer who has been fouled can continue or not, and if his chances have not been seriously jeopardized as a result of the foul may order the bout continued after a reasonable interval set by the referee, who shall so instruct the timekeeper.

Gloves

In all contests the gloves used must weigh not less than eight (8) ounces each.

Gloves shall be examined by the Inspector. If padding is found to be misplaced or lumpy, or if gloves are found to be imperfect, other gloves shall be substituted before the contests starts.

INDEX

(Note: Includes only the world champions)

Akins, Virgil, 220
Ali, Muhammad (Cassius Clay), 1-2, 61, 67-71, 73-76, 78-80, 114, 116, 118, 123
Allen, Terry, 312, 315, 319
Ambers, Lou, 56, 156, 205, 212, 244, 246-249
Angott, Sammy, 173-175, 215, 249-251, 253, 277
Anzya, Romero, 304
Apostoli, Fred, 104, 106, 147, 151, 155-157, 160-161, 203-204
Archibald, Joey, 56, 277-280
Armstrong, Henry, 161, 175, 210-215, 246-248, 251, 253, 277, 279, 298, 310
Attell, Abe, 232, 236, 243, 268-271, 281-283, 290-291

Backus, Billy, 223
Baer, Max, 1-2, 36, 39-41, 43-45, 47, 49-50, 63, 97, 100, 102
Barry, Jimmy, 289, 300
Bartolo, Sal, 280
Basilio, Carmen, 172, 175, 181-186, 201, 216, 219-220
Bass, Benny, 211, 244, 246, 274, 276
Bassey, Hogan, 283, 285-286
Battalino, Bat, 208, 274-276, 283, 295
Becerra, Jose, 300-302
Belanger, Al (Frenchie), 310-311
Benvenuti, Nino, 123, 187-188, 222
Berlenbach, Paul, 94-97, 145, 175
Bettina, Melio, 103-104, 106, 109, 155, 157
Borkorsor, Venice, 320
Bowker, Joe, 290-291
Braddock, Jim, 1, 40-41, 43-48, 97, 100-101, 201
Bratton, Johnny, 216-217, 219, 250
Britton, Jack, 144, 162, 195-200, 240
Brouillard, Lou, 103, 108, 147-148, 202-203

Brown, Jackie, 312-313
Brown, Joe, 220, 256, 258
Brown, Panama Al, 259, 295-296
Buchanan, Ken, 259-260
Buff, Johnny, 293-294, 310
Burns, Tommy, 2, 15-18, 63, 83, 195
Burruni, Sal, 318-320

Canzoneri, Tony, 141, 205, 208, 243-247, 253, 274, 282-283, 293, 295
Carnera, Primo, 1-2, 20, 35, 38-41, 43-45, 47, 63, 65, 80, 97, 100, 293
Carpentier, Georges, 27, 86, 88-92, 96-97, 134-135, 169, 197, 228
Carruthers, Jimmy, 219-220, 254, 256-258, 285
Castillo, Chucho, 303-304
Cerdan, Marcel, 91, 165, 169-171, 228
Chambers, Arthur, 224-225, 235
Charles, Ezzard, 1, 49-52, 55, 58, 109, 112
Chionoi, C., 320
Chip, George, 82, 135-136, 138
Chocolate, Kid, 116, 216-217, 244, 275-276, 295, 311
Christoforidis, Anton, 104, 107-109
Cochrane, Freddie (Red), 215-216, 249
Cohen, Robert, 300
Cokes, Curtis, 222-223
Conn, Billy, 50-51, 104-109, 117, 155, 157, 160, 166, 203, 215
Corbett, James J., 1-2, 4-15, 17, 29, 44, 46-48, 63, 82-84, 86, 99-100, 102, 104, 126, 190, 225, 228, 268
Corbett II, Young, 232, 241, 265-266, 268
Corbett III, Young, 203-204
Coulon, Johnny, 291, 295

INDEX

Criqui, Eugene, 6, 228, 270-272
Cruz, Carlos, 259

Dade, Harold, 257, 297-299
D'Agata, Mario, 300
Delaney, Jack, 95-97, 100, 102, 175
DeMarco, Paddy, 219-220, 254, 258, 284
DeMarco, Tony, 185, 219, 220, 258
Dempsey, Jack, 1-2, 12, 17, 21-23, 25-31, 33, 35, 41, 44-50, 52, 55-58, 63, 65, 74, 86, 88-91, 97, 100, 103, 106, 109-111, 113, 116, 127-128, 136-140, 144, 148, 153, 157, 165, 171, 181, 193, 214, 220, 231, 256, 258, 266-268, 273
Dempsey, Jack (Nonpareil), 8-9, 124-125, 190, 225, 227
Dillon, Jack, 84-86, 135, 138, 195
Dixon, George, 228-229, 263-266, 268, 289-290, 298
Downes, Terry, 123, 185-186
Dundee, Joe, 148, 201
Dundee, Johnny, 6, 239, 242-244, 271-273, 282, 295
Dundee, Vince, 104, 148-149, 154, 160-161, 202
Duran, Roberto, 260

Ebihara, H., 318
Erne, Frank, 227-230, 265-266
Escobar, Sixto, 156, 279, 296-297

Famechon, Johnny, 287-288, 302, 304
Ferns, Rube, 193-194
Fields, Jackie, 201-204, 209, 243, 274
Fitzsimmons, Bob, 1-2, 6-13, 15, 17-18, 46-48, 63, 82-83, 86, 114, 125-126, 142, 197, 306
Flowers, Tiger, 95-97, 102, 136, 138, 141-142, 144
Forbes, Harry, 267, 290
Foreman, George, 1, 2, 68, 72, 75, 77-80, 117
Foster, Bob, 75, 117, 123
Frazier, Joe, 70, 73-78, 123
Freeman, Tommy, 202-203
Fullmer, Gene, 69, 123, 172, 175, 180-182, 184, 186-187, 221

Gans, Joe, 12, 162, 194-195, 212, 228-233, 241, 244, 267-268, 276
Garcia, Ceferino, 151, 155-156, 161, 203, 208, 210, 212
Gardner, George, 8, 82, 194
Gavilan, Kid, 175, 185, 201, 216-219
Genaro, Frankie, 294-295, 305, 310-312
Giardello, Joey, 123, 181, 185-187
Goldstein, Abe, 294-295
Goodrich, Jimmy, 242-243
Graham, Bushy, 295, 311-312
Graziano, Rocky, 48, 74, 161-170, 173, 175, 216
Greb, Harry, 23, 30-31, 48, 68, 74, 84, 86, 96-97, 101, 135-141, 145-146, 203, 213-214, 248, 268
Griffith, Emile, 123, 181, 187-188, 221-222
Griffo, Young, 225, 261, 263-265, 276

Halimi, Alphonse, 300-302
Harada, Fighting, 287, 302-303, 318
Harris, Harry, 289-290
Herman, Pete, 244, 291-294, 296, 306, 308
Herrera, Rafael, 304
Hostak, Al, 155, 157, 159-160, 166

Jack, Beau, 215, 217, 250-253
Jeby, Ben, 147-148, 202
Jeffra, Harry, 156, 278-279, 296
Jeffries, Jim, 1-2, 5-7, 11-15, 17-18, 21, 30, 46-48, 52, 63, 65, 81-82, 125, 133, 276
Jenkins, Lew, 185, 215, 246, 248-250
Jofre, Eder, 302
Johansson, Ingemar, 2, 61-63, 65-66
Johnson, Harold, 110, 117-118, 120

Johnson, Jack, 1, 6, 11-12, 15-21, 30, 46-48, 52, 63, 75, 82-83, 85, 116, 128, 130-131, 214, 276
Jones, Gorilla, 146-147, 151
Jordan, Don, 220-221

Kane, Peter, 312-314
Kansas, Rocky, 239, 242-243
Kaplan, Louis (Kid), 273-274, 283
Ketchel, Stanley, 12, 17-18, 48, 74, 82-83, 86, 126-135, 162, 180, 195, 269, 308
Kid, Dixie (Aaron Brown), 194
Kilbane, Johnny, 239, 242, 269-272, 291
Kingpetch, Pone, 302, 318-319
Klaus, Frank, 134-136, 138, 195
Krieger, Solly, 104, 108, 155, 159-160

LaBarba, Fidel, 141, 203, 207, 275-276, 295, 310-311
Laguna, Ismael, 258-260
LaMotta, Jake, 165, 169-172, 174-175, 182, 215
Latzo, Pete, 97, 100, 101, 141, 144, 200-201
Lavigne, George (Kid), 225, 227-228, 262, 265
Leonard, Benny, 12, 30, 44, 140, 146, 198, 204, 209, 212, 236-244, 270, 272, 276, 280, 308
Levinsky, Battling, 30, 84-89, 138, 195
Lewis, John Henry, 101-104
Lewis, Ted (Kid), 91, 162, 195-199
Liston, Sonny, 2, 61, 66-68, 70
Loughran, Tommy, 39, 44, 91, 95, 97-100, 103, 120, 139-140, 201
Louis, Joe, 1-2, 17, 22, 35-36, 38, 43, 45-53, 55, 58, 75, 80, 86, 96, 103-107, 156-157, 166-167, 214, 298
Lynch, Benny, 313-314
Lynch, Joe, 292-296, 306

McAuliffe, Jack, 125, 225, 227, 263, 300
McCoy, Al, 97, 106, 135-136
McCoy, Kid, 81, 126, 190-192, 195
McGovern, Terry, 228, 241, 265-268, 290
McGowan, Walter, 319-320
McLarnin, Jimmy, 148, 153, 202, 204-205, 207-209, 241, 243-244, 246, 274, 295, 310-311
McTigue, Mike, 93-97, 100, 138, 141, 145
Mandell, Sammy, 242-243, 274
Marciano, Rocky, 1-2, 51-52, 55-61, 65, 74, 112, 114, 153, 165, 178, 180, 182, 214, 225, 300
Marino, Dado, 315
Marino, Tony, 296
Martin, Eddie (Cannonball), 258, 294-295
Matthews, Matty, 192-193
Maxim, Joey, 55, 61, 109-114, 116, 120, 175
Mellody, Honey, 194-195
Miller, Freddie, 101, 246, 275-277
Mills, Freddie, 109-110, 112-114
Monaghan, Rinty, 314-315
Montana, Small, 305, 312-314
Montgomery, Bob, 215, 248-254
Monzon, Carlos, 188
Moore, Archie, 17, 58, 61, 65, 70, 72, 78, 113-117, 177-178, 214
Moore, Davey, 259, 286-287
Murphy, Billy (Torpedo), 261-263

Napoles, Jose, 222-223
Neil, Frankie, 290
Nelson, Battling, 162, 194, 212, 229-235, 237, 266, 268, 276

O'Brien, Philadelphia Jack, 15, 82-83, 127-129, 190, 194-195, 274
O'Dowd, Mike, 135-136, 138, 198
Olin, Bob, 101, 103
Olivares, Ruben, 303-304
Olson, Bobo, 121-122, 172, 175, 177-180, 182, 219

INDEX

Ortiz, Carlos, 256-260
Ortiz, Manuel, 297-299, 315
Overlin, Ken, 151, 161

Pace, George, 297
Papke, Billy, 12, 127, 131-136, 162, 195
Paret, Benny, 121, 181, 187, 220-221
Pastrano, Willie, 69, 118, 120-122, 185
Paterson, Jackie, 314
Patterson, Floyd, 2, 58, 60-63, 65-70, 112, 114, 121
Pender, Paul, 121, 185-186
Pep, Willie, 250, 259, 276, 279-285
Perez, Pascual, 315, 317-318
Perez, Victor (Young), 310, 312, 318
Pinder, Enrique, 304
Pladner, Emile, 310-311

Ramos, Armando, 259-260
Ramos, Sugar, 286-287
Risko, Babe, 104, 148-149, 151-154
Ritchie, Willie, 234-237, 239, 241
Robinson, Sugar Ray, 48, 112, 121, 165-167, 170-186, 213-215, 217, 219, 222, 281
Rodriguez, Luis, 187, 221-222
Root, Jack, 81-82
Rose, Lionel, 302-304
Rosenberg, Charley, 295
Rosenbloom, Maxie, 97, 100-103, 141, 201, 243
Ross, Barney, 156, 161, 201, 204-205, 208-213, 244, 280
Routis, Andre, 228, 246, 274
Ryan, Tommy, 125-126, 130, 190, 192, 295

Saddler, Sandy, 214, 257-258, 280-285
Salas, Lauro, 220, 254, 256-258, 284
Saldivar, Vicente, 287-288
Salica, Lou, 296-298
Salvarria, E., 320
Sanchez, Clemente, 288
Sangchilli, Baltazar, 296
Sarron, Petey, 211, 250, 277
Saxton, Johnny, 184-185, 217, 219-220
Scalzo, Petey, 280
Schmeling, Max, 2, 35-37, 40-41, 43-48, 53, 63, 145, 274
Schwartz, Izzy, 243, 295, 311-312
Servo, Marty, 56, 174-175, 216
Sharkey, Jack, 1, 32-37, 39, 41, 44-45, 47, 56, 63, 95-97, 100, 145, 214
Shibata, Kuniaki, 288
Shirai, Yoshio, 315, 317
Siki, Battling, 88, 91-94, 96

Singer, Al, 204, 209, 243-244, 274, 276
Slattery, Jimmy, 96-97, 100-103, 120, 201
Smith, Mysterious Billy, 125-126, 189-190, 193-194, 265
Smith, Solly, 228, 262, 265
Smith, Wallace (Bud), 219, 254, 256, 258
Soose, Billy, 161, 163, 166
Steele, Freddie, 19-20, 108-109, 147-149, 151-157, 159-161, 279
Sullivan, Dave, 265, 311
Sullivan, John L., 1-8, 10, 16, 44, 46-47, 63, 65, 104, 225, 228, 232
Sullivan, Twin, 129, 135, 194-195

Taylor, Arnold, 304
Taylor, Bud, 207, 294-295, 311
Terranova, Phil, 279-281
Thil, Marcel, 146-147, 156, 202
Thompson, Young Jack, 201-203
Tiger, Dick, 122-123, 181, 187
Torres, Efren, 320
Torres, Jose Luis, 120-122, 221
Toweel, Vic, 299-300
Tunney, Gene, 1-2, 6-7, 16, 26-33, 36, 40-41, 44-45, 47-48, 55-57, 63, 70, 86, 91, 97, 106, 120, 136, 138-140, 145-146, 156, 181, 256, 300, 308
Turpin, Randy, 165, 171-172, 175-177

Villa, Pancho, 207, 294-295, 305, 308, 310, 314, 318

Walcott, Jersey Joe, 47, 51-53, 55-56, 96, 112, 117
Walcott, Joe, 11, 82, 190, 193-194, 227, 232, 265
Walker, Mickey, 74, 95-97, 100-101, 126, 139, 141-142, 144-146, 151, 198-200, 203, 215
Walsh, Jimmy, 291
Weir, Ike, 261-262
Welsh, Freddie, 196, 234-236, 242, 268, 306
Wilde, Jimmy, 196, 236, 292, 294, 305-308, 310, 313-314
Willard, Jess, 1, 18, 20-23, 38, 63, 89, 231, 273
Williams, Ike, 185, 217, 250, 252-254, 285
Williams, Kid, 271, 291-292, 294-295
Wilson, Johnny, 97, 135-136, 138, 140
Wolgast, Ad, 232-235, 237, 242, 268
Wolgast, Midget, 305, 312-313
Wright, Chalky, 211, 278-283

Yarosz, Teddy, 104, 148-149

Zale, Tony, 91, 159, 161-166, 169, 182
Zivic, Fritzie, 104, 173, 175, 212-216, 247, 249, 251
Zurita, Juan, 251, 253-254

WITHDRAWN

```
920                    79-07014
Mc
McCallum, John Dennis.
The encyclopedia of world boxing
    champions since 1882.
```

DATE DUE

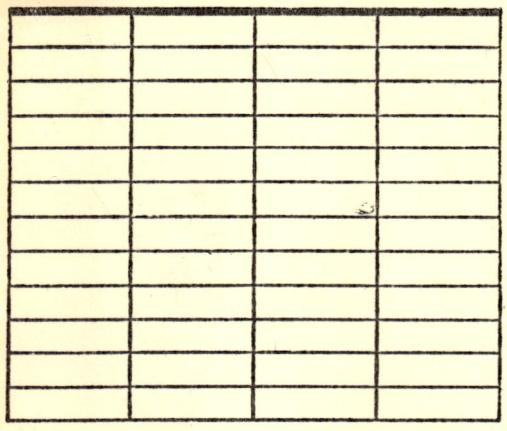

SANBUSKY PUBLIC LIBRARY